# #MakeoverMonday

# #MakeoverMonday

Improving How We Visualize and Analyze
Data, One Chart at a Time

**Andy Kriebel**
*Head Coach, The Information Lab Data School*

**Eva Murray**
*Head of Business Intelligence, Exasol*

WILEY

Cover image: Andy Kriebel
Cover design: I FOR IDEAS (i-for-ideas.com)

Published by John Wiley & Sons, Inc., Hoboken, New Jersey.
Published simultaneously in Canada.

For general information on our other products and services or for technical support, please contact our Customer Care Department within the United States at (800) 762–2974, outside the United States at (317) 572–3993, or fax (317) 572–4002.

Wiley publishes in a variety of print and electronic formats and by print-on-demand. Some material included with standard print versions of this book may not be included in e-books or in print-on-demand. If this book refers to media such as a CD or DVD that is not included in the version you purchased, you may download this material at http://booksupport.wiley.com. For more information about Wiley products, visit www.wiley.com.

A catalogue record for this book is available from the Library of Congress

ISBN 978-1-119-51077-2 (Paper)
ISBN 978-1-119-51072-7 (ePDF)
ISBN 978-1-119-51079-6 (ePub)

Printed in the United States of America.

V10004342_090618

# Contents

## Part III

# Foreword

The world of data is changing rapidly. We can talk about machine learning, artificial intelligence, and automation as much as we want, but what will always be needed is the ability to communicate insights. Only a creative being, a human, fluent in the language of data, can do this effectively. Only a human can combine the skills of data wrangler, communicator, designer, and artist to create visualizations that convey emotion, create an impact, and influence opinions.

Learning to be that kind of person is more vital today than ever.

There are hundreds of books about the principles of data literacy, packed full of examples. From those, you will learn the theory and principles of data literacy. What this book shows is how to build a framework for you to practice. To be an expert in any field requires practice, and this book, along with all the weekly Makeover Monday projects, gives you the framework you need to become one.

In this book you will find hundreds of examples of makeovers, made by people like you: everyday data warriors, trying to make sense of the world through data. You will learn how to develop your own skills and become as fluent as some of the most advanced authors featured in the book.

The Makeover Monday project began its growth as an experiment between Andy and me in 2016. After a year, I stepped back, and Eva Murray stepped in. Together, the two of them expanded the project greatly, and this book is the culmination of their efforts. Now everybody—even those not partaking every week—gets to benefit. Watching the project grow over the years has been truly inspiring; Eva, Andy, and I had no idea Makeover Monday could become so popular. To see the impact on individual people as they develop a portfolio, get involved in a community, and even get new jobs has been a great honor.

I can think of no better guides to help you on your journey than Andy and Eva, two people who are experts in the field, superb teachers, and true community builders.

I hope this book inspires you as it has the thousands of people who have been involved in Makeover Monday so far.

Andy Cotgreave
Brill, England
June 2018

# Acknowledgments

## From Andy and Eva

First and foremost, we must thank the Makeover Monday Community. Without all of you, the project and this book would not exist. Your constant participation and enthusiasm keeps us going. We enjoy seeing you evolve in your development and watching your careers flourish.

We'd like to thank Tableau Software, and specifically the Tableau Public team, for their support in helping the project grow and for providing a free sharing platform. We'd also like to thank data.world for providing a platform for sharing the data and creating an excellent discussion forum. While Tableau has been the most prominent tool used for Makeover Monday, we're very excited to see more and more visualizations from Power BI, Yellowfin, Google Data Studio, and R. The more tools we are all exposed to, the better we will become as data analysts. Thank you also to Bright-TALK, who provided us with a webinar channel that gives us a direct connection to our community for sharing feedback, discussing visualizations, and presenting about various data-related topics.

We'd like to thank Bill Falloon and Purvi Patel from Wiley for taking a chance on us first-time authors and for helping us navigate the book-writing process. Without your continuous, positive support, we would have never gotten this across the finish line.

We also want to thank Andy Cotgreave for his support and advice throughout the book-writing process and for introducing us to Wiley. Andy's contributions in 2016 helped launch Makeover Monday into what it is today.

We'd like to thank Pablo Gomez and his team at iForIdeas for creating the Makeover Monday branding. The cover you created looks amazing! Thank you for all of your support, attention to detail, and recommendations throughout the process. This book looks great because of you!

In addition to those listed above, we would like to thank everyone who helped make this book possible: Adam Crahen, Ann Jackson, Carl Allchin, Carsten Weidmann, Charlie Hutcheson, Cole Knaflic, Deborah Thomas, Donna Coles, Emma Whyte, Jeff Shaffer, Luke Stoughton, Maureen Stone, Pablo Sáenz d Tejada, Pooja Ghandi, Ryan Sleeper, Sean Jackson, Tim Ngwena.

The cover design of this book is based on a visualization Andy created for a Makeover Monday challenge of the artwork from the Tate Collection.

Special thanks to the team at iForIdeas who turned Andy's visualization into a stunning cover image as well as a visual identity for Makeover Monday.

## From Andy

Thank you, Eva, for being an incredible partner on this journey. You've pushed me to grow in ways I never knew existed and have filled me with encouragement and positivity. You've brought so much to this project, pushed me to write this book, and you do an amazing job of keeping us both organized and keeping me in check.

I'd like to thank The Information Lab, The Data School, and Tom Brown for supporting my Makeover Monday hobby and giving me the time to help others grow. Your support has been incredibly influential in helping Makeover Monday flourish.

I'd like to thank Jonathan MacDonald and Craig Bloodworth from The Information Lab for supporting the Makeover Monday website infrastructure. Calling Jonathan while he's on holiday to fix a website I crashed tells you all you need to know about him as a person. Thank you, Craig, for using TIL resources to give Makeover Monday a reliable home on the internet.

I'd like to thank Tim Ngwena for his support in helping produce high-resolution images. Thank you for your wizardry and for being so patient with me.

Finally, and most importantly, I'd like to thank my wife, Beth, and our four amazing children, Michael, Oscar, Elizabeth, and Henry, for their support throughout the writing of this book. Thank you for giving me the time and space to get this done when I needed it most. We've sacrificed many nights and weekends together to get this done. It's been many years now that I've been addicted to data visualization and you have never wavered in your support.

## From Eva

Thank you, Andy, for taking a gamble and asking me to join you in running the Makeover Monday project. While I underestimated the impact it would have on my life and my career, I love being part of this and having a platform for helping others grow their skills and develop their careers. Thank you for encouraging me to tackle the things that scare me and for saying yes to almost all of my ideas, even if they result in more work for us initially. Makeover Monday has been transformational, not just for many of our community members, but for me as well.

I'd like to thank Exasol and Aaron Auld for supporting my involvement with the data visualization and analytics community and for encouraging me to do what I love doing. Thank you for also giving me the opportunity to host and travel for live Makeover Monday events, which have been a great way to connect with the participants of our project.

I'd like to thank the local community and user group leaders who invited us to meet their people through Makeover Monday live events. What you do in your communities and organizations extends the work we do and takes the resources to many more people than we can reach by ourselves. Thank you for being such advocates for Makeover Monday and for helping others to grow, learn, and develop their skills. We appreciate all you do, Fiona Gordon, Josh Tapley, Kai-Ming Cheah, Michael Mixon, Neil Richards, Sarah Bartlett, Simon Beaumont.

Last but not least, thanks to my family and friends for being supportive and understanding and for patiently accepting that my availability between work, book writing, and cycling was much less than usual. Having you cheer me on along the way helped me through this writing process and on my path of becoming an author.

# About the Authors

## Andy Kriebel
Head Coach, The Information Lab Data School

Andy, a member of the Tableau Zen Master Hall of Fame, began using Tableau in April 2007. Since then, it has been Andy's mission to help as many people as possible to see and understand their data with Tableau, which is the focus of his role as Head Coach at The Information Lab's Data School. In August 2009, he launched vizwiz.com, which is credited as the first ever Tableau-related blog and provides examples of data visualization best practices, methods for improving existing work, and tips and tricks with Tableau. He writes or has written three weekly series: Makeover Monday (along with Eva Murray), Tableau Tip Tuesday, and Workout Wednesday (along with Emma Whyte).

Andy writes every week about great data visualizations he finds around the web on his other website Data Viz Done Right (datavizdoneright.com) and he is one-half of the Dear Data Two project along with Jeffrey Shaffer (dear-data-two.com).

In addition to his recognized expertise in data visualization and Tableau, Andy is frequently invited to speak at conferences around the world. Prior to his role at The Information Lab, Andy ran the Tableau Center of Excellence at Facebook, providing data visualization and data analysis training at Facebook offices globally. Andy was also the first Tableau user at Coca-Cola before he was recruited to Facebook.

Websites: vizwiz.com    makeovermonday.co.uk
Twitter: @VizWizBI
Facebook: facebook.com/vizwiz/
YouTube: youtube.com/user/kriebela/
Tableau: public.tableau.com/profile/andy.kriebel

## Eva Murray

Head of Business Intelligence, Exasol

Eva joined the field of Business Intelligence and Data Visualization in 2013 while living and working in Australia. After moving to Germany in 2016, she is now part of Exasol's management team, responsible for executing the company's data-driven strategy and developing an Analytics Center of Excellence. Eva is passionate about bringing data to more people and creating educational content and collaboration opportunities for data analysts across the world to build a community of like-minded professionals who drive action and change.

Eva is a Tableau Ambassador and 2018 Tableau Zen Master, has co-hosted the popular social data project Makeover Monday since January 2017, and blogs at trimydata.com, where she writes about her three passions: Tableau, Travel, and Triathlon.

Eva has successfully built her profile in the data visualization and Tableau community, starting in Australia, where she worked as a Tableau trainer and consultant, helping large organizations improve their analytics environments. Since moving to Europe, Eva has spoken at a number of international conferences and analytics events and was a judge for Tableau's inaugural Iron Viz Europe contest.

Websites: trimydata.com    makeovermonday.co.uk
Twitter: @TriMyData
Tableau Public: public.tableau.com/profile/eva.murray

# Part I

# Introduction

"Practice makes perfect." Our parents, teachers and coaches have said this simple phrase ever since we were old enough to think for ourselves. And we all know now that if you want to be great at anything, you have to practice, over and over and over again. Whether it is data visualization, golf, or underwater basket weaving, in order to be great you have to dedicate time to perfecting your craft. On top of practice, you need to engage with a community that can help you learn, provide you with feedback, and inspire you. This is what Makeover Monday is all about. Makeover Monday will help you go from good to great at data visualization, data analysis, communication, and storytelling, as long as you make the effort, week after week.

## What Is Makeover Monday?

Makeover Monday, the social data project, started in January 2016 as a collaboration between me (Andy Kriebel) and Andy Cotgreave. Makeover Monday as a concept, however, had been around for several years as a weekly project I did by myself to advance my learning and practice my craft.

Makeover Monday is simple: take an existing chart and make it better. The goal is straightforward: improve how we visualize and analyze data, one chart at a time. Here is how it works:

1. Eva Murray (my partner from January 2017) and I find charts that we think do not communicate information as effectively as they could.

2. We prepare the necessary data for each chart so that people can focus on visualizing and analyzing the data (without the need to prepare it first), thus eliminating a big barrier to participation.

3. The original visualization and data, along with the source article, are posted on our website on Sundays.

4. Throughout the week, participants create their own chart, dashboard, or story, publish it to the web, and share it via our data. world page (data.world) and Twitter.

5. In addition to members of the community giving one another feedback, Eva and I run a weekly webinar to provide live feedback.

6. People iterate on the feedback and republish.

7. Each week we identify our favorite visualizations, a few lessons learned, and summarize the week in a blog post on Friday.

8. It starts all over again two days later.

Makeover Monday is open to everyone. Maybe you are just getting started and need a place to practice data visualization or basic data analysis. Maybe you have years of experience and want to improve your storytelling, communication skills, or learn advanced techniques. Wherever you are in your career as a data analyst, Makeover Monday has a place for you.

## How Did Makeover Monday Start?

I started using Tableau Software on 11 April 2007 and immediately began reading all I could to understand the fundamental data visualization principles that Tableau was built upon. Based on a recommendation, the first book I read was Stephen Few's *Information Dashboard Design: The Effective Visual Communication of Data* (O'Reilly Media, 2006). The idea that really stuck with me was how Stephen would teach his readers by reviewing poorly designed charts, indicating what did not work and how he would visualize it differently.

I read the book cover to cover in a day and was blown away that I had not heard anything about data visualization before. I knew at this moment that my world had changed. This was the work I wanted to do.

Fast-forward to August 2009. I noticed that not many people were writing about data visualization and I believed that writing about what I was learning would help make the concepts stick and help me improve faster. VizWiz.com was born and I started doing "makeovers." The first blog post I wrote was a makeover of a pie chart similar to the one in Figure I.1 about the RBIs (runs batted in; baseball) contributed by New York Yankees players:

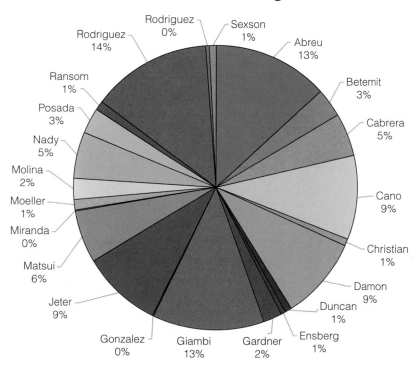

**2008 Yankees Batting Runs**

**FIGURE I.1** The alphabetical sorting of the pie chart makes ranking the players difficult.

Following Few's style, I asked a simple question:

Which player had the fifth most RBIs?

Given the design of this chart, particularly with its alphabetical sort order, finding the fifth-highest player takes too long. When visualizing data, I wanted to aim for simplicity and make it easy for my audience to understand the data. With that in mind, I created the simple bar chart in Figure I.2 as my first makeover.

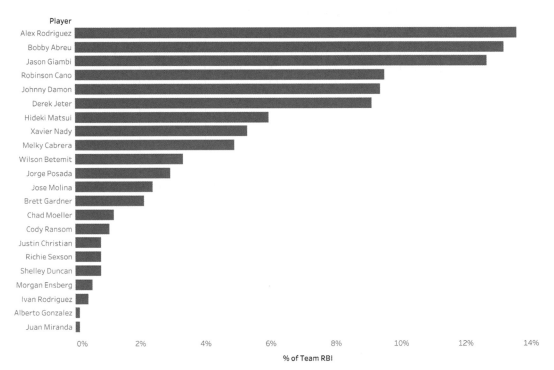

**FIGURE I.2** A bar chart is much better for representing the ranking of the players.

I explained how displaying the data as a bar chart, sorted by the team RBI percentage from highest to lowest, makes answering the same question much easier. All the reader needs to do is scan down to the fifth bar and see that Johnny Damon had the fifth most RBIs for the Yankees in 2008.

The core principle I was following was to make the charts as simple as possible, as quickly as possible, often timeboxing the makeovers to 60 minutes. Giving myself an hour to create a better, more effective chart for a specific topic forced me to make quick design decisions and to be satisfied with charts that were not "perfect" when it came to advanced design.

## The Community Project

Six years and hundreds of makeovers later, my friend Emily Kund noticed that nearly all of the makeovers that I had been posting were on Mondays. Emily is a huge fan of alliterations and suggested that I start calling the weekly series "Makeover Monday." On 28 April 2014, Makeover Monday officially became a project, even though it was still a one-man show.

### The Andys: Makeover Monday 2016

I continued creating these makeovers week after week until November 2015, when Andy Cotgreave, Technical Evangelist at Tableau and author of *The Big Book of Dashboards*, reached out and asked if he could join me each week. Andy C found that, although he was a Tableau employee, he was not exploring data as much as he used to. He committed to do every weekly makeover with me throughout 2016.

Here is how it worked. I posted a data set every week and Andy and I would each visualize the data and post it on our blogs (Andy C's is at gravyanecdote.com). We followed the three-part review format that I had been using:

1.  What works with the original chart?

2.  What could be improved?

3.  What did we do to make it better?

This format helped with consistency, conciseness, and focus. It also helped us each understand the thought process of the other. Andy Cotgreave then had the idea to open it up to the "Tableau Community" by setting up a website (makeovermonday.co.uk), posting the data sets there each week, along with a link to the original visualization to make over, then sharing the details on Twitter (Figure I.3).

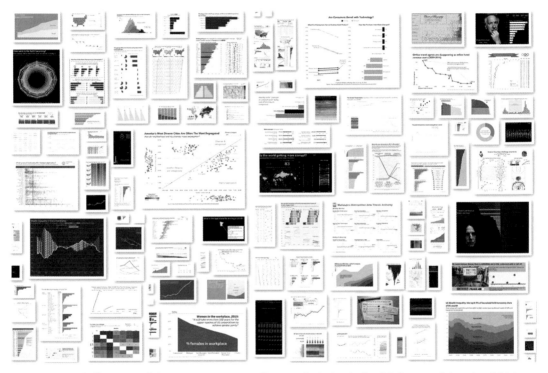

**FIGURE I.3**   Collection of the images created by Andy & Andy for Makeover Monday 2016.

And so, 3239 visualizations and 519 contributors later, year one of Makeover Monday was a huge success.

I could not believe it! How did my little way of learning each week go from just me to hundreds of people in a single year? I love how inspired everyone was, how willing they've been to help each other with their eagerness to learn and improve week after week.

So, what did Andy C think?

I was blown away. Andy K and I thought we might just be producing charts and nothing would happen, but within weeks we
were seeing a bunch of people getting involved each week. As
the year developed, more and more people got involved. The
talent, passion, and dedication of the community was the most
rewarding and surprising aspect of 2016.

To say we were blown away by the participation is a massive under-
statement. I actually saved every single visualization created to a
Pinterest board. As the project grew, this became a bigger and
bigger task. Just to keep track of "pinned" and "to be pinned"
visualizations, I had to develop my own system of "liking" Tweets
and saving to Pinterest as each week progressed.

By the end of 2016, 11 people had completed all 52 weeks: me,
Andy C, Adam Crahen, Charlie Hutcheson, Michael Mixon, Neil
Richards, Paul Rau, Pooja Gandhi, Rob Radburn, Shawn Levin, and
Simona Loffredo (Figure I.4).

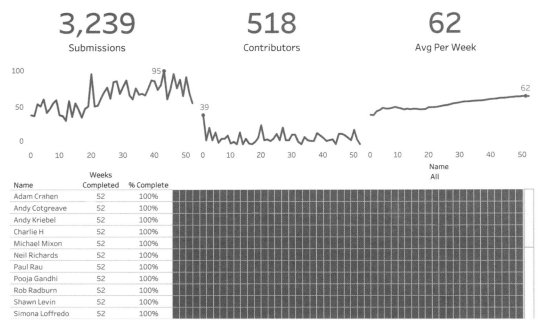

**FIGURE I.4**   Summary of Makeover Monday 2016 with the 100% club.

While this is an amazing effort, I must admit that my favorite participant in the project was 8-year-old Joe Radburn. Joe completed 27 of 52 weeks alongside his dad, Rob. If anyone is set up for a great future in data analysis and visualization, it is Joe. As of this writing, Joe has a portfolio of 38 visualizations.

## The Murray/Cotgreave Swap: Makeover Monday 2017

As Makeover Monday 2016 was winding down, Andy C's year of involvement was coming to an end, so on 23 December 2016, I asked Eva Murray to join me on the project.

Having known Eva for a few years, I was well aware of her passion for Tableau and data visualization. We had a great rapport and, thankfully, she agreed to join me and brought along lots of new ideas and energy. This was the beginning of a great partnership that would see Makeover Monday grow even more in 2017.

How did Eva transition into the world of data? Here is a short description of how she realized that data and data visualization were the things she wanted to focus on in her career:

> I started using Tableau in 2013 and had been fascinated by data visualization since my university years when I studied visual perception in psychology. Working with data, however, was something that remained limited to my day job until my first Tableau Conference in 2015. Suddenly I realized that data, visual analysis, and communicating information were topics I wanted to explore further, and I discovered a passion I shared with countless other data enthusiasts around the globe.

> Very soon after my first few times of "playing with data" in Tableau, I realized that I wanted to make data the focus of my career and I never looked back. Today I am fortunate to be surrounded by colleagues, friends, and an ever-growing community of people who help organizations improve how they use data, share their knowledge freely, and improve how information is communicated.

The project changed a bit in 2017 because I was no longer to be the sole creator of the data sets: Eva and I agreed to alternate weeks (Figure I.5). Some of the ideas Eva brought to the project included the following.

**FIGURE I.5**   Collection of the images created by Andy & Eva for Makeover Monday 2017.

*Weekly Summaries*

Eva suggested that whoever was responsible for a particular week's topic and data set should write a recap of how the week went and pick a few favorites. After settling into a rhythm, these weekly blog posts included lessons learned (which serve as the foundation for this book) and a list of favorites. There was no limit to the number of lessons learned; whatever we saw that required calling out, both good and bad, was summarized and examples provided. This has given the community another way to learn, supported by great examples from the community.

*Makeover Monday Live*

Eva and I hosted live sessions around the world to introduce Makeover Monday to as many people as possible. The on-tour events proved extremely popular and culminated at the Tableau Conference in Las Vegas with more than 500 attendees in the room and 200+ having to be turned away because there was no more space to seat them. Five hundred people came just to visualize data (Figure I.6)—amazing!

**FIGURE I.6**   500 people attended Makeover Monday Live at Tableau Conference 2017.

During live sessions, we introduce Makeover Monday, show the chart to make over, provide access to the data, give the attendees an hour to visualize the data, and ask a few people to present their work.

*Viz Review*

Ultimately, we want everyone who participates in Makeover Monday to focus on their learning. Often people ask for feedback about their visualizations. However, given the hundreds of visualizations that are created each week, Twitter became an inefficient and very time-consuming channel for giving feedback to lots of people.

After running a number of data visualization webinars for BrightTALK, Eva was able to secure a dedicated channel for Makeover Monday. Now that we had a platform for sharing, Eva suggested that we run a weekly webinar called "Makeover Monday Viz Review" in which people could submit their visualizations for a live review by us.

These have proven very popular and it has been a fantastic way for people to improve their skills. Given the feedback provided, participants would make some changes, post their updates, and learn along the way.

For us it has been a very effective and enjoyable way to review visualizations, because instead of trying to provide constructive and comprehensive feedback in a 280-character tweet, we can now spend a couple of minutes on each submission. This allows us to give better feedback and personally address each participant. Those joining the webinar live can also ask questions, resulting in better interactions between us and the community.

*The Community*

To recognize the major contributors to Makeover Monday, we created a community page on the website, highlighting 22 blogs written by the community for the community. These people do amazing work and give their time freely, and their efforts deserve to be recognized.

Makeover Monday changes people's professional lives. By participating week after week, you create an impressive portfolio of different types of visualizations and demonstrate progression, and this can serve as your CV. It is becoming more and more important to potential employers to see what you have done rather than where you went to school. Nothing has made us prouder than the 19 people who've told us how Makeover Monday has helped them find a new job. But really, we merely provided the platform and structure around it; they still had to do the work.

Tableau Zen Masters are "teachers, masters, and collaborators," and the 2018 class of Tableau Zen Masters is filled with people who participate in Makeover Monday nearly every week. Makeover Monday helps them master Tableau, collaborate with the community, and teach other their techniques through blog posts.

The 2018 Tableau Iron Viz Europe finalists are all regular Makeover Monday participants who acknowledged the contribution this project has made in shaping their skills, style, and progression as data analysts over the past few years.

## The Next Phase: Makeover Monday 2018

Going into 2018, there were so many participants and it was taking so much of our time that optimization and simplification were critical to the project's continued success. Some of these key changes included:

1. Partnering with data.world to host the data sets and discussions. This social data platform allows more people to access the data and, most importantly, allows for much richer discussions because discussion forums are structured to be user-friendly and do not come with a 280-character limit.

2. Makeover Monday Enterprise Edition: This involves working with organizations to run their own internal weekly Makeover Monday Live sessions for their people. The key benefit here is to allow people to work with data that they do not use day to day and to free up their creativity. Inevitably, this will make them better analysts, thus providing benefits to both the individual and the organization.

3. Up to 2018, Makeover Monday was primarily a Tableau project. However, there is no reason other tools should not be used and we encourage analysts with any tool to join us. The benefits for them are the same, irrespective of the software they use. This is another area where working with data.world has helped us, because their platform makes access for any tool simple and easy.

For me, these changes were essential if I wanted to keep working on this project and still enjoy it. I was bordering on burnout from putting so many hours into it on top of my day job. I had weeks when I was frustrated, uninterested, uninspired, and, frankly, just did not feel like creating a chart. But I knew I was helping so many people by continuing the project and being consistent in the work I put into it. Helping people is what gets me up in the morning. Seeing people grow inspires me and helps reenergize me.

I think there is so much more we can do to help change the way people look at data. I know there is a ton of growth I can do myself. I want to help people become more data literate. I want to change people's lives by helping them develop the skills that can land them their dream job. And I want what I have learned to permeate through the next several generations of great data analysts.

How did Eva feel about the changes and updates we made in 2018?

When 2018 started I felt the pressure (from myself) to continue innovating in the project and driving additional changes and improvements. With this book and a number of other ideas, I knew I was not going to get bored anytime soon, and equally there was the thought of whether I had taken on a bit too much.

On the days when I do not have the time or motivation to create a visualization, I still do it and focus on a simple, clear message that requires a small amount of effort. When executed well, it is perfectly acceptable and not every week's submission needs to be elaborate in its analysis and/or design. Reminding myself of the messages I can send to the community through my work and consistency helps get me through those weeks when my own participation is more challenging.

Like Andy, I truly enjoy helping people, particularly helping them to get better at what they are already doing and fine-tuning their skills in a way that takes them to the next level in their careers. I see myself as an enabler and Makeover Monday has been a great platform to enable learning and growth for our community.

The growth of the project itself has reached the point where any changes we make need to be well thought through to ensure they make things easier for the community and for us in running the project.

## Pillars of Makeover Monday

After reading about the history of Makeover Monday, you now understand that it started out as a small and personal exercise by Andy to improve his skills and grew from there into the most popular social data project in the world. The people who participate come from a variety of professional and academic backgrounds and use different tools and techniques to analyze and visualize the data.

Participation can be beneficial in many ways that go beyond simply creating a more effective chart. Makeover Monday helps people learn technical skills, improve their data literacy, build a portfolio of their work, and interact with a professional network, and gives them opportunities to demonstrate leadership. By participating, we are confident that you, our new and existing community members, can grow your professional capabilities as analysts, data scientists, designers, and storytellers.

### Developing Technical Skills

The people who participate regularly tell us that they have gained a lot of technical skills by practicing data visualization and analysis on a regular basis. For Makeover Monday, we publish different data every week, giving the community an unfamiliar data set to work with.

Publishing your work on forums and social media will push you to seek out learning opportunities. It becomes apparent very quickly when someone learns and grows, and when they improve their skills week after week. It has been a privilege for us to watch people develop their skills over time.

Someone who developed quickly and built strong data visualization and analysis skills is Sarah Bartlett, who started participating in Makeover Monday in 2016. Figures I.7 and I.8 show her early

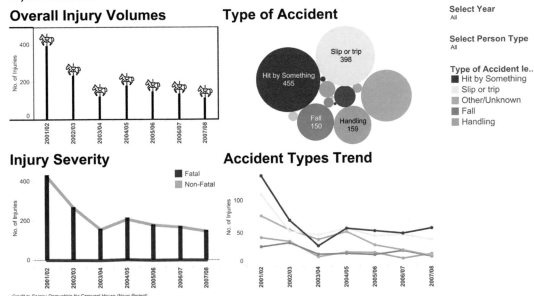

FIGURE I.7   Example of Sarah Bartlett's early work.

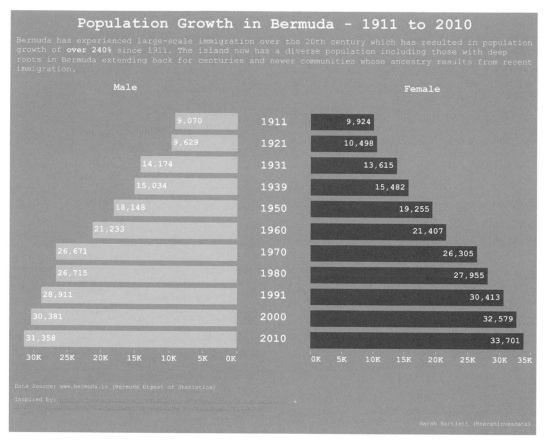

**FIGURE I.8** Example of Sarah Bartlett's early work.

work, followed by more recent visualizations she created, as seen in Figures I.9 and I.10.

Many participants set themselves a time limit and commit to being done by a certain date. Time constraints, consistency, and commitment to regular practice are great for improving your skills. Your chances of success increase exponentially when you make a habit of regularly working on the things you enjoy and want to improve upon. Simon Beaumont, NHS Head of Information at Southern Health, says:

# Eradicating Malaria in Southern Province, Zambia

Malaria is both preventable and treatable but it is a complicated disease whose prevention and control requires multiple interventions. Zambia has made strides in malaria prevention and control in the last few years. However, it still kills more children under the age of five than any other disease or illness. Malaria affects more than 4 million Zambians annually, accounting for approximately 30 percent of outpatient visits and resulting in almost **8,000 deaths** each year.

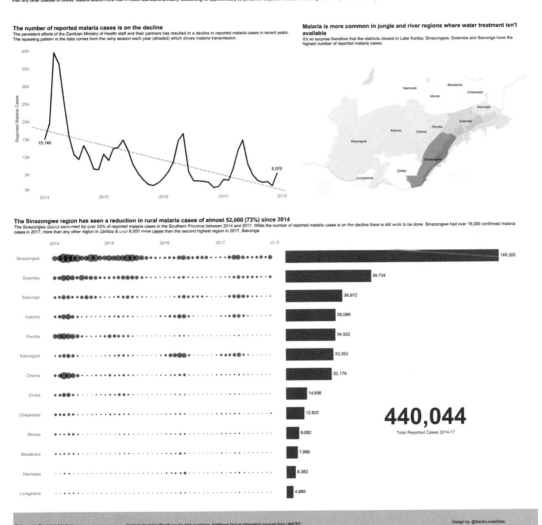

**The number of reported malaria cases is on the decline**
The persistent efforts of the Zambian Ministry of Health staff and their partners has resulted in a decline in reported malaria cases in recent years. The repeating pattern in the data comes from the rainy season each year (shaded) which drives malaria transmission.

**Malaria is more common in jungle and river regions where water treatment isn't available**
It's no surprise therefore that the districts closest to Lake Kariba; Sinazongwe, Gwembe and Siavonga have the highest number of reported malaria cases.

**The Sinazongwe region has seen a reduction in rural malaria cases of almost 52,000 (73%) since 2014**
The Sinazongwe district accounted for over 33% of reported malaria cases in the Southern Province between 2014 and 2017. While the number of reported malaria cases is on the decline there is still work to be done. Sinazongwe had over 18,000 confirmed malaria cases in 2017, more than any other region in Zambia & over 8,000 more cases than the second highest region in 2017, Siavonga.

**440,044**
Total Reported Cases 2014-17

Data source: Simulated data from _____. Contact jdrummey@path.org for data questions. Additional factual information sourced from UNICEF.

Design by: @SarahLovesData

**FIGURE I.9** Example of Sarah Bartlett's more recent work.

## Forget Vodka, Eastern Europeans are increasingly turning to Whiskey as their tipple of choice

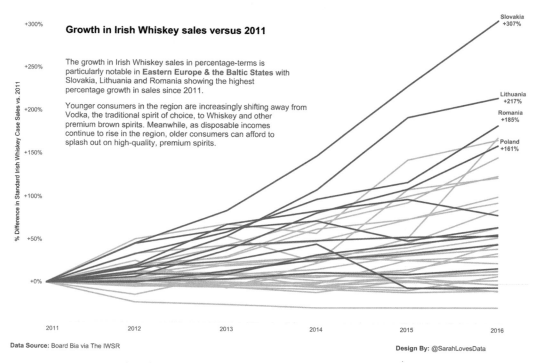

**FIGURE I.10**   Example of Sarah Bartlett's more recent work.

Continuous learning and improvement is at the heart of our Southern Health Tableau Centre of Excellence. Makeover Monday provides a safe, nonjudgmental environment within which our analysts can identify visualisation best practice and to explore new techniques and approaches. We actively encourage our analysts to participate in Makeover Monday on a weekly basis; by doing so not only has our technical knowledge and expertise expanded but our professional networks have also increased, providing our analysts with a source of constant inspiration and guidance.

Those who gain the most from this project participate every week, seek feedback and iterate, keep an open mind, and are receptive to different ideas. Not every week has to be a giant leap forward;

simply focusing on a certain aspect of data analysis and visualization that you would like to improve is a good way to make significant progress over time. One week you may focus on trying a new technique, then your focus shifts to becoming a better designer or storyteller. The week after you could take a minimalist approach and remove as much as possible from the visualization without changing the story.

Take the skills you develop in Makeover Monday back to your day job and improve the way information is communicated in your own organization.

Kai-Ming Cheah, Senior Manager for Visualisation & Analytics at Westpac Group in Sydney, Australia, states:

> Our team host a regular Makeover Monday session as part of our operating rhythm and invite Tableau Desktops users across the group to join. It's a fantastic opportunity to meet new people, learn something new not only about Tableau but interesting topics too. It takes practice, practice and more practice to be good at something; data visualisation is no different.

## Building a Data Visualization Portfolio

As the proliferation of data increases, so does the demand for people with the skills to analyze it. It is an exciting time to be an analyst, filled with options and opportunities. Companies seeking to discover more about their customers, suppliers, and partners have a need for talented, skilled people who can analyze data and effectively communicate the insights.

While it is critical that you continue to improve your technical skills, it is also important to showcase your work. Those looking for skilled people to join their team need to see what you are capable of, how strong your analysis skills are, and how your data visualization skills have developed. Creating a data visualization portfolio allows potential employers to understand your ability to communicate information and insights clearly and succinctly and how well you design your data visualizations.

This portfolio, with some of the work Eva created for Makeover Monday (Figure I.11), gives people an overview of the different topics and designs and the ability to explore them further. Embedding the visualizations in her blog and linking them means people can find more information about the approach to each makeover.

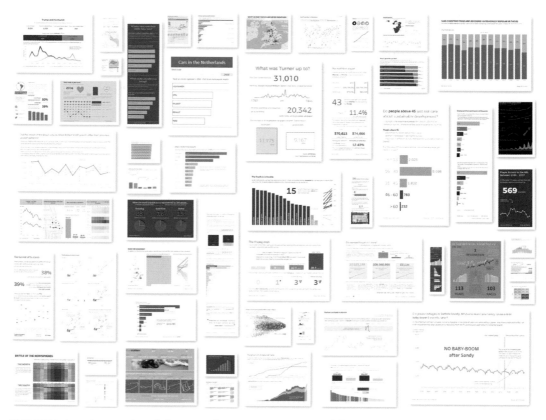

**FIGURE I.11**   A sample of the visualizations Eva created for Makeover Monday 2017.

Good written communication skills are essential as well. Consider writing a blog where you share your data analysis experiences. You can write about things like:

- Step-by-step instructions for reproducing your work
- Different concepts and challenges of data analysis

- Limitations of existing charts that you have improved on through Makeover Monday
- New techniques you have tried

Writing and communication skills are essential for a successful career as an analyst. By blogging, you will get regular practice and you will improve how you communicate your messages. A blog can help you teach others and lets you also provide a bigger context for your analytical work. No one will benefit more from blogging than you will. It is very rewarding to look back and realize how much content you have created and how much you have learned through that experience.

Josh Tapley, Director of Data Visualization at Comcast, sums up the value of developing a portfolio best:

> For most people, Makeover Monday is a tremendous opportunity to practice data visualization and get free coaching from some of the sharpest minds in the industry. For hiring managers like myself, it gives us the ability to see how someone has progressed their skills over a short period of time, how they can react and respond to new data on a tight deadline, and insight into their overall creativity. At this point, I've hired half of our data visualization team based on portfolios built off of Makeover Monday exercises.

We have already outlined the benefits of regular analysis and visualization practice through Makeover Monday and a blog can be developed in the same way. As with any new habit, it is important to commit to a certain cadence in order to create content regularly and build up momentum. Consider blogging about Makeover Monday. Discuss the things that work well and those that could be improved in the original visualization. Follow that with an overview of your own approach and wrap up the blog post with your visualization. This format instills consistency and practice and provides regular content for your audience. If you were to write regularly about your Makeover Monday visualizations, you could end up with 52 blog articles every year.

In addition to writing about Makeover Monday, Andy writes articles focusing on data visualization techniques and showcases outstanding data visualizations created by other authors. Eva writes personal articles about professional development, career advice, travel, triathlon, and racing. There are plenty of directions you can take your blog. As you become more experienced and have a weekly rhythm established, you may want to challenge yourself to add other topics to your blog. This keeps you challenged and motivated, and helps you continue to improve your communication skills.

For further inspiration on data visualization portfolios and blogging, have a look at Part III, "The Community," where we showcase the outstanding efforts by some of Makeover Monday's key contributors.

## Learning and Inspiration

Beyond the personal benefits of participating in Makeover Monday, there is the opportunity to inspire others through your work. Much like when you were a beginner, there are those who are just getting started and your work may help them in their journey in data visualization.

Every week, we receive hundreds of visualizations of the same data set and each submission is unique. While every participant creates their own submission, they get to see countless other approaches for the same data. Some take a different analytical angle; others create a different design or come up with quirky stories. Quite often we see techniques that many had not previously considered. Each week the project becomes a source of inspiration for the entire community.

Not everyone who participates in Makeover Monday has access to the tools, learning resources, and technical courses they need to build their skills. Makeover Monday helps these people by:

1. Making data easy to access
2. Providing guidance

3. Recapping each week with a summary blog detailing lessons learned

4. Hosting free live events

5. Networking and learning from each other

6. Helping others grow and develop

Makeover Monday is a great starting point and catalyst for your career if you take full advantage of the resources provided. Equally, if you simply like to practice data visualization and storytelling, you can utilize the project for that purpose.

## Networking

Makeover Monday is a global community. Some of us travel frequently for business, giving us opportunities to interact with like-minded professionals. Others may not have the opportunity to travel for personal or business reasons, but this does not mean they are not interested in opportunities to connect with others, to exchange ideas, and to meet personally.

To promote networking among community members, we have hosted over 20 live events since the beginning of 2017 in cities around Europe and in selected locations in the US and Australia. The community's reception of these events is a testament to their passion and motivation for continuous learning and their desire to meet those with whom they have previously connected only online.

Everyone at these live events is seeking to get better at data visualization. They are united by this common goal and shared interest. Some people get to meet those who have inspired them, have the chance to ask them questions in person, and thank them for their inspiration.

At the live events, the main session is a 60-minute exercise to visualize the data set of that particular week. The result is organized chaos, conversations among people at each table as they tackle the data together, and a frantic last 10 minutes as attendees scramble to finish their work. We want people to do more than visualize a data set at these events, though. Both of us enjoy nudging or pushing people outside their comfort zone because that is where they will experience the biggest growth.

Following the 60-minute exercise, we ask people to volunteer to present their work to the rest of the group. At some events the setting is very small and personal and presenting your visualization to a couple dozen people does not seem so scary. We did, however, have a very large event in Las Vegas at the 2017 Tableau Conference where the room was filled with over 500 people. Presenting to an audience of that size makes most people feel rather uncomfortable and intimidated, yet we still had half a dozen participants come up to the stage and present their work.

During these presentations, it does not matter whether a visualization is finished and polished. What makes the presentation exercise helpful is that it gives people an opportunity to publicly show their work, explain their approach, talk through the challenges, and, most importantly, to practice talking in front of a large audience.

When giving a live demo, keep in mind the following:

- Take a few moments before your presentation to calm your nerves with a breathing exercise if you feel anxious.
- Slow down your pace so your audience can follow along on the screen, taking conscious breaks between talking points can help you with this.
- Choose deliberate actions for every talking point and become familiar with the order in which you are presenting them.
- Reduce the complexity of what you are showing to improve the audience's understanding.

People who come to these events go away with a new level of confidence in their work and in their abilities as analysts, as well as a drive to participate and to challenge themselves more. Because of the shared interest in Makeover Monday, starting a conversation at these live events is easy. People typically sit in groups around tables and very quickly start building connections and talking about data and visualization.

We are committed to enabling our community to host live events as well. These events do not depend on our physical presence and can easily be created at a local level by someone taking on that responsibility. In Part III we will outline our recipe for success when it comes to creating, hosting, and running live Makeover Monday events, whether they are open for anyone to join locally or as part of continuous learning and development programs within organizations.

## Demonstrating Leadership

Week after week, the Makeover Monday community grows, and new people join the project. New participants mean there is a need for more support from us to get them started. While we make every effort to provide resources for people so they can help themselves, there are always questions. More and more we need to rely on other community members to help us provide feedback.

We are grateful for the leadership qualities of our more experienced participants, who patiently guide newcomers, answer questions, provide constructive feedback, and point people to helpful resources. These people form the backbone of Makeover Monday, contributing every week, and creating great examples of analysis, visualization, and storytelling. The guidance and support provided by these community leaders are crucial to keeping Makeover Monday on a path of success and growth.

What started off as Andy's personal project to practice data visualization has become a platform for hundreds of people to become better analysts, tell impactful data stories, improve data literacy, and find opportunities to change their careers and guide others to do the same.

## Making an Impact

Finally, Makeover Monday has provided a channel for making an impact in the wider community through collaborations with humanitarian causes. While most weeks focus on data sets and visualizations that are in need of a makeover, in 2017 we started collaborations for special causes.

The first collaboration was with Viz for Social Good, a project run by Chloe Tseng and the Inter-American Development Bank (IADB) to highlight challenges of young Latin American people in the job market. While Makeover Monday has a weekly cadence and focuses on telling better data stories for a specific data set, Viz for Social Good connects nonprofits and charities with data analysts and visualization experts to highlight societal issues and challenges. In this project, Makeover Monday was able to provide a forum for participants using the data from the IADB to highlight issues in youth unemployment.

We were immensely impressed and encouraged by the enthusiasm of the wider community and enjoyed introducing our community to Viz for Social Good, helping Chloe to broaden her network of contributors for future causes.

Makeover Monday and Viz for Social Good also collaborated on a project for the United Nations Sustainable Development Goals (SDG) Action Campaign. The efforts by our joint communities impressed the team at the UN and they displayed a number of visualizations prominently at an exhibition during the UN General Assembly in New York in September 2017.

Seeing the community embrace these collaboration efforts has been very encouraging and made us more comfortable with introducing data sets with more challenging topics. In order to avoid material that had the potential to divide opinions and challenge people's fundamental beliefs, we had initially used data sets that were interesting but not necessarily controversial.

Before the collaborations, topics such as the water footprint of the standard Western diet, or meat consumption in the US, might have felt like we were leaning out the window a bit too far. However, we have been encouraged by the professional approach people have taken to these topics, visualizing data sets that made people rethink their daily behaviors and unsettle their assumptions.

We saw several great examples of visualizations with actionable insights and calls to action that went beyond simply being informed. These visualizations would present a clear opportunity for people to make a change to their behaviors, resulting in a lower impact on their environment. We can use our platform to share impactful work and to bring awareness to a larger number of people.

Collaborations with social and humanitarian causes are a way for participants to see that their work is not just about building a visualization and improving the original chart. The collaborations help people learn how to:

- Effectively communicate analysis
- Create user-centric designs
- Practice thoughtful storytelling

Combined, these can result in a contribution to our society that can change people's minds, raise their awareness and open their hearts to issues and causes that urgently need to be addressed.

## How to Use this book

We have divided this book into 12 chapters. Much like the weekly recaps, the chapters are broadly aligned to two main categories:

1. Analysis
2. Design and storytelling

If you are new to data visualization, we recommend that you read the book cover to cover in order to take in the fundamentals that we have learned and helped others learn by running this project. This will give you enough breadth across concepts and depth for each topic to apply to your own work, enabling you to become a better data analyst.

If you have some experience with data visualization and data analysis, you can use the book as a reference guide by identifying the chapters that are most relevant to your needs and reading those sections. We expect that most people will gravitate to using the book in this manner and will refer to specific lessons as they encounter similar problems in their day-to-day work.

In this book we may use the terms "data visualization," "dashboard," and "data story" interchangeably to describe the work created. In this book:

- Data visualization relates to individual charts as well as a larger layout, including multiple charts, such as an infographic.
- Dashboards are not just typical business dashboards displaying key performance indicators. They can include an arrangement of charts, filters, parameters, and more that result in an overall visualization.
- Data stories are visualizations where each element is connected to the others through text, annotations, and visual connectors such as lines or arrows, and where an overall flow from start to finish has been created by the author.

With these broad descriptions in mind, the focus of this book is not on whether something is a dashboard, a visualization, or a data story, but rather how you can most effectively communicate information through the format you have chosen for your data visualization.

We hope you enjoy the book, learn from it, and become the best data analyst you can be. Remember, though, becoming great does not happen overnight; if you want to be great, you need patience, dedication and practice—a lot of practice! Makeover Monday provides a platform for you to go from good to great.

If you have any questions, you can reach us on Twitter at @VizWizBI (Andy Kriebel), @TriMyData (Eva Murray), or by email at info@makeovermonday.co.uk.

# Part II

## Chapter One

# Habits of a Good Data Analyst

By working with different data sets each week, Makeover Monday is a unique opportunity for participants to develop analytical skills that can be used in real life. Working with constantly changing topics, data sizes, and data complexity forces you to be considerate and deliberate about your analysis and helps you develop the skills to make you better at your job. This chapter covers the common characteristics of the best data analysis we have seen in Makeover Monday.

## Approaching Unfamiliar Data

Over the course of 52 weeks, you will find 52 completely different data sets. It is almost impossible to have the knowledge to understand all 52 topics immediately. When faced with this situation, you need to have tools in your arsenal to help you overcome this deficit quickly.

While Makeover Monday is a great opportunity to practice data visualization and data analysis, it is also a chance to simulate real-life business scenarios. When specific requirements or guidelines are provided, considering those requirements for your makeover is a good idea. Think about it this way: if you are given specific requirements at work or specific questions that need to be answered as part of your analysis, will you ignore them? If you do, what will happen? I bet the outcome will not be in your favor. So why not treat Makeover Monday the same way and practice real-life business scenarios with a different data set every week?

In the corporate world, when you kick off any kind of dashboard project, you should engage with stakeholders, meet with the people who will be using it, the people who own and/or govern the data, and others to get the full picture before you start analyzing and visualizing the data.

When it comes to producing something of value for your (internal or external) customer, ask yourself:

- What does the customer need?
- What do they want to know?
- Are there specific guidelines when it comes to style?
- How can I give them more than they asked for? Are there additional insights in the data of which they may not be aware?
- How do I communicate with my customer? Do I need to confirm any additional information before presenting my work?

Occasionally we provide specific requirements for a data set to give our community an opportunity to practice the above approach. When we do, consider treating it just like a work project. You are allowed to explore the data and find your own insights, while considering the requirements provided.

A good data analyst can identify and understand the requirements. A great data analyst will ask questions when they do not clearly understand. It can be difficult to ask questions in a virtual environment like Makeover Monday, but the advantage is that Makeover Monday provides a safe space to ask lots of questions. If you take what you have learned, you will feel more comfortable asking questions when working with stakeholders in your company and it will become much easier.

## Identify the Challenges

A good place to start when working with unfamiliar data is to identify the challenges you are facing. When we say identify, we literally mean writing the challenges down. Nearly every chart you see will be embedded within an article or story of some sort. Read the article. It is likely to have a lot of information that will give you enough context to get started.

Once you have read the article, write down the keywords, write down the definitions, and identify any acronyms and what they mean. This list can go on and on. The more challenges you identify, the less of a struggle it will be to work with unfamiliar data.

For example, we used a data set for the NCAA basketball tournament. Eva did not know what the scores meant or how the tournament was structured, so she researched it. Eva looked at regional clusters, different seeds, rounds, and trends, and she created time series charts, bar charts, scatter plots, heat maps, highlight tables, box and whisker plots, and bump charts. You name it, she tried them all. She looked at winning margins, upsets, and number of wins by team, and continued her analysis until she found something that (i) made sense to her, (ii) she could explain to someone else who does not know basketball, and (iii) was simple. The result was the simple timeline visualization in Figure 1.1.

## Gain Insights from Metadata

When creating a data visualization, we are often tempted to begin exploring the data immediately rather than focusing on doing analysis first. It is beneficial to first get familiar with the data itself. Use the following questions as a guide to becoming familiar with the data.

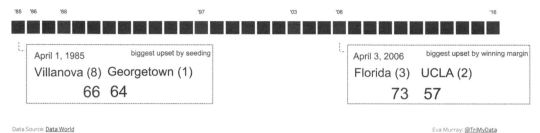

FIGURE 1.1    Upsets in the NCAA basketball tournament championship game.

### What Data Types Are in the Data set?

Data types include numeric values, date fields, text fields, Boolean fields, spatial objects, and so on. Knowing the data types before starting your analysis helps you during the analytical process. If a field is translated as text that should be numeric, now is the time to change it. If there are specific default aggregations (for example, one of your metrics should always be calculated as an average), set these up as default. Give fields more understandable names, so they are clearer and easier to work with.

### What Range of Values Do the Fields Contain?

A text field containing product categories may hold less than a dozen different values, while a field of individual product names may include hundreds or thousands of different values. Understanding the possible values or range for each field helps you get a better feel for the data. Become familiar with the data by sampling the first few rows of the data set.

### Is the Data Complete?

Identifying missing or incomplete data is critical for accurate analysis. For example, when working with dates, first check the range of dates, then look for any missing dates. Comparing years, quarters, or months is challenging and could be inaccurate if some dates are missing.

With geographical data, check for missing locations. For example, if you have state-level data for the United States, check to see if all states are accounted for in the data. If there are some missing, verify whether that is to be expected or if there is a problem. Decide what to do if there is indeed a problem. Make certain you understand the impact of proceeding with incomplete data. If the data set should have data for every state and you do not notice it, then you could make assumptions about aggregations at the region or country level that are incorrect.

## Explore the Data

Once you have some context, begin exploring the data. What do the field names mean? How much variety do the fields have? Is there a data hierarchy? What happens when I compare data across fields? Does one field affect another?

These are all very simple questions to ask and even simpler to answer. Explore the data by building lots and lots of charts. Remember, you are ultimately a data analyst. A good data analyst needs to be able to explore the data to find a story or an insight.

In Figure 1.2, Daniel Caroli chose to compare one field to another. He saw distributions in the data and thought to compare ages across years. Daniel used *all* of the data and included a box plot as a summary to help give context. He made it easier to understand by including some simple text. This is a great example of making the complex simple when working with unfamiliar data.

Once you have a grasp on the fields, focus on the metrics. How varied are they? Is there a wide or narrow distribution? What do the metrics mean? What is the proper way to aggregate the data? Can the data even be aggregated? Are there relationships between the metrics?

One trap people fell into with data about the top 500 YouTube gaming channels was to confuse YouTube *views* with YouTube *videos*. Views and videos are *not* the same thing. One video can be viewed many times, yet some people used views and videos interchangeably. This is a clear sign that the data analyst did not take the time

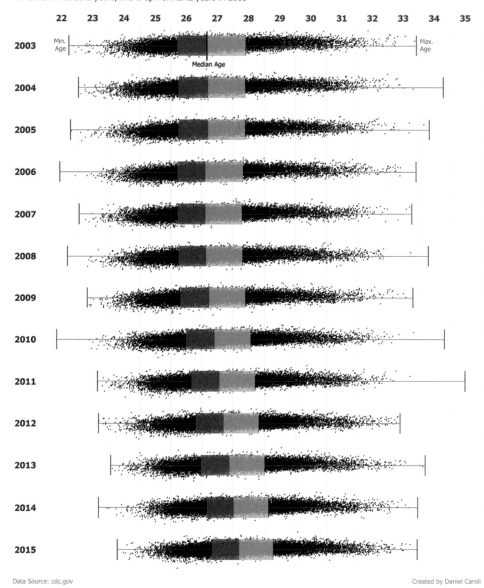

**FIGURE 1.2**   Median age of mothers in the United States when giving birth.

to *understand* the data. Understanding the data is fundamental to ensuring your analysis is correct.

In his visualization (Figure 1.3), Marc Soares demonstrated how to compare metrics effectively, how to research a topic to provide sufficient context, and how to explain the topic to his audience.

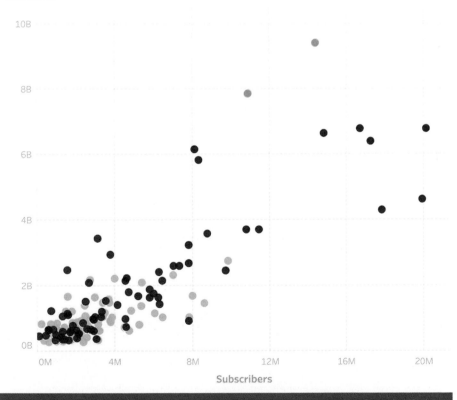

**The Most Influential YouTube Gaming Channels**

The Social Blade rating system aims to measure a channel's influence based on a variety of metrics, including video views and subscribers.

YouTube channels with a rating of **A+**, **A**, or **A-** are considered very influential.

**Total Subscribers and Video Views of channels rated A- or higher by Social Blade**

Video Views

Created by Marc Soares (@soarmarc)                    Source: SocialBlade.com

**FIGURE 1.3**  Scatterplot of YouTube views vs. channel subscribers.

If you want to be great at data analysis, you have to practice, you have to be able to explore and understand the data to find insights, and you have to communicate your findings well.

Charlie Hutcheson has created over 100 Makeover Monday visualizations and through this practice has developed excellent analytical skills. He demonstrated this particularly well when visualizing life expectancy data (Figure 1.4). He explored the data, found some

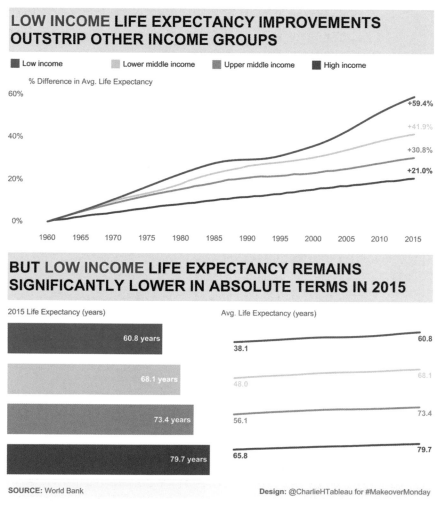

**FIGURE 1.4**   Analysis of life expectancy for different income levels.

insights, then used his data visualization and storytelling skills to communicate his findings succinctly, clearly, and simply.

Now that you have taken the time to read the article for context and explored the fields and metrics to gain more understanding, it is time to think about how to most effectively simplify the data.

### Remove Unnecessary Fields

Consider a wide data set, that is, a data set that has a lot of fields and metrics. After you have taken the time to understand which data is important, remove all of the fields you do not need.

The data set about Chicago taxi trips was both wide (19 columns) and tall (105 million rows). It is very unlikely that you will need all 19 columns and all 105M rows. Pooja Gandhi limited the data set to only three fields and four metrics, yet she was able to create a stunning visualization that shows the when and where of Chicago taxi trips, as can be seen in Figure 1.5.

### Focus on a Subset of the Data

Closely related to eliminating the fields you do not need is reducing the complexity of the data through filtering or limiting the data set. For example, in week 16 of 2017, we challenged everyone to visualize 784 million records of UK medical prescriptions. There is no good way to visualize this much data in a single chart, so to create an effective design you are almost forced to focus on a subset of the data. In Figure 1.6, Adam Crahen focused his analysis on a single drug compared to other drugs, with the number of prescriptions aggregated up to the monthly level.

Through the use of highlighting, Adam intentionally guides his audience to the data the analysis is about. He uses color in his title to clarify what the line represents, reducing clutter by eliminating the need for a legend. Ultimately, the highlighting helps provide focus.

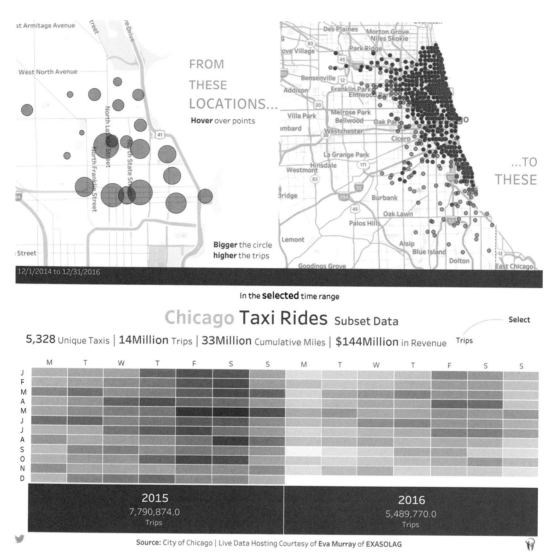

FIGURE 1.5   Visualization of Chicago taxi trips by Pooja Gandhi.

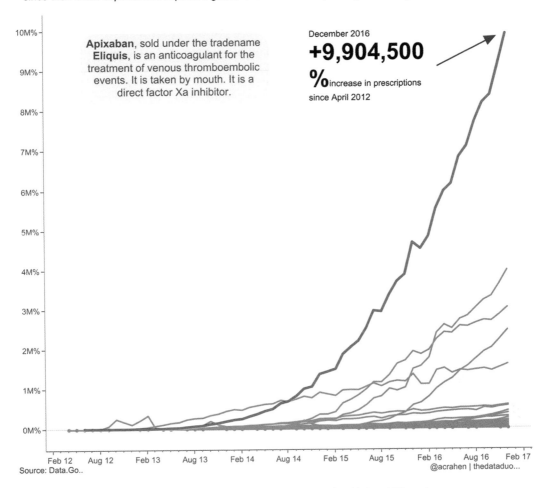

**FIGURE 1.6**   The growth of Apixaban prescriptions in the United Kingdom.

The idea with highlighting is to move the focus to one particular field while keeping all others in scope but moving them to the background. Sean Miller used highlighting to effectively allow his audience to pick one state's income distribution and compare that state to all others, as seen in Figure 1.7. Essentially Sean is viewing a subset of the data to create simplicity.

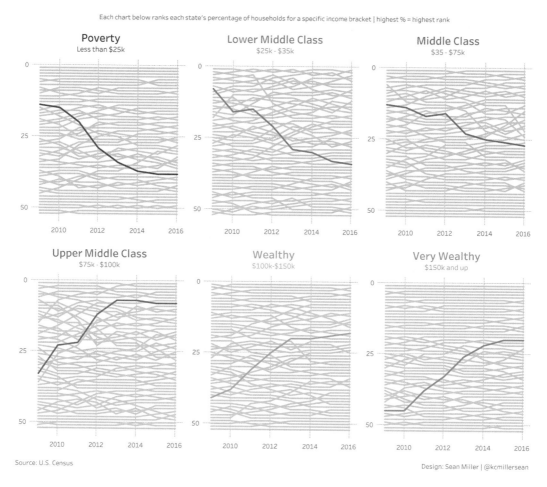

**Where does North Dakota rank in each income bracket over time?**

Highlight a State
North Dakota

Each chart below ranks each state's percentage of households for a specific income bracket | highest % = highest rank

Poverty
Less than $25k

Lower Middle Class
$25k - $35k

Middle Class
$35 - $75k

Upper Middle Class
$75k - $100k

Wealthy
$100k-$150k

Very Wealthy
$150k and up

Source: U.S. Census

Design: Sean Miller | @kcmillersean

**FIGURE 1.7**   Example of combining highlighting and context.

## Analysis versus Visualization

Visualizing every data point in a data set will not necessarily add to our understanding of the data. We have to be able to differentiate between **analysis** and **visualization**.

Yes, we need to make use of all the available data to identify out-liers and trends, to build more accurate analytical and predictive models, and to increase the certainty of our assumptions and con-clusions. Visualizations, however, should represent our findings in a way the audience can comprehend easily and quickly. For example, the audience does not need to see every data point as dots on a map or every product in the product portfolio in a scatter plot. Often, aggregated data or a representative sample of the data is sufficient to support the analysis.

Design the visualizations so that they provide *enough* information to focus the audience on the insights, such as certain trends or out-liers. Combining aggregate level analysis with detailed information should be done with care.

In Figure 1.8 about air quality in the United States, Pooja Gandhi combines aggregated analysis via the tile map and heatmap, while providing detailed data at the county level in the dot plot in the lower half of her visualization.

Pooja provides a state filter to reduce the complexity. Within each year (i.e., the vertical panes dividing the data into bands), a sin-gle dot represents a county. The horizontal distribution of the data points shows increasing levels of ozone measurements and the growth in the number of readings and measurement stations over time, from left to right.

Pooja very effectively combined the two concepts of analysis and visualization. The top half of her dashboard has an analytical and exploratory focus, while the bottom half provides an impactful visual representation of the data to show changes over time.

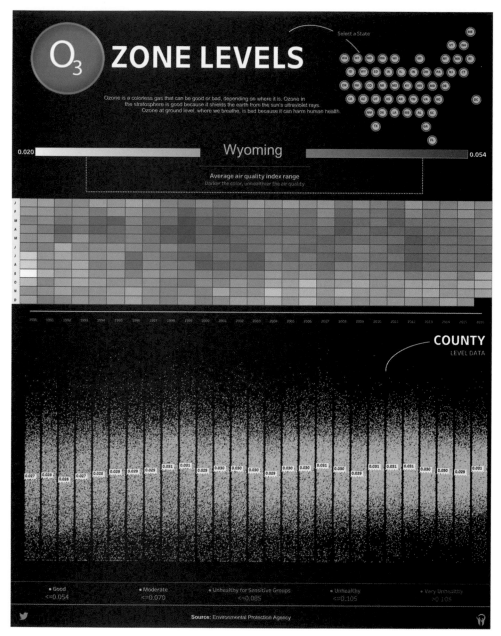

**FIGURE 1.8**   Combine multiple charts to allow aggregate and detailed analysis.

## Take Your Time

While we encourage people not to spend more than an hour on Makeover Monday each week, we do not want you to think that you should rush through your analysis. By taking your time, slowing down, and thinking through the analysis, you will create better work.

Complicated data sets take time to understand, especially those that are wide and tall. Some data sets are more difficult to understand than others. In those cases, take your time to really understand the data. Analysis takes time. Make sure your calculations are accurate. Verify your numbers. Slow down.

Not taking the necessary amount of time to work through your analysis thoroughly, step by step, can easily lead to incorrect assumptions. One of our challenges involved a very simple data set about German car production, including production and export numbers per month for passenger cars and trucks.

Does that data tell you anything about sales? Not really. It does not tell you how many cars were sold and neither does it tell you when people buy cars in Germany. Some people saw that production decreased during August and December compared to the other months. Yet too many people did not bother to try to understand *why* production drops during those months. Germans probably take holidays during August, but maybe it is also a conscious choice by the manufacturer to reduce production output during that month. Those are possible explanations, but not definite conclusions.

Be careful with the statements you add into your visualizations. You could be right, but you could also be way off. Either way, confirm.

# Build Context Through Additional Research

Many data sets warrant additional research to get a clearer picture of the data. For Makeover Monday, we provide participants with an article that gives the story behind the data. This can be a short news story, a longer opinion piece, or even an academic research paper. We encourage everyone to use that information to help them understand the context of the data, and to learn about the data collection process and the intention behind the original visualization that is being used as the basis for the makeover.

While a number of people dive straight into data visualization as soon as the data is published, we find that those who read the available article often find the analysis process easier and are able to show the insights they find more clearly. They use the context, the data definitions, and the available commentary to enhance and strengthen their story.

If you want to build your skills as an analyst, we strongly recommend setting time aside for research to support your data analysis and visualization. Here are some steps you can take to approach a data set and gain a deeper understanding of its topic and background.

## Read the Available Information

Most charts, dashboards, and data visualizations do not exist in isolation. Rather, they are part of a larger data story, news article, blog, forum discussion, white paper, academic research paper, or other publication. Take the time to read and understand the information supporting the chart and take note of key information including:

*Purpose of the Study: Investigation or Analysis*
- Why was the data collected in the first place and by whom?
- Does the purpose give you ideas for building your own data story?
- Is there an interesting insight in the origins of the research that you can use to guide your analysis?

*Definitions of Key Metrics and Dimensions*

- What do the different field names mean and what does this tell you about the values they contain?
- Are there any assumptions stated with regard to specific values?
- Are there comments on data quality and completeness?

*Data Collection Process*

- How, when, and where was data collected?
- How reliable are the data collection methods that were used? For example, is data being collected by highly reliable sensors that automatically send data to a database, or is the data collected through questionnaires filled in manually by study participants?
- How was the data processed and treated following the collection and storage in the database?

*Insights Shared in the Article*

- What are the key messages and conclusions shared by the original authors?
- Are there any claims that are unsubstantiated and that you can target in your analysis?
- Are there data points the original authors were unable to explain or that they disregarded in their work?

These questions are intended to guide you and not to prescribe a strict process to follow. They should encourage you to dig a little further in your analysis and to ensure that your conclusions are based on sufficient research given the available information.

## Seek Additional Information

Aside from the initial research, it can be helpful to seek out information from secondary sources, such as those used by the original authors or commentary included with the original analysis. Doing this research gives you an idea of the type of information that influenced the original research and lets you understand the critique that others may have already written about the data you are about to analyze.

For data sets that provide lots of options for analysis and visualization, spend a little extra time to get a more comprehensive understanding of the topic, the data implications, and the work already done by others. This will save you time in the long run as you build your research and analytical skills while creating stronger arguments to support your analysis.

## Find Insights

Every week, the Makeover Monday data is ripe for analysis. Consider applying analytical thinking to your work. What is the data *really* telling you? What can you add to the conversation? What are the unknown unknowns? Thinking like this will help you move from being a good data analyst to a great data analyst.

Sean Hughes, in analyzing the salaries of the Obama and Trump administrations (Figure 1.9), went through 15 iterations, exploring the fields and grouping them in all sorts of ways before settling on comparing salaries by gender in the two administrations. Sean took the salaries and binned them into $30 000 increments. Lastly Sean used colors associated with the political parties, gave the chart a clear title and subtitle, and included a reference line for context.

By looking at the data from multiple perspectives, Sean was able to identify insights that were not immediately obvious. Sean has organized the chart in a way that clearly shows the differences between the administrations. He uses colors that are associated with the political parties and a subtitle that explains what he found.

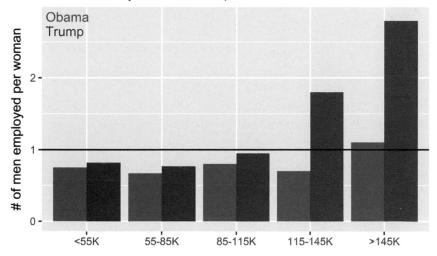

**Pay (dis)parity by gender in the White House**

More women work in low-wage positions. Higher-wage positions are dominated by men in the Trump White house.

FIGURE 1.9   Comparison of White House salaries by Sean Hughes.

## Educating Your Audience

When we gave our community data about solar eclipses, this provided a great opportunity for finding insights and teaching the audience about a topic that fascinates many people. This data set was great for exploring and made it possible to use visual analysis as a way to find a story.

It was a chance to explore how to:

- Put different metrics and fields into the view and manipulate them for unique visualizations so that fascinating patterns could emerge
- Swap axes and understand how this changes the visuals and makes a story more impactful or changes its focus
- Size and color fields to see what happens

Many participants were able to identify patterns and find insights in the data that resulted in informative and stunning visualizations. In Figure 1.10, Marc Reid taught his audience about solar eclipses through his interactive visualization. He showed patterns in the data and used those patterns as the focus of his work.

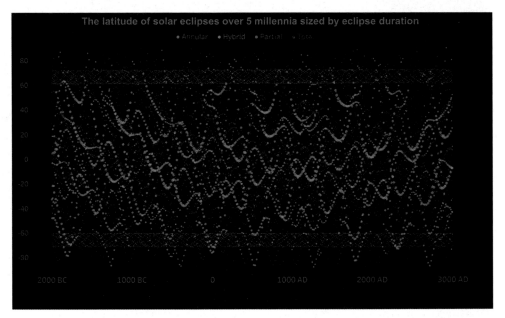

**FIGURE 1.10**   Plot of solar eclipses by Marc Reid.

Sebastián's visualization in Figure 1.11 revealed Saros cycles in the data, which made for a really great visualization of the pattern throughout the series and over time. He also added a number of explanations to help his audience better understand the life cycle of a solar eclipse, turning his dashboard into an interactive astronomy lesson.

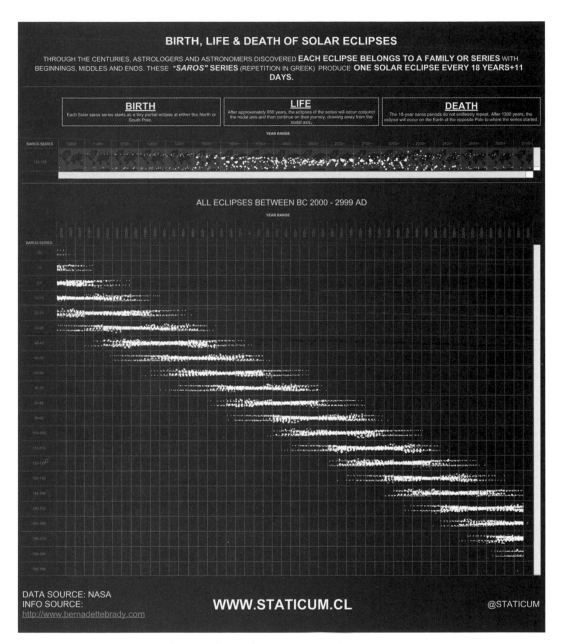

**FIGURE 1.11**　Design can be used to educate your audience.

## Communicate Clearly

Great data analysts are exceptional communicators. They make the complex simple by taking their insights and displaying them clearly and effectively to a broad audience. Rarely are people born as great communicators; even more rare is someone who is innately great at communicating data. Storytelling is a skill we can all learn. Books like Cole Nussbaumer Knaflic's *Storytelling with Data* (Wiley, 2015) help teach the basics of communicating data effectively.

Combining theoretical learning with books and practical learning through projects like Makeover Monday creates a platform to practice clear and effective communication of information through data visualization.

This can be a daunting challenge when the subject is very "niche" and your audience might not be familiar with it. Take week four of 2018 as an example, when Eva posted a data set about turkey vultures.

- What are turkey vultures?
- Why should we care about their migration patterns?
- What do the patterns even mean?

When you communicate your insights clearly, it can pull your audience in. The best compliment from those viewing your data visualizations is if they start caring about a topic previously unfamiliar to them and possibly even take actions to make a difference.

Lindsay Betzendahl created the stunning visualization in Figure 1.12 to explain turkey vultures and their migration patterns simply.

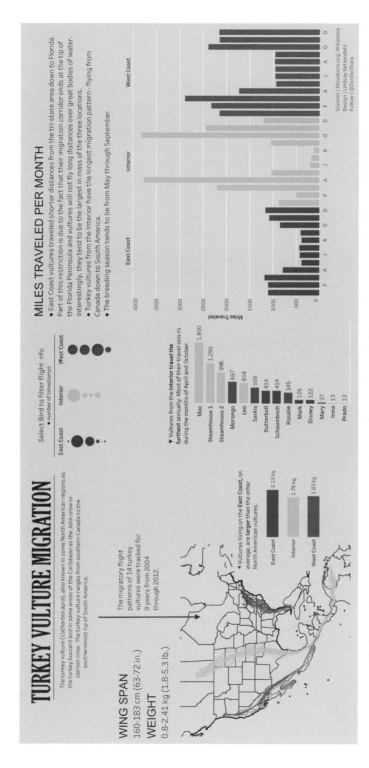

FIGURE 1.12  Turkey vulture migration patterns by Lindsay Betzendahl.

Lindsey communicated clearly by:

- Using the subtitle to explain the subject
- Including basic characteristics of the birds
- Using annotations to highlight specific insights
- Including additional information as context through a series of bullet points
- Using consistent, simple, soft colors that help the audience connect the analytical components

In the same week, Klaus Schulte taught us about one of the three nonmigratory birds in the data set (see Figure 1.13).

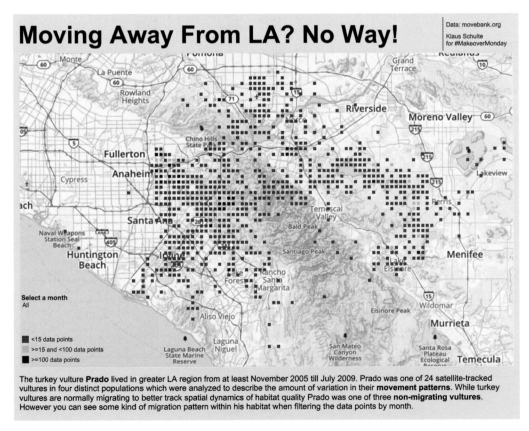

**FIGURE 1.13**   Simplify the data to communicate the analysis more effectively.

Klaus communicated clearly by:

- Summarizing his analysis in the footer
- Choosing colors that are easy to distinguish from each other
- Telling his audience how to interact
- Using simple shapes that frame the visualization

## Ask Questions

The final characteristic common to those highly effective data analysts in the Makeover Monday community is having the confidence to ask questions. Through our day-to-day work and our engagement with the data visualization community we often come across people who clearly do not understand a particular topic as well as they would like to, yet they are afraid to ask questions. Typically, we are told this is because they do not want to look unknowledgeable, but, for us, asking questions shows curiosity and it is this curiosity that separates great data analysts from everyone else. They want to know the "why" and they will continue to ask questions and explore the data until they feel like they know why.

When we gave the Makeover Monday community a data set about the ethnicity of players in Major League Baseball (MLB), Mike Cisneros wanted to provide additional contextual information. How does MLB compare with other major sports leagues in America? He wanted to know the "how" and the "why" of baseball's demographics. What he found, by researching and including additional data, was that Major League Soccer, where more than 28% of players are African-American or Black international athletes, was the most ethnically balanced league in North American professional sports. The design of his visualization in Figure 1.14 effectively supports and highlights his findings.

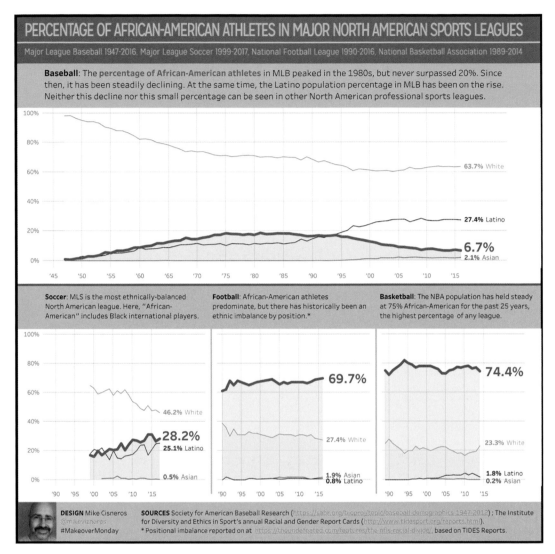

**FIGURE 1.14** Comparison of ethnicities across major sports leagues in North America.

Great data analysts do not settle for reporting a single number. They will dig deeper to provide context. Paweł Wróblewski, when visualizing data about personality types (Figure 1.15), could have simply reported the results of the Myers–Briggs personality test. However, he wanted the reader to be able to compare their own personality type with the rest of the United States. By doing so,

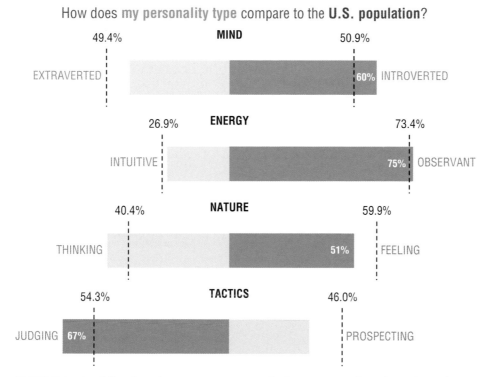

**FIGURE 1.15** Allowing the user to answer their own question draw them into the analysis.

Paweł gave the reader more context. He answered the question "compared to what?"

The Makeover Monday community has struggled at times with asking questions. For one week we provided data about Andy's marathon and Eva's triathlon and a list of questions we were curious to know the answers to, yet very few people bothered to ask us any questions. It was clear early into the week that many people did not understand the data and saw our list of questions as requirements and actually opted out of tackling the data altogether or focused on something "safe" instead.

If you are unsure about any aspect of a data set or the context provided, you have to ask question to get clarification. This applies in your professional environment at work and also for projects like

Makeover Monday where we do not expect people to understand everything every single week. If your boss does not appreciate you asking questions, then you probably need a new boss. Curiosity should be celebrated, especially for analysts. Without curiosity, analysts will simply regurgitate the numbers in the data.

It is obvious from his visualization (Figure 1.16) and its storytelling that Joel Gluck was curious about the topic of the water footprint of the foods we eat. Joel clearly wanted to know *why*. He did additional research and called out the main contributors to water usage as well as other harmful impacts on the planet caused by our food choices. By going further into the topic and making it his personal goal to share his insights in a way that will make his audience think and act, Joel showed that as an analyst he can take the given data far beyond reporting numbers.

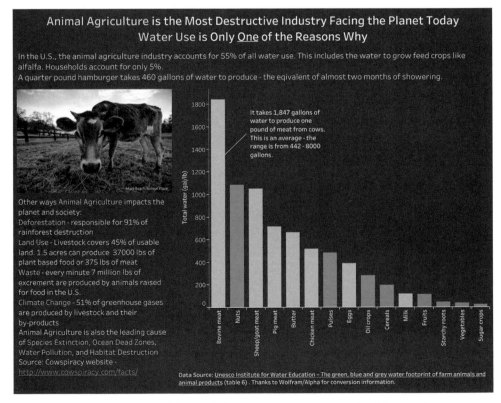

**FIGURE 1.16**   Including additional data is an effective method for explaining the why.

## Summary

Becoming a good data analyst takes practice, diligence, and dedication. It will not come easy and it will take a long time. One of the most satisfying experiences is when you can look back on your previous work, see a progression in your analytical skills, and appreciate how far you have come. This chapter outlined five key habits to help you become a good data analyst:

1. *Grasp unfamiliar data*. Create your own systematic approach to exploring the data in order to understand what it is trying to tell you.

2. *Take your time*. Speeding through the analysis will lead to mistakes and incorrect conclusions. Give yourself enough time to thoroughly understand the data.

3. *Find insights*. Once you understand the data, you will be in a position to develop insights. Take those insights and use them to educate your audience.

4. *Communicate clearly*. If you have done great analysis and you communicate it poorly, the analysis will not have the desired impact. It is critical to develop exceptional communication skills.

5. *Ask questions*. If you have questions or you do not understand, you have to get over your insecurities and ask. The more questions you ask, the better your questions will become. The better your questions become, the better your analysis will be.

By developing these habits, you will improve by leaps and bounds. The more consistent your habits become, the more effective you will be as a data analyst.

## Chapter Two

# Data Quality and Accuracy

Every data set poses challenges and potential pitfalls when it comes to data quality and data accuracy. The challenges faced in Makeover Monday can be grouped into five main categories:

1. Dealing with missing or incomplete data

2. Overcounting data

3. Sense-checking data

4. Is the data aggregable?

5. Substantiating claims with data

This chapter will look into each of these points in detail, with specific examples that demonstrate common mistakes people are likely to make and how to avoid and correct those mistakes.

## Working with Incomplete Data

Data sets, especially those publicly available, need to be looked at with a critical lens. Data could be missing, the range of the data set may be incomplete, or data might be duplicated. How should you handle these situations? How do you identify these problems in the first place? Once you have identified the problems, is it safe to use incomplete data for comparisons?

### Incomplete Data

When we provided a data set about the number of iPhones sold over time, many people looked at units sold over time, similar to Figure 2.1.

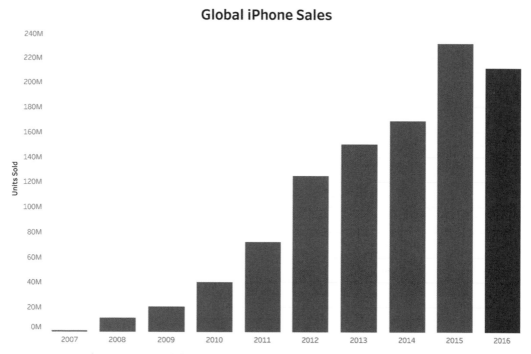

**FIGURE 2.1**   iPhone units sold by year.

Displaying the data by year shows an annual increase from 2008 to 2015 and then a decrease in 2016. Maybe you then want to look at the year over year change, as in Figure 2.2.

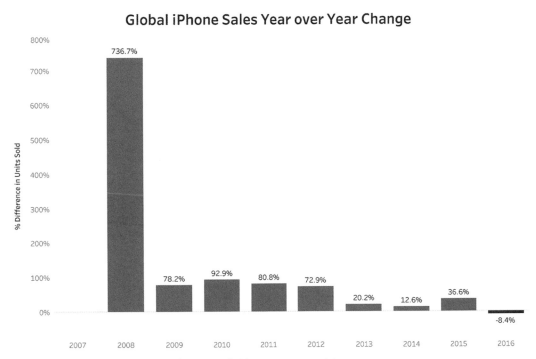

**FIGURE 2.2**   Year over year change of iPhone units sold.

Many people saw the massive increase in 2008, stopped there, and called it job done. However, is this data complete? Indeed, it is not.

Figure 2.3 shows that by taking a few seconds to look at units sold by quarter, you can see a problem.

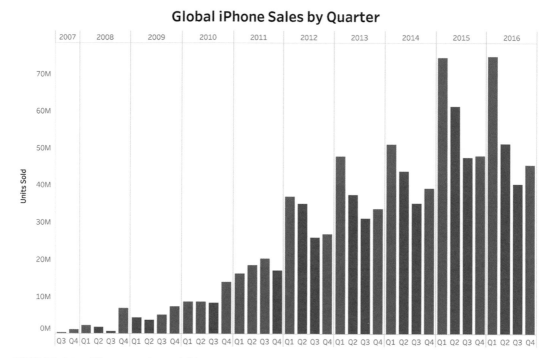

**FIGURE 2.3**   iPhone units sold by quarter.

Looking at the data by quarter clearly shows that the data for 2007 only includes Q3 and Q4; therefore you cannot compare 2007–2008. A key part of everyone's analysis has to be a thorough check of the data at different levels to identify incomplete data and then determine what to do. Perhaps you filter by a date range or you bin the data; each of these will help identify patterns, missing data, or outliers. In this case, analyzing the data by quarter makes sense, whereas looking at it by year does not.

One way to address the missing data is to compare the sales for each quarter by year (Figure 2.4). This helps you understand how the quarters compare to each other within each year.

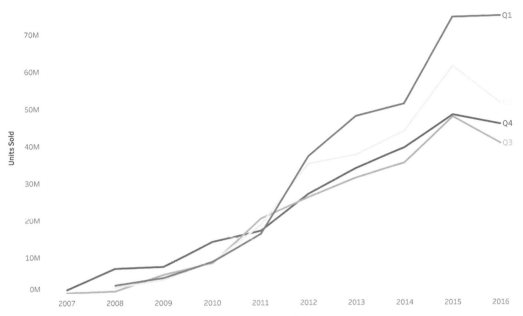

## Did Global iPhone Sales Peak in 2015?

The first quarter of every year (Oct-Dec) has been the best performing quarter for the company since 2012 by the number of iPhones sold.

**FIGURE 2.4**   Comparing quarterly iPhone units sold by year.

By visualizing the data this way, you can see that Q1 does not begin until 2008. Displaying the data by quarter by year also helps you determine which quarter had the most sales in each year.

We can consider another example of incomplete data. Andy gave the Makeover Monday community his American Express spending data for 2016 and challenged them to find something insightful. Many people liked these mobile-friendly dashboards from Shawn Levin (Figure 2.5) and Ravi Mistry (Figure 2.6):

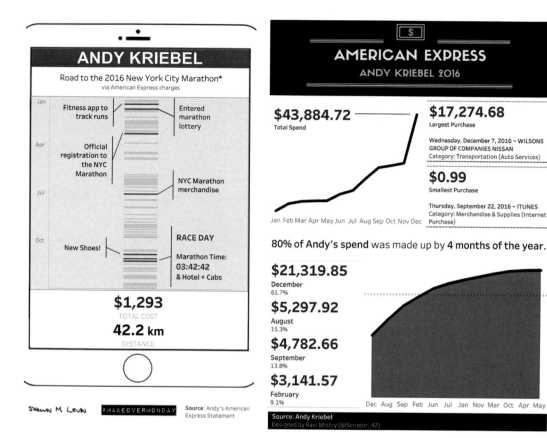

**FIGURE 2.5** Andy's American Express spending by Shawn Levin.

**FIGURE 2.6** Andy's American Express spending by Ravi Mistry.

Both visualizations effectively take into account the data provided. They make it clear that this was Andy's American Express spending—nothing more, nothing less. While each dashboard shows general spending summaries, they did not assume this was *all* of Andy's spending.

However, no one asked Andy if the data was complete. Did the data represent *all* of his purchases? No, it did not, yet some people created graphics that implied that the data was representative of all of his spending. It would have been easy to ask whether Andy only used his American Express in certain circumstances. Making assumptions that this was all of his spending is inaccurate because the data does not support that claim.

To reiterate the point, consider LinkedIn's ranking of the professional skills that are most in demand by employers around the world. The data set had numerous gaps. For example, in 2016 there were far fewer jobs listed than in 2014 and 2015, yet people used this incomplete data for comparison purposes.

There are a few basic strategies that can be used to address problems like this:

1. Remove incomplete years.

2. Do not automatically exclude nulls and outliers for convenience.

3. Use proper text descriptions based on what is being visualized.

Matt Chambers elegantly overcame these problems, as seen in Figure 2.7, by creating a simple dot plot. Matt's visualization is uncluttered, clear, concise, and visually appealing. It shows where skills were ranked compared to the global average and clearly identifies gaps by country and specific skill.

## Missing Data

Handling missing data correctly can be a daunting challenge. In a Tour de France data set we provided, it was important to notice that at a yearly level there was no data during the years of World War I and II, and there were no winners for the years 1999–2005, because results were voided due to doping.

As an analyst, you need to consider those "gaps" in the data.

- How do they impact your story?
- Do you point the gaps out or do you hide them? If you choose to hide them, is this the right thing to do?
- How do you communicate the gaps to your audience?

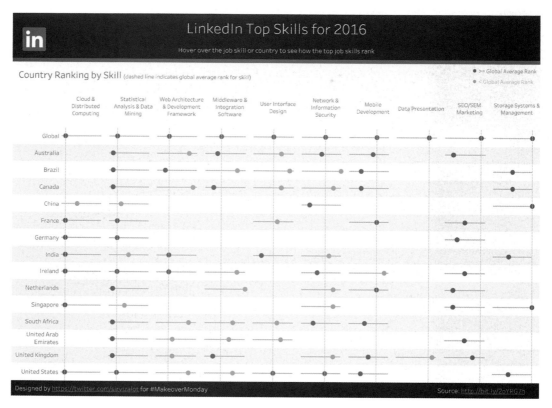

**FIGURE 2.7**    LinkedIn ranking of professional skills by Matt Chambers.

It is important to ensure that any chart visualizing incomplete data does not leave the reader with the impression that the data indeed exists. How then do you ensure that the reader is not misled? One technique is to show the missing data as gaps and include annotations to explain the missing data, as Adam Crahen did.

In his visualization of the Tour de France results (Figure 2.8), Adam showed the two World Wars as actual gaps where the lines did not connect, and he annotated these areas with the text "World War I" and "World War II."

**FIGURE 2.8**  Gaps and annotations help make it clear that data is missing.

## Excluding Data

Often, when working with missing data, you have to make a decision on what to do with those missing data points. What if you have data that comprises actuals, actuals and estimates, and forecast data? A Makeover Monday data set about per capita consumption of poultry and livestock in the US included all of these scenarios in one data set. The data set started with the year 1960 and ended with 2018. There were a couple of gotchas:

1. There is no data for the years 1961–1964. What should you do? Should you include or exclude 1960? If you want to look at the rate of change, what year should you calculate the difference from?

2. The year 2017 included actuals and estimates; 2018 was a forecast. Should you include these?

Natasha Kurakina's initial version (Figure 2.9) started by: (1) including the gaps in the year, and (2) excluding the estimates and forecast.

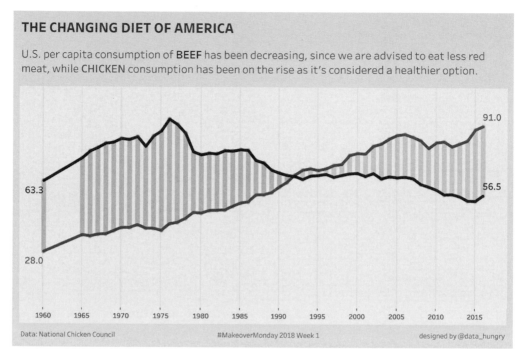

**FIGURE 2.9**   Comparison of beef and chicken consumption for all years.

Much like Adam, Natasha's design effectively shows the gap between 1960 and 1965 by connecting the lines for beef and chicken vertically. However, given that there is only one year of data before the gap starts, would it be more effective to exclude 1960?

By excluding 1960, the visualization (Figure 2.10) looks cleaner and tells a more effective story. It will not leave the audience wondering why a single year was included before a large gap and what the gap might mean.

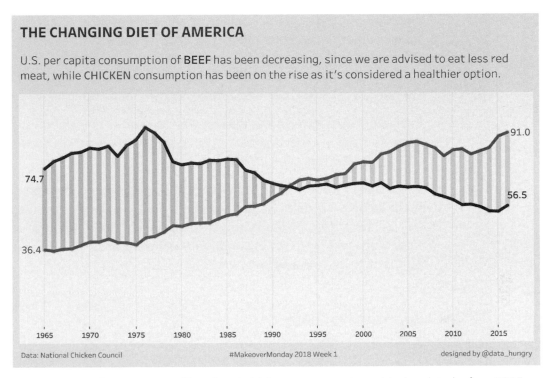

**THE CHANGING DIET OF AMERICA**

U.S. per capita consumption of **BEEF** has been decreasing, since we are advised to eat less red meat, while **CHICKEN** consumption has been on the rise as it's considered a healthier option.

Data: National Chicken Council          #MakeoverMonday 2018 Week 1          designed by @data_hungry

**FIGURE 2.10**   Comparison of beef and chicken consumption with the data before 1965 removed.

## Tips for Working with Incomplete or Missing Data

To summarize, here are a few recommendations for handling incomplete or missing data:

1. Always determine the lowest level of granularity in the data. If it is time series data, what is the smallest increment of time? Is it at the minute or second level or is at the quarterly level? Understanding this will help you make design and aggregation decisions and communicate your insights clearly.

2. Compare your data *only* at the level that is common to the range you want to include. For example, if you want to compare years, then only include the complete years. Consider the chart showing iPhone sales earlier in this chapter. Since 2007 is not a complete year, it should not be compared to 2008 in its totality.

3. If something looks like an outlier when you visualize it, it could be an outlier, it could be caused by missing data, or it could be an interesting insight. Whichever the case, investigate it further to verify, especially if you want to build your analysis around it. Do not rely only on your first impression and assumptions.

4. Excluding data can be the easiest way to deal with incomplete data. Perhaps you have gaps in your data. Maybe it makes sense to exclude the data before the gap.

5. Avoid setting the missing values to zero. Zero is not the same thing as missing data. By assigning the missing points a value, you will be communicating to your audience that, for example, sales were zero and not missing. Very different assumptions will be made from those values.

## Overcounting Data

It is critical to pay attention to the granularity in your data and to explore the data so that you have a firm grasp on what the fields are composed of. Doing this will help you determine if your data is hierarchical, if it needs to be split, or if the data can even be aggregated.

Consider the visualization about medals won in the Southeast Asian Games. Figure 2.11 shows a quick count of the medals won by year.

Is this accurate? You will not know unless you verify the data. The problem here is that in team sports, each person who won a medal on the team is listed individually. In other words, if a team has four members, that will appear in the data as four medals. If you want to count the number of events won by country, is this accurate? Definitely not. The medals won should be counted by event, not by individual. If you do not count the medals accurately, then you are implying that a gold won by a team of five members should be given more credit than an individual winning a medal in an individual sport.

## Medals Won in the SEA Games

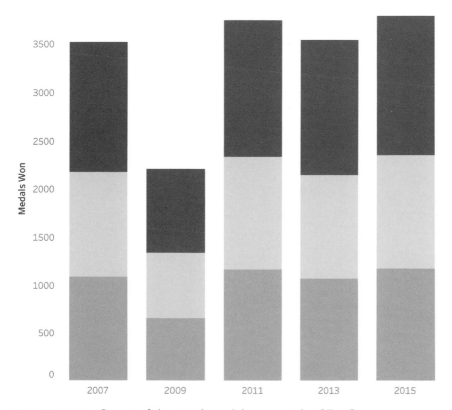

**FIGURE 2.11**    Count of the total medals won at the SEA Games.

Look at your data thoroughly to pick up on these specific charac-teristics in the data. Ask yourself whether the results you are seeing sound reasonable and question them until you have verified that they are in fact correct. When you see that Thailand has won 3583 medals over five competitions, you should really be questioning the data because even with no knowledge of the Southeast Asia Games (SEA Games), this number just seems far too high to be realistic. By counting the number of medals won by event, you get medal counts that make sense (Figure 2.12).

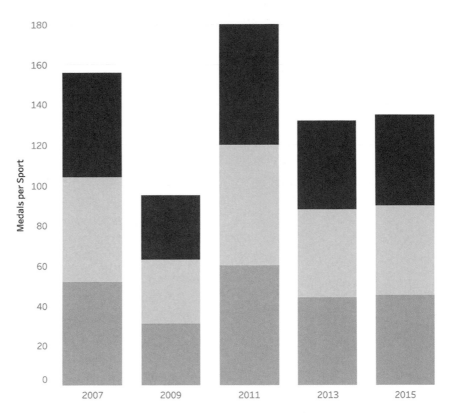

**FIGURE 2.12**  Count of medals won by event at the SEA Games.

## Sense-Checking Data

Assuming you are somewhat familiar with the subject of the data, how can you determine if the data is correct? In his article "Common sense checks for quantitative data,"[1] Adam Grimes calls this the "TLAR test."

TLAR stands for "that looks about right" and is a quick "back of the envelope" type of check we should do with any analysis—it is

[1] adamhgrimes.com/common-sense-checks-quantitative-data/, 30 August 2016.

a way to apply common sense tests to quantitative data. I would do this type of analysis at least twice in the process: first, with the raw data, and second with any final results.

What we are looking for, first of all, are things that just do not make sense or are too good to be true. It takes some experience to know what is too good to be true, but if you ever ignore this common sense check you will be sorry.

When it comes to Makeover Monday, every data set is new, every data set can be misinterpreted, every data set should be looked at with the TLAR test in mind. In fact, this applies to every analytical project you undertake. If something does not seem right or if something is too good to be true, then it probably is.

## Trump's Tweets

When he provided data that included all of Donald Trump's tweets, Andy added a timestamp to each tweet by including hours and minutes. Andy made a mistake by creating a timestamp calculation that returned the hour in am/pm format, whereas it should have returned the hour of the day. Several people published their work without noticing this error, and when creating visualizations by hour of the day, it looked like Trump never tweeted during certain hours of the day. Less activity during certain hours could be right, but no activity at all during those hours just does not seem realistic given Trump's social media engagement. In the end, it is the responsibility of the analyst to question the data.

Those who did notice the problem easily corrected the data by setting all of the tweets to a standard time of Universal Time Coordinated (UTC), since it is not really possible to account for Trump's location for each tweet. By leaving the data in UTC, Mike Cisneros was able to create the stunning radial charts in Figure 2.13 that reveal interesting tweeting patterns.

# Tweet Around the Clock: Donald Trump on Twitter

Trump spent the early 2010s **learning how best to utilize the reach and power of the Twitter platform.**
It paid off during his campaign, through **high levels of engagement with his audience.**

The radial charts here show each individual recorded tweet. The innermost circle shows the first day of the month; the outermost shows the last. The angle is a 24-hour clock; read clockwise. The top of the circle is midnight; the bottom of the circle is 12 noon. **Click on a year to see it expanded below.**

| 2010 | 2011 | 2012 | 2013 | 2014 | 2015 | 2016 |

DJT's tweeting began in mid 2009, but it was **confined largely to business hours: between 9am and 5pm ET,** and he **rarely (if ever) retweeted anybody.**
In 2013, his tweeting became a 24-hour endeavor, and he began retweeting more frequently. Although there is overlap, there is a distinct time window difference in his tweeting: original tweets **mostly happen between 5am and 11pm ET, while** retweets **happen most often between 5pm and 9am ET.**
It makes sense that this way, he (and/or his staff) can maintain round-the-clock engagement with his audience, without having to generate 100% original content.

## All **7,530** Trump Tweets From **2015**

Larger circles show tweets with higher engagement levels (likes and retweets).
**Click on any individual tweet to read the text.**

■ Original Trump Tweet
■ Retweet From Other User

### 2015 Month-By-Month

J    F    M    A
M    J    J    A
S    O    N    D

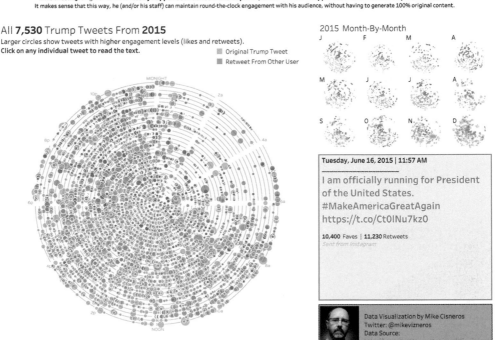

**Tuesday, June 16, 2015 | 11:57 AM**
———————————————
I am officially running for President
of the United States.
#MakeAmericaGreatAgain
https://t.co/Ct0INu7kz0

**10,400** Faves | **11,230** Retweets
*Sent from Instagram*

Data Visualization by Mike Cisneros
Twitter: @mikevizneros
Data Source:

**FIGURE 2.13**   Trump's Tweets by Mike Cisneros.

Mike is a well-established data analyst in the Makeover Monday community who pays attention to small details. He looks at the data and asks, "Does this look about right?" before he makes any assumptions or definitive statements about the data.

Check your data. Make sure the numbers stack up. If you are unsure, ask. Do a bit more analysis. Despite all of your attempts, if you really cannot confirm the accuracy of the data, then perhaps it is time to change your analysis. It is better to stop and start again than it is to make a claim that is wrong.

## Is Puerto Rico a State?

The US household income distribution data used in early 2018 included Puerto Rico. The column was named "State," but Puerto Rico is not a state. How should you handle this? Start with Adam Grimes's advice: does the data pass the TLAR test? Puerto Rico is a huge outlier in the data set, and many people noticed that and focused their visualizations on Puerto Rico like the visualization in Figure 2.14 by Simon Beaumont.

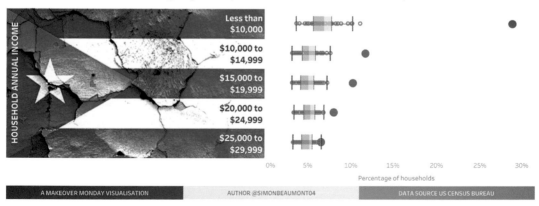

**FIGURE 2.14**   Dot plot of household income by state.

Simon directly called out Puerto Rico as an outlier. Great! Insights! But wait, read the subtitle: "Looking at the household income of American States." Puerto Rico is not a state. When you see outliers, this should make you question and verify the data. You then have a choice: Do you include or exclude the outlier? In this case, if you are set on using the word "state" in your visualization, then you should exclude Puerto Rico.

If you want to focus on Puerto Rico, do not refer to it as a state, and build your story with different descriptions. The challenge here was not incorrect data and Simon's analysis was still valid; it was simply the description that weakened the story. We pointed this out to Simon, who immediately updated his visualization to include the right description to read, "American States & Territories," resulting in a better representation of the data and the topic.

## Is the Data Aggregable?

Lots of data sets that we provide for Makeover Monday are pre-aggregated. Often this data comes in the form of percentages or indexes. When you have data that is pre-aggregated, how should you treat further aggregations? And can you even aggregate the data further?

### Adult Obesity in the United States

A data set about obesity rates in the United States led Andy to analyze the obesity rates by age in his home state of Pennsylvania (Figure 2.15).

Because the data is at the lowest level of detail (i.e., annual data by age group), presenting the obesity rate as an aggregation works. What if you want to look at the overall obesity rate for each state? You could start by removing Age Group from the

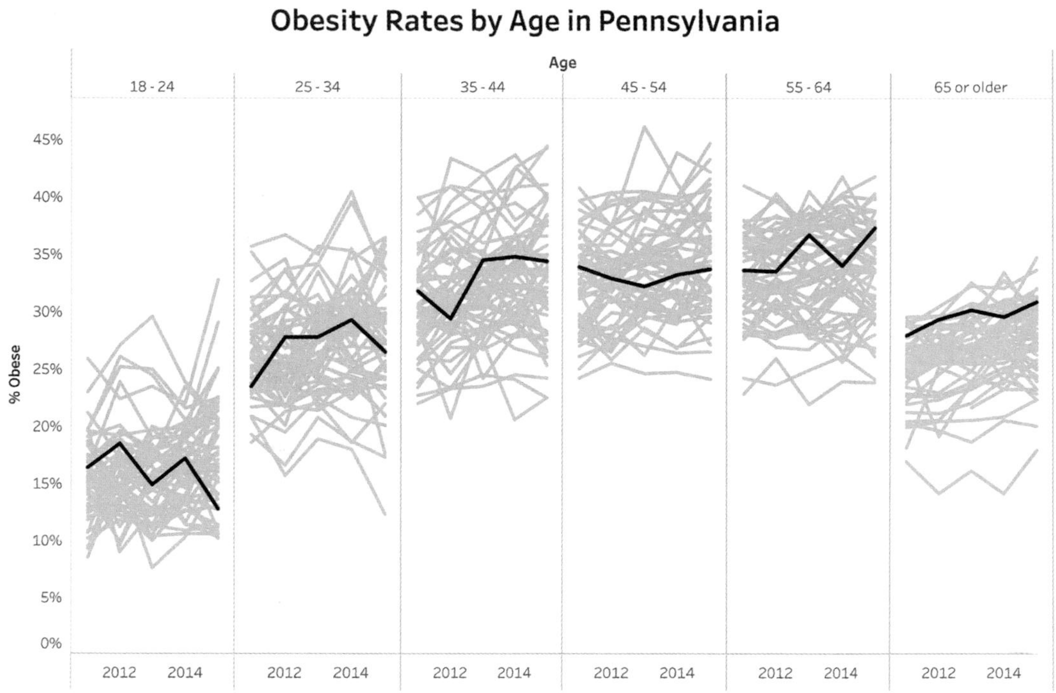

## Obesity Rates by Age in Pennsylvania

**FIGURE 2.15**  Obesity rates by age group in Pennsylvania compared to all other states.

view and making the obesity rate an average across all ages, as in Figure 2.16.

Is this accurate? Is it mathematically correct to take percentages and average them? Not in this case, because the sample sizes are different (i.e., different age groups had different numbers of people included in them). Therefore, you need to calculate a weighted average:

$$SUM([\% \ Obese] * [Sample \ Size]) \div SUM([Sample \ Size])$$

Now you have a mathematically correct obesity rate and your visualization can be sliced and diced in any manner using the new calculation and you can be confident in the accuracy of the numbers. While the incorrect average obesity rate for Pennsylvania

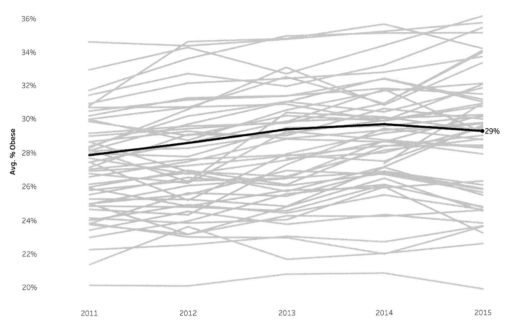

**Average Obesity Rate in Pennsylvania**

**FIGURE 2.16**   Average obesity rate by state by year.

across all age groups in the previous chart was 29%, the chart in Figure 2.17 uses the weighted average and results in 32%. Quite a difference!

The key when working with pre-aggregated data is to understand at what level the data is pre-aggregated. From there, if you have sample sizes, like in the example above, you should calculate a weighted average. However, if you do not have sample sizes, then you should neither aggregate the data to a higher level nor should you take an average of the percentages. Both of these will result in inaccurate data, which in turn may inadvertently harm your reputation as a data analyst.

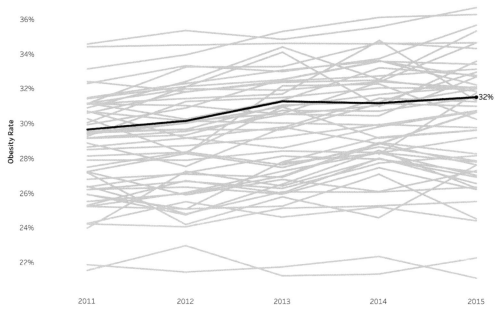

**FIGURE 2.17**   Properly aggregated obesity rate by state by year.

## Averages of Averages

The Domestic and International Tourism Spend in New Zealand data that we used for week four 2017 contained a few potential challenges for those who did not look closely at the data:

1.  There was a region named "Total (all TLAs)" that represented the total and it was mixed in with all of the other regions.

2.  The data was an index, which is calculated as a weighted number for each region, month, and visitor type.

3.  When using indexes in a data set, using an average aggregation is appropriate as long as you only use it at the individual region, month, and visitor type level (i.e., the lowest granularity of the data). You cannot use an average of the average to represent the total.

A few people made the mistake of using an average of the average. Why is this a problem? To understand this better, we need to explain the concept of "averages of averages," why they do not calculate accurately, and how people should be using them.

### How do you Calculate a Weighted Profit Ratio?

We will use coffee sales data to explain this concept. To calculate a Profit Ratio (profit compared to sales), use the formula:

$$SUM([Profit]) \div SUM([Sales])$$

This is the correct way to represent the overall profit ratio. The first two columns in Figure 2.18 are the profit and sales numbers while the third column, Profit Ratio, uses the formula above.

| Product | Profit | Sales | Profit Ratio |
|---|---|---|---|
| Amaretto | 4,890 | 26,269 | 18.6% |
| Caffe Latte | 11,375 | 35,899 | 31.7% |
| Caffe Mocha | 17,678 | 84,904 | 20.8% |
| Chamomile | 27,231 | 75,578 | 36.0% |
| Colombian | 55,804 | 128,311 | 43.5% |
| Darjeeling | 29,053 | 73,151 | 39.7% |
| Decaf Espresso | 29,502 | 78,162 | 37.7% |
| Decaf Irish Cream | 13,989 | 62,248 | 22.5% |
| Earl Grey | 24,164 | 66,772 | 36.2% |
| Green Tea | -231 | 32,850 | -0.7% |
| Lemon | 29,869 | 95,926 | 31.1% |
| Mint | 6,154 | 35,710 | 17.2% |
| Regular Espresso | 10,065 | 24,031 | 41.9% |
| Grand Total | **259,543** | **819,811** | **31.7%** |

**FIGURE 2.18**   Using the correct formula to calculate a profit ratio.

Using this formula, notice how the Grand Total is a weighted calculation. The overall profit ratio is the sum of all profits divided by the sum of all sales.

$$259,543 \div 819,811 = 31.7\%$$

If the Profit Ratio Grand Total cell is changed to an average, notice how the result changes to 28.9% in Figure 2.19.

| Product | Profit | Sales | Profit Ratio |
|---|---|---|---|
| Amaretto | 4,890 | 26,269 | 18.6% |
| Caffe Latte | 11,375 | 35,899 | 31.7% |
| Caffe Mocha | 17,678 | 84,904 | 20.8% |
| Chamomile | 27,231 | 75,578 | 36.0% |
| Colombian | 55,804 | 128,311 | 43.5% |
| Darjeeling | 29,053 | 73,151 | 39.7% |
| Decaf Espresso | 29,502 | 78,162 | 37.7% |
| Decaf Irish Cream | 13,989 | 62,248 | 22.5% |
| Earl Grey | 24,164 | 66,772 | 36.2% |
| Green Tea | -231 | 32,850 | -0.7% |
| Lemon | 29,869 | 95,926 | 31.1% |
| Mint | 6,154 | 35,710 | 17.2% |
| Regular Espresso | 10,065 | 24,031 | 41.9% |
| Grand Total | 259,543 | 819,811 | 28.9% |

**FIGURE 2.19** An incorrect overall profit ratio resulting from averaging the individual profit ratios.

In this case you are adding together each of the profit ratios and dividing by the number of products. This means you are adding the percentage figures and dividing them by the number of rows in the table, rather than using the grand total profit and dividing it by the grand total sales. The result is:

$$376.3 \div 13 = 28.9\%$$

This is an inaccurate overall profit ratio calculation.

*A Makeover Monday Mistake*

When analyzing New Zealand tourism spending data, some people did not look closely enough at the data. They did not notice the line item named "Total (all TLAs)" in the Region column that provided the overall index. Many people included this as if it were any other region. This is like comparing world level results to individual country results.

When using indexes in this data set, using an average aggregation is appropriate as long as you use it only at the individual region level. In the example in Figure 2.20, consider the average index for each region for April 2016.

1.  The Grand Total is calculated as an average.

2.  The Total region is included.

| Region | Visitor Type | |
| --- | --- | --- |
| | Domestic | International |
| Grand Total | 106.1 | 103.3 |
| Total (all TLAs) | 106.0 | 99.6 |
| Ashburton District | 114.7 | 102.1 |
| Auckland | 108.6 | 100.2 |
| Buller District | 97.6 | 101.1 |
| Carterton District | 102.9 | 97.7 |
| Central Hawke's Bay District | 107.9 | 68.5 |
| Central Otago District | 106.0 | 116.5 |
| Christchurch City | 97.3 | 76.8 |
| Clutha District | 106.6 | 104.0 |
| Dunedin City | 102.4 | 96.2 |

**FIGURE 2.20**   Table of tourism spending in districts in New Zealand.

The first mistake people made is that they included the Total region in the overall average. Notice how the grand total in the top row differs from the Total region. The data set included the Total region index already and that is the index people should be using instead of creating their own. Why? Because the statisticians who created the data set created the total (all region) index at the right level of aggregation already, taking into account the sample size. Without knowing the sample size, you cannot accurately calculate the total index with the data you have.

Displaying the data visually, as in Figure 2.21, makes the difference even more apparent.

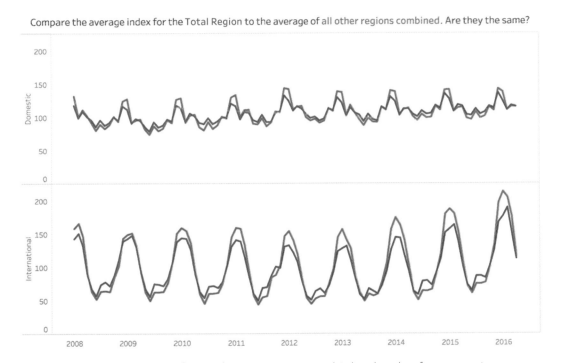

Compare the average index for the Total Region to the average of all other regions combined. Are they the same?

**FIGURE 2.21**   An average of an index is inaccurate at higher levels of aggregation.

Analyze first, build your visualization later. Look at the fields and metrics you are using. Can they be aggregated? Do the aggregations make sense? Ask yourself these questions and you will be more likely to avoid incorrect assumptions and aggregations that give you inaccurate results.

## Substantiating Claims with Data

Sometimes a visualization will have a catchy title, yet the content does not deliver on the title. Either the title makes a claim that is not substantiated, or it contains a question that is not actually answered in the visualization.

Using a question as a title is a great way to guide the audience. The question helps you ensure that your charts respond directly to the question and when they do not, you can remove them. And that is the main point: You need to answer the question. If the data is not conclusive, say so. Give an explanation that relates back to your title and close the loop so that your audience is informed and gets the complete picture included in your analysis.

For Makeover Monday we provided a data set about potato production in Europe. The selling price included in the data was a wholesale price per 100 kg. No other pricing information was provided. Therefore, you cannot assume anything about consumer prices, that is, the prices you pay for potatoes in the supermarket. What farmers receive on the agricultural market for their potato crops does not let you directly relate this information to end consumer prices, because there are many layers in between, and price decreases on the wholesale market may not be passed on directly to the end consumer. In this case, you should stick to statements about wholesale prices and their behavior, without drawing conclusions to consumer prices.

Through his analysis in Figure 2.22, Luke Stoughton demonstrated that he took the time to understand the data, to find something he wanted to focus on, and to make conclusions based on the data itself and its properties, rather than just visualizing something randomly.

# The 2013 Potato Crisis

**In 2013 potato prices soared to unprecedented heights...**

**...a 37% increase in average price from 2012 meant everyone's favourite root vegetable was on the way to being a luxury item!**

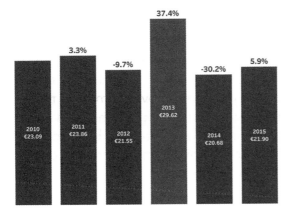

**But which countries were hit hardest by soaring spuds?**

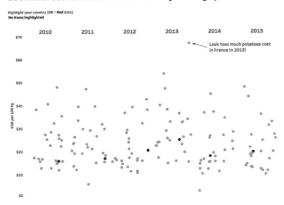

**Why could this be?**

**The answer lies with the main area of production which dropped significantly from 2012 to 1,761,000 hectares, a move of -69%!**

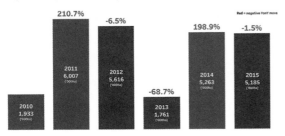

**FIGURE 2.22**    Analysis of potato prices in Europe by Luke Stoughton.

## Summary

Data quality and accuracy are key concepts that every data analyst must thoroughly understand and take into account when working with data. To become a great data analyst, you must be able to identify and deal with incomplete data and work to identify the data quality and accuracy issues in a data set.

While you are honing this skill, you will learn about data aggregations, overcounting, sense-checking, and drawing conclusions. Data analysis is more than crunching numbers; it is about finding insights, identifying the unknown unknowns, and presenting the data in a simple yet deep enough way so that your audience can understand your insights and make decisions.

## Chapter Three

# Know and Understand the Data

Plotting numbers on a chart does not make you a data analyst. Knowing and understanding your data before you communicate it to your audience does. Understanding data is challenging and this chapter is designed to help you understand these important ideas:

- The concept of data aggregation
- How to effectively communicate metrics to your audience
- How to identify and correct mistakes in your analysis
- How to understand and present time series data

## Using Appropriate Aggregations

Aggregated data is data combined from several measurements for the purpose of summarization.[1] Some of the uses for data aggregation include:

- Understanding higher-level groupings of the data (e.g., sales per region vs. each individual transaction)
- Reducing query times
- Finding patterns, trends, and outliers
- Providing a starting point for deeper data analysis (i.e., identifying problems at a higher level and then drilling into the data to find the specific problem)

This section will help you understand whether data can be aggregated, some basic aggregation methods, and things to watch out for.

### Can the Data Be Aggregated?

When working with aggregation, it is important to avoid metrics that aggregate data that is already aggregated. What does this mean?

Aggregating summarized data to a higher level will often work. However, there are aggregations you cannot aggregate further without additional data. It takes time and practice to understand data aggregation. To aid you on your journey, here are four frequent aggregation mistakes to avoid as a data analyst.

#### Average of Percentages

Combining several data points into a single value is the most obvious way to aggregate data. However, not all data can be summarized. Figure 3.1 shows response rates to a survey question:

---

[1] en.wikipedia.org/wiki/Aggregate_data

| | Social Strata | | |
|---|---|---|---|
| Reason | Middle class | Poor | Rich people |
| abilities, talents | 8.0% | 7.0% | 13.0% |
| connections to the right people | 32.0% | 39.0% | 9.0% |
| cunning, cheating | 21.0% | 32.0% | 11.0% |
| entreprenurial spirit, courage | 16.0% | 16.0% | 27.0% |
| fortune, good luck | 15.0% | 12.0% | 13.0% |
| good education, high qualification | 33.0% | 18.0% | 28.0% |
| hard work | 27.0% | 16.0% | 38.0% |
| presence of initial capital | 23.0% | 27.0% | 15.0% |

**FIGURE 3.1**  Pre-aggregated data.

The data in this case is pre-aggregated; that is, the percentages represent the number of people who specified a reason in a social class divided by the total number of people surveyed. Since this is the lowest level of data provided, the numbers are represented accurately.

A common mistake people make is to combine (or aggregate) these measurements even further. For example, you may want to know the overall percentage of people who gave abilities and talents as their reason. The natural thing to do is to remove social strata from the table and take an average across the entire surveyed population. This results in the table shown in Figure 3.2.

This table tells you that, on average, 9% of people responded that abilities and talents was a reason for success. But this is not accurate because you have not considered the sample size. Taking an average of an average (the original percentage) does not result in a weighted average, which takes into account the sample size (i.e., the number of people from each social stratum who responded to the survey).

If the survey questioned 100 poor people, 200 middle-class people, and 300 rich people, then you could calculate the weighted average by taking each individual percentage, multiplying it by the number of responses, then dividing that result by the overall number of responses.

$$\frac{\Sigma \ (Response \ Rate * People \ surveyed)}{\Sigma \ People \ surveyed}$$

Using this weighted calculation, you can now calculate the correct overall average, as seen in Figure 3.3.

| Reason | |
|---|---|
| abilities, talents | 9% |
| connections to the right people | 27% |
| cunning, cheating | 21% |
| entreprenurial spirit, courage | 20% |
| fortune, good luck | 13% |
| good education, high qualification | 26% |
| hard work | 27% |
| presence of initial capital | 22% |

FIGURE 3.2   Unweighted average of response rates.

| Reason | |
|---|---|
| abilities, talents | 10.3% |
| connections to the right people | 21.7% |
| cunning, cheating | 17.8% |
| entreprenurial spirit, courage | 21.5% |
| fortune, good luck | 13.5% |
| good education, high qualification | 28.0% |
| hard work | 30.7% |
| presence of initial capital | 19.7% |

FIGURE 3.3   Weighted average of response rates.

Knowing when your data can and cannot be aggregated is critical to performing accurate analysis. As you can see from these aggregated tables, the numbers differ between the *unweighted* and *weighted average*. If your data is pre-aggregated and you are not provided with the sample size, aggregating the data further could yield inaccurate numbers.

*Average of Averages*

As mentioned previously, aggregating an average to a higher level without appropriately weighting the data could lead to inaccurate representation of the data. Consider Figure 3.4, which Andy created about internet usage trends around the world.

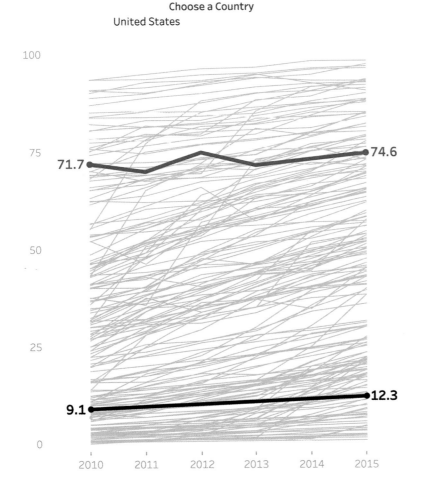

By 2015, internet access increased by **+2.9** people per 100 in **United States** compared to a **+3.2** increase worldwide.

**Choose a Country**
United States

Source: Knoema World Data Atlas                    Designed: @VizWizBI

**FIGURE 3.4**    Internet access per capita by country.

This data set contains pre-aggregated data of internet usage per 100 people per year per country. Essentially this data can be presented as percentages since its base is 100 people. Looking at an individual country per year provides an accurate picture, because the data was given at that granularity.

However, there is a mistake in calculating worldwide internet usage. The worldwide average was calculated as a straight average of all of the countries for each year. Why is this a problem? It does not account for the population of each country and therefore it is not weighted.

For example, Iceland has the highest internet usage per 100 people, but it also has a tiny population compared to China, with the largest population, which finds itself in the middle of the countries listed when it comes to internet usage penetration. Giving Iceland the same weight as China when calculating the overall internet usage is wrong and inaccurate. The population of each country should be included in the overall calculation in order to provide an accurate representation of the worldwide internet access per 100 people. In this case, the worldwide average should be removed from the visualization.

### Percentages of Percentages

For the dataset about the drinking habits of British people, many Makeover Monday participants focused on the year-over-year change. The data was already provided as percentages, so when calculating year over year change, in order to show accurate results you should use the difference, not the percent difference.

The chart in Figure 3.5 is filtered to one age band and one question. Creating a calculation that is the difference from each year compared to the very first year shows that in 2016, 14% fewer people aged 16–24 "drank alcohol in the last week" (based on the question in the survey) compared to 2005. Every single year from 2006 onward relates its result back to the value of 2005, which forms the baseline, showing that overall alcohol consumption appears to be trending down.

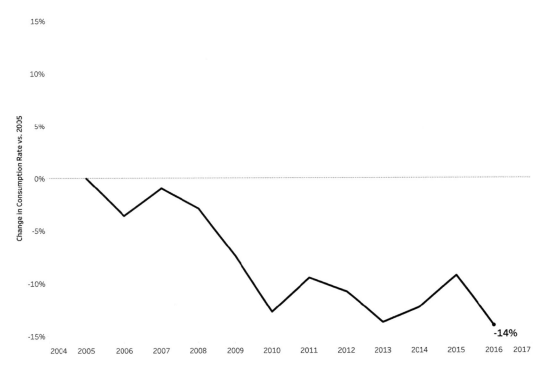

**FIGURE 3.5**   Alcohol consumption rate in Britain compared to 2005.

Compare that to Figure 3.6, where, instead of using absolute change (difference from 2005) we have applied a relative change calculation: the *% difference* of each year compared to 2005. This implies that in 2016, 23% fewer people aged 16–24 "drank alcohol in the last week" compared to 2005.

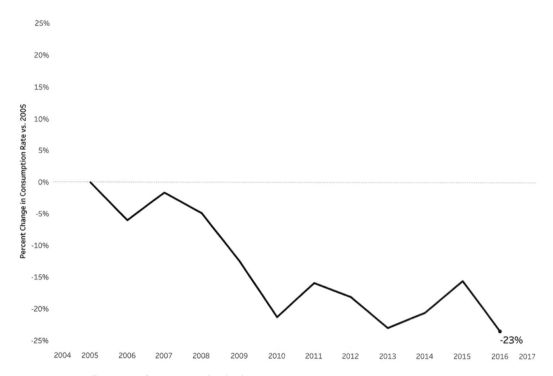

**FIGURE 3.6**   Percent change in alcohol consumption rate in Britain compared to 2005.

Calculating the percent change between two percentages is not completely inaccurate, but it can be very misleading. Instead, you should use the absolute change when you are working with percentages and want to show the difference between two points in time.

*Making Comparisons with Ranks*

Ranks do not explain how much one item varies from another. Ranked data is ordinal; that is, the data is categorical and has a sequence (e.g., who finished the race first, second, and third). That's it! Ranked data can be used for showing the order of the data points.

Consider Figure 3.7, which shows the rank of sales for each region across product categories.

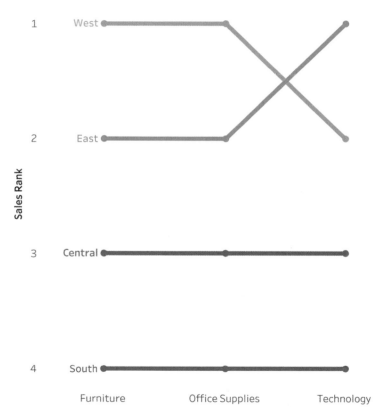

**FIGURE 3.7**   Rank of regions by sales by product category.

Figure 3.7 tells you which region ranked first, second, third, and fourth for a given product category, no more, no less.

If a box plot is added to show the variance between the data, as in Figure 3.8, you see that the statistical median (i.e., the place where the two gray areas meet in the box plot) within each category is identical. This means that the variance between the ranks is identical, as would be expected with ordinal data. In other words, you cannot make assumptions about the true variance between the regions (i.e., by how much sales vary from one region to the next).

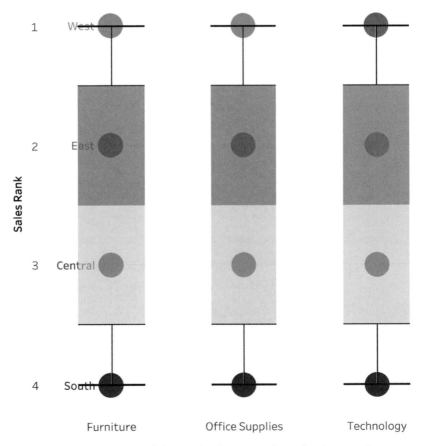

**FIGURE 3.8**    Box plot of the rank of regions by sales by product category.

If you look at the actual sales values instead of the rank of sales, you start to gain an understanding of the variance across the regions. You can now see in Figure 3.9 how much better one region performs in monetary terms compared to another region.

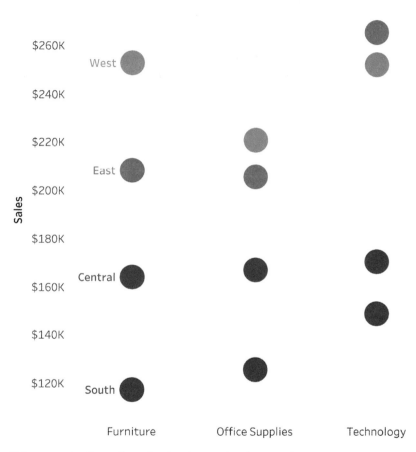

**FIGURE 3.9**   Dot plot of sales by region by product category.

By adding a box plot in Figure 3.10, it is now easier to see the variance across the regions within each category and also which category has the highest median (technology).

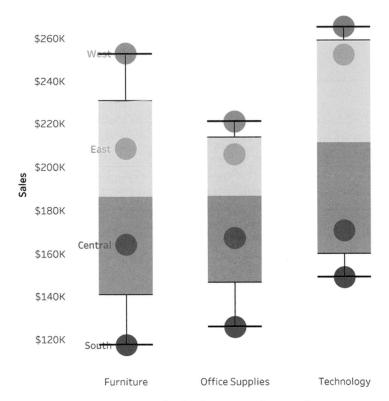

**FIGURE 3.10**   Box plot of sales by region by product category.

When working with ranked data, you cannot make inferences about the variance in the data; all you can say with certainty is which item is ranked higher than the others, not how much higher. When you have ranked data of a sprint race at the Olympics, you can say who came first, second, and third, but without the underlying detail, you cannot say how much faster one person was compared to the next.

## Basic Aggregation Types

This section covers the four most common aggregation types that we have observed during the Makeover Monday project. The definition of the aggregation and the formulas for creating each calculation are included, as well as an example of a chart for each type of aggregation.

### Summarization

You have gathered all of your sales data and now you need to understand total sales at various levels of aggregation. Perhaps you need to understand sales by month or sales by region or which products are selling the most. Each of these requires a basic summarization; that is, you add the sales together for each member of a field, as in Figure 3.11.

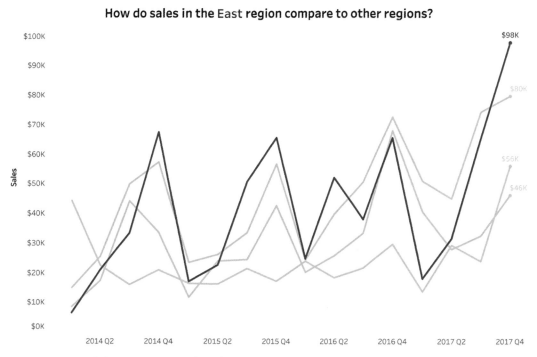

**FIGURE 3.11**   Sales summarized to the region and quarter level.

Formula

$$\sum each\ individual\ value$$

Example Chart

Figure 3.11 shows the sales summarized by region, year and quarter.

### Average/Mean

An average represents a typical number for a group of things. For example, on average it rains three days per week. In everyday talk, people use the word "average" as a good indicator, meaning that some of the values are above the average and some are below.

When an analyst calculates an average, what they are really calculating is the mean. The mean is calculated by summarizing the values in the set and then dividing by the number of values that comprise the set.

Formula

$$\frac{\sum each\ individual\ value}{n}\ where\ n = number\ of\ values\ in\ the\ data\ set$$

Example Chart

In Figure 3.12 we want to know the average number of RBIs (runs batted in) across all players.

### Median

Median and mean are often confused. While the mean provides the mathematical average, the median returns the middle value in a data set when the values are arranged from smallest to largest.

## What is the average number of RBIs per position?

| Pos | RBI | Players | Avg. RBI |
|-----|-----|---------|----------|
| RF | 100 | 1 | 100.0 |
| 2B | 72 | 1 | 72.0 |
| SS | 69 | 1 | 69.0 |
| LF | 111 | 2 | 55.5 |
| 3B | 107 | 2 | 53.5 |
| DH | 45 | 1 | 45.0 |
| 1B | 122 | 3 | 40.7 |
| CF | 37 | 1 | 37.0 |
| OF | 16 | 1 | 16.0 |
| C | 30 | 3 | 10.0 |
| UT | 40 | 4 | 10.0 |
| IF | 9 | 2 | 4.5 |

**FIGURE 3.12**   Table of average RBIs per player.

If there is an odd number of values, then the median represents the value exactly in the middle of the data set. For example, if there are seven values ordered from smallest to largest, then the median would be the fourth value in the data set.

If there is an even number of values, then the median is the average of the two values in the middle. If there are eight values, then the median would be the average of the fourth and the fifth values.

Formula

*Median = value of ((n + 1)/2)th data point in an ordered set*[2]

---

[2] en.wikipedia.org/wiki/Median

**What is the median RBIs for all players?**

| # | Player | RBI | Median |
|---|--------|-----|--------|
| 1 | Alberto Gonzalez | 1 | 20 |
| 2 | Juan Miranda | 1 | 20 |
| 3 | Ivan Rodriguez | 3 | 20 |
| 4 | Morgan Ensberg | 4 | 20 |
| 5 | Justin Christian | 6 | 20 |
| 6 | Richie Sexson | 6 | 20 |
| 7 | Shelley Duncan | 6 | 20 |
| 8 | Cody Ransom | 8 | 20 |
| 9 | Chad Moeller | 9 | 20 |
| 10 | Brett Gardner | 16 | 20 |
| 11 | Jose Molina | 18 | 20 |
| 12 | Jorge Posada | 22 | 20 |
| 13 | Wilson Betemit | 25 | 20 |
| 14 | Melky Cabrera | 37 | 20 |
| 15 | Xavier Nady | 40 | 20 |
| 16 | Hideki Matsui | 45 | 20 |
| 17 | Derek Jeter | 69 | 20 |
| 18 | Johnny Damon | 71 | 20 |
| 19 | Robinson Cano | 72 | 20 |
| 20 | Jason Giambi | 96 | 20 |
| 21 | Bobby Abreu | 100 | 20 |
| 22 | Alex Rodriguez | 103 | 20 |

**FIGURE 3.13**   Table of median RBIs across all players.

## Example Chart

Figure 3.13 shows the median number of RBIs across all players.

1. Summarize the RBIs per player (i.e., how many RBIs does each player have?).

2. Sort the players from smallest to largest RBI (or largest to smallest).

3. Count the number of players, add one, and then divide by two: (22 players + 1) / 2 = 11.5.

4. Since there is an even number of players, to get the median you need to average the RBI values for the players in the 11th and 12th positions in the order: (18 + 22)/2 = 20.

### Count (Distinct)

Counting is the action of finding the number of elements of a finite data set.[3] For example:

- How many players are on a team for each season?
- Who are the female engineers employed by an organization each month?
- How many SKUs (stock-keeping units) are in the product portfolio?

To count the unique items in a data set, you typically use a *distinct* function: count the number of elements in a data set, but count each element only once. For example:

- How many unique first names are there for all players in the league?
- How many days have at least one sale?
- How many unique customers did we reach during last year's marketing campaign?

Counting the distinct elements avoids incorrectly inflating the numbers. Using the marketing campaign example, to get the number of customers reached, you do not want to count a single customer multiple times even if we contacted them every month and therefore there are 12 records in the data set for that customer.

---

[3] en.wikipedia.org/wiki/Counting

Formula

$$Count = \sum Observations\ in\ a\ set$$

*Given the set ['blue', 'red', 'blue', 'yellow', 'blue', 'red'], count = 6*

$$Count\ Distinct = \sum Unique\ Observations\ in\ a\ set$$

*Given the set ['blue', 'red', 'blue', 'yellow', 'blue', 'red'], count distinct = 3*

Example Chart

If you want to know how frequently products are sold in each product category, you should count all of the products each time they had a sale, as shown in Figure 3.14.

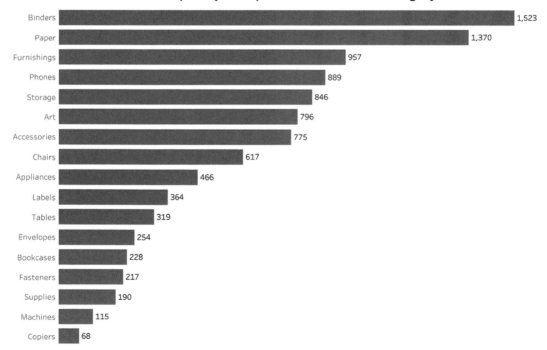

**FIGURE 3.14**   Bar chart of a count of products sold.

However, if you want to know how many unique products sold in each category, you need to change the measurement to a distinct count. Notice in Figure 3.15 how the order of the product categories changed based on the number of distinct products sold.

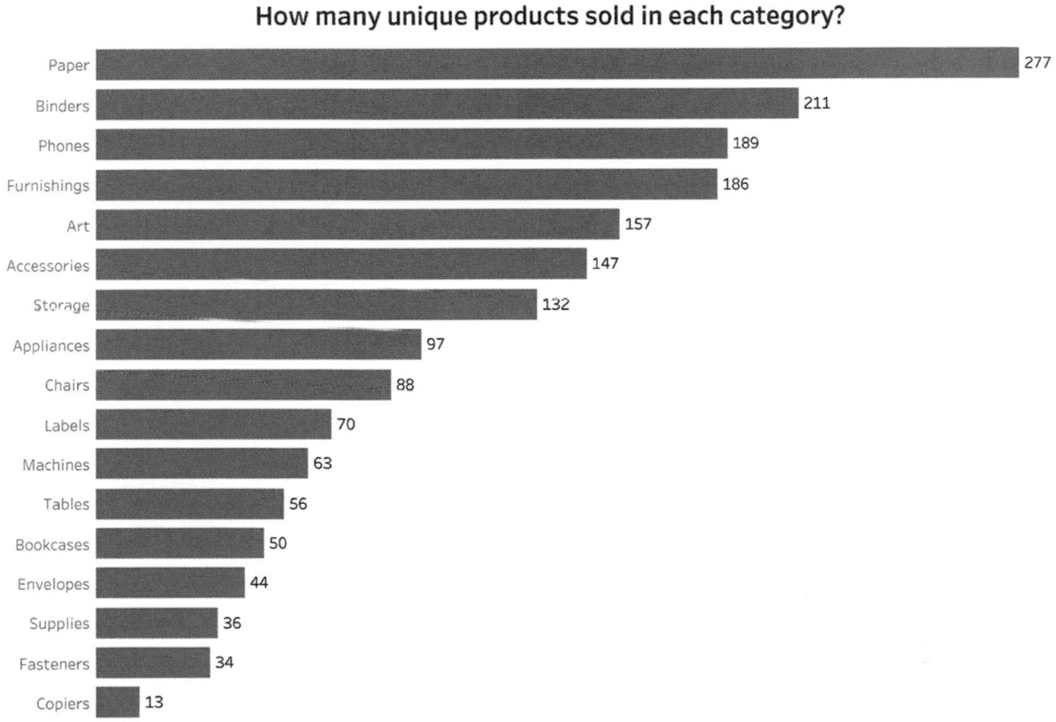

**How many unique products sold in each category?**

|  |  |
|---|---|
| Paper | 277 |
| Binders | 211 |
| Phones | 189 |
| Furnishings | 186 |
| Art | 157 |
| Accessories | 147 |
| Storage | 132 |
| Appliances | 97 |
| Chairs | 88 |
| Labels | 70 |
| Machines | 63 |
| Tables | 56 |
| Bookcases | 50 |
| Envelopes | 44 |
| Supplies | 36 |
| Fasteners | 34 |
| Copiers | 13 |

**FIGURE 3.15**   Bar chart of unique products sold.

Count and count distinct are used to answer different questions. Use count when you need to know the total number of items in a set. Use count distinct when you are interested in the unique number of items in a set.

## Explaining Metrics

Include information for viewers of your visualizations who do not have any background on the topic and need some guidance to interpret the data. If it is a metric the audience is probably not familiar with, take the time to explain how it is calculated and what it means. If you have taken a standard calculation and changed it slightly to fit the purpose, be sure to point that out to the audience. In the end, you want your audience to quickly understand what you created. Using complex metrics will only hinder interpretation.

## Know Your Audience

When you create a data visualization, you rarely create something for yourself and instead focus on other users. Unless you know your audience, you are likely to fall short with your communication. If you know exactly who your audience is, great! However, it is rare that you will know everyone who will view your work. It is likely you will have to account for an unknown audience; whether it is online or in your organization, someone you gave a report to may show it to others you never considered as your target audience.

### Tips for Identifying Your Audience

A little bit of research can go a long way toward understanding your audience and their needs. Consider making a short list of the people who may be in your audience. Try to be as specific as possible and then do some research about them. If you are presenting to upper-level management, ask others in the organization what is important to them. If you are presenting to a team of analysts, it is likely you will go into a lot more detail than you would for an overview report to the board of directors. Either way, taking some time to get to know your audience will help you communicate more effectively.

If you are addressing a mixed audience, your communication will most likely need to be targeted at the most senior person or the decision maker. Design your analysis for them; you can always follow up with the rest of the team later.

Once you have enough information about your audience, make note of their different needs and use these insights as a guideline for your analysis. If you create something that is not on that list of needs, keep it off your final output; you can always provide it on request. Do not add something that could confuse your audience. Finally, review your work with someone who can give you unbiased feedback. Particularly useful is someone who does not know about the content and is honest with you; if you make your analysis understandable to them, then you have probably communicated the information very well.

## Using Appropriate Metrics

When aggregating data, it is important to consider the base metric. Take a look at Figure 3.16, a line chart of BMW and Mercedes car prices by month.

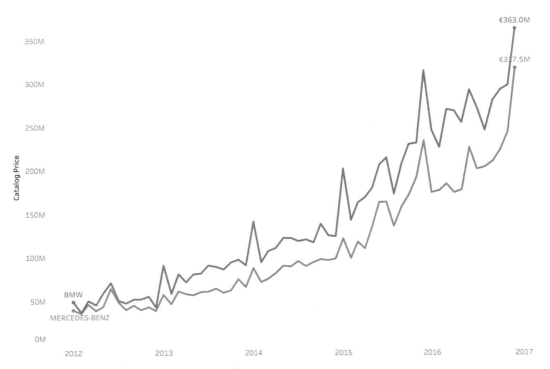

**FIGURE 3.16**  Total BMW and Mercedes-Benz prices over time.

It should be obvious that a car does not cost €300+ million. The purpose of this chart is to compare the prices of BMW to Mercedes over time, but the data, as presented, is not normalized by the number of cars sold. Data is often presented in this manner because the analyst did not take the time to understand the data and to identify an appropriate metric.

Since this data is about car prices, it does not make sense to summarize the prices. When you want to compare the prices of car models, you should probably look at the median or average price. When you do that, as in Figure 3.17, the prices are easy to understand, and effective comparisons can be made.

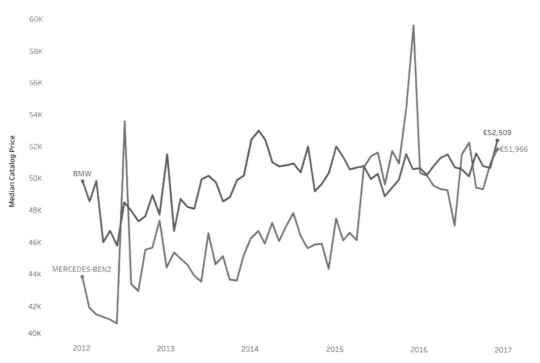

**FIGURE 3.17**   Median BMW and Mercedes-Benz prices over time.

## Creating New Metrics to Tell a Different Story

When approaching an analytical project, you are often presented with a limited set of metrics. Any great data analyst will see this as an opportunity to redefine or restructure the data in order to interpret it in a different way. Reshaping the data provides you with a new structure of fields and metrics that can potentially be used in ways that give you more options for analyzing the data.

Consider Figure 3.18, which examines visitor history to US National Memorials. A common way to look at this data is to plot the cumulative number of visitors over time.

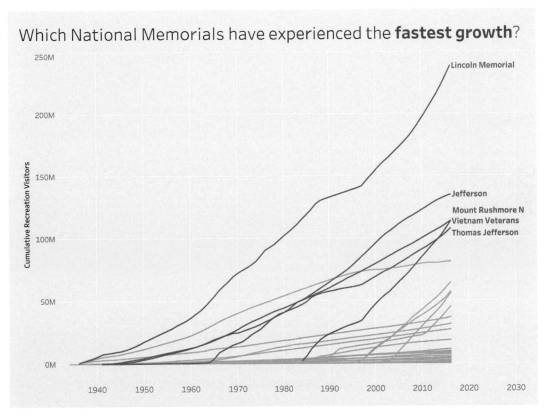

**FIGURE 3.18** Cumulative visitors to National Memorials.

There is nothing wrong with this metric; however, Shawn Levin took a different approach in Figure 3.19 by creating a metric for how "old" each park was. This metric was not originally in the data set, so he needed to create a calculation to include it.

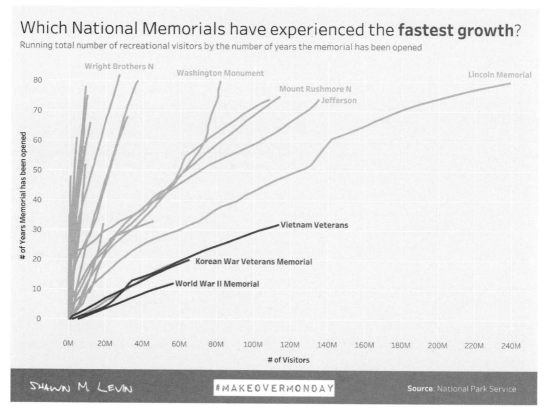

**FIGURE 3.19**   Cumulative visitors to National Memorials since they opened.

This is a subtle change, and when presented in the way that Shawn did, a different story can be told. When you are exploring your data, look for alternate views of the data; you just may find a more interesting insight.

## Identifying and Correcting Mistakes

When we gave the community global warming data to analyze, one of the first visualizations posted came from Charlie Hutcheson (Figure 3.20).

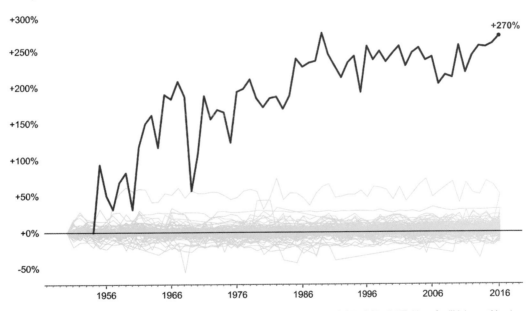

**FIGURE 3.20**   Relative temperature change by country.

While the design looks great, this visualization suffered from a flaw: it showed relative change instead of absolute change. Since this visualization focused on temperatures, what really is relative change?

What does it mean for something be 20% hotter? And 20% hotter in °C is very different to 20% hotter in °F. Relative change is the percentage change of the absolute variance to a prior period.

On the other hand, absolute change is the difference to a prior period. When analyzing temperature change, absolute change is more understandable to the audience. We know what +10°F or −5°C feels like. Charlie took this feedback into account and revised his visualization in Figure 3.21; +10°F is much easier to understand than +270%.

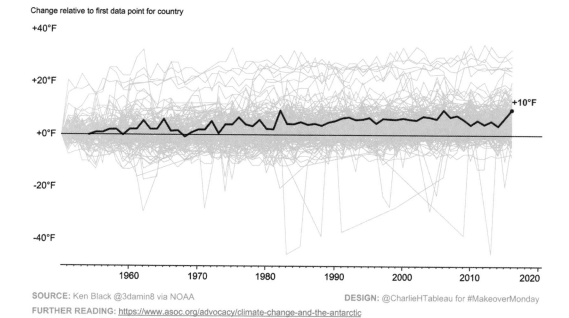

FIGURE 3.21    Absolute temperature change by country.

While Charlie's visualization related to using a confusing metric, the dashboard Rahul Singh created in Figure 3.22 used an incorrect aggregation. The data about medal winners in the Southeast Asian Games (SEA Games) included every medal won by every individual and team.

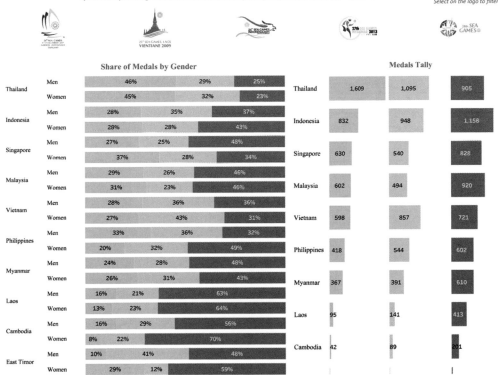

*The Southeast Asian Games (also known as the SEA Games) is a biennial multi-sport event involving participants from the current 11 countries of Southeast Asia. The games are under regulation of the Southeast Asian Games Federation with supervision by the International Olympic Committee (IOC) and the Olympic Council of Asia. The following dashboard looks into how the participating nations have performed between 2009 and 2015.*

*Select on the logo to filter*

**FIGURE 3.22**   Duplicated count of medals won in the SEA Games.

Look at the bars on the right side. According to this chart, Thailand won 1609 medals as a country across five years. That is nearly 322 medals per year. A quick analysis of the data set indicates there are only 75 unique sports. So how can a country win more medals than events that exist? Obviously, they cannot. The issue is that every medal for every individual was counted as part of the total medal count for a country. However, the official medal counts are by event.

By counting the unique number of sports for each medal type, you get an accurate count of the number of medals won by each country. Figure 3.23 shows the accurate medal counts.

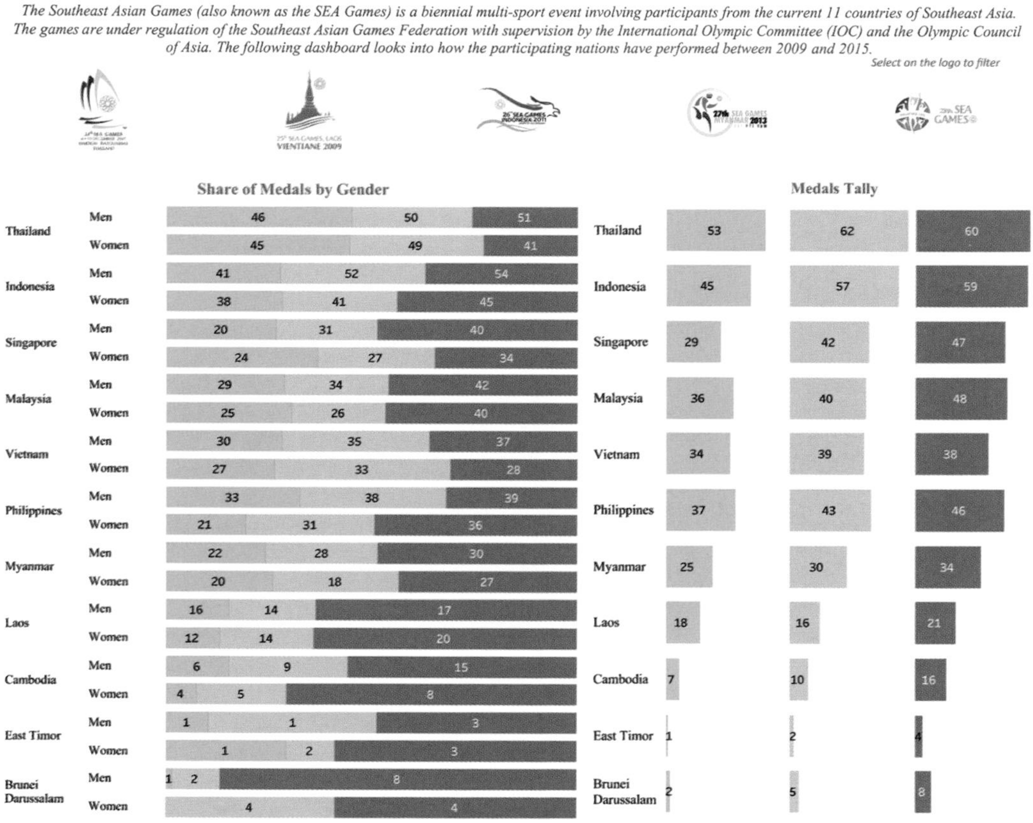
The Southeast Asian Games (also known as the SEA Games) is a biennial multi-sport event involving participants from the current 11 countries of Southeast Asia. The games are under regulation of the Southeast Asian Games Federation with supervision by the International Olympic Committee (IOC) and the Olympic Council of Asia. The following dashboard looks into how the participating nations have performed between 2009 and 2015.
Select on the logo to filter
VIENTIANE 2009
Share of Medals by Gender
Medals Tally
Thailand
Indonesia
Singapore
Malaysia
Vietnam
Philippines
Myanmar
Laos
Cambodia
East Timor
Brunei Darussalam
Men
Women

FIGURE 3.23 Correct count of medals won in the SEA Games.

As a data analyst, you need to have a sense for when something does not look quite right. You need to be able to spot outliers quickly and investigate their validity. Take time to explore the data and do some research about the topic. Simple steps like this will help you avoid basic mistakes.

## Time Series Analysis

A time series is a sequence of values, usually taken in equally spaced intervals. Typical examples include:

- Sales by month
- Users added to an app by year
- Heart rate per minute
- GPS location by second
- Stock price per hour
- Electricity used per day

Essentially, anything with a time dimension, measured in regular intervals, can be used for time series analysis. This section will introduce you to common methods for analyzing and visualizing time series data.

---

[4] onlinecourses.science.psu.edu/stat510/node/47

## Univariate Time Series

A univariate time series is a sequence of measurements of a single variable collected over time.[4] As shown in Figure 3.24, observations of $CO_2$ concentration are a single variable collected over time.

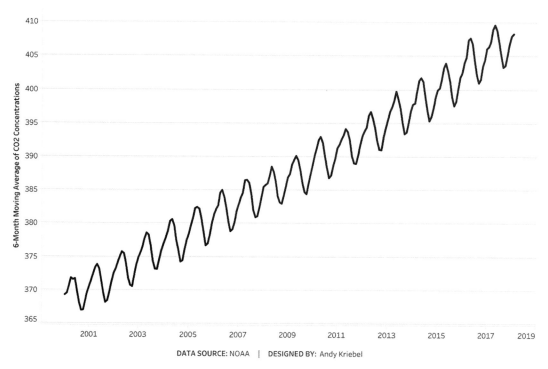

DATA SOURCE: NOAA   |   DESIGNED BY: Andy Kriebel

**FIGURE 3.24**   Time series plot of $CO_2$ concentration.

When analyzing univariate time series, you may be able to quickly see trends, as in the linear trend in Figure 3.25. Adding a linear trend line while observing the R-squared helps you confirm if the data points are well approximated.

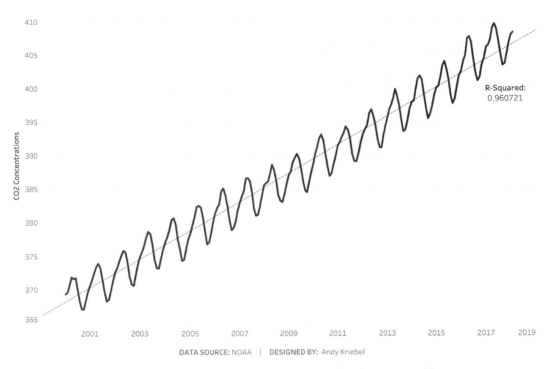

**FIGURE 3.25**   Time series plot of $CO_2$ concentration with a linear trend line.

## Visualizing Seasonality

If you are interested in seasonality, you can plot a date part (e.g., month) on the x-axis and add a line for each year, as in Figure 3.26.

The data has consistent patterns across all of the years, with the $CO_2$ concentration peaking in May, decreasing until September, then rising again until the following May. The design of the chart also shows a consistent increase of $CO_2$ concentrations over time as more recent years have higher $CO_2$ concentration levels than earlier years.

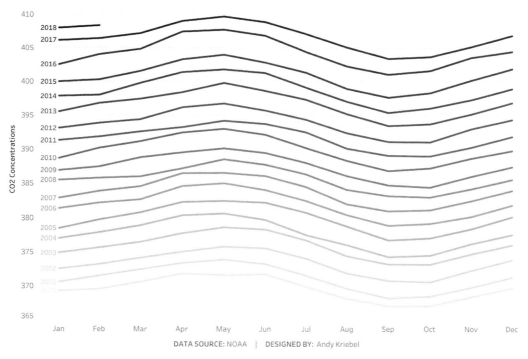

**FIGURE 3.26**   Seasonality plot of $CO_2$ concentration.

Displaying the data in a box plot, as in Figure 3.27, reveals the consistent distribution of the years within the months (lowest to highest data point as depicted by gray and black circles), the pattern of the median (where the two gray shaded boxes meet), and the consistent width of the interquartile range (the range from the bottom of the gray box to the top of the lighter gray box).

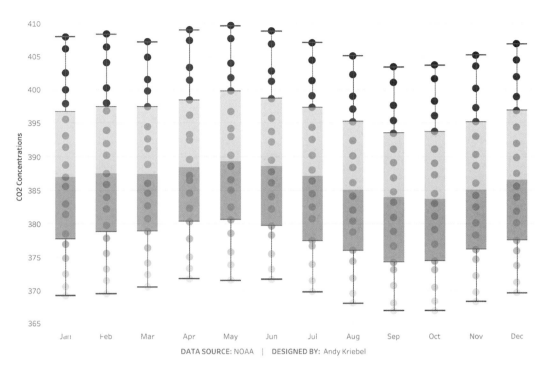

**FIGURE 3.27**   Box plot of $CO_2$ concentration.

However, the drawback of the box plot is that it tends to hide the values due to its design. The gray shaded boxes cover some of the data points, making them hard to identify. Figure 3.28 uses lines for more effective display of the median, 25th percentile, and 75th percentile, ensuring the focus is on the spread.

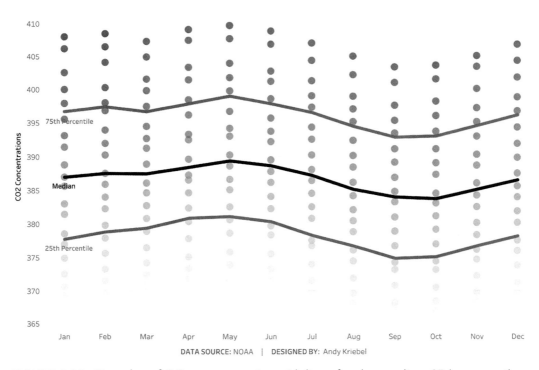

**FIGURE 3.28**   Dot plot of $CO_2$ concentration with lines for the median, 25th percentile, and 75th percentile.

Finally, comparing each individual month to the average for the year normalizes the data and creates an index for each year (i.e., a variance from the mean). In Figure 3.29, the zero line represents the yearly average, while the black lines are plotted along the months for each year. This display shows the variation from that average (i.e., how much one month differs when compared to the average).

This method for visualizing time series data confirms the systematic nature of $CO_2$ concentration.

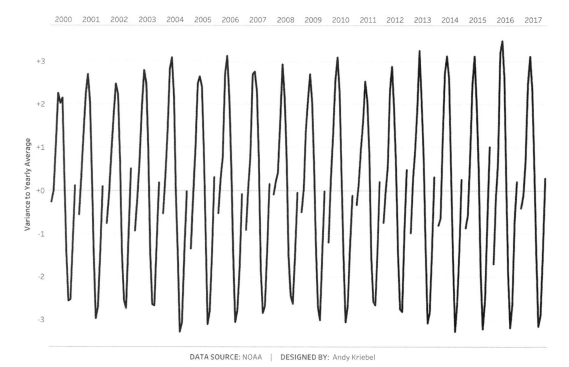

DATA SOURCE: NOAA | DESIGNED BY: Andy Kriebel

**FIGURE 3.29** Monthly CO$_2$ concentration.

## Using Moving Averages for Smoothing

Smoothing is a technique that can be used to remove some of the variation in short-term data in favor of emphasizing long-term trends. One of the most common methods is moving average smoothing. Typically, a moving average is the unweighted mean of a series of preceding data points. In many cases, the moving average will also include the current data point. For example, a six-month moving average would be the average of values from the current month and the previous five months.

In the sample data set of $CO_2$ concentration, you may want to smooth the data over a period of time by adding a moving average. Applying a six-month moving average to the data (i.e., the current month value plus the values for the previous five months divided by six) gives you a much smoother visualization, as demonstrated in Figure 3.30.

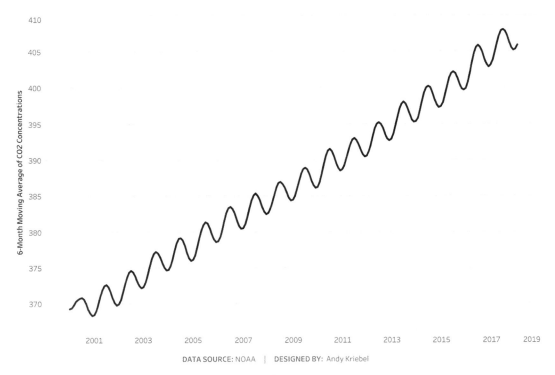

DATA SOURCE: NOAA  |  DESIGNED BY: Andy Kriebel

**FIGURE 3.30**   Six-month moving average of $CO_2$ concentration.

## Variance from a Point in Time

Comparing data to a fixed point in time allows the audience to understand magnitude of change. For example, Figure 3.31 shows how home prices have changed since the first month that data was available.

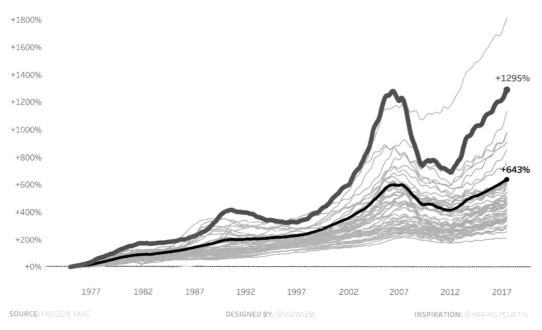

**FIGURE 3.31**   Change in home prices compared to the first time period.

This type of variance analysis allows you to compare change to any point in time. On 30 December 2008, the Case–Shiller home price index reported its largest price drop in its history.[5] Visually plotting time series data against a point in time reveals patterns relative to that period, thus allowing the reader to understand growth and decline before and after the given point in time.

Giving your audience the flexibility to pick and choose their reference point, as has been done in Figure 3.32, allows them to compare values across any time periods that are of particular interest to them.

---

[5] en.wikipedia.org/wiki/United_States_housing_bubble

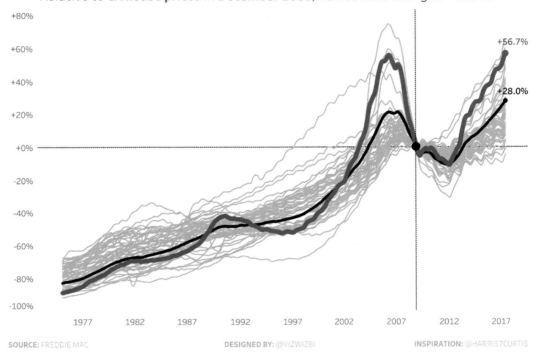

**FIGURE 3.32**   Change in home prices compared to a selected time period.

In addition, allowing the user to choose a state to highlight makes it more contextual. Including a black line for the US average shows how all of the states compare to the nation.

## Cycle Plots

A cycle plot (Cleveland, Dunn, and Terpenning, 1978) shows both the cycle or trend and the month-of-the-year effect.[6] A standard line chart will display year and then month on the x-axis and a metric on the y-axis. Figure 3.33 represents the median ozone level across the United States by month for a number of years.

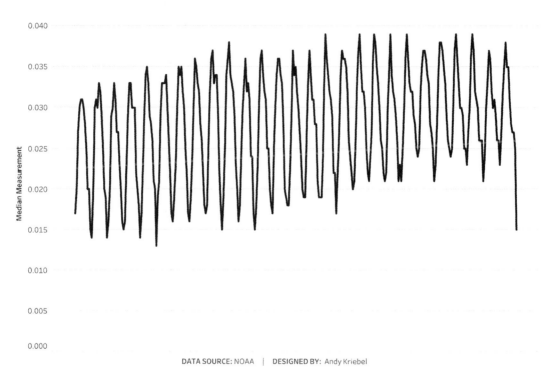

DATA SOURCE: NOAA   |   DESIGNED BY: Andy Kriebel

**FIGURE 3.33**  Monthly $CO_2$ concentration.

---

[6] Naomi B. Robbins, Ph.D., Visual Business Intelligence Newsletter, January 2008.

A cycle plot will flip the two parts of the date field. While Figure 3.33 displays months within each year, a cycle plot, as in Figure 3.34, will display years within each month. Once that display is created, add a line for the average across all years for each month and you have a cycle plot.

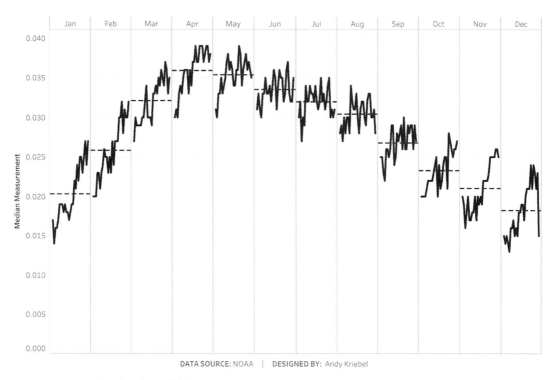

DATA SOURCE: NOAA   |   DESIGNED BY: Andy Kriebel

**FIGURE 3.34**   Cycle plot of $CO_2$ concentration.

The cycle plot shows you that April has the highest median ozone level, which was much more difficult to see in the original view. You can also see that, generally speaking, ozone levels have increased in most months over the years as many of the lines within each month are trending upward (i.e., from bottom left to top right).

## Calendar Heat Map

Heat maps are effective visualizations for seeing concentrations as well as patterns. Adding time series to a heat map can also reveal seasonality that may not be obvious otherwise. As we saw in the previous section, $CO_2$ levels are highest in the US from April until June. See Figure 3.35.

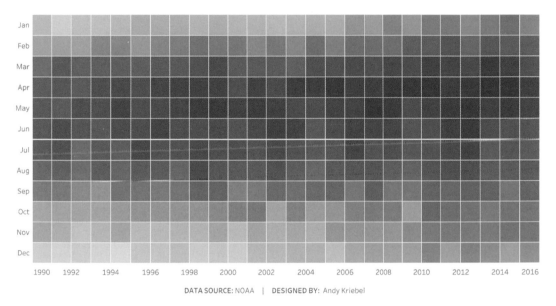

DATA SOURCE: NOAA  |  DESIGNED BY: Andy Kriebel

**FIGURE 3.35**   Heat map of median $CO_2$ levels.

Presenting this data as a heat map instead of a cycle plot reveals a pattern you may not have noticed before: $CO_2$ levels have steadily increased since 1990. You can see this by the gradual darkening of the heat map as you read it from left to right.

Figure 3.36 reduces the data to the state of Colorado, revealing an even more striking increase.

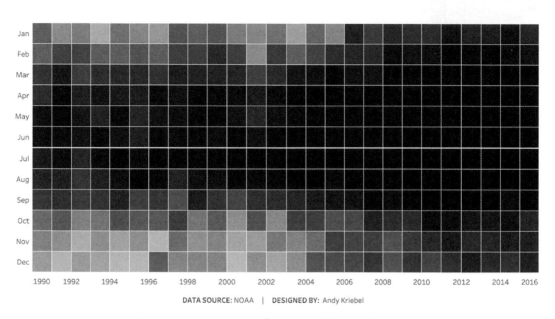

DATA SOURCE: NOAA  |  DESIGNED BY: Andy Kriebel

**FIGURE 3.36**  Heat map of median $CO_2$ levels in Colorado.

Figure 3.37, shows decreases in Florida in the summer, likely because people who live there seasonally retreat from the heat (and take their cars with them).

Consider calendar heat maps as an alternative time series visualization. They can be very effective at revealing hidden patterns in your data.

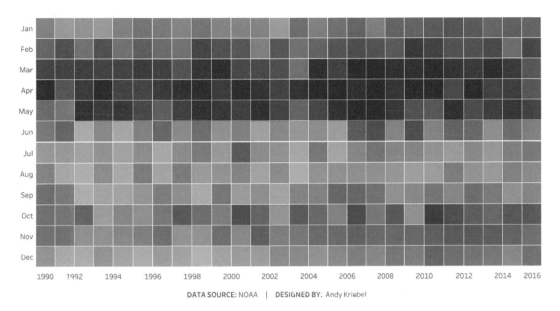

**FIGURE 3.37** Heat map of median $CO_2$ levels in Florida.

## Summary

Throughout this chapter we have provided some basic advice for how to become a more effective data analyst by really knowing and understanding your data. You should now understand:

1. What data aggregation means, how you can aggregate data, and when you should avoid aggregating data that is already aggregated

2. How to identify your audience and how to communicate metrics clearly to them

3. How to identify and correct a mistake in your analysis

4. The basics of time series analysis and effective visual representations of time series data

These lessons are easy to incorporate into your daily analytical work. All it takes is attention to detail and an honest assessment of your own work.

Chapter Four

# Keep It Simple

Keeping it simple can relate to various aspects of your work, be it design, storytelling, or analysis. Before providing guidance on how you can meld simplicity into your work, let us define what we mean.

## What Is Simplicity?

Simplicity for data visualization often focuses on minimizing the number of elements that do not add value to your display. These include borders, gridlines, axes lines, and boxes, which can easily distract from your core message. This recommendation also relates to the information itself. You should strive to create a visualization that focuses on specific aspects of the data, rather than including all fields and metrics but not saying much about any of them.

A broader definition describes simplicity as *the state of being simple, uncomplicated, or uncompounded; freedom from pretense or guile; directness of expression.*[1]

---

[1] merriam-webster.com/dictionary/simplicity

With data visualizations, you typically aim to communicate information, ideally in a way that makes it accessible quickly and easily for the audience. Sometimes, including additional visual indicators, such as icons or images, can enhance a design. However, if overused, they can distract from the core message.

This chapter focuses on different types of simplicity as they relate to data visualization, specifically:

- Simplicity in design
- Simplicity in analysis
- Simplicity in storytelling

## Simplicity in Design

Simplicity in design can be recognized in visualizations that are clear, easy to understand, uncluttered, and impactful. Nonessential items are removed from these visualizations so that the data stands out, giving it space and removing distractions. Simplicity in design pays careful attention to the overall layout and positioning of individual components, the balance of charts and text elements, and the choice of colors, fonts, and icons, as well as the clarity with which all of these elements communicate to the audience.

The following sections provide examples and recommendations relating to these items to help you simplify your own designs.

### Simplicity in Layout and Positioning

Whether you are visualizing data, designing dashboards, or telling data stories, there is a lot of flexibility when it comes to layout, sizing, and positioning. Most of these choices will, and should, be driven by the needs of the audience and stakeholders.

*Devices Dictate Your Layout*

In most organizations, the majority of information presented digitally will be consumed on laptops and desktop computers. When
you create data visualizations for an audience using standard computer screens, size your dashboards accordingly and keep to a format that does not go beyond the dimensions of a typical laptop
in your organization. Predetermine the size of your dashboard so
you have full control over its layout and the positioning of different
charts and text elements.

Most of the dashboards you design are likely to be in landscape
format. Take care not to let them extend beyond the width of the
screen because scrolling horizontally—as opposed to vertically—is
not intuitive for most people.

Increasingly, dashboards are viewed on mobile devices such as
phones and tablets. Interactivity through touch brings different
design challenges. If your audience is likely to view visualizations on
their mobile phones, you need to ensure that the number and size
of the various charts, text boxes, and the white space around them
suit the smaller screen size. The interactivity through touch, and the
sizing of titles, subtitles, and annotations, as well as a vertical flow,
also need to be taken into account for when users scroll. "Designing for Mobile" is discussed in more detail in Chapter 6.

*Horizontal and Vertical Layouts*

The flow of your visualization significantly influences your overall
layout. Landscape format is suitable and most commonly used to
show all of the information on a single page. This allows elements to
be arranged easily and effectively, guiding the viewer's eye across
the page from left to right and top to bottom, a natural reading
direction. A dashboard with a width-to-height ratio of 4 : 3 or 16 : 9
can fill up a screen nicely, maximizing the available space.

When we asked our community to visualize survey results of the characteristics people from different nationalities prefer in a romantic partner, Leonid Koyfman created a very straightforward dashboard in Excel (Figure 4.1), using a horizontal layout and strong, bold colors to show his findings.

**Personality** is the single **most important** characteristic in a romantic partner, say half of Brits. Surprisingly, **amount of money** is **least important**.

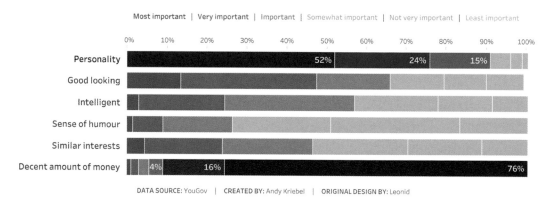

**FIGURE 4.1**   Horizontal layout that fills the space nicely.

For a horizontal stacked bar chart like Figure 4.1, a landscape format works well, because it gives each bar enough space and allows the characteristics to be displayed in an easy-to-read fashion. If this bar chart were half the current width, the individual response categories would not be as easy to differentiate because they would be much closer together.

A portrait layout, where the height is larger than the width, is commonly used for a visualization that unfolds through a series of steps and charts. It typically starts with an introduction at the top and moves through key findings until reaching the conclusion at the bottom. Infographic-style dashboards and chronological flows can make for very compelling portrait layouts, following a Z-pattern from the top left to the bottom right of the page. While a horizontal timeline conveys the notion of time very well, it may not be the only chart you want to use in your overall visualization. The vertical layout can help you take your audience through the different stages of your visualization.

The visualization in Figure 4.2 from Athan Mavrantonis of air quality data from US-based measuring stations was created in a portrait format. Athan showed how ozone levels have changed over the years and within each year on a month-by-month basis, guiding the eye from top left to bottom right down the view.

The repetition of the US map for every month and year keeps this visualization simple and allows Athan's audience to understand patterns as their eyes move down the page from one month to the next and across the page to see the changes over time.

Placing the color legend and definition of ozone at the top of the page helps the audience understand the key elements of the visualization up front. This is followed with small multiple maps that highlight the points in time at which ozone concentrations are most dangerous for our health. The visuals are followed by another two text elements: one focusing on answering the question "So what?" and the other providing practical tips for the readers who want to protect themselves from the harmful ozone. Athan's layout choices frame the visualization with explanations and insights.

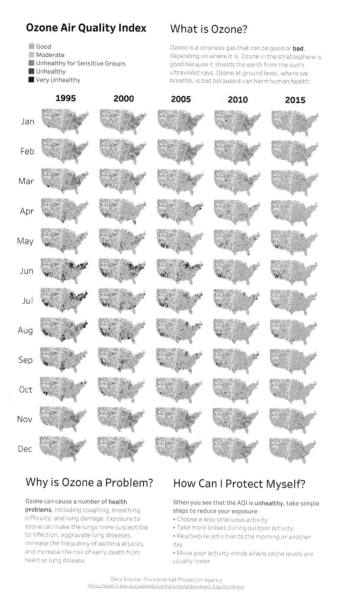

**Ozone Air Quality Index**

- Good
- Moderate
- Unhealthy for Sensitive Groups
- Unhealthy
- Very Unhealthy

**What is Ozone?**

Ozone is a colorless gas that can be good or **bad**, depending on where it is. Ozone in the stratosphere is good because it shields the earth from the sun's ultraviolet rays. Ozone at ground level, where we breathe, is bad because it can harm human health.

|       | 1995 | 2000 | 2005 | 2010 | 2015 |
|-------|------|------|------|------|------|
| Jan   |      |      |      |      |      |
| Feb   |      |      |      |      |      |
| Mar   |      |      |      |      |      |
| Apr   |      |      |      |      |      |
| May   |      |      |      |      |      |
| Jun   |      |      |      |      |      |
| Jul   |      |      |      |      |      |
| Aug   |      |      |      |      |      |
| Sep   |      |      |      |      |      |
| Oct   |      |      |      |      |      |
| Nov   |      |      |      |      |      |
| Dec   |      |      |      |      |      |

**Why is Ozone a Problem?**

Ozone can cause a number of **health problems**, including coughing, breathing difficulty, and lung damage. Exposure to ozone can make the lungs more susceptible to infection, aggravate lung diseases, increase the frequency of asthma attacks, and increase the risk of early death from heart or lung disease.

**How Can I Protect Myself?**

When you see that the AQI is **unhealthy**, take simple steps to reduce your exposure:
- Choose a less-strenuous activity
- Take more breaks during outdoor activity
- Reschedule activities to the morning or another day
- Move your activity inside where ozone levels are usually lower

Data Source: Enviromental Protection Agency
https://aqsdr1.epa.gov/aqsweb/aqstmp/airdata/download_files.html#Raw

Designed by @amavrantonis for #MakeoverMonday

**FIGURE 4.2**   Vertical layout that flows down the page.

*Using White Space*

White space gives the charts and text elements of your visualization room to breathe, resulting in a cleaner look and feel. Think of it like effective pauses and silence in a speech. A well-planned pause can strengthen the argument someone just made. A pause can increase tension or apprehension. It can draw an audience in further, making them want to hear the rest of the story. Pauses set the scene for whatever comes next. White space, as the visual equivalent of a pause, helps your audience to focus on the next part of the story.

If your visualization contains a number of elements and pieces of information together, white space helps remove unnecessary distractions. Ideally, the charts are designed in a way that gives your audience clarity and lets them understand the key insights very quickly. Color choices, highlighting, annotations, and other ways of drawing attention to your findings help in the process. By leaving white or blank space around your charts, you are able to keep the focus of your audience on the key message rather than distracting or confusing them.

When the Makeover Monday community looked at life expectancy data by the World Health Organization, Colin Wojtowycz created a visualization that uses white space very effectively, as seen in Figure 4.3.

Colin could have filled the white space in his visualization with text, filters, or additional charts. Instead, Colin chose to focus on a single country and visualized the significant drop in life expectancy during the genocide in 1994 in Rwanda. His design is impactful enough to make curious viewers do their own research to find the story behind the drop.

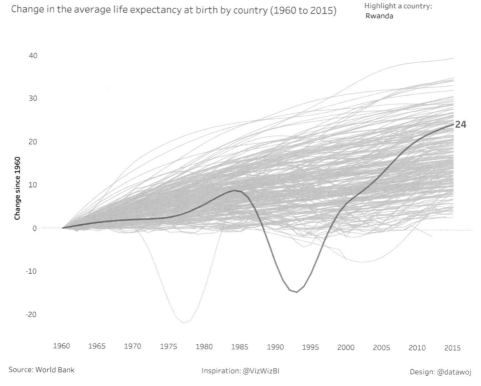

### How has life expectancy in Rwanda changed since 1960?

Change in the average life expectancy at birth by country (1960 to 2015)     Highlight a country: Rwanda

Source: World Bank                 Inspiration: @VizWizBI                 Design: @datawoj

**FIGURE 4.3**   White space helps provide focus on the important data.

### Intuitive Design

An intuitive design helps your audience understand quickly by being clear and easy to follow, and using familiar elements, such as colors and shapes. To assess whether your design is intuitive, ask yourself the following questions:

- Am I allowing my audience to read the visualization in a logical and natural order? Would those without any background knowledge or guidance follow this path? Does the visualization flow in a natural reading pattern from the top left to the bottom right?

- Do the colors logically fit the data? For example, should a solemn or serious topic be visualized using muted or dark colors?

When representing female and male categories, do the colors form associations to gender?

- Are the titles, filters, legends, and controls placed in areas that make them easy to find without getting in the way?
- Does the design build trust with the audience? If the title is in the form of a question, is this question answered by the analysis and the conclusions? Alternatively, if the title is making a claim, does the data back it up?

Go through some of these questions as you design your next visualization to ensure what you create is straightforward and intuitive.

### Reducing Charts and Text

It can be very tempting to create visualizations using as much of the available data as possible; it is tempting to choose a variety of charts to highlight different perspectives. A typical Makeover Monday visualization will have two or three charts, yet out of those there is a single chart that provides the insight really well, while the other charts are seemingly included to fill a gap. If the analysis can be told using a single chart, then that is what you should stick to. Any additional elements need a good reason for being there and should enhance, not distract from, the original insights.

This may mean that you may need to adjust the format of the final visualization and reduce it in size if a single chart does not take up as much space. Alternatively, consider using some of the available space to annotate the chart as a way of guiding the audience through the analysis. Keep in mind that these annotations should be succinct and add valuable information. As you read in the previous section, white space can be a useful and intentional choice in your design to present your analysis.

In Figure 4.4, Matt Francis used a single chart to visualize the changes in US meat consumption over the last few decades. Given that he created a single visualization instead of a collection of three or more charts on one page, Matt annotated the line chart and used reference bands to highlight his findings.

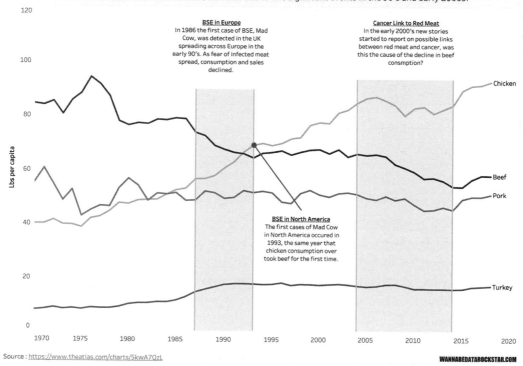

**FIGURE 4.4**  A single chart can be enough to reveal the analysis.

Adding annotations and reference bands helps clarify the possible reasons for a noticeable change in the pattern. In Matt's visualization, two key points were worth calling out:

1. The point in time when chicken consumption overtook that of beef

2. The period of a significant decline in beef and pork consumption, coinciding with an increase in chicken consumption

*Balancing Charts and Text*

Simple and effective design means that you must carefully consider the right balance of charts, text objects (e.g., titles, subtitles, annotations, footnotes), and interactivity. There is no one rule that stipulates the perfect balance of visualization to text. Some visualizations are highly effective and use the minimum amount of text. On the other hand, a text-heavy infographic can still be informative, engaging, and impactful.

To achieve simplicity, ask yourself:

- Does a chart or text box make a topic, a statement, or an insight easier to understand?
- Would a particular chart benefit from a small number of annotations explaining specific data points?
- Can filters and controls be replaced by interactivity so that user selections in one chart update other areas of the visualization?
- Are color, size, or shape legends necessary or can you avoid them by explaining these elements in subtitles, descriptions, or the axis?

When you design data visualizations that will stand on their own, you need to provide a different level of information compared to visualizations that are presented by a person who can add commentary and descriptions.

For standalone visualizations where the audience is often unknown, the type of data and the topic it relates to will often influence the amount of detail you need to provide. Some topics and data sets are more complicated and may require additional explanations that can be best achieved through descriptions and annotations. Other topics are basic enough for a single bar chart with a well-chosen title to tell the entire story.

Figures 4.5 and 4.6 showcase these two different approaches, yet both visualizations are excellent examples of simplicity and effectiveness. Figure 4.5, by Rob Radburn, analyzes the geographical patterns of prescriptions for asthma medication in England.

# The geography of high dose inhaled steroids to treat asthma across England

In the UK, around **5.4 million people** are currently receiving treatment for asthma, and tragically, three people die every day because of asthma attacks. Research shows that two thirds of asthma deaths are preventable. Some people with asthma are prescribed a preventer inhaler. They contain a low dose of steroid medicine called **corticosteroids.** However latest guidance on the treatment of asthma recommends that patients should be maintained at the lowest possible dose of inhaled corticosteroid.

Using a definition from the www.openprescribing.net, the viz below compares the prescribing of **high dose inhaled corticosteroids** with prescribing of **all inhaled corticosteroids** using the practise postcode for **2015.** There is wide variation in prescribing of high doses across England, particularly in the north of the country.

Let's be clear, there may be good reasons why a practice is prescribing more or less of something than other practices in the country. We don't have access to medical records. I'm not a doctor.

But the differences may highlight some issues - different prescribing cultures across the country, asthma not being as well managed as it should be, better detection, or simply more of the conditions that 'cause' asthma. Although it's difficult to say for sure what causes asthma. The viz poses more questions than it answers.

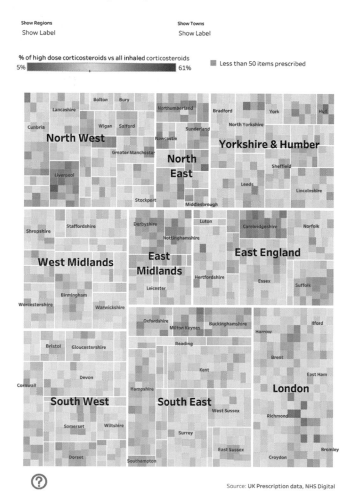

Source: UK Prescription data, NHS Digital

**FIGURE 4.5**   Geographic treemap of high dosage inhaled steroids.

**FIGURE 4.6** A well-chosen title and simple visualizations can tell an effective story.

Rob used a single visualization to showcase the geographical patterns in the data through a treemap that is aligned to the geographical regions of England. He included four paragraphs of descriptive text to highlight the risks surrounding high-dosage inhaled steroids.

When he analyzed data about the world as 100 people in Figure 4.6, Athan Mavrantonis focused on using colors, large numbers, only a few words, and two simple visualizations to put the data into a more meaningful context for his audience.

## Simplicity in Colors and Icons

While the previous sections focused on overall simplicity and effectiveness for data visualizations, when it comes to colors and icons, there are three things that can make your visualizations anything but easy to understand:

1. Too much color

2. Too many colors

3. Too many icons

## Colors

Colors in data visualization play a big role in communicating your message. They can enhance your visualization significantly by drawing attention to certain aspects, to outliers or growth, to loss, to specific regions. However, too much color can distract and confuse. Using color sparingly will help your audience understand the key message. There are very few situations in which using many colors in a single visualization will work well. When you want your viewers to understand the significance of something, it is important to make that something stand out from the rest.

## Icons and Images

By using images and icons in moderation, you can enhance your work and make certain topics appeal to an audience more easily. Images and icons can result in faster recognition and comprehension (e.g., using a flag for a country or a logo for a team). However, if you have many different icons and images in your visualization, you may leave your audience confused, because it can be difficult to differentiate between the objects and their purpose.

When you use icons and images, it is also important that these are easy to recognize. If you know your audience, you may be able to make assumptions about their familiarity with specific logos, flags, and commonly used symbols. If you do not know who your audience is, such as when publishing your work online, be conservative in your assumptions and use only icons that would be recognized and understood easily by everyone. Examples include:

- Symbols for women and men
- Traffic signs
- Small information icons, such as a lowercase "i"
- Signs with transport symbols such as planes, cars, or bicycles

Before you create a visualization with lots of icons and images, consider that their use can make your work difficult to understand. Not every data visualization needs to be thought of in a business context and not every topic needs to be presented in a formal and serious design. However, each visualization should represent your ability, as an analyst, to identify the key insights, build a story around them, and communicate it effectively.

Keeping your visualization clean and uncluttered, adding color to highlight or draw attention, and using icons and images sparingly will make it easier for your audience to follow your visualization and gain insights from it. The straightforward visualization in Figure 4.7 by Alicia Bembenek uses color effectively and manages to tell a clear story without any icons or images.

Alicia created a dot plot to show the progression of internet usage by country over time. The pattern allows the audience to see quickly that all countries move in the same direction, with some reaching higher penetration of internet usage at an earlier stage than others.

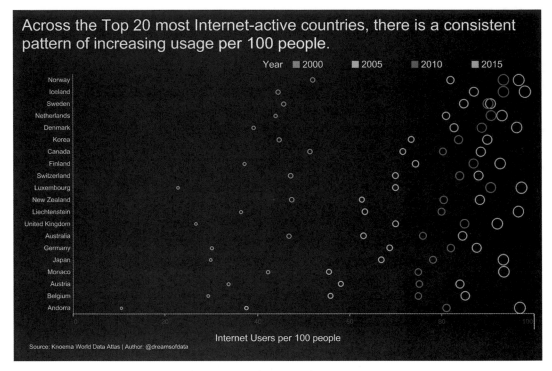

Across the Top 20 most Internet-active countries, there is a consistent pattern of increasing usage per 100 people.

Year ■ 2000 ■ 2005 ■ 2010 ■ 2015

Internet Users per 100 people

Source: Knoema World Data Atlas | Author: @dreamsofdata

**FIGURE 4.7** Example of using color to highlight and removing unnecessary details.

## Simplicity in Analysis

Every analyst has their own way of approaching an unknown data set. Some focus on the numbers first, while others go straight into building charts and graphs. Some analyze the metadata, while others want to focus on the data that is in each field. When you find yourself looking at unfamiliar data, you want to avoid feeling overwhelmed and instead feel excited to explore, to analyze, to ask questions, and to find answers that you can share with your audience.

Chapter 3, "Know and Understand the Data," goes into detail around becoming familiar with your data set. The following section provides a number of suggestions to help you through your analysis. For new and less experienced analysts, these suggestions can be helpful to avoid getting lost among the noise in the data and instead help you find the story in the data.

## Getting Started with New Data

Typically, when you approach a new data set you will know something about it and the purpose of the analysis. For example:

- What type of data is it? Is it survey data? Does it come from sensor measurements? Is it a set of summary statistics or detailed transaction-level records? There is an endless array of possibilities.
- What is the topic of the data? Are you looking at economic data from different countries around the world? Is it feedback results from a student survey or individual transactions of a payment system?
- Who is the audience? Are you creating analysis and visualizations for an unknown online audience or is your audience inside your organization?
- What tools do you have available for exploring and visualizing the data? Is the data clean and prepared for you or do you have to do further data preparation work to make it ready for analysis? Do you have visual analytics software to speed up your analysis process? Are you constrained to using tools that require you to wrangle numbers and limit the type of analysis you can do?

These questions are a set of the parameters within which you will undertake your analysis and they determine how far you can take the data. So how do you start your analysis of a new data set?

## Start Simple

Different data sets allow for different types of analyses. Starting simple is a good way to approach a new topic and get a better understanding of the data. With a rich data set containing very granular data over a long period of time, you could work with predictions and forecasts. However, a better way to approach the analysis would be to start identifying trends over time. If you are new to data analysis and visualization—and even for those who are experienced—start from a high level and work your way into the detail.

For time-based data this could mean looking at the data across the years, drilling into quarters and months to see whether interesting trends and patterns emerge. Once you understand the summary level, you can work on defining some of the questions you want to explore further. For example:

- Are there specific dates that differ from the rest across all years? If you look at air traffic data, public holidays probably stand out because of increased flight traffic before, during, and after these days.
- Does a specific trend over a period of several years hold true across decades? Has the situation improved over time or did it get worse? When looking at environmental data like carbon emissions, you may notice lower levels many decades ago, followed by a strong increase and then a gradual decline as measures are put in place to reduce carbon emissions.
- Is there a specific time of the day that differs from the remaining hours? Are there one or two weekdays that stand out compared to rest of the week? Commuter data typically shows very specific patterns around time of day and day of the week and such patterns are worth exploring.

Visual analysis of data gives you the ability to ask and answer questions quickly. Along the way you will find more questions and hopefully more answers. As you work through the data set this way, make sure to save the different steps and perspectives, so that when the time comes for putting together your visualization, you can evaluate which charts or ideas are best to include.

### Know When to Stop

What if you hit a dead end? What if you have a hunch and you spend significant time exploring the data and cannot get to the answer? Is it all a waste of time? Certainly not. These situations can be frustrating because you may get wedded to a particular idea and do not want to let it go and move on. However, moving on is exactly what you need to do.

If the story turns out not to be a real story and your hypotheses are not confirmed, it is okay to put your original ideas aside instead of backing up your hypothesis with weak arguments and data that does not stand up to real analytical scrutiny. Do not be afraid to acknowledge that there may not be any interesting insights in a particular data set.

## Simplicity in Storytelling

How do you tell a story that is easy to understand? How do you tell a complex story in a way that is accessible for your audience? Moving beyond the design and analysis into the area of storytelling is another important aspect of the overall idea of keeping things simple. This section provides tips for finding insights and focusing on the key message.

### Finding Insights

The first part of creating a story is to have something worth talking about. By following the analysis recommendations in the previous section, you will have a couple of angles that comprise the basis of your story. While analysis is about finding those interesting insights in a data set, storytelling is about bringing them into a form that you can communicate to your audience.

While it can take some time to find a story in a data set, you can easily create impactful visualizations from the first insights you come across. Sticking to basic and easy-to-understand insights while making enough time to practice regularly is perfectly fine. To help you find a story in your data, consider the following:

- What do you notice?
- Are there obvious outliers?
- Are there trends that are immediately apparent?
- Are there possible correlations between two metrics?
- Are there interesting clusters in your data?
- Are there repetitive patterns in the data, such as seasonal spikes or troughs?

Any one of these observations can be a story in itself. Naturally, you can combine the findings and bring them all together, but this bears the risk of having disparate stories that may be difficult to integrate. Instead, pick one story and stick to it, while completing it in a reasonable amount of time.

One of the very memorable challenges we gave the Makeover Monday community was data about the migration paths of two dozen turkey vultures in North and South America. Klaus Schulte found a story in the data of a single bird and turned it into the visualization in Figure 4.8.

Klaus's focus on the data of turkey vulture Prado meant he could go deeper into a subset of the data and spend his time analyzing the migration patterns around the LA region where this nonmigratory bird moves during different times of the year.

A focus on simplicity in storytelling by choosing one specific topic in a larger data set is a good reminder that you do not have to use all the data all the time. Using a subset is fine and can make for an interesting analysis and visualization as a result.

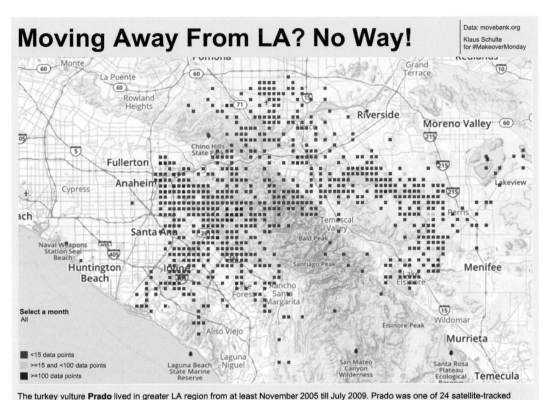

**FIGURE 4.8**  Simplifying the data can help simplify the story.

## Focusing on a Key Message

Highlighting your key message through the effective and minimal use of color and by creating a clean overall design can strengthen the impact it will have on your audience. If you focus on a single insight, make sure it stands out, make sure it is well supported by the data, make sure the analysis is sound, and then bring it all to life through thoughtful formatting and attention to all the small details that make a visualization exceptional.

In Figure 4.9, Joe Kristo visualized data about the highest-paid jobs in Australia and the difference in pay for men and women. He focused his analysis and resulting visualization on those jobs where women earn more than men.

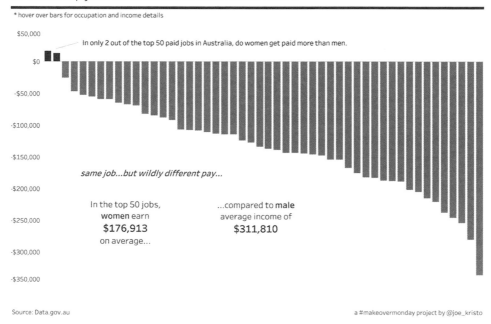

The **Top 50 highest paid jobs** in Australia.

In which top jobs do **women earn more** than men?

**FIGURE 4.9**   Example of a clean, simple design with minimal colors.

The bar chart and the clean formatting help his audience to see the two jobs he highlights in red on the far-left side, where women are paid more than men. The remaining gray bars show the pay differential that favors men.

## Summary

Keeping visualizations simple by practicing simplicity in analysis, design, and storytelling requires ongoing work; it is worth the effort because it will help you become more effective at communicating information. This chapter provided a number of suggestions to help you find a focus for your analysis and to turn it into a great visualization. Take some of them into your next data project and they will help you work more efficiently to get to your insights.

When it comes to simplicity, try removing some of the embellishments from your visualization in order to bring more clarity to your message. Less is certainly more when designing effective data visualizations and most topics benefit from a clean-looking layout that makes the data the focus of your analysis.

## Chapter Five

# Attention to Detail

Among all of the skills required to be a good data analyst, attention to detail ranks near the top. When you work with data, you cannot afford to overlook details that point to outliers or anomalies or interesting trends and patterns. Paying attention to all characteristics of the data you are working with and how it is presented is critical for success. This chapter looks at the various parts that come together in a great visualization, demonstrating attention to the finest detail.

We encourage people to treat Makeover Monday as a fun project and a testing ground for their ideas and creativity. Every visualization they publish becomes part of their portfolio and reflects their abilities as analysts. This does not mean that every visualization has to be an outstanding, in-depth, comprehensive analysis. What it does mean is that when you pay attention to detail, it shows.

It can be obvious to an audience when care has been taken during analysis and design to ensure that it is supported with facts, laid out in a logical order, and allows the audience to gain insights or to be informed. Taking care means that various aspects of the overall design have been considered, a thorough spell check has been done, formatting is consistent, and attributions have been given for images and data sources.

Consider Figure 5.1, a visualization by Michael Mixon of historical results from Le Tour de France.

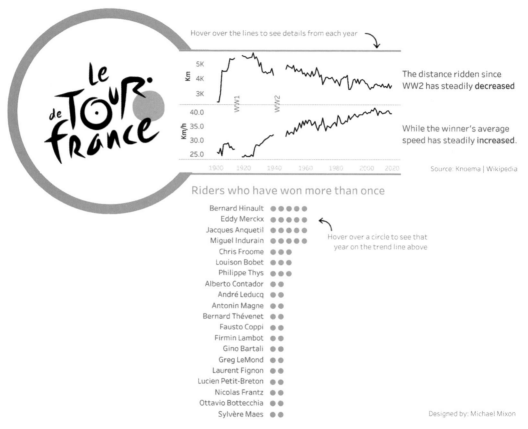

**FIGURE 5.1**   Visual history of Le Tour de France.

At first glance Michael's visualization may look simple: a couple of line charts, a unit chart, and some text boxes. Upon exploring the tool tips and interactivity, however, the various layers of information Michael has worked into the visualization and the focus on the details reveal the care he has put into his work.

- Applying gray shading to indicate there was no race due to World Wars I and II

- Using line charts that resemble elevation profiles to go with the theme of the data
- Small instructional text boxes indicate how to interact with the visualization
- Data source is stated where the data is displayed
- Designer credit is positioned in the bottom right corner

The overall design with the yellow circle at the left, the rectangular chart in the middle, and text boxes on the right resemble the chain and chainrings on a bicycle. The circular pattern flows into the unit chart where yellow circles indicate the number of times a rider has won the race. All of these elements blended together make everything work as one visualization.

Mastering attention to detail only happens when you get the basics right first. The following sections focus on those foundations.

## Typos

It is very easy to make minor errors when creating data visualizations, especially when you use text elements that rely on manually added words. Typographical errors can reduce the impact of your work, making it appear unpolished, unprofessional, or even sloppy.

There are a number of reasons why you may make such mistakes. You might:

- Be in a rush
- Not know how to spell a certain word
- Be suffering from dyslexia
- Be creating a visualization in a second language

The audience, however, generally does not care about the reasons for your mistakes; all they see are the errors on the page, likely leading them to assume that you did not take enough care to produce work that is free from typos and spelling mistakes. Aside from these fairly harmless considerations, typos may completely change the meaning of words, resulting in confusing titles and an audience that might tune out because what they are looking at does not make sense.

Before publishing your work, conduct a thorough check for typographical errors. The result is a more polished, credible visualization. A useful technique for checking your work is to read the text backward, starting from the last word to the first. This makes every word stand alone, prevents the brain from naturally filling in the gaps, and helps identify mistakes much more easily. While proofreading an entire book backward may not sound appealing, applying this technique to a sentence or two is certainly doable and a good way to identify any remaining typos.

## Punctuation

Whether there is a missing comma or an unnecessary exclamation mark drawing attention to something that is not actually that important, punctuation plays a role in how people read and understand text. Punctuation can change the meaning of a sentence dramatically, so you need to pay careful attention to it to avoid misunderstandings.

In data visualization, text is typically written in relatively short paragraphs or single-line sentences. To check how well a passage of text flows, read it aloud and read it slowly, making use of pauses as indicated by the punctuation. Reading aloud helps identify any missing or superfluous marks, such as periods (full stops), commas, or parentheses.

## Formatting

After ensuring your text is clear of typos, grammatical errors, and punctuation mistakes, spend time focusing on formatting. Formatting helps your audience easily consume the information you present and has the ability to provide a great first impression.

This section covers formatting from two different angles:

1. Chart formatting
2. Overall formatting

Chart formatting is more about the effective design of a chart through formatting choices, while dashboard or visualization formatting relates to elements that bring several charts, text boxes, and titles together effectively.

## Formatting Charts Effectively

Generally, removing clutter and nondata ink ("Above all else show the data")[1] is a good idea to help your message stand out and for the information to be consumed more easily. At a summary level, this can include any of the following:

- Removing gridlines, borders, and divider lines
- Removing shading of titles and labels
- Replacing legends by adjusting the color and size of text in titles
- Choosing colors that are easy to differentiate, carry meaning, and are used sparingly
- Ensuring charts are sized correctly and have the right width-to-height ratio so as to not distort the data

### Line Charts

A line chart without any labels can still convey information about the trends in the data and the general behavior of the metric, such as whether there are increases, decreases, or plateaus and when fluctuations occur. It is easier for an audience to quickly understand the details of a chart, however, when clear labels are included to specify the units of a measure.

---

[1] Edward Tufte, 1983.

When analyzing gold and oil price correlations, as in Figure 5.2, Pablo Gomez used three different line charts to show the timeline of how prices changed over time.

# GOLD & OIL PRICE CORRELATION

## How much Oil can you buy with an ounce of Gold?

Over the past 35 years, the relationship between **Gold** and **Oil** shows that on average, for every ounce of **Gold** you can purchase just **over 16 barrels of crude Oil.**

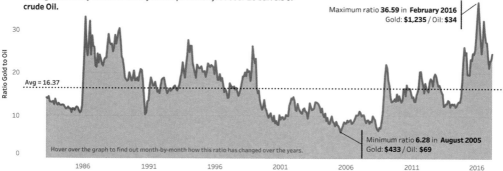

Maximum ratio **36.59** in **February 2016**
Gold: **$1,235** / Oil: **$34**

Avg = 16.37

Hover over the graph to find out month-by-month how this ratio has changed over the years.

Minimum ratio **6.28** in **August 2005**
Gold: **$433** / Oil: **$69**

*Ratio Gold to Oil* — 30, 20, 10, 0
1986　1991　1996　2001　2006　2011　2016

## Five Key Moments in Oil & Gold Relationship

### Oil & Gold Partnership
The price of oil plays a crucial role in the determination of the price of gold. They are both commodities and like gold, the price of crude oil is determined in the US dollar. When the US dollar rises, dollar-denominated assets usually drop in price, as investors of other currencies find dollar-denominated assets more expensive.

### Oil Price since 1983
Hover over the graph for more information

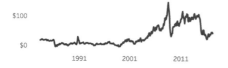

$100
$0
1991　2001　2011

### Aug 2011 ... Gold rockets high
Gold climbs back to record highs, this time to a peak of **$1,814** driven by a weaker dollar, economic uncertainty and amid fears that the global recovery is running out of steam.

### 37 Years of Gold Price
Hover over the graph for more information

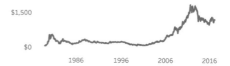

$1,500
$0
1986　1996　2006　2016

### A Decade of Oil highs and lows
In the mid 2000's the combination of declining production and surging Asian demand send prices to record highs but in **2008** the global financial crisis causes a bubble-bursting sell-off. Prices plummet 78.1% from July to December.

**FIGURE 5.2**　Example of minimalist line charts.

Pablo paid particular attention to the formatting:

- The price in dollars is represented on the y-axis of the two smaller charts at the bottom.
- The unit of measure is clearly stated in the subtitle; for gold the price relates to ounces, for oil the price relates to barrels.

As an alternative to labeling the axis with the actual unit of measurement, Pablo could have included the unit in the subtitle for each chart and only provided the numbers on the axis. This would still give his audience the important details, but it may look repetitive.

*Bar Charts*

When it comes to labeling the units on a bar chart, you need to find the balance between keeping a clean and simple design and providing sufficient information for the audience. In Figure 5.3, Steve Wood used stacked bar charts to visualize air quality data in the US. Each horizontal bar represents a state, divided into three panes: 1995, 2005, and 2015. The columns show the time of day and the labels guide the audience to understand how data changes from left to right. The inclusion of AM and PM in his unit labels on the x-axis make it very easy for the audience to interpret the visualization and to understand how air quality changes throughout the day.

In Figure 5.4, Charlie Hutcheson visualized medal tallies from the Southeast Asia Games as a horizontal bar chart, using color for highlighting and labels to show the value.

Designing bar charts this way removed the need to display an axis. Showing the label on the maximum medal tally for each year provides a reference point for the nonlabeled bars. By labeling the ends of a bar, Charlie created a clean, easy-to-understand visualization.

## Ozone air quality in the United States by time of day

Ground level ozone can be bad for us. What times of the day are we most at risk? These heat maps show the maximum level of ozone recorded per state at various times of the day over two decades. The charts do <u>not</u> show the frequency of the maximums, which may have been isolated and/or infrequent. Nevertheless we can see that exposure is generally greater in the afternoon.

Levels: ▪ Good  ▪ Moderate  ▪ Unhealthy for sensitive groups  ▪ Unhealthy  ▪ Very unhealthy

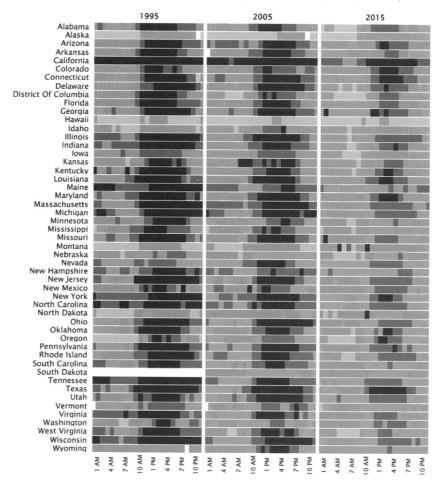

Source: www.epa.gov/outdoor-air-quality-data via www.makeovermonday.co.uk | #MakeoverMonday is a community data visualisation project. Refer to the website, twitter feed and blog links to join discussions about the strengths and weaknesses of the original chart, data set and participants makeovers. The charts above are not intended as medical advice.

**FIGURE 5.3**   Removing labels from the bars created an uncluttered look.

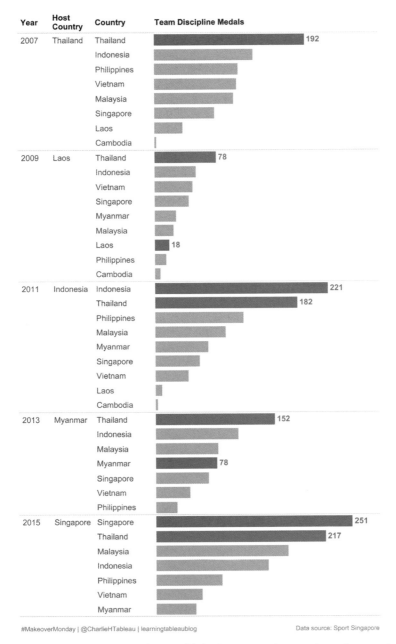

**FIGURE 5.4** Using color and labels sparingly on a bar chart to indicate the important data.

*Dual Axis Charts*

Dual axis charts are typically created to show:

1. Two metrics on two separate axes in the same chart (e.g., snow-fall levels vs. temperature)

2. Two metrics with different measurement units

3. Two metrics with the same measurement unit, but on different scales

4. The correlation between two metrics

If you use the same metric twice to create a dual axis, it is essential that you synchronize the axes to ensure the data points are on the same scale. In other cases, you may want to keep unsynchronized axes if you use different scales or metrics in combination. While axis synchronization may happen by default in your data visualization tool, some tools will make the two axis scales different from each other even when they represent the same metric. It is a good habit always to double-check that the axes are synchronized to ensure your visualization does not look misleading or confusing and does not impact your credibility with the audience.

Figures 5.5 and 5.6 show the consumption of poultry and livestock. Figure 5.5 has two axes with two different metrics that have not been synchronized. Both metrics show consumption in pounds, meaning they are the same unit, and therefore should be scaled the same. Figure 5.6 shows synchronized axes, completely changing the story.

Look at Figures 5.5 and 5.6 in comparison. What kind of story would you tell for the first versus the second?

CONSUMPTION OF **BEEF** VERSUS **COMMERCIAL FISH AND SHELLFISH**

**FIGURE 5.5**   Example of unsynchronized axes using the same unit (lbs).

CONSUMPTION OF **BEEF** VERSUS **COMMERCIAL FISH AND SHELLFISH**

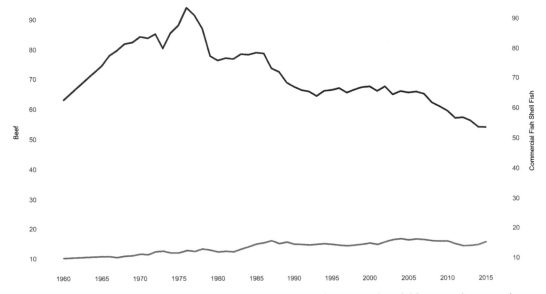

**FIGURE 5.6**   When using the same unit on two axes, the axes should be synchronized.

*Tile Maps*

Tile maps require extra considerations for formatting, particularly because they are a different way to present data compared to more familiar choropleth and bubble maps. The benefit of using a tile map is that it allocates equal size to each geographical element regardless of its actual physical size. This makes geographically smaller and larger states easier to compare. You can read in more detail about this chart type in Chapters 7 ("Trying New Things") and 10 ("Choosing the Right Chart Type").

Figure 5.7 is a dashboard Eva created using tile maps to visualize US household income distribution from 2009 to 2016. The most visually appealing tile maps combine the following characteristics:

• Use a single shape (like the hexagons in Figure 5.7).
• Keep shapes close together, leaving a small white gap that helps differentiate the geographical areas.
• Tessellate shapes to ensure a snug fit. Notice how the hexagons in Figure 5.7 are rotated to ensure a tighter fit.
• On larger tile maps, place geographical information (e.g., state abbreviations) or data values inside each tile.

Pay special attention to the orientation of tile maps. Is each tile in its logical place? Is the map sized correctly? For example, when you create a state-level tile map of the US, the ratio of height to width needs to be appropriate to keep the overall shape of the US recognizable.

An easy way to check the impression your tile map can have on your audience is to get out of your chair, take a step back from your screen, and look at the overall design. This helps you identify obvious mistakes and gives you an appreciation for what your audience sees when they first look at your work.

# US HOUSEHOLD INCOME DISTRIBUTION

## Income levels by state from 2009 - 2016

Data from the US Census Bureau shows that in the years since the Global Financial Crisis, income levels in a number of states have improved.

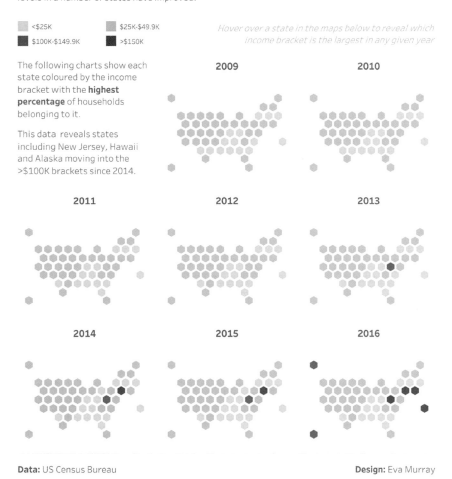

■ <$25K          ■ $25K-$49.9K

■ $100K-$149.9K  ■ >$150K

*Hover over a state in the maps below to reveal which income bracket is the largest in any given year*

The following charts show each state coloured by the income bracket with the **highest percentage** of households belonging to it.

This data reveals states including New Jersey, Hawaii and Alaska moving into the >$100K brackets since 2014.

2009    2010

2011    2012    2013

2014    2015    2016

**Data:** US Census Bureau                 **Design:** Eva Murray

**FIGURE 5.7**   Small multiple-tile map.

## Universal Formatting

Formatting plays an important role in creating data visualizations that effectively communicate information and provide actionable insights. It helps to have an overall theme or format for your work. This section covers the following aspects related to the overall formatting of your visualization:

- Background colors
- Fonts
- Alignment
- Labels
- Lines
- Visibility

### *Background Colors*

Ensure that the background is consistently formatted across the entire visualization. Strive to achieve a consistent overall look and feel by choosing colors for shading and the background that work well together.

Figure 5.8 represents a dashboard where the charts, titles, and text boxes have different shading and background colors, resulting in a visualization that looks too busy.

By contrast, using a consistent approach to background colors results in a dashboard that flows more easily without the breaks created by the formatting of different sections, as in Figure 5.9.

### *Fonts*

Generally speaking, when it comes to formatting, simplicity, consistency, and less variety work best. For fonts, limiting yourself to a single font for the entire visualization, or one font for the title plus a font for the rest of the visualization, will typically result in a

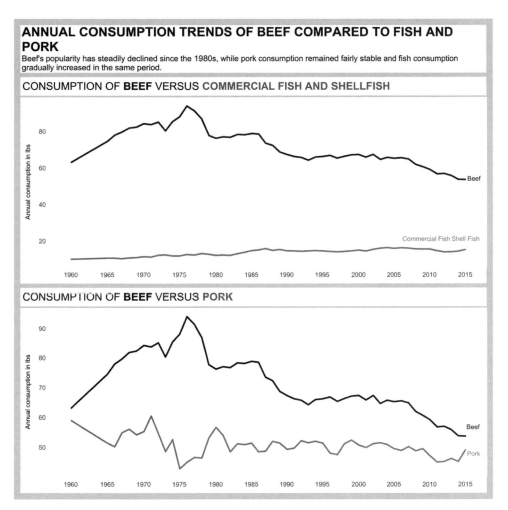

**ANNUAL CONSUMPTION TRENDS OF BEEF COMPARED TO FISH AND PORK**

Beef's popularity has steadily declined since the 1980s, while pork consumption remained fairly stable and fish consumption gradually increased in the same period.

CONSUMPTION OF **BEEF** VERSUS COMMERCIAL FISH AND SHELLFISH

CONSUMPTION OF **BEEF** VERSUS PORK

**FIGURE 5.8** Example of too many different background colors.

consistent and professional-looking product. Formatting the color, capitalization, font size, and font weight can be a very effective approach to structuring your visualization. As with anything you want to highlight, this only works if very few elements are formatted to stand out, otherwise everything is competing for attention.

**ANNUAL CONSUMPTION TRENDS OF BEEF COMPARED TO FISH AND
PORK**

Beef's popularity has steadily declined since the 1980s, while pork consumption remained fairly stable and fish consumption
gradually increased in the same period.

CONSUMPTION OF **BEEF** VERSUS COMMERCIAL FISH AND SHELLFISH

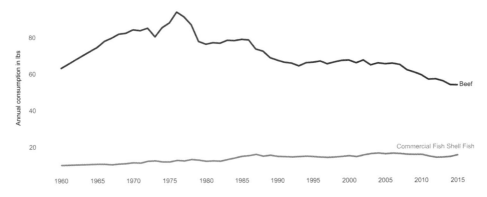

CONSUMPTION OF **BEEF** VERSUS PORK

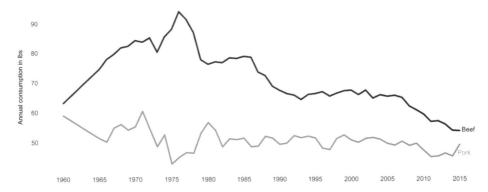

**FIGURE 5.9**   Example of simple background colors.

While visualizing survey data, Naledi Hollbrügge created the dashboard in Figure 5.10 to visualize policy makers' responses for a survey about issues facing women and girls. The following uses of text
formatting makes this dashboard design work well:

- Using a large font size for the title
- Applying color to the text in the subtitle to define the colors that
  are used in the visualization
- Limiting the design to two different colors to convey the meaning

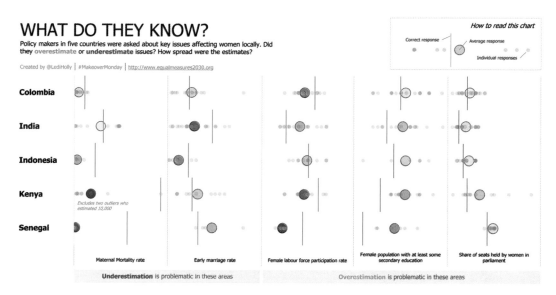

**FIGURE 5.10**  Example of effective use of color, fonts, and formatting.

- Using gray text for information that is less important
- Using bold fonts for country names to make them easy to read
- Using italics to indicate instructions

Make text elements more effective during the design process by asking a few questions:

1. Does the text need to be colored, bolded, or italicized?

2. What if some of the formatting is removed? Will the necessary words still stand out?

3. Does a single font or multiple fonts work better?

4. Is the text displayed in a single block or have you used paragraphs and spacing to make it easy to read?

5. What is the balance of text versus charts? Is it appropriate for the topic?

6. Does the visualization meet the style intended?

7. Do the fonts and formatting display well on different screen sizes?

This is simply a starting point, a collection of questions that can guide the design process. As always with learning, it is important to experiment, to try things out, and to iterate to improve your visualization. This applies not only to your chart choices, but also to your font selections.

### Alignment

When all the elements of a visualization are properly aligned, the result is much more appealing to the audience. Alignment includes the overall layout of your data visualization, as well as the positioning of charts, text boxes, labels, titles, annotations, icons, and so on. Considering the location of each element on the page and ensuring they are neatly aligned shows that the author has paid attention to those details and is aware of their impact.

For long-form dashboards, it helps if the charts are neatly aligned and not offset left or right from one another. Figure 5.11 from Pooja Gandhi shows a well-structured, long-form dashboard that flows from a high-level summary to a detailed breakdown. The alignment of every line and text box is deliberate and adjusted with pixel-perfect precision to ensure the lines guide the audience through the visualization most effectively. The positioning of text, titles, and large numbers brings attention to each part of the analysis. The end result looks polished and professional and gives credibility to her skills as a data analyst.

### Labels

When placed correctly, labels can be a very effective way to add information to charts. In Figure 5.12, Rodrigo Calloni created a dashboard with six line charts: one summary index and five detailed indices. He used labels to give his audience the values of each line's start and end points.

Adding labels to the first and last value of each line help the audience understand the changes for each index over time. He included an option to highlight a specific country, so that viewers could

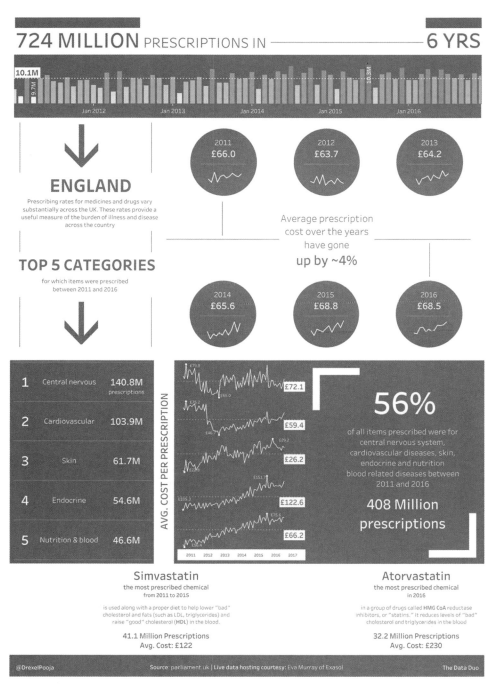

**FIGURE 5.11**    Perfect alignment helps guide the audience.

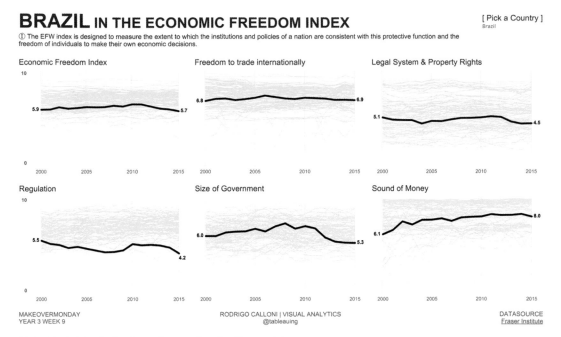

**BRAZIL IN THE ECONOMIC FREEDOM INDEX**

[ Pick a Country ]
Brazil

① The EFW index is designed to measure the extent to which the institutions and policies of a nation are consistent with this protective function and the freedom of individuals to make their own economic decisions.

MAKEOVERMONDAY
YEAR 3 WEEK 9

RODRIGO CALLONI | VISUAL ANALYTICS
@tableauing

DATASOURCE
Fraser Institute

**FIGURE 5.12** Labeling the ends of a line adds context.

choose a country they were interested in and have labels change accordingly.

Figure 5.13, created by Amar Donthala, demonstrates how effectively placed labels provide focus on the important insights in the visualization. The labels are only displayed for the selected nationality and show up inside the circles. This provides an additional reference point for the circles, as well as their distance from the average (dotted line) and gives the audience a sense of the distribution. The labels allow the audience to easily understand the approximate value of the gray circles without needing to refer back to the y-axis.

### Lines

Dashboards vary in size, layout, and complexity, with some consisting of a single chart and a few text elements, while others combine multiple charts across different sections. More complex

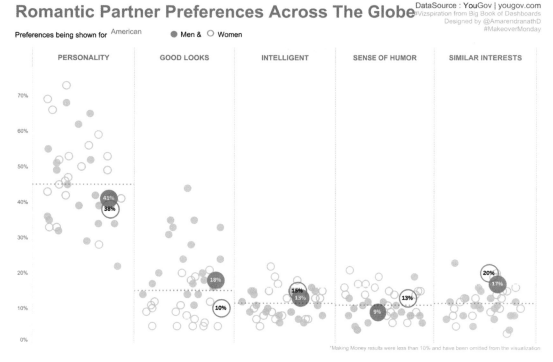

**FIGURE 5.13** Labeling specific data points provides focus.

visualizations require a well-structured layout to ensure the visualization flows easily. Section dividers, arrows, connecting lines, and borders act as effective visual elements to structure the visualization and help the viewer understand the information provided.

In Figure 5.14, Michael Mixon used different types of lines to connect the parts of his visualization in order to guide the audience through his findings. To enhance his visualization, Michael used the following line formatting techniques:

- A horizontal line under the title separates it from the rest of the view.
- Dashed square brackets encapsulate the key insights.
- Short, dashed lines connect the labels for the minimum and maximum values.
- A shaded reference band represents the Great Recession.
- A thick line connects the labels of the measurements (gold and oil price) while also serving as a color legend.

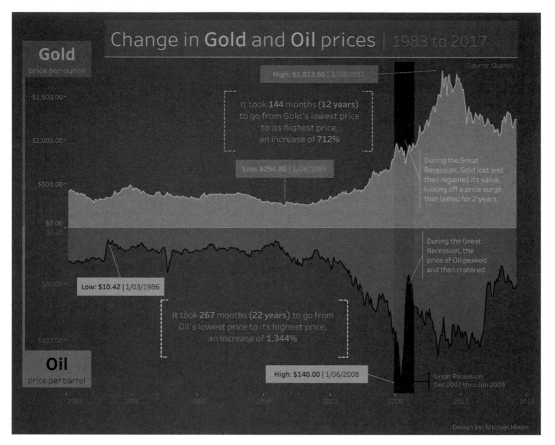

**FIGURE 5.14**   Example of using lines to connect sections.

Overall, the use of lines is expertly executed. Each line deliberately guides the audience through the analysis.

## Visibility

All of the elements in a visualization should be easy to see, read, and compare. They should not be made less visible by poor color choices, difficult-to-read fonts, misalignment, and overlapping text. When your audience looks at a visualization, they should not have to expend any unnecessary effort to see what is being presenting to them.

Consider Figure 5.15 by David Hoskins, which shows the prevalence of different dietary requirements around the world. All of the elements of his visualization (the title and subtitle, the filter, the instructions, the chart, and the footer) are easy to see and nothing is obstructed, freeing up the audience to take in the relevant information. David deliberately displayed lines along the x-axis that guide the eye rather than competing for attention, resulting in a clean overall look.

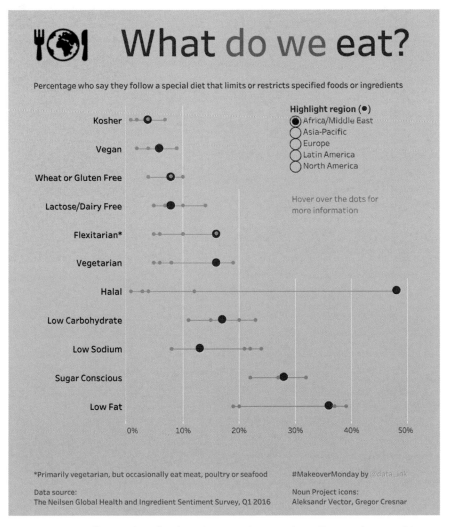

**FIGURE 5.15** Example of color choices that work well together, making them easy to read.

The goal should be to ensure that your audience can see the necessary information and insights as clearly as possible. Otherwise, your viewers may quickly switch off and navigate away. Remove any barriers that could hinder your audience's understanding.

## Crediting Images and Data Sources

The credit to data and image sources, and those that inspired your work, is typically confined to a footer at the bottom of your dashboard. The credit section is highly important and needs to be included in every visualization, irrespective of whether the analysis was done for an internal or external stakeholder.

For Makeover Monday, we publish each week's data set with a link to the source. Most visualizations reference the sources and some people have developed a specific footer design to blend with the rest of the visualization. Keep in mind that content like icons, images, and photos available on the internet are not necessarily available for reuse. Some Makeover Monday topics lend themselves to the use of a few small icons or the inclusion of an image that reflects the design and emotion communicated in the visualization. Only when these are explicitly labeled for reuse, should they be included; attribution to the creator must be given.

When images and icons are used, the following needs to be considered:

1. Did you create the icon or image yourself? In this case you are free to use it as you choose, provided it does not breach copyright or trademark laws.

2. Did you pay for the icon or image? In this case the license you paid for will dictate the type of usage available to you and the attribution you need to give.

3. Did you find the image online? It will be very difficult to discern whether a random picture can be used in a visualization. If possible, contact the creator of the image directly and if that is not possible, find a different picture that is permitted for reuse.

For her visualization of the UK pet population in Figure 5.16, Sarah Burnett used a number of animal icons that she created herself. This is the best way to ensure that you are able to use an image or icon in your work. Sarah properly stated in the footer that the images were her own and also listed the data source as well as her name.

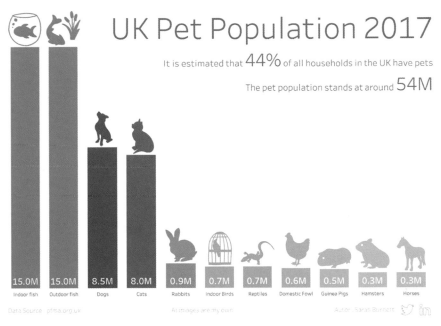

**FIGURE 5.16** When using icons, either create them yourself or give credit as dictated by the creator.

## Summary

Taking into account the formatting of charts, as well as the format of the overall visualization, is just as much a part of creating great work as using effective language that is free from grammatical or typographical errors. Stating your sources clearly and correctly and using only images that you have the license to use ensures your work is credible and professional.

The suggestions in this chapter will help you develop well-rounded skills that take your designs to the next level and make you stand out as an analyst who delivers valuable insights *and* communicates them effectively through language, visual analysis, and thoughtful design.

## Chapter Six

# Designing for the Audience

As a data visualization designer, you must know your audience if you want your work to be viewed, understood, appreciated, and potentially used as a basis for decision making. Along with the design skills you develop over time and the technical skills that are required to conduct the initial analysis, it is important to put yourself in the shoes of the audience and ask, "What do they need?"

As previously mentioned, stating the dashboard title in the form of a question, ideally a question the audience wants answered, is a great way to start as it will help focus the analysis and subsequent design. The audience comes in two forms:

1. Those you already know, like your boss, your department, or your organization as a whole

2. A completely unknown audience, for example, the people who come across the work you publish online

It is this latter audience that we design for in Makeover Monday. Not knowing who will see, consume, and interact with your visualizations presents its own set of challenges.

After reading this chapter, you will have strategies for:

1. Creating an effective design

2. Designing for mobile

3. Using visual cues for additional information

4. Using icons and shapes

5. Storytelling

6. Reviewing your work to improve its quality

## Creating an Effective Design

The more you know about your audience and their preferences, the easier it will be to create an engaging design. If they prefer simple charts, create simple charts. If they prefer flashy and fancy visual designs, even if it comes at the expense of telling a clear story, then you may need to create those advanced visuals.

Today's audience typically prefers a single-page, at-a-glance type of dashboard that allows for quick decision making. Ultimately if your work is engaging, your audience will love it. If they are not engaged, that falls back on you as the designer. Before you start creating your design, it helps to think through and plan the design.

### What Is the Purpose?

Any project starts with a goal. If you do not know the goal or the aim of your project, then you are not ready to start. Go back and ask more questions, do additional research on the topic—whatever it takes to be able to communicate the goal easily. Once you know the goal, you will be in a better position to determine the purpose of the piece. Some of the considerations you should make include:

- Is your visualization supporting decision making?
- What are the most important metrics?
- How will you provide context to those metrics?
- What defines good or bad?
- Where will your work be seen? Online? In a static presentation slide deck?
- Who will deliver the message and how? Will the analysis be presented in person and does the presenter know all the aspects of your design (e.g., interactivity, drill-down and filters)?
- How much time does your audience have? Do they get to ask questions?
- Are there any limitations or special considerations of your audience like colorblindness, language, or data literacy level?

*Washington D.C. Metro Scorecard*

For Makeover Monday, Lindsey Poulter created the scorecard in Figure 6.1 about the Washington D.C. Metro system.

Can we clearly identify the purpose? Let's go back to some of the considerations above.

*Does the Visualization Support Decision Making?*
- The design is organized, clean, and easy to read. Using "cards" allows each metric to be considered individually.
- Including the values on the bars aids in comprehension yet does not distract.
- The timelines are consistent across all of the metrics.

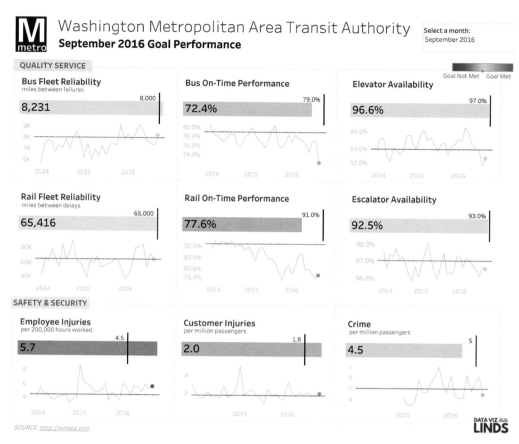

**FIGURE 6.1**   Performance dashboard for the Washington D.C. Metro.

*What are the Most Important Metrics?*

- Sectioning the dashboard by "Quality Service" and "Safety & Security" allows the users to focus on the metrics that are important to them.

- Then within each section, the metrics are listed in a "z" pattern from most important to least important.

*Do the Metrics Have Proper Context?*

- Including a reference line and labeling it for the goal helps the audience understand performance.
- Each metric has a clear, simple title. Subtitles are included as needed to aid comprehension.
- Including a dot on the end of each line and color-coding it allows the reader to determine good or bad performance in the most recent period.
- Including a goal line on each of the line charts allows the reader to find patterns of consistent over- or underperformance.

*Identifying What Defines Good or Bad*

- Color-coding the bars by above/below the goal makes problems easy to spot.
- Really good labeling on the color legend helps to clarify information.

*Where Will Your Work Be Seen?*

- Lindsey knew her audience was the Makeover Monday community on Twitter, so she designed it so that it could be seen and understood as a static image, meaning that its effectiveness does not depend on interactivity.
- She provided click-through so the audience could interact if they desired.
- Her work could have just as easily been done by and for the D.C. Metro itself. This is a great example of an actionable dashboard that would help them provide better services and identify where to deploy more resources.

## Who Is the Audience?

For Makeover Monday, the audience is nearly always online. When considering this audience, an effective visualization will need to be understood as a static image. If it cannot be understood without interaction, then the designer did not take the time to understand *who* the audience is and *where* they will consume the visualization. Many people engage while on the move using their smartphones, so a static image is easy to access and does not come with the risk of display issues in browsers or other apps.

When you start a data visualization project, it is quite rare that *you* are the audience; you are typically designing for someone else and they will likely have a different comprehension level than you do about the topic.

### Do They Have Knowledge about the Topic Already?

If so, then it is usually okay to use acronyms and metrics that are not understood outside of this audience. If they have little or no knowledge about the topic, then you need to educate them with your design, for example, through well-placed annotations, footnotes, and descriptions.

### How Numerically Literate Are They?

The less literate the audience, the more basic your design and metrics need to be. Typically, the higher up in an organization the people are, the simpler you need to make the metrics, because your audience is less familiar with detail and more interested in the impact of key high-level metrics across the organization. If a metric is not easily understood within an organization, use it with caution.

### What Are Their Needs?

Is your audience full of senior-level executives with little time? Are you creating something for a product manager with deep insight into the product? What if the audience is made up mostly of data analysts? Each of these audiences has different needs that must be taken into consideration.

### What Do They Want to Find Out?

Depending on the audience, they may only care about a single number and/or how it compares to a prior period or a goal. Perhaps they want to see trends over time to identify patterns. The list of what they want to find out goes on and on. Interview the audience, ask them questions. By asking questions, you will begin setting their expectations and confirming in the audience's mind that you care about delivering a high-quality end product.

## Sketching

Too often we receive a data set, jump into our data visualization tool of choice, and create something without a whole lot of thought or planning. If this is you, then you should include sketching as part of your design process. Why is sketching an important part of the process?

> Sketches help to convey ideas, demonstrate functionality, visualize user flow, and illustrate anything that requires human interaction. Sketching helps discover potential issues and solutions early, prior to starting the design and development stages.[1]

Assuming you know the purpose and audience for your visualization and have done the associated research to understand the problem you are trying to solve, you are ready to start sketching. Sketching is noncommittal; that is, you are not obligated to produce anything you draw. This frees up your creativity, allows you to get lots of ideas out of your brain, and helps you determine which parts may or may not work in the final output.

-----------

[1] The Role of Sketching in the Design Process. DNN Software. 4 January 2017.

*Tips for Fast Sketching*

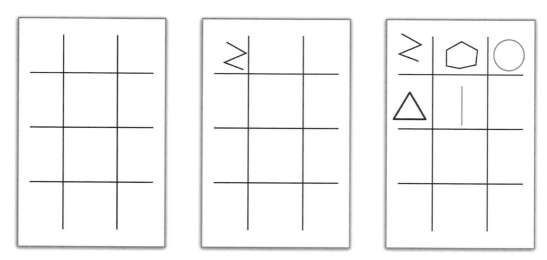

**FIGURE 6.2** Sketching grid by Caroline Beavon.

1. If you have A2 (17″ × 22″) or flipchart paper, use that. Start by creating a 3 × 4 grid of any size (Figure 6.2).

2. Create a sketch in every square. Each sketch should be related to the data you have and what you are trying to communicate. For example, if you want to show a ranking of the top five products, sketch a basic bar chart. Or if you want to show sales over time, draw a simple line chart. Maybe it is a key performance indicator (KPI) and you just need a big number.

3. Time-box this activity; the idea is to do something quick, not exhaustive.

## Planning the Layout

Once you have gone through a few iterations of sketching, from abstract to rough to refined, you should now be ready to completely flush out your design before moving to the computer. Creating a data visualization is similar to considering the components of a book in that a visualization tends to have a pretty structured set of elements.

1. Header or title

2. Subtitle or introduction

3. One or more sections

4. Charts and graphs within each section

5. Explanatory text or annotations

6. Footer

Do you need all of these elements in every design? Of course not. However, the more structured and repetitive the process, the easier and faster it will be to create the end product.

Now that you have refined your sketches, transfer them onto sticky notes and grab another sheet of big paper. Each sticky note should have one chart or one data point or one block of text. It is time to start laying out the design.

1. Write a nice big title on the paper; consider writing it in the form of a question.

2. Consider adding a smaller-sized subtitle that explains what the visualization is about.

3. Group the sticky notes together. You can organize the groups by the data they refer to or by the type of metric like KPIs or perhaps by the chart type. The idea is to group things that belong together. Repeat until you and your team are satisfied.

4. Once you have the groups, it may be worthwhile to assign each group a sticky note color. This means redrawing some of the notes, but it will save time in the long run.

5. Organize the sticky note groups from most important to least important and, keeping them in their groups, arrange them in the Z-Pattern.

6. Depending on the number of groups, draw a grid on the paper so that there are sections for each set of sticky notes.

7. Transfer the sticky notes onto the paper and arrange each section separately. Within each section, again consider what is the most and least important. Place the most important chart or piece of information on the upper left.

8. Iterate on the layout a few times if needed. Consider removing notes that do not help answer the question in the title. Removing some notes will reduce clutter and result in a cleaner design.

9. Draw annotations or additional text directly on the paper. These do not have to be accurate or detailed; they are serving as placeholders. The intent is to see if they add to the visualization. If they do not, scribble them out or erase them.

10. Finally, add a footer with credits, sources, and so on.

Now that you are done with the planning, tape the big paper up on a wall and take a few big steps back. Can you still understand the design even though you are farther away? If so, great; you have likely created an effective design. If not, identify what does not work and make changes until it becomes more effective.

Your analog dashboard is now ready to be reproduced digitally. At this point, as you are building the final charts, text, and so on, you may decide to change your mind on the chart choices, colors, and even the layout. The whole idea of sketching is to make the digital process faster. Even if you must change a few things, the overall concept will likely stay the same.

Consider the visualization by Athan Mavrantonis in Figure 6.3.

What effective design choices did he make?

- The title tells us exactly what the visualization is about.
- There are clear section breaks. Athan uses gray shading to distinguish one section from another.
- Each section has a clear title.
- None of the charts are complicated. He used a heatmap, a scatter plot, a stacked bar chart and a map. His typical audience members understand how to read these.

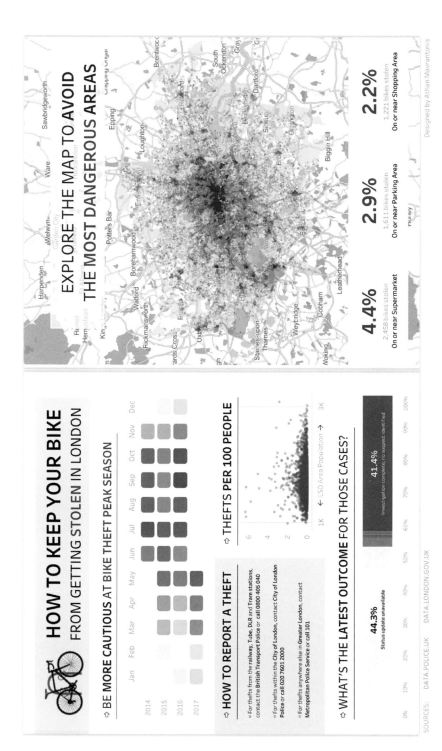

**FIGURE 6.3** Dashboard of stolen bikes in London.

- There are big numbers as KPIs below the map with smaller text below each number for context.
- The colors consistently represent the same values; the darker the red, the more bikes were stolen.
- The footer cites the sources and credits the designer.

You cannot create a design like this without planning it first. By following this basic process, deliberately and diligently, you will become a better designer. It takes practice. It takes discipline. It takes patience. Being great at anything does not come easy; the work you put in will be worth it, though. As you improve your skills and your designs, your reputation as an analyst will improve along with it.

## Designing for Mobile

Designing data visualizations for mobile devices is not easy. How do you design for a small screen size yet still provide enough information and make the different parts large enough? Should you design long or wide? How do you account for touch screens? What different display choices do you need to make compared to a full-size screen? How many colors are okay to use?

The list of questions and considerations does not stop there, so in this section, we will provide some basic tips and strategies we have learned through Makeover Monday to help you overcome these design challenges.

### Know Your Audience

Mobile users expect a different experience than desktop users. Before setting out to create a mobile data visualization, ask yourself (or better yet ask your audience) a few basic questions:

- How will they be using it and how is information shared?
- Do they expect interactivity?

- Will this be used merely for reporting or will they need to be able to answer their own questions through interactivity?
- What are the most important metrics?

Once you have gathered this information, you are ready to embark on your design. Follow the principles outlined in the section above. Draw with pen and paper. Rearrange the design with sticky notes. This will help you "see" the design before you sit in front of the computer.

## Information Displays

You are now ready to take the sticky notes and turn them into visualizations. Thinking about the audience and what they really need will help you design the most effective information displays.

### *Charts versus Text*

For example, typically we will display sales over time with a line chart.

However, when a user is accessing the data on a mobile device, all they might care about is the most recent sales and how that compares to the previous period. Therefore, a simple number may be preferred over a chart.

### *Filters and User Controls*

When designing a dashboard for a desktop screen, we are tempted to allow users to see all of the options they can select at once. When designing for mobile, though, we need to optimize the available space and limit the number of objects on the screen. This might mean swapping charts for metrics, as in Figures 6.4 and 6.5. Other forms of simplicity include removing unnecessary charts, simplifying or removing text and titles, removing legends, and/or incorporating them into chart titles.

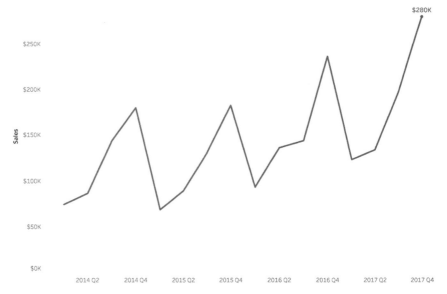

**FIGURE 6.4**   Line chart of sales over time.

# Q4 2017 Sales

# $280,054

## +42.7%

**FIGURE 6.5**   Big numbers are great for KPIs. Include context if possible.

Radio buttons are a typical filter display. This type of filter allows the user to pick one option at a time while allowing them to see all the available options. The disadvantage of this display is that radio button filters take up a lot of space—space we do not have on mobile devices. A more effective display would be a selection filter. These save space, are easy to use on touch devices, and are familiar to users. (See Figure 6.6.)

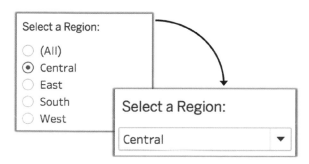

**FIGURE 6.6**   Selection filters take up less space than radio button filters, making them more accessible on mobile devices.

*Example of an Effective Mobile Design*

In the mobile-first design about German auto production in Figure 6.7, Robert Crocker used big text, included context and simple charts, excluded color legends in favor of coloring the text, and used selections that are touch-friendly to make the most of the limited space available.

## Color Choices

Desktop displays allow us to include color legends, display many colors for a single chart, and have different color legends for different charts. Mobile designs require simplicity and minimal colors, where colors emphasize what is important.

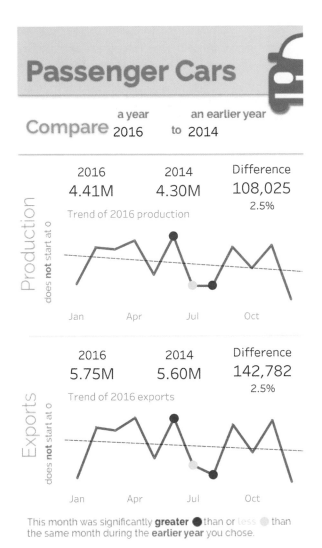

**FIGURE 6.7**   German auto production mobile dashboard.

*Contrast*

The colors used in mobile designs need to contrast enough to work in high- and low-visibility environments. In Figure 6.8, the colors are of a similar hue, making them hard to distinguish from one another.

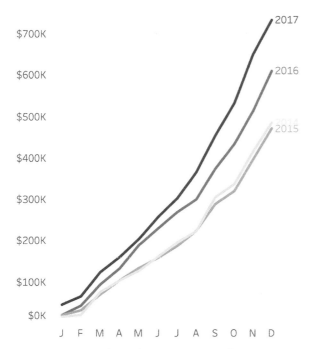

**FIGURE 6.8**   Colors that are too similar to one another to work on mobile devices.

Instead, consider high-contrast colors as in Figure 6.9. Orange and blue contrast more effectively, making it easier for the user to distinguish the two years.

If you need inspiration, look at the official colors for any professional sports team. They intentionally use high-contrast colors to make the uniforms stand out. In the line chart in Figure 6.9, the number of lines was also reduced to focus on the most relevant data since it is likely that the focus would be on comparing the most recent two years.

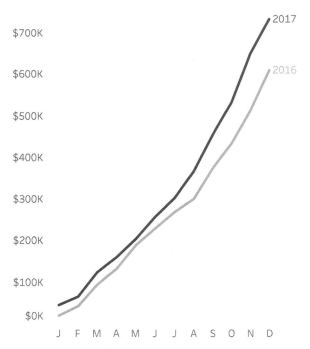

**FIGURE 6.9**   High-contrast colors work well on mobile devices.

### *Highlighting*

Highlighting is an effective alternative to high-contrast colors. The purpose of data visualization is to make it easier for the audience to understand the data. Highlighting can be used to draw attention to something important, emphasize a significant data point, or put focus on what you want the audience to notice first.

Let us assume that our sales team is responsible for the East region. We need to understand where the East ranks compared to the other regions and we want the team to know that quickly. We can use highlighting to ensure the audience sees what is important to them, as in Figure 6.10.

# Using Visual Cues for Additional Information

Visual cues are simple images or text that provide additional information to the user that is not essential to the main visualization. Visual cues serve as supplementary context for a topic.

Consider Figure 6.13 created by David Krupp. David placed a question mark icon in the upper right corner to provide:

- Data explanations
- Instructions on how to navigate and use the dashboard
- Information about what the comparisons mean and how to interpret them
- Guidance on how to understand the candlestick chart

**FIGURE 6.13** Information icons are useful for providing extra information to the audience.

Including all of this information on the dashboard would be distracting and consume a fair amount of space, so David moved it out of the way and made it available as a user hovers over or clicks on the question mark. He did not exclude the information; he merely chose to make it available on demand.

## Using Icons and Shapes

Adding pictographs to your visualizations can make them more appealing and help the audience more easily understand the message you are trying to convey. In Figure 6.14, Pablo Gomez used footprint icons to represent each of the water types from the data set and to connect the image of a footprint to the topic: water footprint of different foods.

**FIGURE 6.14** Icons can help relate the data to the topic.

There were three water types in the data (blue, gray, and green), so Pablo associated those colors with each footprint, used text in the available space that was not taken up by the chart to describe each water footprint and use dashed lines to separate them neatly.

## Proper Attributions

Pablo created the footprint icons himself, so there is no need for him to credit anyone. However, if you are using icons created by someone else or a service like FlatIcon, then it is critical that you follow their protocol for crediting the creators; otherwise, you are effectively stealing someone else's creative work. Credit any and all of the sources in the footer like Louise Shorten did in Figure 6.15.

## Go Easy on the Shapes

While we need to give credit for the shapes we use and ensure they are connected to the analysis, we must take care and use them sparingly. In the same way that using too many colors can be distracting for your audience, too many icons or shapes can have the same effect.

The visualization in Figure 6.16 looks at the ranking of Major League Baseball teams across various statistics for the 2017 season.

There are 30 teams in the Major Leagues, hence there are 30 logos. And while this might look intuitive to the person who created it, the audience will not be able to glean any insights because the visualization is simply too busy with so many icons and lines. You could get around this by allowing the user to highlight their favorite team and then have the graph show only the logo for that team.

If you are going to use icons, limit the number you use, consider the audience, and evaluate the effort you are asking the audience to make in order to understand your visualization.

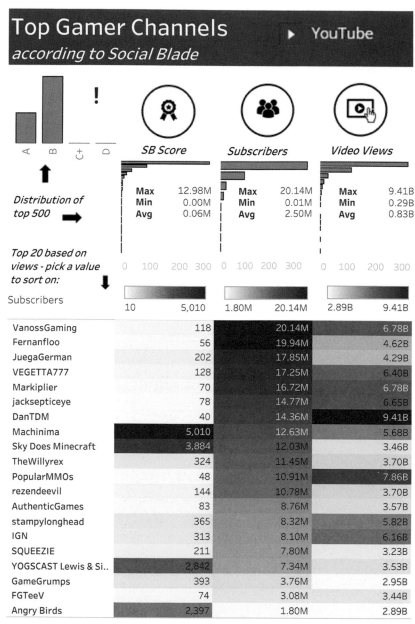

FIGURE 6.15   Example of proper image attribution.

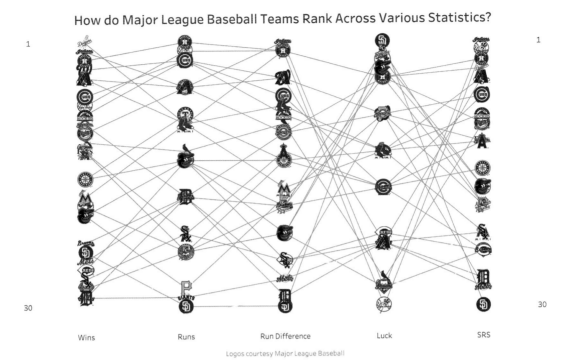

**FIGURE 6.16** Too many icons create a cluttered mess.

## Storytelling

We have given you tips and suggestions on structuring your design, from layout considerations to mobile formats, and the inclusion of visual cues, icons, and shapes. Bringing it all together in a coherent story is an essential step to achieving a design that informs your audience and gives them something of value that they enjoy.

### Finding a Story and Sticking to It

Sometimes we fall into the trap of using all the available data, turn it into visualizations, and do not end up with a structured, coherent story that is easy for our audience to comprehend. To achieve an effective design, it is a good idea to choose a specific angle or use

**Guatemala** boasts the **highest employment rate** of **LATAM** countries in the **15-24** age group

But **863,366 Guatemalan** "nininis" are "**neither in education, nor working, nor looking for work**"

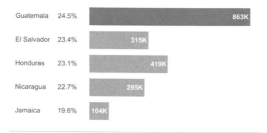

**Lack of educational opportunities** results in **gender stereotyping**, with girls prepared for "**housekeeping**". A clear difference is seen between male and female employment rates.

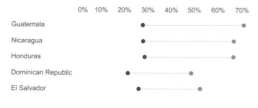

Which directly influences the number of "**nininis**" in ..

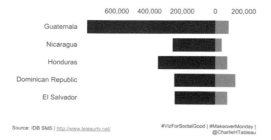

Source: IDB SMS | http://www.telesurtv.net/          #VizForSocialGood | #MakeoverMonday | @CharlieHTableau

**FIGURE 6.17**   Choosing a subset of the data can make a story more focused.

a subset of the data and build a story from there. We do not have to use the entire data set and it is actually helpful to really pin down something we find particularly interesting and go deeper into it, rather than creating something general and nondescript.

Charlie Hutcheson created the mobile-friendly visualization in Figure 6.17, focusing on the employment challenges of young people in Guatemala. The data set covered most South American nations and Charlie could have simply created an overview dashboard with high-level information. He chose to focus on a single country and go into deeper detail. This helped him develop a strong story with interesting insights, which flows from the beginning at the top to the end down the page.

## Long-Form Storytelling

Long-form storytelling, an approach taken in many infographics, is an excellent way to present data and take the audience on a journey. Consider Figure 6.18, a long-form dashboard about Tourism for Berlin and Brandenburg from Sarah Bartlett.

Sarah starts with an introduction to the topic, sets the scene by describing the state of Brandenburg, and shares high-level statistics. She goes on to focus on a specific district, incorporating a map before going into more detailed analysis of the tourism data. Sarah takes the reader on a journey down the page as if you are reading a story. Like any good writer, she starts with an introduction, then adds more and more detail to the story as you scroll down, before concluding with information about who stays the longest.

When you have a data set that contains rich levels of detail for you to work with, it may be suited for a long-form dashboard. While this type of design will require a bit of additional research to add information and context, the results can be very impactful.

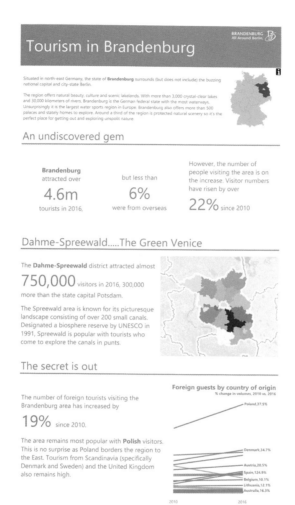

## Tourism in Brandenburg

BRANDENBURG
All Around Berlin.

Situated in north-east Germany, the state of **Brandenburg** surrounds (but does not include) the buzzing national capital and city-state Berlin.

The region offers natural beauty, culture and scenic lakelands. With more than 3,000 crystal-clear lakes and 30,000 kilometers of rivers, Brandenburg is the German federal state with the most waterways. Unsurprisingly it is the largest water sports region in Europe. Brandenburg also offers more than 500 palaces and stately homes to explore. Around a third of the region is protected natural scenery so it's the perfect place for getting out and exploring unspoilt nature.

### An undiscovered gem

**Brandenburg**
attracted over

### 4.6m
tourists in 2016,

but less than

### 6%
were from overseas

However, the number of people visiting the area is on the increase. Visitor numbers have risen by over

### 22% since 2010

### Dahme-Spreewald.....The Green Venice

The **Dahme-Spreewald** district attracted almost

### 750,000 visitors in 2016, 300,000
more than the state capital Potsdam.

The Spreewald area is known for its picturesque landscape consisting of over 200 small canals. Designated a biosphere reserve by UNESCO in 1991, Spreewald is popular with tourists who come to explore the canals in punts.

### The secret is out

The number of foreign tourists visiting the Brandenburg area has increased by

### 19% since 2010.

The area remains most popular with **Polish** visitors. This is no surprise as Poland borders the region to the East. Tourism from Scandinavia (specifically Denmark and Sweden) and the United Kingdom also remains high.

**Foreign guests by country of origin**
% change in volumes, 2010 vs. 2016

Poland, 37.5%
Denmark, 34.7%
Austria, 20.5%
Spain, 124.9%
Belgium, 10.1%
Lithuania, 12.1%
Australia, 16.3%

2010          2016

### Who stays the longest?

The average visitor to Brandenburg stays for

### 3 nights.

Visitors from **Romania** stayed in Brandenburg for an average of

### 6 nights
over the 2010 to 2016 period while visitors from Sweden only stayed for an average of 2 nights.

**Average nights stayed per guest**
2010-2016

| | |
|---|---|
| Romania | 6 |
| Brazil | 5 |
| India | 5 |
| Hungary | 4 |
| Slovenia | 4 |
| China & Hong Kong | 4 |
| Greece | 4 |
| Bulgaria | 4 |
| Croatia | 4 |
| Poland | 3 |

Data source: Statistik Berlin Brandenburg          @SarahLovesData

**FIGURE 6.18** Long-form visualization can be useful for guiding the audience through the analysis.

## Think Like a Data Journalist

Storytelling can often be thought of as data journalism. How can you take a data set, investigate, analyze, research, and communicate the insights? This requires continuous and regular practice, a bit of inspiration, and a willingness to learn.

Figure 6.19 by Mike Cisneros is a visual news story about life expectancy at birth. He lets the user pick the story they want to see and the visualization updates according to what they choose.

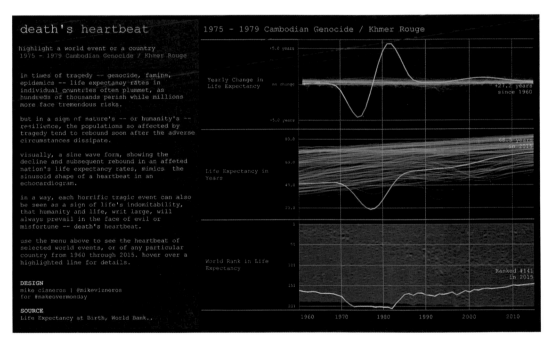

**FIGURE 6.19**   Life expectancy at birth by Mike Cisneros.

On the left side of his visualization, Mike describes the pattern in the data for the events that were selected. On the right side, his audience can see and understand what the data is showing based on these explanations and descriptions. This is a very effective way to communicate insights and educate the audience.

## Reviewing Your Work to Improve Its Quality

Before you publish your work, spend some time reviewing it. Stepping back and reviewing your work with a critical eye allows you to:

1.  Find errors or omissions
2.  Ensure simplicity
3.  Test for bugs
4.  Put yourself in the shoes of the audience

This section will provide tips and strategies for reviewing your work.

### Take a Step Back

The easiest and quickest way to "test" your visualization is to step away from the screen. You can do this in many ways, for example:

- Literally get out of your chair and take a few steps back so that you cannot touch the screen or the computer.
- Look away for a few seconds, then look back at your screen and pay attention to where your eyes are drawn.

Both of these techniques allow your brain to "reset" itself and consider the visualization anew. When you step back, ask yourself a few questions:

- Does this visualization tell the story in the most effective way?
- Is there anything (lines, words, labels, logos, images, etc.) I can remove or simplify, while still keeping the overall message the same?
- Is the layout intuitive and does it support or possibly enhance the story?

This does not take much time and it provides a lot of value. Give it a try.

## Ask a Friend

Ask a friend what they think, preferably someone who does not work in the field of data visualization and does not know much about the topic. The benefits of this include feedback about:

- *Insights*. Did they say back to you what you intended them to understand?
- *Usability*. Did they click where you wanted them to? Did they use an unexpected combination of interactions?
- *Honesty*. We can typically count on friends and family to be very honest with us.

Do not take their feedback personally. They are not critiquing you; they are critiquing the visualization. Listen to them. Do not interrupt. Hear what they have to say. Then incorporate their feedback and ask them again.

## Viz Review

Each week, we review visualizations on a webinar specifically designed for feedback. This is an opt-in session, so we only review work that people want feedback on. We are often seeing these visualizations for the first time, so you will get our initial impressions. Each review covers:

- Overall design
- Use of text in titles, subtitles, and annotations
- Font choices
- Effective use of color
- Depth and accuracy of the analysis

These sessions are designed to help anyone interested in improving their skills. However, if you want feedback, it is expected that you will listen to the feedback, take it on board, and iterate. This does not mean you have to agree with all of the feedback, but you should take it into consideration. After all, you asked for the feedback in the first place.

For more information about techniques for applying feedback, flip to Chapter 8, "Iterate to Improve."

## Summary

Your visualizations will be most effective when they are designed with the audience in mind. Ask yourself who will consume the information, what message you want to share, and what assumptions you can make about your audience's knowledge of a topic. Do you want them to interact with your visualization and delve deeper into the data, or are you providing them with an overview of your findings?

Tailor your visualization to your audience and give them the information and context they need to understand your key message.

## Chapter Seven

# Trying New Things

Makeover Monday offers participants the chance to work with an unknown data set every week and gives them many opportunities to be creative and try new things. This can include:

- Developing chart types they have not used before
- Learning a new technique to build visually compelling charts
- Improving their design skills
- Building a visualization that unfolds step-by-step

In our community, we have a number of members who have developed their own style and often this inspires others. We have also noticed certain trends emerge over the course of the project. For example, when a participant creates a novel or unusual chart, we see the same chart being replicated over the next few weeks. The ability for everyone to share their work in our online community means beginners and advanced analysts alike learn from their peers and are able to apply best practices that inspire them.

While not every chart type works for every data set, trying something new is an opportunity to learn and refine your skills. This can include focusing on color choice, layout, storytelling, highlighting, annotating, or creating an audience-centric design. It also provides an opportunity to develop your overall style and voice.

Most people know and understand the importance of giving credit where credit is due. You do it regularly in daily life, be it at work, university, or during a speech at a family event. When it comes to data visualization, you *must* credit the work of others when you use it for the benefit of your own work. While you can read more about citing your sources in Chapter 5, it is generally important to recognize those who have inspired your work.

Slavik Glazyrin was inspired by Cole Knaflic and tagged her in his tweet when he published his visualization of ethnicity distribution in Major League Baseball (Figure 7.1).

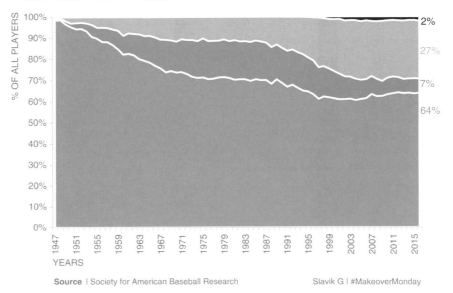

**FIGURE 7.1**   Ethnicity distribution in Major League Baseball, by Slavik Glazyrin.

A simple statement of attribution is a great way to acknowledge those who created the original design, color palette, or layout. It is gestures like these that encourage influencers to continue sharing their knowledge and skills with the wider community.

Some examples of inspiration from the Makeover Monday community include:

- Using a particular color palette that someone else created
- Replicating someone's formatting style, such as lines to connect different objects visually or using a specific font combination
- Emulating a specific chart type and following someone's instructions for creating it
- Taking the analysis someone else did, including their insights, and turning it into a different design
- Practicing a certain type of storytelling, like Slavik did when he emulated Cole's *clean storytelling* approach above

Many analysts and data visualization experts are passionate about their work and put a lot of effort into creating compelling visualizations for their audiences. It can be frustrating for them to see their work replicated without any attribution to the original author.

We ask our community to ensure they give credit to those who have inspired their work. This does not have to be as formal as academic citations; a short acknowledgement, footnote, or comment can suffice. We recommend that you include such credits on the visualization itself, so they remain visible even when your work is taken away from the context of a blog, forum post, or tweet.

## Developing a Sharing Culture

Social media, and the sharing capabilities it provides, helps to facilitate the learning process for the entire Makeover Monday community. In our project, we have novices and experts alike sharing their work, writing detailed instructions for others to learn from, and providing feedback and suggestions to others. Without these contributions it would be far more difficult to enable the type of progress we have seen with so many of the analysts participating week after week.

While not everyone in the community blogs and posts their submissions for download, we encourage everyone to move toward this sharing culture because everything we give back to the community helps others improve. The following sections highlight designs from Makeover Monday that have inspired others.

## Circular Charts

Taking a new approach to visualizing differences between categories, Adam Crahen created a circular histogram in Figure 7.2, looking at gender disparity for salaries in Australia.

**FIGURE 7.2**  Circular chart of gender salary disparity in Australia, by Adam Crahen.

The visualization received a lot of attention in the community and we have since seen numerous circular histograms appear for a variety of topics and data sets since. For example, the chart in Figure 7.3 by Jamie Smyth visualizes the proportion of African American players in Major League Baseball since 1947.

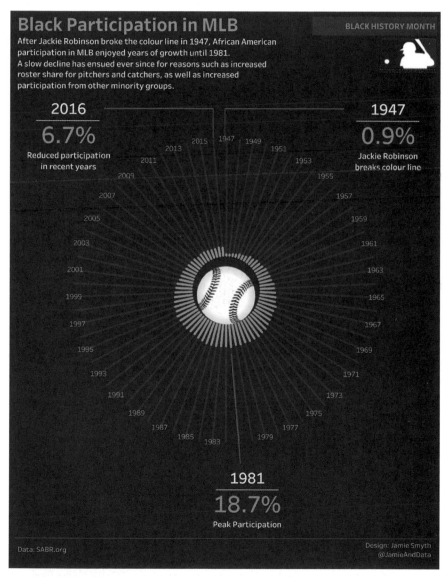

**FIGURE 7.3**    Circular time plot, by Jamie Smyth.

## Images from Dot Plots

Figure 7.4 from Curtis Harris used President Trump's tweets to create an image of Trump's face. The data showed tweets versus retweets and their impact from the time prior to his candidacy until early 2017.

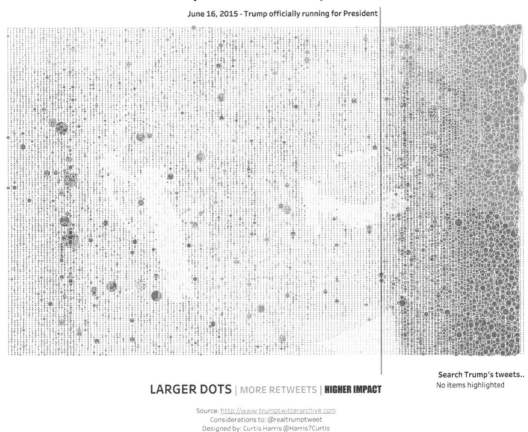

**FIGURE 7.4** Trump's face revealed through a series of tweets, by Curtis Harris.

## Patterns and Shapes

When we asked the community to visualize data from 5000 years of solar eclipses, Athan Mavrantonis created Figure 7.5 to look at the

Gamma values of each eclipse, which describes the centrality of the shadow cast by the eclipse.

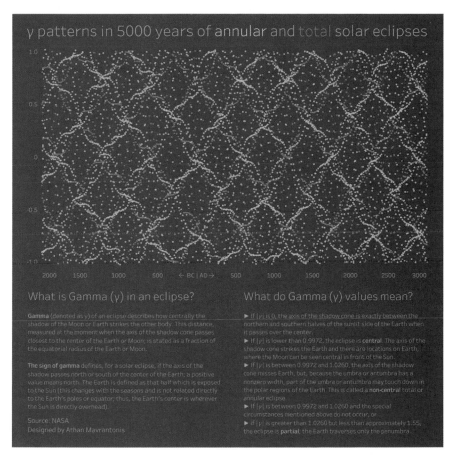

**FIGURE 7.5** Gamma pattern of solar eclipses, by Athan Mavrantonis.

The visualization shows a beautiful pattern in the data, and the use of different colors for annular versus total eclipses supports the regularity and symmetry of the pattern.

Mike Cisneros visualized the same data in Figure 7.6 to identify the best position for seeing the eclipse, depending on the latitude of the sun.

**FIGURE 7.6** How to find the best place to see an eclipse, by Mike Cisneros.

## Waffle Charts

Waffle charts are a great way to visualize percentages of a total and to make really large numbers more relatable. They are a type of visualization that has become increasingly popular within our community. We first saw them appear in the Makeover Monday project in early 2017 when a data set on employment growth in G7 countries contained percentage values, and participants used a template Andy had shared a few months prior on his blog.

Pooja Gandhi created the waffle chart in Figure 7.7.

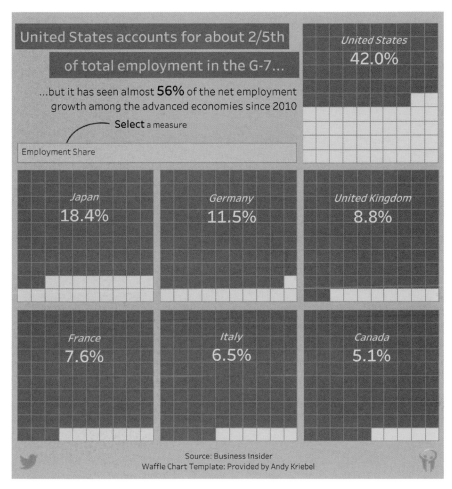

**FIGURE 7.7** Waffle chart of G-7 employment, by Pooja Gandhi.

Pooja used a bright yellow color to shade the relevant number of squares representing the percentage, with the total of each panel's squares summing up to 100. The yellow squares stand out noticeably against the dark gray background.

Charlie Hutcheson used a data set about the world as 100 people to create the simple yet impactful waffle chart in Figure 7.8 to capture the most significant issues still affecting major parts of the population.

Charlie used a basic color palette with red employed to draw attention to poverty, malnutrition, and starvation.

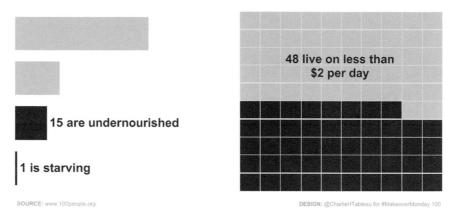

**IF THE WORLD WERE 100 PEOPLE...**

48 live on less than
$2 per day

15 are undernourished

1 is starving

SOURCE: www.100people.org                    DESIGN: @CharlieHTableau for #MakeoverMonday 100

**FIGURE 7.8**   Waffle chart of 100 people, by Charlie Hutcheson.

## Tile Maps

Tile maps reduce each geographic area to the same shape and size while maintaining their relative spatial positions. Since these visualizations first emerged in the Makeover Monday community, many tile maps were created based on the instructions by Matt Chambers. Andy blogged about and created a video on how to produce these types of maps and the community embraced tile maps, especially when it comes to visualizing US-based data.

The benefit of using a tile map is that you can avoid the Alaska effect of filled maps, where large states like Alaska make the results appear skewed because of scaling required to show the entire country.

Tile maps are also a useful alternative to filled maps because filled maps can become unsuitable when trying to identify data for small states. When you use color to represent values on a filled map, variances in large versus small states can be difficult to distinguish because of the different shape and size of each state.

With tile maps, the entire map can fit into a smaller space because the focus is not on exact geographical coordinates and instead on providing a basic view of the entire geographic location at a glance. Tile maps are very suitable for countries with states or regions of different sizes to highlight particular characteristics of a population, location, and changes over time, as can be seen in Figure 7.9.

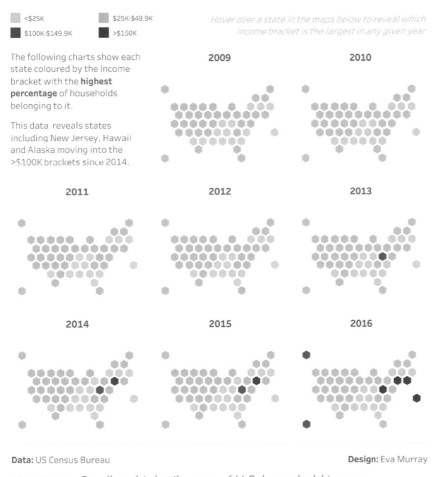

## US HOUSEHOLD INCOME DISTRIBUTION
### Income levels by state from 2009 - 2016
Data from the US Census Bureau shows that in the years since the Global Financial Crisis, income levels in a number of states have improved.

■ <$25K     ■ $25K-$49.9K
■ $100K-$149.9K     ■ >$150K

*Hover over a state in the maps below to reveal which income bracket is the largest in any given year*

The following charts show each state coloured by the income bracket with the **highest percentage** of households belonging to it.

This data reveals states including New Jersey, Hawaii and Alaska moving into the >$100K brackets since 2014.

2009    2010

2011    2012    2013

2014    2015    2016

**Data:** US Census Bureau                 **Design:** Eva Murray

**FIGURE 7.9**  Small multiple tile map of U.S. household income.

The Makeover Monday community has used tile maps extensively and has also gone beyond the template for the US and created tile maps for other countries and regions. Figures 7.10–12, all created by Neil Richards, are examples of tile maps that have inspired others and will hopefully inspire you, too, to create different types of maps.

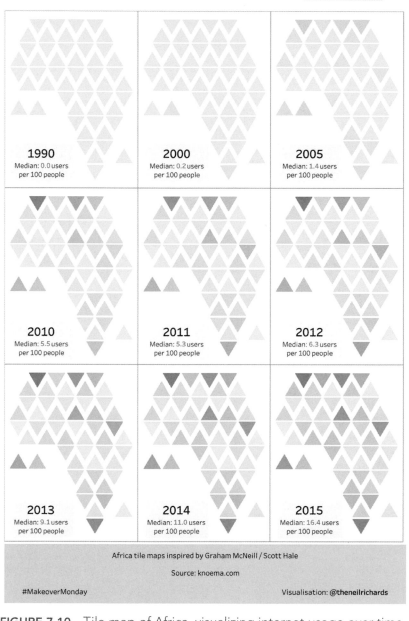

**FIGURE 7.10**   Tile map of Africa, visualizing internet usage over time between 1990 and 2015.

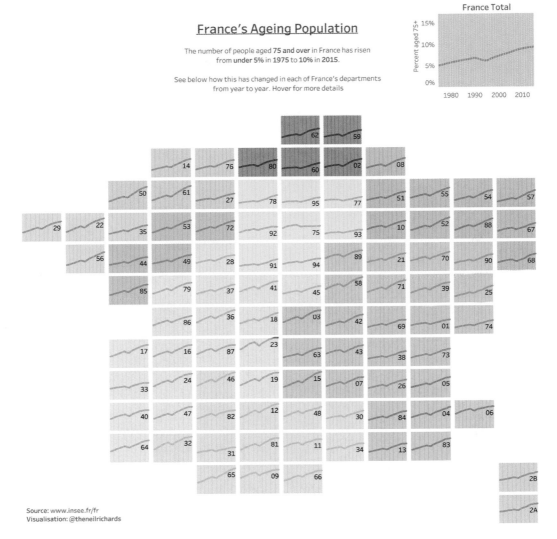

Source: www.insee.fr/fr
Visualisation: @theneilrichards

**FIGURE 7.11**   Line chart tile map of France's population.

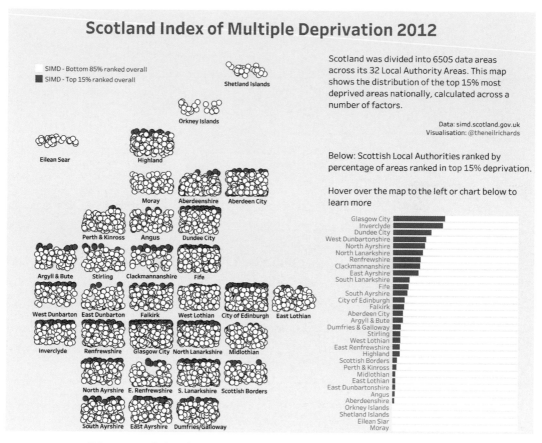

**FIGURE 7.12**   Tile map of the deprivation index of Scottish local authorities.

## Borders and Lines

Guiding your audience through a visualization helps them understand where and how to interact and read a chart. Pooja Gandhi uses borders and lines very effectively to guide her audience through her analysis. This lets her connect different text components and charts used to support the overall flow while minimizing complexity.

Pooja's visualization of crude oil and gold prices in Figure 7.13 is an excellent display of her techniques using lines. Pooja created a compelling dashboard comparing the price changes of the two commodities, using lines to break up the dashboard into components and to annotate certain data points and insights.

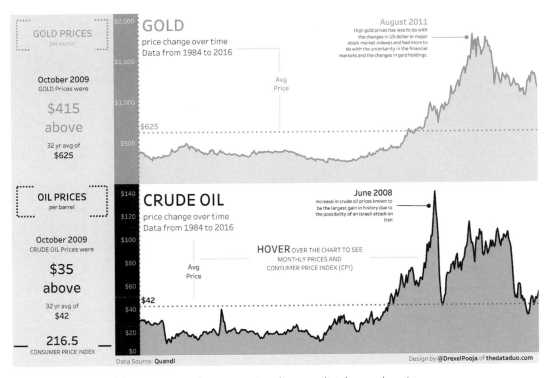

**FIGURE 7.13** Gold prices vs. oil prices using line to divide up the view.

The mix of dotted lines, solid lines, and lines that are broken up by text boxes provides variety and connects different components of the display. Dotted lines are used to indicate per-barrel versus per-ounce prices, while annotations and labels are connected with solid lines. For annotations, an additional dot at the end of each line helps link the commentary to its data point.

In Figure 7.14, Chantilly Jaggernauth shows a timeline of Jackie Robinson's career and the impact of African American players on Major League Baseball.

Chantilly uses colors and lines very effectively, staying within the familiar MLB color palette. Her use of lines to connect the years on a timeline allows her audience to easily follow the flow from the top of the page to the bottom. Individual callouts break up the page, add variety, and highlight points of particular interest. The line chart at the bottom shows the participation rates of African American

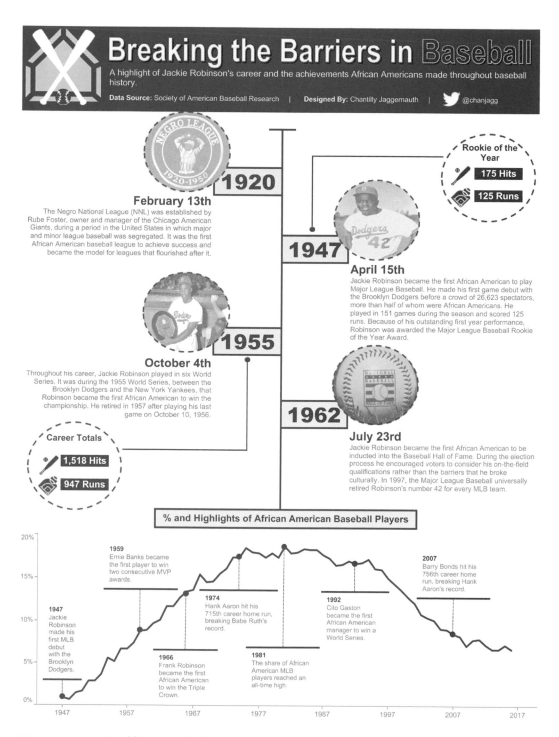

# Breaking the Barriers in Baseball

A highlight of Jackie Robinson's career and the achievements African Americans made throughout baseball history.

**Data Source:** Society of American Baseball Research    |    **Designed By:** Chantilly Jaggernauth    |    🐦 @chanjagg

**1920**

## February 13th

The Negro National League (NNL) was established by Rube Foster, owner and manager of the Chicago American Giants, during a period in the United States in which major and minor league baseball was segregated. It was the first African American baseball league to achieve success and became the model for leagues that flourished after it.

**1947**

**Rookie of the Year**

175 Hits

125 Runs

## April 15th

Jackie Robinson became the first African American to play Major League Baseball. He made his first game debut with the Brooklyn Dodgers before a crowd of 26,623 spectators, more than half of whom were African Americans. He played in 151 games during the season and scored 125 runs. Because of his outstanding first year performance, Robinson was awarded the Major League Baseball Rookie of the Year Award.

**1955**

## October 4th

Throughout his career, Jackie Robinson played in six World Series. It was during the 1955 World Series, between the Brooklyn Dodgers and the New York Yankees, that Robinson became the first African American to win the championship. He retired in 1957 after playing his last game on October 10, 1956.

**Career Totals**

1,518 Hits

947 Runs

**1962**

## July 23rd

Jackie Robinson became the first African American to be inducted into the Baseball Hall of Fame. During the election process he encouraged voters to consider his on-the-field qualifications rather than the barriers that he broke culturally. In 1997, the Major League Baseball universally retired Robinson's number 42 for every MLB team.

### % and Highlights of African American Baseball Players

**1947**
Jackie Robinson made his first MLB debut with the Brooklyn Dodgers.

**1959**
Ernie Banks became the first player to win two consecutive MVP awards.

**1966**
Frank Robinson became the first African American to win the Triple Crown.

**1974**
Hank Aaron hit his 715th career home run, breaking Babe Ruth's record.

**1981**
The share of African American MLB players reached an all-time high.

**1992**
Cito Gaston became the first African American manager to win a World Series.

**2007**
Barry Bonds hit his 756th career home run, breaking Hank Aaron's record.

**FIGURE 7.14**   Visual history of African American players in Major League Baseball.

players over time. Chantilly also uses annotations to relate this data back to the first part of her visualization, focusing on achievements by African American players.

## Summary

Trying new things and putting what you have learned into practice are two great ways to improve your skills in data analysis and data visualization. The examples in this chapter are a small showcase of the ideas and approaches created by the Makeover Monday community. We encourage you to take all of the visuals you find in this book as inspiration and not to stop there. There are many data sets available on our website to test different chart types and techniques. Go beyond the book and let the work of others inspire and influence how you communicate data.

## Chapter Eight

# Iterate to Improve

Data visualizations are never "done"; you merely get to a point where you think they are "good enough" and consider them complete. This chapter will provide advice about iterating through your work, giving and receiving feedback, and the benefits of iteration.

## Why Iterate?

In Chapter 6, we provided tips for identifying your audience and getting to know their needs. Once you have identified those needs, you should generate lots of ideas, and then it is time to build a prototype. You then review or test the design with your audience, get feedback, and iterate on your work. Once you have a new prototype built, the process starts over again.

The earlier you start this feedback loop, the more cost-effective it will be. Working through this feedback loop with the audience early is also beneficial because they will understand that it is only a prototype, so they will focus more on the functionality than the design, thus resulting in a more usable product in the end.

## Agile Data Visualization

Nearly every data analysis or dashboard design project starts like Figure 8.1.[1]

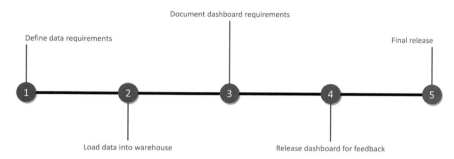

**FIGURE 8.1**    A waterfall approach to data visualization projects.

This is often called waterfall development; that is, you do not start the next process until the previous stage has finished, continuing until you get to the end. This is great if everything in the project is perfect, but how often does that happen? Almost never. Requirements change, the data is not correct or complete, the development takes longer than expected. The list of obstacles to overcome is endless.

The problem with waterfall development is that once something breaks down, you have to go back to the beginning and start again. This is not sustainable if you want to get a lot of work done and you want your projects to be a success.

If you follow a waterfall process and do not get feedback until the end of your project, you will find it highly likely that people will not use your dashboard. Why? Because it may not be the dashboard they needed and probably does not address the reasons the project was started in the first place.

---

[1] From Data to Insight, Chris Love, The Information Lab, 3 March 2016.

How can you give your end users something of value when you do not know their definition of value and have not checked whether what you created suits them? The solution is to go on a journey together, and the result almost certainly will not be a direct journey like it was above. It will probably look somewhat like the "squiggle" in Figure 8.2, adapted from the original by Damian Newman:[2]

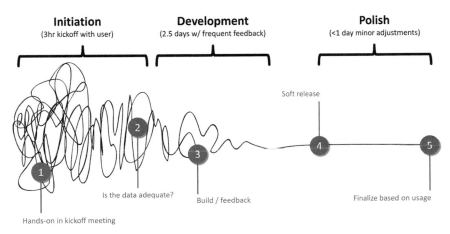

**FIGURE 8.2**  An agile approach to data visualization projects.

This process is proven and effective. This is the process that has been followed by the Data School for over 100 projects and the failure rate is 0%. That's right—every project has been a success, largely due to following this "squiggle" development process. There are three simple phases that make it work.

*Initiation*

*Time*: Three hours.

*Who*: Project owner, users, developers.

*Purpose*: Determine scope and sketch ideas with stakeholders.

---

[2] That Squiggle of the Design Process, Damien Newman, ReVision Lab.

*Details*: Start every project with a kickoff meeting. The project owner should be able to clearly communicate the questions they want answers to. Having the project owner list a set of questions removes them from the design process (no more "Build me a pie chart, please") and gets them thinking about the insights they are seeking.

Users, developers, and the project owner should get involved in prototyping and sketching designs so that everyone is clear on what can be delivered.

*Decisions*: At the end of the initiation phase, there should be enough information to determine whether the data is available and in the right format to deliver the project. If not, then the initiation phase should continue until the scope is appropriately sized based on the data available.

*Outcomes*: A prototype or wireframe that all stakeholders agree to which provides the basis for the deliverables of the project.

*Development*

*Time*: Two to three days.

*Who*: Developers.

*Purpose*: Build, test alternate visualization techniques, design user interface that can be changed and adjusted as needed.

*Details*: Dedicated work on the deliverables by the developer, including daily feedback sessions with a subset of users. Create a time-boxed, structured daily schedule to keep the team motivated and the project moving forward. The daily feedback loop ensures that no work gets too far outside the scope without time to correct the direction.

*Decisions*: At the end of the development phase, there should be enough information to determine whether there is a viable product to be released for final feedback.

*Outcomes*: All stakeholders get daily reassurance that the project will be delivered as expected. A beta version of the work for feedback by users to be provided within one work week.

*Polish*

*Time*: Less than one day.

*Who*: Developers.

*Purpose*: Deliver final visualization.

*Details*: Incorporate final feedback; ensure details like tooltips, formatting, and color are addressed. Conduct peer review session. Verify accuracy of final calculations.

*Decisions*: By the end of the polish phase, the team should determine if the product goes into production.

*Outcomes*: A final release of the visualization to stakeholders.

## Examples of Effective Iteration

Most people we know agree that this development method works extremely well, yet few organizations implement iterative processes and get stuck in a never-ending cycle of development. Each week, we host a live webinar where we provide feedback on visualizations to the Makeover Monday community. Similar to the development loop above, users seek feedback and iterate on their work.

We typically recommend, above all other suggestions, a simplification of the design, with fewer colors; clearer instructions, titles, and descriptions; and a general decluttering of dashboards. We sometimes also have to address incorrect treatment of data, such as aggregation issues or misrepresenting the data.

Below is a series of before and after images from people who have iterated through feedback (Figures 8.3–8.16).

## Louise Heath: The Price of Oil versus Gold

*Before*

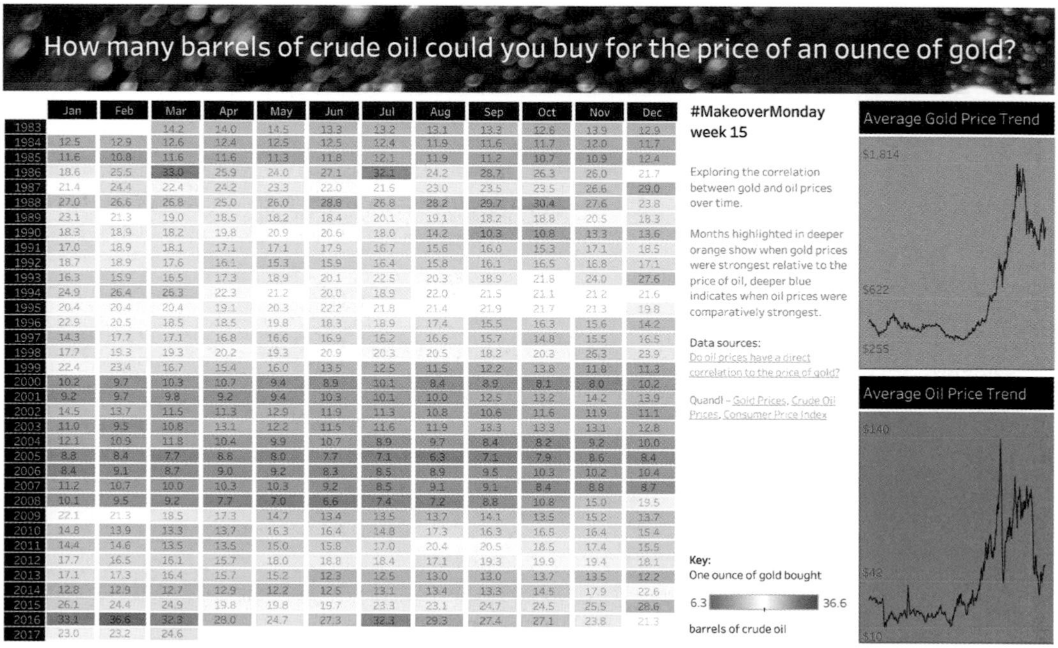

How many barrels of crude oil could you buy for the price of an ounce of gold?

| | Jan | Feb | Mar | Apr | May | Jun | Jul | Aug | Sep | Oct | Nov | Dec |
|---|---|---|---|---|---|---|---|---|---|---|---|---|
| 1983 | | | 14.2 | 14.0 | 14.5 | 13.3 | 13.2 | 13.1 | 13.3 | 12.6 | 13.9 | 12.9 |
| 1984 | 12.5 | 12.9 | 12.6 | 12.4 | 12.5 | 12.5 | 12.4 | 11.9 | 11.6 | 11.7 | 12.0 | 11.7 |
| 1985 | 11.6 | 10.8 | 11.6 | 11.6 | 11.3 | 11.8 | 12.1 | 11.9 | 11.2 | 10.7 | 10.9 | 12.1 |
| 1986 | 18.6 | 25.5 | 33.0 | 25.9 | 24.0 | 27.1 | 32.1 | 24.2 | 28.7 | 26.3 | 26.0 | 21.7 |
| 1987 | 21.4 | 24.4 | 22.4 | 24.2 | 23.3 | 22.0 | 21.5 | 23.0 | 23.5 | 23.5 | 26.6 | 29.0 |
| 1988 | 27.0 | 26.6 | 25.8 | 25.0 | 26.0 | 28.8 | 26.8 | 28.2 | 29.7 | 30.4 | 27.6 | 23.8 |
| 1989 | 23.1 | 21.3 | 19.0 | 18.5 | 18.2 | 18.4 | 20.1 | 19.1 | 18.2 | 18.8 | 20.5 | 18.3 |
| 1990 | 18.3 | 18.9 | 18.2 | 19.8 | 20.9 | 20.6 | 18.0 | 14.2 | 10.3 | 10.8 | 13.3 | 13.6 |
| 1991 | 17.0 | 18.9 | 18.1 | 17.1 | 17.1 | 17.9 | 16.7 | 15.6 | 16.0 | 15.3 | 17.1 | 18.5 |
| 1992 | 18.7 | 18.9 | 17.6 | 16.1 | 15.3 | 15.9 | 16.4 | 15.8 | 16.1 | 16.5 | 16.8 | 17.1 |
| 1993 | 16.3 | 15.9 | 16.5 | 17.3 | 18.9 | 20.1 | 22.5 | 20.3 | 18.9 | 21.8 | 24.0 | 27.6 |
| 1994 | 24.9 | 26.4 | 26.3 | 22.3 | 21.2 | 20.0 | 18.9 | 22.0 | 21.5 | 21.1 | 21.2 | 21.6 |
| 1995 | 20.4 | 20.4 | 20.4 | 19.1 | 20.3 | 22.2 | 21.8 | 21.4 | 21.9 | 21.7 | 21.3 | 19.8 |
| 1996 | 22.9 | 20.5 | 18.5 | 18.5 | 19.8 | 18.3 | 18.9 | 17.4 | 15.5 | 16.3 | 15.6 | 14.2 |
| 1997 | 14.3 | 17.7 | 17.1 | 16.8 | 16.6 | 16.9 | 16.2 | 16.6 | 15.7 | 14.8 | 15.5 | 16.5 |
| 1998 | 17.7 | 19.3 | 19.3 | 20.2 | 19.3 | 20.9 | 20.3 | 20.5 | 18.2 | 20.3 | 26.3 | 23.9 |
| 1999 | 22.4 | 23.4 | 16.7 | 15.4 | 16.0 | 13.5 | 12.5 | 11.5 | 12.2 | 13.8 | 11.8 | 11.3 |
| 2000 | 10.2 | 9.7 | 10.3 | 10.7 | 9.4 | 8.9 | 10.1 | 8.4 | 8.9 | 8.1 | 8.0 | 10.2 |
| 2001 | 9.2 | 9.7 | 9.8 | 9.2 | 9.4 | 10.3 | 10.1 | 10.0 | 12.5 | 13.2 | 14.2 | 13.9 |
| 2002 | 14.5 | 13.7 | 11.5 | 11.3 | 12.9 | 11.9 | 11.3 | 10.8 | 10.6 | 11.6 | 11.9 | 11.1 |
| 2003 | 11.0 | 9.5 | 10.8 | 13.1 | 12.2 | 11.5 | 11.6 | 11.9 | 13.3 | 13.3 | 13.1 | 12.8 |
| 2004 | 12.1 | 10.5 | 11.8 | 10.4 | 9.9 | 10.7 | 8.9 | 9.7 | 8.4 | 8.2 | 9.2 | 10.0 |
| 2005 | 8.8 | 8.4 | 7.7 | 8.8 | 8.0 | 7.7 | 7.1 | 6.3 | 7.1 | 7.9 | 8.6 | 8.4 |
| 2006 | 8.4 | 9.1 | 8.7 | 9.0 | 9.2 | 8.3 | 8.5 | 8.9 | 9.5 | 10.3 | 10.2 | 10.4 |
| 2007 | 11.2 | 10.7 | 10.0 | 10.3 | 10.3 | 9.2 | 8.5 | 9.1 | 9.1 | 8.4 | 8.8 | 8.7 |
| 2008 | 10.1 | 9.5 | 9.2 | 7.7 | 7.0 | 6.6 | 7.4 | 7.2 | 8.8 | 10.8 | 15.0 | 19.5 |
| 2009 | 22.1 | 21.3 | 18.5 | 17.3 | 14.7 | 13.4 | 13.5 | 13.7 | 14.1 | 13.5 | 15.2 | 13.7 |
| 2010 | 14.8 | 13.9 | 13.3 | 13.7 | 16.3 | 16.4 | 14.8 | 17.3 | 16.3 | 16.5 | 16.4 | 15.4 |
| 2011 | 14.4 | 14.6 | 13.5 | 13.5 | 15.0 | 15.8 | 17.0 | 20.4 | 20.5 | 18.5 | 17.4 | 15.5 |
| 2012 | 17.7 | 16.5 | 16.1 | 15.7 | 18.0 | 18.8 | 18.4 | 17.1 | 19.3 | 19.9 | 19.4 | 18.1 |
| 2013 | 17.1 | 17.3 | 16.4 | 15.7 | 15.2 | 12.3 | 12.5 | 13.0 | 13.0 | 13.7 | 13.5 | 12.2 |
| 2014 | 12.8 | 12.9 | 12.7 | 12.9 | 12.5 | 12.5 | 13.1 | 13.4 | 13.3 | 14.5 | 17.9 | 22.6 |
| 2015 | 26.1 | 24.4 | 24.9 | 19.8 | 19.8 | 19.7 | 23.3 | 23.1 | 24.7 | 24.5 | 25.5 | 28.6 |
| 2016 | 33.1 | 36.6 | 32.3 | 28.0 | 24.7 | 27.3 | 32.1 | 29.3 | 27.4 | 27.1 | 23.8 | 21.3 |
| 2017 | 23.0 | 23.2 | 24.6 | | | | | | | | | |

**#MakeoverMonday week 15**

Exploring the correlation between gold and oil prices over time.

Months highlighted in deeper orange show when gold prices were strongest relative to the price of oil, deeper blue indicates when oil prices were comparatively strongest.

Data sources:
Do oil prices have a direct correlation to the price of gold?

Quandl - Gold Prices, Crude Oil Prices, Consumer Price Index

Key:
One ounce of gold bought
6.3  36.6
barrels of crude oil

Average Gold Price Trend
$1,814
$622
$255

Average Oil Price Trend
$140
$42
$10

**FIGURE 8.3** A very "busy" visualization comparing the price of crude oil and gold.

*After*

## The relationship between oil & gold prices

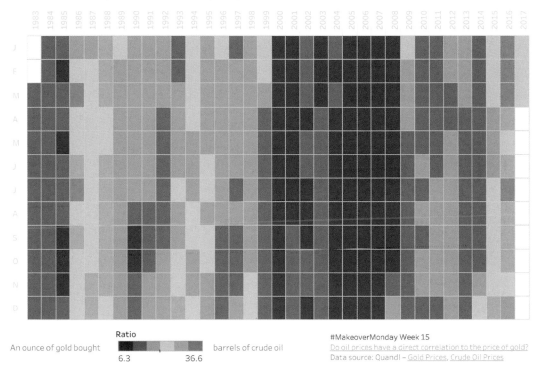

FIGURE 8.4    A much simpler way of showing the relationship between oil and gold prices.

*Effective Changes*

- Colors were softened, and text was removed from the heatmap to move the focus to the patterns in the colors.
- Line charts and background images were removed to reduce clutter.
- Heatmap is now the sole focus of the analysis.

## Wale Ilori: Air Quality Above America

*Before*

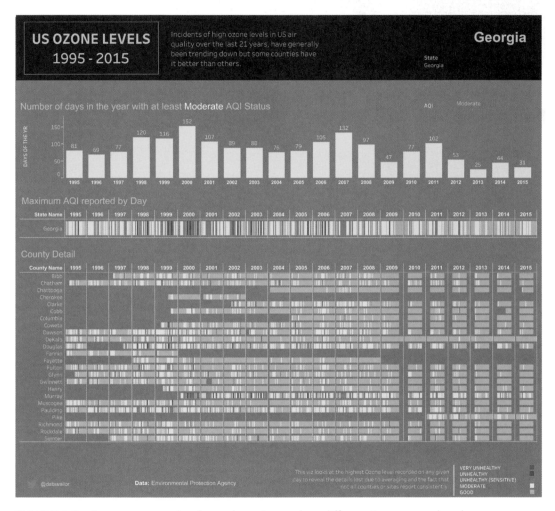

**FIGURE 8.5**   A green-to-red color palette is used to differentiate ozone levels.

*After*

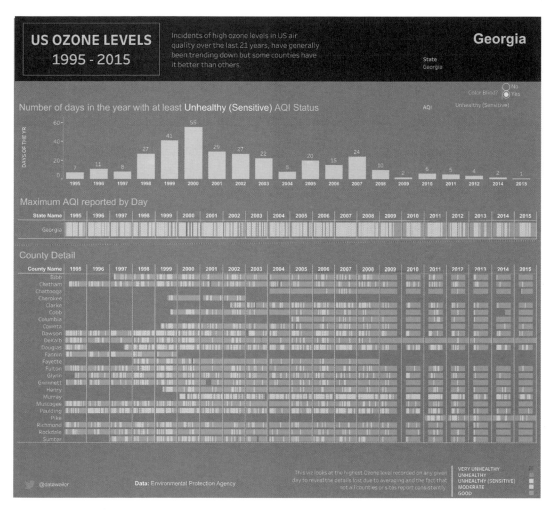

**FIGURE 8.6**  A blue-to-red color palette makes this visualization colorblindness friendly.

*Effective Changes*

• Colors have been adjusted for colorblindness.

## Paul Griffith: Le Tour de France

*Before*

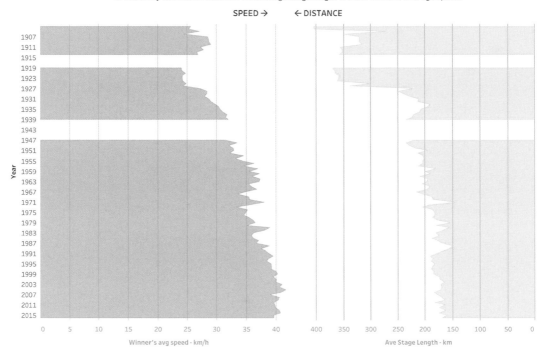

**FIGURE 8.7** An eye-catching but difficult to read vertical timeline.

*After*

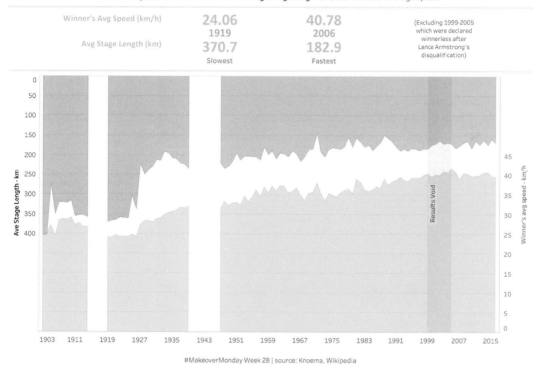

FIGURE 8.8    The horizontal timeline creates a more intuitive design that is easier to comprehend.

*Effective Changes*

• Chart was rotated so that time reads left to right.
• Big numbers were added to summarize the findings.

Rodrigo Calloni: India's Broken Toilets

*Before*

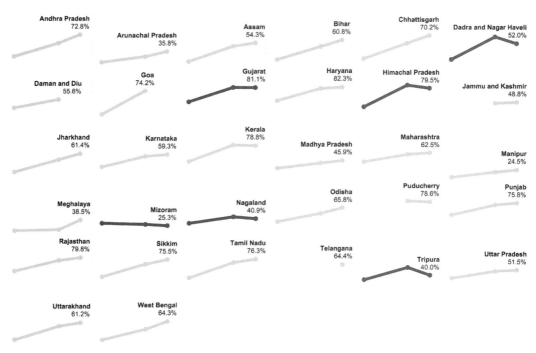

# The **GIRLs BROKEN TOILET** problem in **INDIA**

In India efforts are being made to improve girls toilet availability in schools. The scenario improved from **2010**, however between **2014 and 2016** some States are showing **DECREASE** in availability of working toilets for female students.

a #makeovermonday design by Rodrigo Calloni | @tableauing

Datasource: Annual Status of Education Report

**FIGURE 8.9**   Small multiple line charts without zero lines make it difficult to compare different states.

*After*

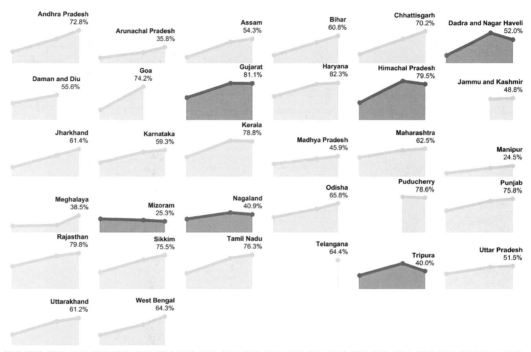

Datasource: Annual Status of Education Report

**FIGURE 8.10**  Small multiple area charts with a clear zero line make comparisons easier and show changes more clearly.

*Effective Changes*

- Chart was changed to an area chart to ensure the emphasis is on the problem areas.

## Sarah Bartlett: The Timing of Baby Making

*Before*

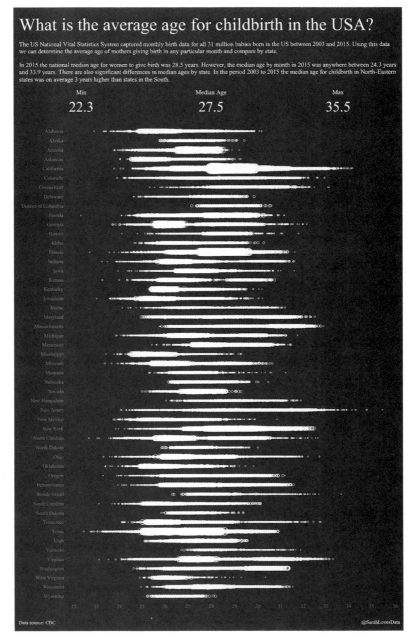

**FIGURE 8.11** The single color of the dot plot reduces the visibility of differences between states.

*After*

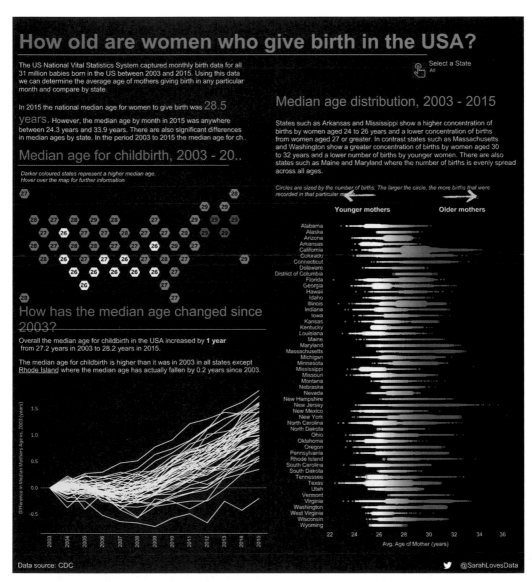

**FIGURE 8.12** Applying a diverging color palette highlights differences and trends more clearly.

*Effective Changes*

- Hex map and line charts were added to enhance the analysis.
- Colors were changed to diverging to make the patterns more obvious.

Daniel Caroli: The UK Economy Since the Brexit Vote

*Before*

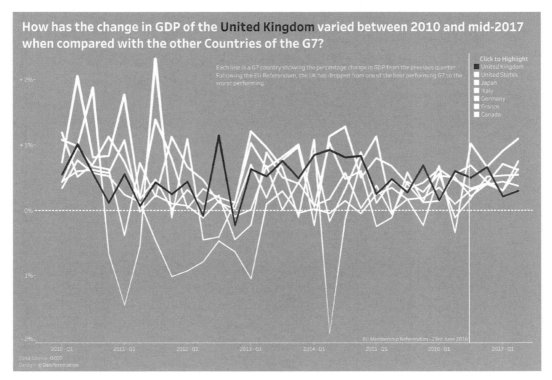

**FIGURE 8.13**   White lines with changing thickness for non-UK countries reduce the impact of the pink line representing the UK.

*After*

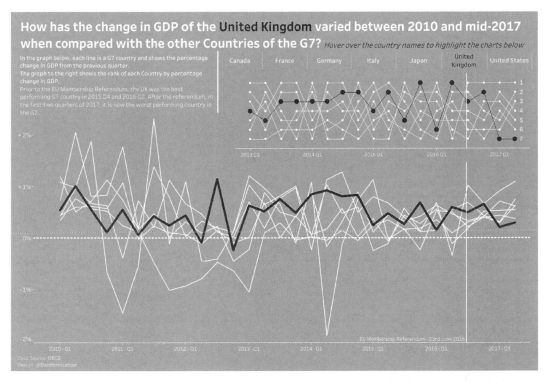

**FIGURE 8.14** Reducing the thickness of all non-UK country lines helps focus on the key message about the UK GDP.

*Effective Changes*

- Bump chart was added to emphasize rankings.
- Size of lines was made consistent.
- Legend was removed because it was already incorporated in the title.

Adolfo Hernandez: Baseball Demographics, 1947–2016

*Before*

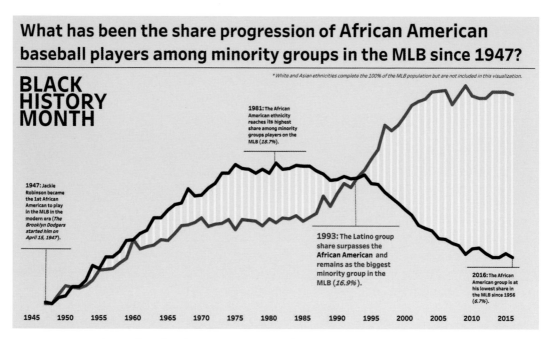

**What has been the share progression of African American baseball players among minority groups in the MLB since 1947?**

BLACK HISTORY MONTH

*White and Asian ethnicities complete the 100% of the MLB population but are not included in this visualization.*

1981: The African American ethnicity reaches its highest share among minority groups players on the MLB (*18.7%*).

1947: Jackie Robinson became the 1st African American to play in the MLB in the modern era (*The Brooklyn Dodgers started him on April 15, 1947*).

1993: The Latino group share surpasses the **African American** and remains as the biggest minority group in the MLB (*16.9%*).

2016: The African American group is at his lowest share in the MLB since 1956 (*6.7%*).

1945   1950   1955   1960   1965   1970   1975   1980   1985   1990   1995   2000   2005   2010   2015

**FIGURE 8.15**   The yellow background is uncomfortably bright.

*After*

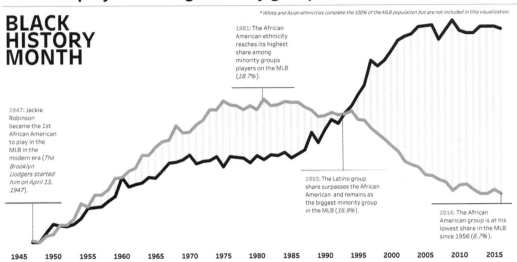

**What has been the share progression of** African American **baseball players among minority groups in the MLB since 1947?**

*\* White and Asian ethnicities complete the 100% of the MLB population but are not included in this visualization.*

BLACK
HISTORY
MONTH

1981: The African American ethnicity reaches its highest share among minority groups players on the MLB (*18.7%*).

1947: Jackie Robinson became the 1st African American to play in the MLB in the modern era (*The Brooklyn Dodgers started him on April 15, 1947*).

1993: The Latino group share surpasses the African American and remains as the biggest minority group in the MLB (*16.9%*).

2016: The African American group is at his lowest share in the MLB since 1956 (*6.7%*).

1945  1950  1955  1960  1965  1970  1975  1980  1985  1990  1995  2000  2005  2010  2015

**FIGURE 8.16**   The light gray background and light and dark blue lines result in a more professional appearance.

*Effective Changes*

- Colors were made softer to make it easier to read.

## Giving and Receiving Feedback

Feedback is information about reactions to a product, a person's performance of a task, and the like, which is used as a basis for improvement.[3] In data visualization, feedback is about reactions to the visualization, how well it communicates information, how it can be more effective, and the overall design.

If you are giving feedback, be mindful of the person receiving it and make it constructive and encouraging. If you have asked for feedback, be prepared to listen and not view it as personal criticism. When receiving feedback about your data visualization, it is your choice which feedback to accept and which to reject, but it is important to understand that the feedback is about your work, not about you as a person.

For Makeover Monday, each participant has the option to receive feedback on the data.world website in the discussion posts, as well as during the weekly Viz Review webinar and on Twitter. The key is having the courage to ask for it. As mentioned before, no visualization is ever "done"; the feedback loop helps you make your visualization more effective and communicate more clearly.

### Giving Effective Feedback

For Makeover Monday and data visualization in general, effective feedback is that which is clearly heard and understood.[4] As the provider of feedback, those are the only areas that are within your control. The recipient will ultimately determine which parts of the feedback to accept or reject in order to improve their work.

The process for providing feedback can be broken down into a few simple steps.

---

[3] Google dictionary – google.co.uk/search?q=feedback
[4] Adapted from *Giving and Receiving Feedback* by Skills You Need, skillsyouneed.com/ips/feedback.html

*Feedback Should Be About the Work, Not the Person*

First, we recommend that you provide feedback only when it is requested. If you provide feedback to someone who has not asked for it, it is possible that the recipient will find it offensive and might question your motive for providing feedback.

If you are asked to provide feedback, it is critical that you remember to keep the feedback based on the work. Think back to the first visualization you created when you got started in data visualization, and provide the feedback as if someone were providing you feedback at that time. Really focus on their work and be objective.

*Feedback Should Describe Your Opinion*

After all, you do not know the opinion of anyone else. You only know your reaction or what you thought. Presenting feedback as your opinion makes it much easier for the recipient to hear and accept it, even if the feedback is negative yet constructive. Similar to how the creator has no control over what you thought, you have no insight into the intention of their design. Keeping the feedback focused on the end product will make the feedback much more acceptable.

*Feedback Should Be Specific*

If you start by telling someone that "everything is poor," you can easily demoralize them and discourage them from seeking your feedback again. Think about the specific feedback you can provide. Perhaps you think there are too many colors in the visualization competing for your attention. Provide feedback exactly about where there is too much color and how color could be used more effectively. Giving the designer specific feedback and a suggestion for changes is constructive and helpful.

As an example, consider the Makeover Monday data set about arrests of NFL (National Football League) players. Since there are 32 teams in the NFL, it is easy to fall into the trap of using too many colors when you are showing all 32 teams in the same chart. Many teams have colors that are very similar, making it difficult to distinguish them from one another.

It is okay to show all 32 teams at once; however, when you do, consider using highlighting to either (i) focus on a team you want your audience to focus on, or (ii) allow your audience to pick a team themselves. If you want to look at cumulative arrests by team across the seasons from 2000 to 2017, you could assign each team's official color to the team name and create a view like Figure 8.17:

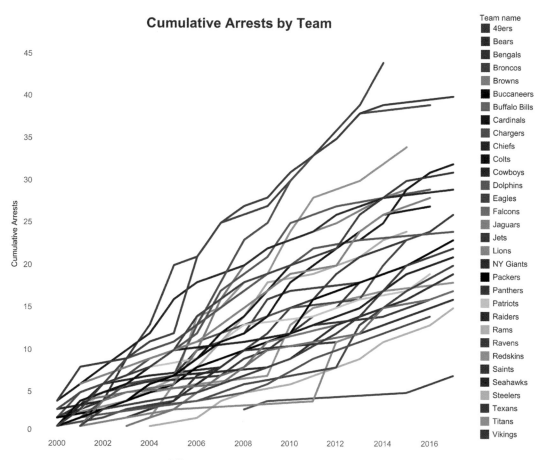

**FIGURE 8.17** Assigning a different color to each team creates a busy visualization with very similar-looking lines throughout.

Many of these colors blend together. Instead, consider Figure 8.18, which allows the user to highlight their favorite team.

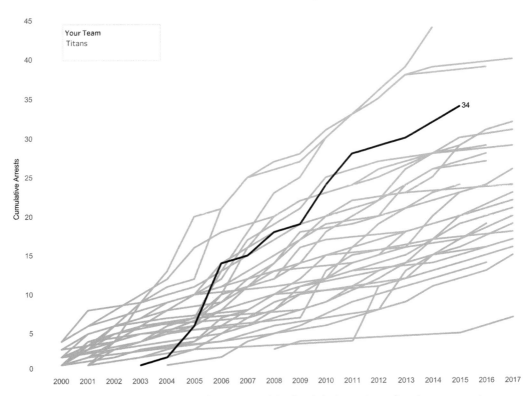

**FIGURE 8.18**  Highlighting a single team in black while keeping all other teams in gray ensures focus without losing context.

Now that the visualization is much less cluttered, the user can focus on what they are interested in, and thus they will be more engaged. In general, if you are ever unsure whether you are using too much color, you probably are. If you need a second opinion, ask someone who does not know anything about the data. Can they see what you want them to see?

When providing feedback, the more specific, the better. It is much easier to understand and act on specific feedback. For example, suggesting that a design would be more effective with fewer colors while suggesting highlighting as an alternative is constructive and will likely help the author create a better visualization.

### *Feedback Should Be Timely*

Feedback needs to be given in a timely manner while it is still appropriate to take action, rather than providing suggestions on work from many months ago. If you have been asked to give feedback and have something to share, do not keep the person waiting. Keep in mind, though, that your feedback should be specific and actionable.

## Receiving Feedback

If you ask for feedback, be prepared to receive it, consider which comments you agree with, take note of the suggestions you disagree with, and act upon the feedback provided. Constructive critique by others is an opportunity to learn and improve, so take advantage of it. Also keep in mind that acknowledging feedback is the right and courteous thing to do. Even if you do not agree with the suggestions, thank the person for taking the time to review your work, for putting thought into their comments and making the effort to help you improve. For people who give you feedback, it is satisfying and exciting to see you improve.

Receiving feedback can be difficult and it may feel like you are being criticized personally rather than in response to your work. If someone says something about you as a person, do your best to ignore them and do not react impulsively. Focus on the constructive feedback you have received and use it to improve your work. The most important skill in receiving feedback is listening. When someone gives you suggestions, focus on listening to their points, rather than thinking about how you are going to respond or defend yourself.

## Acting Upon Feedback

Consider Figure 8.19 from Sarah Burnett, who had asked for feedback on her work during a Viz Review webinar.

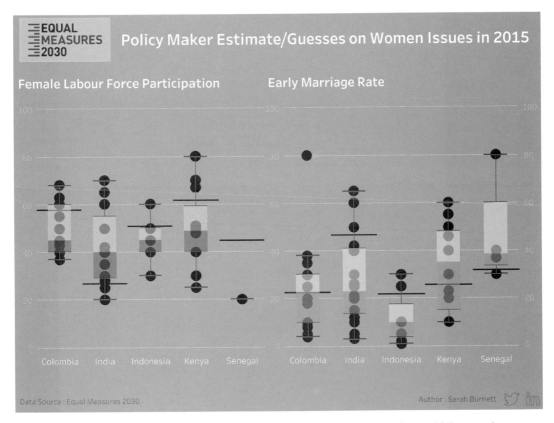

**FIGURE 8.19** A deep turquoise background makes the dark purple and blue circles difficult to see.

We provided some feedback:

1. What value do the whiskers on the box plot add?

2. Consider a reference band that spans +/− 20% from the correct answer as this range was meaningful to the stakeholder, the Equal Measures 2030 campaign team.

3. Change the scale to percentages instead of absolute numbers.

4. The turquoise background is too strong and makes it challenging to focus on the data and the message.

5. Include a description in the subtitle that explains what the visualization is about.

Note that none of this feedback is about Sarah as a person; it is about her work. The feedback is our opinion. The feedback is specific, timely, and actionable. In other words, the feedback is effective, and Sarah was able to take a short amount of time to create a more informative visualization (Figure 8.20).

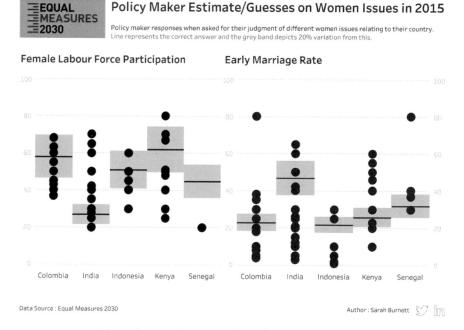

**FIGURE 8.20** The white background lets the data stand out more easily and makes labels easier to read.

Sarah was open to feedback; she asked for it. She used the feedback as a way to learn and improve. She understands that the feedback will help her become better at analyzing and visualizing data and will help her communicate information more effectively.

Once you receive feedback that has helped you, you will be able to provide effective feedback to others because you know the style of feedback that has helped you.

## Summary

Being open to feedback and iterating on your work is an essential skill if you want to learn, grow, and become a better data analyst and data visualization designer. Learning how to properly communicate feedback takes practice, much like developing any other skill. In this chapter, you have learned:

1. How iterating during a project will help you deliver outputs faster and with higher quality

2. What examples of effective iterations look like

3. How to give and receive feedback

None of this is complicated; these things can be subtle and may go unnoticed when you look at just the surface of your work and processes. It is natural to make mistakes along the way; no one gets it right all the time. What is important is that you continue to develop your communication skills along with your technical skills. In today's market, those two skills in combination are critical for success not just as a data analyst but as an effective member of any organization and team.

## Chapter Nine

# Effective Use of Color

Most of the chart examples used in this book include color to help bring a topic to life, draw your attention, highlight specific insights, or evoke emotion. Using color in data visualization is an effective way to better communicate your message and to make your work more impactful.

In this chapter, you will learn best practices for using color in data visualization. More specifically, this chapter will help you understand how you can use color to:

- Evoke emotions
- Create associations
- Highlight key findings and data points

# The Significance of Color in Data Visualization

Color has long been used to communicate information and convey emotions. Color theory[1] became a topic through the work of Leone Battista Alberti and Leonardo Da Vinci in the fifteenth century before being formalized through Isaac Newton's theory of color in 1704. We can acknowledge that the concepts introduced by these influencers informed many of the ways we think about color today.

Color is used to influence people in advertisements and product packaging, and to capture their attention through various channels. In data visualization, you can utilize the research on the effectiveness of color to help influence the processing and understanding of information.

## How Color Is Used to Tell Stories

Children's books use color in storytelling. There are lush green meadows where cows graze, while a dog runs after a butterfly. It is a colorful display to draw children into the story and help them discover all the objects on a page. It enables children to learn how colors help the parts of a story fit together. You can use the ideas behind children's stories and apply them to data visualization in a business context.

Stories are a natural way for humans to communicate information. Thousands of years ago, before we had books and paper to capture data and display information, stories were the only way to transfer knowledge from one generation to the next.

Your audience will likely respond very positively to a captivating story, one they understand easily and can follow along, a story that

---

[1] en.wikipedia.org/wiki/Color_theory

informs them and shares critical insights that help them make decisions and take actions.

Whether you create data visualizations as a hobby, for social impact, in your day job, or for all these reasons, practicing your storytelling skills and enhancing them through the effective use of color will help you communicate your message more clearly to your audience.

In the following sections we will introduce the parallels between data visualization and storytelling and how you can use color to tell a better story.

NOTE: The next few sections assume that the default background color for data visualizations is white. Any other colors in the text are specified as required.

## Using Color to Evoke Emotions

> They may forget what you said, but they will never forget how you made them feel.
>
> —*Carl W. Buehner*

Creating data visualizations that evoke emotions in your audience will make your work more memorable, give you a greater chance to influence people, and ensure that they take action or make changes based on your findings and recommendations.

In business, concepts like responsibility, ownership, urgency, and pride evoke emotion. For example, if your analysis shows that there is a large untapped opportunity to close a major deal with an existing customer by the end of this quarter, you can use color to give your audience a sense of urgency and communicate the need to act quickly.

In the following sections we have assumed a typical Western view, which associates certain colors with certain meanings and emotions. Emotional colors are very culturally defined and what is seen as an alarming color in the Western world (i.e., red) is perceived as a celebratory color in many parts of Asia.

Diving into the cultural context of emotional color would go far beyond the limitations of this chapter, so please read the following pages with the assumption of a North American and European perspective.

## Positive Results and Emotions

For good things, you will typically want to use bright, positive colors, such as blue and green. In business, green is often representative of positive results and gives people confidence that things are going well. Pinks and purples, as opposed to reds, are also often used to show positive outcomes. On dark backgrounds, white can be featured as a positive color. These colors work well by themselves or in combination with lighter hues or neutral grays.

In Figure 9.1, Shawn Levin visualized iPhone sales over time, showing the performance of the product in a simple line chart, specifically highlighting the difference between sales of various iPhone models. Shawn uses green boxes and white upward arrows showing positive performance and white in the line chart to show the total sales figures across years and quarters. The white line works well on the black background and the gray shading below the line ensures the chart stands out.

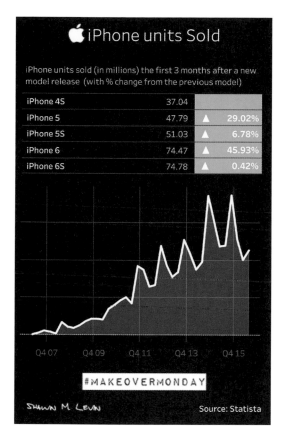

**FIGURE 9.1** Using a basic line chart to show iPhone units sold over time.

In her visualization of tourism trends in New Zealand (Figure 9.2), Aline Leonard used two shades of green to specify domestic versus international visitors. Aline's visualization evokes positive connotations and the colors she uses help reveal the pattern in the data.

## Negative Results and Emotions

Color can be a key factor in communicating negative results and emotions. The best colors to use for conveying negative results are

# Tourism Trends of New Zealand

Variation of domestic and **international** tourism between the seasons by region

Tourism is measured by RTI. RTI measures the change in level of expenditure of both international and domestic travellers in New Zealand by region. Reference line (100) is average month in 2008.

Select a region
Buller District

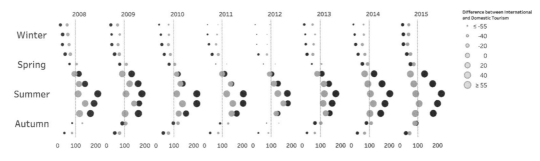

Source: NZ Ministry of Business, Innovation and Employment.
#MakeOverMonday 4 designed by @alileo84

**FIGURE 9.2**   A simple color palette shows domestic versus international tourism trends of New Zealand.

red, orange, black, and gray. These contrast well with neutral and positive colors.

In a financial context, red usually depicts losses, expenses above a certain threshold, or below-target results. In a social, environmental, or health context, dark colors typically evoke a somber, sad tone. Haiping Kuang created the visualization in Figure 9.3 of German car exports between 2008 and 2017. She used red to highlight the months when car exports dropped below prior year values. Red is used in the line charts to indicate the decline of exports during 2009 and to show that truck exports took a longer time to recover to prerecession levels than passenger cars.

# STORY OF GERMAN CAR EXPORTS

**(2008Q1-2017Q1)**

**Germany** is one the of leading countries for automobile exports worldwide. From 2008Q1 to 2017Q1, Germany has produced **53.9M** cars (both passenger cars and trucks), with **76%** exported internationally. It's a heavy export-based business model. Therefore, any change in the international market would affect the business significantly.

During the recession of 2008-2009, with a fall in external demand for manufactured goods and automobiles, the German car export ratio declined to **61%.** Passenger car exports have recovered from the fall the year after, while Truck exports struggled for years until 2015.

**53.9M**
Production

**40.8M**
Exports

**76%**
Exports Ratio

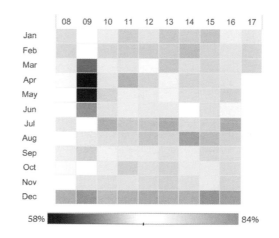

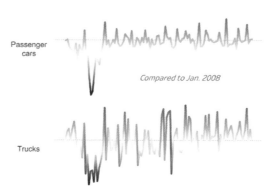

**FIGURE 9.3**  Red color highlights the impact of recession on German car exports between 2008 and 2017.

Figure 9.4, from Rosario Gauna, analyzes the likelihood of UK workers being replaced by robots, using color effectively to highlight negative findings. Her use of red to call out the key findings focuses

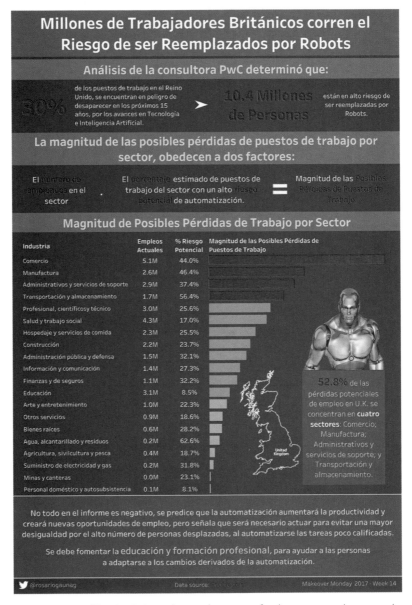

**FIGURE 9.4** Key insights about the use of robots to replace workers are accentuated with red color on dark background.

the audience on those insights. While the title sets the scene, the red elements on a black background stand out strongly and direct the audience's attention.

## Using Color to Create Associations

We previously discussed how colors can evoke emotions in an audience. Companies around the world use this knowledge to their advantage, which makes you naturally associate colors with brands like Coca-Cola, for example.

Aside from brands, we also associate colors with countries, topics, and themes. The following section shows you how to use color for creating associations in three areas:

1. Brands

2. Topics and themes

3. Linking fields across charts

### Color Associations with Brands

The example of Coca-Cola probably made you think of the color red, because that is the main color of their logo. For Makeover Monday we have used several data sets that were associated with brands and the resulting visualizations predictably featured the colors associated with those brands.

Apple as a brand is associated with the colors white, black, and silver, and the concept of clean, minimalist design. In Figure 9.5, Michael Mixon's choice of black with a gray font and a white to blue color palette for units sold creates a strong visual connection with the Apple brand. Like Apple's products, the visualization has a minimalist and uncluttered design.

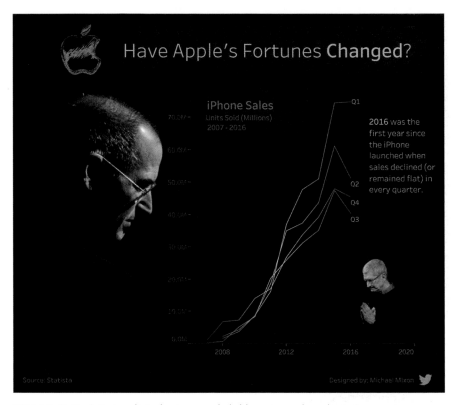

**FIGURE 9.5**  Minimalist design and deliberate color choices create associations with Apple as a brand.

The Makeover Monday topic of "Top 500 YouTube Gaming Channels" featured a number of visualizations with the red and black colors found in the YouTube logo. The creative, lighthearted design from Mike Cisneros in Figure 9.6 combined a long-form layout with interactive dashboard elements, balancing the colors so the YouTube red would not be overwhelming.

Mike used the YouTube red sparingly. In the title, red reflects the YouTube logo. Red is then repeated in the instructions. The other colors used are more muted shades of red, where Mike reduced the saturation of the red color. If the circles in the scatterplot had been bright red as well, then the audience would likely struggle to

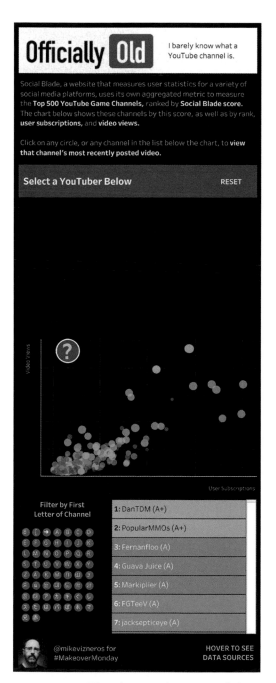

**FIGURE 9.6** The design elements of this visualization lead to fast brand recognition with YouTube.

understand what they should focus on and the different elements would compete for attention. Using pastel colors helps avoid this problem.

## Color Associations with Topics

When communicating information, data, and insights, using colors associated with the topic will help your audience understand the message more easily. It came as no surprise when we provided a data set about bee colony loss, that many dashboards contained yellow, gold, and black.

The visualization in Figure 9.7 by Sean Ramsdale stood out for its clean design and very visual representation of the data. The total

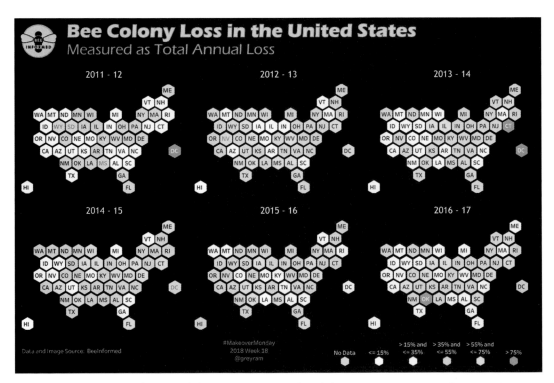

**FIGURE 9.7**   Using colors and shapes associated with bees creates a visualization that forms strong associations with the topic.

annual bee colony loss was represented by different shades of yellow, from a golden hue to a very pale, almost white color.

The colors chosen were deliberate and work well with the topic. The hexagon map suits the association with honeycombs and allows for an easy representation of the United States. The prominent title, and the subtle color legends, provide a nice frame for the visualization.

It often makes sense to use colors associated with the topic because the colors put the subject matter and the visual representation of the data in harmony with each other. Your audience will be more likely to focus on your key messages because they do not have to overcome a disconnect between the topic and the way you have visualized it.

Any nature topic, such as the analysis of National Park visitors in the US, will probably make people think of nature colors like browns and greens, oranges and blues, or anything to do with the earth, the sky, rivers, mountains, plants, and animals. As an example, as seen in Figure 9.8, Chantilly Jaggernauth created a beautiful visualization, providing an overview of the parks across the United States and a more detailed breakdown for the top 10 national parks.

The colors were chosen deliberately to feel like a nature theme. The placement of lines to split total visitors and yearly average for each of the top 10 parks, and the addition of horizontal bars in brown and green to divide the page into sections, mean the information is more easily consumed as the audience can work their way down the page section by section.

American baseball is often associated with the colors on the logo of Major League Baseball (MLB). When visualizing baseball demographics in MLB since the middle of the twentieth century, many visualizations used blue, red, and white as the main colors. Chantilly

**FIGURE 9.8** Using a palette that reflects nature's colors makes the topic visually more accessible.

Jaggernauth produced an insightful infographic (Figure 9.9) showing a timeline of the involvement of African American players in baseball and highlighting Jackie Robinson's career.

Years are consistently labeled in red, the vertical timeline and the line in the chart at the bottom are in blue, and specific achievements or notable events are represented with images that have dotted circular lines drawing attention to them. The design is easy to read, makes the story relatable, and adds richness to the insights. The colors Chantilly used in her design are an obvious choice for the MLB

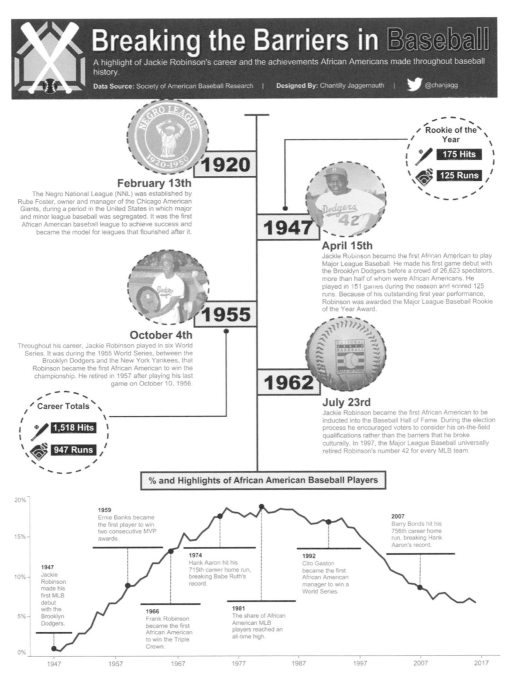

**FIGURE 9.9** Selecting colors, shapes, and images that are generally recognized as baseball-related supports fast recognition by the audience.

topic and work well together, while also being easy to differentiate. The balance of blue and red compared to white ensures there is no overload of color and color remains meaningful.

## Color Associations Across Multiple Charts

You can use colors to create a strong connection between the different elements of your visualizations. It is good practice to apply color deliberately and sparingly to specific fields that you want to focus on in your dashboard and to let those colors highlight the important aspects of your data throughout the visualization. If your dashboard contains a number of charts that visualize related data, you can connect these visuals by applying color to specific fields or metrics. In Figure 9.10, David Eldersveld created a dashboard about the European Union potato sector and compared the five primary EU producers to other countries.

The choice of colors in this visualization very easily highlights the two groups of countries being compared and shows David's audience how these two groups differ across a number of key indicators of potato production.

Other examples of using two colors—one color for a specific field and second color for all other data points—include dashboards that focus on the performance of one product versus all other products, one team versus all other teams in the league, or one region in a business compared to the remaining regions. There are numerous use cases and we encourage you to try this approach to create effective linkages between the different elements of your visualization. Keeping a consistent meaning attached to the colors you use helps your audience follow your story more easily from start to finish.

Exploring the European Union Potato Sector
Nearly 2/3 of potatoes harvested in the EU come from only five of the 28 member states
5 Primary EU Producers
Other EU Producers
18M
38M
2010
21M
42M
2011
17M
37M
2012
18M
36M
2013
19M
40M
2014
17M
36M
2015
15M
38M
2016
Germany consistently ranks as the top producer
2010 2011 2012 2013 2014 2015 2016
Potato Harvest in Tonnes
Germany 10.2M
Poland 8.3M
France 6.9M
Netherlands 6.6M
United Kingdom 5.7M
(alongside Poland, France, the Netherlands, and the UK)
28.7% Other
19.3% Germany
15.7% Poland
13.0% France
12.5% Netherlands
10.8% United King...
Which it achieves not only through greater planting area, but also with efficient use of that land
Planted Land (x1000 Hectares)
Poland 320
Germany 236
Romania 185
France 166
Netherlands 158
Tonnes Yielded per Hectare
Germany 43.2
Netherlands 42.7
Austria 36.1
Sweden 35.7
Luxembourg 30.4
@dataveld
Data: Eurostat

**FIGURE 9.10** Consistent colors linked to specific groups of countries guide the audience through the analysis across multiple charts.

## Using Color to Highlight

Using colors to highlight specific data points or insights helps show your audience how specific data points differ from the rest. Kate Brown analyzed the cost of meals at different pubs for a popular chain of pubs in the UK and the Republic of Ireland, shown in Figure 9.11.

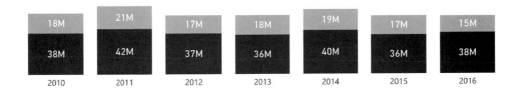

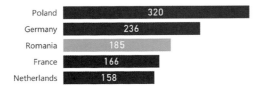

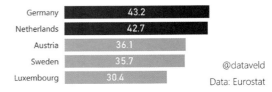

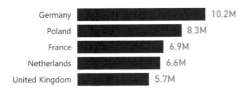

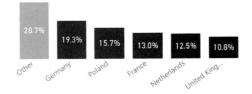

# One Owner, Different Pubs, Different Prices

JD Wetherspoon has **893** pubs across the UK and Republic of Ireland. All of these pubs have the same menu, however, prices vary across their locations. To get a sense of the pricing structure the Financial Times sampled the same meal in **213** different pubs.

The meal consisted of a Chicken Tikka, an Empire Burger, a Doom, and a Moretti. There were **130** different prices for this meal and a **£10.96** difference between the most and least expensive meal.

**Price Range for the Meal**

The most common price point for the sampled meal was between £25 and £25.99. There are 107 pubs in that price range.

**Why are there Different Prices?**

Wetherspoons's explains the diffent pricing with this:

*"For various reasons, such as rents, rates, staffing, local competition and so on, food and drinks prices may vary per pub. This tends to be the case with all pubs, in general. What we do try to achieve, however, is having the lowest prices, on average, in each location where we operate."*

Use the map to see the areas where the price of the meal was above or below the average for the 213 sampled pubs.

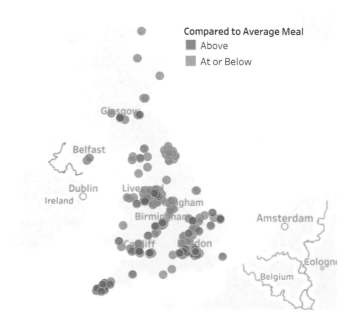

created by @katebrown_5 for #makeovermonday                     data source Financial Times

**FIGURE 9.11**    Specific data points are highlighted in red against all other data points.

Kate showed those pubs that charged above-average prices for a meal and used red circles to highlight the locations.

The audience can easily see the clusters of more expensive pubs as well as their proximity to the cheaper locations. The horizontal bar serves as a color legend and shows the range of prices.

## Best Practices for Using Color

So far, this chapter has shown how color can be used for storytelling and for bringing the key insights into focus. Before applying the ideas from previous sections to your own work, there are some best practices to keep in mind.

### Less Is More

Too often, dashboards are designed with too many different colors. Including lots of colors together creates a lot of noise in the visualization, keeping any single color from standing out and insights can easily get lost.

Consider Figure 9.12 of cumulative sales across different cities in New Zealand. Because the colors create confusion, a few simple questions cannot be answered:

- Is the highest-performing city Auckland or Rotorua? (Both are blue.)
- Which city is represented by the horizontal brown line at $5000?
- Which two cities are represented by the two brown lines among the top performers? Are they Wellington and Hamilton? Or is Paraparaumu a possible option?

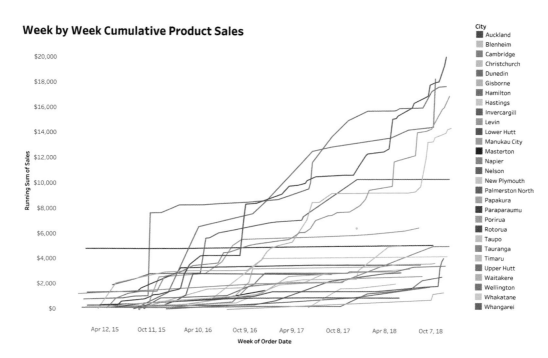

**FIGURE 9.12** The meaning of colors is unclear and confusing because a number of colors are applied to different cities.

The colors in this visualization create confusion and get in the way of effectively conveying insights. This multitude of colors means your audience has to work hard to look back and forth between the graph and the color legend to make sense of the information provided. If you want to make data visualization available to a broader audience, you need to make information accessible and easy to understand.

Monochrome colors are used effectively in Figure 9.13 to highlight the poor-performing stores in Paraparaumu. Paraparaumu is now the focus of the analysis and stands out against the remaining cities, which are shown in gray to provide context. The color of the line is noted by the bold font in the title and the small label next to the line.

Cumulative Sales in **Paraparaumu** have only grown by NZ$407 in the four year period between January 2014 and December 2017

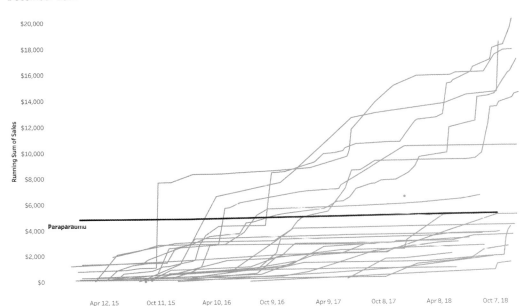

**FIGURE 9.13**   Reducing colors allows a single city to be highlighted effectively.

If you want to compare two cities against all other cities, they can be highlighted with two distinct and well-contrasting colors while all other cities are represented by gray lines, as in Figure 9.14.

Again, the title is used as a color legend and the two colors chosen have a strong contrast with each other, while also being easy to differentiate from the gray lines representing all other cities.

## Considerations for Color Blindness

Color blindness is a vision deficiency that effects on average 8% of men and 0.5% of women worldwide,[2] making it a significant enough

---

[2] colourblindawareness.org/colour-blindness

**Wellington** and **Hamilton** have shown consistent growth in their sales figures over the years to become part of the top three performing cities overall.

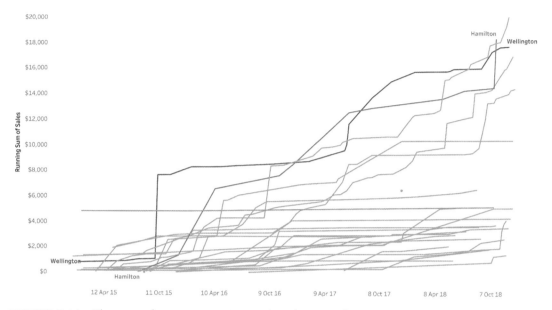

**FIGURE 9.14**   The use of two contrasting colors for specific cities allows an easy comparison, while gray lines indicate all other cities for context.

challenge to consider when it comes to communicating information. This is especially true for data visualization since color plays such an important role when visualizing information for an audience.

There are different forms of color blindness, which, at a general level, can be categorized as follows:

1. Deuteranomaly, where people are less sensitive to green light, because the medium-wavelength cones are defective, resulting in a "green weakness," which makes it difficult for people to differentiate hues of red, orange, yellow, and green.

2. Protanomaly, where people are less sensitive to red light, because the long-wavelength cones in their retina are defective. Protans have trouble with red-green distinctions as well as green-orange.

3. Tritanomaly, where people are less sensitive to blue light, because their short-wavelength cones are defective. These people struggle to differentiate between blues and greens and yellows and reds.

Deuteranomaly is the most common form of color blindness.[3] People affected by protanomaly or deuteranomaly suffer from what is commonly described as red-green color blindness and struggle to differentiate between hues of red and green, brown and orange.

In the context of data visualization, using red and green together in a chart to represent bad and good results could easily be misinterpreted by people with these two types of color blindness. How many financial dashboards have you seen with numbers, bars, lines, or circles in red and green, aiming to alert the audience about negative and positive results? If those colors are perceived as very similar shades of gray or brownish gray by people with color blindness, how does this affect their understanding of the results?

There are helpful tools available online, such as the Chromatic Vision Simulator,[4] which allow you to upload an image of your work to see what it looks like for people with different types of color blindness. It is also important to have color palettes available that are color-blind friendly. Jeffrey Shaffer from Data + Science has written a very helpful article on his blog on how to design color palettes yourself.[5]

## Using Background Colors

Most of the dashboards and data visualizations you see use a white background. However, we have seen a trend in Makeover Monday toward other background colors, the most common being black.

---

[3] colourblindawareness.org/colour-blindness
[4] asada.tukusi.ne.jp/webCVS/index.html
[5] dataplusscience.com/DataVizRuleColor.html

The typical use case for applying a different background color is for linking the topic to the design. Serious topics, such as wars, illnesses, death rates, and inequality, lend themselves to darker visualizations with black or dark gray backgrounds.

It is important to keep in mind that colors are perceived differently on different backgrounds. You need to ensure that regardless of the background color you use, your visualization is easy to read, and the information is communicated clearly.

In her visualization of solar eclipse data (Figure 9.15), Angie Chen used a black background and plotted individual data points in a warm golden hue.

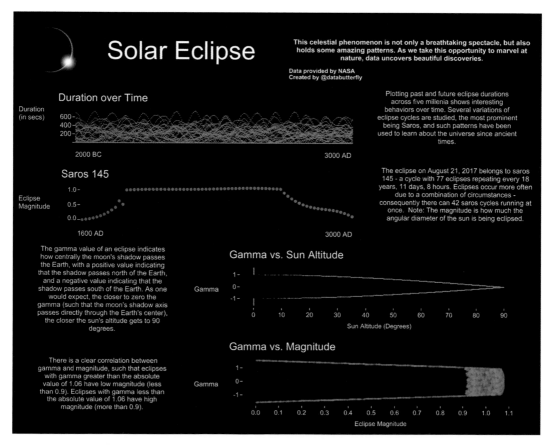

**FIGURE 9.15**  A black background was used for the topic of solar eclipses.

If you change the visualization to a white background, making the necessary adjustments for the text from white to black, you get Figure 9.16.

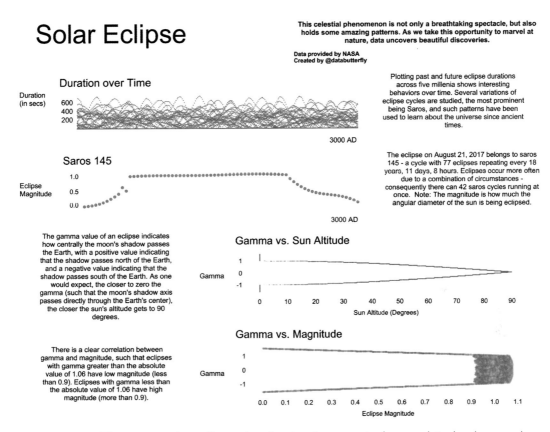

## Solar Eclipse

This celestial phenomenon is not only a breathtaking spectacle, but also holds some amazing patterns. As we take this opportunity to marvel at nature, data uncovers beautiful discoveries.

Data provided by NASA
Created by @databutterfly

### Duration over Time

Duration (in secs)
600
400
200

3000 AD

Plotting past and future eclipse durations across five millenia shows interesting behaviors over time. Several variations of eclipse cycles are studied, the most prominent being Saros, and such patterns have been used to learn about the universe since ancient times.

### Saros 145

Eclipse Magnitude
1.0
0.5
0.0

3000 AD

The eclipse on August 21, 2017 belongs to saros 145 - a cycle with 77 eclipses repeating every 18 years, 11 days, 8 hours. Eclipses occur more often due to a combination of circumstances - consequently there can 42 saros cycles running at once.  Note: The magnitude is how much the angular diameter of the sun is being eclipsed.

The gamma value of an eclipse indicates how centrally the moon's shadow passes the Earth, with a positive value indicating that the shadow passes north of the Earth, and a negative value indicating that the shadow passes south of the Earth. As one would expect, the closer to zero the gamma (such that the moon's shadow axis passes directly through the Earth's center), the closer the sun's altitude gets to 90 degrees.

### Gamma vs. Sun Altitude

Gamma
1
0
-1

0    10    20    30    40    50    60    70    80    90
Sun Altitude (Degrees)

There is a clear correlation between gamma and magnitude, such that eclipses with gamma greater than the absolute value of 1.06 have low magnitude (less than 0.9). Eclipses with gamma less than the absolute value of 1.06 have high magnitude (more than 0.9).

### Gamma vs. Magnitude

Gamma
1
0
-1

0.0   0.1   0.2   0.3   0.4   0.5   0.6   0.7   0.8   0.9   1.0   1.1
Eclipse Magnitude

**FIGURE 9.16**   The same solar eclipse visualization is presented on a white background.

The visualization still works well, but the overall perception of the two dashboards is very different. The version with the white background does not convey the astronomical nature of the topic as well as the dark background does.

When analyzing economic freedom data (Figure 9.17), Steve Fenn emulated the *Financial Times* chart design style, using their color palette with a beige background and a unique color for each of the different columns in his dashboard.

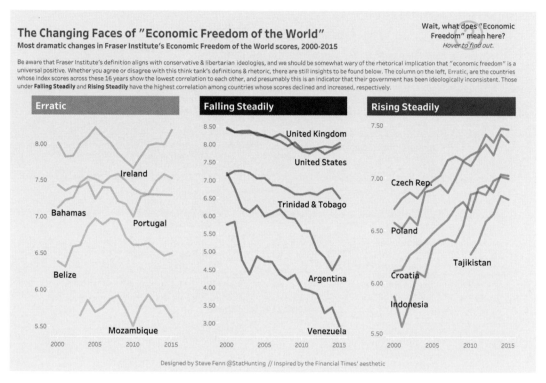

**FIGURE 9.17**    The beige background was inspired by the *Financial Times Style Guide.*

With the topic being about economics and financial matters, this design approach worked very well, resulting in a recognizable visualization. The gray, burgundy, and dark blue can be easily distinguished from the background, and the black text font is easy to read.

In Figure 9.18, the visualization definitely still works well on the white background, but it does not trigger associations with the *Financial Times*. The colors do not appear as warm as they did on the beige background, changing the overall feel of the dashboard.

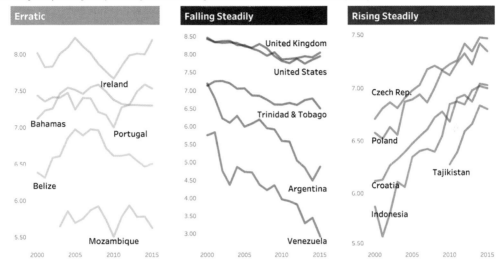

**The Changing Faces of "Economic Freedom of the World"**

Most dramatic changes in Fraser Institute's Economic Freedom of the World scores, 2000-2015

Be aware that Fraser Institute's definition aligns with conservative & libertarian ideologies, and we should be somewhat wary of the rhetorical implication that "economic freedom" is a universal positive. Whether you agree or disagree with this think tank's definitions & rhetoric, there are still insights to be found below. The column on the left, Erratic, are the countries whose index scores across these 16 years show the lowest correlation to each other, and presumably this is an indicator that their government has been ideologically inconsistent. Those under **Falling Steadily** and **Rising Steadily** have the highest correlation among countries whose scores declined and increased, respectively.

Designed by Steve Fenn @StatHunting // Inspired by the Financial Times' aesthetic

**FIGURE 9.18**  Notice how the visualization changes when the background color is removed. Removing the beige background leaves no association with the original design inspiration.

As you have seen in Figures 9.15–9.18, background colors change the appearance and the perception of a visualization. Sometimes this is very subtle, while other times it is much more noticeable. Stay clear of bright background colors that make your visualization difficult to read, are hard on the eyes, and look unprofessional.

## Using Text as a Color Legend

Applying color to the relevant words in a title or subtitle removes the need for a separate color legend. In Figure 9.19, Mark Bradbourne visualized meat consumption data for the US and colored the words "Poultry" and "Red Meat" in the same colors as their respective lines in the chart.

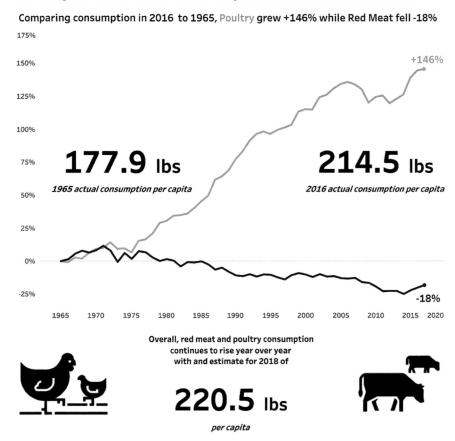

**FIGURE 9.19** Colors applied to the words "poultry" and "red meat" in the subtitle work as a color legend.

In Figure 9.20, Adam Crahen took a similar approach when highlighting the rapid growth of prescriptions for the drug Apixaban. At a glance, Adam's audience can tell that orange and Apixaban are related, given the coloring of the text in the title and the color of the line. Using the color in the title also eliminates the need for a color legend, thus removing elements from the visualization.

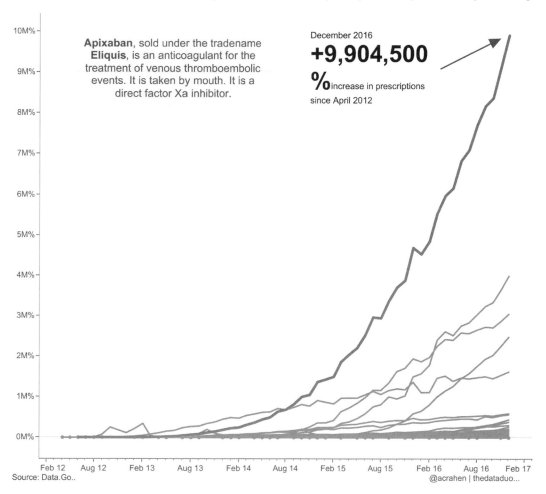

**Apixaban** was approved in Europe on April 20, 2012
since then it has experienced explosive growth in the number of prescriptions compared to every other drug

**Apixaban**, sold under the tradename **Eliquis**, is an anticoagulant for the treatment of venous thromboembolic events. It is taken by mouth. It is a direct factor Xa inhibitor.

December 2016
**+9,904,500**
**%**increase in prescriptions
since April 2012

Source: Data.Go..

@acrahen | thedataduo...

**FIGURE 9.20**   The orange line represents a specific drug, which is made clear by applying the same color to the drug's name in the title.

As you apply color to text, keep in mind that the audience can get confused if you color too many words. If you have more than about three colors, then a color legend will be easier to read and understand.

## Summary

Color is a great tool for conveying information quickly and effectively and to draw your audience into your visualization. Using color sparingly makes it more meaningful and can highlight your key insights effortlessly. Look at each visualization you create with a critical eye, and take a step back (literally and figuratively) to see the complete picture. Let the overall impression of your visualization sink in for a few minutes and decide whether your use of color is as effective as it can be.

Make deliberate color choices to evoke emotions in your audience. Do you want your visualization to have a specific emotional tone and is this conveyed through your color choices? When it comes to storytelling, have you chosen specific colors for particular fields to tell your story in a way that flows from start to finish with clarity and consistency? Using color to create linkages between different parts and concepts in your visualization as well as between individual charts helps to bring your overall design together.

## Chapter Ten

# Choosing the Right Chart Type

Understanding the purpose of different chart types will help you decide which visualization to use for your data in order to communicate information most effectively. Bar charts and line charts are well documented in most data visualization books and you will find them in most of the chapters of this book as well. This chapter will focus on the charts that are not discussed as often, several of which have sparked a lot of discussion in the Makeover Monday community. Each chart type will have four sections:

1. Purpose

2. Description

3. Examples

4. Alternatives

There are several examples of each chart type and then alternatives that can be used in a similar situation. This chapter can be used as a visual reference library for these chart types. By the end of this chapter, you should have a better understanding of why certain charts work better than others. Finally, we will provide resources that describe chart best practices in detail.

## Area Charts

### Purpose

Show cumulative trends over time of one or more attributes of a field.

### Description

Area charts are line charts that are typically stacked on top of one another, creating a cumulative view. The area below each line is filled down to the section below, with the lowermost section filled down to the zero axis. Area charts are useful for understanding:

1. The contribution to the total

2. The trend of the lowermost segment

3. The trend of the total, which is represented as the top of the area chart

Area charts are problematic when trying to evaluate the trend of contribution of any segment other than the lowermost segment as each segment's pattern is affected by the contribution of every other segment below it. See examples in Figures 10.1–10.5.

## Examples

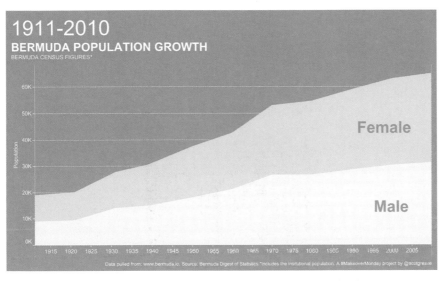

**FIGURE 10.1**   A stacked area chart makes the total and the lowermost attribute (male) easy to understand but can hinder our understanding of trends for other attributes (female).

**FIGURE 10.2**   Individual area charts show trends for each National Park clearly and their proximity allows for comparisons between parks.

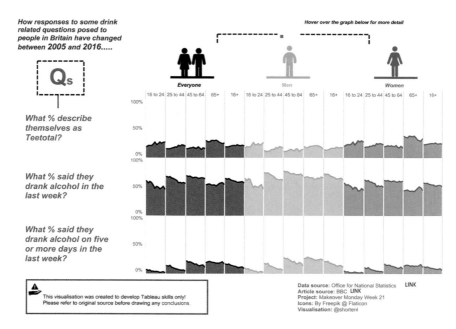

**FIGURE 10.3** Individual area charts color coded by category let the audience compare differences quickly.

## Alternatives

### What's on your dinner plate?

Since 1965, per capita **beef** consumption in the United States has steadily decreased, chicken consumption has significantly increased, and poultry consumption has slightly decreased.

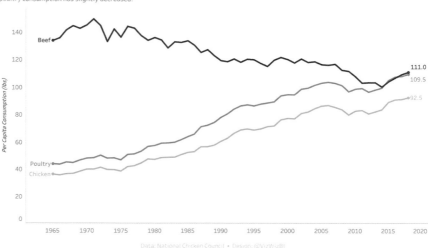

**FIGURE 10.4** A line chart highlights only the actual data points without the shading of the area below the line and helps to compare different categories.

### What's on your dinner plate?

Since 1965, per capita **beef** consumption in the United States has steadily decreased, chicken consumption has significantly increased, and poultry consumption has slightly decreased.

**FIGURE 10.5**   A percent of total area chart gives the top and bottom area a horizontal reference line (0% and 100%), which helps identify trends.

## Stacked Bar Charts

### Purpose

Show how members of a field contribute to the total.

### Description

When attributes of a field are placed above one another in a bar chart, the top of the bar represents the overall total. Stacked bars are useful for understanding the contribution of segments to the total bar. Stacked bars are most effective when they allow for comparison of common parts across multiple segments.

Stacked bar charts are best when displayed vertically and should contain no more than two to three segments. Including more segments makes the chart harder to understand and hinders meaningful comparisons between segments. See examples in Figures 10.6–10.11.

## Examples

### The Change in **Red Meat** & Poultry Consumption in the US

In 1965 consumption of red meat in the US far exceeded poultry with 134 pounds eaten per person against 44 pounds.
The proportion of red meat eaten continued to rise until 1968, since then the proportion has been slowly decreasing.

In 2015, whilst the total amount of meat eaten has increased to 209 pounds, the proportion of red meat has dropped just below 50%.

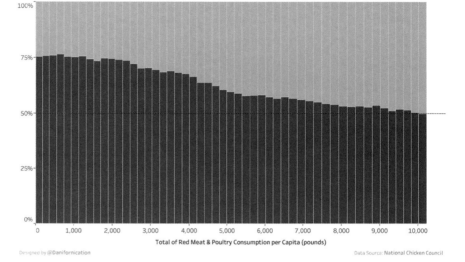

Designed by @Danifornication

Data Source: **National Chicken Council**

**FIGURE 10.6**   A stacked bar chart scaled to 100% shows the contributions of two categories to the total very clearly.

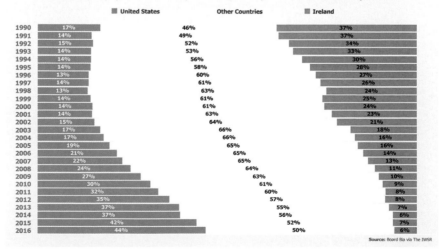

**FIGURE 10.7**   Comparing the contribution of the white bars is difficult because their starting point depends on the differing length of the green bars.

**THE SECRET OF SUCCESS**

What do representatives of different social strata think is the **main reason for their success?**

| | Poor<br>**Connections to the right people** | Middle Class<br>**Education and qualifications** | Rich People<br>**Hard work** |
|---|---|---|---|
| abilities, talents | 7% | 8% | 13% |
| connections to the right people | 39% | 32% | 9% |
| cunning, cheating | 32% | 21% | 11% |
| entreprenurial spirit, courage | 16% | 16% | 27% |
| fortune, good luck | 12% | 15% | 13% |
| good education, high qualification | 18% | 33% | 28% |
| hard work | 16% | 27% | 38% |
| presence of initial capital | 27% | 23% | 15% |

Source: visual.ly/secret-success | @shivraji

**FIGURE 10.8** Using gray reference bars sized to 100% gives your data the appearance to "fill up" the reference bars.

## Alternatives

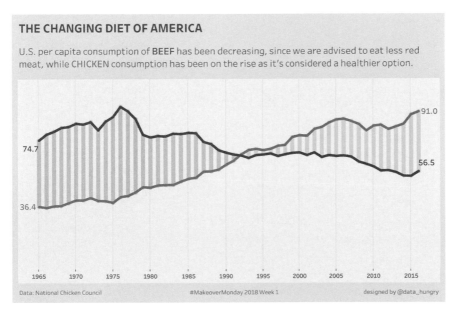

**THE CHANGING DIET OF AMERICA**

U.S. per capita consumption of **BEEF** has been decreasing, since we are advised to eat less red meat, while CHICKEN consumption has been on the rise as it's considered a healthier option.

74.7
91.0
56.5
36.4

1965  1970  1975  1980  1985  1990  1995  2000  2005  2010  2015

Data: National Chicken Council          #MakeoverMonday 2018 Week 1          designed by @data_hungry

**FIGURE 10.9** Vertical bars between two lines of a line chart highlight the differences between the two categories.

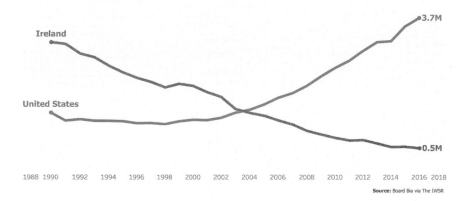

## The Growth of Irish Whisky Sales in the United States

In 1990, just **17%** of Irish Whisky cases were sold to the United States, by 2016 this had increased to **44%**. Meanwhile, the proportion of Irish Whisky cases sold domestically has decreased from **37%** to just **6%**.

**FIGURE 10.10** In a line chart, trends over time become easier to see than in a bar chart and comparisons between lines can be made with ease.

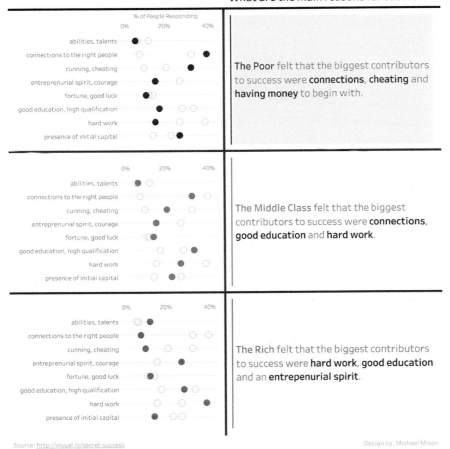

**FIGURE 10.11**  A dot plot moves the focus to the rank of each member within each category.

## Diverging Bar Charts

### Purpose

Show the spread of negative and positive values (e.g., customer sentiment regarding a product) or compare two attributes of a field along a common scale (e.g., male versus female by age).

### Description

Diverging bar charts can be a good alternative to side-by-side bars or stacked bars. The bars point in opposite directions typically along a continuous scale (e.g., age, salary, year). When the chart splits a single field into two parts (e.g., Republican versus Democratic voters by income level), the chart is also known as a spine chart. See examples in Figures 10.12–10.18.

As a best practice, ensure that both sides of the chart are scaled the same, otherwise the reader might misinterpret the data.

## Examples

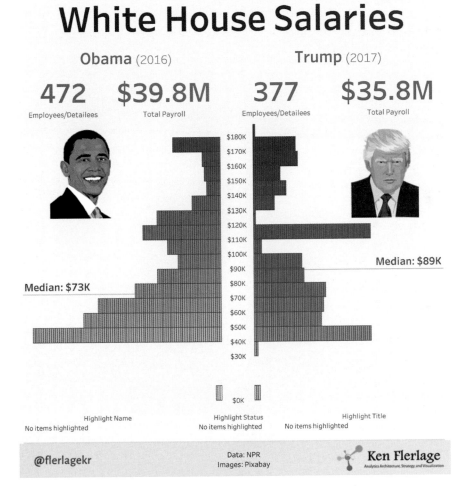

**FIGURE 10.12**  A diverging bar chart is useful when visualizing two opposing concepts, such as two political parties.

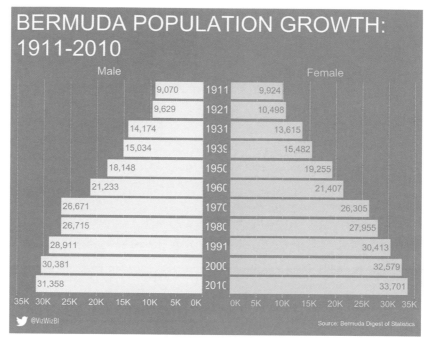

**FIGURE 10.13** Labeling each bar with its numerical value makes the data more precise.

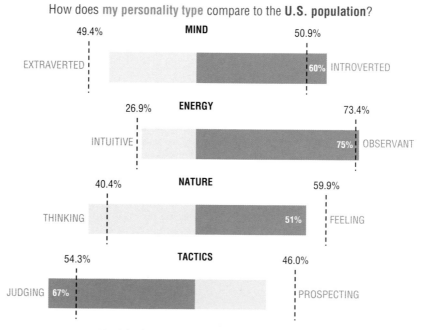

**FIGURE 10.14** Highlighting in a diverging bar chart helps bring focus to the larger segment.

Alternatives

# The Global Intensity of Migration

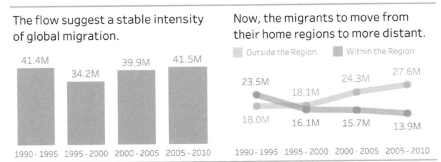

The flow suggest a stable intensity of global migration.

Now, the migrants to move from their home regions to more distant.

## Migration into & out between ten world regions (2005-2010)

Select Period: 2005-2010

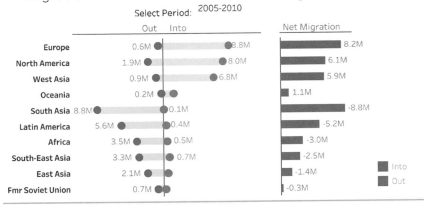

## Top 20 largest country-to-country flows (2005-2010)

| Country Origin → Destination | | Country Origin → Destination | |
|---|---|---|---|
| Mexico → United States | 1,957,397 | Philippines → United States | 373,024 |
| India → United Arab Emirates | 1,149,965 | Myanmar → Thailand | 368,832 |
| India → United States | 701,242 | Indonesia → Malaysia | 346,048 |
| Bangladesh → United Arab Emirates | 646,729 | Kazakhstan → Russia | 307,495 |
| Bangladesh → India | 630,451 | Uzbekistan → Russia | 299,656 |
| China → United States | 615,536 | India → Qatar | 297,570 |
| Bangladesh → Saudi Arabia | 523,342 | Tanzania → Burundi | 294,595 |
| Zimbabwe → South Africa | 495,779 | Pakistan → Saudi Arabia | 285,441 |
| Pakistan → United Arab Emirates | 494,846 | El Salvador → United States | 268,935 |
| Malaysia → Singapore | 395,727 | Afghanistan → Iran | 266,595 |

**FIGURE 10.15** Shading the area between two dots in a diverging dot plot highlights the differences between the sides effectively.

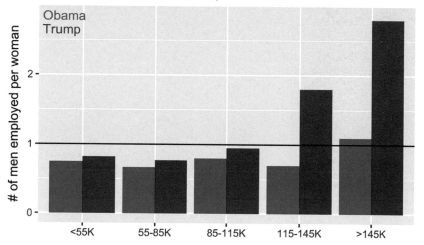

## Pay (dis)parity by gender in the White House

More women work in low-wage positions. Higher-wage positions are dominated by men in the Trump White house.

**FIGURE 10.16**  Grouping bars that should be compared together makes analysis of differences between two or more categories easier.

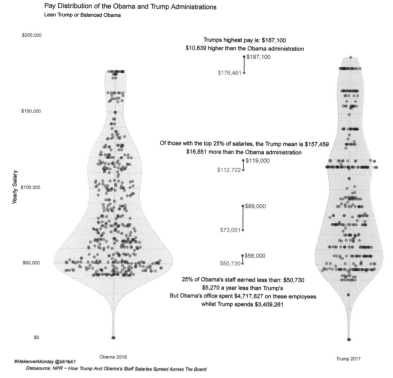

**FIGURE 10.17**  A violin plot is an effective way to visualize overall distribution of data and the detailed data points.

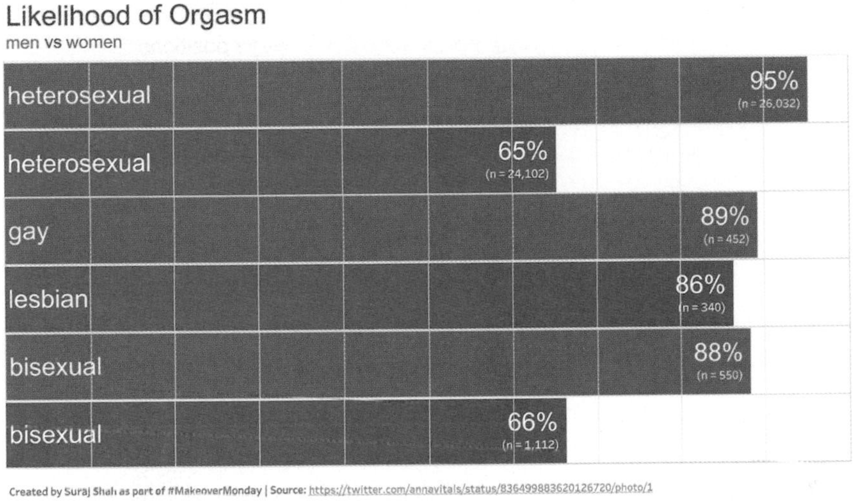

## Likelihood of Orgasm
men vs women

| | | | |
|---|---|---|---|
| heterosexual | | | 95% (n = 26,032) |
| heterosexual | | 65% (n = 24,102) | |
| gay | | 89% (n = 452) | |
| lesbian | | 86% (n = 340) | |
| bisexual | | 88% (n = 550) | |
| bisexual | | 66% (n = 1,112) | |

Created by Suraj Shah as part of #MakeoverMonday | Source: https://twitter.com/annavitals/status/836499883620126720/photo/1

**FIGURE 10.18**   Vertical lines break these bars into 10% segments and help with comparisons across categories.

## Filled Maps

### Purpose

Proportionally shade geographical areas by a data variable; also known as choropleth maps and thematic maps.

### Description

Filled maps are used when the location of the data is the most important. Map locations are predefined and data is typically displayed as a proportion of a single variable to all geographical areas displayed or as a ratio of two variables within each area.

Filled maps are a popular visual display of data as they are familiar to the average user and visually pleasing. While data of a single variable can be displayed (e.g., population), a preferred visual display would have a common baseline (e.g., income per capita). Small geographical areas can be hard to compare to larger areas on filled maps. For example, comparing the color of Rhode Island to Texas in Figure 10.19 is harder on the user and because Texas is larger, it will be perceived as darker even if the values are the same.

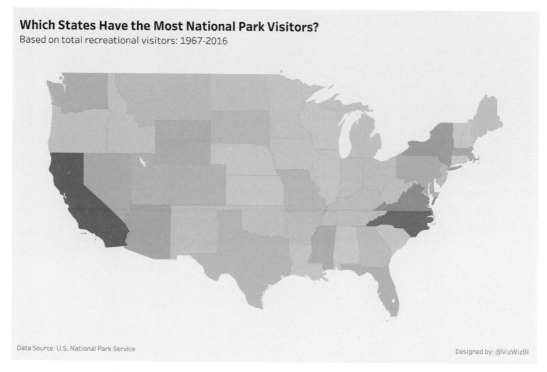

**FIGURE 10.19**   Filled maps make it difficult to see and compare small areas to large areas, because larger regions or states typically dominate the map.

If using a single variable that is always either positive or negative (e.g., number of visitors to national parks), then hues of a single color are preferred from light to dark or dark to light. If the variable spans a common midpoint (e.g., profit above or below zero), then a diverging scale of two colors is useful to distinguish the range of colors. See examples in Figures 10.20 and 10.21.

## Examples

### Where have the most bikes been stolen?

**FIGURE 10.20** A single color in different levels of intensity is applied for a single metric in this filled map to show impact on different regions.

**Worst** states to drive

**& Best**

DESIGNED BY: @yake_84

|  | Worst Drivers | Best Drivers |
| --- | --- | --- |
| Rank | | |
| Fatalities per 100M Miles | | |
| Careless Driving | | |
| Drunk Driving | | |
| Speeding | | |
| Failure to Obey Laws | | |

**FIGURE 10.21**   A diverging color palette can be used when a clear midpoint exists for the measurements in the data, such as the classification of good and bad drivers in this map.

## Alternatives

There are many ways to visualize geographic data either to display distribution patterns more effectively or to give the different areas equal weight. See examples in Figures 10.22–10.26.

*Bubble Map*

# The Land of the Walking Dead
Death Penalty Executions in the United States

Just **5%** of counties in the United States are responsible for **73%** of executions since 1976, but the rate of execution is half what it was at the start of the 21st century. This is due in large part to the cost of lethal injection drugs and the lack of supply as pharmaceutical companies worldwide have cut off supplies.

DESIGNED BY: @VizWizBI

DATA SOURCE: Death Penalty Information Center

**FIGURE 10.22** Bubble plots are useful for showing geographic distribution of the data. Bubbles are sized by a single, common metric.

*Time Series Tile Map*

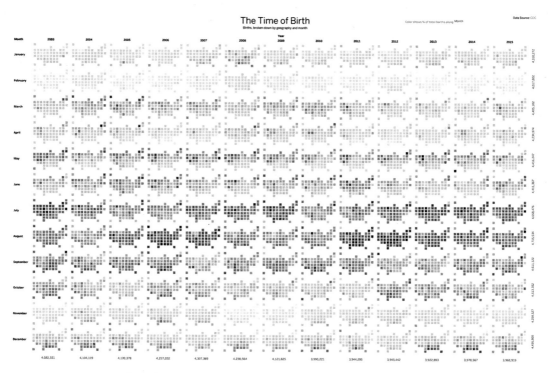

**FIGURE 10.23**  Small multiple-tile maps present patterns over time (left to right) and throughout the seasons (top to bottom).

*Tile Map Waffle Chart*

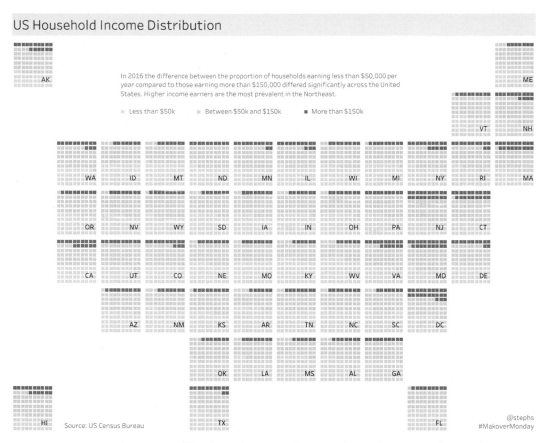

**FIGURE 10.24**  A tile map waffle chart shows each state through an equally sized square, filled according to a single metric.

*Tile Map Bar Chart*

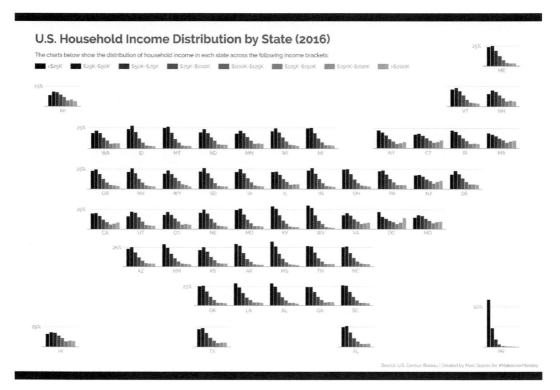

**FIGURE 10.25** The tile map bar chart also gives each state an equally sized space and effectively highlights income distribution through colors and bar length.

*Hex Map*

# US HOUSEHOLD INCOME DISTRIBUTION

## Income levels by state from 2009 - 2016

Data from the US Census Bureau shows that in the years since the Global Financial Crisis, income levels in a number of states have improved.

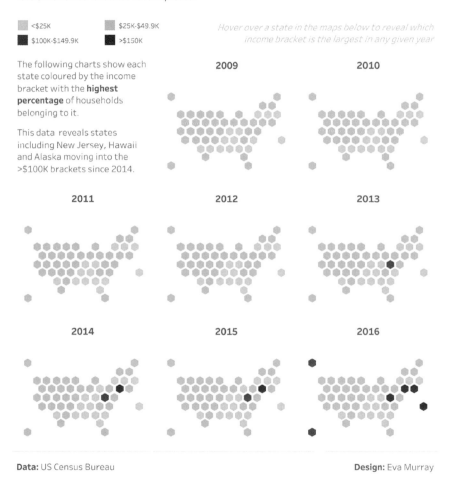

| | |
|---|---|
| ▢ <$25K | ▢ $25K-$49.9K |
| ◼ $100K-$149.9K | ◼ >$150K |

*Hover over a state in the maps below to reveal which income bracket is the largest in any given year*

The following charts show each state coloured by the income bracket with the **highest percentage** of households belonging to it.

This data reveals states including New Jersey, Hawaii and Alaska moving into the >$100K brackets since 2014.

2009

2010

2011

2012

2013

2014

2015

2016

**Data:** US Census Bureau                **Design:** Eva Murray

**FIGURE 10.26**   Multiple hexagon maps show changes over time, allocating an equally sized hexagon shape for each state.

### *Cartogram Map*

A cartogram, as seen in Figure 10.27, is a map in which some thematic mapping variable—such as travel time, population, or gross national product—is substituted for land area or distance. The geometry or space of the map is distorted in order to convey the information of this alternate variable.[1]

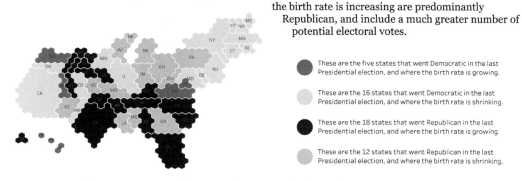

The Electoral Map of the United States, in cartogram form, shows the proportional representation of each state in the U.S. Senate and House of Representatives, which is also the number of electoral votes Presidential candidates receive for winning that state's popular vote. From this chart, it is clear to see that the states where the birth rate is increasing are predominantly Republican, and include a much greater number of potential electoral votes.

These are the five states that went Democratic in the last Presidential election, and where the birth rate is growing.

These are the 16 states that went Democratic in the last Presidential election, and where the birth rate is shrinking.

These are the 18 states that went Republican in the last Presidential election, and where the birth rate is growing.

These are the 12 states that went Republican in the last Presidential election, and where the birth rate is shrinking.

**FIGURE 10.27**   This cartogram shows each state clearly while sizing them according to the number of electoral votes.

## Donut and Pie Charts

### Purpose

Donut and pie charts are designed to show how individual subsegments divide up an entire segment, typically referred to as parts-to-whole.

---

[1] en.wikipedia.org/wiki/Cartogram

## Description

The area of each segment represents the proportion of each segment to the whole. All of the segments added together must total 100%. If designed properly, pie charts can provide quick insight into the distribution of the data, with focus on the largest segment.

There are many drawbacks to pie charts:

- Displaying more than a few values forces the size of each slice to become smaller, thus more difficult to compare. To avoid this, consider limiting pies to two or three slices for easy interpretation. Consider bar charts as an alternative for comparing segments.
- Accurate comparisons are difficult, especially across multiple pie charts. It is difficult for the human eye to distinguish the area of slices of a pie. Consider 100% stacked bar charts as an alternative.
- Pie charts require a legend or labeling, all of which takes up a lot of space. A bar chart takes up less space and does not require an additional legend to aid comprehension.
- Comparing the size of an area is more difficult than comparing length. Consider bar charts as an alternative.

The only difference in design between a pie chart and a donut chart is that the donut chart has a hole in the middle, typically reserved for a large summary figure. In addition to the drawbacks of pie charts, donut charts force the reader to compare the length of the arcs. This is especially difficult across multiple donut charts. See examples in Figures 10.28 and 10.29.

## Examples

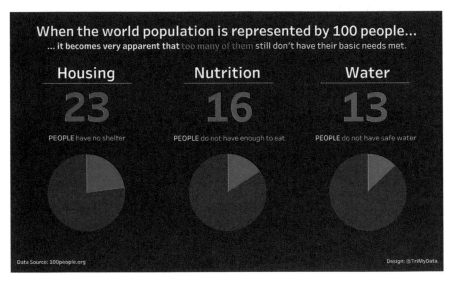

**FIGURE 10.28**   Pie charts with only two segments can show each category contribution clearly.

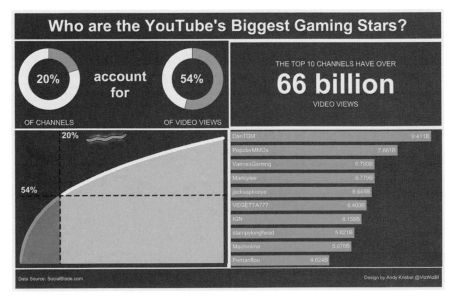

**FIGURE 10.29**   Adding large numbers in a donut chart with two segments gives exact values to each section.

## Alternatives

Figures 10.30–10.32 show some alternatives to donut and pie charts.

**Personality** is the single **most important** characteristic in a romantic partner, say half of Brits. Surprisingly, **amount of money** is **least important**.

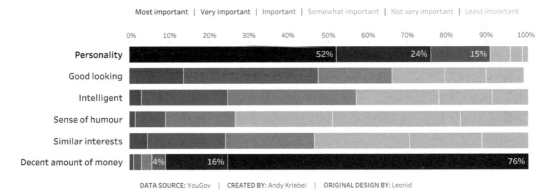

**Survey results: men and women**

Thinking about your personal preferences in a romantic partner, how would you prioritise each of the following characteristics?

Most important | Very important | Important | Somewhat important | Not very important | Least important

DATA SOURCE: YouGov | CREATED BY: Andy Kriebel | ORIGINAL DESIGN BY: Leonid

**FIGURE 10.30**    A stacked bar chart sized to 100% works better than a pie or donut chart for data with more than two or three attributes.

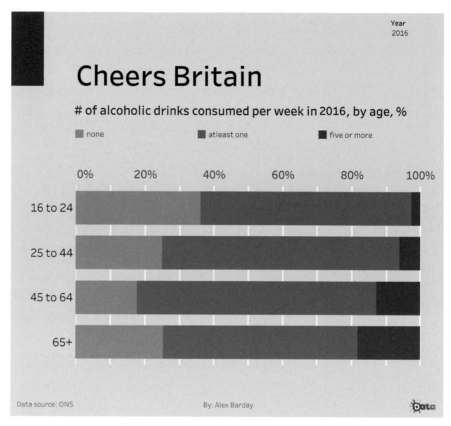

**FIGURE 10.31** A stacked bar chart with a color gradient based on a single metric works well to show results across age groups.

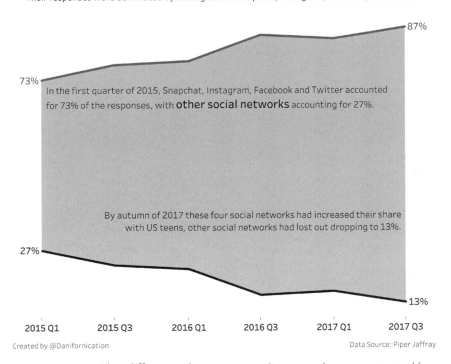

## The Rise in Dominance of the
### Big Four Social Networks

US teens were asked which social network they consider their favourite
Their responses were dominated by the big four of Snapchat, Instagram, Facebook, and Twitter

87%

73%

In the first quarter of 2015, Snapchat, Instagram, Facebook and Twitter accounted
for 73% of the responses, with **other social networks** accounting for 27%.

By autumn of 2017 these four social networks had increased their share
with US teens, other social networks had lost out dropping to 13%.

27%

13%

| 2015 Q1 | 2015 Q3 | 2016 Q1 | 2016 Q3 | 2017 Q1 | 2017 Q3 |

Created by @Danifornication                            Data Source: Piper Jaffray

**FIGURE 10.32**    The difference between two lines can be accentuated by shading the area between the lines.

A heat map like Figure 10.33 focuses more on the patterns in the data and increases the data-to-ink ratio (Figures 10.34 and 10.35).

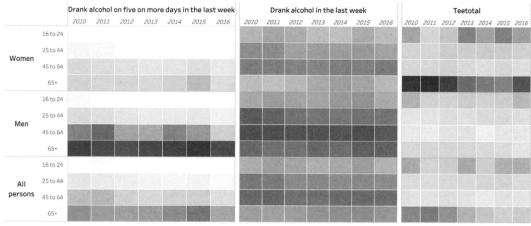

**FIGURE 10.33**   A heatmap focuses more on the patterns in the data and increases the data-to-ink ratio.

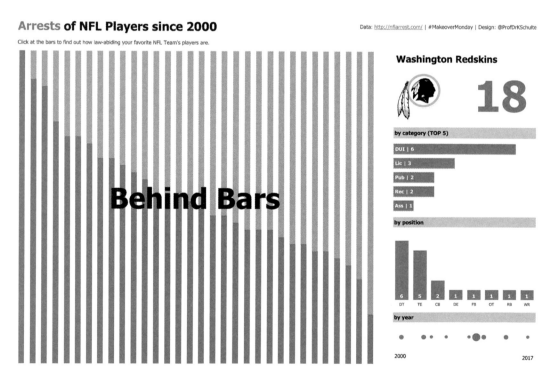

**FIGURE 10.34**   Stacked bars sized to 100% and colored in two distinct colors allow for easy comparisons and show trends.

# It's o-fish-ial!

UK pet population in 2017 dominated by denizens of ..

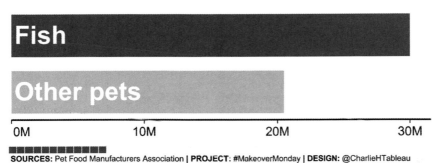

**SOURCES:** Pet Food Manufacturers Association | **PROJECT:** #MakeoverMonday | **DESIGN:** @CharlieHTableau

**FIGURE 10.35**    Bars sized by a specific metric clearly show which segments make the largest contributions to a total and allow for quick comparisons between segments.

## Packed Bubble Charts

### Purpose

Packed bubble charts, commonly referred to as bubble charts, display each attribute of a field as a circle, packed together as tightly as possible within the available space, with the size of the bubble representing the relative values of each attribute.

### Description

In most cases, bubble charts provide a means to communicate two fields:

1. What each bubble represents (categorical data like products or states)

2. The value of each bubble scaled in proportion to every other bubble (continuous data like sales or number of customers)

Bubble charts in their simplest form have these two fields, which essentially means that the larger the bubble, the larger the value. A third field could be used for color to represent discrete data (e.g., regions) or continuous data (e.g., profit ratio). Bubble charts can be a useful way to quickly spot large outliers.

There are a few basic rules to follow when creating bubble charts.

- If including labels, ensure they fit inside the bubble. If the label does not fit, do not display it.
- Size the bubbles according to their area, not their diameter.
- Use shapes that make sizes as easy as possible to compare, preferably circles rather than squares or other marks.

Drawbacks of bubble charts include:

- Comparing the area of the circles is extremely difficult.
- The location of the bubble is determined by the available space. Sorting is controlled by an algorithm and does not contribute to helping your end user process the view.
- If the metric contains negative values, size cannot be used to represent the values.

## Examples

Figures 10.36–10.38.

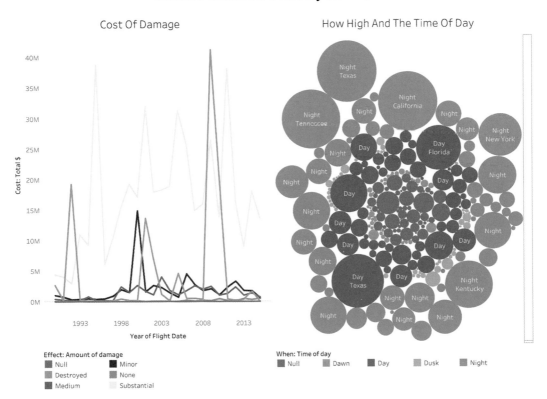

**FIGURE 10.36**  Comparing the size of bubbles or circles is much harder than comparing bars or rectangles.

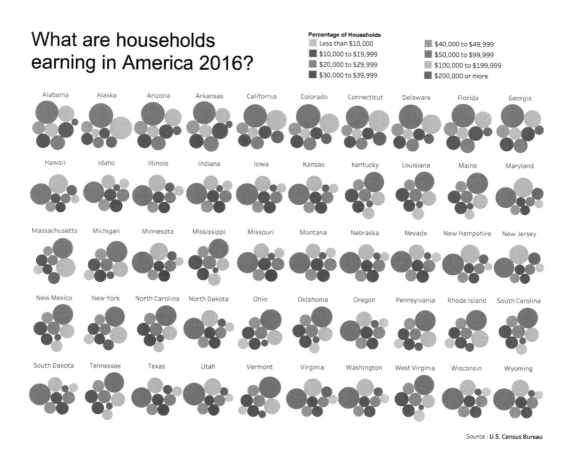

**FIGURE 10.37** Small multiple-bubble charts are difficult to compare because the circles change their location to fill the available space.

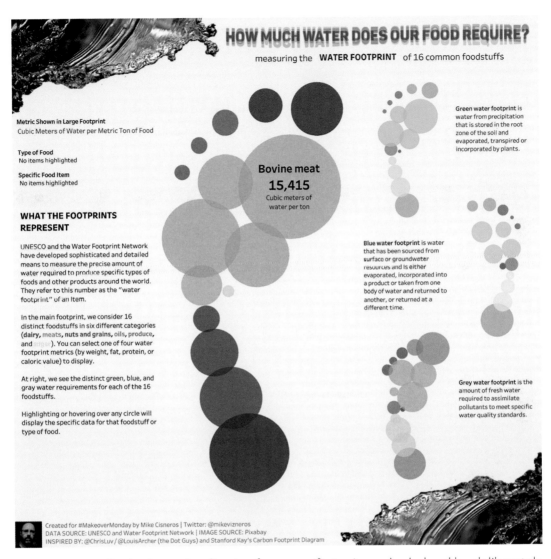

**FIGURE 10.38** Designing a visualization for a specific topic can be helped by deliberately placing circles and bubbles to create greater shapes.

Alternatives

Figures 10.39 and 10.40.

# The Most Influential YouTube Gaming Channels

The Social Blade rating system aims to measure a channel's influence based on a variety of metrics, including video views and subscribers.

YouTube channels with a rating of **A+**, **A**, or A- are considered very influential.

**Total Subscribers and Video Views of channels rated A- or higher by Social Blade**

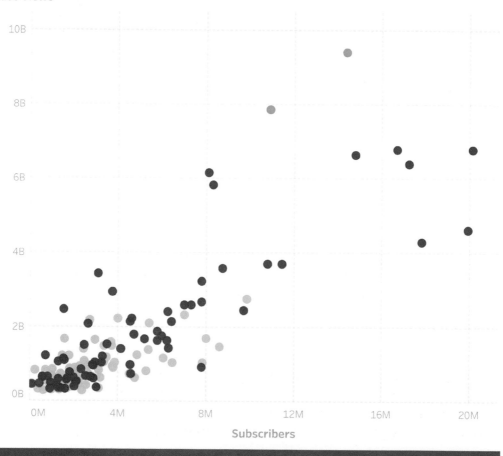

Created by Marc Soares (@soarmarc)                      Source: SocialBlade.com

**FIGURE 10.39**   A scatterplot is an effective way to visualize the relationship between two metrics.

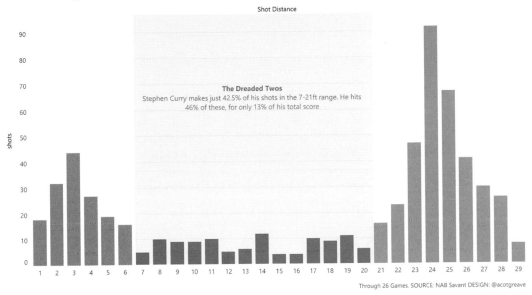

**The NBA's greatest shooter hates mid-range jump shots**

FIGURE 10.40 A histogram can be used to highlight how your data is distributed.

## Treemaps

### Purpose

Treemaps display hierarchical data in a single space that is split up into a series of rectangles. The size and position of each rectangle is determined by the proportion of a quantitative variable that each rectangle represents as part of the total quantitative variable.

### Description

Treemaps are an alternative for displaying parts-to-whole data, typically where there is a hierarchical relationship in the data (e.g., a tree diagram). Each grouping of rectangles inside the treemap represents a category, with each rectangle inside each category representing the next level down in the hierarchy. The rectangles are displayed as a nested relationship. Each rectangle is sized by its proportion of the total. The rectangles are arranged via a tiling algorithm in the software that, ideally, organizes the rectangles from largest proportion to smallest. See examples in Figures 10.41–10.47.

The proportion each rectangle represents is determined by its area. Therefore, the larger the rectangle, the bigger the rectangle's share of the total. Treemaps are useful for quickly understanding the overall hierarchy of the data and helping you identify which section is the largest based on its position in the chart.

Drawbacks of treemaps include:

- Negative values are difficult to represent.
- Comparisons of rectangles that are not next to each other is difficult.
- Users have no control over the order of the rectangles because they are determined by the tiling algorithm.

## Examples

### Apple made more than $45 billion in net income in 2016.

Of the 25 companies that make the most profit per second, Apple accounts for 12% of the net income.

DATA SOURCE: TitleMax                                    DESIGNED BY: @VizWizBI

**FIGURE 10.41** Treemaps with a clear focus on a single section make the key message more accessible for the audience.

# The geography of high dose inhaled steroids to treat asthma across England

In the UK, around **5.4 million people** are currently receiving treatment for asthma, and tragically, three people die every day because of asthma attacks. Research shows that two thirds of asthma deaths are preventable. Some people with asthma are prescribed a preventer inhaler. They contain a low dose of steroid medicine called **corticosteroids.** However latest guidance on the treatment of asthma recommends that patients should be maintained at the lowest possible dose of inhaled corticosteroid.

Using a definition from the www.openprescribing.net, the viz below compares the prescribing of **high dose inhaled corticosteroids** with prescribing of **all inhaled corticosteroids** using the practise postcode for 2015. There is wide variation in prescribing of high doses across England, particularly in the north of the country.

Let's be clear, there may be good reasons why a practice is prescribing more or less of something than other practices in the country. We don't have access to medical records. I'm not a doctor.

But the differences may highlight some issues - different prescribing cultures across the country, asthma not being as well managed as it should be, better detection, or simply more of the conditions that 'cause' asthma. Although it's difficult to say for sure what causes asthma. The viz poses more questions than it answers.

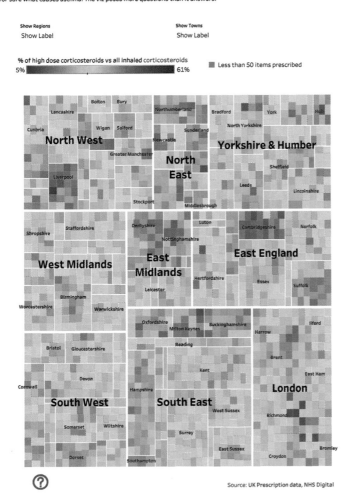

Source: UK Prescription data, NHS Digital

**FIGURE 10.42**  Applying a diverging color palette to a treemap that is structured geographically highlights problem areas effectively.

# He kicked him *where*?

### How Different Media Outlets Get Around Saying "Groin"

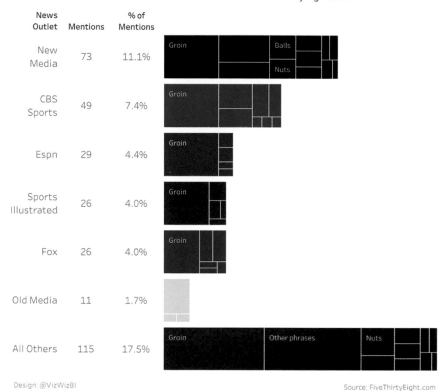

| News Outlet | Mentions | % of Mentions |
|---|---|---|
| New Media | 73 | 11.1% |
| CBS Sports | 49 | 7.4% |
| Espn | 29 | 4.4% |
| Sports Illustrated | 26 | 4.0% |
| Fox | 26 | 4.0% |
| Old Media | 11 | 1.7% |
| All Others | 115 | 17.5% |

Design: @VizWizBI

Source: FiveThirtyEight.com

**FIGURE 10.43** A treemap bar chart shows the ranking of each top-level segment, while providing a ranking of the subsegments within each bar.

## Alternatives

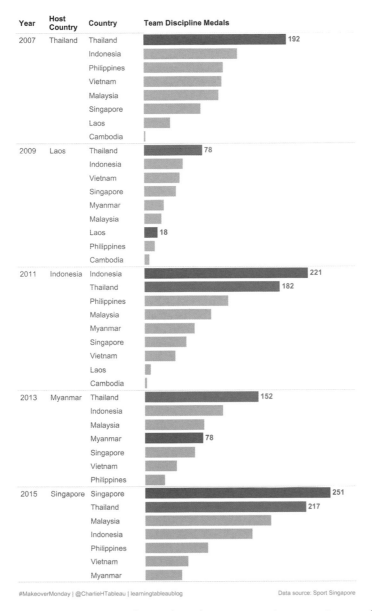

**The host nation or Thailand win most Team Discipline medals at the Southeast Asia Games**

**FIGURE 10.44** Bar charts that show categories over time make it easy to compare different attributes, especially when color highlighting is used.

**FIGURE 10.45**    Color highlighting to show the largest bar helps when sorting by size does not apply.

## Was it good for you too?

*The likelihood of orgasm for women and men depending on the type of relationship they're in...*

Picture yourself sitting at a table with a number of different couples. You all order your meals and your heterosexual male friends tuck in, munch their way through entrees, mains and desserts, while your heterosexual and bisexual female friends get their food taken away after eating just two thirds of their meals... Sounds pretty unfair, doesn't it?

When it comes to **orgasms**, the statistics aren't great either for the women involved, no matter what kind of relationship they're in...

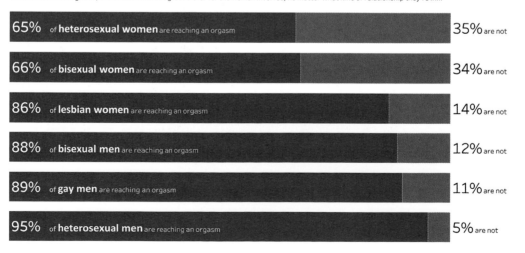

**FIGURE 10.46**    Stacked bars sized to 100% with labels for both segments provide clear and specific answers.

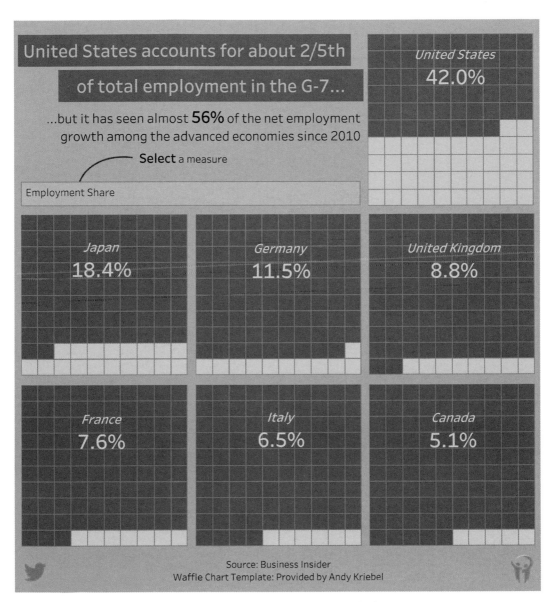

**FIGURE 10.47** A waffle chart focuses more on each individual segment.

## Slopegraphs

### Purpose

Slopegraphs, first invented by Edward Tufte, are typically used to show change between two time periods. They can also be used to show change between any two points.

### Description

Slopegraphs are line charts, except they include only two periods; therefore, they ignore the time between the two periods to accentuate the change, or slope, between the two periods. Slopegraphs are useful if you want the reader to compare only the start and the end of a specific period. The ends of the lines are typically labeled, and the lines colored by either absolute change, relative change, or positive versus negative change (i.e., two colors). See examples in Figures 10.48–10.53.

Other common use cases for slopegraphs include:

- Comparing the difference between two data populations
- Comparing the rank of two data populations
- Comparing the proportion of two data populations

# Growth Rates of Irish Whiskey Consumed in the United States

While growth rates of Standard Quality Whiskey have been more or less constant over the decades  growth rates of **Premium Quality Whiskey** seem to be much more affected by external effects such as financial and political crisis. Thus growth rates of Premium Quality Whiskey behave similar to those of luxury products while Standard Quality Whiskey seems to be more like a (growing) basic need for people in the US.

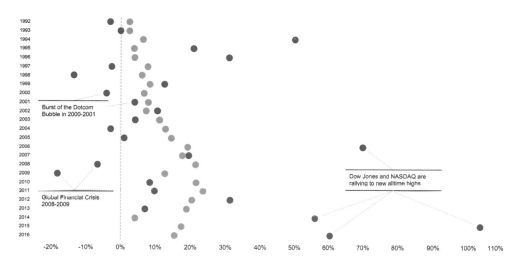

Data Source: https://twitter.com/Bordbia

Design: Klaus Schulte for #MakeoverMonday

**FIGURE 10.52**  A dot plot focuses on the position rather than the slope of the difference.

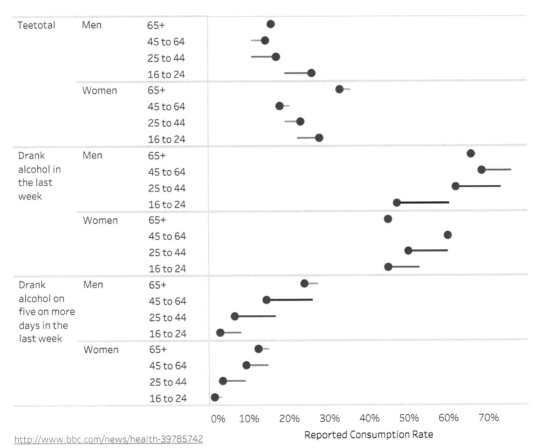

# Changes in UK Drinking Habits 2006 to 2016

Circles show 2016 reported rates, end of lines show 2006 reported rates

http://www.bbc.com/news/health-39785742

**FIGURE 10.53** Connecting individual dots to lines in the direction of change between two points in time shows each age group's development over time.

## Connected Scatterplots

### Purpose

Connected scatterplots show two variables in a scatterplot and connect the points as a line over time.

### Description

Connected scatterplots are nothing more than scatterplots with each data point in the scatterplot represented along a time dimension. One data variable is on each axis, a single dot is displayed for each member of the time series, and the dots are connected via a line in the sequence of the time series. These charts are useful for identifying correlated movement patterns between the two variables. See examples in Figures 10.54–10.61.

If it is difficult to follow the sequence of the line and/or no overall pattern emerges, consider an alternative visualization.

## Examples

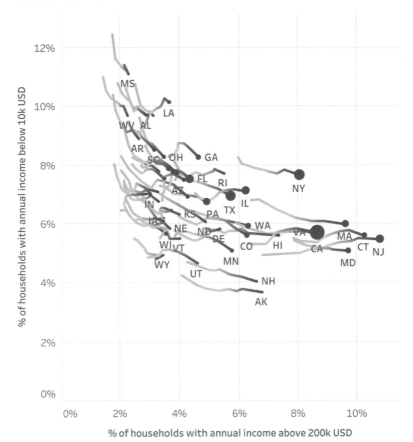

There are **more extremely rich** households and **less poor** ones in the US.

**How % of rich and poor households changed between 2009 and 2016?**

The greener the line, the more recent the year. Size of the bubble is proportional to the number of households with income above 200k USD in 2016.

Highlight State
No items highlighted

DESIGN: @BartPopeda
DATA SOURCE: U.S. Census Bureau

**FIGURE 10.54** A scatterplot with a line connecting the dots of each attribute over the years shows most states progressing to more households being in higher income brackets.

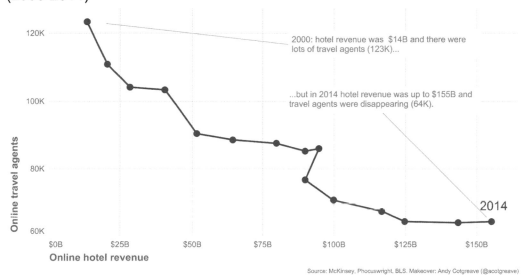

Online travel agents are disappearing as online hotel revenue soars (2000-2014)

2000: hotel revenue was $14B and there were lots of travel agents (123K)...

...but in 2014 hotel revenue was up to $155B and travel agents were disappearing (64K).

2014

Online travel agents

Online hotel revenue

Source: McKinsey, Phocuswright, BLS. Makeover: Andy Cotgreave (@acotgreave)

**FIGURE 10.55** Clearly labeling the start and end point of a line in a connected scatterplot accentuates the development over time.

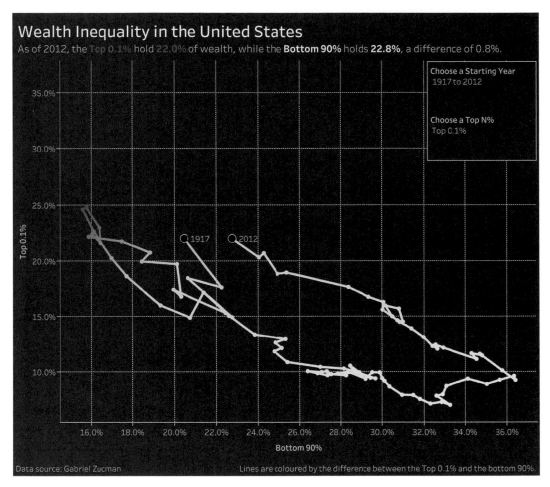

**FIGURE 10.56**   While this connected scatterplot shows dramatic changes over the years, the start and end point of the data are fairly close together as highlighted by their labels.

## Alternatives

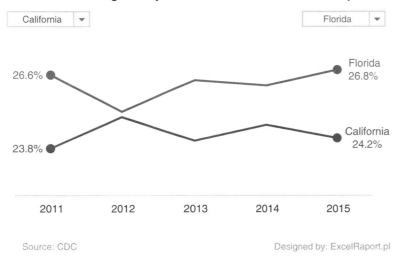

FIGURE 10.57 A simple line chart focuses your audience's attention on the trends over time.

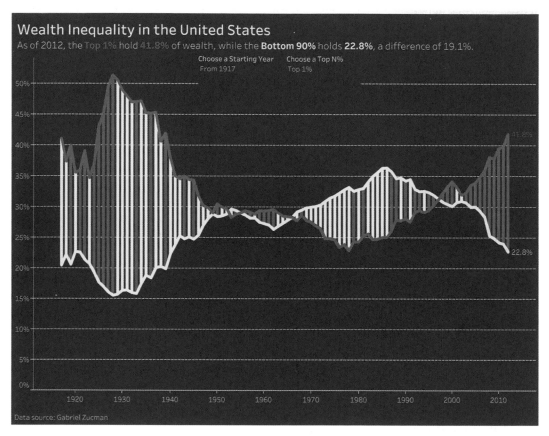

**FIGURE 10.58**   Adding vertical lines or bars between two lines accentuates the magnitude of the difference between the two lines.

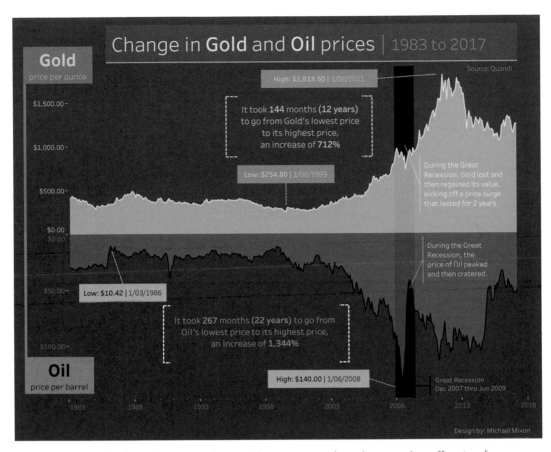

**Gold**
price per ounce

Change in **Gold** and **Oil** prices | 1983 to 2017

Source: Quandl

High: $1,813.50 | 1/08/2011

$1,500.00 –

It took **144** months **(12 years)** to go from Gold's lowest price to its highest price, an increase of **712%**

$1,000.00 –

During the Great Recession, Gold lost and then regained its value, kicking off a price surge that lasted for 2 years.

Low: $254.80 | 1/08/1999

$500.00 –

$0.00
$0.00

During the Great Recession, the price of Oil peaked and then cratered.

$50.00 –

Low: $10.42 | 1/03/1986

It took **267** months **(22 years)** to go from Oil's lowest price to its highest price, an increase of **1,344%**

$100.00 –

**Oil**
price per barrel

High: $140.00 | 1/06/2008

Great Recession
Dec 2007 thru Jun 2009

1983   1988   1993   1998   2003   2008   2013   2018

Design by: Michael Mixon

**FIGURE 10.59**   A diverging area chart with a common baseline can be effective for showing the different trends of two attributes over time.

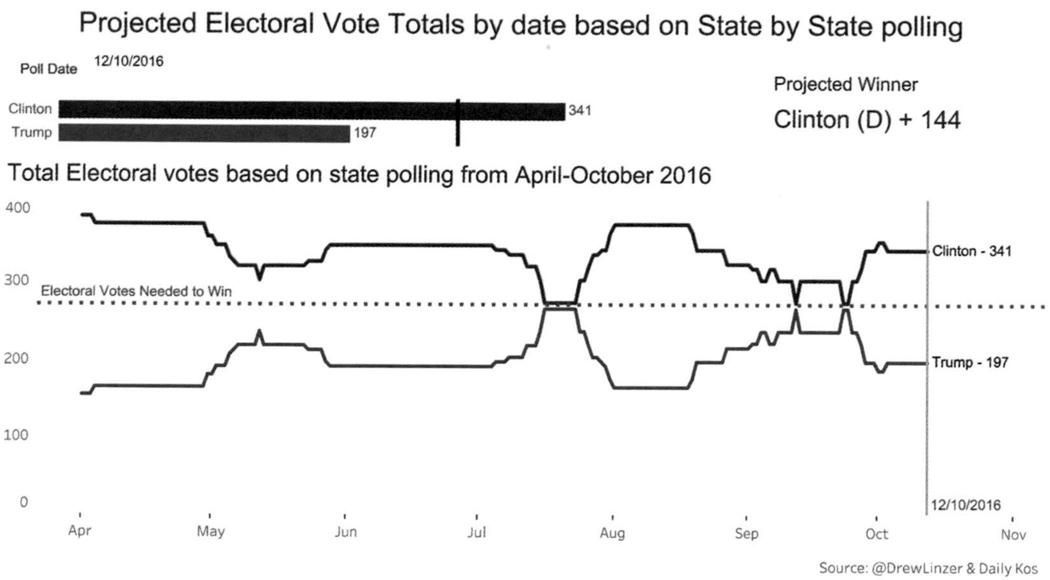
Projected Electoral Vote Totals by date based on State by State polling
Poll Date 12/10/2016
Projected Winner
Clinton (D) + 144
Clinton
341
Trump
197
Total Electoral votes based on state polling from April-October 2016
400
300
Electoral Votes Needed to Win
200
100
0
Clinton - 341
Trump - 197
12/10/2016
Apr
May
Jun
Jul
Aug
Sep
Oct
Nov
Source: @DrewLinzer & Daily Kos

**FIGURE 10.60** A diverging line chart highlights the differing or similar patterns of two attributes across the same variable.

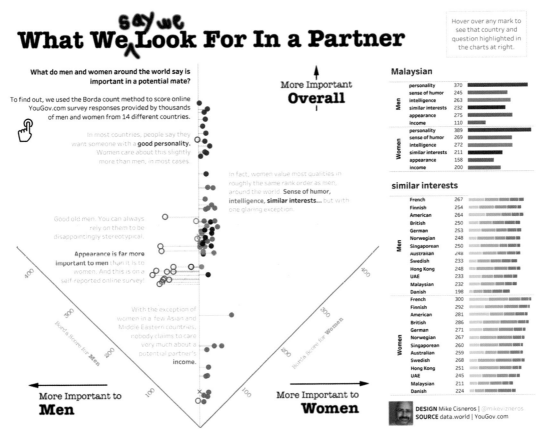

**FIGURE 10.61** This dot plot highlights criteria that are more important for women compared to men and also indicates the overall importance.

## Circular Histograms

### Purpose

A circular histogram is used for displaying data around a circle as a series of bars with the bar length representing a data variable. See examples in Figures 10.62–10.68.

## Description

Circular histograms are similar to time series bar charts, except the bars extend outward from the edge of an inner circle. For easiest comprehension, begin the plot at the 12 o'clock position and continue clockwise around the circle in chronological or continuous order. Circular plots can also be used for comparing two elements of a single field or for ranked data. The bars should be spaced so that the number of bars wraps entirely around the inner circle once.

Drawbacks of circular histograms include:

- Patterns can be difficult to identify.
- Comparing the length of bars that are not next to each other is challenging.
- It is confusing for readers who are unfamiliar with the chart type.

## Examples

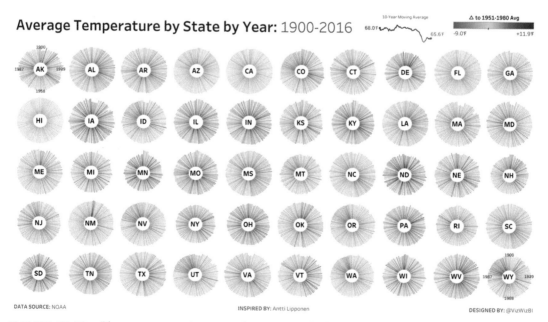

**FIGURE 10.62**  Changes over time are shown in a clockwise order in this circular histogram, which displays all the data at one time.

**FIGURE 10.63** This circular histogram highlights outliers in the data with lines that are far longer than most other lines.

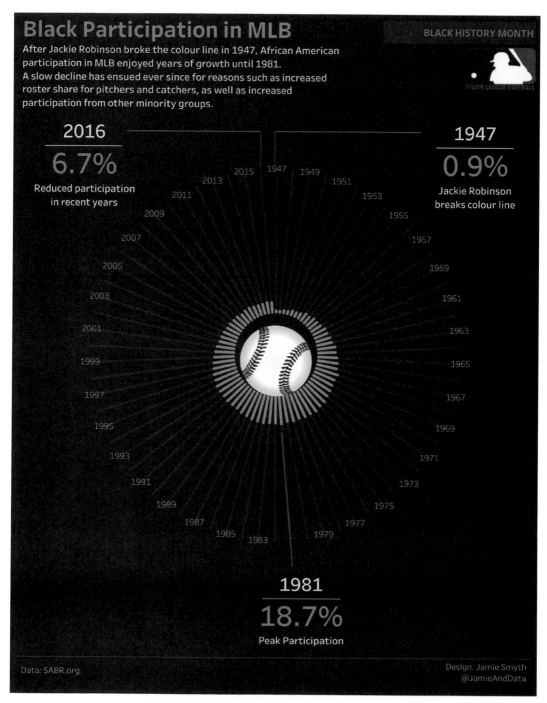

**FIGURE 10.64** With bar length representing the magnitude of black participation, and labels for key points in time, this circular histogram clearly indicates changes over the years.

Alternatives

# Global Peace Index
Tracking trends of the world's leading measure of peacefulness

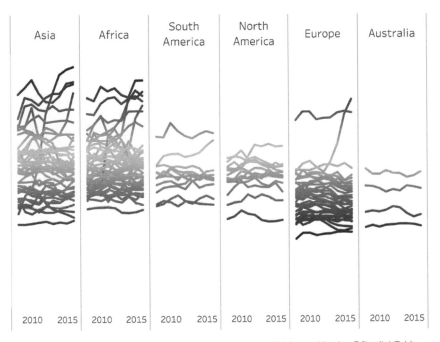

**FIGURE 10.65**  Line charts can be used to effectively show patterns in the data across multiple regions at once.

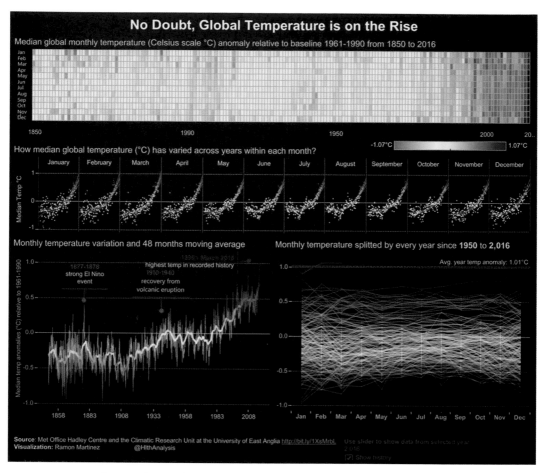

**FIGURE 10.66** Giving the audience multiple visualizations of the same data provides a comprehensive picture of trends, changes, and key findings.

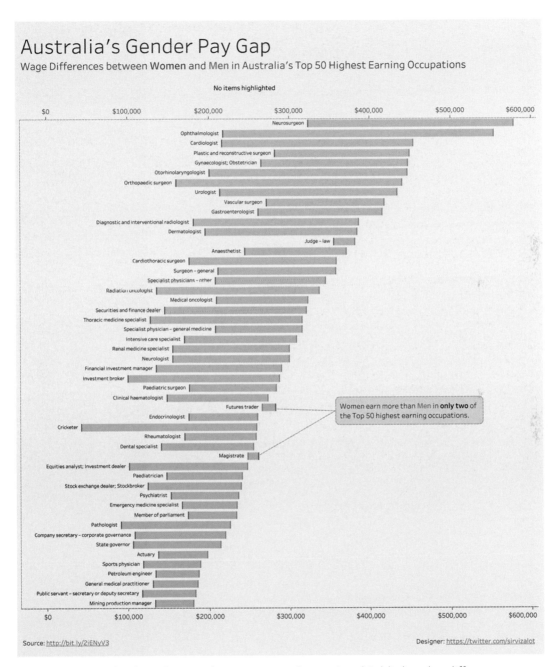

**FIGURE 10.67**  Shading the area between two data points highlights the differences between two attributes.

Ozone Daily AQI Values in Los Angeles takes the **highest values** from May to September

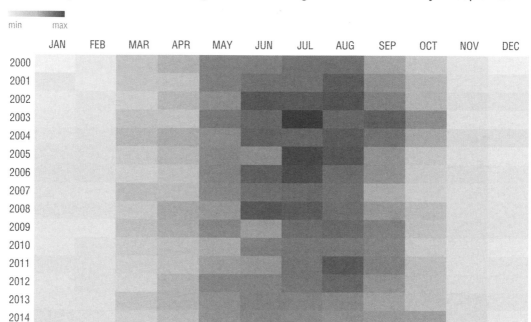

Source: EPA

Designed by: ExcelRaport.pl

**FIGURE 10.68**   Seasonal trends and changes over time are easy to spot in a heatmap coloring values by a single variable.

## Radial Bar Charts

### Purpose

Radial bar charts are bar charts plotted on a polar coordinate system.

### Description

Similar to a bar chart, radial bar charts are used for showing comparisons of categorical data elements. Radial bar charts are most effective when they represent parts-to-whole relationships with the radial chart starting and ending at 12 o'clock as the

0% and 100% marks. The bar should be sorted from outside to inside from the largest value to smallest value. See examples in Figures 10.69–10.74.

Drawbacks of radial bar charts include:

- Comparisons are more difficult than with a regular bar chart, because curved bars are harder to compare to each other than straight bars
- Bars on the outside use more data ink than an arc on the inside of a similar percentage, thus looking longer

Examples

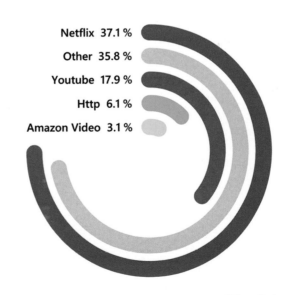

## America's Biggest Bandwidth Hogs

On Monday 7th December 2015, broadband services company **Sandvine** released data showing how video streaming utterly dominates the internet. During peak hours in North America, 70% of all bandwidth going from providers to consumers (that's "downstream" bandwidth) was taken up by video.

**Netflix** is the biggest bandwidth hog of the bunch, making up more than **37%** of all downstream traffic during peak hours. Google's **YouTube** is a distant second, with about **18%**. All non-video web services combined (HTTP) take up only **6%** of all downstream bandwidth.

Netflix  37.1 %
Other  35.8 %
Youtube  17.9 %
Http  6.1 %
Amazon Video  3.1 %

#MakeoverMonday
@thoang1000
www.toanhoang.com

**FIGURE 10.69**  Radial bar charts can be easy to understand but can distort the viewer's perception of the data.

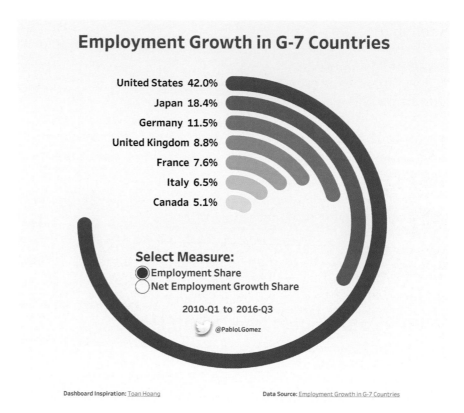

**FIGURE 10.70**    While the outer bar dominates this view, the chart provides an overall impression of each bar's contribution to the whole.

## Alternatives

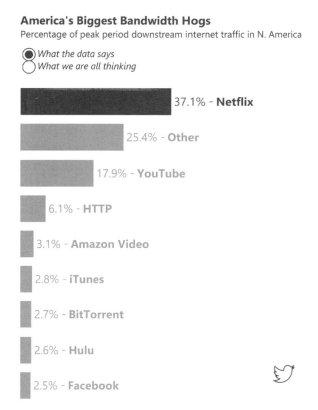

**America's Biggest Bandwidth Hogs**
Percentage of peak period downstream internet traffic in N. America

⦿ *What the data says*
◯ *What we are all thinking*

37.1% - **Netflix**

25.4% - **Other**

17.9% - **YouTube**

6.1% - **HTTP**

3.1% - **Amazon Video**

2.8% - **iTunes**

2.7% - **BitTorrent**

2.6% - **Hulu**

2.5% - **Facebook**

**FIGURE 10.71**  Straight rectangular bars are more effective because they do not require the audience to interpret the curvature of the bars as in a radial bar chart.

**FIGURE 10.72**   A dot plot with shading that indicates the minimum and maximum value shows the spread of the data as well as the value of each attribute.

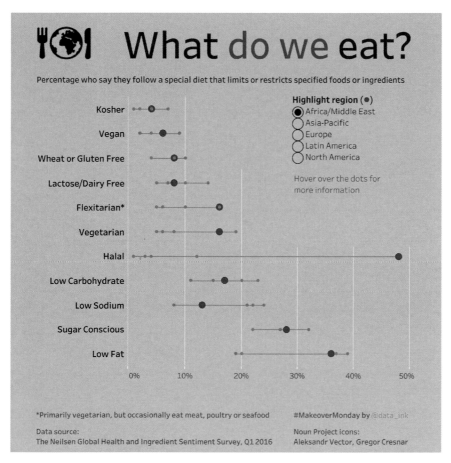

**FIGURE 10.73** Connecting the data points in a dot plot with a line shows the spread of the data. Adding nonselected data as small gray circles provides context.

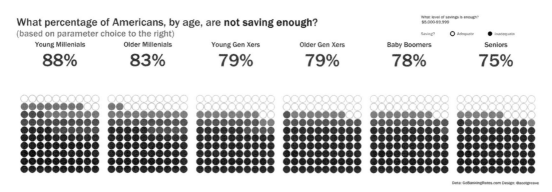

**FIGURE 10.74** A unit chart sized to 100% is easy to understand and can be enhanced with large numbers showing the actual value for each age group.

## Resources

Below is a list of resources that we often use for charting best practices and charting ideas. These resources provide a short description of the chart's purpose and the type of data that is best suited for the chart.

- Financial Times Visual Vocabulary: ft.com/vocabulary
- The Data Viz Project: datavizproject.com
- The Data Visualization Catalogue: datavizcatalogue.com
- Chart Chooser Cards–Stephanie Evergreen: chartchoosercards.com
- Chart Chooser Diagram–Andrew Abela: ExtremePresentation.com

## Summary

The number of chart types available to display data can be overwhelming. After reading this chapter, you should have a better grasp of which charts to use in which situations and have gained inspiration from the visualizations we provided and their alternatives. This chapter does not cover all types; rather it is focused on those that are not discussed as often in the data visualization community. Some of the charts might be considered controversial or unconventional; however, we have provided well-executed examples that demonstrate when these charts can work.

Trying new chart types will help you learn by forcing you to develop new skills and techniques. Ultimately, the process of continuous learning will make you better at communicating information, it will develop your data visualization knowledge, and it will help you become a better data analyst.

## Chapter Eleven

# Effective Use of Text

Visual analysis means more than building a number of charts. It involves the use of text in titles, subtitles, labels, annotations, tooltips, footers, and so on to effectively communicate your insights and inform your audience. Text can elicit emotions and help ensure that your readers fully understand the impact and meaning of your findings.

In this chapter, you will learn how to use text elements to more effectively communicate your message by:

- Creating effective titles and subtitles
- Communicating your key message
- Guiding your audience through clear instructions and explanations

## Effective Titles and Subtitles

The title of your visualization is typically the first thing your audience notices about your work. This title needs to draw them in and give them a snippet of what is to come, and can be used to inform them of your key message. Different data analyses lend themselves to different types of titles. For some data sets, an intriguing question or a provocative statement can work. Regardless of the type of title you use, it should not mislead your audience or impact your credibility.

This section covers four different types of titles:

- Using questions as titles
- Making definitive statements
- Using descriptive titles
- Working with quirky, funny, or poetic titles

For each of these concepts, you will see examples of how titles work in the real world and in the context of the data analysis supporting them.

## Using Questions as Titles

A question in your title tells your audience what they can expect to find the answer to in your visualization. Using a clear question in your title and answering that question will make data more accessible for your audience.

In Figure 11.1, Nish Goel analyzed data about the World Economic Freedom Index. His title reads "Which Countries Have the Biggest Decline in Economic Freedom from 2000–2015?"

This title works very well for the following reasons:

- The question is very specific.
  - "Which countries" informs the audience that they are looking at country-level data.
  - "Biggest Decline" tells the audience that the analysis focuses on those countries that have decreased most significantly in the given time period.

# Which Countries Have the Biggest Decline in Economic Freedom from 2000-2015?

Both **Argentina** and **Venezuela** have steeply declined in economic freedom over the last 16 years.....

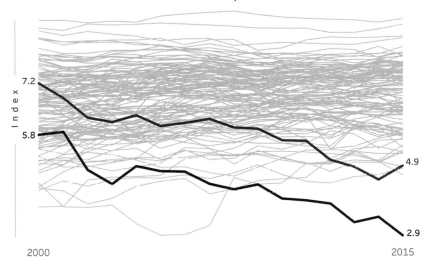

......however **Argentina** has seen the biggest drop in economic freedom ranking out of the 123 countries

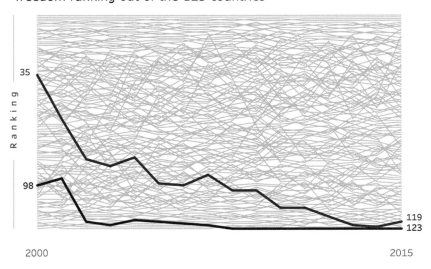

**DATA SOURCE:** Fraser Institute          **DESIGNED BY:** @thevizlover

**FIGURE 11.1**   With a title in form of a question, this visualization guides the audience to look for and find the answer in the data.

- ◆ "Economic Freedom" indicates the topic.
- ◆ "2000–2015" provides a timeframe for the data.
- Whether the viewer is a layperson or an expert, the title sets the expectations for the type of answer the visualizations will provide.
- The title is supported by the data and insights.
- The individual chart titles, which spell out the findings in plain English sentences, provide the answer to the primary question.

In Figure 11.2, Matt Francis analyzed US meat consumption, asking, "Did Mad Cow and Cancer Scares Harm US Beef Consumption?"

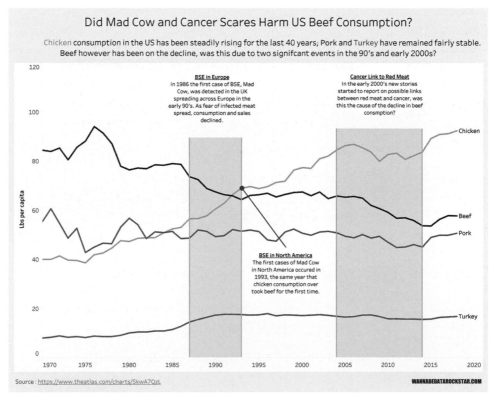

**FIGURE 11.2**  Questions in titles encourage your audience to take a position and see if the data supports their view.

Matt's title is supported by a clarifying statement about the four different types of meat visualized in the chart. He further asks whether the decline of beef is due to the emergence of mad cow disease and the link of cancer to red meat consumption.

While we cannot definitely answer the question in the title of Matt's visualization, the audience is guided through his analysis and can make the judgment for themselves, given the indicators in the data. In this case the title works well to engage the audience to come to their own conclusions and to consume the information provided to them.

## Making Definitive Statements

As an alternative to the use of questions to gain your audience's interest, clear and definitive statements can make for very effective titles. In data visualizations, definitive statements in titles can be used to clearly communicate your message and key insights upfront. It is essential that you follow this up with analysis that backs up your statement to avoid any confusion for your audience.

Kate Brown visualized Winter Olympics data and focused on the success of the Netherlands in speedskating (Figure 11.3). Kate states, "The Netherlands Dominated Speed Skating at the 2014 Winter Olympics."

Her visualization backs up her claim in the following ways:

- She provides a brief explanation of the key findings in the data.
  - Dutch speed skaters won 23 Olympic medals in 2014.
  - 63% of the total medals in that sport were won by the Netherlands.
  - Three medals were won by the second most successful team.

The Netherlands Dominated Speedskating at the 2014 Winter Olympics

The Netherlands's speedskaters won **23 Olympic medals in 2014**. This was **63%** of the total medals awarded in speedskating. Poland, the 2nd place team won 3 medals.

Medals by Country

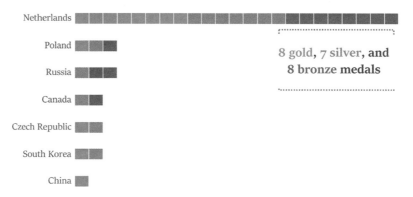

Percent of Medals won by the Netherlands by Year

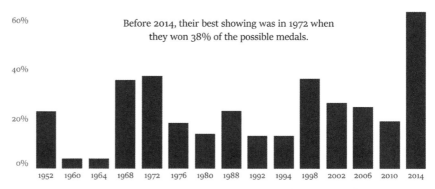

created by: @katebrown_5 for #makeovermonday
data source: Sports-Reference.com icon: the noun project

**FIGURE 11.3**   Making a clear statement in your title sets the tone for your analysis and highlights your insights from the start.

- Kate adds a basic unit chart comparing the seven nations who won medals in speed skating in 2014 in order to show the dominance of the Netherlands.
- She gives an overview of the Dutch medal tally by games in speed skating.

It is almost impossible to disagree with the claim Kate put into her title. The Netherlands really did dominate speed skating at the 2014 Winter Olympics.

## Using Descriptive Titles

The most commonly used type of title seen in Makeover Monday has a short description of the analysis. The way this differs from definitive statements is that descriptive titles do not make a claim and instead give an overview of the analysis to come. Sometimes you simply do not have the data to support a specific claim, so instead you can describe what your analysis shows or what the data is about.

As seen in Figure 11.4, Rob Radburn created a geographical treemap highlighting asthma medication prescriptions in the UK in 2015. His analysis focused on high-dose inhaled steroids and his title makes this clear: "The geography of high-dose inhaled steroids to treat asthma across England."

Rob's title shows his audience what he focused on:

- "The geography of" gives you an idea that his analysis provides geographical insights.
- The phrase "high-dose inhaled steroids to treat asthma" tells you that this visualization focuses on medication for asthma.
- "Across England" sets the geographical context.

# The geography of high dose inhaled steroids to treat asthma across England

In the UK, around **5.4 million people** are currently receiving treatment for asthma, and tragically, three people die every day because of asthma attacks. Research shows that two thirds of asthma deaths are preventable. Some people with asthma are prescribed a preventer inhaler. They contain a low dose of steroid medicine called **corticosteroids**. However latest guidance on the treatment of asthma recommends that patients should be maintained at the lowest possible dose of inhaled corticosteroid.

Using a definition from the www.openprescribing.net, the viz below compares the prescribing of **high dose inhaled corticosteroids** with prescribing of **all inhaled corticosteroids** using the practise postcode for **2015**. There is wide variation in prescribing of high doses across England, particularly in the north of the country.

Let's be clear, there may be good reasons why a practice is prescribing more or less of something than other practices in the country. We don't have access to medical records. I'm not a doctor.

But the differences may highlight some issues - different prescribing cultures across the country, asthma not being as well managed as it should be, better detection, or simply more of the conditions that 'cause' asthma. Although it's difficult to say for sure what causes asthma. The viz poses more questions than it answers.

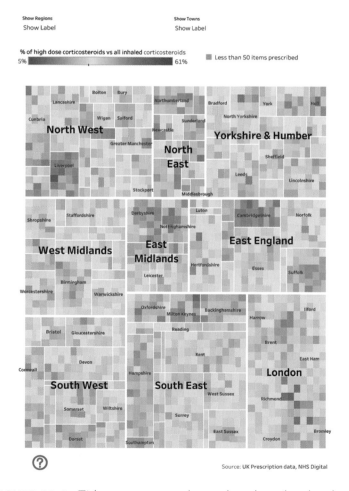

**FIGURE 11.4** Titles are commonly used to describe the data set and the visualization.

The title, combined with the additional text, sets the scene for the audience to better understand the visualization.

## Working with Quirky, Funny, and Poetic Titles

Some data visualization topics give room for a bit of humor. Charlie Hutcheson analyzed pet ownership data in the UK and created Figure 11.5 with the title "It's o-fish-ial" as a play on words to show that fish are the most numerous pets in the UK.

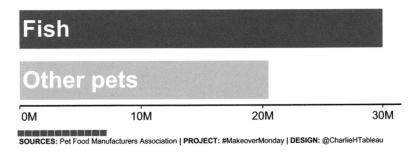

# It's o-fish-ial!
UK pet population in 2017 dominated by denizens of the deep

**Fish**

**Other pets**

| 0M | 10M | 20M | 30M |

SOURCES: Pet Food Manufacturers Association | **PROJECT:** #MakeoverMonday | **DESIGN:** @CharlieHTableau

**FIGURE 11.5**   Many topics in Makeover Monday leave room for creative titles that make your audience smile.

In this context, a quirky title is absolutely fine to use because not every data visualization needs to be serious. Charlie added a simple bar chart showing that fish are more plentiful in numbers than all other pets combined and describes them in the subtitle as "denizens of the deep," carrying the same humorous message throughout the visualization.

Completing two Makeover Monday challenges at once, Mike Cisneros combined the data sets from two weeks, one about the EU potato sector and one about Andy's credit card spending, into the single dashboard in Figure 11.6 with the title "Potato Kriebel."

**FIGURE 11.6** Not all analysis has to be serious and a humorous title supported by imagery brings out the lightheartedness of this visualization.

Humor is reflected in the choice of Andy's picture, overlaid with two potatoes on his hands. The analysis itself goes into further detail about Andy's credit card spending and how many potatoes he could have purchased for the amount he spent in 2016. The two topics have nothing to do with each other, making the combination of the data sets funny in a bizarre kind of way.

These types of headlines evoke curiosity and encourage people to look at your visualization.

## Delivering on Your Promises

Once you choose a great title, make sure your visualization delivers on the promise of your headline. Ask yourself:

1. Do my analysis and conclusions actually support the claim in my title?

2. Does the analysis answer the question from the title?

3. Is it easy to find the answer?

Your title draws your audience in; it makes a statement in some way that invites the readers to spend time looking at the work you created. Make sure that when they leave, they have answers to their questions, they are informed, and they have gained new knowledge or confirmed existing hypotheses. It is an opportunity for you to make them feel confident in your abilities as an analyst and to build trust and credibility as you impress them with your analysis, design, and storytelling.

## What Is Your Key Message?

With every visualization ask yourself: What is the key message? If it takes a while to figure out what you wanted to communicate, then the message has probably not been visualized clearly and simply.

To ensure your key message gets through, consider the following recommendations:

1. Assume your audience does not know anything about the topic or the data set.

2. Assume your audience does not know how to work with interactive visualizations and will need some guidance on how to use your visualization.

3. State your key insights and conclusions very clearly to ensure your audience knows exactly what you are showing them.

These suggestions help to create data visualizations that are easy to understand for the average person with little background knowledge. Instead of simply visualizing data and building charts, make an effort to communicate information effectively in visual and text form to help your audience understand and use your visualization.

## State Your Message

The easiest way to ensure that your audience knows what your visualization shows is to tell them clearly. In Figure 11.7, Emily Chen

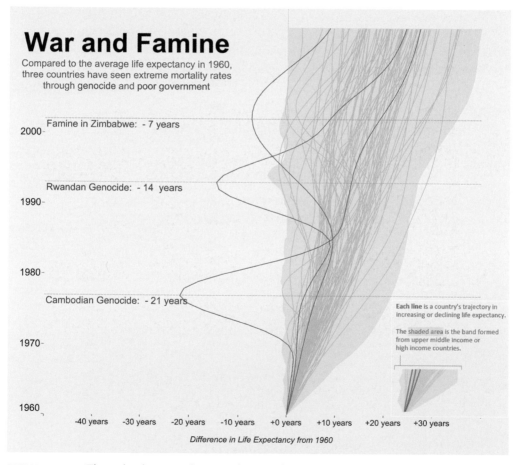

**FIGURE 11.7**   The subtitle is an element that can be used to effectively state your key message, reflecting the insights you derived from your analysis.

visualized life expectancy and highlighted three countries to show how they deviate from all other countries in the data set.

Emily's subtitle clearly states what she found in her analysis: genocide and poor government led to extreme mortality rates in the countries highlighted.

As seen in Figure 11.8, Shawn Levin also took this approach to show the correlation he found between geographical location and obesity in the US.

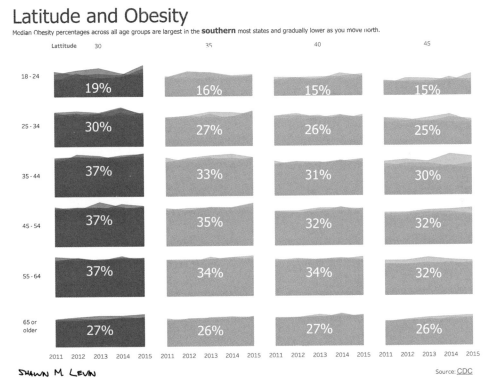

## Latitude and Obesity

Median Obesity percentages across all age groups are largest in the **southern** most states and gradually lower as you move north.

SHAWN M. LEVIN

Source: CDC

**FIGURE 11.8**  The subtitle states the key message, supports the short title, and summarizes the analysis visualized in multiple area charts.

Shawn's visualization is called "Latitude and Obesity" and his subtitle reads: "Median Obesity percentages across all age groups are largest in the southern most states and gradually lower as you move north." The audience can quickly understand that Shawn analyzed the commonalities between states according to their latitude and that he found a stable pattern across age groups.

Both Emily and Shawn used their subtitles to clearly state their focus on one particular insight in the data.

## Semantics Matter

Language plays an important role for communicating effectively and a deliberate choice of words is essential to frame your message clearly. Titles, subtitles, and descriptions can be misinterpreted because authors are too vague.

Figure 11.9, created by Charlie Hutcheson, visualizes the basic level of accessibility in Singapore in red in his stacked bar chart. He

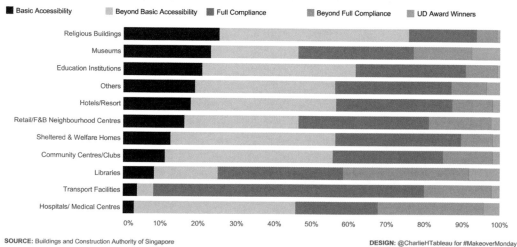

**FIGURE 11.9**   Being very specific in your title or subtitle helps your audience to understand your findings easily.

concluded that religious buildings perform poorly compared to other buildings when it comes to accessibility.

You will notice that he used a very specific title and a descriptive subtitle to explain his findings. These clarify exactly what he analyzed and the conclusions he came to. Had he chosen a title like "Religious buildings in Singapore are hard to access," the meaning would be completely different.

When you choose a vague title, it leaves the visualization open to misinterpretation. Ensure that your analysis is visualized in a way that does not lead to misinterpretations and misunderstandings. As you create visualizations, ask for feedback regarding your title, subtitle, and descriptions. Ask your peers, friends, or family if your text communicates the key message clearly and ask which parts are difficult to understand. Having this feedback will help you create visualizations that are comprehensive and polished.

## Big Ass Numbers

Using very large numbers in visualizations is a great way to highlight the key metrics and focus on specific figures. They provide an opportunity to bring actual data values back into a visualization, and to focus on selected numbers and why they matter.

In Figure 11.10, Sebastián Soto Vera used Big Ass Numbers (BANs) in his analysis of the UK pet population. He highlighted the large number of birds in captivity, drawing attention to the issue of birds being kept in cages.

After seeing the title, your eyes are immediately drawn to the large number of 700 000 caged birds, on which Sebastián built the narrative of his data story.

**FIGURE 11.10** A single large number in a visualization draws the audience's attention and provides the focus for the key message.

Paul Morgan used BANs with great effect in his visualization of US Winter Olympic performances (Figure 11.11).

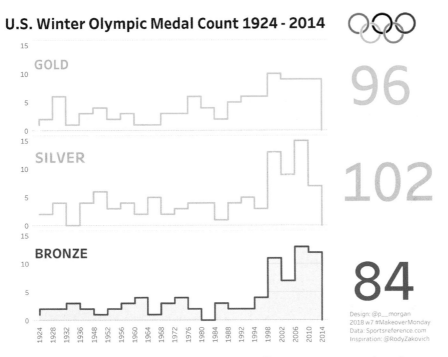

**FIGURE 11.11**   Large numbers provide an effective summary of each medal count in this visualization.

The large totals on the right side gives a quick overview of the medals won by the US over the years.

Curtis Harris built an interactive dashboard (Figure 11.12), where the audience could enter their date of birth and the age at which they expect to die. Based on these entries, Curtis uses BANs to show how many solar eclipses already happened in a person's life and how many are remaining.

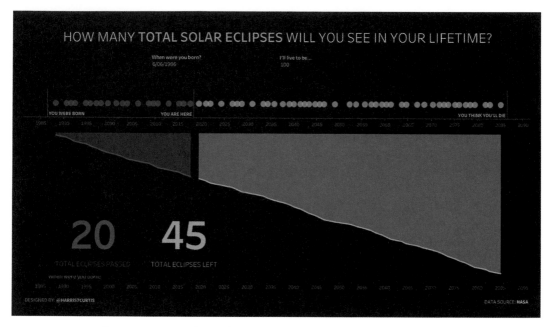

**FIGURE 11.12**   Dynamic BANs based on user selections show the impact of the parameter changes and highlight the most important metrics.

The large numbers are a focal area in the bottom left corner of his visualization and provide nice concrete figures that are relatable.

For BANs to be most effective, they need to become part of the overall design and stand out without looking out of place. In each example in this section, the large numbers are part of the visualization and blend in with the remaining elements on the page. Bringing these kinds of layouts together harmoniously will require a bit of practice and are a great way to enhance your analysis.

## Call to Action

If you want your audience to engage, include a clear call to action. Makeover Monday participants have taken important topics around education, employment, public sanitation, climate change, and food choices and included strong calls to action so their audience would act on their new knowledge.

A very simple yet impactful dashboard, as seen in Figure 11.13, came from Klaus Schulte's analysis of Indian school children's access to functioning toilets.

## How likely is it that a girl is finding a proper toilet at school in India?

Check out a State:

Nagaland

# 41%

If you think that's **not enough** please support and donate for 'Toilets & Water for school children' (especially in rural) India!

Link to the Global Giving Projekt

Data: Annual Status of Education Report          Design: @ProfDrKSchulte

**FIGURE 11.13**   Including a call to action for your audience to donate, sign a petition, access further information, and so on can make your visualization very impactful.

Klaus combined a question in his title with a BAN to answer that question before his call to action. He encourages his audience to donate to the Global Giving Project to help improve sanitation facilities for school children in India.

Especially for social impact topics, a call to action can make your analysis transformative, allowing you to become an agent of change by combining your analytical and design skills to take your audience one step further. Data visualizations do not always have to be neutral and formal. Bringing emotion into your work, especially for topics that matter to you personally, is a great way to create impactful visualizations that address your audience at a different level.

## Instructions and Explanations

Supporting your headline with instructions on how to interact with the data or with explanations that define metrics and technical terms can make your visualization more effective at communicating your intended message. Instructions can be simple statements like "click on the map to filter" or "select a country to see its data." When the text is placed near the relevant filters, charts, or buttons, you help your audience find their way around your dashboard and understand how to use the interactive elements.

In general, be very specific with your instructions and assume that your audience has no experience with interactive dashboards. Including instructions in different places on the page helps you communicate to all members of your audience. It is easy to forget to include instructions in your visualization, because for you it may be obvious how to use the interactive elements and find your way around a dashboard. For your audience this may not be so clear. So before you share your work, take a moment to evaluate the guidance you have provided for the users of your visualization.

### Filters

People who regularly use dashboards will likely be used to applying filters to limit the results shown in a visualization. When you include filters to enable interactivity, it is important to add instructions on how to use them. Otherwise, those who are unfamiliar with filters will never explore the data this way, resulting in a missed opportunity to engage with your viewers.

Charlie Hutcheson visualized Formula E race results, as seen in Figure 11.14, and added a filter for race venue and date in the top right corner of the dashboard. His instruction reads, "Select race venue and date," encouraging his audience to explore the dashboard.

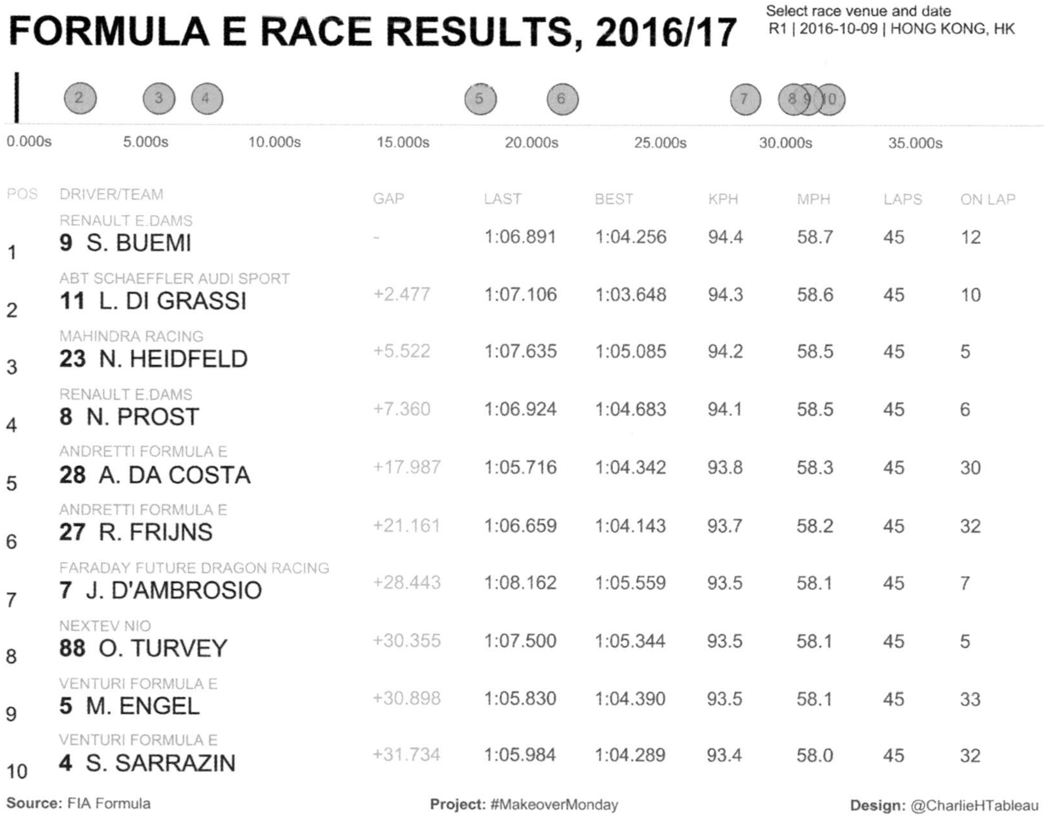

# FORMULA E RACE RESULTS, 2016/17

Select race venue and date
R1 | 2016-10-09 | HONG KONG, HK

| POS | DRIVER/TEAM | GAP | LAST | BEST | KPH | MPH | LAPS | ON LAP |
|---|---|---|---|---|---|---|---|---|
| 1 | RENAULT E.DAMS **9** S. BUEMI | – | 1:06.891 | 1:04.256 | 94.4 | 58.7 | 45 | 12 |
| 2 | ABT SCHAEFFLER AUDI SPORT **11** L. DI GRASSI | +2.477 | 1:07.106 | 1:03.648 | 94.3 | 58.6 | 45 | 10 |
| 3 | MAHINDRA RACING **23** N. HEIDFELD | +5.522 | 1:07.635 | 1:05.085 | 94.2 | 58.5 | 45 | 5 |
| 4 | RENAULT E.DAMS **8** N. PROST | +7.360 | 1:06.924 | 1:04.683 | 94.1 | 58.5 | 45 | 6 |
| 5 | ANDRETTI FORMULA E **28** A. DA COSTA | +17.987 | 1:05.716 | 1:04.342 | 93.8 | 58.3 | 45 | 30 |
| 6 | ANDRETTI FORMULA E **27** R. FRIJNS | +21.161 | 1:06.659 | 1:04.143 | 93.7 | 58.2 | 45 | 32 |
| 7 | FARADAY FUTURE DRAGON RACING **7** J. D'AMBROSIO | +28.443 | 1:08.162 | 1:05.559 | 93.5 | 58.1 | 45 | 7 |
| 8 | NEXTEV NIO **88** O. TURVEY | +30.355 | 1:07.500 | 1:05.344 | 93.5 | 58.1 | 45 | 5 |
| 9 | VENTURI FORMULA E **5** M. ENGEL | +30.898 | 1:05.830 | 1:04.390 | 93.5 | 58.1 | 45 | 33 |
| 10 | VENTURI FORMULA E **4** S. SARRAZIN | +31.734 | 1:05.984 | 1:04.289 | 93.4 | 58.0 | 45 | 32 |

**Source:** FIA Formula          **Project:** #MakeoverMonday          **Design:** @CharlieHTableau

**FIGURE 11.14** Adding simple instructions to your visualization encourages your audience to interact with the visualization and explore the data further.

If motor racing fans were to use Charlie's dashboard, they may filter the results to show a recent race. This makes the dashboard relevant for the individual audience members.

### Hover Interactivity

Filters are probably the most well-known type of interactions people use on dashboards and many data visualization tools offer additional layers of interactivity. In Figure 11.15, Lawer Akrofi visualized

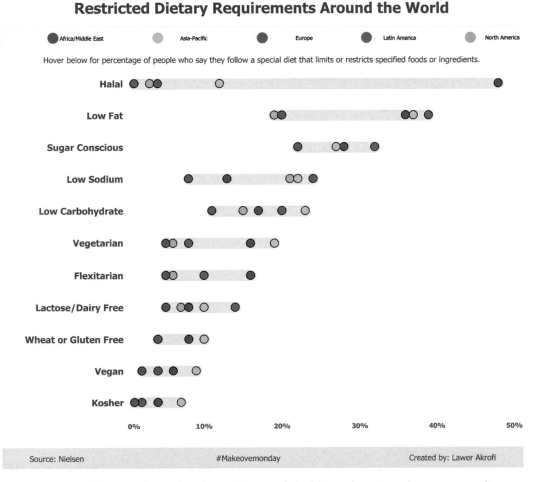

**FIGURE 11.15** Clear and concise descriptions of dashboard actions show your audience that more information can be accessed by through interactivity on the visualization.

restricted dietary requirements around the world and added an option to highlight as you hover over the color legend. There is also the option to hover over a specific data point to see the percentage of people following a diet displayed in the tooltip.

Lawer's brief instruction below the color legend informs the audience that there is more information available if they hover over different parts of the dashboard.

## Explanations

While instructions tell your audience *how* to interact with your visualization, explanations actually describe the data, the results of your analysis, and your findings. In data visualization, a very descriptive, text-heavy approach can be counterproductive to visual analysis and data exploration. When you combine color or icon legends with descriptions in a single sentence, you save space on the screen and bring different elements of the visualization together. This provides all the relevant context in one place. The audience does not need to look back and forth across the page to find the information that helps them understand the data and your key message.

### Color Legends in Text

Paweł Wróblewski created the highlight table in Figure 11.16 to visualize data about ozone levels in Los Angeles and used his title as a color legend.

By coloring the words "highest values" in the same shade of red that also represents the highest values, the text immediately communicates the meaning of the color.

Ozone Daily AQI Values in Los Angeles takes the **highest values** from May to September

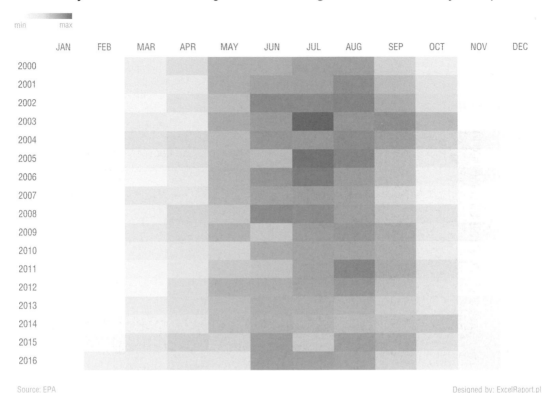

**FIGURE 11.16**  Coloring specific parts of the title to correspond with the visualization gives your audience an immediate understanding of the significance of the color chosen.

Consider Figure 11.17 from Jamie Briggs, who analyzed data about the Tate art collection. His title is a summary statement to show the dominance in numbers of J.M.W. Turner's paintings compared to all other artists.

Jamie highlights this effectively by coloring all references to Turner in the same shade of blue as the bar chart. The title describes the key finding in a single sentence and intuitively explains the colors used in the visualization. Repeating the blue color for Turner in the descriptive text on the right further enhances the focus of the visualization.

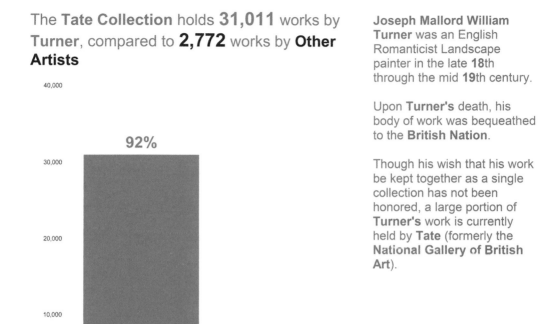

The **Tate Collection** holds **31,011** works by Turner, compared to **2,772** works by **Other Artists**

**Joseph Mallord William Turner** was an English Romanticist Landscape painter in the late **18**th through the mid **19**th century.

Upon **Turner's** death, his body of work was bequeathed to the **British Nation**.

Though his wish that his work be kept together as a single collection has not been honored, a large portion of **Turner's** work is currently held by **Tate** (formerly the **National Gallery of British Art**).

By Source, Fair use,
https://en.wikipedia.org/w/index.php?curid=50936222

Design: Jamie Briggs (@indented)
MakeoverMonday, 2017 week 24 | http://www.makeovermonday.co.uk/

Data Source: https://github.com/tategallery/collection
http://research.kraeutli.com/index.php/2013/11/the-tate-collection-on-github/

**FIGURE 11.17**   Applying two different colors to the title text relates artists clearly to their respective bars in the bar chart.

## Annotations

Annotations are small sections of text, a few words, or a short sentence, placed inside your visualization and associated with specific data points. They are commonly used to highlight outliers, describe a particular point in time, or show how a data point contributes to an interesting insight.

As seen in Figure 11.18, Shawn Levin created a vertical timeline of Andy's credit card spending and used annotations that outline the "Road to the 2016 New York City Marathon."

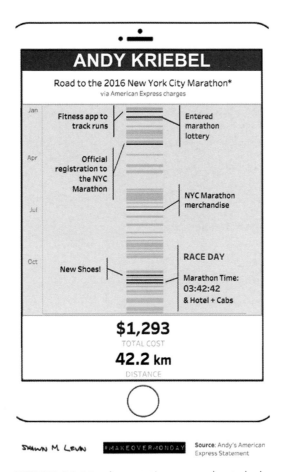

**FIGURE 11.18**   Annotating your charts helps guide your audience through different parts of your analysis and the key data points in your visualization.

Shawn investigated the spending categories and looked at running-related purchases that could be linked to the New York Marathon. Shawn added annotations only to the relevant data points, while other purchases throughout the year are visualized using gray lines for context.

Lindsey Poulter visualized data for the NCAA Basketball Tournament in the US in Figure 11.19, using historical data to show what seeded teams made it to the Final Four stage of the competition.

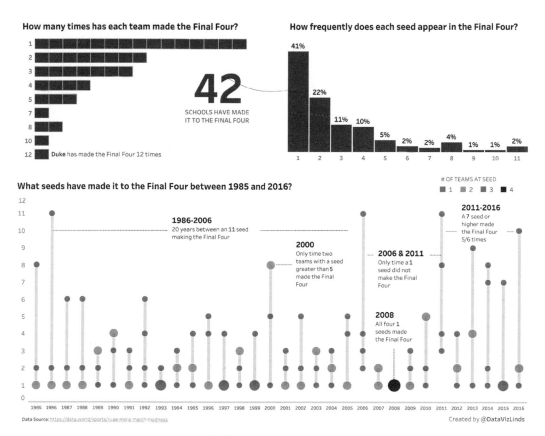

**FIGURE 11.19**   Annotations typically focus on the most important, interesting, or surprising data points and provide contextual information for your audience.

Lindsey's use of annotations in the timeline are an excellent example of how insights and further information can be added for specific data points and timeframes. Without these annotations the audience may be left wondering *so what*? By including the additional text, Lindsey helps the audience understand the data and the context.

*Labels*

Labels can be used as reference points in your visualization and allow you to remove gridlines and axis lines. When you do not need or want to use annotations in your work, labels can be a good alternative for highlighting specific values in your data.

Colin Wojtowycz analyzed data on drug exporting nations in Figure 11.20 and created a simple bar chart using labels for the data values at the end of each bar.

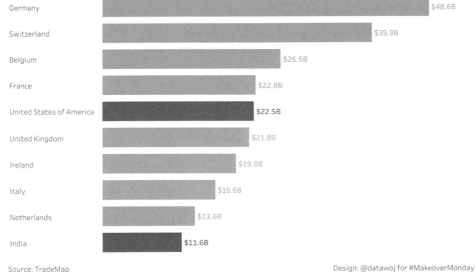

**In 2016, the USA and India were the only non-European countries in the top 10 exporters of drugs and medicines**

Top 10 exporting countries of drugs and medicines in $USD in 2016

| | |
|---|---|
| Germany | $48.6B |
| Switzerland | $39.9B |
| Belgium | $26.5B |
| France | $22.8B |
| United States of America | $22.5B |
| United Kingdom | $21.8B |
| Ireland | $19.8B |
| Italy | $16.6B |
| Netherlands | $13.6B |
| India | $11.6B |

Source: TradeMap                                    Design: @datawoj for #MakeoverMonday

**FIGURE 11.20**   Stating the actual values of different data points adds precision and shows the contribution of each attribute.

Adding labels meant that Colin could remove all lines from the chart, while still allowing his audience to know which values the bars represent.

In Figure 11.21, Charlie Hutcheson considered data about the usage of social media platforms by teenagers in the US and visualized it using a bar chart to compare Snapchat's dominance over the other social networks.

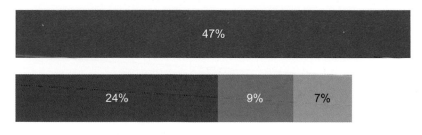

**US teens rank Snapchat as favourite social network**
More than **Instagram, Facebook** and **Twitter** - combined!

47%

24%    9%    7%

Source: Piper Jaffray                    Design: @CharlieHTableau for #MakeoverMonday

**FIGURE 11.21**   Percentage-of-total labels give the audience a better understanding of the significance of Snapchat compared to the other social networks.

His inclusion of labels on the bars, especially the stacked bar chart that combines Instagram, Facebook, and Twitter, helps relate the apps to one another. Note that Colin and Charlie also used colors on the text in their titles and subtitles to explain the colors of the bars in their visualizations.

You do not have to label every data point or category in your visualization. In fact, this could result in a very "busy"-looking dashboard. It is important to find the balance between labeling those points that help your audience better understand your message and keeping the visualization uncluttered, so your viewers can focus on the essential aspects.

*Tooltips*

Tooltips can provide useful layers of information when you want to give your audience additional information without adding it directly into your visualization. Sarah Bartlett formatted her tooltips to make them responsive, engaging, and impactful. Her infographic (Figure 11.22) about US birth statistics is an example of great use of tooltips.

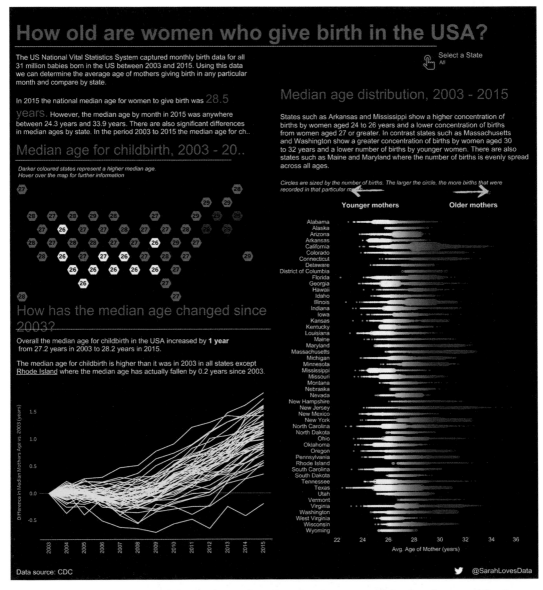

**FIGURE 11.22** Text is used throughout this visualization to explain the data and findings and make the analysis more accessible for the audience.

The dashboard itself provides a very comprehensive overview of the data that is supplemented by dynamic tooltips that appear whenever you hover over data points in one of the three charts. See Figure 11.23. The "median age for childbirth" tile map is supported by a tooltip that displays the median age of mothers when giving birth.

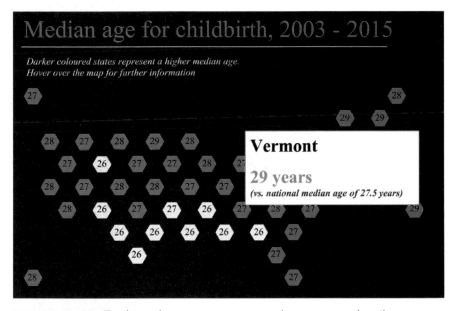

**FIGURE 11.23** Tooltips that appear as a user hovers over the tile map show additional information for each state.

The median age distribution chart shows the number of births (one circle for each birth) across a range of ages displayed on the x-axis. The tooltip includes additional information in a couple of plain English sentences. This helps provide the context in which the data needs to be understood. See Figure 11.24.

Tooltips are a neat way to make your visualization stand out and show your analysis and design skills at various levels of detail in your work. Make sure that you inform your audience somewhere on your visualization that additional information is available when they hover over a data point.

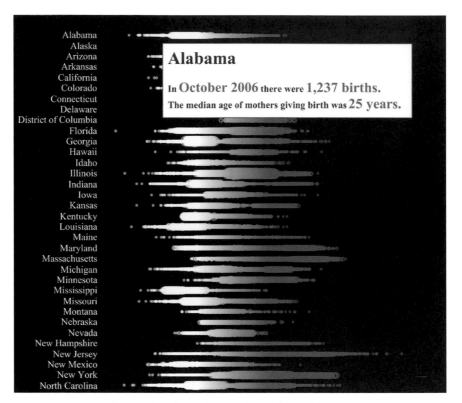

**FIGURE 11.24**   The tooltip lists the total number of births per month and the median age of the mother. This information is provided in complete English sentences.

## Summary

In this chapter we focused on the effective use of text to let your insights shine and your visualization tell a story that captivates your audience. By using titles, subtitles, large numbers, calls to action, explanatory text, instructions, labels, and tooltips, you can help communicate information clearly to your audience. Use text sparingly and deliberately. Consider removing text and see if it changes your message. If the message changes, then put the text back. If removing the text does not impact the key message, then leave it out.

## Chapter Twelve

# Using Context to Inform

Providing your audience with context about the data, the subject, and the impact of your findings helps them draw meaningful conclusions and understand the relevance of your analysis. When you work with data and spend time analyzing and visualizing it, you need to ensure you give your audience enough background information to set the scene. If you jump straight into the detail, you will lose your audience very quickly and leave them confused, uninspired, and potentially misinformed.

For Makeover Monday, we select data sets from a variety of topics and urge our participants to give their audience sufficient context, because if the subject is unfamiliar to our community, it is probably unfamiliar to their audience as well.

This chapter describes why context is important, how you can communicate context easily, and how context allows you to inform your audience more effectively.

## The Importance of Context

In everyday life, you come across numbers constantly. People tell you how tall their children are, friends talk about the results of a football match, and the news reports on the latest company revenues. Numbers are just numbers, though, and they do not mean much in isolation.

Rather than accepting the numbers as facts and the partial information they offer, you should ask probing questions to put these numbers into context. This will help you understand whether the results are good, bad, or as expected.

Here are some simple examples of adding context to numbers:

- My five-year-old daughter is 44" tall.
  - Is that taller or shorter than the typical five-year-old girl?
  - How much has she grown in the past six months?
  - Is she taller than you were at that age?
- The Golden State Warriors beat the Cleveland Cavaliers 108:85.
  - How does this compare to the last times these two teams played each other?
  - What is their average score per match?
  - What did the bookmakers suggest the final score would be?
- In 2017, Microsoft reported revenues of 89.95 billion USD.
  - Is this result better than the previous year?
  - What was the overall profit?
  - How does this result compare to their rivals?
  - How did the stock market view the results? Did the share price rise?

There are numerous angles to take on any piece of information and different audiences will have different interests and questions about your work. Providing context with your visualization allows you to show your audience how you want your work to be understood, what information you worked with, what you focused on, and how the different parts of your analysis work together.

## Lack of Context

Before you dive into the usefulness of contextual information, look at what happens to your understanding when no context is provided. For this purpose, consider Figure 12.1, a stripped-down version of one of Andy's visualizations. All information aside from the title and the line chart has been stripped off.

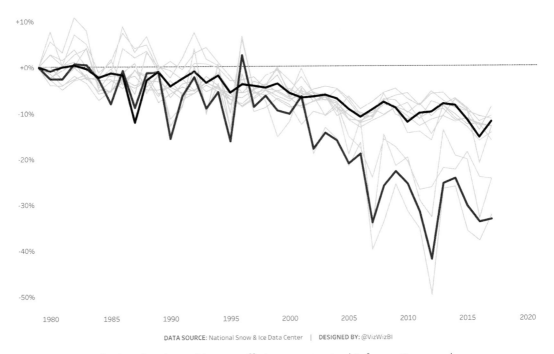

**FIGURE 12.1** A visualization without sufficient contextual information can leave your audience confused as to what your message is.

Does this chart provide you with valuable insights? You can make the following assumptions:

1. The topic is the melting ice in the Arctic.

2. The lines in the chart are going down with noticeable spikes.

3. There are a black and a red line and a number of gray lines.

Because context is not provided, you cannot answer any of the following questions from this visualization:

- What do the colors of the different lines mean?
- How can I identify the summer months referred to in the title?
- What do the percentages on the y-axis represent?
- Are things getting worse over time, and if so, how much worse are they now compared to when measurements began?
- What is the significance of the starting point of the lines? Why do they all meet at the far left?

Not having the relevant context available makes it difficult for us to understand the full picture and to truly appreciate what the author of a visualization wants to communicate.

In the following sections, we will gradually add contextual details to show you how they help you communicate information more effectively.

## Using Simple Metrics

Simplicity is important for communicating effectively, especially when the topic is new for the audience or is complex and needs to be broken down into easy-to-understand components. Complicated metrics require mental gymnastics to understand them. And even then you sometimes do not know what exactly the creator wanted to achieve with a particular metric.

Using basic metrics that are easy to understand will help you get your point across and encourage your audience to interact with your work. Comparing metrics such as sales or profit gives your audience proper context to understand what has been presented.

Figure 12.2 builds on Andy's previous visualization by adding a simple metric that compares the extent of Arctic sea ice in each year to 1979, the first year that the data was collected. Does adding this small amount of contextual information back into the visualization help improve your understanding?

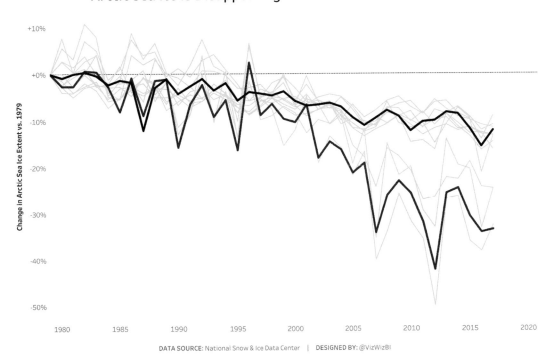

FIGURE 12.2    Metrics that are easy to understand and labeled clearly help you communicate your message to your audience

The only additional information is the axis label for the y-axis. It reads "Change in Arctic Sea Ice Extent vs. 1979." This small axis label alone allows us to answer two of our original questions:

1. What do the percentages on the y-axis represent?
   *Answer:* The percentages represent the change compared to 1979. This is expressed in percentages, with positive numbers showing more ice and negative numbers showing less ice than in 1979.

2. What is the significance of the starting point of the lines? Why do they all meet at the far left?
   *Answer:* All the lines start at 1979, which is the first year for which data was available in this data set. From there the lines diverge as the data is compared to 1979.

How can you answer the remaining questions? We'll gradually complete Andy's dashboard over the remainder of this chapter by continuing to add a few more elements of contextual information.

## Big Ass Numbers

Big Ass Numbers (BANs), which you can also read about in Chapter 11, "Effective Use of Text," are large numbers on a visualization that capture your audience's attention and let you make a precise statement. BANs can be a great supportive element in your visualization, when done well as part of the overall design.

### Ineffective Example

We challenged the Makeover Monday community to visualize data about the Tate collection of artworks. Eva created the image seen in Figure 12.3, focusing on the artworks created by J.M.W. Turner.

While Eva included BANs to show the sheer volume of artworks created by Turner, there are actually four large numbers, all competing for attention. A single BAN would have worked much better, with the remaining numbers turned into unit charts.

# What was Turner up to?

The Tate Collection lists

# 31,010

items by **Joseph Mallord William Turner** that were created between

1787 ——————————— and ——————————— 1844

Of these paintings and drawings,
an astonishing

# 20,342

were done using **graphite on paper**

---

For the layout of his **graphite on paper** artwork Turner favors

PORTRAIT     over     LANDSCAPE

11,175
titles

9,167
titles

Design: @TriMyData
Data: Tate Collection on GitHub

**FIGURE 12.3** Using multiple BANs in different sizes and font colors across your visualization makes them less effective as they compete for attention.

*Effective Example*

When you add BANs to Andy's visualization, as in Figure 12.4, they enhance the understanding of the chart and give the audience useful context.

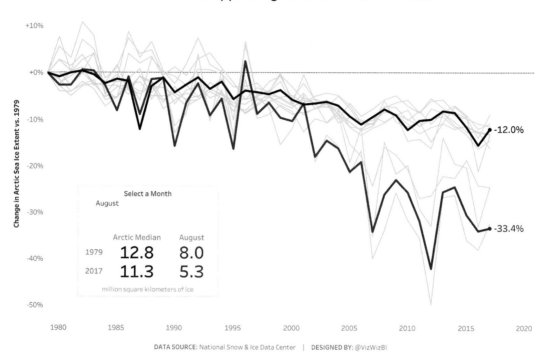

FIGURE 12.4   Adding well-positioned BANs in your visualization shows your audience what to focus on and aids their understanding.

Having the right amount of information displayed with BANs and labeling the end of the black and red lines highlights the key figures based on a selection the audience can make. When choosing a particular month additional black and red BANs show the difference between the Arctic median (black line and black number) and the median of the chosen month (red line and red number), in this case August. The viewer's eyes are immediately drawn to these numbers. The stark difference between the black and the red numbers helps Andy make his visualization more impactful.

## Color Coding

Using colors is another effective way to add context and provide additional information in your visualization. It is important not to overdo it, though. Use color sparingly yet deliberately, so that it has maximum impact.

### Ineffective Example

Too often we have seen visualizations similar to Figure 12.5 that use an abundance of colors.

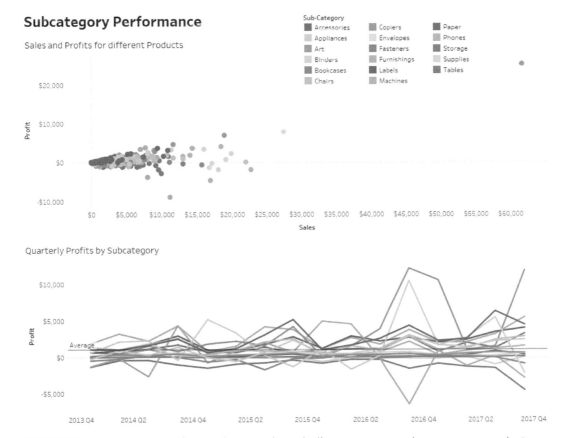

**FIGURE 12.5**  Using more than a dozen colors challenges your audience to move their eyes constantly between chart and color legend to make sense of the data.

The use of color to show different subcategories results in a scatterplot and a line chart with 17 different colors. That is not helpful for anyone looking at this visualization, especially if you ask yourself questions like:

- Which subcategories were profitable?
- Were there any quarters during which all subcategories were profitable?
- Which subcategory sold the most?

Too many colors result in an increased cognitive load because the users of your visualization need to remember the meaning of each color as they scan the page. By changing the color to show profitability in the existing two charts, they would be more effective at providing a quick overview of the results. Alternatively, color could be applied to a single subcategory to show its performance against all other subcategories.

*Effective Example*

In Andy's visualization, colors are used sparingly with most of the lines in the chart being gray and only two lines being highlighted: one in black and one in red. Figure 12.6 adds a color legend to the visualization, helping to quickly explain the meaning of black and red lines.

The color legend reminds us that the black line is the median across all months, while the red line represents the month chosen. Using the color for the highlighted month helps the audience explore the visualization because when you change the month, the visualization changes to reflect the color to focus on. Having a single highlight color, one reference color (black), and one context color (gray) means you know what to focus on immediately. Repeating the red and black across the lines, the color legend, and the box with the BANs helps reinforce the message.

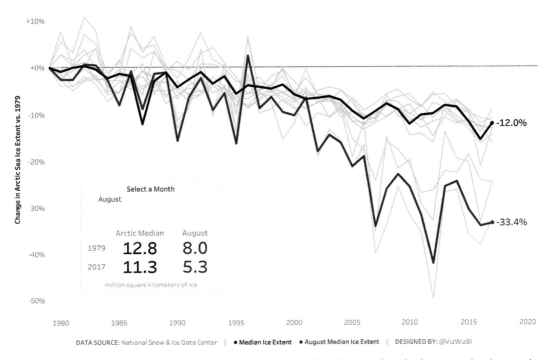

FIGURE 12.6   Applying minimal color to highlight the data and including a color legend creates clarity for your audience.

The color legend allows us to answer an additional question from the list we compiled earlier:

- What do the colors of the different lines mean?
  *Answer*: The black line shows the median ice extent, while the red line shows the median ice extent for a chosen month, in this case August.

## Reference Lines

Reference lines provide a point to which you compare any other results. Common use cases for reference lines are:

- Revenue of the previous quarter or year
- Points scored during the last season
- Target units sold
- Median house price for a country
- Average sales across a year

Reference lines are an excellent way to put any number into context. When visualizing data, your audience wants to know whether a result is good or bad, what it means to them, and so on. A reference line can give them this information by showing where their sports team is compared to their performance in the previous season. Your CFO will be interested to know how the current quarter's revenue compares to the previous quarter and the same quarter in the previous year, and the like.

### Ineffective Example

It can be very helpful to include a reference line in your visualization, yet some reference lines are neither clear nor allow for insights.

Using the colorful line chart from the previous section again, we have added *average profit* as a reference line in Figure 12.7. You may find it difficult even to see that reference line because it is thin, gray, and does not stand out against all of the colors. Additionally, with so much variation in the profit figures of each subcategory, an average is not very meaningful.

Quarterly Profits by Subcategory

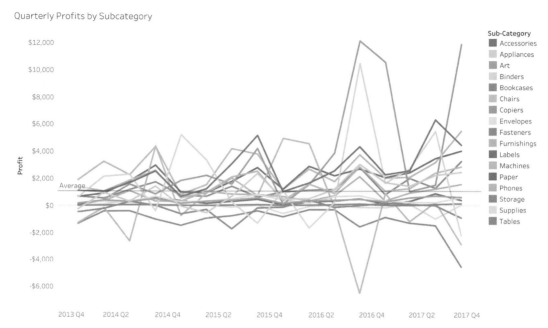

**FIGURE 12.7**   The reference line becomes almost invisible among the multitude of colored lines and is therefore ineffective at providing contextual information.

## Effective Example

Consider Andy's dashboard again as seen in Figure 12.8. The black reference line shows the median ice extent. This is effective because the median, as the middle value of the data, gives a reference point that is not skewed by extreme points in the data. The reference line helps us see how much of an impact the higher temperatures have on the ice melting (the lines further below the black line) and that the overall ice extent is decreasing, as shown by the downward trend of the black line as well as the label of −12%.

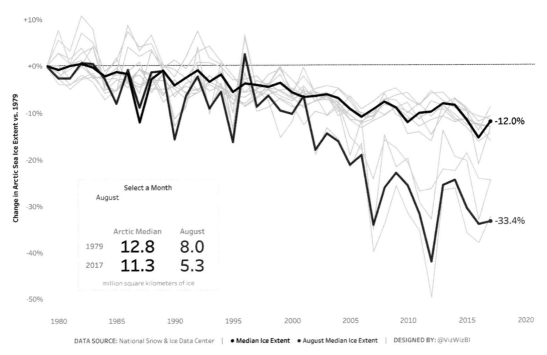

**FIGURE 12.8** The black reference line is darker and thicker than the gray lines and can easily be compared to the red line.

When you use a reference line, make sure the metric you choose is logical in the context of your analysis and insights. Letting your reference line stand out, like Andy did, helps provide context for your audience, which in turn allows them to better understand your insights. For the melting Arctic ice, you can see that the median extent has decreased by 12% since 1979, and you will probably be even more shocked to see that the August decrease has reached 33.4% in 2017 compared to 1979!

## Tooltips

Tooltips are an effective way to provide contextual information to your audience in an interactive visualization without cluttering up your charts. Tooltips are the little boxes with information or additional charts that appear as you move your mouse over an interactive visualization.

### Ineffective Example

In the performance dashboard for various subcategories in Figure 12.9, you can see poorly executed tooltips.

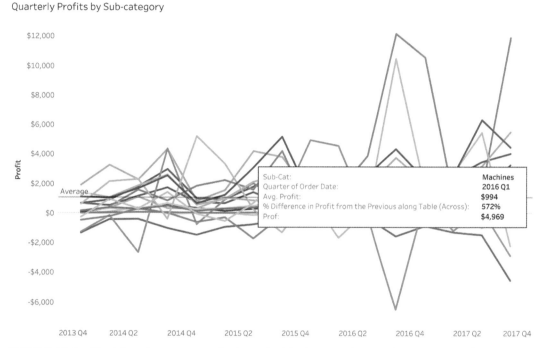

FIGURE 12.9    Tooltips that are not designed with the user in mind are a wasted opportunity to provide additional information for your audience.

The tooltip shows the key metrics, but the formatting is poor, the descriptions are abbreviated, and the alignment makes the tooltip difficult to read. A few basic tidy-ups would make this much more effective. Do not neglect your tooltips when you publish your visualizations.

*Effective Example*

In Figure 12.10, Andy chose to update his tooltips to achieve consistency with the overall design of his visualization and to provide information about those data points that were not labeled in his view (i.e., the gray lines).

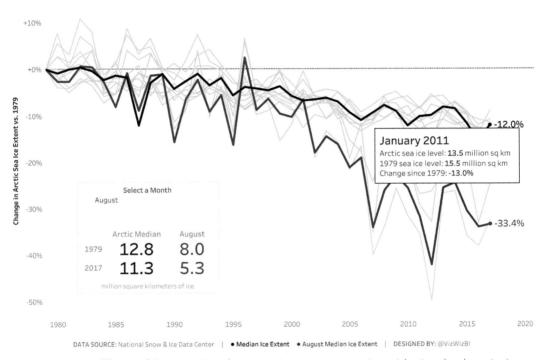

### Arctic Sea Ice is Disappearing Fastest in Summer Months

> January 2011
> Arctic sea ice level: **13.5** million sq km
> 1979 sea ice level: **15.5** million sq km
> Change since 1979: **-13.0%**

-12.0%

-33.4%

Select a Month
August

|        | Arctic Median | August |
|--------|---------------|--------|
| 1979   | **12.8**      | **8.0** |
| 2017   | **11.3**      | **5.3** |

million square kilometers of ice

DATA SOURCE: National Snow & Ice Data Center   |   ● Median Ice Extent   ● August Median Ice Extent   |   DESIGNED BY: @VizWizBI

**FIGURE 12.10**   The tooltip contains the most important metrics with simple descriptions and clearly states the month and year of the data point.

The interactive tooltips provide information about actual sea ice levels, as well as the change since 1979. By adding this contextual information, Andy provides the same details for all lines, just at different levels of interactivity. Most importantly, his viewers can see the month and year of each data point to help identify the months with the largest decrease of ice (those clustered around the red August line) and those months that are closely aligned to the median.

You can now answer a further question:

- How can I identify the summer months referred to in the title?
  *Answer*: The control with the title "Select a Month" lets the audience identify a particular month. By hovering over the gray lines with a similar pattern to August, the summer months can be identified via the information provided in the tooltip and the line you hover over will be highlighted against the remaining months.

## Subtitles

While the title for a visualization sets the scene, a subtitle provides additional information in a short sentence or two, further guiding your audience and aiding their understanding of your analysis. A subtitle can feature your key insights, describe the data set, explain how the data was collected, and serve as a place to explain the colors and metrics used.

### Ineffective Example

An ineffective subtitle represents a lost opportunity to inform your audience and to provoke their curiosity in a subject. In Figure 12.11, the subtitle does not add any value that you could not gain simply from looking at the axis labels.

The subtitle merely states the obvious; it names the metrics contained in the dashboard (profit and sales) and the field by which the data is broken down (subcategory). A more effective subtitle would include summary insights.

## Subcategory Performance
Profits and Sales for Product Subcategories

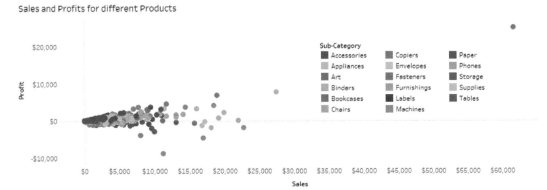

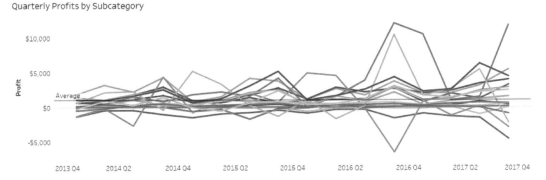

**FIGURE 12.11**    The subtitle is used to state the metrics and fields used in the charts, instead of stating some of the insights from the analysis.

### Effective Example

In Figure 12.12, Andy used the subtitle in his visualization to explain the key findings to his audience in three straightforward sentences.

The subtitle explains:

- The amount of Arctic sea ice that has disappeared between 1979 and 2017.
- The analysis relates every month and year back to 1979.

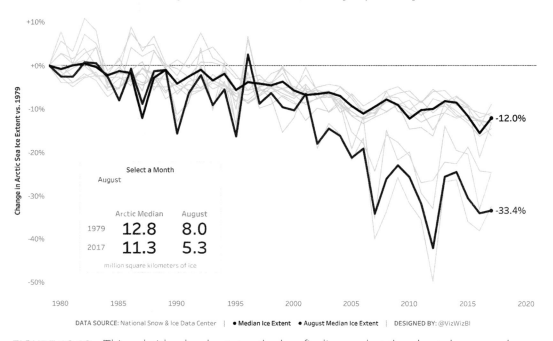

**FIGURE 12.12**   This subtitle clearly states the key findings, what the chart shows, and what the results mean for the environment.

- There is a link between warmer summers and the accelerated decrease of sea ice.
- In general, less ice equals warmer weather, which equals accelerated melting of ice.

In dashboards using scientific data like Andy's, it is helpful to use the subtitle as a description, outlining in plain English what the significant findings were so that an audience of laypeople can gain value and better understanding of the topic from the analysis and visualization.

## Methods for Communicating Context

Now that you have thoroughly dissected Andy's visualization of melting Arctic ice, look at a few more methods for communicating context. The following section goes through a variety of visualizations on different topics, each showing an ineffective chart or dashboard first, followed by an effective example.

### Indicators and Arrows

Indicators and arrows are commonly used in dashboards to quickly show performance against a reference point. For example, if the quarterly revenue figures are below target, a downward arrow, colored in red, can be placed next to charts or numbers to indicate, at a glance, whether a result is good or bad.

*Ineffective Example*

In Figure 12.13, indicator arrows were used to show whether profits were positive or negative at an annual basis for different regions in Italy. Giving your audience this first impression can be helpful, but if you stop there, your viewers will wonder what they should do with this information.

The arrows provide an overall impression of the performance of each region, showing profits as green upward arrows and losses as red downward arrows. However, this information should be extended to include some additional detail. For example:

- How big were the profits and losses for each region and what were the contributions to the overall Italian market?
- Given that you are looking at the annual results, did each region trade for all periods during each year?
- Which cities or products contributed to the performance?

Indicators alone will rarely be effective in communicating your message to the audience. By including additional information for context, you will provide a more complete picture.

# Profit for Italian Regions

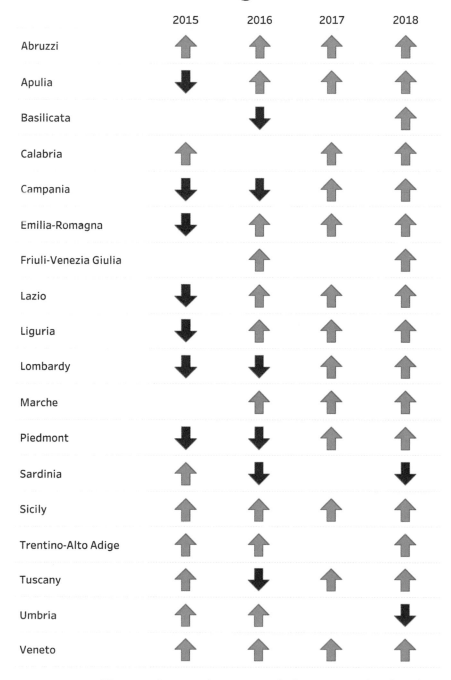

**FIGURE 12.13**  These indicators do not specify the magnitude of profits or losses and how the different regions compare to each other.

*Effective Example*

Figure 12.14 uses arrows to indicate whether a result is positive or negative. Amar Donthala shows that meat consumption trends are increasing for chicken and turkey but decreasing for beef and pork.

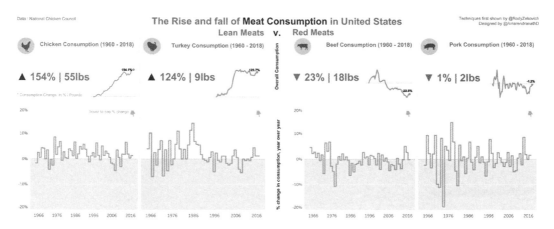

**FIGURE 12.14**   Indicators are more effective in combination with percentage figures and actual consumption statistics.

Amar listed the percentage values to show how much consumption has grown or declined for a given meat product. The downward or upward arrow next to those numbers makes it clear whether it was growth or decline and this is further visually supported by the small sparkline next to the total numbers, showing how the consumption developed over time.

## Comparing Time Periods

Comparing the performance between specific points in time is a useful method to add context for time series data. For example, profit achieved in one quarter can be compared to profit achieved in a previous quarter or to the same quarter in the previous year.

*Ineffective Example*

Figure 12.15 contains information about the profits achieved by different departments from Q1 2014 through Q4 2017.

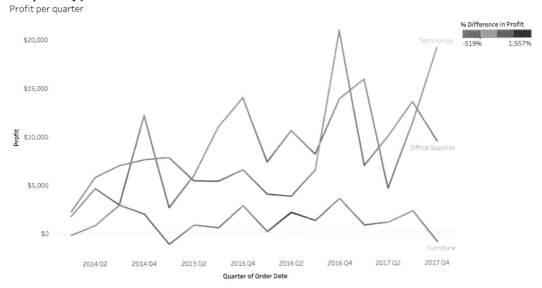

**Did quarterly profits increase or decrease?**

Profit per quarter

**FIGURE 12.15**   Comparing quarterly results on a single continuous timeline is difficult because quarterly differences are not as easy to see.

While the colors indicate whether profits decreased or increased from one quarter to the next, there is limited value in this information alone and quarterly results could be displayed differently to focus more on profits. A simple change of the view, as in Figure 12.16, allows us to look at each quarter's performance over time. Color has been applied to the product category to differentiate those lines more clearly.

**Did quarterly profits increase or decrease?**

Profit per quarter

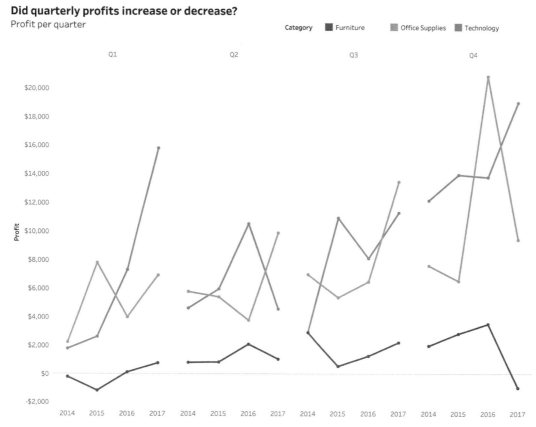

**FIGURE 12.16**   Dividing the chart into quarters and showing performance over the years makes the comparison of quarters easier.

### Effective Example

Using date and time fields to add context to your visualization can work really well, as you can see in Andy's visualization of UK economic growth in Figure 12.17.

Quarterly analysis is a relevant and logical way to approach economic and financial data. There are commonalities for each quarter in the UK (e.g., Q3 features the summer slowdown, while Q4 includes the busy Christmas and holiday season).

## Which Quarter Performs Best in the UK Economy?

At +0.64% growth, **Q3** has the highest **average quarterly growth** in the UK. Comparing the **change vs. the previous quarter** to the historical average, **Q4** outperforms by the largest margin.

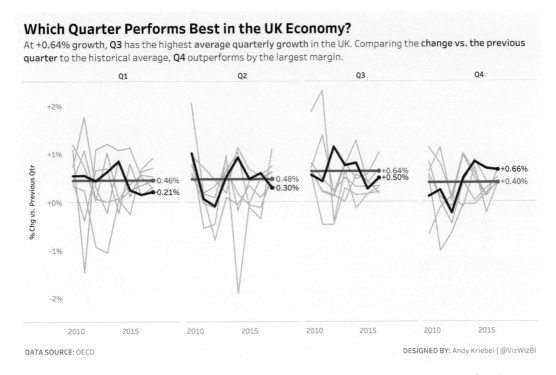

**DATA SOURCE:** OECD

**DESIGNED BY:** Andy Kriebel | @VizWizBI

**FIGURE 12.17** Economic performance is often viewed in quarters to account for the impact of summer months and holiday seasons.

Andy added other G7 countries for context in gray, highlighted the average quarterly growth for the UK in blue, and used red to indicate the change to the previous quarter.

## Normalizing the Data

Data is often not normalized, for instance when you analyze country-level data for different metrics. Normalizing data brings values that are on different scales into a common range.[1] What this means for country-level data is that every metric should be on a per capita

---
[1] en.wikipedia.org/wiki/Normalization_(statistics)

basis. This makes the results comparable across countries regardless of a nation's population (e.g., you can now compare China and Luxembourg for different indicators).

### Ineffective Example

In Figure 12.18, the lines correspond to the total ecological consumption per country since 1961. The design highlights China as an outlier.

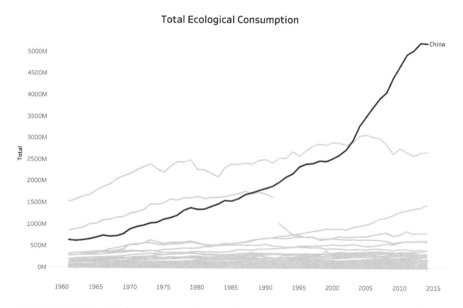

**FIGURE 12.18**   Without normalizing the data, very populous nations like China and India will appear as outliers for resource consumption at a total level.

Note that the data is the total consumption for each country. China has the largest population in the world, therefore you would expect China to have the largest ecological consumption. A more effective way to communicate the data is to represent the consumption on a per capita basis, as in Figure 12.19.

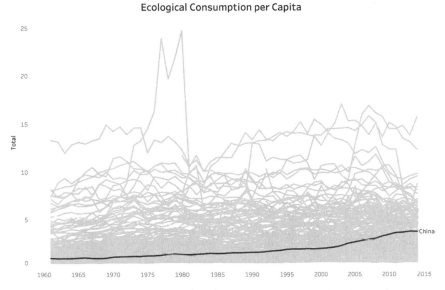

**FIGURE 12.19**   At a per capita level, comparing countries is much more appropriate and the results for China now appear very differently.

Normalizing the data gives a completely different picture. China is actually near the bottom half on the basis of consumption per capita.

*Effective Example*

In her visualization of different countries' ecological footprint and biocapacity, as seen in Figure 12.20, Luisa Bez used per capita indicators so that her audience can easily compare the results of different countries.

Comparing the total impact of countries would skew the results because very populous countries will have more negative results simply based on the number of people living in each country. Luisa analyzed the data on a per capita basis to make the countries more comparable.

### Are we exceeding the Earth's resources?

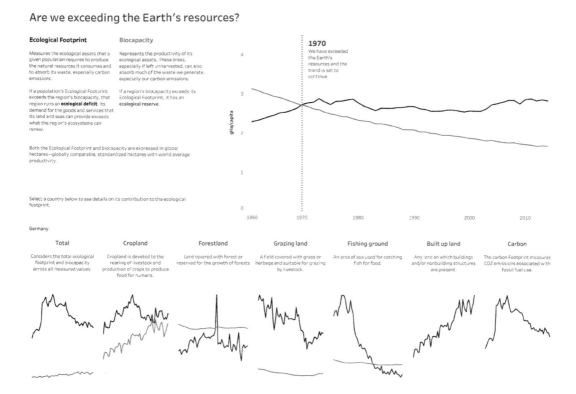

**Ecological Footprint**

Measures the ecological assets that a given population requires to produce the natural resources it consumes and to absorb its waste, especially carbon emissions.

If a population's Ecological Footprint exceeds the region's biocapacity, that region runs an **ecological deficit**. Its demand for the goods and services that its land and seas can provide exceeds what the region's ecosystems can renew.

Both the Ecological Footprint and biocapacity are expressed in global hectares—globally comparable, standardized hectares with world average productivity.

Select a country below to see details on its contribution to the ecological footprint.

**Biocapacity**

Represents the productivity of its ecological assets. These areas, especially if left unharvested, can also absorb much of the waste we generate, especially our carbon emissions.

If a region's biocapacity exceeds its Ecological Footprint, it has an **ecological reserve**.

**1970**
We have exceeded the Earth's resources and the trend is set to continue

Germany

| Total | Cropland | Forestland | Grazing land | Fishing ground | Built up land | Carbon |
|---|---|---|---|---|---|---|
| Considers the total ecological footprint and biocapacity across all measured values. | Cropland is devoted to the rearing of livestock and production of crops to produce food for humans. | Land covered with forest or reserved for the growth of forests | A field covered with grass or herbage and suitable for grazing by livestock. | An area of sea used for catching fish for food. | Any land on which buildings and/or nonbuilding structures are present. | The carbon Footprint measures CO2 emissions associated with fossil fuel use. |

**Source:** Global Footprint Network

**Designed by:** Luisa Bez

**FIGURE 12.20** Highlighting detailed metrics at a per capita level for an individual country creates a country profile that can be compared to a benchmark.

## Supplementing the Data

For Makeover Monday we provide a single data set each week. The data can be used as is or additional data sources can be used to supplement the data set. Including additional data allows participants to delve deeper into a particular analysis and find additional insights or context to make their analysis more impactful.

### Ineffective Example

Supplementing data just for the sake of it and drawing conclusions that are not substantiated creates the risk of losing credibility. Sometimes there simply is not an insightful story in a data set and adding more data just makes things worse. In these situations, pick a clear story. If it does not make sense to supplement the original data with more information, do not feel compelled to do so.

### Effective Example

In Figure 12.21, Gina Reynolds used additional data when she visualized the prices of meals at Wetherspoon pubs in the UK. By supplementing her data with geographical information about the distance of a pub relative to Big Ben in the heart of London, she was able to show a clear decrease in prices the further away a pub was located from Big Ben.

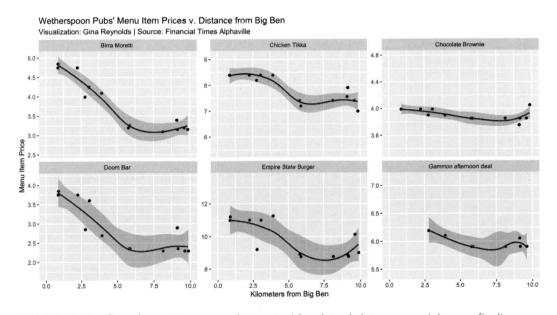

**FIGURE 12.21**  Supplementing your data set with related data can enrich your findings and make them more relevant for your audience.

Supplementing a data set with interesting data to enrich your visualization can be very effective in communicating a stronger message.

## Summary

When you give your audience sufficient context alongside your data visualization, you help them understand your message more easily. Effective ways to achieve this include:

- Simple metrics communicated through large numbers
- Color coding and highlighting
- Reference lines
- Tooltips
- Subtitles

You can also choose additional techniques for providing context in your data including:

- Comparing time periods
- Adding indicators and arrows
- Normalizing the data
- Supplementing your data with further information

Next time you create a data visualization, look at each element and ask yourself, "Compared to what"? If you cannot answer this question, then you have a clear indication that you need to add more context.

# Part III

# The Community

Makeover Monday has grown far beyond the sharing of data sets and visualizations on a weekly basis. The success of the project is due to the community that has embraced the ideas, suggestions, and processes so enthusiastically. The steady growth of the community has shaped the way we run the project. New ideas that are introduced or existing processes that changed are a response to or in anticipation of what will benefit the Makeover Monday community the most. Fundamentally, the project is designed to help you learn, improve, develop, and excel at becoming a better data analyst.

This chapter is an acknowledgment of the many long-term contributors who have helped make Makeover Monday much more successful than the two of us could have achieved on our own. Beyond their consistent contributions, these people have stepped up to help others. Each week brings new participants, and this group has been incredibly helpful with their guidance and coaching.

## Long-Term Contributors

The following is a gallery of the long-term contributors, those who have stayed loyal to the project and engaged with the community since the early days of Makeover Monday. For each person's portrait, we have included their picture, contact details, a statement about their involvement with Makeover Monday, and their favorite visualization from their Makeover Monday portfolio. We encourage you to check out their profiles and their visualizations for inspiration, ideas, and tips on what you can do with the data you are working with.

Adam Crahen. Visualize No Malaria.

Twitter: @acrahen
Website: thedataduo.com
Participant since: week 7, 2016

### In Adam's words:

Makeover Monday is an amazing data viz project and should be considered by anyone trying to hone their craft. I became addicted to the improvements I could see from week to week while participating. It offers a great variety of unique takes on the same data that you can learn from. While practicing, you build a portfolio of work, demonstrate dedication, become visible in the data viz community, and inspire others. I think Makeover Monday opens many doors, including access to experts in the field and building professional contacts for the future. Makeover Monday definitely played a role in helping me find a great new job at Pluralsight.

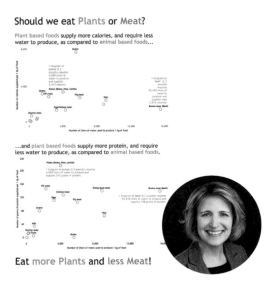

Alicia Bembenek. The Water Footprint of Our Food.

Twitter: @dreamsofdata
Website: dreamsofdatablog.wordpress.com
Participant since: week 21, 2017

### In Alicia's words:

Participating in Makeover Monday has helped me both professionally and personally. On a professional level, I was able to learn and practice new skills, build a portfolio, and share what I learned on my blog. Makeover Monday gave me visibility in the data viz community and I have been contacted with career opportunities as a result of that. On a personal level, the feedback I received through Makeover Monday has given me greater confidence in myself and my abilities. I have also gained new friendships with other Makeover Monday enthusiasts, and it has been wonderful to connect with others and share our experiences and challenges.

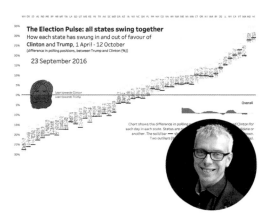

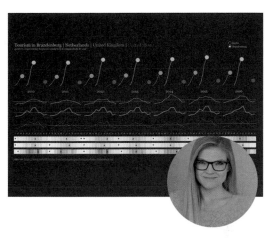

Andy Cotgreave. US Election Tracker.

Twitter: @acotgreave
Website: gravyanecdote.com
Participant since: week 1, 2016

**In Andy's words:**

Makeover Monday is the best data viz project in the world. Seeing hundreds of perspectives on a single data set each week is incredibly valuable. I've also been thrilled to see so many develop their skills over the time they've done Makeover Monday. Makeover Monday generates debate, too. People can try out new techniques and discuss them.

Ann Jackson. Tourism in Brandenburg.

Twitter: @AnnUJackson
Website: jacksontwo.com
Participant since: week 47, 2016

**In Ann's words:**

Makeover Monday is hands down one of the most challenging and rewarding initiatives I've been a part of. It provides the opportunity to express creativity, grow technically, rapidly receive feedback, and connect with peers globally. Contributing to this social project has helped connect me with other individuals, grow my leadership skills, and evangelize my passion for data visualization. It's been an unforgettable experience seeing the exponential impact it has had to those surrounding the project.

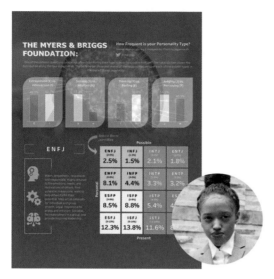

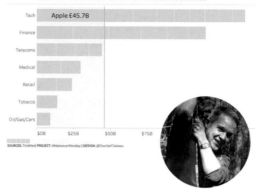

Chantilly Jaggernauth. How Frequent Is Your Personality Type?

Twitter: @chanjagg
Website: chanjagg.com
Participant since: week 38, 2016

**In Chantilly's words:**

Makeover Monday is the greatest and easiest community project to get involved with. I was first introduced to Makeover Monday by an interviewer for a job that I was seeking. At the time I had no idea about the project nor did I have a Tableau Public account. It was after that interview that I researched Makeover Monday, saw the amazing visualizations, and decided to get started on creating my own. The first Makeover Monday viz that I published was picked as Tableau's Viz of the Day. In short, Makeover Monday was the starting point of my community journey. It has enabled my design skills, my collaboration skills, and even my networking skills. To this day, Makeover Monday was the largest building block in both my professional and my personal brand.

Charlie Hutcheson. Apple's Net Income.

Twitter: @CharlieHTableau
Website: learningtableaublog.wordpress.com
Participant since: week 1, 2016

**In Charlie's words:**

Makeover Monday was a core part of my Tableau development and I'm genuinely proud to have participated in every single week. Free practice with clean data, appraised by industry experts who support the initiative in their own time. It's a ludicrously selfless exercise by Andy, Eva, and Andy C before. Phenomenal.

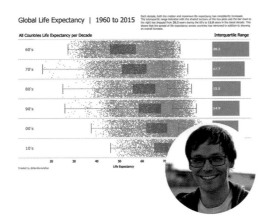

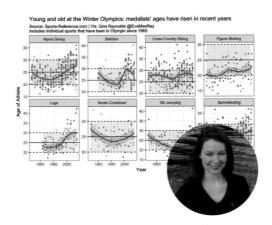

Daniel Caroli. Global Life Expectancy.

Twitter: @Danifornication
Website: datavsfood.wordpress.com/
Participant since: week 27, 2016

### In Daniel's words:

Makeover Monday is fantastic. This project has not only helped me to improve my skills as an analyst and a designer, but I also have so much fun taking part each week. So many people in the community give so much to this project. Week after week it's a joy to see what everyone has created from a single data set. In one week, you see countless detailed analyses, works of art, and more often than not a combination of the two. I don't know where else you'd find a community with such a wealth of skills and knowledge that is continuously improving.

Gina Reynolds. The Winter Olympic Games.

Twitter: @EvaMaeRey
Website: sites.google.com/site/evangelinemreynolds/
Participant since: week 50, 2016

### In Gina's words:

Makeover Monday has given me an opportunity to focus just on visualization. Sometimes, data visualization comes at the end of a much bigger data project, involving collection, cleaning, and analysis. Once you get to the visualization step, I think it is easy to be a bit burned out by the back-end of projects and be less self-demanding when it comes to visually communicating the results. Makeover Monday's delivery of clean data sets with the task of designing a single visualization has given me thinking space to focus on how to effectively design visualization lessons that I can of course take back to other data projects! The community of interested participants is also very motivating. Eva and Andy's feedback is encouraging and honest!

Joe Radburn. The Joey YouTube Verdicts.

Twitter: @joe_radburn
Participant since: week 9, 2016

### In Joe's words:

Makeover Monday is a fun thing to do and it helps me learn how to use Tableau and data.

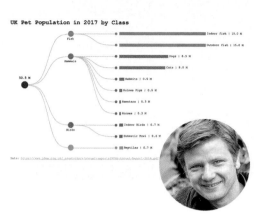

Klaus Schulte. The UK Pet Population.

Twitter: @ProfDrKSchulte
Website: vizjockey.com
Participant since: week 28, 2017

### In Klaus's words:

In July 2017, I was new to Tableau and Twitter. It did not take long time to realize that Makeover Monday was perfect for me to work on my Tableau skills in a continuous way. Most of the things I have learned about data visualization to date were only possible thanks to Makeover Monday and the incredible efforts of Eva and Andy. Moreover, I am very happy that I have become a part of this amazing community.

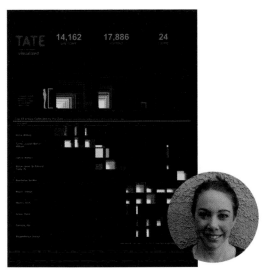

Lilach Manheim. The Tate Collection.

Twitter: @lilachmanheim
Website: databard.wordpress.com
Participant since: week 3, 2016

### In Lilach's words:

Participating in Makeover Monday was *the thing* that really helped me feel like I was part of the Tableau community. It is so hard not to get lost in the crowd on Tableau Public, especially when you're just starting out. Having such amazing support from the community was the confidence boost I needed to play and stretch my vizzing skills in directions that I couldn't really experiment with at work. And to participate in IronViz and the Tableau Fringe Fest!

Louise Shorten. Trends of Youth Employment in Latin America.

Twitter: @shortenl
Website: gettingvizzywithit.blog/
Participant since: week 41, 2016

### In Louise's words:

I have really enjoyed taking part in Makeover Monday since I discovered it in 2016. It has allowed me to connect with a group of inspirational and talented people with a common passion for data visualization. I've learned a huge amount from the community and deepened my knowledge of Tableau along the way. Prior to participating in the project, my exposure to the Tableau community was limited and I feel I've benefitted both personally and professionally from my involvement.

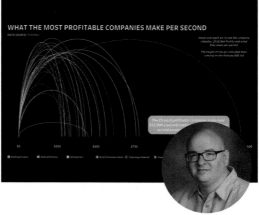

Marc Soares. Household Income
Distribution in the US.

Twitter: @Marc_Soares
Website: marcsoares.ca
Participant since: week 41, 2016

**In Marc's words:**

Makeover Monday has helped develop
and refine my skills in data visualization and
storytelling. I continue to learn new techniques
each week in Tableau and Google Data Studio.
The community has become an invaluable
resource of knowledge, expertise, and
inspiration.

Mark Bradbourne. What the Most
Profitable Companies Make per Second.

Twitter: @markbradbourne
Website: markbradbourne.com
Participant since: week 26, 2016

**In Mark's words:**

Makeover Monday has been and continues
to be the greatest thing I've done for skill
development over the course of my entire
career. It's been a data playground for
experimentation and learning, and I've
been able to bring those elements into
my "professional" life, making me a better
developer overall. Aside from the technical
skills, it's also taught me about the importance
of feedback, iteration, and community. The
community's willingness to support and teach
only makes the program that much more
effective. Through the process I've built a
portfolio that shows my skills, growth, and
development and it has led to the opportunities
that I am enjoying today.

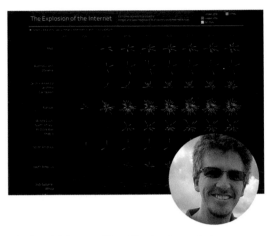

Michael Mixon. The Explosion of the Internet.

Twitter: @mix_pix
Website: mixpixviz.blogspot.com/
Participant since: week 3, 2016

### In Michael's words:

Makeover Monday provided me with an opportunity to connect more with the Tableau community and to stretch my creativity in data visualization. Prior to Makeover Monday, I was using Tableau almost exclusively for work-related projects. Not only could I not share those visualizations outside of work, but they tended to be fairly limited in design latitude. With Makeover Monday, I could try new design ideas, learn new approaches to data challenges, and, most importantly, share them with a community from which I could get feedback and inspiration. I think I can say with absolute confidence that I would not be a Zen Master today if it weren't for Makeover Monday. The project impacted me so much that I even wrote it a love letter. :-) mixpixviz.blogspot.com/2016/08/a-love-letter-of-sorts-to-makeover.html

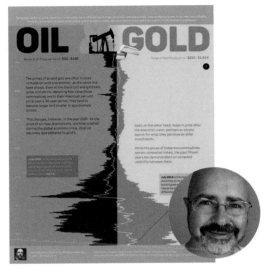

Mike Cisneros. Oil and Gold.

Twitter: @MikeVizneros
Website: mikevizneros.com
Participant since: week 5, 2016

### In Mike's words:

The value of the community aspect of Makeover Monday can't be overstated. First off, there's the discipline it instilled, of encouraging/forcing me to attempt every set in every week, even when I wasn't taken by the data. Then there was the knowledge that other people would see my work and understand the challenges of the underlying data, because they themselves had attempted it; and I would get to see all of their efforts, and learn new techniques in analysis, in design, in functionality, and in technical approaches. It brought me closer to other people in the wider data visualization community *and* made me a better designer *and* taught me new ways of thinking about data. It has been an invaluable part of my professional development.

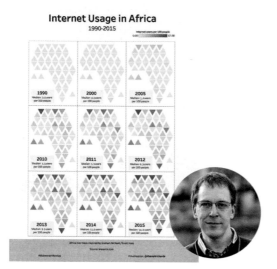

Neil Richards. Internet Usage in Africa.

Twitter: @theneilrichards
Website: questionsindataviz.com
Participant since: week 1, 2016

### In Neil's words:

Makeover Monday is a free data set every week with which to explore and practice your visualization skills. For the first several weeks I made a point of learning and practicing a new technique every week, and as a result, two years later, I had a wide variety of over 100 public visualizations from the simple to the experimental, forming my own personal portfolio with each image, documenting a stage in my journey with Tableau. Better still, as you are participating, so are many dozens around the world who are ready to collaborate, give feedback, critique, advise, and congratulate with you. I don't think there's a better community data visualization project out there – many rainy Sunday afternoons in the UK have been spent eagerly awaiting the latest data set and wondering what challenge lies ahead!

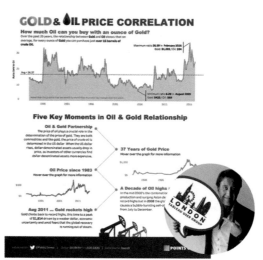

Pablo Gomez. Gold and Oil Price Correlation.

Twitter: @PabloLGomez
Website: pointsofviz.com
Participant since: week 37, 2016

### In Pablo's words:

Makeover Monday has completely transformed the way I visualize data. Every week is a different challenge, every week there is something new to learn. Both Eva and Andy have constantly helped develop and improve my skills in data visualization and storytelling. It's been an amazing journey and Makeover Monday has been part of the driving force helping us to become great data viz experts.

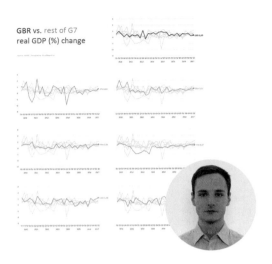

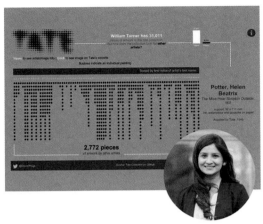

Paweł Wróblewski. GDP Change in Great Britain and the rest of the G7 countries.

Twitter: @ExcelRaport
Website: excelraport.pl/
Participant since: week 30, 2016

**In Paweł's words:**

Makeover Monday is a great data viz project that allows you to visualize data using many different tools (all of my visualizations are created in Excel). Thanks to Makeover Monday I got to know many different types of charts that allow me to present data effectively. In the Makeover Monday community, I met many very talented people whose visuals inspired me to constantly deepen my knowledge. Thanks Eva and Andy for your hard work and passion for data visualization!

Pooja Gandhi. The Tate Collection.

Twitter: @DrexelPooja
Website: thedataduo.com
Participant since: week 5, 2016

**In Pooja's words:**

Makeover Monday has given me the opportunity to make connections with the broader community, helped me build an interactive data visualization portfolio, and helped me land a fantastic job. I love that I can use my creative freedom and build visuals that I don't normally get to create at work. It has played a huge role in the development of my personal brand and professional accomplishments.

Rob Radburn. Police Killings in the US in 2015.

Twitter: @robradburn
Website: adventuresinviz.com
Participant since: week 1, 2016

### In Rob's words:

Makeover Monday became an obsession for me in 2016. I loved the demands of producing a viz every week with different data sets. The community showed me new types of charts, new ways to design, and new ways to analyze data. And I got to viz with my son. The best part? I got to know some great people.

Rosario Gauna. Top Skills According to LinkedIn.

Twitter: @rosariogaunag
Website: rosariogaunag.wordpress.com/
Participant since: week 40, 2016

### In Rosario's words:

Makeover Monday has been an invaluable source for my learning. Each week is an enriching experience to appreciate the multiple perspectives elaborated by the members of the community on the analyzed topic. Each new challenge offers me the possibility to learn, to experiment, to test ideas and develop new ones, and to improve my skills. It has also given me the opportunity to meet people who have become my source of inspiration. In addition to being talented, they are amazing generous people, always willing to share their knowledge. I especially thank Eva and Andy for their dedication and effort to this great project. Makeover Monday has been a unique and special experience in my life, since besides being a cornerstone in the development of my skills in data visualization, it has allowed me to make friends with wonderful people from all over the world.

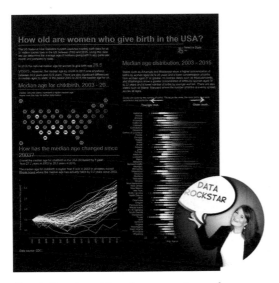

Sarah Bartlett. The Average Age of Childbirth in the USA.

Twitter: @sarahlovesdata
Website: sarahlovesdata.co.uk
Participant since: week 9, 2016

### In Sarah's words:

Makeover Monday is a project very close to my heart. I started participating in Makeover Monday at the beginning of my Tableau journey and without this project I am certain I would not be where I am today. As well as improving my confidence, Makeover Monday has enabled me to build a portfolio of work to demonstrate my Tableau skills and has connected me with people from all over the world, many of whom I now consider friends.

Sean Miller. Household Income in the US.

Twitter: @kcmillersean
Website: mydatamusingsblog.wordpress.com
Participant since: week 4, 2016

### In Sean's words:

Makeover Monday is awesome. When Andy and Andy started it in 2016, I was still relatively new to Tableau Public and Tableau in general. The Andys did such a great job encouraging people to join and take part. More than anything, I enjoy how Makeover Monday is a learning platform. It has never had a competition edge and that is so important. I have learned so much over the past several years that I've been able to take directly to my role in my professional career.

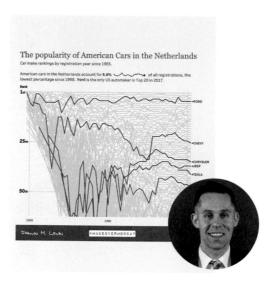

Sebastián Soto Vera. Le Tour de France.

Twitter: @staticum
Website: staticum.cl
Participant since: week 2, 2017

**In Sebastián's words:**

Makeover Monday was and continues to be a tremendous space to share my passion for data visualization. I was used to generating formal reports, so the possibility of innovating around data visualization within the company in which I worked was not something that was valued very much. Makeover Monday is a free and creative space, deeply welcoming and tremendously enriching for me, both personally and professionally. Thanks to what I have learned and to the recognition of the community, I consider Makeover Monday a better way to guide my professional development in this area. In September 2017, I quit my job while preparing for an opportunity in data analysis and visualization. Currently I own a small consulting company dedicated to data topics. Also, I have a new half-time job in a company as Chief of Analysis and Data Visualization. All of the above encouraged me to enroll in a diploma in data visualization. Finally, I just want to say thanks to the entire #MakeoverMonday community, especially Eva and Andy for this great space.

Shawn Levin. The Popularity of American Cars in the Netherlands.

Twitter: @shawnmlevin
Website: shawnmlevin.com
Participant since: week 8, 2016

**In Shawn's words:**

I started Makeover Monday as a fun way to create and share data visualizations. My participation has helped shape my career by providing a channel for deliberate practice, constructive feedback, and community. As a result of my participation in Makeover Monday, I now have the opportunity to teach these best practices to students at Temple University.

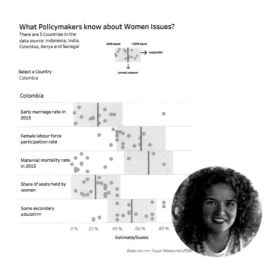

Simona Loffredo. What Policy Makers Know about Women's Issues.

Twitter: @simonaloffredo2
Website: thevizconnoisseur.wordpress.com/
Participant since: week 1, 2016

### In Simona's words:

Makeover Monday means a lot to me; it is my weekly appointment and I rarely miss it! What I like is that it makes me feel part of the community and every week I get a "free" new data set to play with without time constraints. I feel like I will never get bored!

Steve Fenn. Winter Athletes in their Prime.

Twitter: @StatHunting
Participant since: week 2, 2016

### In Steve's words:

I learn things from Makeover Monday even in weeks when I don't contribute. It's always interesting to compare the approaches all these talented people take with the same data. Every time I teach a Tableau class I recommend that my students check out Makeover Monday, even if they're not ready to contribute right away.

## Educators

A significant milestone for us was when we heard that some university lecturers had started using Makeover Monday as a way for their students to practice their data analysis, data visualization, and communication skills. These professors use the work their students create for credits in their courses and appreciate the reliable and consistent availability of data sets, feedback, examples, ideas, and the many sources of inspiration the Makeover Monday community provides.

In early 2017, we virtually attended a data visualization user group at St. Joseph's University in Philadelphia, where we spoke to over 60 students about Makeover Monday, its purpose and history, and the benefits people can gain from participating. With more and more university courses making data analysis and data visualization a focus of the coursework, Makeover Monday is an easy way for students to access data, visualization examples, and industry experts. This gives them a good chance of landing an exciting job as an analyst once they graduate.

## Employers

Companies are always recruiting talented data analysts to join their teams. More and more companies are scouting talent from the Makeover Monday community based on the data visualization portfolios people have built. These companies are looking for people who have developed over time. Team leaders and heads of departments engage with participants to identify their interest in a new role and pave the way for a transition to a job in analytics with a strong focus on visualization.

Never delete your old work even if it includes visualizations you are not proud of. It is important to employers that you demonstrate your progression. They look for things like:

- What have you learned over time?
- How has your style developed and become more refined?

- What makes your visualizations different from the others?
- Do you scratch the surface or go deep into a topic?
- How do you use words, colors, and layout to structure a visualization and guide your audience through the analysis?

Some portfolios are a mix of different chart types because the author chose to learn new chart types as often as possible. Other portfolios show a clear progression from playful experimentation to polished, business-ready dashboards that any CEO would be glad to get their hands on. It is not the end result that matters; what is important is the journey you have been on to develop your skills.

## Organizations

Aside from individuals looking for new employees, organizations have also embraced Makeover Monday to build internal communities of analysts. Large corporates from Singapore to Sydney to Silicon Valley have given their people the time to come together and work on Makeover Monday challenges.

Organizations have told us they have seen the following gains by giving their teams time to work on Makeover Monday each week:

- *Bringing together analysts* from different parts of the organization who may not know one another, let alone know about the shared skills and passion for data visualization.
- *Using nonbusiness data sets* to allow their people to think creatively in a safe environment, free from the scrutiny of corporate standards.
- *Low barriers to entry*, as the data sets are already prepared, allowing their teams to focus on the analysis, visualization, and storytelling aspect of their work.
- *A well-established feedback process* for everyone in the community, which people can join, and organizations can emulate internally.
- *A "live-event" format* that can be used on a weekly basis to practice analysis, visualization, and presentation skills.

Having someone dedicated to leading Makeover Monday internally at an organization helps make the process smoother and the adoption more successful. Ask us for help in getting Makeover Monday established in your organization.

## Nonprofits

In 2017, we started collaborating with nonprofit organizations to give our participants an opportunity to have an impact with their work. Our collaborations with the Inter-American Development Bank, the United Nations, and PATH.org provided these nonprofits the chance to crowdsource data visualizations on specific topics and tap into the pool of talented, passionate analysts who were eager to get involved.

For nonprofit organizations who often work with very limited financial resources to achieve their goals, being able to access the Makeover Monday community and gain insights into their data in just a few days is invaluable. We have enjoyed the collaborations and will continue to engage with organizations who are interested in our project and have a specific need for our community to work on.

## Social Impact

Beyond nonprofit organizations, we have also used data sets that have a social impact in such areas as:

- Income inequality
- Air quality
- Environmental issues like water footprint
- Animal products
- Health
- Life expectancy
- Bee colony declines

These social impact topics have been exciting, have broadened the horizons of many participants, and have made the community stronger and larger than before.

## Makeover Monday Live Events

In the introduction, we told you about some of the live events we ran in 2017, and we continue to bring people together whenever possible by hosting live Makeover Monday events. We also encourage our participants to host their own events. Anyone can get an event off the ground and bring people together to share ideas, help each other, work together, analyze and visualize data, and present the results back to the group.

The ingredients for success are simple. If you want to plan and host your own Makeover Monday live event, this is what you need:

- A room with tables and chairs to seat everyone
- Internet connection and the ability to access the data sets
- A few interested people
- A projector or TV screen
- 90 minutes of uninterrupted time
- Music and snacks also nice to have

This has proven to be a successful format. It inspires people and helps them connect with their community.

This is how we run the live events:

- For the first ten minutes, we present information to the group about Makeover Monday, what the project is, how it developed over time, and how the weekly process works. We also talk about the benefits of participating regularly. You can find all the benefits in the introduction under the section "Pillars of Makeover Monday."

- We then show people how to find the data and give them 60 minutes to work on their makeovers.
- During these 60 minutes we play music for a bit of background noise to help create a relaxed atmosphere. We offer our help to anyone who needs it. We walk around and check in on people.
- People can work by themselves or in teams of two or three. Small teams work well to accelerate learning. Working in groups also helps participants get to know each other and helps them to build their network.
- Once the 60 minutes are over, we ask people to volunteer to present their makeovers. We have never struggled to find volunteers and with the right level of encouragement (and coaxing) you will have at least a couple of participants showing their work to the rest of the group. This often results in others volunteering.

In the end, people will have worked with an unfamiliar data set, practiced their analysis and visualization skills, and had an opportunity to present their work to an audience. These are all valuable skills to practice and, when done on a regular basis, will strongly enhance the individual and collective capabilities of the people in your organization.

## Makeover Monday Enterprise Edition

Over the past couple of years, we have had increasing interest from organizations to run workshops to help their teams move to the next level of visual analytics and build even stronger professional communities internally. These interactions have led us to develop Makeover Monday Enterprise Edition, a concept aimed at corporations and larger organizations that want to go beyond establishing Makeover Monday and apply the concepts to the way they build their internal communities and facilitate ongoing development.

To help these organizations, we have developed a workshop program, facilitated by us, that takes all of the successful building blocks from Makeover Monday and applies them to a corporate setting. We take into account the unique geographical, organizational, cultural, language, and time zone challenges that today's globally operating organizations face and provide a solution that allows them to create an internal analytics community that brings together people with common skills and passion for data analysis.

Contact us for more information through our website: makeovermonday.co.uk.

# Source Lines

Figure I.1 Data from ESPN

Figure I.2 Data from ESPN

Figure I.7 Credit to Sergey Demushkin for Carousel House (Noun Project)

Figure I.8 Data from Bermuda Digest of Statistics www.bermuda.io

Figure I.9 Simulated data from visualizenomalaria.org

Figure I.10 Board Bia via the IWSR

Figure 1.1 Data from Data World

Figure 1.2 Data from cdc.gov

Figure 1.3 Data from SocialBlade.com

Figure 1.4 Data from World Bank

Figure 1.5 Data from City of Chicago

Figure 1.6 Data from Data Go..

Figure 1.7 Data from US Census

Figure 1.8 Data from Environmental Protection Agency

Figure 1.11 Data source NASA; info source www.bernadettebrady.com

Figure 1.12 Data from Movebank.org, Wikipedia

Figure 1.13 Data from Movebank.org

Figure 1.14 Data from Society for American Baseball Research, The Institute for Diversity and Ethics in Sport's annual Racial and Gender Report Cards, TIDES Reports

Figure 1.15 Data from Unesco Institute for Water Education

Figure 2.5 Data from Andy's American Express Statement

Figure 2.6 Data from Andy Kriebel

Figure 2.7 Data from bit.ly/2oYRG7h

Figure 2.8 Data from Knoema / Wi..

Figure 2.9 Data from National Chicken Council

Figure 2.10 Data from National Chicken Council

Figure 2.11 Data from trumptwitterarchive. com/#/

Figure 2.14 Data from US Census Bureau

Figure 3.4 Data from Knoema World Data Atlas

Figure 3.5 Data from Office of National Statistics

Figure 3.6 Data from Office of National Statistics

Figure 3.12 Data from Major League Baseball

Figure 3.13 Data from Major League Baseball

Figure 3.16 Data from Verband der Automobilindustrie

Figure 3.17 Data from Verband der Automobilindustrie

Figure 3.18 Data from National Park Service

Figure 3.19 Data from National Park Service

Figure 3.20 Data from NOAA

Figure 3.21 Data from NOAA

Figure 3.22 Data from Sport Singapore

Figure 3.23 Data from Sport Singapore

Figure 3.24 Data from NOAA

Figure 3.25 Data from NOAA

Figure 3.26 Data from NOAA

Figure 3.27 Data from NOAA

Figure 3.28 Data from NOAA

Figure 3.29 Data from NOAA

Figure 3.30 Data from NOAA

Figure 3.31 Data from Freddie Mac

Figure 3.32 Data from Freddie Mac

Figure 3.33 Data from NOAA

Figure 3.34 Data from NOAA

Figure 3.35 Data from NOAA

Figure 3.36 Data from NOAA

Figure 3.37 Data from NOAA

Figure 4.1 Data from YouGov

Figure 4.2 Data from Environmental Protection Agency

Figure 4.3 Data from World Bank

Figure 4.4 Data from National Chicken Council

Figure 4.5 Data from NHS

Figure 4.6 Data from 100people.org

Figure 4.7 Data from Knoema World Data Atlas

Figure 4.8 Data from Movebank.org

Figure 4.9 Data from data.gov.au

Figure 5.1 Data from Knoema

Figure 5.2 Data from Quandl

Figure 5.3 Data from the EPA

Figure 5.4 Data from Sport Singapore

Figure 5.5 Data from National Chicken Council

Figure 5.6 Data from National Chicken Council

Figure 5.7 Data from US Census Bureau

Figure 5.8 Data from National Chicken Council

Figure 5.9 Data from National Chicken Council

Figure 5.10 Data from Equal Measures 2030

Figure 5.11 Data from NHS

Figure 5.12 Data from Fraser Institute

Figure 5.13 Data from YouGov

Figure 5.14 Data from Quandl

Figure 5.15 Data from Nielsen

Figure 5.16 Data from Pet Food Manufacturers Association

Figure 6.1 Data from Washington Metropolitan Area Transit Authority

Figure 6.3 Data from data.police.uk

Figure 6.7 Data from VDA

Figure 6.12 Data from College Board

Figure 6.13 Data from New Zealand Ministry of Business, Innovation and Employment

Figure 6.14 Data from UNESCO

Figure 6.15 Data from Social Blade

Figure 6.16 Data from Major League Baseball

Figure 6.17 Data from IDB SMS

Figure 6.18 Data from Statistik Berlin Brandenburg

Figure 6.19 Data from World Bank

Figure 7.1 Data from Society for American Baseball Research

Figure 7.2 Data from womensagenda.com.au

Figure 7.3 Data from SABR.org

Figure 7.4 Data from trumptwitterarchive.com

Figure 7.5 Data from NASA

Figure 7.6 Data from NASA Eclipse 2017 eclipse2017.nasa.gov

Figure 7.7 Data from Business Insider

Figure 7.8 Data from 100people.org

Figure 7.9 Data from US Census Bureau

Figure 7.10 Data from knoema.com

Figure 7.11 Data from www.insee.fr/fr

Figure 7.12 Data from simd.scotland.gov.uk

Figure 7.13 Data from Quandl

Figure 7.14 Data from Society of American Baseball Research

Figure 8.3 Data from Quandl

Figure 8.4 Data from Quandl

Figure 8.5 Data from EPA

Figure 8.6 Data from EPA

Figure 8.7 Data from Knoema and Wikipedia

Figure 8.8 Data from Knoema and Wikipedia

Figure 8.9 Data from ASER Centre

Figure 10.50 Data from YouGov

Figure 10.51 Data from blogs.ft.com/ftdata/2016/09/17/datawatch-satisfaction-with-transport-in-eu-cities/

Figure 10.52 Data from twitter.com/Bordbia

Figure 10.53 Data from www.bbc.com/news/health-39785742

Figure 10.54 Data from US Census Bureau

Figure 10.55 Data from McKinsey, Phocuswright, BLS

Figure 10.56 Data from Gabriel Zucman

Figure 10.57 Data from CDC

Figure 10.58 Data from Gabriel Zucman

Figure 10.59 Data from Quandl

Figure 10.60 Data from @DrewLinzer & Daily Kos

Figure 10.61 Data from data.world / YouGov.com

Figure 10.62 Data from NOAA

Figure 10.63 Data from womensagenda.com.au

Figure 10.64 Data from SABR.org

Figure 10.65 Data from www.visionofhumanity.org

Figure 10.66 Data from Met Office Hadley Centre and the Climatic Research Unit at the University of East Anglia bit.ly/1XsMrbL

Figure 10.67 Data from bit.ly/2iENyV3

Figure 10.68 Data from EPA

Figure 10.70 Data from Employment Growth in G-7 Countries

Figure 10.73 Data from The Nielsen Global Health and Ingredient Sentiment Survey, Q1 2016

Figure 10.74 Data from GoBankingRates.com

Figure 11.1 Data from Fraser Institute

Figure 11.2 Data from www.theatlas.com/charts/SkwA7QzL

Figure 11.3 Data from Sports-Reference.com

Figure 11.4 UK Prescription data, NHS Digital

Figure 11.5 Pet Food Manufacturers Association

Figure 11.6 The EU Potato Sector

Figure 11.8 Data from CDC

Figure 11.9 Data from Buildings and Construction Authority of Singapore

Figure 11.10 Data from pfma.org.uk and www.staticum.cl

Figure 11.11 Data from Sportsreference.com

Figure 11.12 Data from NASA

Figure 11.13 Data from Annual Status of Education Report

Figure 11.14 Data from FIA Formula

Figure 11.15 Data from Nielsen

Figure 11.16 Data from EPA

Figure 11.17 Data from github.com/tategallery.collection

Figure 11.18 Data from Andy's American Express Statement

Figure 11.19 Data from data.world/sports/ncaa-means-march-madness

Figure 11.20 Data from TradeMap

Figure 11.21 Data from Piper Jaffray

Figure 11.22 Data from CDC

Figure 12.1 Data from National Snow & Ice Data Center

Figure 12.2 Data from National Snow & Ice Data Center

Figure 12.3 Data from Tate Collection on GitHub

Figure 12.4 Data from National Snow & Ice Data Center

Figure 12.6 Data from National Snow & Ice Data Center

Figure 12.8 Data from National Snow & Ice Data Center

Figure 12.10 Data from National Snow & Ice Data Center

Figure 12.12 Data from National Snow & Ice Data Center

Figure 12.14 Data from National Chicken Council

Figure 12.17 Data from OECD

Figure 12.20 Data from Global Footprint Network

# Index

**Caravaggio** Catherine Puglisi

**For Bill**

Phaidon Press Limited, Regent's Wharf, All Saints Street, London N1 9PA

Phaidon Press Inc., 180 Varick Street, New York, NY 10014

www.phaidon.com

First published 1998

Reprinted in paperback 2000 (twice), 2002, 2003, 2004, 2005, 2006

©1998 Phaidon Press Limited

ISBN 0 7148 3966 3

A CIP record for this publication is available from the British Library

Printed in Hong Kong

Frontispiece

Ottavio Leoni, **Portrait of Caravaggio** (detail), *c.*1621–5; red and black chalk with white heightening on blue paper, 23.4 × 16.3 cm, Biblioteca Marucelliana, Florence

# Preface

Caravaggio has enjoyed widespread admiration as an accepted Old Master since his rescue from oblivion and opprobrium at the start of this century. The phenomenal increase in his popularity, already notable forty years ago, has skyrocketed among the broad public in just the past fifteen years. His current renown is greatest, of course, in Italy, where he now resides in the mythic pantheon of artistic giants. Reflecting his newly won status as a national cultural monument along with Bernini and Maria Montessori is the reproduction of his portrait and two of his works on the 100,000-lire banknote, in circulation since the early 1980s; and the fact that several of his secular pictures have turned up routinely in Italian advertising for commercial products like wine or as decoration on luxury goods, such as a recent Trussardi shawl reproducing Caravaggio's *Musicians*, is further proof that his art has attained canonical status. Moreover, the greatest news sensation during the trial of former prime minister Giulio Andreotti in Rome in the autumn of 1996 was a former Mafioso's testimony revealing that the Mob was in fact responsible for the unresolved theft of Caravaggio's altarpiece of the *Nativity*.

For the Anglo-American public, Caravaggio's appeal rests not only on his often shocking imagery but also on his romantic persona. Like the artist's early critics, his modern audience cannot resist viewing the art through the filter of his tempestuous and tragic life. The potent alliance of artistic creativity and violence has fascinated writers and spawned works of fiction revolving around the painter. The latest in the crime genre, Margaret Truman's *Murder at the National Gallery* (1996) features Caravaggio's horrific *Medusa* on the dust jacket and, within, depicts him as a crazy murderer with uncounted homicides to his name, who painted not only violent death but also incest and rape, which the author incredibly adds to his repertoire to pique jaded readers. Caravaggio's life and art resonate in a recent novel of a different class, Michael Ondaatje's *The English Patient*, winner of the Booker Prize in 1992. One of the four protagonists, David Caravaggio, bears the painter's name, criminal record and tormented state of mind. Victim of a violent mutilation, this character's fictional plight is at once inspired by, and enkindles, the author's reflections on Caravaggio's *David and Goliath*.

These fictions represent a small and specialized segment in the full-blown industry of Caravaggio publications. Art historians primarily account for the mushrooming of books, dissertations, articles and exhibition catalogues, but significantly amplifying this production are essays by non-specialists. His paintings have engaged diverse commentators including the critic Arthur Danto, the philosopher David Carrier, the semiologist Louis Marin, the psychoanalyst John Gedo, the literary critic Mieke Bal and the artist Frank Stella. No other Italian seventeenth-century painter has succeeded in making the 'crossover' from the confines of Baroque studies into the arena of modern criticism.

Given the glut of the market, how does an author justify another general book on Caravaggio? The truth is that since the appearance in 1983 of Howard Hibbard's excellent and then definitive book, a wealth of fresh material has emerged. The rediscovery of two lost masterpieces and of a surprising number of documents unearthed in the Roman, Neapolitan and Maltese archives has immeasurably enriched our understanding of Caravaggio's art, and has called for some readjustments to the established outline of his life and career. Systematic restoration and scientific analyses of many of the painter's works have recovered the pristine quality of individual pictures, yielded some unexpected results, and led to a spirited discussion of his working methods. Intensified research into the history of early Baroque Italy has brought alive the religious, social and cultural world in which Caravaggio lived and worked. This book attempts to gather and make accessible the results of these scattered studies, integrating them into a fresh narrative and explanation of the painter's life and art. My primary aim in these pages is to characterize Caravaggio's artistic development, define the uniqueness of his art, and understand its historical role in the renewal of painting *c.*1600.

Many publications of the past decade and a half have deepened my own understanding of Caravaggio. Without wanting to slight important contributions, I can single out here only those few that have had a significant impact on my thinking. Mina Gregori's essays, especially in her two major exhibition catalogues of 1985 and 1991, have provided me with the most comprehensive, current account of Caravaggio's artistic formation and development. Challenging prior assumptions, she has forced me to ponder hard about the limits of his *œuvre*. Presented in exemplary publications by, respectively, Denis Mahon and Sergio Benedetti, the rediscovered *Cardsharps* and *Betrayal of Christ* have also been instrumental in redefining Caravaggio's art. The ongoing campaign of restoration and scientific investigation of individual paintings has resolved other questions of connoisseurship, resulting in convincing reattributions, such as the Capitoline *Fortune-Teller* and *Saint John the Baptist*, and the *Narcissus*. The increased body of technical material has cast light on

Caravaggio's working methods, a subject analysed by Keith Christiansen and Roberta Lapucci, upon whose work I have gratefully relied in my Epilogue.

An earlier generation of writers established years ago the main outline of Caravaggio's artistic career in Rome, and into that profile I have tried to integrate the surprising amount of new information that fills gaps and sharpens details about his personal life, as well as his social and artistic milieu. One representative example is Randolph Parks's discovery of the contract for the *Death of the Virgin*, which names for the first time its patron, Laerzio Cherubini, and forces us to reconsider the sequence of Caravaggio's Roman altarpieces. Concurrently, Pamela Askew's monograph on the *Death of the Virgin* explicates the imagery of the painting and delves into the issues surrounding its rejection. My summary of Caravaggio's Roman residences, his intimate circle and his brushes with the law capitalizes on the recent research of Maurizio Marini and Sandro Corradini, and also on the provocative, albeit unreliable, findings of Riccardo Bassani and Fiora Bellini. Caravaggio the man now emerges more fully amidst the resurrected identities of his models, the courtesan Fillide Melandroni, his 'woman' Lena or Maddalena Antognetti, and his acquaintance and fated victim, Ranuccio Tomassoni. The keen detective work of Francesca Cappelletti and Laura Testa has notably added to our knowledge of Caravaggio's Roman patrons with the addition of Marchese Ciriaco Mattei, and Creighton Gilbert has resuscitated the personality of Ciriaco's brother Cardinal Girolamo.

Of the various current studies exploring the tastes and cultural world of the artist's private patrons, several articles by Franca Trinchieri Camiz linking trends in early music to Caravaggio's genre pictures have helped to elucidate their original meaning and reception. That an extensive network of patronage nurtured and protected the artist not only in Rome but also later in exile is a case persuasively presented by Maurizio Calvesi. Concentrating rather on Caravaggio's formal concerns and solutions, Janis Bell has astutely investigated colour and light in his Roman pictures.

Caravaggio's exile in Malta and Sicily has drawn unprecedented attention in recent publications focusing on his last artistic phase. If I have been able to throw more light than previous authors on his movements and activities during this period, it is thanks to Vincenzo Pacelli's studies of Neapolitan commissions, and to the archival research and writings of Dominic Cutajar, John Azzopardi, Stefania Macioce, and of David Stone on the painter's stay in Malta. For my account of Caravaggio's death, I have relied on Pacelli's and Marini's investigations and canny readings of documentary and circumstantial evidence. Recent books on the artist by Held, Peter, and Seong-Doo became available too late to be taken into account in my text, but are cited in the bibliography.

My interpretation of Caravaggio's art, developed in the last years of this century, is of course founded upon those of many decades of distinguished art historians, beginning with Roberto Longhi's seminal contribution. The monographs of Maurizio Calvesi and Ferdinando Bologna offer the latest explanations of the painter's work and personality. Although unconvinced by Calvesi's final image of the painter as a learned theologian and by Bologna's view of him as an empirical scientist, many of the insights which make these two books so notable have found their way into my discussion.

While researching and writing this book, my understanding of Caravaggio has evolved so as to encompass more than his familiar reputation as the archetypical creative genius and the painter of the *Bacchus* and the *Calling of Saint Matthew*, highlighted in survey courses on art history. I have tried to show a fully three-dimensional man, unexpectedly sociable as well as irascible, resourceful and resilient, and wholly engaged by his art. With the complete rehabilitation of his late paintings, the artistic development that I have traced embraces an impressive range of expression from his early beguiling themes of love and transience, to his mature religious works alternately capturing explosive violence and spiritual introspection, to his late tragic images imbued with compassion and personal hope of redemption. Caravaggio's astonishing achievement is that in spite of the flaws in his character and the adversities he faced, in the brief span of less than two decades he transformed himself into one of the greatest painters in Western art.

Research for this book was in part funded by a Rutgers University Research Council Grant and was made possible by a sabbatical. The Rutgers Art Library provided unflagging assistance, for which I especially thank Beryl Smith and Roger Smith. Jeffrey Rudell at the American Academy in Rome helped facilitate viewing works *in situ*.

I thank too the many art historians, museum curators, and private collectors who kindly assisted me, including Gioacchino Barbera, Camillo Borghese, Dominic Cutajar, Diane DeGrazia, Rolando Dionisi, Elena Fumigalli, Frima Fox Hofrichter, Alice Jarrard, Stéphane Loire, Constance Lowenthal, Tod Marder, Nicoletta Odescalchi, Christina Olsen, Louise Rice, Richard Spear, David Stone, Janis Tomlinson, Rossella Vodret, Mariët Westerman, and Carolyn Wood. I would also like to acknowledge the enthusiastic support of my students in undergraduate and graduate seminars. I am as ever indebted to Italian friends for their warm hospitality: Franca Lolli, Rudi Rooms and Giancarla Baldini, and Teresa Caponsacco.

Special thanks are owed to several individuals for their time and stimulating conversations: Franca Trinchieri Camiz, Denis Mahon, Maurizio Marini, Sarah Blake McHam, Anthony Panzera, Ubaldo Vitali, and in particular, Claudio Marangon, for the great sensitivity with which he translated the primary material in the Appendix. Keith Christiansen's ready help honed my thinking at various stages and especially improved my Epilogue. I would like to express deep gratitude to Donald Posner, without whose generosity and encouragement the book would not have been written, and who graciously read the text, offering numerous valuable suggestions.

Dorothy and Peter Cleaves were welcome companions in Syracuse and, along with Raphael and Arianna, gamely bore the summer heat in Gozo and Valletta. Finally, I dedicate this book to my husband William Barcham, who masterminded our Maltese adventure, and whose critical advice was essential throughout.

October 1997

Part One

From Lombardy to Rome 1571–1600

Chapter 1  **Lombard Roots**

Two of Caravaggio's self-portraits frame the opening and close of his artistic career. The *Self-Portrait as Bacchus* (Pl. 1) records his appearance when about twenty-two years old, shortly after he settled in Rome, whereas *David With the Head of Goliath* (Pl. 2) records his likeness at the age of thirty-nine or so. Stylistically disparate, both paintings disconcert us, and for different reasons. In the earlier work, the painter's self-scrutiny produced a study from life of the turn of his head, the bared shoulder, the crown of ivy, and the two peaches and cluster of grapes on the table. Although the attributes of the pagan god of wine and divine inspiration fit awkwardly and the pallor of the subject's complexion looks sickly, this classical and allegorical guise asserts traditional notions about artistic creativity. In the later painting, the artist portrayed himself as one of the protagonists in the Bible story but, contrary to convention, as villain rather than hero. Even more disquieting is the fact that Caravaggio projected his features on to Goliath's already severed and bleeding head, gruesome with its glazed eyes, gaping mouth and bloodied forehead. Only sixteen years at most separate the two self-portraits, but during their course Caravaggio forged an extraordinary art that broke with the past. Notoriety jostled with fame, however, and his identification with the destroyed giant chillingly evokes the capital sentence for murder which haunted him during his last four years in exile.

The main events of Caravaggio's life and career are well known from documents relating to his family, apprenticeship, and later escapades in Rome, from contracts for artistic commissions and inventories of patrons and collectors, and from several seventeenth-century biographies. This seeming wealth of information is at times contradictory: it fails to clarify the details of his artistic formation and earliest activity, and sheds little light on the content of the paintings. And it must be remembered that apart from the terse statements recorded in the legal proceedings in which Caravaggio became involved in 1603, all of the painter's views come down to us once removed, filtered through his contemporaries' sensibilities and biases.

Michelangelo Merisi was born in 1571, probably in Milan. Caravaggio, the name by which he came to be called, was his family's home town, 43 kilometres to the east of Milan. His parents, Fermo Merisi, already a widower with an infant daughter, and Lucia Aratori, had married at the beginning of the year, on 14 January, in a country church just outside Caravaggio. The exact date of Michelangelo's birth is undocumented, but circumstantial evidence points persuasively to 29 September, the feast day of Saint Michael the Archangel.[1] His early childhood must have been relatively comfortable as his father owned property in the town, possessed some capital, and held the job of steward to Francesco I Sforza, the Marchese of Caravaggio.[2] Sforza came from a Milanese family that descended from the Renaissance Duke of Milan, Ludovico il Moro; his wife, Costanza Colonna, who assumed the marquisate of Caravaggio after her husband's death in 1583,

Overleaf
**1 Self-Portrait as Bacchus** (Pl. 23), detail of head
**2 David with the Head of Goliath** (Pl. 180), detail of head of Goliath

came from an even older Roman family and was the daughter of Marcantonio II Colonna, the victorious naval commander at the Battle of Lepanto. The Marchese's presence as a witness at the wedding of Fermo and Lucia attests to the good relations between the Marquis and his steward. The service of Michelangelo's father to the Sforza and Colonna secured for the Merisi the protection of these powerful families, which the painter enjoyed throughout his life.

As Sforza and his household were in residence in his Milanese palace near the cathedral at the time of Michelangelo's birth, Fermo and Lucia lived nearby in the heart of the old city and raised their eldest son there, along with his younger brothers Giovanni Battista (born in 1572) and Giovan Pietro (birth date unknown), and his younger sister Caterina (born in 1574), until the plague of 1576 forced the family to flee Milan for the illusory security of Caravaggio. They and others returning to the countryside carried the contagion with them, and in 1577, Michelangelo, now six years old, lost first an uncle and, a few months later, both his father and grandfather within a day of each other. Lucia assumed responsibility for the children, moving into her father's home in Caravaggio. Given the family's social status and economic means, the likelihood is that Michelangelo spent some part of the next seven years attending grammar school. A later, autograph receipt for a Roman commission confirms his writing ability and, later still, Baglione's libel case against Caravaggio in 1603 presupposed that he wrote the offensive verses. Moreover, the dozen books inventoried in his house in 1605 offer strong evidence of his literacy.[3]

By 6 April 1584 at the latest, Michelangelo was back in Milan, for on that day the almost thirteen-year-old boy was apprenticed there to the painter Simone Peterzano (c.1540–c.1596). When the four-year term of the apprenticeship expired, Michelangelo moved back to Caravaggio, where he remained from 1589 to 1592. With the cash he raised from selling land from his small paternal inheritance he may have financed study trips to nearby cities in Lombardy, and possibly as far afield as Venice, to round off his artistic education. After his mother's death in late 1590, the departure for Rome of his only living uncle Ludovico, and the sale of his last share in his father's legacy in May 1592, Michelangelo left Northern Italy for good. No documents sustain the later reports of Mancini and Bellori that he left Milan under a cloud after spending a year in prison for what would have been the earliest of his criminal offences.[4]

Caravaggio spent his first twenty-one years, more than half of his life as it turned out, in Lombardy. During this crucial period, and particularly during the years of his adolescence, he underwent formative experiences for his future artistic career. But apart from sketching the bare bones of biographical data – birth, parentage, apprenticeship – his biographers skim over the pre-Roman years, leaving to modern scholars the task of reconstructing a hypothetical yet plausible portrait of the artist as a young man. Late sixteenth-century Lombardy where

**3** Map of Italy in the late 16th century

Caravaggio grew up was peaceful and prosperous, but beneath the surface lay a recent turbulent history, an unpopular political system, and religious ferment.[5] At the time of the painter's birth, the region stretched from the Alps to the Po river and was bordered on the north by the Habsburg Empire, on the west by the Duchy of Savoy, on the south by the Republic of Genoa and the Grand Duchy of Tuscany, and on the east by the Republic of Venice (Pl. 3). Because of its geographical location, Lombardy suffered in the sixteenth century from the expansionist goals of the rival European powers – France, the Habsburgs, and the Papacy – and saw war, famines and plagues. It finally lost its political independence with the Habsburg Emperor Charles V's abdication in 1556, for his son Philip II of Spain inherited what had been the Duchy of Milan, and Milan became the seat of Spanish rule, presided over by a Spanish governor and controlled by a large Spanish army quartered throughout the province, which also included such cities as Cremona, Pavia and Lodi. In the 1570s and 1580s the corruption and abuses of the foreign occupiers, which eventually plunged Milan into decline in the seventeenth century, had not yet stifled the city's economy and culture.

Archbishop Carlo Borromeo (1538–84, Pl. 4) exercised the juridical and moral authority of the Catholic Church in Milan, counterbalancing Spanish rule.[6] Regarded in his own lifetime as the embodiment of a Counter-Reformation bishop and canonized in 1610, Borromeo had been instrumental in internal reform of the Church, especially in the convocation of the third and last session of the Council of Trent, which had met on and off between 1545 and 1563 to codify official doctrine. In obedience to the Tridentine decrees, from 1565 he occupied his own see in Milan and, until his death in 1584, radically reformed local religious houses. Borromeo's saintly reputation derived from his personal immersion in the widespread spiritual renewal that was revitalizing Catholicism and that found inspiration in the asceticism and mysticism of the other great sixteenth-century reformers, Ignatius Loyola, Teresa of Avila and Philip Neri.

**4** Agostino Carracci, **Portrait of Carlo Borromeo**, 1585; engraving, 48.1 × 34.1 cm

As part of his reform programme, Borromeo directed ecclesiastical artistic policy in the archdiocese of Milan. The use and efficacy of devotional images were reaffirmed at the last Tridentine session in 1563 in a decree establishing general guidelines on religious art and entrusting specific policy to local bishops. Borromeo actively promoted the construction, renovation, and decoration of Milanese churches, and like his fellow archbishop in Bologna, Gabriele Paleotti (1522–97), contributed to the new literature on sacred art with his treatise on church architecture of 1577.[7]

The particular religious and artistic climate of Borromean Milan formed the backdrop to Caravaggio's youth. The Archbishop's pastoral voice would certainly have reached Michelangelo's consciousness, as his uncle Ludovico was a priest serving in the archdiocese of Milan, and his brother Giovanni Battista was tonsured in 1583, the first step to priesthood, in the adjacent diocese of Cremona. The Merisi family's association with the Sforza–Colonna household provided another, albeit indirect, link to the Archbishop in that the Marchesa, Costanza Colonna, was related by marriage to Carlo Borromeo, with whom she corresponded.[8] When Borromeo died in November 1584, Caravaggio had been living in Milan as an apprentice for the past eight months. Since Peterzano and other Milanese workshops had fulfilled Borromeo's call for frescoes and altarpieces to decorate the city's churches, the Archbishop's death must have had some effect on Caravaggio's workplace, if only at an economic level.

Caravaggio was the first in his family to take up painting. Bellori recounted that the boy, when helping his father with a building job in Milan, made glue for some fresco painters and decided to join them in order to study painting. He added that Caravaggio forged ahead for four or five years, making portraits, before his alleged flight from Milan. Mancini's biography only mentioned in general terms a period of study in Milan that lasted seven or eight years. Baglione pointed out that the aspiring painter had to move to Milan to find a distinguished master.[9] Yet the town of Caravaggio, like many Italian provincial centres, boasted its own artistic heritage from the early sixteenth century that perhaps first stimulated the young Michelangelo's decision to become a painter. The town's most famous native son was Polidoro Caldara, known as Polidoro da Caravaggio (c.1500–43), who had moved to Rome and established a high reputation throughout the peninsula. The churches of SS. Fermo e Rustico and of San Bernardino were decorated in the first quarter of the century with altar paintings and frescoes by local painters who also worked in Cremona, Brescia and Milan. By mid-century, most of these artists had died, and Bernardino Campi (1522–91) came from Cremona to continue the fresco decoration in the Chapel of the Holy Sacrament in SS. Fermo e Rustico. Campi subsequently returned and stayed long enough to finish the chapel in 1571, the very year of Caravaggio's birth. A few years later, Archbishop Borromeo sent Pellegrino Tibaldi (1527–96), who was serving as architect of the cathedral of Milan, to take charge of renovations to the sanctuary of the Madonna di Caravaggio.[10]

Caravaggio's contract with Peterzano stipulated that he would live with the master, who would teach him everything necessary to becoming an independent painter within the four-year term.[11] A quick look at the artistic situation in Milan at the end of the sixteenth century helps to explain his family's choice of Peterzano, who is virtually unknown today except as the teacher of his more famous pupil.

By about 1550, the Milanese school had stagnated; the two prevailing artistic currents were alternately retrospective and imported. The former derived partly from North Italian art of the preceding century and partly from Leonardo da Vinci, while the latter expounded a version of Central Italian Mannerism modelled after the late works of Michelangelo. Borromeo's patronage of Pellegrino Tibaldi helped to ensure that 'Michelangelism' dominated ecclesiastical art during Caravaggio's youth in the 1570s and 1580s.[12] Although Peterzano was born in Bergamo and trained under Titian in Venice, he conformed to this prevailing Roman aesthetic, painting monumental and gracefully

**5** Simone Peterzano, **Persian Sibyl**, 1578–82; fresco, Certosa di S. Garegnano, Milan posed muscular figures. Moreover, he was friends with its two leading Milanese exponents: Giovanni Paolo Lomazzo (1538–1600) and Ambrogio Figino (1548–1608). By the time of Caravaggio's apprenticeship, Lomazzo had been forced by blindness to abandon painting; however, he dedicated himself to his theoretical writings and kept abreast of the latest artistic developments, lauding Peterzano in his *Trattato dell'arte de la pittura* (1584). Figino, Lomazzo's former pupil, also adopted an academic style allied to Central Italian Mannerism and built a career comparable with that of Peterzano. Undoubtedly aware of the Milanese prejudice against native painters, Peterzano vaunted his Bergamasque origins and Venetian artistic education. By 1584, he had been in Milan over a decade, and his solid reputation rested on his Milanese altarpieces and frescoes.[13]

In Peterzano's studio, Caravaggio presumably learned the basics of drawing and of painting in fresco and oil. None of Caravaggio's youthful frescoes from the Lombard period survive or have been identified and, given his later avoidance of that medium, he may have chafed at the exacting requirements of fresco. Unfortunately, nothing is known of Peterzano's artistic projects between 1584 and 1587, the period when Caravaggio was in his studio. If the master did not have any fresco projects in hand at that time, his apprentice's understanding of the

medium may have been more theoretical than technical, which might further account for his later exclusion from such projects in Rome.[14]

On the surface, Caravaggio's art has little in common with his teacher's crammed compositions in which artificially posed figures gesticulate wildly against landscape settings. But close inspection of Peterzano's works betrays numerous links. In the first place, Caravaggio stored up compositional ideas for future reference; for example, Peterzano's Garegnano fresco of the *Persian Sibyl* (Pl. 5) served as the source for the *Self-Portrait as Bacchus* (Pl. 23). In addition, he focused selectively on the Lombard, as opposed to Central Italian, lessons inherent in Peterzano's art. Looking beyond the schematic and turgid designs of the frescoes, he noted scattered realistic episodes in which Peterzano inserted one or a pair of peasants with strongly individualized traits.[15]

When imitating his master's figures, Caravaggio also learned and extended a standard Lombard practice. For certain paradigmatic attitudes, such as the youth looking over his shoulder and raising his hand to his face, Lombard painters commonly consulted prints, especially after Raphael and Michelangelo, and then set up a model in that same attitude in order to study the pose from life. But unlike his teacher and Lombard predecessors, Caravaggio painted directly from the model without further refinement. His later claim that nature alone was his model was hyperbolic; throughout his career he in fact adopted many poses and compositional motifs from Lombard pictorial sources and from prints after a wide range of artists.[16]

Finally, Caravaggio's apprenticeship coincided with Peterzano's shift towards a direct and prosaic devout style in his altarpieces, a late form of Mannerism that responded to the Tridentine call for a reform of religious painting, so fully endorsed by Carlo Borromeo. His teacher's contemporary altarpieces (Pl. 6) reflected reformed Mannerism, in which solemn figures enact the traditional events of the Gospels in simplified and austere compositions. But the icy rigidity of Peterzano's late works was only a limited solution to the call for reform of religious imagery, and one which Caravaggio reacted against. In the final analysis, Caravaggio's apprenticeship gave him more than just basic skills, but the evidence of even his earliest paintings proves that he rejected the Mannerist premisses of Peterzano's art.

In this period of study stretching four years beyond his apprenticeship, to 1592, Caravaggio immersed himself in a broad spectrum of Lombard art in Milan and nearby in Brescia, Bergamo and Cremona. The view that a Lombard pictorial tradition existed independently from

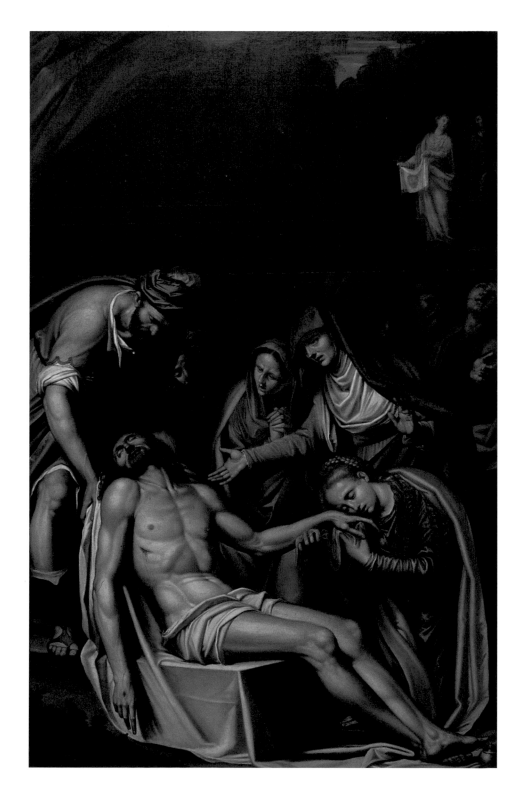

**6** Simone Peterzano, **Entombment**, *c.*1573–8;  oil on canvas, 290 × 185 cm, S. Fedele, Milan

26

**7** Antonio Campi, **Beheading of the Baptist**, 1571;  oil on canvas, 280 × 192 cm, S. Paolo, Milan

Central Italian or Venetian art was first argued at the end of the sixteenth century and has been reaffirmed in this century. Simply put, the Lombard master Vincenzo Foppa (c.1428–1515) bequeathed a heritage of naturalism to his successors that was reinforced by the art and writings of Leonardo da Vinci, who was claimed as an honorary Lombard.[17] Distinctive to this regional school are the primacy of the effects of natural light and the communication of intense human expression. As these ingredients, which are fundamental to Caravaggio's art, pepper the works of major and minor Lombard painters in varying degrees, the list of his precursors has grown in recent years to include painters whose influence on his artistic formation ranges from direct to passing and even remote. The raw naturalism and immediacy of Caravaggio's art, its play of light and dark, and its radical reinterpretation of both secular and sacred religious subject-matter can be found in four members of the school whose works had a significant role in shaping these essential elements: Giovanni Gerolamo Savoldo (c.1480–c.1548), Alessandro Bonvicino, called Moretto, of Brescia (c.1498–1554), and Antonio (1523–87) and Vincenzo Campi (1530/5–91). The Campi brothers were of course alive and active in Milan during Caravaggio's youth, while almost three generations separated him from Savoldo and Moretto. The Campi's paintings, however, were indebted to these older Brescian masters and were the likely intermediary between them and Caravaggio.[18]

Antonio Campi's altarpieces for Milanese churches dating from between 1571 and 1584 set an immediate example for the dramatic use of light. In the *Beheading of the Baptist* (Pl. 7), and *Saint Catherine Visited in Prison* (Pl. 8), he placed the sacred story in a darkened interior from which emerge shadowy figures lit selectively by an internal source of light. The *Saint Catherine*, a *tour de force* in which Antonio demonstrated the effects of artificial (torch), natural (moon), and divine light, caused a stir that could not have been lost on the young Caravaggio. The novelty of the picture incurred Lomazzo's disgust, expressed in verses entitled 'against a modern painter'. But the Spanish governor of Milan, Charles of Aragon, was sufficiently impressed by Antonio's

**8** Antonio Campi, **Saint Catherine Visited in Prison**, 1584; oil on canvas, 400 × 500 cm, S. Angelo, Milan

painting to honour him with a visit to his studio. Antonio's high status in the artistic circles of Milan was further cemented by a recently conferred knighthood, an honour that Caravaggio sought to attain in his last years.[19] Caravaggio remembered and imitated the dramatic impact of Antonio's contrast of light and dark in his first large-scale and public work in Rome. The psychological intensity of Caravaggio's works is not matched in Antonio Campi's art, however, but finds a more direct precedent in Antonio's own source, Savoldo.

Four of Savoldo's paintings, which hung in the Mint at Milan in Caravaggio's youth, had been celebrated in Giorgio Vasari's vivid phrase, 'pictures of night and fire'. The *Saint Matthew and the Angel* (Pl. 9) from this group is lit by the identical trio of light sources with which Antonio Campi isolated the principal episodes in *Saint Catherine*. The soft glow of light emanating from a candle on the table in the foreground reveals the evangelist's vision of the angel, and the curtain of darkness makes their intimate dialogue inaudible to the people in the tiny scenes in the background. Savoldo's use of a half-length format and the device of a table marking the edge of the picture plane sets his saint and angel directly before us, implicating us as eavesdroppers of their spiritual exchange. To achieve a similar immediacy, this format and the table device were adopted by Caravaggio in many of his early Roman easel pictures. Like Savoldo, Caravaggio used light to convey the communication between man and God in the *Calling of Saint Matthew* (Pl. 82), but unlike the Brescian painter, and Antonio Campi too for that matter, he rarely included the source of light within the painting.

The common model for Savoldo's and Antonio Campi's adoption of a strongly contrasted lighting, and perhaps for Caravaggio as well, lies in Leonardo da Vinci's art and theories of the early sixteenth century. Leonardo's two Milanese sojourns left a small but influential body of work and established a wide following of painters who for decades imitated his manner and copied his designs. Caravaggio himself later appropriated figural motifs from Leonardo: the angel's pointing finger in his *Sacrifice of Isaac* (Pl. 118) cites the *Virgin of the Rocks* (Paris, Louvre), the outflung arms of Christ's disciple in his earlier version of the *Supper at Emmaus* (Pl. 110) calls to mind Saint James the Less in the *Last Supper* (Milan, S. Maria delle Grazie), and Leonardesque prototypes also influenced the beardless Christ in the *Supper at Emmaus*.[20]

**9** Giovanni Gerolamo Savoldo, **Saint Matthew and the Angel**, 1533–5; oil on canvas, 93.3 × 124.5 cm, Metropolitan Museum of Art, New York

Beyond compositional and figural motifs, Caravaggio's naturalism and *chiaroscuro* would seem to embody Leonardo's theories about the primacy of nature, and the central role of light, colour and expression in painting. Leonardo's recognition of the interdependence of colour and light, and his invention of a dark mode to give sculptural relief to the human figure, had radically transformed the artistic practices of the preceding century and profoundly affected sixteenth-century painting. In the 1580s, these theories circulated in Milan through the writings of Lomazzo, which expounded on Leonardo's views on light, colour and expression. Caravaggio either absorbed these ideas directly from Lomazzo or acquired them at second hand from his workshop experience in Milan and from his study of Lombard painters, such as Antonio Campi and Savoldo.[21]

Caravaggio's commitment to naturalism also evokes Leonardo's precepts, but here too Lombard precedents in the works of Vincenzo Campi and Moretto provide the link. Vincenzo, younger than Antonio, dispensed with the mannered grace of his brother's altarpieces in favour of greater naturalism. In his two versions of *Christ Nailed to the Cross* (Pls. 10, 11) of the 1570s, the juxtaposition of the suffering victim and the callous executioners inspired Caravaggio's similar treatment in the *Crucifixion of Saint Peter* (Pl. 89). Vincenzo used steep foreshortening to close the gap between fictive and the viewer's space, and his unidealized figures and realistically drawn objects – hammer, nails, rope – drive home the spectacle of human brutality. But despite their impressive immediacy, the impact of Vincenzo's altar paintings is diluted by the muddy compositions, abrupt shifts in scale, and clumsy, even ugly figures.

**10** Vincenzo Campi, **Christ Nailed to the Cross**, 1575; oil on canvas, 136.5 × 196.5 cm, Certosa, Pavia

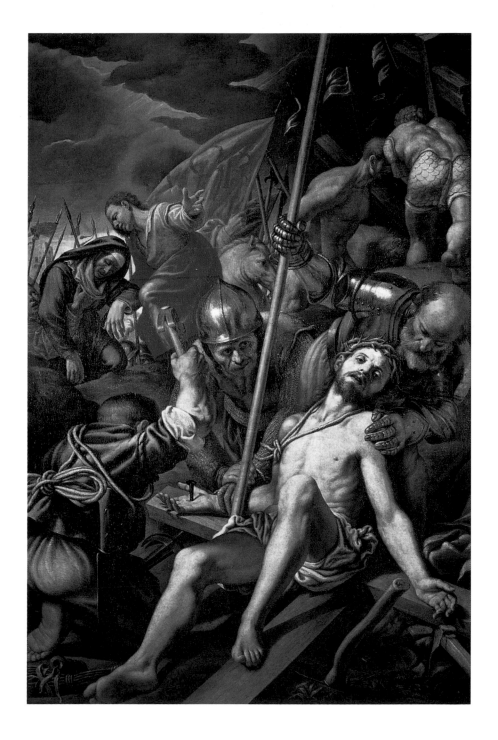

**11** Vincenzo Campi, **Christ Nailed to the Cross**, 1577; oil on canvas, 210 × 141 cm, Prado, Madrid

Moretto's lucid designs and imposing figures provided Caravaggio with a corrective to Vincenzo's provincial shortcomings. His altar painting of the *Supper in the House of Simon* (Pl. 12), still hanging in a Brescian parish church, distils this Gospel story into a private, modest supper. The closely framed composition reinforces the sense that the essentials of the story alone are represented. Naturalistic devices comprise a checklist of Caravaggism *avant la lettre*: dim interior, blank backdrop, a shaft of light entering along a diagonal from the right, biblical robes for Christ and Simon versus modern dress for Mary Magdalen and the two servants, and some simple, realistic still-life objects on a table. Based on live models, Moretto's cast consists of solid individuals whose faces are stamped by strong character. Again and again in his *œuvre*, Moretto clothed saints in humble human guise. His portrayal of the evangelist *Saint Luke* (Pl. 13), for the Chapel of the Sacrament in the cathedral of Brescia, shows a muscular, balding man, intent on his writing. Moretto's example, more than Peterzano's types, informs Caravaggio's conception of Matthew, and for that matter, of Jerome, Mary Magdalen, Catherine of Alexandria, and so forth. Of course, Caravaggio went further and imbued his saints with the realism reserved by Moretto, as well as Savoldo, for specific portraits of donors or other individuals in the guise of saints.

The preoccupation of Lombard artists with creating convincing religious imagery generated a category of artistic enterprise singular to the region: the decoration of alpine

**12** Alessandro Bonvicino, Il Moretto, **Supper in the House of Simon**, 1550–4; oil on canvas, 207 × 140 cm, S. Maria in Calchera, Brescia

**13** Alessandro Bonvicino, Il Moretto, **Saint Luke**, 1530–5; oil on canvas, 210 × 90 cm, Duomo Vecchio, Brescia

**14** Gaudenzio Ferrari, **Crucifixion**, *c.*1520–6; wood, terracotta and fresco, Sacromonte, Varallo

shrines or 'sacred mountains' ('sacri monti'). At the sanctuary at Varallo, the most spectacular example, small chapels wind up the hill to the main church. On their climb to the top, pilgrims paused on the threshold of each to pray in front of 'tableaux vivants' of life-sized painted terracotta statues with real hair and clothing who enacted the successive stages of Christ's Passion against frescoed panoramic backdrops (Pl. 14). Expressive faces and gestures charged the sculpted and painted figures, moving the worshipper to pity. Just before his death in 1584, Carlo Borromeo made his second pilgrimage to Varallo, setting a pious example to the Milanese populace.[22]

Lombard art moulded Caravaggio's approach to secular as well as religious themes. Although, according to Bellori, he started out as a portraitist in Milan, he first caught the attention of his Roman public with genre pictures. The dependence of portraiture and genre on the here and now lowered the critical status of these artistic categories in the hierarchy of traditional subject-matter for Italian painters. While portraiture and genre sank to the bottom, calling as they did merely for technical competence, history painting presided at the summit, for it exalted the noble deeds of heroes, heroines and saints, and it affirmed the artist's intellectual stature. Nevertheless, a steady demand for portraits from all manner of clients obliged even the most committed history painters to produce a portrait or two, but they shunned genre, leaving it to specialists.

Not surprisingly for a tradition rooted in naturalism, Lombard artists excelled in portraiture: compelling likenesses immortalize the sitters of Moretto and Savoldo and, moreover, of the major Bergamasque masters, Lorenzo Lotto (1480–1556/7) and Moretto's pupil, Giovanni Battista Moroni (1520/4–78).[23] Beyond the mapping of face and social status, their portraits reveal an individual's personality through veristic description of clothing, background and props, often with symbolic meaning. While dynamic poses animate the figures, frank gazes and eloquent gestures command our attention. Strangely, these characteristics appear only sporadically in Caravaggio's few extant portraits. Instead, the personages of his secular and sacred themes project the same convincing presence as do the portraits of his Lombard predecessors. Based as they are on live models, Caravaggio's anonymous boys, pagan deities, saints, Madonnas, and even bystanders closely resemble portraits of specific people who have assumed a role for the painter. But whereas in the older masters' allegorical

portrait, such as Moretto's *Portrait of a Woman as Saint Agnes* (Pl. 15), the disguise exposes rather than hides an aspect of the sitter's identity, the dress and attributes of Caravaggio's models mask their real identities under a fictive, if plausible, alias. Furthermore, in his altarpieces that juxtapose individualized figures in contemporary clothing with more generic types in biblical dress, Caravaggio's confrontation of now and then, of profane and sacred, imitates but moves beyond the earlier Lombard tradition of combining an actual portrait with a divine image, as exemplified by Moretto's *Apparition of the Madonna to the Deaf-Mute Filippo Viotti* (Pl. 16).

Despite its low critical standing, Lombard painters also took up genre painting at the end of the sixteenth century. Leonardo's legacy in Milan and the importation of northern examples stimulated native painters, including Figino, who painted at least one independent still life, and maybe Peterzano, in whose workshop were produced oil sketches of peapods and cherries in imitation of Leonardo.[24] The genre painting of Vincenzo Campi, however, was the most significant during the young Caravaggio's artistic formation. In the 1580s, Vincenzo painted a series of canvases combining figures and fruit, fish, poultry and cheese. Versions could be seen in the artist's native Cremona, and the wealth and prestige of the client for one series, the Függer family of Germany, must have impressed Campi's fellow artists and critics.[25]

**15** Alessandro Bonvicino, Il Moretto, **Portrait of a Woman as Saint Agnes**, *c*.1540; oil on canvas, 88.5 × 71.5 cm, private collection, Switzerland

**16** Alessandro Bonvicino, Il Moretto, **Apparition of the Madonna to the Deaf-Mute Filippo Viotti**, *c.*1534; oil on canvas, 122 × 177 cm, Santuario, Paitone (Brescia)

In the *Fruitseller* (Pl. 17), a young woman amidst a lavish array of fruits and vegetables looks directly out at us, one hand dangling a bunch of grapes, the other cradling a lap full of peaches. In addition to conveying the colours, forms, and textures of each fruit and the various receptacles, Vincenzo heightened the fruitseller's sensuality with customary connotations of fecundity. This mingling of naturalistic observation, allegorical meaning and sexual overtones set an influential example for Caravaggio's early Roman paintings.

During the four years of study following his apprenticeship, or between his last recorded presence in his home town in May 1592 and his assumed arrival in Rome that same year, Caravaggio had time to visit Venice. Whether or not he did so and the larger issue of the role of Venetian painting in his formation remain vexing questions. The only early evidence for such a trip comes from Bellori's assertion, dating sixty years after the painter's death, that Caravaggio went to Venice after leaving Milan and there discovered the art of Giorgione (1477/8–1510).[26] Venice was the most vital artistic centre in North Italy throughout the sixteenth century, and Lombard artists like Peterzano, Lotto and Savoldo had gravitated there to study and to work. During Caravaggio's youth, the political territory of the Republic of Venice encompassed the former Lombard cities of Brescia and Bergamo, and cultural and artistic exchange brought the two regions into close contact. Caravaggio's initial exposure to Venetian painting would have been in Milan, where major works by Titian, Tintoretto and Jacopo Bassano could be seen. His appetite whetted, the likelihood is that as an aspiring Lombard artist with some time and money, he seized the chance to see for himself the sights and famous pictures of Venice.

Caravaggio's *œuvre*, however, reveals only limited links with Venetian art. Bellori's claim that Caravaggio discovered Giorgione in Venice rested on his identification of certain elements in the early works as Giorgionesque: the sweet and pure colouring, the tempered shadows, and the use of a few tones to render natural form. Having annotated Baglione's earlier biography of Caravaggio, Bellori knew that Giorgione's name had been invoked by one critic upon the unveiling of the Contarelli Chapel. On that occasion, the strong *chiaroscuro* in Caravaggio's *Calling of Saint Matthew* (Pl. 82) was probably judged as representative of the North Italian painterly tradition, and perhaps the plumed caps and striped doublets of Matthew's companions reminded Roman viewers of Giorgionesque types. Such features in Caravaggio's early works, however, can also be explained by the phenomenon of 'Giorgionism'. Savoldo and other Lombard painters served as transmitters of Giorgione's 'sweetness' of colouring, romantic attire, allegorical themes of love and music, and also emulated his dreamy youths. Caravaggio's own assimilation of Giorgionism did not extend to the pastoral landscape, and as for his *chiaroscuro*, it more likely derived from Leonardo's heritage.[27]

**17** Vincenzo Campi, **Fruitseller**, *c.*1580–1; oil on canvas, 145 × 215 cm, Brera, Milan

Caravaggio's debt to Titian is explicit in one instance: the composition of the *Martyrdom of Saint Matthew* (Pl. 76), imitates Titian's *Martyrdom of Saint Peter Martyr* (Pl. 78), which hung in SS. Giovanni e Paolo in Venice until its almost complete destruction by fire in the nineteenth century. But as Titian's composition was disseminated in engravings during his lifetime, Caravaggio did not need to travel to Venice to see the original. Even if he did, he restricted his attention to the dramatic potential of Titian's figurative design and had no use in the Contarelli Chapel or elsewhere for the importance assigned to the landscape by the Venetian master. Furthermore, Titian's loose

brushwork or his colour with its glazes, blended and reflected tones did not influence Caravaggio's handling of paint, and quintessentially Titianesque themes, such as the female nude, are absent from Caravaggio's *œuvre*.

Of Titian's younger compatriots who were still alive in the 1580s, only Jacopo Bassano (d. 1592) and Tintoretto (d. 1594) painted works showing pronounced affinities with Caravaggio's art. Although no specific painting by Bassano can be cited as a direct model for Caravaggio, his biblical interpretations (cf. *Adoration of the Shepherds*, Pl. 18) broke with Italian tradition in recasting the stories with humble, usually peasant characters, in pastoral settings warmed by natural light. Bassano's rustic types in barnyards or fields seldom stray into Caravaggio's art, which is set primarily indoors and peopled by urban dwellers. Yet the farm horse in the *Conversion of Saint Paul* (Pl. 86) or the shepherds and animals in the late *Adoration of the Shepherds* (Pl. 165) are successors to Bassano's peasants and animals.

Unlike the art of Bassano, Tintoretto's work supplied specific compositional motifs for Caravaggio's works, and his influence extended further still. Although Tintoretto's visible brushstrokes and sketchy finish are techniques found sparingly in Caravaggio's handling of paint, his dramatic lighting offered a valuable model that reinforced and even superseded Antonio Campi's and Savoldo's nocturnes. Completed as recently as 1581, Tintoretto's decoration of the Scuola Grande di San Rocco presented an entire ensemble in which supernatural light flashes across deeply shadowed scenes and acts as a dynamic agent of spiritual revelation. As Tintoretto's effects of light cannot be fully understood from engravings, Caravaggio could only have absorbed this lesson at first hand in Venice.[28]

Apart from these specific links, Caravaggio's working procedure bears general similarities to Venetian tradition. Throughout his career, Caravaggio dispensed with the standard practice of making preliminary compositional drawings and figure studies preparatory to a painting. Instead he roughed out his design directly on the canvas or 'alla prima', correcting it as he went along. This approach departs from the training that he must have received from Peterzano who, as a large corpus of extant drawings attests, prepared his frescoes and altarpieces in careful studies.[29] Nor was Peterzano unique in this in Milan, for graphic evidence also exists for the methods of Figino and the Campi. Their procedure conforms to Central Italian theory based on Neoplatonic thought about artistic creation: namely that drawing (*disegno*) represents the first step in translating the artist's divinely inspired idea (*disegno interno*) into its external expression in a painting. However, the Venetian painterly tradition put colour (*colore*) before *disegno*, and artists like Titian and Tintoretto often conceived their compositions 'alla prima', on occasion making drawings to study natural light or to fix a pose.

During this artistic gestation of eight years, Caravaggio acquired practical skills and a substantial familiarity with modern North Italian painting. By now twenty-one and with both parents dead, he decided to move to Rome in order to follow in the path of the many Lombard artists before him who had sought work and fame there. Caravaggio set off for the papal capital some time after 11 May 1592, the date on which he was last recorded in his home town.

Chapter 2 **Rome**

Arriving in Rome in late 1592 or early in 1593, Caravaggio struggled for the next three years to earn a living and build a career. He had no money and no fixed address, and so his small inheritance must have been depleted. Hard as these times were, his Lombard contacts probably eased the way for him somewhat. His uncle Ludovico, a priest, had already moved to Rome and was an obvious first recourse. Perhaps with his uncle's help, Caravaggio met his first host, Monsignor Pandolfo Pucci from Recanati in the Marches. Pucci was steward to Camilla Peretti, sister of Pope Sixtus V and a relative by marriage of the family of Costanza Colonna, the Marchesa of the town of Caravaggio. In return for his board, Caravaggio was forced to do work that was distasteful to him, as well as to paint replicas of devotional pictures. Finally disgusted by too many suppers of nothing but salad from 'Monsignor Insalata', as he nicknamed the stingy prelate, Caravaggio bolted from Pucci's service after a few months.

The room let to him by Pucci was the first of many Caravaggio lived in as he moved around Rome, restlessly it would seem, from prelates' households to painters' studios. After leaving Pucci, he joined the studio of Lorenzo, an otherwise forgotten Sicilian painter, for whom he churned out three heads a day. Around this time, he probably did similar hack work for the painter Antiveduto Grammatica (1571–1626), whose reputation rested largely on series of portraits of famous men. At some point, Caravaggio switched to the prestigious workshop of the brothers Giuseppe (1568–1640) and Bernardino (1571–1622) Cesari, where he lasted as long as eight months. Around 1595, he again changed lodgings, moving into the palace of another Monsignor, Fantin Petrignani (1540–1600) in the parish of S. Salvatore in Campo.[1]

The city in which he now made his home was very different from Milan, with its cold and grey skies, foreign overlords and mercantile economy. From early Christian times, Rome had a unique dual identity as the political capital of the Papal States and spiritual capital of Western Christendom. By the end of the sixteenth century, the efforts of reform-minded popes had reconsolidated papal power after the religious upheaval of the Protestant Reformation and the political trauma of the Sack of Rome (1527). The short reign of Sixtus V (1585–90) especially strengthened the papacy's now unprecedented power by reinvigorating the damaged, demoralized and depopulated capital both spiritually and materially. Sixtus limited the number of cardinals in the Sacred College to seventy and reorganized the papal government, or the Curia as it was known. While the Curia administered spiritual matters and oversaw its own temporal interests, the Roman Senate, composed of elected officials, managed civic affairs involving citizenship, commerce, law enforcement, city-wide festivals and the urban fabric. Papal and municipal jurisdiction overlapped, however, with ultimate authority residing in the Pope.[2]

The territory of the Papal States too had notably expanded after the annexation of Bologna (1506) and of Ferrara (1598). In 1600, the papacy was a major physical presence on the Italian peninsula, its rule extending into northern Italy where its secure borders met the Venetian state on the east and the Duchy of Modena on the west. The papacy's international relations were helped by the dramatic conversion of Henri IV of France from Protestantism in 1595, and pan-European peace was promised three years later by the papal mediation of a treaty between France and Spain.

Caravaggio reached Rome in time to witness its emergence as a splendid capital, thanks to a number of ambitious urban projects initiated by Sixtus V. The Pope conceived a network of spacious avenues connecting major Christian monuments and opening long vistas culminating in squares adorned with ancient obelisks and modern fountains; his scheme of renewal also included the repair and extension of the old aqueducts, enabling new neighbourhoods to be settled. A visitor returning to Rome in 1590, after the lapse of a decade, declared that he scarcely recognized the city which seemed to him to have been reborn from the ashes.[3]

In 1592, Clement VIII became Pope and began a thirteen-year period of stability, growth and prosperity that exactly coincided with Caravaggio's career in the capital. The surge in construction that transformed the urban fabric of Rome in the second half of the sixteenth century continued under Clement: new churches and palaces rose alongside earlier projects, while many older structures were enlarged or renovated. Rome of the late sixteenth century was arguably the most cosmopolitan city in Europe, boasting a unique mix of inhabitants. Comparatively small in 1527, its population had doubled to almost 110,000 by 1600. The teeming papal capital drew immigrants and visitors from all over Italy – Milanese, Genoese, Florentines – and its international affairs attracted many foreigners. Men far outnumbered women, and ecclesiastics accounted for almost ten per cent of residents. The overwhelming proportion of men, many of them single, explains the profusion of prostitutes. But a constant influx of pilgrims also crowded the city; their numbers soared to around half a million for Holy Year in 1600.[4]

Joining the artists, architects and artisans who moved to Rome to seize the unparalleled opportunities for employment, Caravaggio served both ecclesiastical and lay patrons for the most part attached to the papal bureaucracy and representing both the city's old, baronial families and its new arrivals. Princely cardinals, titled nobility, rich bankers and jurists were all commissioning works of art at this time and assembling private art collections to enhance their elegant city palaces. Caravaggio's wealthiest and most powerful patrons maintained lavish households with liveried retinues and expensive carriages, a luxurious solution to the practical need for crossing the city with its new and broad thoroughfares. The Pope and his family, enriching themselves through nepotism, presided at the very top of what was a singularly open social structure. The magnificence and pomp of the papal court and its capital ostensibly reflected the greater glory of God.

Yet Clement VIII, while embracing outward ceremony, was pious and ascetic in his personal conduct and set a high moral tone for his household and the city. Upon his election as Pope, he immediately turned his attention to one of several worrisome urban problems: the ubiquity of prostitutes. After a vain attempt to banish them, he succeeded in confining most to neighbourhoods out of his sight. More grave than the threat posed by prostitutes, however, was the assault on the Catholic faith by diverse heretics: under Clement, Caravaggio could have witnessed both the jailing of Tommaso Campanella and Giordano Bruno's fiery pyre in the Campo de' Fiori. Perhaps, a year earlier in 1599, he might have stood among the crowd to watch the beheading of the young noblewoman Beatrice Cenci whom Clement refused to pardon for patricide, along with her stepmother and brother – a sensational spectacle of papal severity.[5]

The Pope's scrutiny also fell on indecent ecclesiastical art and, during pastoral visits to Roman churches, he ordered images with nude or scantily clad figures to be covered or removed. His censorship of sacred art safeguarded decorum in the representation of saints and biblical narrative.[6] Clement's righteous outlook goes far to explain the rejection of the first version of Caravaggio's *Saint Matthew and the Angel* (Pl. 94) for S. Luigi dei Francesi. But the portrayal of the evangelist, judged indecorous for a public setting, found a welcome home in a private art collection, testifying to the range, and even the dichotomy, of attitudes towards religious painting in Rome *c.*1600. In sum, the restored prestige of the Church and the renewed energy of its leaders, the wealth and aspirations of the élite, the rich heritage of antiquity and of the Renaissance, the cosmopolitan population and the current building boom, all of these factors fed the creative vitality of Rome on

46

the brink of a new century and ripe for the genesis of new artistic forms.

Upon arriving in Rome, Caravaggio must have marvelled at the great wealth of contemporary art in the city, which surpassed anything he had seen in Milan in terms of sheer volume, monumentality and variety of styles. His attention would have gravitated especially towards paintings produced under papal auspices. Three artists, older than Caravaggio by a generation, had worked on papal projects before his arrival in the city and still held respected positions at the end of the century: Girolamo Muziano (1532–92), Federico Barocci (c.1535–1612), and Federico Zuccaro (c.1542–1609). Although all three had been shaped by Mannerism, they developed distinctive and influential styles which contributed to the naturalistic trends in painting that were gathering momentum before the turn of the century.[7]

The Brescian-born Muziano was the first of the three to come to Rome, in 1549, later earning papal patronage under Gregory XIII (1572–85). In his altarpieces inspired by Counter-Reformation piety, the naturalistic lighting and spacious landscape settings betray his Lombard origins and Venetian training, and distinguish his art from late Mannerism. Although Caravaggio arrived in Rome after Muziano's death, the latter's artistic legacy later proved valuable in the commission for the Contarelli Chapel.

Barocci and Zuccaro, both from the Marches, worked on the frescoes in the Casino of Pius IV in the early 1560s. Returning home to the ducal court at Urbino, Barocci continued to fulfil Roman commissions, and his later patronage by the Roman Oratory brought two of his mature altarpieces to Rome. In 1586, six years before Caravaggio's arrival, artists had lined up for three days to admire Barocci's *Visitation* in the Chiesa Nuova (Pl. 19), and perhaps the well-known story of Philip Neri's rapture in front of the painting was still passed around. Although the ideality and painterly brushwork of Barocci's art are essentially different from Caravaggio's, its dynamism, human warmth and domestic intimacy presented a vivid contrast to much contemporary Roman painting, and we can imagine that it struck a sympathetic chord in the young Lombard painter.

**19** Federico Barocci, **Visitation**, 1586; oil on canvas, 285 × 187 cm, S. Maria in Vallicella (Chiesa Nuova), Rome

**20** Federico Zuccaro, **The Archangels Worshipping the Trinity**, *c.*1590–4; Il Gesù, Rome

The third artist of this important trio, Zuccaro, had emerged in the 1580s as Sixtus V's favourite painter and was in charge of numerous papal projects. However, he subsequently fell out of favour and was excluded from Clement's official projects; Zuccaro worked instead for ecclesiastical and private patrons, as well as on the erudite frescoes in his own house. By the 1590s, he had evolved a deliberately simplified style, and a post-Tridentine severity and clarity stamp his altarpiece (Pl. 20) and frescoes of c.1590–4 in the Cappella degli Angeli of Il Gesù, the Jesuits' mother church. Zuccaro is the only painter of the older generation for whom there survives a record of direct contact with Caravaggio: his reaction to Caravaggio's work was reported by Baglione and, in his deposition for the 1603 libel suit, Caravaggio stated

that he was friendly with Zuccaro and regarded him as one of the good artists in the city. Despite Zuccaro's marginalized position *vis-à-vis* papal patronage, his prestige had remained high among artists in Rome because of his role as founder and first *principe* of the Academy of St Luke, the painters' guild.

The Academy first opened its doors to Roman artists in November 1593; in lectures delivered there Zuccaro expounded the theoretical bases of the discipline and argued that the artist's intellectual inspiration separated painting from the manual crafts. Caravaggio would certainly have known many of the academicians who attended the first meetings and may have done so himself if he is to be identified with the 'Michele da Milano' recorded as present in 1593. His full name appears in late-seventeenth-century copies of the Academy attendance rolls, and his portrait hangs in the palace of the institution alongside those of other members, even though his anti-academic biases argue against any active commitment to its ideals and, in 1600, he assaulted one of the Academy's pupils. He none the less must have weighed the potential advantages of membership for professional advancement, especially as Federico Borromeo, the Cardinal Protector of the Academy, was a Milanese, Carlo Borromeo's nephew and a relative of the Marchesa di Caravaggio. A few years later sponsorship of the Academy transferred from Borromeo to Cardinal Del Monte, who, at that very moment, was welcoming Caravaggio into his household; surely the painter realized his self-interests lay in respecting his new patron's influential position in the artistic establishment.[8]

Among living Italian painters closer in age to Caravaggio, the most eminent was Giuseppe Cesari. Caravaggio's eight-month stint in his workshop, some time between 1593 and 1595, fell just when Cesari had emerged as the leading painter in the city. That Caravaggio entered into association with such an eminent artist so quickly suggests that he came recommended and that he pursued the highest professional ambitions.

Cesari's studio exposed Caravaggio to the artistic style most in favour in official circles. Reformed Mannerism characterizes his work, exemplified by the *Raising of Lazarus* (Pl. 21); here Cesari designed a balanced and symmetrical composition defined by a plausible architectural space, in which Christ and Lazarus occupy front centre stage. Both the composition and the figures depend on Raphael's frescoes in the Vatican Palace, which had become the paradigm of history painting for Mannerist artists in Rome and Florence. The *Raising* displays a command of the human figure, and the refined poses and fluid handling delighted seventeenth-century commentators, who esteemed the grace of Cesari's art.[9] Lacking, however, is any convincing drama; the generically handsome protagonists and well-behaved crowd enact the Gospel story with ceremonial but expressionless dignity.

**21** Giuseppe Cesari, Il Cavaliere d'Arpino, **Raising of Lazarus**, *c.*1593; oil on canvas, 76 × 98 cm, Galleria Nazionale d'Arte Antica, Rome

50

**22** Giovanni Baglione, **The Emperor Constantine Investing the Lateran with Treasure**, 1600; fresco, S. Giovanni in Laterano, Rome

Working under Cesari, Caravaggio could have been asked to participate in any one of the major fresco projects then under way in the workshop. But if it is true, as Bellori says, that Caravaggio grew frustrated at not painting the human figure and being restricted to flowers and fruits, the likelihood is that he had little if any role in these works, despite a few early claims to the contrary.[10] Indeed, upon Cesari's appointment to supervise the large papal projects at the Lateran and St Peter's in 1599, Caravaggio was not among those invited to participate. In directing the artistic team that collaborated on these Clementine decorations, Cesari imposed a unified, 'official' style on a diverse group of painters.[11] As exemplified in the Lateran transept (Pl. 22), legible and rhythmically measured narratives inspired by Raphael's compositions solemnly celebrate Church history. We can picture Caravaggio impressed by the sheer grandeur of the Lateran decoration but we know, with the advantage of hindsight, that he found the bland uniformity of most official Clementine art of little use for his own work. Such major enterprises demanded skilled frescoists, and perhaps his lack of experience in this medium told against him. Furthermore, the half-length figures that typify his early Roman easel pictures do not demonstrate the mastery of pictorial narrative vital to the papal cycles and which he acquired only later. Despite its limitations, Caravaggio's experience in Cesari's studio must have been invaluable for its affiliation with the Roman artistic establishment, for introducing him to the most prestigious contemporary artistic projects, and for useful contacts with future patrons.[12]

The Central Italian tradition, embodied in Cesari's art, was the main artistic lesson available to Caravaggio in his first three years in Rome. For any young artist arriving in the capital in the late sixteenth century, the customary curriculum covered the ancient ruins and statues, followed by the works of the High Renaissance masters, Michelangelo and especially Raphael. That Caravaggio's open disregard for this prescribed programme shocked his contemporaries is clear from his biographers. Bellori, who upheld the classical ideal of beauty in his writings, remarked on Caravaggio's 'not only ignoring but even despising the most excellent marbles of the ancients and the famous paintings of Raphael', in this early period in Rome. When shown ancient sculptures by Phidias and Glycon, Caravaggio supposedly dismissed them and pointed instead to a crowd of people. There, he declared, were sufficient models for his brush. Even if this particular episode never happened, Caravaggio must have made some such public show of this attitude, for, according to other critics, his disdain for ancient statuary prevented him from selecting the best in nature and condemned him to being a mere transcriber of reality. Baglione, who disliked his rival for personal reasons, attributed this unorthodox approach to the painter's 'sarcastic and haughty personality', claiming that arrogance led him at times to 'speak badly of all the painters of the past and present, no matter how distinguished they were'.[13]

No one would argue today that Caravaggio's paintings have the realism of snapshots, and his familiarity with ancient and Renaissance art has often been demonstrated. None the less, his early biographers rightly recognized that the imitation of traditional models in his paintings was minimal in contrast to the practice of contemporary artists. The theoretical implications were radical because at issue was the classical ideal of painting as it had evolved since the fifteenth century: the painter's vocation was to invent an art that mirrored divine creation; guided by the best examples in the art of the past, he was to improve upon nature through the process of selection. The motives underlying Caravaggio's belligerence towards this venerable ideal cannot easily be understood; a vehemently independent spirit must have played some part, as Baglione suspected. Already in Milan, Caravaggio had rejected his teacher's authority in the spheres of drawing and fresco painting. But he had studied his Lombard forebears closely, and his stylistic allegiance to that naturalistic tradition, all the more precious in the foreign Roman environment, may well have predisposed him to challenge the supremacy of the artistic canon he met there in his first years.

The first pictures Caravaggio painted in Rome immediately set him apart from the artistic mainstream. On the testimony of the early biographies, a small group of works can be assigned to 1593–5: *Self-Portrait as Bacchus* (Pl. 23), *Boy Peeling a Fruit* (Pl. 25), *Boy Bitten by a*

*Lizard* (Pls. 26, 31), *Boy with a Basket of Fruit* (Pl. 24), *Penitent Magdalen* (Pl. 32), *Cardsharps* (Pl. 35), and the *Fortune-Teller* (Pl. 37). Two of these – the *Self-Portrait* and the *Boy with a Basket of Fruit* – were confiscated from Cesari in a legal settlement in 1607, along with other paintings, and given by Pope Paul V to his nephew Cardinal Scipione Borghese; their presence in Cesari's studio, as well as their youthful style, suggests that Caravaggio had executed them while employed by Cesari.[14] Clouding any reconstruction of Caravaggio's earliest activity in Rome, however, are debates over authenticity and chronology posed by the lack of documentary evidence and the existence of competing versions of *Boy Peeling a Fruit*, *Boy Bitten by a Lizard*, and the *Fortune-Teller*. On the positive side, the fortuitous rediscovery of the original *Cardsharps* and the restoration of the Capitoline *Fortune-Teller* have helped to create a clearer profile of the youthful Caravaggio.

Dazzling in their illusionism and originality, the *Boy with a Basket of Fruit* and *Boy Bitten by a Lizard* are Caravaggio's most striking juvenilia. Along with the *Self-Portrait as Bacchus* and *Boy Peeling a Fruit*, they focus on a youth holding still-life objects or posed next to them; these four canvases all have modest dimensions, a half-length format, a bright and neutral background, and, of course, compelling physicality of figure and objects. The antecedents for their still lifes and allegorical implications lie in Lombard painting, but in Rome of the 1590s they represented a novelty for contemporary viewers in several ways.

One fresh aspect in particular was the prominent still life, a principal element in Caravaggio's youthful works and one which his biographers praised. Enthusing over a certain vase of flowers, which he said was one of many Caravaggio painted while working for Cesari, Bellori noted such effects as the transparency of the glass vessel and the water within, the reflections of a window in the room, and the freshness of dewdrops scattered on the flowers. Unfortunately, this painting is lost, and no other independent still life from Caravaggio's earliest phase of activity has been satisfactorily identified. Although he may have painted relatively few still lifes in contrast to Flemish contemporaries active in Rome in the last decade of the sixteenth century, none the less the early sources emphasize his talent in this category of subject-matter. Bellori even asserted that Caravaggio's convincing imitation of fruits and flowers had created a new fashion for still life. In his earliest genre pictures, such as the *Boy with a Basket of Fruit*, the care lavished on the still life, and its visual and thematic significance, confirm that Caravaggio was in fact one of the first Italian painters to pay serious attention to still life and to put flowers, fruits, and vegetables on an equal footing with the figure.[15]

While the young Caravaggio profited from his naturalistic skills in still life, he could not entirely escape from contemporary artistic attitudes. An ambivalence on his part can be detected in his supposed 'deep frustration' at being forced to paint only still life and not the figure in Cesari's studio. At the same time he maintained that 'good still life painting required as much of his artistry as good figure painting'.[16] This declaration surely carried a polemical edge, because the mere imitation of fruits and flowers could never claim the same exalted status enjoyed by figure painting in the hierarchy of artistic genres since the early Italian Renaissance. By his late Roman years, Caravaggio did stop painting vases of flowers and arrangements of fruit but it was the altered nature of his commissions, rather than any theoretical shift on his part, which accounted for the change. In his religious subject-matter, another class of still life had come to occupy his attention: books, skulls, swords and shovels. These objects anchor his mature religious works to reality and find their antecedents in the roses and grapes of his early easel paintings.

**23  Self-Portrait as Bacchus**, *c.*1593–4;  oil on canvas, 66 × 52 cm, Galleria Borghese, Rome

Beyond the unprecedented role of still life, Caravaggio's earliest genre pictures impressed viewers for the naturalism and expressiveness of their figures. Critics remarked that he painted directly from life, studying his own features in the mirror for the *Self-Portrait as Bacchus* and *Boy Bitten by a Lizard*. But exactly what other connotations Caravaggio's earliest genre pictures conjured up for viewers is harder to fathom. The seventeenth-century sources are silent on Caravaggio's singular imagery, and modern specialists continue to ponder its elusive allegorical and even erotic implications.

The argument that these works have no more content than meets the eye has become a minority viewpoint. A current fashion is to unravel the hidden meaning of each by seeking clues in glances and gestures, and in the floral and vegetal species on display. One of the most recondite modern interpretations is the startling claim that Caravaggio hid allegories of Christian redemption in his young boys' activities.[17] The *Boy Peeling a Fruit* would thus be a surrogate for Christ who purifies humanity's sinful soul, and in the *Self-Portrait as Bacchus*, Caravaggio would have represented himself as imitator of the resurrected Christ. The proposition that a seemingly secular painting supports a Christian reading is by no means outlandish in the religious climate of late-sixteenth-century Italy. However, in view of their impact, either singly or as a group, and the lack of any evidence, whether internal or external, Caravaggio's images of young boys belie Christian interpretations.

Caravaggio's early pictorial imagery lends itself instead to seasonal and sensory associations, as has been frequently suggested. From

24 **Boy with a Basket of Fruit**, *c.*1593–4; oil on canvas, 70 × 67 cm, Galleria Borghese, Rome

his Lombard study years, his traditional training under Peterzano, and his eight-month stint in Cesari's conventional studio, he would surely have been familiar with the standard allegorical themes found in North Italian genre paintings. Bassano produced more than one such series beginning in the 1570s and, a decade later, Vincenzo Campi painted two sets of genre scenes with symbolic allusions. One of Campi's cycles, which includes a kitchen and two market scenes, and the *Fruitseller* (Pl. 17), contains allusions to the Four Elements. In both Bassano's and Campi's series, the theme provided a loose unity and offered a light symbolic gloss to the primary content of the imagery: peasants at work, the display of foodstuffs, the landscape and bawdy humour.[18]

When set within this allegorical context, Caravaggio's choice of fruit in the *Boy with a Basket of Fruit* can be described as autumnal, and the pagan deity in *Self-Portrait as Bacchus* personifies that same season. In *Boy Bitten by a Lizard*, the sense of touch is vividly illustrated, while the *Boy Peeling a Fruit* might allude to taste.[19] However, the fruits in the boy's basket do not all ripen in autumn; Bacchus's identity as the god of wine can convey other equally plausible messages of bacchic pleasures; and the boy peeling a fruit is not *tasting* it. Furthermore, as the dimensional and compositional disparities of these early genre pictures preclude their grouping as cycles or even pairs, the individual canvases would have to stand alone, shed of their usual context. Pertinent to remember is that Caravaggio's early works may well have elicited unintended associations in viewers' minds. Before Del Monte's patronage, none of Caravaggio's works were painted on commission. How Cesari came to own the *Self-Portrait as Bacchus* and *Boy with a Basket of Fruit* is unknown, and what appealed to him

**25 Boy Peeling a Fruit** (attributed), *c.*1593–4; oil on canvas, 75.5 × 64.4 cm, private collection, Rome

then or what might interest a modern audience today cannot necessarily be attributed to Caravaggio himself. The elusiveness of the symbolism in Caravaggio's youthful genre pictures suggests that he was less concerned to convey allegories of the seasons or the senses than to simulate – even stimulate – sensory experience through the descriptive naturalism of the fruits and flowers as well as the figures he painted.[20]

In *Boy Bitten by a Lizard*, Caravaggio concentrated primarily on the portrayal of human emotion. Unlike earlier, didactic representations of the Sense of Touch, as in the widely disseminated print of 1561 after Frans Floris (Pl. 27), the boy's reaction to what he touches is far more pictorially important than the act of touching itself. His brow contracts and his mouth opens in pain; his right hand tenses from the bite while, in reflex, his left hand flies up. Through the youth's exaggerated recoil at the lizard's bite – painful but neither poisonous nor fatal – Caravaggio first explored dramatic facial expression and bodily gesture, two fundamental elements in his subsequent visualization of narrative subjects. In so doing, he was less interested in an allegory of touch than in testing his observations from the model against analogous representations in sixteenth-century painting across Northern Italy and in Leonardo da Vinci's theories about the importance of expression in art. Mimetic exercises in extremes of expression had inspired images such as Sofonisba Anguissola's *Child Bitten by a Crab* (Pl. 28). Violent and instantaneous, the response of Caravaggio's boy is also transitory and, as such, grounded in real experience.[21]

While stressing Caravaggio's recourse to live models, his biographers make no comment about his exclusive use of youths, another

**26 Boy Bitten by a Lizard**, *c*.1593–4;  oil on canvas, 66 × 49.5 cm, National Gallery, London

factor setting the early genre pictures apart from contemporary painting. The *Self-Portrait as Bacchus* is by necessity male, but the same does not hold for the choice of a boy as protagonist in the other three paintings. The prosaic rationale that poverty forced Caravaggio to use himself and his friends as models, though unproblematic in the case of the *Boy Peeling a Fruit*, inadequately accounts for the appearance of the male figures in *Boy with a Basket of Fruit* and the *Boy Bitten by a Lizard*.[22] Both boys' shirts inexplicably slip down, baring their right shoulders which are thrust forward. Accentuating the ambiguous appeal of these paintings are the direct gazes of both, the fruit-selling boy's tilted head and parted lips, and the other boy's luscious mass of curls and the rose tucked behind his ear.

The erotic charge in this imagery has especially piqued modern curiosity about the sexual preferences of Caravaggio and his audience.[23] As might be expected from such a slippery and potent topic, opinions vary widely as to both Caravaggio's intent and his viewers' response. Only conflicting evidence about the painter's sexuality can be culled from the early sources, warning us to beware of oversimplifying the private life of this complex personality. Caravaggio never married and, as far as is known, he had no children. His presumed homosexuality hinges on the use of the word *bardassa* in a remark made by a witness in the 1603 libel suit brought against him by Baglione. The witness applied the word to a boy whom Caravaggio and Onorio Longhi, his friend and co-defendant, had asked to distribute their libellous writings. Although *bardassa* can in fact mean male lover, this witness does not seem to have been insinuating a male *ménage à trois* but was more likely using the word in its alternative, non-sexual meaning of 'urchin'.[24]

62

Reports of Caravaggio's relations with women come a few years later. In 1605 the Roman police records cite a certain Lena, who was identified as 'Caravaggio's woman' and the cause of an argument between him and the plaintiff. Another reference to Caravaggio and women was made by Mancini, whose presence in Rome during Caravaggio's lifetime is now documented; he stated that the model for Mary in the *Death of the Virgin* was a 'courtesan loved by Caravaggio'.[25]

Two still later claims imply that Caravaggio's attraction to women did not preclude an interest in boys. The first, dating to about 1650 – forty years after his death – was made in an entry in the travel diary of the English connoisseur Richard Symonds, who noted that Caravaggio's male model for the *Cupid* (Pl. 106) 'laid with him'. The second arises from an incident reported in Messina. Caravaggio allegedly left the town after assaulting a teacher suspicious about his spending so much time 'watching the poses of schoolboys at play'. Although dating to more than a century later, this report cited exact names and places, which suggests that the tale was passed down through local oral tradition.[26]

Beyond reflecting Caravaggio's personal tastes, his effeminate youths perhaps deliberately pandered to a gay Roman market, as has been proposed. But although prelates or other Romans with homosexual proclivities might have responded favourably to Caravaggio's pretty youths, the proposition remains speculative in that the *Boy Bitten by a Lizard* was sold on the market, and *Boy with a Basket of Fruit* may or may not have been painted for Cesari, its later owner. As for Cardinal Del Monte's personality, I will return to that subject in the next chapter.

Can we draw any conclusions about the overt sensuality of the youths in *Boy with a Basket of Fruit* and *Boy Bitten by a Lizard*?

27  Cornelis Cort after Frans Floris, **Allegory of Touch**, 1561;  engraving, 20.2 × 26.7 cm
28  Sofonisba Anguissola, **Child Bitten by a Crab**, c.1554;  black chalk, 33.3 × 38.5 cm, Capodimonte, Naples

The former offers his fruit with uncalled-for passion, and the latter resembles a distraught lover. Reducing either, however, to the status of a homosexual icon flattens the richness of the imagery and presupposes that our own biases about gender and sexuality prevailed in early Baroque Rome. But the very existence of exclusive categories of homosexuality and heterosexuality in the pre-modern period has been challenged by cultural historians.[27] Moreover, the cultivated élite of Caravaggio's day had deeply imbibed classical culture, in which love

between men and boys held an honoured place and did not preclude relations between men and women. The seductive appeal of Caravaggio's beautiful boys, then, might well have been directed simultaneously to viewers of different sexual persuasions. The androgyny of the youths certainly embodies an antique ideal of beauty, which had resurfaced widely in painting and sculpture from the early Renaissance. Before Caravaggio, Leonardo da Vinci had painted comely youths with ringlets and softly rounded bodies, and Giorgione and his imitators had depicted sweet-faced dreamy boys.[28]

In *Boy with a Basket of Fruit* and *Boy Bitten by a Lizard*, Caravaggio filtered the eroticism through a refining lens and elevated his boys above their humble origins. This process of refinement is all the more striking in contrast to such imitations as Bartolomeo Manfredi's *Fruitseller* (Pl. 29) or the anonymous *Boy Bitten by a Crayfish* (Pl. 30). Unlike those banal scenes, Caravaggio's idealized boys juxtaposed with the fruits of nature call up poetic conceits of the transitory nature of youth. Still-life painting in itself often inspires meditation on the course of time and the regenerative cycle of birth, life and death.[29] Wilting grape leaves, notched pear leaves, and a blemished apple contrast with the fresh-

**29** Bartolomeo Manfredi, **Fruitseller**, *c.*1615–20; oil on canvas, 116 × 158 cm, Pushkin Museum, Moscow

faced youth in *Boy with a Basket of Fruit*. In the *Boy Bitten by a Lizard*, the nasty surprise hidden amidst the fruit acts as a metaphor for the inevitable passage from innocence to experience, and the green, ripening, and ripened cherries on the table reinforce the eternal message that everyone must grow up. That process can be as painful as it is unavoidable, and the lizard's bite foretells the disillusionments of adulthood. The theme that bitter knowledge lies in wait for unsuspecting youth was perhaps also intended as an underlying meaning in *Boy Peeling a Fruit*, if the fruit is actually a sour-tasting orange or bergamot, as it has been identified.[30]

Caravaggio's evocation of fleeting youth may also reflect classical literature, specifically the lyric verses of Horace and Ovid, which were reinterpreted in his day in the poetry of Giambattista Marino and others. That Caravaggio himself knew this literature is possible; he first came into contact with literary circles through his great friend, the painter Prospero Orsi, whose brother Aurelio was a distinguished poet; later he became friends with Marino.[31] Although only Caravaggio's cultured admirers could and did delight in

**65**

**30** Anonymous, **Boy Bitten by a Crayfish**, 17th century; oil on canvas, 96 × 73 cm, Musée des Beaux-Arts, Strasbourg

uncovering specific analogies with classical literature in these paintings which inspired their own epigraphs in verse, a wide audience surely appreciated his expression of the universal themes of vibrant youth, awakening sexuality, the mutability of nature and the poignancy of ageing.

Though professional success did not come instantly, Caravaggio's first genre pictures soon became fashionable, as early copies attest. As many as ten versions of the *Boy Peeling a Fruit* survive; Caravaggio's original has yet to be identified, although several canvases of the highest quality have competing claims. Likewise, the *Boy Bitten by a Lizard* exists in two versions, almost identical in size, that have generated heated debate among connoisseurs about their respective authenticity. Subtle changes in light, colour and mood, accentuated by its abraded condition, differentiate the painting in London (Pl. 26) from the canvas in Florence (Pl. 31). In the latter picture, the heightened contrast of light and dark and the boy's more pained expression suggest that it was painted after the more colourful and softer London painting. Only very recently, and as a result of technical analyses, has it been proposed that both paintings be accepted as originals by Caravaggio. That the artist might have copied his own paintings goes against the grain of cherished assumptions about his working directly from the model in front of him. If both versions were to prove autograph, then Caravaggio must have repeated himself, as did many of his contemporaries, to satisfy a client's request. Yet, despite the few noted differences, the overriding similarity of the two paintings makes them unique as a pair for Caravaggio who, when repeating the same subject, tended to introduce significant variations in the second

**31 Boy Bitten by a Lizard** (attributed), *c.*1593–4; oil on canvas, 65.8 × 52.3 cm, Roberto Longhi Foundation, Florence

versions, as in the *Fortune-Teller* (Pl. 38), *Lute-Player* (Pl. 195), and *Supper at Emmaus* (Pl. 130). Most likely, then, Caravaggio asked or authorized an assistant to produce the Florentine copy of his original, the London *Boy Bitten by a Lizard*, when his own fame stimulated demand among collectors for his early pictures. This conclusion, however, requires us to revise the established view that Caravaggio had no assistants.[32]

The *Penitent Magdalen* (Pl. 32), one of Caravaggio's first known religious subjects, shares with the genre pictures a close observation of the model, a fresh approach to subject-matter, in this instance traditional, and a lyrical mood. Similarities in composition, colour and lighting link all of these youthful works, and when set next to the *Boy Peeling a Fruit*, the Magdalen's bowed pose and joined hands mirror the boy's portrayal. But Caravaggio here set himself the challenge of placing a full-length, seated figure in an interior, moving the model further back from the picture plane and avoiding the cramped space of the *Self-Portrait as Bacchus*. The original owner of the *Penitent Magdalen* is unknown, but if circumstantial evidence proves correct, the painting belonged to Cardinal Pietro Aldobrandini, nephew of Pope Clement VIII.[33]

In representing Mary Magdalen, Caravaggio took up a theme with a long textual and visual history. Devotional images of the saint generally followed two traditions. The first and most widespread type portrays Mary as a penitent hermit in the wilderness where she had retreated for the last twenty years of her life. Typically shown in a landscape setting, she is a beautiful woman with long tresses

**32 Penitent Magdalen**, *c.*1593–4; oil on canvas, 122.5 × 98.5 cm, Galleria Doria Pamphilj, Rome

covering her nudity, who prays before a crucifix and meditates upon a skull, as in Annibale's etching of 1591, *Mary Magdalen in the Wilderness* (Pl. 33), which is dated just prior to Caravaggio's painting. Exemplifying the second type is Piero di Cosimo's painting *Magdalen* (Pl. 34) of an elegantly attired woman who is reading and can be identified by the small unguent jar on the table beside her. This type inspired portraits of women in the Magdalen's guise and, in some cases, such as Savoldo's *Magdalen* (London, National Gallery) of the 1530s, ambiguity arises as to the secular versus the sacred content.[34]

Interested in neither the idealized female nude, the imagined wilderness, nor standard Christian symbols of death and salvation, Caravaggio portrayed his *Penitent Magadalen* in a portrait-like image. Bellori in fact stressed his study of the model from life: '[Caravaggio] painted a young girl seated on a chair, with her hands in her lap in the act of drying her hair, he portrayed her in a room and, adding a small ointment jar, with jewellery and gems, on the floor, he pretended that she was the Magdalen.'[35] But in contrast to other representations that dwell on the former courtesan's worldly appearance, Caravaggio's saint has left her hair undone, no longer wears her jewels, and slumps down in her chair.

Not only does the naturalism of the painting set it apart, but so too does Caravaggio's subtle study of the Magdalen's passage from sin to enlightenment. For unlike earlier devotional images, such as Donatello's powerful sculpture of the emaciated penitent, this Magdalen is undergoing conversion and has not yet entirely abandoned society. With eyes closed and hands cradled in her lap, her whole body turns inward to absorb the divine message so eloquently symbolized by the wedge of light piercing the darkened room. Her posture indicates passive acceptance of the future, while the lone tear wetting the side of her nose and the humble chair she occupies express her past shame, embodied in the cast-off gold and pearls. The quiet introspection of the *Penitent Magdalen* and

**33** Annibale Carracci, **Mary Magdalen in the Wilderness**, 1591; etching and engraving, 22.3 × 16 cm

the violent reaction in the *Boy Bitten by a Lizard* are Caravaggio's first essays in the emotional polarities that return as leitmotifs in his art.

In the *Fortune-Teller* and the *Cardsharps*, the young Caravaggio faced the challenge of composing narrative works with more than one figure. Although long known through its many copies and an old photograph, the original *Cardsharps* (Pl. 35), newly recovered, enhances our understanding of this earliest period. And complementing this remarkable find is the recent addition of the *Fortune-Teller* (Pl. 37), in the Pinacoteca Capitolina in Rome, to Caravaggio's earliest autograph works. The *Fortune-Teller* is painted on a reused canvas, already roughed out with a Madonna in prayer; visible in X-rays, this image closely resembles Cesari's type of Madonnas, implying that Caravaggio repainted the canvas during his stay in Cesari's studio or soon after.[36]

Of different dimensions and so not intended to hang as pendants, the *Fortune-Teller* and *Cardsharps* are none the less alike in style and content. Both share a horizontal format, which closely frames three-quarter-length figures against a blank backdrop – a narrative formula

**34**  Piero di Cosimo, **Magdalen**, *c.*1500–5;  oil on wood, 72 × 53 cm, Galleria Nazionale d'Arte Antica, Rome
Overleaf **35 Cardsharps**, *c.*1594–5;  oil on canvas, 94.2 × 131.3 cm, Kimbell Art Museum, Fort Worth

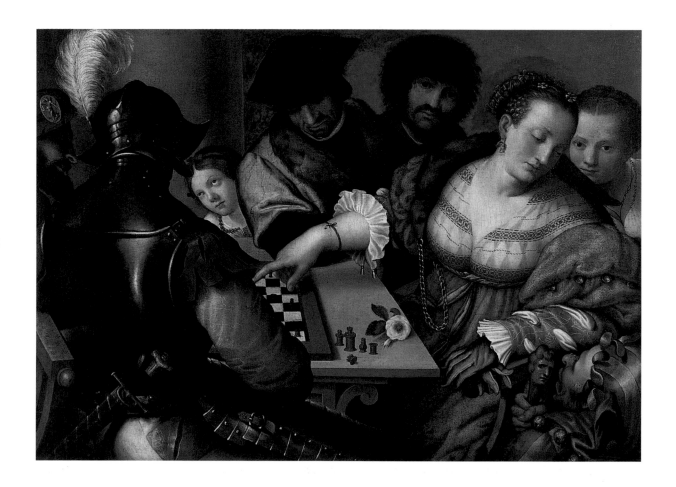

**36** Giulio Campi, **Chess Game**, *c.*1535; oil on canvas, 90 × 127 cm, Musei Civici, Turin

known to Caravaggio from Lombard and Venetian examples.[37] However, the simple alignment of gypsy and youth in the *Fortune-Teller* suggests that its execution slightly preceded that of the *Cardsharps*, whose space is measured by a table marking recession into depth, thereby forming a more complex figural arrangement. Caravaggio introduced other spatial devices to bring the card-players close to us, such as the projecting backgammon board, the positioning of the deceitful youth standing on the near side of the table, and the foreshortening of his right hand, which forces us to be privy to his guilty act.

Bright and colourful, the *Cardsharps* and the *Fortune-Teller* typify the vivacity of Caravaggio's earliest works, 'without those shadows as he later used', as Bellori put it. Bellori further noted that the players' clothing in the former work did not look artificial, so true to life were the colours; Baglione likewise singled out the beautiful colouring in the *Fortune-Teller*. Unlike the palette of strong primary colours characterizing Central Italian painting of the early sixteenth century or the high-keyed and shot colours of Mannerist art, Caravaggio adopted a Lombard range of burgundies and ochres, using white and black to outline a silhouette or delimit a plane, and adding, as in the *Cardsharps*, the unexpected accent of the salmon-coloured feather. His choice and juxtaposition of tones, and his application of broad swatches of intense hue not only heighten the immediacy of his models but, combined with the illusionistic compositional and spatial devices, invest the figures with unprecedented tangibility.[38]

In contrast to the classicizing garb in his first genre paintings, in the *Fortune-Teller* Caravaggio used contemporary clothing to individualize his characters and reinforce the narrative. Not only her art but her attire serve to identify the fortune-teller as a gypsy; the turban, full-sleeved blouse, and mantle tied up at the shoulder reappear in depictions of gypsies from the fifteenth century on.[39] Her victim is smartly dressed in a damask doublet, bordered in black with matching sleeves, and handsomely lined. His lace collar and cuffs, plumed hat and sword with gloves stuffed in the hilt characterize him as a *bravo*, or mercenary soldier. Similarly, in the *Cardsharps*, both the young cheat and the older man wear a form of military dress; the garish yellow of the latter's sleeve surely connoted deceit, traditionally associated with that colour. An added touch of realism is provided by this gambler's ripped glove, a trick of the trade for feeling marked cards. The other card-player's higher rung in society is conveyed by his fine, dark velvet hat and jacket that clash with his opponents' flashy and motley clothing.[40]

Overleaf **37 Fortune-Teller**, *c*.1594–5; oil on canvas, 115 × 150 cm, Pinacoteca Capitolina, Rome

In each picture, Caravaggio explored the theme of a well-off young man being duped. Given the unregenerate pursuits of such feckless youths, the moral is unmistakable, and the gambling in the *Cardsharps*, like the gypsy's seductiveness, brings to mind the excesses of the Prodigal Son in the biblical parable. The image of fleeting youth also echoes here in the disillusionment that awaits the pair of inexperienced adolescents. Caravaggio shied away from blatant moralizing, however. His gypsy is young and pretty, as well as unexpectedly neat, and does not arouse the same immediate suspicions as her counterparts in northern prints and paintings, who are often joined by cutpurses. Only the very attentive viewer can spot her surreptitious theft of the young man's ring as she smilingly foretells his future.

Avoiding any overt allegorical allusions, Caravaggio studied his card-players with seeming objectivity, in the manner of Lucas van Leyden's chess-players or card-players, or Giulio Campi's *Chess Game* (Pl. 36). Yet the elimination of bystanders and the neutral backdrop detach Caravaggio's two scenes from daily existence, lending credence to Bellori's reconstruction of the origins of the *Fortune-Teller* in which Caravaggio invited a gypsy from the street into his studio. The staged look of both works reflects Caravaggio's recourse to contemporary theatre and the stock characters and situations of the *commedia dell'arte*, in addition to northern pictorial and literary sources. In time, Caravaggio's *Fortune-Teller* and the *Cardsharps* became his most popular paintings, inspiring numerous imitations and many copies.[41]

When he painted the second and more charming version of the *Fortune-Teller* (Pl. 38), perhaps five years later, Caravaggio used a different, rounder-faced model for the youth and modified details of his clothing. But one of the most conspicuous changes – the thick and wavy feather in the boy's cap – is mostly the work of a seventeenth-century restorer, who added a horizontal strip at the top and repaired damages suffered by the canvas in its transport to Paris. The slight adjustments in the poses of the figures reveal Caravaggio's increased skill in foreshortening, evident in the gypsy's left arm and hand, and his arrangement of the mantle enveloping the young man in a sweeping circle demonstrates a heightened sense of graceful line. Although significantly smaller in size, the later version projects greater depth and breadth, again attesting to Caravaggio's technical development in the few years separating the two canvases.

After three years in the capital, artistic success still eluded Caravaggio. His attempt at professional independence had reduced him to dire straits and, compounding his troubles, he was kicked in the leg by a horse badly enough to be hospitalized at the Ospedale della Consolatione. Watching his money dwindle and his clothes wear out, he was forced by necessity to sell his paintings for a pittance.[42]

Caravaggio must have derived some consolation in his misery from the friendships he forged with other artists: the painters Prospero Orsi (c.1558–1633) and Mario Minniti (1577–1640), and the architect Onorio Longhi (1569–1619). Nicknamed 'Prosperino degli grotteschi' after his specialization in painting ornamental motifs or 'grotesques', Orsi came from Lombardy and, in Rome, lived in the same piazza as one of Caravaggio's early landlords, Monsignor Petrignani. The older, more established painter, Orsi, assumed the role of agent, or henchman as Baglione acerbically remarked, for his younger compatriot. Closer in age to Caravaggio, Longhi shared his Lombard background, while Minniti, who was a southerner from Syracuse in Sicily, was also a recent arrival in the capital. All three remained Caravaggio's close friends; when needing help later in life, he counted on both Orsi and Minniti, and Longhi was at his side at the fateful murder that closed his Roman career.[43]

Finally some artists, perhaps even these friends, came to his aid, arranging for him to market his work through a dealer, a certain Maestro Valentino, who had a gallery near the church of S. Luigi dei Francesi.[44] Surely motivated in part by compassion, or pity as Baglione would have it, these fellow artists may also have wished to support Caravaggio's innovative art. The *Cardsharps*, and presumably the *Fortune-Teller*, soon attracted a buyer, Cardinal Del Monte, who at the same time invited Caravaggio to join his household.

Overleaf **38 Fortune-Teller**, *c.*1598–9; oil on canvas, 99 × 131 cm, Louvre, Paris

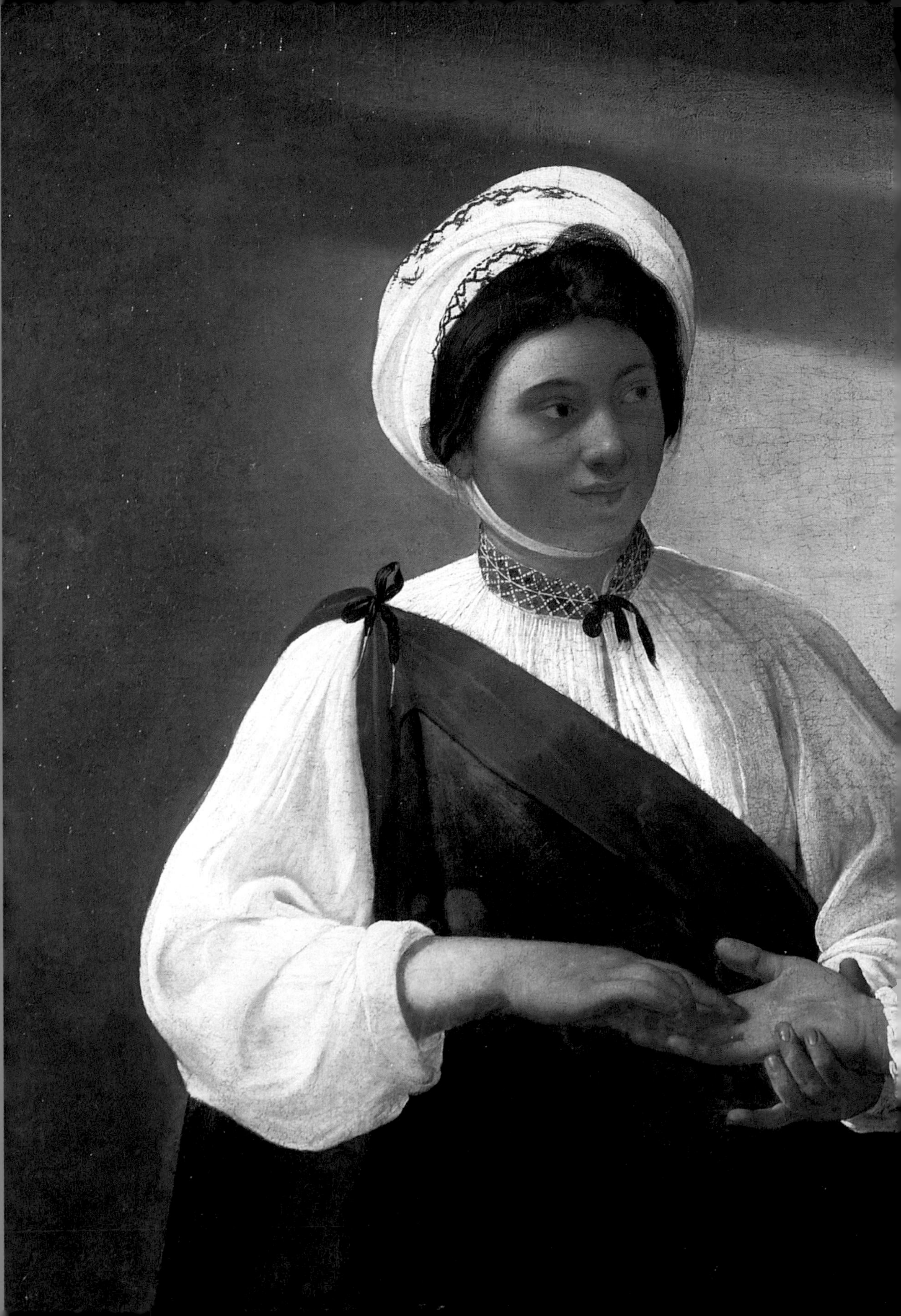

Chapter 3  **In Cardinal del Monte's Household**

On a summer evening in 1597, Caravaggio and his friend Orsi heard and partly saw an assault as they were walking to a local tavern for dinner. Witnesses called in an ensuing criminal investigation positively identified Caravaggio as Cardinal Del Monte's painter and clarified his role as a bystander rather than a participant. Recently discovered, their depositions present a vivid description of Caravaggio that strikingly matches and fills out what is known of his appearance from his own self-portrait just two years later in the *Martyrdom of Saint Matthew* (Pl. 79) and in Ottavio Leoni's portrait (frontispiece): 'a big young man of about twenty or twenty-five years with a straggly, black beard, heavy-set with thick eyebrows and dark eyes, who wears black clothing, somewhat dishevelled [and] who dons a pair of black stockings, somewhat tattered [and] who wears his full head of hair long and falling forward'. Although Caravaggio was fully exonerated, the incident hints at his own violent propensities. One witness stated he had formerly treated Caravaggio for a wound from a fight, and Orsi himself asserted Caravaggio had been armed that night, as was his habit.[1]

A year later the police arrested Caravaggio and threw him into gaol on the charge of illegally carrying a sword (Appendix IV). The following morning, before the judge, he defended his right to do so, arguing that he was 'painter of the Cardinal Del Monte', from whom he drew a salary for himself and his servant, and in whose palace he lived. No longer a starving artist, Caravaggio had become a protected member of an eminent prelate's household. This upward move guaranteed his financial security and freed him from the vagaries of the market-place. Moreover, as 'painter of Cardinal Del Monte', Caravaggio enjoyed a higher social status than before, assuming the airs of

**39** Antonio Tempesta, **map of Rome**, 1593;
detail showing: **1** Palazzo Madama; **2** Piazza Navona; **3** S. Luigi dei Francesi; **4** Palazzo Giustiniani; **5** Chiesa Nuova; **6** S. Agostino; **7** Palazzo Firenze

a gentleman employing a servant and wearing a sword. In reality, he had no legal right to bear arms. Just as the mere mention of Del Monte's name had allayed the authorities' suspicions in the investigation of the previous summer, on this occasion, too, the charge was dropped on the strength of Caravaggio's statement to the authorities; Del Monte's name afforded protection for those in his service.[2]

Caravaggio had been living in Del Monte's palace possibly since late 1595. By the 1590s Del Monte's income was comfortable, yet not especially high, and his retinue numbered only fifty. Of the Cardinal's two official residences, the Palazzo Firenze (near the site of the former Roman harbour of the Ripetta) and the Palazzo Madama (next door to San Luigi dei Francesi and the present seat of the Italian Senate), the latter is where Del Monte was recorded as living at this time and so is the more likely location of Caravaggio's apartment (Pl. 39). In addition to other family properties in Rome, Del Monte also bought a country house at Porta Pinciana in 1596, which Caravaggio came to know through working upon a commission there.[3]

Caravaggio remained in Del Monte's service for five or six years; he still identified himself as a member of the Cardinal's household in October 1601, when he was again arrested for carrying a sword. Because the paintings made specifically for the Cardinal seemingly date to the years in his home, Caravaggio was presumably expected to execute a certain number of pictures for his patron in return for lodgings and a stipend. Even after he had left Del Monte's service, Caravaggio did not stray far from his former protector, in 1603 renting a house next door to the Palazzo Firenze.[4]

Twenty-four years Caravaggio's senior, Francesco Maria Bourbon Del Monte (Pl. 40) was born in Venice in 1549, into a noble family originating from Pesaro. Groomed from adolescence for an ecclesiastical career, Del Monte settled in Rome in the mid-1570s and, soon after his thirtieth birthday, entered the service of Cardinal Ferdinand de' Medici. In 1588, when Ferdinand renounced his cardinal's hat to become Grand Duke of Tuscany, he prevailed upon Sixtus V to appoint Del Monte as his successor in the Sacred College. As the Grand Duke's most trusted representative, the new Cardinal assumed an influential position at the papal court, reporting regularly to Florence on politics and promoting Tuscan interests in Rome. As a loyal Medici servant, he belonged to the pro-French, rather than the Hispanophile faction in Rome, yet he managed to maintain relations with both groups, a testimony to his diplomatic skills. A cardinal in Rome for almost forty years, Del Monte devoted himself, on the one hand, to his ecclesiastical responsibilities in the Curia and political services to the Medici, and to his personal tastes in music, science and art on the other. Conventionally devout and a benefactor of numerous charitable foundations, Del Monte was best known, however, as a 'lover of pleasures and leisure'.[5]

The Cardinal's profile as shrewd diplomat, pious bishop and patron of music and art was shared by many of his fellow cardinals at the end of the sixteenth century. But his activities in science and the arts were not merely public symbols of rank, as was often the case. They reflected instead his keen interest in new developments in those fields; one contemporary report spoke of his 'study of singular things and knowledge of harmonies and songs'.[6] Prompted by the work of his older brother Guidubaldo, a distinguished scientist, Del Monte followed the latest discoveries and became an early and ardent supporter of Galileo, who gave him a telescope. Furthermore, he performed medicinal and alchemical experiments in his own fully equipped laboratory in town, as well as in the one at his villa. Also active as a patron of music in the 1590s, he headed the papal Congregation for reform of liturgical music from 1594 and served as Vice-Protector, and later Protector, of the Sistine Choir, the all-male papal ensemble. He collected musical instruments and scores, and, like any well-bred

**40**  Ottavio Leoni, Portrait of Cardinal Francesco Maria del Monte, 1616;  black chalk with white heightening on blue paper, 22.9 × 16.5 cm,
John and Mable Ringling Museum of Art, Sarasota

gentleman, played the guitar and sang; at home and at his fellow cardinals' palaces, he hosted or attended private musical entertainments.[7]

Del Monte held official positions as co-protector of the Academy of St Luke and as a member of the Fabbrica di San Pietro, the papal commission for building projects at St Peter's. His own collection, which was inventoried after his death in 1626, contained a number of notable works by contemporary painters, in addition to the obligatory devotional pictures and antiquities. The inventory reveals that his taste extended to classicizing painters, such as the Carracci and their followers, Reni, Albani, and Guercino, as well as to the naturalistic work of Scipione Pulzone, Carlo Saraceni, Battistello Caracciolo, Jusepe Ribera, Jan Brueghel and, of course, Caravaggio. Del Monte's passion for commissioning modern works of art and using his resources to support new trends furthered the careers of young artists under his tutelage.[8]

What Caravaggio painted for his patron can be deduced in part from the early sources and the evidence of Del Monte's estate inventory. Besides the *Cardsharps* and *Fortune-Teller* which Del Monte acquired, at least five other pictures have been traced, and can be identified as the *Musicians* (Pl. 41), the second version of the *Lute-Player* (Pl. 195), *Saint Catherine of Alexandria* (Pl. 63), *Saint John the Baptist* (Pl. 107), and the *Medusa* (Pl. 54). In addition to these easel paintings, one decorative commission for a ceiling in oils in Del Monte's villa at Porta Pinciana, representing *Jupiter, Neptune and Pluto* (Pl. 55), was described by Bellori as attributed to Caravaggio.[9]

87

Several other pictures can be assigned to Caravaggio's 'Del Montean years'; as some were evidently painted for other clients, his service to the Cardinal did not exclude outside commissions. Among these, he repeated both the theme of the *Fortune-Teller*, as we saw in the previous chapter, and also that of the *Lute-Player*. Thematic and stylistic similarities also link two mythological and four sacred works with Del Monte's pictures, implying a coeval date: *Bacchus* (Pl. 50) and *Narcissus* (Pl. 53); *Rest on the Flight into Egypt* (Pl. 59), *Saint Francis in Ecstasy* (Pl. 61), *Judith Beheading Holofernes* (Pl. 69), and *Conversion of Mary Magdalen* (Pl. 67). Finally, Caravaggio also painted a few portraits, only two of which have been convincingly identified – *Portrait of Fillide* (Pl. 66) and *Portrait of Maffeo Barberini* (Pl. 146); the latter work and the issue of Caravaggio as portraitist will be taken up more fully in Chapter 6.

The *Musicians*, the first picture that, by Baglione's telling, Caravaggio made expressly for Cardinal Del Monte, offers an excellent introduction to the paintings from this period. A lutenist and horn-player gaze out of the picture and prepare to play, while their fellow musician, turning his back to us, studies his score. The boy on the left, part of the ensemble yet not a musician, is intent on picking grapes. Caravaggio here devised a more complex composition than in his previous works, with as many as four figures, and also broached a more

Overleaf **41 Musicians**, *c.*1595;  oil on canvas, 87.9 × 115.9 cm, Metropolitan Museum of Art, New York

88

sophisticated theme, while preserving many of the stylistic elements of the *Cardsharps*, which had originally caught the Cardinal's attention. The handsome young musicians belong to the same family as the earliest genre pictures, and the same models, or their close relatives, probably posed for Caravaggio. His own features are recognizable in the horn-player (Pl. 42), looking out at us over his shoulder as in the earlier *Self-Portrait as Bacchus* (Pl. 23).

The *Musicians* inaugurates a series of dramatic easel paintings with dense, half-length compositions and leading to the full-length and multi-figured compositions in his later public commissions. The painting is also characterized by a growing attention to depth, especially in the foreshortenings of figures, instruments and musical scores. These and similar spatial exercises mark Caravaggio's art from the time of his association with Del Monte and can be related to the Cardinal's own interest in the subject. In the 1590s, Del Monte's brother, Guidubaldo, was writing an extensive treatise on perspective, which he dedicated to the cardinal.[10]

Caravaggio's entrance to a refined cultural milieu in the cardinal's palace is reflected in the subject-matter and imagery of the *Musicians*. The substitution of a lute, violin, horn and musical scores for fruits and vegetables is especially telling. Given Del Monte's active involvement in the contemporary musical world, he surely chose the theme, intending the picture for his private collection, which came to include at least four other paintings entitled 'Musica'.[11]

For the *Musicians*, Caravaggio drew upon his North Italian artistic inheritance, rich in scenes of men alone or in the company of women

**42 Musicians** (Pl. 41), detail of horn-player

playing music, in contemporary dress or costumed in allegorical or mythical guise. For example, either the *Concert* (Pl. 43) by Callisto Piazza, an early sixteenth-century Lombard artist, or a work like it, served Caravaggio as a prototype for his format and closely cropped composition. Another similar feature is the crowded grouping of the figures in a shallow space whose front edge is marked by a table and the back of the figure pushed up against the picture plane. For the strictly male composition of the ensemble and the allegorical allusions, however, Caravaggio might have recalled Titian's *Concert* (Pl. 44), evoking the three ages of man, or the Bergamasque painter Giovanni Cariani's trio, celebrating friendship (Pl. 45). The sensuality of Caravaggio's languorous lutenist and alluring horn-player also find precedents in the Venetian and Lombard pictorial tradition, along with the ardent males engaging the beholder in Giorgione's *Impassioned Singer* (Pl. 46), or in Cariani's *Lute-Player* (Musée des Beaux-Arts, Strasbourg).

The vaguely classicizing garb of Caravaggio's musicians and his portrayal of the boy picking grapes inject the seeming genre scene with allegorical meaning. This nude figure's wings and a quiver of arrows can be discerned upon close inspection, thus identifying him as the pagan god Cupid.[12] Love's coupling with music has a long visual and literary tradition. In Piazza's *Concert*, love-making is suggested by the close physical proximity of the female lutenist and the elegantly

**43** Callisto Piazza, **Concert**, *c.*1520–30;  oil on wood, 90.4 × 90.4 cm, Philadelphia Museum of Art, John G. Johnson Collection

**44** Titian, **Concert**, *c.*1510–12; oil on canvas, 108 × 122 cm, Palazzo Pitti, Florence

**45** Giovanni Cariani, **A Concert**, *c*.1506–10;  oil on canvas, 92 × 130 cm, National Gallery of Art, Washington DC

attired gentleman; the lady's décolletage casts her as a courtesan, and the angled placement of her admirer's dagger makes clear his intentions. In contrast, Caravaggio avoids such an explicit reference. The grapes Cupid picks intimate the intoxicating pleasures of music when combined with wine. Caravaggio was surely following the suggestion in Cesare Ripa's iconographical handbook for painters, first published in Rome in 1593, that 'Music' can be depicted by a large carafe of wine, because 'music was invented to make man happy, as does wine, and moreover, good wine does a lot for the melodiousness of the voice'. The impassioned expressions of his two instrumentalists imply that music acts as an aphrodisiac when mixed with wine. That the lute-player is tuning up, rather than playing, would have conveyed further symbolism to anyone steeped in a humanist education: the harmony arrived at by tuning was believed to reflect the harmony of the universe.[13]

**95**

Music again inspired the theme for Caravaggio's two compositions of a young singer who accompanies himself on the lute. The first version (Pl. 47) was painted for the Genoese patrician, Marchese Vincenzo Giustiniani, like Del Monte a connoisseur of painting and music and, moreover, one of Caravaggio's most ardent patrons. Del Monte soon wanted a similar painting for himself, and a variant was produced (Pl. 195) which has recently been rediscovered.

Unlike the relationship between Caravaggio's two *Fortune-Tellers*, the second of which is the more proficient, the reverse is true for the *Lute-Players*; Del Monte's version is not only cruder than Giustiniani's exquisite painting but also presents disturbing weaknesses in its execution, which have denied it universal acceptance as an autograph work. As X-rays demonstrate, the composition was copied, probably mechanically, from the Giustiniani canvas. The still life was then painted out and replaced with two new instruments, and other small variations were introduced in the lutenist's costume, his lute, the scores, and in other details. Skilled as the painter was who scrupulously rendered the instruments, he cannot have been Caravaggio himself, for close examination betrays the skewed proportions of the figure's

**46** Giorgione, **Impassioned Singer**, *c*.1507; oil on canvas, 102 × 78 cm, Galleria Borghese, Rome
Overleaf **47 Lute-Player**, *c*.1595–6; oil on canvas, 94 × 119 cm, Hermitage, Saint Petersburg

head and body, the schematic description of the folds in his shirtsleeve, and the too steeply foreshortened table. The fact that the canvas passed as an original suggests that it was painted in Caravaggio's studio under his supervision and with the endorsement of his patron, whose primary interest was to add another 'Musica' to his collection.

In Giustiniani's *Lute-Player*, an open songbook is turned towards the viewer. The notes are fortunately still legible and have been identified as four madrigals by Jacques Arcadelt, a fashionable Franco-Flemish composer. Omitting the texts of all but one of the songs, the score shows the instrumental accompaniments (*basso continuo*). In Del Monte's version, different madrigals were copied from Arcadelt's popular anthology. Either one or both of Caravaggio's patrons must have supplied these scores, and only they and their cultivated friends would have recognized all of the specific songs. The addition of the spinettina and recorder in Del Monte's version further celebrates his musical tastes. Given their costliness, it is likely that Caravaggio borrowed the models for all the instruments from Del Monte's collection, which included lutes, viols, spinets and guitars, totalling thirty-seven pieces at his death.[14]

Perhaps it was in his patron's palace that Caravaggio himself learned to play the guitar; later, in 1603, his landlady accused him of disturbing the peace by, among other things, playing it with his friends in the alley under her window in the middle of the night. By that time he owned both a guitar and a violin, possibly presents from Del Monte or Giustiniani. In the absence of any evidence

**48** Annibale Carracci, **Portrait of the Lute-Player Mascheroni**, *c.*1593–4;  oil on canvas, 77 × 64 cm, Staatliche Kunstsammlungen, Dresden

that Caravaggio also played the violin, its presence amidst his possessions can be best explained by its use as a prop in his paintings.[15]

The *Lute-Player* is based on a tradition of representations of solo lutenists in sixteenth-century North Italian and Flemish art. The individuality of Caravaggio's youth argues for a portrait, as in Annibale Carracci's *Portrait of the Lute-Player Mascheroni* (Pl. 48), but the contrast between the two works is striking. Unlike the straightforward presentation of Mascheroni as an adult male, Caravaggio's lutenist is a boy with fine features and delicate hands, his hair dressed in ringlets piled on top of his head and tied with a scarf. An amorous mood is deliberately created, especially in Giustiniani's *Lute-Player*, by the boy's soulful expression as he sings the lyrics, 'You know that I love you.' The fleeting beauty of the flowers and the erotic connotations of the ripe pears, figs and cucumber complement his love-song.

The seductive atmosphere of the *Lute-Player*, also present in the *Musicians*, recalls Caravaggio's earlier works and here, too, the sexual ambiguity of the male models has raised the issue of homo-erotic intent. As Caravaggio was addressing a particular patron and ambience, Del Monte's personality has come under modern scrutiny, and his presumed homosexuality is repeatedly invoked as justification for the suggestive imagery. However, Del Monte's alleged taste for boys rests on insinuations made by a hostile contemporary who claimed that, as an old man, that is in the 1620s, Del Monte displayed more than paternal love for the boys under his protection. Less tainted evidence from two decades earlier exists for Del Monte's decidedly heterosexual behaviour. On more than one occasion, he himself fondly reminisced with an old friend about the women they had courted in their youth. Once a cardinal, he did not abandon his former gallantries. In 1597, after dining and gambling with two other cardinals of the same worldly cast, he and his friends continued the evening with music in the company of two courtesans – not an isolated incident as later evidence shows. Of course Del Monte might have simultaneously indulged a taste for boys, but the incriminating testimony cited above is contradicted by a report of 1621 that the seventy-two-year-old cardinal was 'a living corpse … given up entirely to spiritual matters, perhaps so as to make up for the licence of his younger days'. Giustiniani's heterosexuality, on the other hand, has rarely been questioned, partly because he was married and partly because of the previous, mistaken belief that he was not responsible for the original commissioning of the *Lute-Player*.[16]

Without wholly discounting a homo-erotic appeal, historical and cultural factors also inform Caravaggio's imagery, suggesting other possible associations Del Monte and his friends might have entertained in viewing the works. In the ecclesiastical preserve of early Baroque Rome, performers were generally male as women were banned from the public stage by papal decree. On occasion these actors donned costumes to enact allegorical dramas, such as at the presentation of a work by the Florentine composer Emilio de' Cavalieri – one of

Del Monte's circle – at the Chiesa Nuova in Rome in 1600, in which singers holding instruments and 'dressed becomingly' formed a tableaux embodying 'Pleasure'. Thus, the often cited report that Cardinal Del Monte attended a ballet in 1605, at which the dancers were young boys dressed up as women, records a special, but hardly scandalous event, which has parallels on the contemporary Elizabethan and Jacobean stage where boys also played the heroines.[17]

While Caravaggio's models are not specifically dressed up as women, their androgyny endows them with feminine as well as male attributes. This sexual ambiguity has been linked to a particular Italian phenomenon of the period: the castrated boy-singers of the Sistine Choir. One such *castrato*, a Spaniard, Pedro de Montoya, who became a member in 1592, is recorded as living in Cardinal Del Monte's household in 1599 before his return to Spain a year later. Perhaps Caravaggio, who must have known the singer personally and seen him perform in the Cardinal's palace, used Montoya as a model. Because Montoya's age can only be guessed at and no documented portrait is known, we can conclude at most that Caravaggio may have recorded the effeminate physical traits of the fashionable *castrato*.[18]

Contemporary musical practices can also be invoked to explain the expressive sensuality of Caravaggio's musicians. At the end of the sixteenth century, the new fashion was for monody, or solo singing accompanied by instruments. The singer's emotive powers were crucial for interpreting the full affective range of musical texts. In the *Lute-Player*, the youth's open mouth was carefully drawn by Caravaggio to show the position of the tongue touching the bottom teeth (Pl. 49), a vocal technique recommended for solo singers.[19]

**49 Lute-Player** (Pl. 47), detail of head

As well as mirroring current trends in music in Rome, Caravaggio's imagery may also have appealed to the classical tastes of Del Monte and his friends. His musicians are draped or wear loose-fitting white shirts suggestive of ancient attire rather than expressly female or everyday dress, and their androgynous beauty, as already pointed out in Chapter 2, had classical associations. A definite antique context may have even been intended for the *Lute-Player*. His curly locks tied by a scarf, his white, softly draped shirt, and his lips parted in song to show his teeth correspond to the mythological musician Amphion, whose appearance the ancient Greek author Philostratus described in his celebrated *Imagines*. Smitten by Amphion's beauty, the god Hermes gave him a lyre. If this was indeed the textual source, Caravaggio's classically educated viewers might have delighted in his evocation of the classical past and the myth of love in the golden age.[20]

While in Cardinal Del Monte's household, Caravaggio extended his range of subjects to specifically classical themes, producing a remarkable group of mythological paintings. The fact that he styled himself as the pagan god in his early *Self-Portrait as Bacchus* suggests a personal interest in, and familiarity with, mythology. An inclination for such subjects would have been nurtured both by Rome's classical past and by exposure to Del Monte's collection of antiquities.[21]

The *Bacchus* (Pl. 50) stands out from earlier and contemporary mythological works, looking every bit the incarnation of the pagan god. Though one of Caravaggio's best-known canvases, the only early record of it dates to 1618, eight years after his death, when it was bought in Rome for Cosimo II Medici, then Grand Duke of Tuscany.[22]

**50 Bacchus**, *c.*1597;  oil on canvas, 95 × 85 cm, Uffizi, Florence

104

51 Annibale Carracci, **Bacchus**, *c.*1590–1; oil on canvas, 163 × 104 cm, Capodimonte, Naples

With face reddened from drinking and wavy black locks crowned with grapes and vine leaves, a fleshy Bacchus, ancient god of wine and fertility, leans back on his couch at a table on which stands a carafe of wine and a bowl of fruit. Usually a full-length nude in a landscape, as in Annibale Carracci's painting (Pl. 51), the deity in Caravaggio's painting has come inside as if to take the place of honour at a banquet. Having draped a toga-like robe over one shoulder, he is fingering the oversized bow of the black sash keeping it in place. In his other hand he holds the stem of a wine goblet, offering its contents to the viewer. The explicit invitation represents the traditional motif of the proffered glass, which betokens Bacchus's gift of wine to humanity.

The *Bacchus* represents the stylistic climax in Caravaggio's early series of single youths. Increased technical assurance can be seen in the handling of the human figure and the creation of an ambient space by means of the table, couch and the play of light on the wall; his mastery of still life is evident in the reflections and transparency of the glass goblet through which the god's shirt and hand are seen. On the lower right surface of the carafe, he painted a small male head in front of an easel, a self-portrait, perhaps verifying the 'truth' of his transcription of nature. Most striking is the way in which Caravaggio set off the god's luminous skin, the brightest part of the picture, by toning down the white draperies, and surrounding the figure with the earth colours of the leafy crown and still life, accented by spots of autumnal burgundy and dark green; the impact achieved is of an extraordinary colouristic harmony.

Caravaggio's *Bacchus* is still startling in its immediacy and in the insistent presence of the studio model with his farmer's tan and dirty fingernails. In this and other early cabinet pictures, Caravaggio first reinterpreted traditional sacred and mythological themes in the idiom of contemporary life. Just as a young woman had 'played' the Penitent Magdalen, a young man here assumes the role of Bacchus. Caravaggio also emphasized the god's sensuous nature, portraying the feminine as well as masculine qualities of the androgynous divinity.[23] The figure's gaze engages the beholder from under plucked and pencilled eyebrows, in a round, smooth-cheeked face framed by a luxurious mass of black curls. The invitation to partake in drunken revelry is the same as is offered by Annibale Carracci's *Bacchus*, but that Caravaggio's god also makes a promise of amorous pleasures is hinted at by the visual juxtaposition of the hand ready to untie the sash with the glass brimming with wine and the overripening fruit. Lending immediacy to the scene are the air bubbles around the surface of the wine in the carafe, as if to suggest that the god has just set it down after filling his glass. Drink and make love now, Bacchus seems to say, before it is too late.

Caravaggio infused this appeal with a greater sense of urgency through the use of still life; the turning leaves and decaying fruit warn of the inexorable passage of time. If painted originally for the pleasure-loving Del Monte, the image evoked past and present dalliances with the seductive 'Artemisias' and 'Cleopatras' he recalled in his letters. *Bacchus* conveys above all a hedonistic message and an elegiac reminder of the brevity of earthly pleasures, overriding other, more recondite interpretations.[24]

Whereas the extroverted Bacchus solicits the viewer's complicity, Caravaggio's *Narcissus* (Pl. 53), is an emblem of introspection and self-love. The history of this much debated canvas has recently been traced back to the Giordani family of Pesaro, descendants of a close childhood friend of Del Monte. Caravaggio may thus have originally painted the picture for the Cardinal, who later gave it to his old friend.

A handsome but vain young hunter in one of the myths in Ovid's *Metamorphoses* (III, 338–510), Narcissus remained cold to the nymph Echo and was condemned by the gods to fall in love with his own reflection in the water. He pined away because of his unrequited love and

his body was changed into the flower named in his memory. Although in this instance a sixteenth-century print illustrating Ovid's tale served as his starting point (Pl. 52), Caravaggio eliminated its landscape and narrative details, the better to concentrate solely on Narcissus. He dispensed with Bacchus's pseudo-classical costume and here staged the ancient tale in modern dress. As a result, extracted from its classical envelope the image presents a psychological profile of narcissism, as relevant in 1600 as it was in antiquity. The boy, whose pose was studied from life, fills the frame with his crouching form and its reversed image. With a brilliant and characteristic compositional solution, Caravaggio fixed the boy's knee at the exact centre of the canvas, and around this fulcrum he traced a closed circle from the twin arching forms of arms, head, neck and shoulder. This controlling structure creates a perfect visual metaphor for the protagonist's obsessive and fatal infatuation.[25]

Caravaggio's striking *Narcissus* quickly impressed other artists and the pose was imitated by such diverse painters as Domenichino (Palazzo Farnese, Rome, 1603–4), Orazio Gentileschi (*David*, Galleria Spada, Rome, *c.*1610), and Poussin (*Realm of Flora*, Gemäldegalerie, Dresden, 1631). Moreover, the freedom with which Caravaggio interpreted this and all of his mythological themes set an influential precedent for his followers, especially Bartolomeo Manfredi.

106

**52** Tommaso Barlacchi (active *c.*1540–50), **Narcissus**, engraving

**53 Narcissus**, *c.*1597; oil on canvas, 113 × 95 cm, Galleria Nazionale d'Arte Antica, Rome

The most sensational of Caravaggio's mythological pictures, the *Medusa*, (Pl. 54) illustrates its classical subject with shocking vividness and, moreover, on the unusual support of a circular, convex shield. The theme is also taken from the *Metamorphoses* (IV, 770–887) in which Ovid tells how Perseus killed the Gorgon Medusa, a monster with snakes instead of hair, whose horrific appearance turned men to stone. Using the metallic surface of his shield as a mirror, as shown in Annibale Carracci's fresco in the Palazzo Farnese of 1595–6, Perseus severed the monster's head and carried it off as a trophy. The apotropaic power which Medusa's head had exerted since antiquity was revived during the Renaissance in the many battle-shields sporting the snaky apparition. Caravaggio surely knew these frontal, heraldic images engraved upon metal armour.[26]

More stimulating to his imagination, however, would have been Vasari's description of a wooden circular support which Leonardo da Vinci painted with a transfixing Medusa blowing poison from her open mouth, smoke from her nose, and fire from her eyes. The Duke of Milan had bought Leonardo's *Medusa*, and it had later passed into the Medici collections. Del Monte may well have had Leonardo's work in mind when he commissioned from Caravaggio the round wooden shield with Medusa's head. Del Monte intended it as a princely present for another Medici, his friend, Grand Duke Ferdinand of Tuscany, to whom he probably gave it personally when he went to Florence in 1598. Some time after 1601 when the Shah of Persia gave Ferdinand two suits of armour, a central display of paired mounted knights was installed in a hall of the newly reorganized ducal armoury. One of the knights held Caravaggio's shield, which was fitted with leather straps at the back.[27]

In his *Medusa* Caravaggio strove to match the reported realism of Leonardo's lost work, eliminating the potentially awkward fire and smoke but exploiting the expressive features of open mouth and bulging eyes. To capture the extreme emotion, he perhaps studied his own features in the mirror – maybe the very same convex one that appears as a prop in the *Conversion of Mary Magdalen* (Pl. 67); he did own such a mirror, at least by 1605. The blood streaming from the head, which is Caravaggio's invention, signals that decapitation occurred moments before. Medusa's mythological persona and the shield's function as a decorative object mitigate the brutality of this, the first of the painter's several representations of severed heads. Dead, yet alive, terrified, yet horrifying, Caravaggio's *Medusa* exerted a fascination upon its viewers, inspiring poems on the power of art by Murtola and Marino, as well as the artistic homage of Peter Paul Rubens (Kunsthistorisches Museum, Vienna, *c*.1617).[28]

**54 Medusa**, *c*.1598; oil on canvas on wooden shield, diameter 55 cm, Uffizi, Florence

Unique among his mythological subjects for its full-length male nudes, Caravaggio's *Jupiter, Neptune and Pluto* (Pl. 55) is also his only ceiling painting. Believed lost or even dismissed as Bellori's mistaken invention until about twenty-five years ago, the work is now generally accepted as by Caravaggio on the basis of circumstantial and stylistic evidence, and technical information supplied by its recent restoration. The painting remains little known because it is still *in situ* in Del Monte's former country house, known today as the Casino Boncompagni-Ludovisi; moreover, it is not yet widely reproduced in other than specialized journals.

Del Monte's purchase of the property in 1596 provides a *terminus post quem* for the painting. His initial ownership was short-lived, however, as he ceded the land to Cardinal Pietro Aldobrandini a year later; only after he bought it back in April 1599 did he begin major improvements, presumably including Caravaggio's ceiling. The small size and location of the room on the 'piano nobile', or main floor, support the supposition that it functioned as Del Monte's study and not his distillery as Bellori had claimed. Following nineteenth-century renovations, the room, originally only accessible from the Sala di Fama, now serves as a corridor between this main hall, frescoed by Guercino for Cardinal Ludovisi in 1621, and a later addition.[29]

In keeping with Caravaggio's practices, the ceiling is executed not in fresco, a technique that he seems never to have adopted, but in oils. First experimented with in the early Renaissance and exploited increasingly in late sixteenth-century Rome, the medium of oil on plaster allowed painters to transfer the colouristic and lighting effects of easel painting to mural and ceiling commissions.[30]

Within the rectangular format, Caravaggio devised a wheel-like composition. At one end, Jupiter, god of the heavens, flies overhead astride his eagle and with a white drapery swirling about him. Opposite, his two brothers stand paired. The sea god Neptune holds a trident and straddles a seahorse; his bearded face resembles that of Caravaggio, who did wear a beard and moustache, as the description of 1597 attests and as seen in his self-portrait in the *Martyrdom of Saint Matthew* (Pl. 79). Looking towards Neptune is Pluto with a two-pronged fork and his dog Cerberus, guardian of his underworld realm. Dominating the centre of the composition is a large, translucent celestial sphere, crossed by a zodiacal band and containing a dark circle at centre and two shining balls at the poles.

**55  Jupiter, Neptune and Pluto**, *c.*1599–1600;  oil on plaster, 500 × 285 cm, Villa Boncompagni-Ludovisi, Rome

Caravaggio's sources for the steep foreshortening of the figures lie in North Italy. The closest precedent for the 45-degree-angled viewing of Neptune and Pluto, and Jupiter seen from directly beneath, is Giulio Romano's ceiling of *The Sun and the Moon* (Pl. 56), in the Palazzo del Tè in Mantua. The challenges he faced in representing the gods and their complex allegory on a ceiling might have forced Caravaggio to look beyond the live model to artistic precedents such as Giulio's famous frescoes, which he knew either from his early travels or from engravings. The Mantuan prototype, one in a rich North Italian tradition of illusionistic ceilings, offered the most naturalistic solution to the pictorial fiction of figures inhabiting the heavens.[31]

Caravaggio's gods embody the Elements, as Bellori explained. Following tradition, Air, Water, and Earth are personified by Jupiter, Neptune, and Pluto respectively. The specific choice of this triad and their triangular arrangement derive further meaning from the luminous sphere depicted in the centre of the ceiling. The dark globe of earth sits in the middle of the sphere, the lighter ball of the sun is off to the right, and the zodiacal band displaying four visible astrological signs crosses at the left. This imagery, surely related in some way to Del Monte's activities as an amateur scientist, may have alluded to the essential objective of alchemy, the preparation of the so-called Great Work, or elixir of life. Under the auspicious signs of Aries and Taurus – centred on the painted zodiac – the three gods might symbolize the alchemical phases of the transmutation of matter from earth to water to air. Alternatively, or even simultaneously, the celestial sphere can refer to themes appropriate for a suburban villa: the elements as constituents of the material world, the passage of time, and the regenerative power of the sun. These universal ideas are personally brought to bear on the inhabitant of this villa by the intentional placement of the ball of the sun directly above Del Monte's own birth sign, Cancer. The specialized nature of the allegory must have required that Del Monte, who was thoroughly steeped in alchemy, dictate specific instructions to Caravaggio. Given Del Monte's outspoken and lifelong support of the new science and Galileo, the geocentric universe presented in the ceiling is puzzling but perhaps reflects a pre-Copernican phase in his scientific attitudes.[32]

Within the context of ceiling decoration in Rome of the mid-1590s, Caravaggio's painting belongs to the vanguard of illusionistic ceilings and is contemporaneous with the major public example of the type, known to have been admired by Del Monte: the frescoed vault in the Sala Clementina of the Vatican Palace (Pl. 57), by Giovanni (1558–1601) and Cherubino Alberti (1553–1614). The two brothers' decoration

112

**56** Giulio Romano, **The Sun and the Moon**, *c.*1527–34;  frescoed ceiling, Palazzo del Tè, Mantua

**57** Giovanni and Cherubino Alberti, frescoed decoration, 1596–9;  Sala Clementina, Vatican Palace, Rome

exemplified *quadratura* painting, in which architecture was projected illusionistically on to the ceiling by means of perspective and foreshortening, so as to pierce the vault and open up views of a unified expanse of sky. Caravaggio, similarly, painted away his ceiling to reveal the open sky above and foreshortened the figures as if seen from below, but he dispensed with *quadratura*. He was working in a much smaller space, of course; none the less he took one step beyond the Alberti brothers in eliminating the transition between ceiling and walls. The boldness of his design is clear from a comparison with Annibale Carracci's contemporaneous frescoed vault for Cardinal Odoardo Farnese's gallery in the Farnese Palace (Pl. 58), a long, relatively narrow room which housed fine antique statues from the patron's collection. In contrast to Annibale's compartmentalized structure with enframed narratives, composed from the same viewpoint as if they were hung on the wall, Caravaggio set his composition within a fictive frame centred on the barrel-vaulted ceiling, and the foreshortened figures take into account the viewer's vantage point in the room below.[33]

Caravaggio never decorated another ceiling. Perhaps he found easel painting and the relative spontaneity it afforded more congenial, although large size in itself did not daunt him, as is attested by his later, monumental altarpieces. He may have decided on the basis of this one experience that the inherent artificiality of ceiling painting placed too great a strain on his naturalistic concept of painting. Although its isolated setting seemingly limited its influence on subsequent ceiling decoration, Caravaggio's ceiling provided the direct model for Guercino's *Aurora*, executed for the same *casino* in 1621, just over a decade later.[34]

During the years of his residence in Del Monte's palace, Caravaggio also began to paint a significant number of religious subjects, thus addressing the most weighty category of subject-matter in Italian painting and the one that would primarily occupy him for the rest of his career. Five canvases form a cohesive stylistic group, datable between 1595 and 1598–9, and illustrate a variety of sacred themes, two biblical (*Rest on the Flight into Egypt* and *Judith Beheading Holofernes*) and three saintly (*Conversion of Mary Magdalen*, *Saint Francis in Ecstasy* and *Saint Catherine of Alexandria*).

Imaginative and innovative, Caravaggio's early religious works unfold in diverse settings (daytime and night-time landscapes and interiors) and strike moods swinging from serene to disquieting to electrifying. In response to the demands of the subject-matter, he adapted earlier compositional ideas while at the same time expanding his stylistic solutions. As in his *Penitent Magdalen* (Pl. 32), he placed

**58** Annibale Carracci, vault of the gallery, *c.*1598–1601; fresco, Palazzo Farnese, Rome the full-length figure of Saint Catherine in a darkened interior, surrounded by a few realistically drawn attributes, and he composed the stories of the Magdalen's conversion and Judith's heroism in the same way as the *Fortune-Teller* (Pl. 37) or *Cardsharps* (Pl. 35), with three-quarter-length figures standing at the front of a shallow space backed by a blank wall. For the *Rest on the Flight into Egypt* (Pl. 59), and *Saint Francis of Assisi in Ecstasy* (Pl. 61), however, he moved his figures out of doors, painting the first of the few landscapes found in his *œuvre*. Beyond widening his compositional repertory, Caravaggio also introduced the strong contrast of light and dark that distinguishes his mature works; Bellori's observation that in *Saint Catherine of Alexandria* (Pl. 63), Caravaggio was 'already beginning to strengthen the darks' holds true for all the paintings in this group except the *Rest on the Flight*, ostensibly the earliest.[35] Each of these religious works has a novel aspect, illustrating either an unexpected narrative moment or introducing unconventional details. Just as with his early genre pictures, the success of these new inventions can be measured in the many imitations of *Saint Francis in Ecstasy* and *Judith Beheading Holofernes*.

The *Rest on the Flight* was cited by Mancini and Bellori among Caravaggio's earliest uncommissioned works, and its light tonality supports an early dating. But the sophisticated musical content of the picture closely relates it to the *Musicians* and *Lute-Player* for Del Monte and Giustiniani, and so it, too, probably originated in their refined circle.[36]

Sweetest of all his sacred images, *Rest on the Flight into Egypt* depicts a theme that had enjoyed new popularity since the Council of Trent. In flight from Herod's soldiers, the Holy Family pauses to rest before continuing on to Egypt. Caravaggio's Lombard and Venetian artistic sources for his visualization of the scene have often been pointed out. The Madonna's gracefulness and the colourful, bright tonality of the scene recall Lorenzo Lotto's art, and Jacopo Bassano's *Rest on the Flight* (Pinacoteca Ambrosiana, Milan, *c*.1547) has been cited as a direct source.[37] However, Caravaggio did not represent an idealized female type in the Madonna's features but posed the same young redhead who had modelled for the *Penitent Magdalen*. His homespun Joseph, on the other hand, does not depend on a live model but looks back to Savoldo's depictions of male saints, such as the *Prophet Elijah* (National Gallery of Art, Washington DC, *c.*1515–20) for the long grey hair and beard, lined brow, and oversized hands and feet.

Caravaggio turned to other sources for his angelic violinist and for the numerous symbolic details in the painting. Borrowing from a northern pictorial tradition of angels making music for the Holy Family, he transformed what had been a background motif into the pivotal image of his painting. The angel plays sacred music set by another Franco-Flemish composer Noël Baulduin to verses in the Song of Songs ('How fair and pleasant you are, O loved one, delectable maiden', 7:6–8, 10–13). Caravaggio omitted the words, and so the message conveyed through this particular text would have been understood only by his patron and those already familiar with the musical score. Presenting a dialogue between bride and bridegroom, the verses were interpreted allegorically in the sixteenth century as prefiguring the marriage of Christ and the Church. As applied to Caravaggio's *Rest on the Flight*, the Madonna personifies the Church, as was traditional, and the bridegroom is not her mortal husband Joseph, but her divine child. Thus, for the initiated, the bride's love for her spouse along with the bucolic imagery of the biblical verses symbolize faith in salvation and spiritual rebirth.

Even for those viewers lacking musical expertise, the visual imagery contains accessible symbolism. A purposeful connection between the left and right half of the picture is suggested by the contrast of Joseph's shadowed face with the radiance of angel, Madonna and Child. While Joseph rests his feet on bare, stony ground, Mary and the Christ Child sit amidst lush vegetation. Although also weary, Joseph stays awake to prop up the angel's music, as if he represents humanity who must listen attentively to divine scripture in order to hear the promise of salvation. Christian redemption through Christ's Passion is symbolically alluded to in the thorny bush and a tall green reed to Mary's right that foreshadow the mocking of Christ, while above her head, the oak tree recalls the tree of life from which the crucifix was hewn. Wedged between its trunk and her bent head is a laurel bush, the symbol of Christ's victory over death. A possible reference to the eucharistic bread

Overleaf **59 Rest on the Flight into Egypt**, *c.*1595; oil on canvas, 135 × 166.5 cm, Galleria Doria Pamphilj, Rome

and wine may be seen in two details framing the figural grouping: the stalks of wheat and the bottle of wine. These symbolic elements trace a passage from death to resurrection.[38]

Despite its allegorical import, Caravaggio's *Rest on the Flight* primarily evokes a peaceful interlude in the arduous journey. Just as in Barocci's earlier painting of the theme (Pl. 60), Caravaggio lingered on its lyrical possibilities, especially in the graceful angel, whose immaculate white drapery spirals around smooth, sinuous limbs. He also inserted realistic details to make the story ring true. Thus, the angel stands firmly on the ground playing the violin with eyes fixed on the score, across which dangles a spare piece of violin string. The Madonna tenderly cradles her plump baby in an autumnal landscape with oak trees and poplars, based on a real Roman view, not an imaginary one.[39] Joseph rubs one tired foot against the other, and his humble demeanour and straitened circumstances are accentuated by the juxtaposition of his and the donkey's heads and by his travelling gear: the bundle wrapped in a blanket upon which he is sitting and the demijohn plugged with a piece of paper.

Also set in a landscape, Caravaggio's *Saint Francis in Ecstasy* (Pl. 61) is his first nocturnal scene. As it shares common features with the *Rest on the Flight*, the *Cardsharps*, and the *Musicians*, a dating at the start of his residence in Del Monte's household is likely. He evidently did not paint the work for the Cardinal, however, but rather for the banker Ottavio Costa, who commissioned several paintings from him. As in his other early narratives, Caravaggio used a rectangular canvas for a horizontal composition in which the principal figures occupy a shallow foreground space. The model for the angel closely resembles, in both physical type and pose, his sweet-faced Cupid in the *Musicians* and the young noble in the *Cardsharps*. The angel's gentle ministrations to the saint imbue the image with the lyricism not only of the *Rest on the Flight* but of all Caravaggio's early works. Drawing on his Lombard background, Caravaggio recalled Savoldo's and Antonio

**60** Federico Barocci, **Rest on the Flight into Egypt**, 1573; oil on canvas, 133 × 110 cm, Pinacoteca Vaticana, Rome

Campi's nocturnes for the lighting, and Moretto's human saints for Francis's homely face. An early dating also explains certain awkward passages: the lower part of the saint's body lacks substance, and the angel is disproportionately large in relation to the saint.

Though painting a landscape, Caravaggio showed little of the wooded setting beyond a few plants in the foreground and some indistinct trees behind the figures. He concentrated instead on painting a night-time scene, playing with artificial, natural and divine sources of light in the distant camp-fire and the streaked sky, and in the bright beam of light of unidentified origin falling on Francis and the angel along a diagonal path from the upper left. The contrast of the lit and darkened areas in the foreground figures is softer than in the later paintings, and transparent shadows cross the angel's cheek, chest and back without obscuring form.

In *Saint Francis in Ecstasy*, Caravaggio visualized afresh the popular Saint Francis of Assisi, founder of the Franciscan Order in the thirteenth century. Medieval texts narrated the saint's life and his mystical experience known as the stigmatization, which occurred on Monte La Verna, in the Apennines to the east of Florence. When he had gone up the mountain to pray in the company of Brother Leo, Francis saw a vision of a crucified seraph, or six-winged angel, who imprinted on his body the stigmata: Christ's five wounds from the nails of the cross and the lance.

Caravaggio explicitly referred to the stigmatization of Francis by the wound in the saint's chest, setting the scene on a hilltop, the presence of Brother Leo (the hooded figure crouched under a tree in the left middleground of the painting), and the small scene in the

distance where shepherds around a fire point excitedly at streaks of light in the sky. Yet he departed significantly from traditional depictions of the stigmatization, such as Barocci's contemporaneous altarpiece for a Capuchin church in Urbino (Pl. 62). Caravaggio's Francis does not kneel in prayer, as was customary, but falls back in a faint, supported by an angel; missing altogether from the scene are the saint's vision and his four other wounds.

Unconcerned with a faithful illustration of the miracle, Caravaggio instead examined its spiritual meaning. The saint's recumbent pose conveys that Francis suffered a metaphorical death in order to be reborn spiritually in Christ's image. The visual prominence accorded to the wound 'to the heart', the last of the stigmata to appear, expresses the origin of the miracle in the burning love which Francis felt for Christ and which made him privileged to share the pain of the Crucifixion. Emphasizing further the parallel between the lives of Francis and Christ, the figures around the fire evoke the annunciation of Christ's nativity to the shepherds, and the angel's supporting embrace is modelled after representations of the Agony in the Garden and of the Pietà, in which angels sustain Christ. Caravaggio reinterpreted the miracle as an internalized experience, akin to his portrayal of the *Penitent Magdalen* (Pl. 32). Just as he had with the Magdalen, he suggests here that Francis is in the process of conversion, with one eye closed and one fluttering open, and his left hand beginning to feel the imprint of the wound: an image intended to inspire devotion in the beholder.

His depiction of Francis perhaps reflects contemporary veneration of the saint by the Confraternity of the Cordons of Saint Francis, founded in 1585. Supporting a link with this pious organization is the action of the angel hooking his index finger and thumb around the saint's corded belt, although whether or not Ottavio Costa belonged to the Confraternity cannot be determined because of the loss of its lists of membership.[40]

Although Caravaggio's innovative *Saint Francis of Assisi in Ecstasy* exerted immediate influence on painting in Rome, as witnessed in works by Orazio Gentileschi, Baglione, and Albani, his sophisticated conflation of narrative and devotional imagery was not easily understood or imitated. Not until later in the seventeenth century did Giovanni Lanfranco, in the *Ecstasy of Saint Margaret of Cortona* (Palazzo Pitti, Florence), and Bernini, in the *Ecstasy of Saint Teresa* (S. Maria della Vittoria, Rome) and in the *Blessed Ludovica Albertoni* (S. Francesca Romana, Rome), portray saintly visionary experiences in equally tangible terms.[41]

**62** Federico Barocci, **Stigmatization of Saint Francis of Assisi**, *c.*1594–5; oil on canvas, 360 × 245 cm, Galleria Nazionale delle Marche, Urbino

The resplendent *Saint Catherine of Alexandria* (Pl. 63), is Caravaggio's grandest early easel picture and the only extant religious subject undisputably commissioned by Del Monte. By the time of his death, Del Monte owned five paintings with this theme by well-known artists, indicating a special devotion for the saint.[42] Caravaggio's monumental saint and strong *chiaroscuro* suggest a dating for the canvas around 1599, contemporaneous with the *Jupiter, Neptune and Pluto* (Pl. 55) and his first paintings in the Contarelli Chapel. Although he obscured the background, he created a convincing space through his manipulation of light and dark, and through his careful placement of objects within the scene. Thus, depth is marked by the obliquely positioned wheel, the slanting palm, and the sweeping movement of Catherine's flowered mantle. The huge wheel and the saint's thin halo echo the circular composition, accentuated further by the curving border of Catherine's blouse and the lower hem of her dress. New for Caravaggio is the splendour of the saint's dress, mantle and cushion: he heightened the drama of the dark setting by robing his figure in a black velvet dress and using an equally dark, but contrasting midnight-blue, mantle to separate the figure from the background. The sharp light creates shimmering highlights on the gold trim of the dress and picks out the gold-threaded floral design on the mantle, brushed on with surprisingly summary strokes. All the more luminous because of the dark foil are the saint's face, her white blouse, and the red cushion.

Caravaggio must have been familiar with the popular account of Catherine's life in *The Golden Legend*, the medieval collection of saints' lives, which told how the early Christian princess was tortured and martyred in Egypt under the Roman emperor Maxentius (306–12) or Maximinus (308–13). Devotional images of the saint generally represent her with one or more attributes: the wheel, a crown, and the martyr's palm. In her sumptuous attire and the prominence of her attributes, Caravaggio's Catherine fits firmly into the pictorial tradition and is often described as the most straightforward of his religious images. Yet the saint's portrayal differs markedly from previous and contemporary representations.

**63 Saint Catherine of Alexandria**, *c.*1599;  oil on canvas, 173 × 133 cm, Thyssen-Bornemisza Collection, Madrid

128

**64** Guido Reni, **Saint Catherine of Alexandria**, *c.*1606; oil on canvas, 98 × 75 cm, Prado, Madrid
**65** Bernardino Luini, **Saint Catherine of Alexandria**, *c.*1516; oil on wood, 71.3 × 50.8 cm, University Museum, Notre Dame, Ohio

Unlike her counterparts, Caravaggio's Catherine looks directly at us instead of turning her gaze piously towards heaven. The instrument of her torture is not a mere symbolic prop, but has grown alarmingly in size, and the iron spikes, instead of studding the outer part of the wheel, point menacingly at the saint from its inner rim. In place of the martyr's palm, as was customary, Catherine delicately fingers the hilt and blade of a sword lying against her skirt, as if emphasizing its reaffirmed role in her martyrdom. During Caravaggio's early years in Rome, Clement VIII had officially censured an altarpiece in a city church that depicted the saint martyred on the spiked, or 'Catherine', wheel; painters were advised to avoid such historical inaccuracy, for God's intervention had caused the wheel to break *before* the torture, and the instrument of martyrdom was the executioner's sword.[43] A measure of the unconventionality of Caravaggio's image is provided by a comparison with that of Guido Reni (Pl. 64), painted six or seven years later in 1606, and probably a close variant on the painting by Reni which Del Monte owned. Caravaggio's contrasted lighting and naturalistic handling of the saint's clothing provided the model for Reni, but the younger painter shied away from his glaring saint, prominently displayed sword and obtrusive wheel.

The deep colours and realistic depiction of fabrics and clothing relate Caravaggio's *Saint Catherine* to the art of his Lombard precursors. Moreover, the saint's direct gaze recalls the way in which female sitters engage the spectator in allegorical portraits by Moretto and Savoldo (cf. Pl. 15) and, most pertinently, in a *Saint Catherine of Alexandria* by Leonardo's follower, Bernardino Luini (Pl. 65). The accusatory stare of Caravaggio's saint and her commanding full-length presence distinguish her, however, from Luini's demure maiden.

The reappearance of ostensibly the same model in the contemporaneous *Conversion of Mary Magdalen* (Pl. 67) implies that Caravaggio did not intend a portrait in either religious subject. The same woman is yet again portrayed in his *Portrait of Fillide* (Pl. 66), this time without a historical guise, wearing earrings, a bracelet, and a fashionable hairstyle. About eighteen years old in 1599, Fillide Melandroni was the most celebrated of the various courtesans who posed for Caravaggio.[44] In the *Saint Catherine*, the model's forceful personality somewhat compromises the devotional content of the image; the painting has thus justifiably been judged more worldly than pious.

Strong women also take centre stage in Caravaggio's last two religious pictures from this period, the *Conversion of Mary Magdalen* and *Judith Beheading Holofernes* (Pl. 69). The narrative as opposed to devotional subjects inspired not only original but highly charged interpretations from him. Both paintings were rediscovered as recently as the second half of this century. New documentary evidence has confirmed that the *Judith*, like the *Saint Francis*, belonged to Ottavio Costa, whose will pointedly enjoined his heirs never to sell the picture. The *Conversion* was perhaps painted for Olimpia Aldobrandini, the niece of Clement VIII, being first mentioned in a 1606 inventory of her collection.[45]

Although Caravaggio painted the two works for patrons other than Del Monte, stylistic factors indicate that he did so during the very period when he was working on the *Saint Catherine*. The same or a similar model reappears as Mary Magdalen, even wearing the identical black dress, and she has posed for *Judith* too. In all three works, an intense beam of light falls on the heroine, whose figure is thrown into sharp relief by the deeply shadowed interiors. Instead of a single devotional image, however, Caravaggio presented the Magdalen and Judith in narrative compositions similar to the *Cardsharps* and *Fortune-Teller*. But in stark contrast to those earlier, colourful canvases, a taut mood of drama charges these images, largely as a result of the new method of lighting, with its darkened backdrops and pools of shadow masking form.

66 **Portrait of Fillide**, *c*.1598–9; oil on canvas, 66 × 53 cm, formerly Kaiser Friedrich Museum, Berlin (destroyed)

Overleaf **67 Conversion of Mary Magdalen**, *c*.1598–9; oil on canvas, 97.8 × 132.7 cm, Detroit Institute of Arts

132

Not based on any one textual source, the *Conversion of Mary Magdalen* represents the encounter between Martha of Bethany, at the left, and her sister Mary Magdalen. As Martha reproves Mary for her past sins and explains Christ's miracles to her, the Magdalen experiences conversion. A painting in Del Monte's collection, then thought to be by Leonardo da Vinci (Pl. 68), provided Caravaggio with a direct compositional source, but he transformed this static prototype into an eloquent dialogue. The light bathing the Magdalen's face and reflected as a small white square on the convex mirror in Caravaggio's painting signals that, at this moment, divine illumination suffuses her being; in *The Golden Legend*, the Magdalen is hailed as the light-giver who, having absorbed the light, enlightened others. As in the *Saint Francis in Ecstasy*, Caravaggio avoided any physical manifestation of the supernatural, and in the absence of clouds or cherubs, the light embodies divine grace. Two small details also betoken the saint's internal conversion: the orange blossom, which she is clasping, and the gold band on her left ring finger, her only piece of jewellery; both allude to her mystical union with Christ.[46]

The strength of the image derives largely from the antithesis Caravaggio projected in the two sisters' personalities. Whereas the Magdalen's elegant appearance and the cosmetic jar and comb on the table are reminders of her former life of pleasure, Martha's tempered ways can be inferred from her subdued attire. Her bowed position and shadowed profile set off her regally posed sister, whose form dominates the centre of the scene. In his care to recreate real experience, Caravaggio painted a comb lacking a tooth and paid special attention to the reflections in the mirror of the Magdalen's fingers, her ruffled cuff, and touches of red and green from her clothing.

Unfortunately, this canvas has suffered from past over-cleanings, and its damaged state has clouded discussion of its authenticity. Some areas of its surface have been flattened and abraded, as, for example, in Martha's face, which lacks definition, and in the patchy background, where the ground is irregularly exposed. The overall tonal balance has been also been upset, resulting in abrupt breaks between adjacent colours, like the Magdalen's green velvet mantle and left red silk sleeve. Echoes of the original splendour of the picture

**68** Bernardino Luini, **Martha and Mary Magdalen**, *c.*1516; oil on wood, 63.7 × 82.5 cm, San Diego Museum of Art

emanate from a few notable passages, such as the reflections, the delicate flower, the Magdalen's fine gauzy cuffs and decorated bodice. X-rays of the canvas reveal *pentimenti*, lending support to its status as an original rather than a copy, and technical examination has uncovered Caravaggio's characteristic artistic methods.[47]

As shocking today as it must have seemed four hundred years ago, Caravaggio's *Judith Beheading Holofernes* (Pl. 69) is a surprisingly faithful illustration of the biblical story. The Book of Judith from the Apocrypha recounts how the Jewish widow Judith saved her people by seducing and killing Holofernes, the general of the invading army. Alone with him in his tent, Judith seized his sword as soon as he was drunk, and 'she approached to his bed, and took hold of the hair of his head, and said, Strengthen me, O Lord God of Israel, this day. And she smote twice upon his neck with all her might, and she took away his head from him' (Judith 13:7–8). With the head in a sack, she slipped away from the camp under the cover of night.

A personification of fortitude and justice, Judith was a favourite subject in Italian Renaissance art, inspiring a range of interpretations from Donatello's sculpted figure, implacable with divine vengeance (Pl. 70), to Giorgione's exquisitely refined heroine (Hermitage, Saint Petersburg, 1505). Choosing a distinct moment in the narrative, Caravaggio boldly represented Judith slicing Holofernes's neck with his sword. This choice of the climax must have challenged him to consider the question of exactly how a woman decapitated a strong man and to reconstruct the physical as well as the emotional experience.

In the manner of an ancient relief, he aligned the three actors on the lip of a narrow stage and set the scene in Holofernes's tent with the simple props of the bed and red curtain. With arms extended tautly in front of her, Judith grabs at Holofernes's hair with one hand while the other drives in the blade. Screaming as he turns towards his murderer, Holofernes futilely pushes with one hand to get up and clenches his other fist in pain. X-rays of the canvas reveal that Caravaggio adjusted the placement of Holofernes's head after he had drawn from the model; for the sake of verisimilitude he moved it slightly to the right and separated it partially from the torso. Judith's youth and beauty shine all the more in contrast with the wrinkled face of the ugly crone waiting to bag the head and the blood streaming from Holofernes's muscular torso.[48]

The servant's grim countenance and Holofernes's contorted features reveal Caravaggio's skilful command of expression, but Judith's face presents the most impressive study in emotion. A few lines disturb her smooth brow, dark shadows partially obscure her eyes fixed on Holofernes, and her lips are slightly parted. That she is deeply troubled and even repelled by this act is heightened by the arc traced by her

**135**

Overleaf **69 Judith Beheading Holofernes**, *c*.1599; oil on canvas, 145 × 195 cm, Galleria Nazionale d'Arte Antica, Rome

body, curving back from her victim at the shoulders and at the legs where her skirt is swept up. Her blouse, dampened with sweat, and her erect nipples, visible through the thin fabric, manifest the physical and emotional strain. Although later painters surpassed Caravaggio in the narrative realism of the scene, as, for example, Artemisia Gentileschi's Judith who forcibly subdues her struggling adversary with the able assistance of a servant (Pl. 71), none conveyed the psychological ambivalence that endows Caravaggio's Judith with the stature of a tragic heroine.[49]

Some time before June 1601 Caravaggio moved out of Del Monte's palace. While in his patron's household he created a remarkable body of easel pictures. Working for a private clientele on a relatively modest scale, he reinvigorated contemporary art with novel secular themes, audacious portrayals of pagan gods and heroes, and unconventional sacred imagery. Painting directly from the model in defiance of traditional methods, he succeeded in granting his figures the illusion of life to a greater degree than any previous painter.

The years in Del Monte's palace not only nurtured Caravaggio's intellect but the Cardinal's cultural and social set furthered his professional ambitions. Living in the Palazzo Madama exposed him to the world of local politics and international diplomacy, contemporary science and music, and the gracious lifestyle of princely cardinals in the papal capital. Through Del Monte's contacts, Caravaggio met prelates and professionals from the élite governing class, thereby enlarging his circle of patrons to include two men who were to play a significant role in his emerging career, Vincenzo Giustiniani (1564–1637) and Ottavio Costa (1554–1639). Both were Genoese patricians who had settled in Rome where they established themselves as bankers, and they were related by marriage (both their wives were from the Genoese Spinola family). In their artistic patronage, Giustiniani

**138**

**70** Donatello, **Judith and Holofernes**, *c.*1460;  bronze, height 236 cm, Palazzo Vecchio, Florence

and Costa demonstrated remarkable sensitivity to new trends in contemporary painting. Like Del Monte, they showed a precocious taste for Caravaggio's art, but unlike the Cardinal, they had considerable fortunes at their disposal to spend on his increasingly expensive paintings.[50]

Neither Caravaggio's adulthood – he was now in his late twenties – nor his artistic coming-of-age seem to have produced the common effect of calming down his personal behaviour. His arrest in 1598, mentioned at the start of this chapter, was followed by two more serious brushes with the law in 1600. That summer, he wounded a man's hand with a sword blow in Del Monte's own neighbourhood, and in the autumn he assaulted, first with a stick and then with his sword, a young pupil on his way home from the Academy of St Luke.[51] Del Monte himself witnessed the artist's mercurial temperament at first hand when Caravaggio's younger brother Giovanni Battista supposedly called at the palace in search of the painter. When questioned by Del Monte, Caravaggio declared that he had no family, and he later went so far as to disclaim his brother in the Cardinal's presence. Documentary evidence does put Giovanni Battista in Rome between April and December 1599, when Caravaggio was living with Del Monte. For the biographer Mancini, the anecdote exemplified Caravaggio's strange behaviour, proving that he was 'extremely crazy' (*stravagantissimo*). Six years later, in 1605, when Del Monte similarly referred to the painter's 'very crazy mind' (*cervello stravagantissimo*) he may have been alluding to Caravaggio's volatile personality. Yet despite Caravaggio's arrests and 'craziness', there is no indication of any falling-out between the affable patron and the irascible painter; on the contrary, Caravaggio later rented a house next door to the Palazzo Firenze and continued to seek Del Monte's protection when in trouble.[52]

Under Del Monte's protection, Caravaggio attained professional success, evolving from an unknown to a '*famosissimo*' artist.[53] The next years saw a galloping succession of masterful altarpieces and easel pictures that won him immortal fame.

**71** Artemisia Gentileschi, **Judith Beheading Holofernes**, *c*.1612–13; oil on canvas, 158.8 × 125.5 cm, Capodimonte, Naples

Part Two

**Success in Papal Rome** 1600–1606

Chapter 4 **'Most Famous Painter'**

As he approached thirty, Caravaggio entered upon a new and dazzling phase in what promised to be the 'mezzo del cammin' of a long and distinguished artistic career. In the span of seven years between July 1599, the year he signed his first public contract for the canvases in the Contarelli Chapel, and May 1606, when he fled the city for ever, he carried out six public commissions in Roman churches calling for as many as five altarpieces and four lateral paintings. Among these were the masterpieces most closely associated with his name: the *Calling of Saint Matthew*, the *Conversion of Saint Paul*, and the *Death of the Virgin*. These commissions gave Caravaggio the chance to paint, on a monumental scale and for a wide audience, the religious subjects that were central to the Italian artistic tradition since the early Renaissance. This entire group of paintings, except the *Death of the Virgin*, remains in Rome, and six still decorate the spaces for which they were intended.

In the last fifty years, the chronological sequence of Caravaggio's public commissions in Rome has been seemingly established only to be upset by new documentary discoveries, which include, in some instances, actual contracts or records of payments. As this information has not all been assembled in one place, a review of known facts to date for each commission is presented here as a prelude to consideration of the paintings themselves. Especially enlightening has been the identification of nearly all the patrons for Caravaggio's public works, who came primarily from a tight web of wealthy laymen and prelates. The chapels they endowed are found in assorted Roman churches: two Augustinian establishments built in the fifteenth century (S. Maria del Popolo, S. Agostino), and three more recent constructions presided over by two Counter-Reformatory orders, the Discalced Carmelites (S. Maria della Scala) and the Oratorians (Chiesa Nuova), and by French clergy (S. Luigi dei Francesi). A Confraternity, or association of pious laymen, was responsible for commissioning Caravaggio's last Roman altarpiece, whose destination in St Peter's represented the pinnacle of professional success.

Writing almost half a century after Caravaggio's death, the connoisseur Francesco Scannelli hailed the paintings in the Contarelli Chapel in S. Luigi (Pl. 72) as the most impressive of his best works, all on public view in Rome.[1] The church was founded to serve the French community in Rome, and among those financing its completion was Matteu Cointrel, a Frenchman appointed Cardinal in 1583, who is remembered by his Italianized name, Matteo Contarelli. He endowed the chapel for his eventual burial site and commissioned Girolamo Muziano to undertake its artistic decoration in 1565. As outlined in a brief memorandum attached to the contract, he instructed Muziano to paint the altarpiece, walls, and vault of the chapel with six scenes from the life of the apostle and evangelist Matthew, his patron saint.

Upon Contarelli's death in 1585, his executors, the Crescenzi family, assumed responsibility for the chapel. Muziano died in 1592,

apparently without having made a start on the work, while in 1587 the Crescenzi had already hired Jacob Cobaert, a Flemish artist, to sculpt the altarpiece. Giuseppe Cesari was then assigned to paint the vault and walls, but his busy schedule allowed him to carry out only three small frescoed scenes in the vault. As late as 1599, the altarpiece and laterals were still not done, and the congregation of priests at S. Luigi finally lost patience with the Crescenzi and appealed to the Fabbrica di San Pietro, which held jurisdiction over outstanding legacies.

According to Baglione, Cardinal Del Monte recommended Caravaggio for the project, securing him the commission first to paint the *Calling of Saint Matthew* and the *Martyrdom of Saint Matthew* on the side walls and, three years later, *Saint Matthew and the Angel* above the altar. In all likelihood, Del Monte did intervene with the Fabbrica, seizing this ready chance both to advance his painter's career and to further his own Francophile interests by satisfying the French congregation living next door to his palace.[2]

In April 1600, as his work was nearing completion on the Contarelli laterals and three months before receiving the final payment, Caravaggio signed the contract for another large work which he finished by November of that same year. The documents unfortunately reveal neither the subject nor the intended placement of the painting, and the identity of Fabio de Sartis, who ordered it, is a mystery beyond his name and his Sienese origin. None the less, the sizeable dimensions of the painting (*c.*268.2 x 156.5/178.8 cm) and the respectable fee of 200 scudi imply a public commission.[3]

Before undertaking this new canvas, Caravaggio agreed to paint the *Crucifixion of Saint Peter* and the *Conversion of Saint Paul* for the side walls of Monsignor Tiberio Cerasi's funerary chapel at S. Maria del Popolo. Born in 1544, Cerasi practised law at the papal court before shifting course, as he approached fifty, to embark upon an ecclesiastical career. By 1556 his wealth had allowed him to buy his way up to the influential post of Treasurer General to the Apostolic Chamber, which put him in charge of authorizing papal expenditure. Cerasi's position brought him into professional contact with Vincenzo Giustiniani who, as Depositary General to the Apostolic Chamber, received and disbursed funds. Giustiniani in fact figures as the banker in Cerasi's contract with Caravaggio, and it may well be that the Marchese and Monsignor discussed aesthetic as well as financial considerations on this occasion.[4]

**72** View of the Contarelli Chapel, S. Luigi dei Francesi, Rome

In July 1600, Cerasi had capped his social rise with the acquisition of rights to the chapel in S. Maria del Popolo, a virtual pantheon for eminent prelates and nobles from the late fifteenth until the end of the seventeenth century. He appropriated a prominent site in the church, the small chapel immediately to the left of the high altar in the transept (Pl. 73).

In a brilliant act of patronage, Cerasi entrusted the pictorial decoration to the two newest and most talked about painters on the Roman scene, Annibale Carracci and Caravaggio. Annibale was awarded the larger and more highly regarded part of the project, the altarpiece and the frescoes in the vault above. His contract for the *Assumption of the Virgin* remains untraced, but circumstantial evidence suggests that it predated September 1600, the date when Caravaggio agreed to execute the two side paintings within the next eight months. Whereas Annibale's altarpiece honours Mary, to whom the church is dedicated, Caravaggio's works celebrate Peter and Paul, the patron saints of Rome. Cerasi's special devotion to this saintly pair, which he professed in his will, perhaps commemorated his father's attainment of Roman citizenship in 1530.

When Cerasi died on 3 May 1601 Caravaggio's work on the paintings was still in progress. Six months later, on 10 November, the painter signed the receipt for the final instalment of his total fee of 300 scudi. The apparently smooth sequence of events from late September of the preceding year, the date of the contract, is belied by the lapse of fourteen months – five beyond the stipulated deadline – the reduction in price by 100 scudi, and Baglione's startling claim that Caravaggio first executed the two pictures 'in another manner, but as they did not please the patron, Cardinal Sannesio took them for himself'. Caravaggio did in fact substitute two new canvases, the ones now in the chapel, for the originals painted on cypress wood and acquired by Giacomo Sannesio (1551–1621), secretary of the *Consulta* that administered the Papal States, a collector of paintings and a friend of Del Monte. Of the two earlier versions, Caravaggio's *Conversion of Saint Paul* alone survives (Pl. 83). Enough time had passed between Caravaggio's signing of the contract and Cerasi's death for the first panels to have been finished, so presumably the patron himself ordered the replacements. He never lived to see the extraordinary final canvases, which were approved and paid for by his heirs.[5]

146

DEIPARAE
VIRGINI
SACELLVM

This marked the first time Caravaggio redid his own works for a public commission; almost fifteen months later he was to replace another work, the original altarpiece of *Saint Matthew and the Angel* (Pl. 94), for the Contarelli Chapel. In both cases, his initial conceptions failed to please but he had the chance to salvage the situation himself; later, the *Death of the Virgin* (Pl. 98) and the *Madonna dei Palafrenieri* (Pl. 105) were rejected outright. All of his controversial originals found eager buyers among wealthy collectors, however. Although painters suffered such rejections regularly, five instances in a relatively short career suggest that Caravaggio's imagery consistently confounded the expectations of his patrons.[6]

While still at work in the Cerasi Chapel, Caravaggio contracted in June 1601 to paint a large altarpiece representing the *Death of the Virgin* for Laerzio Cherubini's funerary chapel in S. Maria della Scala (Pl. 74). Born in the small town of Norcia in Umbria, Cherubini emigrated to Rome where he built a distinguished legal career, filling various administrative posts for the Curia and, in 1601, becoming Conservator of Rome, one of three elected urban magistrates. He was a devout man and served, among various philanthropic activities, on the governing board of the Casa Pia, a foundation for battered and abandoned wives, which became associated with the adjacent S. Maria della Scala. Completed in 1597, the new church was entrusted to the Discalced Carmelites, a reformed branch of the order founded by Teresa of Avila during the Counter-Reformation. Carmelite devotion to the Virgin Mary, and in particular her death, accounts for the subject of Caravaggio's altarpiece.[7]

In choosing Caravaggio for the commission, Cherubini perhaps hoped for something resembling the Contarelli laterals which he must have known well because his house was just up the street from S. Luigi dei Francesi. He also lived near the Giustiniani palace, and knew both Vincenzo and his brother, Cardinal Benedetto. Like Cherubini, Benedetto helped administer the Casa Pia. In the contract for Caravaggio's altarpiece, Cherubini named Vincenzo to assess the finished work and set the fee.[8]

Until the recent discovery of the contract, the *Death of the Virgin* was always considered to be Caravaggio's last Roman work, dating to 1605–6, and its solemn grandeur has argued against pushing back its completion to June 1602, the promised date of delivery. Whether

**74** View of the Cherubini Chapel, S. Maria della Scala, Rome

Caravaggio met his deadline is not known. Stylistic arguments, though problematic because of the muted colours resulting from yellowed varnish, can be mustered to assign execution of the work over a span of time from June 1601 to 1603, contemporaneous with both versions of *Saint Matthew and the Angel* (Pls. 94, 95) and the *Entombment* (Pl. 91).

On 7 February 1602, a week after rejecting Cobaert's now finished but disappointing sculpture for the Contarelli altar, the congregation of S. Luigi again turned to Caravaggio and asked him to produce a painted altarpiece in its stead. Caravaggio agreed to paint *Saint Matthew and the Angel* and to complete the work by the feast day of Pentecost, which fell three months later on 26 May. The final payment made in September 1602, well beyond the deadline, provides an outside completion date for Caravaggio's first version of the altarpiece. The priests rejected the painting, however, which reputedly 'no one had liked' and which 'had neither decorum nor the appearance of a saint'.[9]

At this critical moment, Vincenzo Giustiniani intervened, snapping up the altarpiece for his private collection and, in exchange, paying Caravaggio to paint a replacement. Giustiniani's eagerness to acquire the rejected version attests to the high esteem in which he held Caravaggio's work; its modest size and cost (150 scudi) also made it an attractive acquisition for a private gallery. The surviving record of payment made to the carpenter for the frame of the altarpiece suggests that the second version was completed by February 1603. As this is the painting now above the altar, the changes made by Caravaggio obviously met with the priests' approval.[10]

Although Caravaggio was probably engaged to paint an altarpiece for the Chiesa Nuova during the last six months of 1601, execution of the *Entombment* can also be plausibly placed during this same period, between 1602 and 1604. In January and February of 1602, the restructuring and renovation of the Vittrice Chapel (Pl. 75), its intended destination, was under way.[11]

In 1602 Pietro Vittrice, the founder of the chapel, had already been dead two years and, as two independent documents affirm, it was his heir and nephew Girolamo Vittrice who commissioned Caravaggio's *Entombment* (Pl. 91) for the altar of the new chapel. On 1 September 1604 Girolamo asked the Oratorians to return the former altarpiece, 'having graciously ordered the new painting by Caravaggio'. Girolamo's request conveniently informs us that the *Entombment* was completed if not in place by September 1604 at the latest.[12]

Little is known about Caravaggio's patron beyond the fact that he had in his possession a version of the *Fortune-Teller* and so must have been an admirer of Caravaggio's work. He does not seem to have enjoyed his uncle's close ties with the Oratorians, and he refused to meet any further expenses for the new chapel. For Caravaggio, the *Entombment* represented an especially prestigious commission as it would hang in the most fashionable Roman church of the day in company with works by the most celebrated contemporary painters, including Barocci (Pl. 19), Cesari, Scipione Pulzone (Pl. 187), and Cristoforo Roncalli.[13]

Meanwhile, in September 1603, the noble Bolognese family of Cavalletti had acquired the rights to a chapel in S. Agostino, which they dedicated to the Madonna di Loreto. Caravaggio's *Madonna di Loreto* (Pl. 102) must have been delivered some time before March 1606, when the Augustinian fathers discussed giving away the painting formerly over the chapel's altar.

Caravaggio's altarpiece celebrated the Marian cult centred around the sanctuary of Loreto in the Marches, the site to which the Virgin Mary's Nazarene house had been miraculously transported by angels after the Turks invaded the Holy Land in the thirteenth century. Two centuries later, the basilica of the Santa Casa di Loreto was constructed around the small wooden house, which became an enormously popular pilgrimage site; Caravaggio's commission in Rome reflects renewed artistic activity at Loreto.[14]

On 1 December 1605 Caravaggio received a down-payment for another commission, the most prestigious yet in his career: the *Madonna dei Palafrenieri* (Pl. 105) for the basilica of St Peter's. The commission came from the Confraternity of *palafrenieri*, gentlemen attendants responsible for a variety of practical and ceremonial duties in the papal household. Their company had claimed a new altar in St Peter's to replace the old one slated for demolition along with the remaining parts of the Early Christian basilica, and decided to commission a 'beautiful new painting'. Although Caravaggio's fame would have sufficed to recommend him, the fact that the *palafrenieri's* Cardinal Protector happened to be Ascanio Colonna, brother of the Marchesa di Caravaggio, must also have helped him to secure the commission. Within four months of receiving his first payment, the painter delivered the altarpiece, signing the receipt for the final settlement of 75 scudi on 8 April 1606. By 14 April at the latest, the *Madonna dei Palafrenieri* hung in St Peter's, as attested by payment to the carpenter for its installation. But not for long. Two days later, workmen removed it to the nearby church of S. Anna dei Palafrenieri, and on 16 June 1606 the *palafrenieri* sold it for 100 scudi (25 scudi more than their payment to Caravaggio) to Cardinal Scipione Borghese, nephew of the newly elected Paul V and an insatiable collector of art.[15]

These six public commissions for Roman churches presented challenges to Caravaggio for which his few earlier easel pictures with religious subjects had hardly prepared him. The new contracts called for a wider range of religious subject-matter, including dramatic narratives with far larger casts, and he now had to compose on a monumental scale for a diverse public forum. At the outset Caravaggio hesitated, testing and discarding different approaches in the lateral paintings for the Contarelli and Cerasi Chapels. His struggle was no secret even in the seventeenth century: Bellori reported that Caravaggio redid his initial design for the *Martyrdom of Saint Matthew*, and

Baglione said the same of the Cerasi paintings.[16] But by late 1601, when both decorations were completed, Caravaggio had reinterpreted their traditional sacred subjects in a highly personal style, in a remarkably short time forging a unique conception of ecclesiastical art which remained constant for the rest of his career.

In the first of these two seminal commissions, for the Contarelli Chapel, Caravaggio probably began with the *Martrydom of Saint Matthew* (Pl. 76), the final episode in the saint's life which took place during his mission to Ethiopia. According to *The Golden Legend*'s account of Matthew's death, King Hirtacus had ordered the apostle to be killed for obstructing his marriage by converting his fiancée to Christianity. Contarelli's own memorandum to Muziano had instructed that the scene was to show:

**154**

*a long and ample place more or less in the form of a temple and, in the upper part, an isolated altar raised up above three, four, or five steps, at which Saint Matthew, dressed in liturgical vestments, is celebrating the Mass. Let him be killed by a few soldiers, and it would be more artful to depict him being killed, having received some wounds, and let him be already fallen or in the act of falling but not yet dead. And in that temple should be a large number of all sorts of men and women, old, young, and babies, mostly praying, and dressed befitting their station and nobility, on benches, rugs and other furnishings and, for the most part, frightened by the event, creating contempt in some and compassion in others.*[17]

Seemingly with Contarelli's original guidelines in hand, Caravaggio worked out an initial composition whose outlines beneath the present painted surface can be reconstructed from X-rays (Pl. 184).

**76 Martyrdom of Saint Matthew**, 1599–1600; oil on canvas, 323 × 343 cm, S. Luigi dei Francesi, Rome

156

**77** Girolamo Muziano, **Martyrdom of Saint Matthew**, 1586–9; oil on plaster, *c.*320 × 350 cm, S. Maria in Aracoeli, Rome

**78** Titian, **Martyrdom of Saint Peter Martyr**, 1528–30; etching by Nicholas Cochin, 1691, 28.5 × 17.2 cm, after lost altarpiece in SS. Giovanni e Paolo, Venice

What emerges most strikingly is that Caravaggio originally approached his first large-scale narrative in an entirely traditional way. Monumental classical architecture centred in the upper part of the canvas would have set the scene in a temple and delimited a measured space for the figures. Standing at right of centre, Matthew faced a trio of soldiers, one of whom is helmeted and seen from the back. Witnesses included a young acolyte and two women: one fallen at the apostle's feet and, to the left of the soldiers, another raising her hand to her cheek. Clearly Caravaggio's first impulse was to think in terms of a Raphaelesque balanced arrangement of figures within an imposing setting, and to adopt a favourite Mannerist device of a centrally placed figure seen from behind. Although he even roughed out his preliminary ideas directly on the canvas, he abandoned a first and perhaps a second design for the radically different solution he subsequently arrived at.[18]

In the final painting, only some shadowy columns, a partly visible altar, and a few steps suggest the temple; Matthew has already been fatally wounded by a lone, semi-nude assassin, and the women have fled the scene. To the crowd of onlookers, Caravaggio added three other half-naked men looming in the foreground.[19] Despite all these changes, he perhaps still drew inspiration from Contarelli's wishes, focusing, however, on other, selected details such as the isolated altar and steps, the dying saint whose blood stains his alb, and the bystanders' frightened reactions. And although he ultimately rejected a Central Italian model for his composition, he did adopt figural motifs from artistic precedents, preferring North Italian sources, such as Muziano's *Martyrdom of Saint Matthew* (Pl. 77) and Titian's *Martyrdom of Saint Peter Martyr* (Pl. 78).[20]

These comparisons only emphasize the degree to which Caravaggio transformed his models. He boldly eliminated any defined setting, a convention by this time in ecclesiastical works. In turn he magnified the figures to fill the frame and arranged them in a centrifugal, wheel-like configuration, with the onlookers radiating

out as so many spokes from the murderer and victim at the hub. Intent on conveying the horror of the deed, he reproduced the gamut of human emotion in the individual facial expressions, poses and gestures, for which he drew on his own earlier works. For the crowd, Caravaggio adapted yet another element from his easel pictures, using studio models dressed in contemporary clothing, so that while the primary action can be imagined taking place long ago in distant Ethiopia, the witnesses with their plumed hats, doublets and lace collars are modern. Pictorial precedents already existed for the intrusion of contemporary figures into a biblical scene, but invariably they were present as portraits of the donors. Here the intention differs, for although the onlookers are not specific individuals in seventeenth-century Rome, they are reminders that the past survives into the present, and all are called upon now, as then, to bear witness to acts of divine revelation.

At the very back of the crowd, one witness is meant to be identified, Caravaggio himself, now twenty-eight and bearded. Running away, he turns back to look on the carnage, his face marked with fear and dismay (Pl. 79). As will be seen, this is the first of several instances in which he inserted himself into a religious work. While Renaissance artists had done likewise, usually as a profession of piety, Caravaggio seems to emphasize his witnessing of the event as if to authenticate the truth to nature of his painted version.

Crucial to Caravaggio's fresh interpretation of the apostle's martyrdom is the strong *chiaroscuro* contrasting the brightly lit figures with the dark background. Having deepened the shadows in his easel paintings of around 1599, he now realized the dramatic potential of tenebrism for his large narrative paintings. As Bellori aptly described this artificial system of lighting, Caravaggio 'never brought any of his figures out into the daylight, but found a way to paint them against the darkness of a closed room, taking a high lamp that hung vertically over the principal part of the body, and leaving the rest in shadow, so as to give force through the power of light and dark.'[21] The darkened backdrop creates a foil for the figures, who project forward with sculptural volume. In the *Martyrdom of Saint Matthew*, the light is most

**79 Martyrdom of Saint Matthew** (Pl. 76), detail showing Caravaggio's self-portrait

brilliant in the middle, focusing attention on the brutal murder, while at the left, flashes of light strike the jumble of onlookers, arbitrarily fixing on a hand, a forehead, or a cheek. The resulting fragmentation of form intensifies the sense of chaos unleashed by the offence against God and humanity.

Turning to the opposite wall, Caravaggio illustrated the decisive moment in Matthew's life when he abandoned his trade as a tax-collector to follow Christ. Here too Contarelli had outlined how the scene should be painted but Caravaggio either did not know of, or ignored, the instructions, which his predecessor Cesari evidently had followed in a preliminary idea for the composition (Pl. 80). Unlike Cesari, Caravaggio interpreted the prescribed setting within the tax office as no more than a table set against a wall under a window. He not only eliminated anecdotal incidents but even reduced the number of Christ's disciples to one, Peter. While his composition instead resembles Cristoforo Roncalli's exactly contemporaneous fresco of the same subject (Pl. 81), he none the less rejected its conception as a daylight scene enacted by idealized and graceful figures within a defined architectural space.[22]

The few changes visible in X-rays suggest that Caravaggio composed the companion piece, the *Calling of Saint Matthew* (Pl. 82), with confidence, presumably gained from the experimentation in the *Martyrdom*. He chose, subtly, to show Matthew undergoing conversion, rather than already converted. The traditional identification of Matthew as the pointing man still carries the most conviction, despite recent arguments to the contrary. With the appropriate age, attire and accessories, this figure indeed points to himself, as is clear from the shadow on his index finger. The transience of the moment is conveyed by Matthew's startled reaction, as if to say, 'You don't mean me!'[23]

Though drawn to Christ, Matthew's individualized features and elegant modern clothes are in pointed contrast to the idealized heads

**81**  Cristoforo Roncalli and assistant, **Calling of Saint Matthew**, 1600;  fresco, Palazzo Caetani, Rome

and biblical robes of the two divine figures, thereby tying him to his past life. The companions of that life, who surround him, appear to have wandered in from Caravaggio's earlier genre pictures, especially the two young men at the far right of the table wearing plumed hats and fancy dress.

Like the *Martyrdom*, the *Calling of Saint Matthew* is distinguished from contemporary Roman painting by its forceful contrast of light and dark. But whereas the lighting has a scattershot effect in the *Martyrdom*, a shaft of light here descends from the upper right in a steady diagonal path, just grazing Christ and flooding on to Matthew's face. The radiance of the light creates a wedge-like pattern on the back wall, a device used by Caravaggio in the *Penitent Magdalen* (Pl. 32) and the *Lute-Player* (Pl. 47). A purely formal device in the latter picture, it takes on the symbolic meaning of enlightenment in the *Penitent Magdalen* and the *Calling of Saint Matthew*. The bottom edge of the wedge forms a line of demarcation between light and shadow and traces a course from Christ to Matthew. The light thus acts as the vehicle of divine illumination penetrating the shadowy realm of unenlightened sinners and effecting Matthew's conversion. Caravaggio also expressed tangibly the saviour's symbolic role as the 'light of the world' (John 8:12) by showing the figure of Christ striding forward from darkness into the light. The theme of divine illumination, is reversed at the far end of the table where the old man's eyeglasses do not extend his vision beyond the money lying there, over which hunches a young man equally blinded by material things.[24]

In the Cerasi Chapel, Caravaggio built upon the innovations of his two lateral paintings in the Contarelli Chapel. But whereas the first

**82 Calling of Saint Matthew**, 1599–1600; oil on canvas, 322 × 340 cm, S. Luigi dei Francesi, Rome

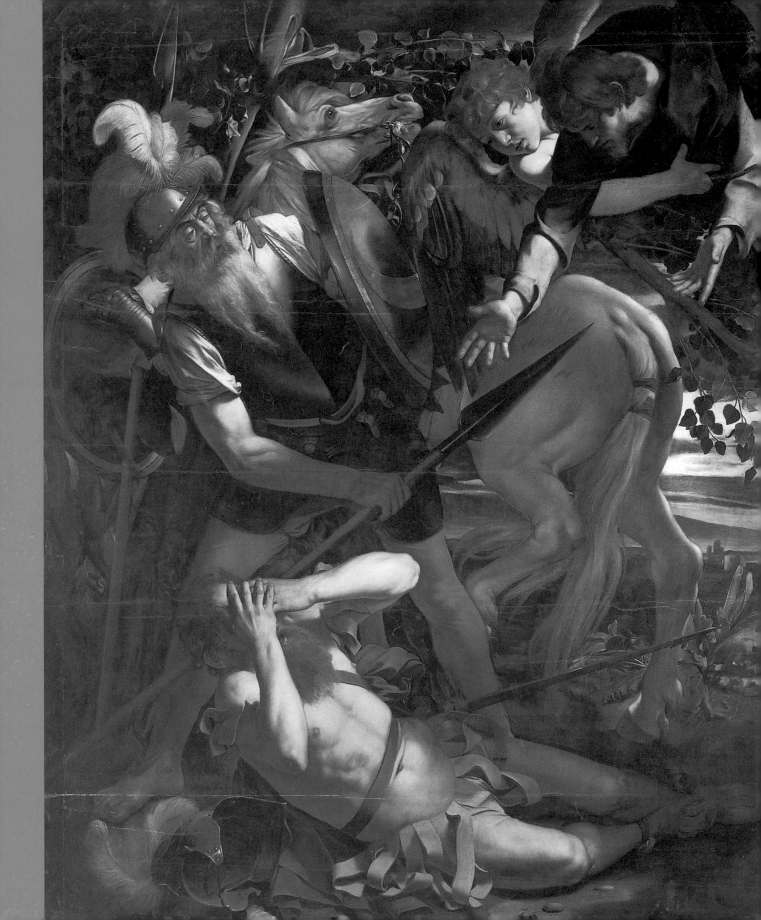

pair retain obvious links to his early secular canvases, the *Conversion of Saint Paul* and the *Crucifixion of Saint Peter* break decisively with his youthful manner, signalling his artistic maturity. That the break was not a clean one is suggested by his redoing of each picture. The startling disparity between the initial conception of the *Conversion of Saint Paul* (Pl. 83) – the only surviving original version – and the definitive altarpiece (Pl. 86) underlines the stylistic shift Caravaggio accomplished in the year between the autumn of 1600 and that of 1601.

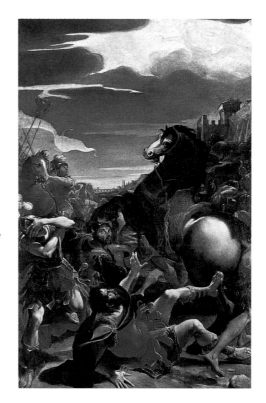

According to the Acts of the Apostles (9:3–9), the Roman official Saul was travelling to Damascus to persecute Christians when a divine light knocked him off his horse and the voice of Christ chastized him. The vision blinded him for three days, after which he converted to Christianity and, newly baptized Paul, preached to the Gentiles. The tumultuous confusion surrounding the miracle of Paul's conversion inspired many painters including Michelangelo and, closer to Caravaggio's day, Ludovico Carracci (Pl. 84). Like his predecessors, Caravaggio initially pictured a landscape in which Paul has just fallen from his rearing horse and gave bodily form to what is only a voice in the Scriptures. Seeking to animate the familiar biblical event, he pushed the action into a shallow foreground space and used the sharply contrasted lighting to strengthen the sculptural volume of forms and for dramatic effect. Furthermore, he painted certain, salient details from life, such as the hands of Paul and Christ and the head of the angel. The general impression made by the work, however, is of a crowded and confused composition that looks more bombastic than convincing. Paul's fussy cuirass increases the sense of sham, along with the plumed helmet and decorative shield of the standing soldier; these distracting elements

**83 Conversion of Saint Paul**, 1600–1; oil on wood, 237 × 189 cm, private collection, Rome

**84** Ludovico Carracci, **Conversion of Saint Paul**, 1587–9; oil on canvas, 279 × 171 cm, Pinacoteca Nazionale, Bologna

166

derive from Caravaggio's Lombard background, recalling, for example, Campi's *Christ Nailed to the Cross* (Pls. 10, 11), painted as much as thirty years earlier. Although impressive and beautifully executed in certain passages, the first version lacks the tight composition and emotional power of its replacement.

Next to nothing of the original work survives in Caravaggio's definitive *Conversion of Saint Paul* (Pl. 86). The heavenly vision has vanished, a younger man with closely cropped beard acts the part of Saul, and an old servant holds the bridle of an almost quieted horse. Limiting the narrative to essentially the saint and horse was not Caravaggio's invention but must have been suggested to him by North Italian tradition in familiar examples by Moretto (Pl. 85) and Parmigianino (Kunsthistorisches Museum, Vienna, *c*.1530). However, Caravaggio went so far as to paint out the trees, plants, and light-streaked sky of the road to Damascus, isolating and shrouding the scene in mysterious darkness. Most astonishing of all is his reinterpretation of the action as a still and hushed event. To communicate Paul's internal upheaval, he drastically reduced visible signs of movement to the saint's open arms and the horse's raised foreleg and foaming mouth, so that all attention focuses on his full acceptance of the heavenly message. The means of its transmission is again light; descending from the upper right-hand corner of the painting, its rays follow a steep diagonal path towards the saint's face and body and, like a powerful magnet, draw his arms upward. Recent cleaning of the canvas reveals that Caravaggio indicated the sparkle of the light by painting minuscule white dots along its trajectory. Thus, in his final version, Caravaggio transformed his initial, literal illustration into an unprecedented conception of the subject, visualizing an individual's response to a transcendental experience.

**85** Alessandro Bonvicino, Il Moretto, **Conversion of Saint Paul**, *c*.1529–30; oil on canvas, 306 × 146 cm, S. Maria presso S. Celso, Milan

**86 Conversion of Saint Paul**, 1600–1; oil on canvas, 230 × 175 cm, S. Maria del Popolo, Rome

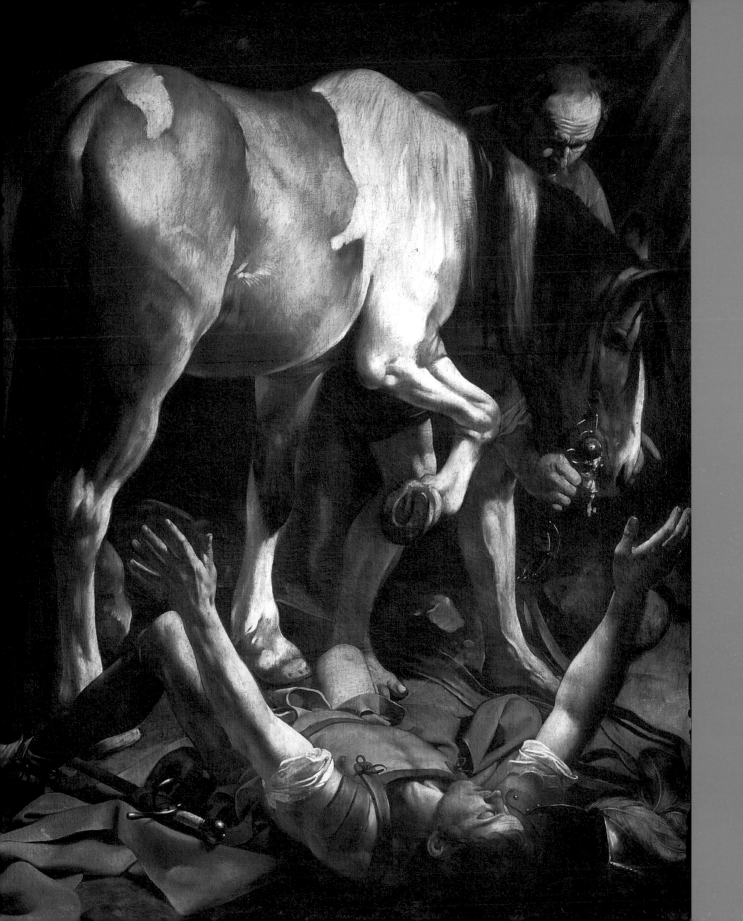

The originality of his invention must have impressed fellow painters such as Roncalli (1522–1626), a highly successful artist in contemporary Rome who was on friendly terms with Caravaggio. In his *Death of Sapphira* (Pl. 87) for St Peter's, Sapphira's steeply foreshortened pose and outstretched arms, and Roncalli's use of a secondary oblique viewpoint resemble Caravaggio's *Conversion* strongly enough to suggest deliberate imitation. Not all viewers were favourably impressed, however; Bellori complained that the narrative 'is entirely without action'.[25]

Caravaggio's *Crucifixion of Saint Peter* (Pl. 89) also relies on minimal means, setting four figures in front of what appears to be a rocky escarpment with some vegetation. Peter was crucified head down, as he declared himself unworthy to die in the same way as Christ. Typically the apostle's martyrdom called for a daytime scene with a crowd of witnesses, as exemplified in Domenico Passignano's altarpiece for St Peter's (Pl. 88).

168

Dispensing with noble architecture and heavenly hosts, Caravaggio instead riveted the viewer's attention on Peter's physical and spiritual trial. The strongest light falls on the saint, and his is the only fully visible face. Caravaggio judiciously excluded all but the most symbolically fraught objects: the prominently placed rock refers to Christ's calling Peter 'the rock' upon which the Church was to be founded. In contrast to Passignano's scenographic visualization, Caravaggio's compositions must have looked cut down and condensed, narrowly covering the main action and glossing over all the particulars of time and place. Paradoxically, the absence of a descriptive ambience does not compromise their arresting immediacy, and both Cerasi pictures carry more conviction than Passignano's discursive altarpiece.

The *Crucifixion of Saint Peter* especially exemplifies the naturalism that amazed Caravaggio's audience then as much as it does now. Its photographic sharpness gives the impression that the action was staged by four models in his studio, much in the way that his critics described. That some posing did take place is suggested by the reddened hand and protruding vein of the man at upper left – characteristics of supporting a heavy weight – and by the bulge of flesh where the jacket cuts the waist of the standing man pulling on the rope. But

**87** Cristoforo Roncalli, **Death of Sapphira**, 1599–1606; oil on slate, 769 × 427.5 cm, S. Maria degli Angeli, Rome

**88** Domenico Passignano, **Crucifixion of Saint Peter**, 1602–5; engraving by Jacques Callot, *c.*1611–16, 10.9 x 7.1 cm, after a lost altarpiece in St Peter's, Rome

Caravaggio simulated rather than reproduced reality. He carefully planned his composition, locking each figure into a geometric design, and arbitrarily imposed a preternaturally still and nocturnal setting. By means of pictorial sleight of hand, he created the persuasive illusion that Peter is nailed to the cross which is being lifted into place. Yet the cross is actually no more than a single board without a crossbeam; the apostle's left arm, therefore, actually stretches along the same beam as the rest of his body.[26]

The figures in both Cerasi laterals have even greater sculptural force than those in the Contarelli canvases and are barely contained within their frames. At the centre of the *Crucifixion of Saint Peter* is a powerful nude torso studied from life but inspired by Michelangelo's art. Another early source served as an example for the monumental animal in the final *Conversion of Saint Paul*: Albrecht Dürer's graphic *œuvre*, which Caravaggio drew upon more than once in his Roman years. He studied the pose and type of Dürer's engraved *Large Horse*, 1505, but then revised the particulars after a real horse.[27] Thus, by the end of 1601, Caravaggio had mastered the weightiness and volume of High Renaissance form, although he successfully disguised his figures' traditional antecedents beneath the individualized and unidealized features of his models.

The particular requirements of the Cerasi commission might also have influenced his new handling of the figure. Not only were the dimensions of the two works smaller than the Contarelli canvases, but their vertical format also discouraged narrative expansiveness. Furthermore, the narrow space of the sanctuary of the chapel dictated an oblique viewing angle. This proved an important factor in his positioning of each apostle along the same diagonal as the spectator's line of vision. Given that the viewer's glance first alights on the dirty feet and rear end of the stooping executioner, Caravaggio may well have slipped in a sly joke.[28]

170

**89 Crucifixion of Saint Peter**, 1600–1; oil on canvas, 230 × 175 cm, S. Maria del Popolo, Rome

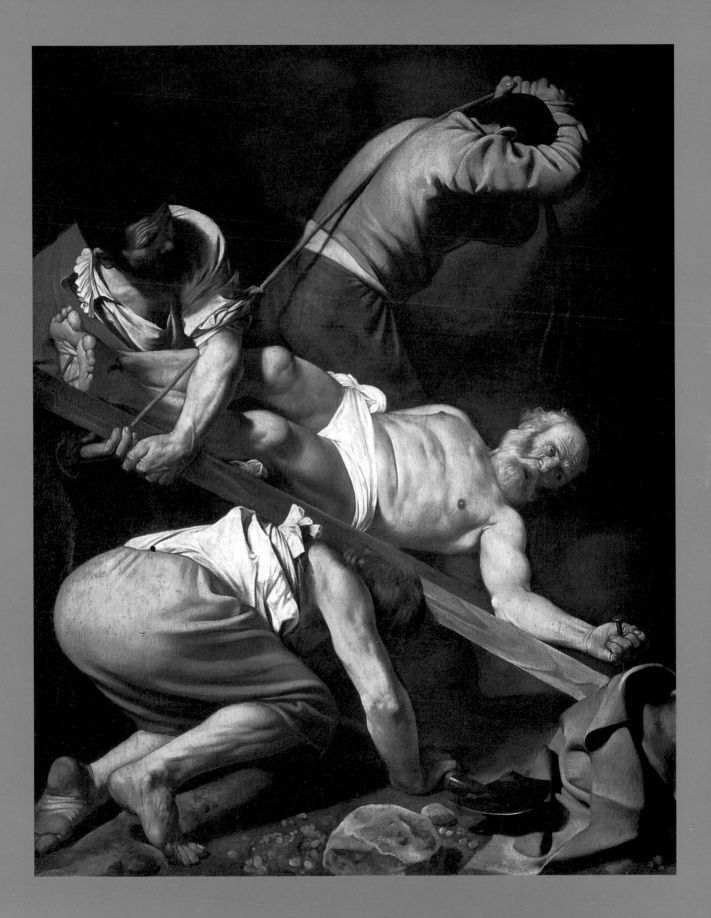

**90** Annibale Carracci, **Assumption of the Virgin**, 1600; oil on wood, 245 × 155 cm, S. Maria del Popolo, Rome

Caravaggio surely recognized, too, that his Cerasi paintings would be assessed alongside Annibale Carracci's altarpiece of the *Assumption of the Virgin* (Pl. 90). Annibale (1560–1609) was the only other painter active in contemporary Rome whose artistic innovations and historical significance equalled Caravaggio's. Together with his cousin Ludovico (1555–1619) and his brother Agostino (1557–1602), Annibale had earlier founded the Carracci Academy in Bologna and inaugurated a naturalistic reform of painting. Settling in Rome by 1595, he entered Cardinal Alessandro Farnese's service. Caravaggio's reaction in 1599 to the unveiling of another of Annibale's public works was reportedly enthusiastic. The story rings true, for Annibale's painting exudes exceptional vitality, unparalleled in this period.[29]

That Caravaggio saw Annibale's *Assumption* before, or while, working on his final paintings is suggested by Paul's extended arms in the *Conversion* mirroring the Virgin Mary's gesture. Just as Annibale squeezed his weighty figures into a shallow space, Caravaggio moved his own figures to the very edges of the frame and up against the picture surface. But whereas Annibale's evenly diffused lighting, high-keyed palette and idealized figures filter his naturalism, Caravaggio's darkened background throws his forms into sharp relief, and his selective, deep colours enhance the lifelikeness of the whole. He further juxtaposed the relative nobility of his apostles with the menial character of the supporting figures, so that common labourers prepare to lift the cross and a poor servant calms the horse.[30]

In his *Entombment* (Pl. 91), Caravaggio took up the venerable theme of Christ's Passion, depicted by all the great Italian artists since Giotto. Caravaggio's aged and veiled Madonna extends her arms behind John and Nicodemus, bent with the load of the dead body, while one of the Marys lowers her head to weep and the other throws up her arms in grief. The observation from life of Christ's unidealized body and Nicodemus's rugged face and ungainly legs is offset by the supremely artful composition. Uniting the densely grouped figures is the diagonal descending from the raised left hand of the woman at the back to the tip of Jesus's shroud spilling over the stone slab. This falling movement strengthens the sense that Christ's dead weight strains his bearers, forcing Nicodemus to grasp his knees in a bear-hug. The *Entombment* fits more squarely within the artistic tradition than Caravaggio's other Roman commissions, perhaps in response to its intended placement over an altar and the demands of his patron and/or the church.

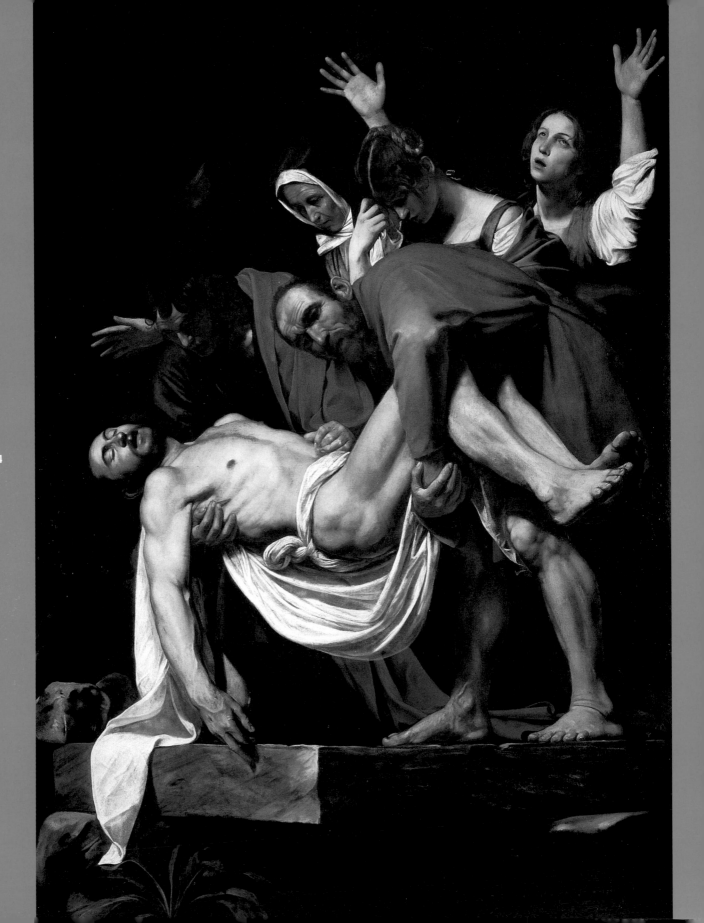

174

Many artistic prototypes, including Peterzano's altarpiece (Pl. 6), must have come to Caravaggio's mind as he planned his composition. Although he seems to have remembered certain details of his former master's painting, he was equally aware of Peterzano's wooden forms and prosaic design. Instead, the model that most engaged him was Michelangelo's *Pietà* (Pl. 92). Michelangelo was one of the few artists Caravaggio ever quoted explicitly, but his homage veered from respectful to ironic, and here betrays a competitive edge. Retaining the bowed head and outstretched hand of Michelangelo's Madonna, Caravaggio depicted her as old, as she must have been, and modified her gesture to one of blessing. As if seeking to match the relief of his sculpted source, Caravaggio modelled Christ's body to appear as three-dimensional as possible. Rejecting the slender build and graceful pose of Michelangelo's figure, Caravaggio portrayed Jesus with a broad physique and accentuated the raised veins on the hanging arm and the prominent hip bone. Not only is Christ's flesh shown as imperfect, but his body is not accorded the customary reverential treatment, for John's bare hands touch his skin directly, and his brusque handling opens the wound in Christ's side. Thus, Caravaggio declared his own virtuosity in demonstrating how Michelangelo could be improved upon by recourse to the ultimate model, nature herself.

92 Michelangelo, **Pietà**, 1498–9; marble, height 175 cm, St Peter's, Rome

91 **Entombment**, *c*.1602–4; oil on canvas, 300 × 203 cm, Pinacoteca Vaticana, Rome

Beyond dramatic effects, Caravaggio sought to reveal the spiritual meaning of his work by centring attention on Christ and visually linking the altarpiece to its physical setting within the Vittrice Chapel. Light shines fullest on Christ's body, further accentuated by the whiteness of the shroud, while pockets of shadow eat into the rest of the figures. The sacramental meaning of the image would have had greatest impact during celebration of the Mass within the chapel (Pl. 75). For when the priest intoned 'This is my body' at the consecration, the eucharistic liturgy was complemented by the visual reminder of Christ's sacrifice in the altarpiece above. As can be seen from its copy now in the chapel, Caravaggio further linked the *Entombment* to actual devotions by calculating the level of the tomb slab to coincide with the head of an officiating priest. More than an effective formal device, the jutting stone of the slab refers to a passage in the Gospel of Matthew (21:42) alluding symbolically to Jesus as the cornerstone of the Church. Thus, Caravaggio's *Entombment* both affirms the Catholic doctrine of transubstantiation, reiterated at the Council of Trent after its denial by the Protestants, and the role of the Church as intermediary between God and the devout.[31]

High critical praise was lavished on Caravaggio's *Entombment*, which his biographers declared equal to the *Calling of Saint Matthew* or even his best public painting. Among its admirers was Peter Paul Rubens, who had the chance to study it closely while working on the paintings for the high altar of the church between 1606 and 1608. With its rationalized action and its restrained expression, Rubens's later free copy (Pl. 93) makes the severe and moving grandeur of Caravaggio's altarpiece all the more evident.[32]

**93** Peter Paul Rubens, **Entombment**, 1613–15; oil on wood, 88.3 × 65.4 cm, National Gallery of Canada, Ottawa

The imagery in Caravaggio's earliest ecclesiastical paintings, from 1599 to 1602, did not incur the disapproval of critics nor presumably of devout viewers. The objection to the original pictures for the Cerasi Chapel was more likely aesthetic than doctrinal. But with the completion of the first *Saint Matthew and the Angel* (Pl. 94) for the Contarelli altar in September 1602, Caravaggio broached the unmarked border between acceptable novelty and threatening unorthodoxy, and hostility grew against his vernacular reinterpretation of sacred subject-matter. Content and not style distinguishes the second *Saint Matthew* (Pl. 95) from the first, even though the two altarpieces superficially appear as antithetical as the two Cerasi *Conversions*. In each, a fully three-dimensional evangelist and angel emerge in a brilliant beam of light slicing the dark interior. Their individual expressions – one agog and the other attentive – are precisely caught. Intent on bringing the scene alive to us, Caravaggio swung out the first Matthew's foot to the edge of the picture plane and, the second time around, he tipped the foot of his stool over the ledge marking the front plane of the painting.

The drastic changes Caravaggio introduced in the second altarpiece, then, can be viewed as his compromise on the appearance of the evangelist and the angel. He had initially envisaged Matthew as seated writing his Gospel in a large book at the dictation of an angel. The bent posture of the burly saint accentuated his bulbous, balding head and thick neck, while his rolled-up sleeves and short tunic exposed hefty arms and equally muscular legs. The strain of concentration wrinkled his brow as he gaped wide-eyed at the Hebrew letters spelling out the beginning of his Gospel. Poised gracefully at his elbow to guide his hand, his heavenly assistant was everything Matthew was not: young and beautiful, with a sinuous body revealed by clinging, transparent fabric.

In the redaction (Pl. 95), Matthew has exchanged his cloddish look for a noble demeanour. His arms and legs hidden by ample robes, he pauses at his table with his pen suspended in the inkpot to heed the angel's words. The pair's former cosy intimacy has yielded to a hierarchical arrangement wherein a now airborne angel dictates from on high, ticking off on his fingers the generations of Christ's genealogy

179

94 **Saint Matthew and the Angel**, *c.*1602; oil on canvas, 223 × 183 cm, formerly Kaiser Friedrich Museum, Berlin (destroyed)

opening Matthew's Gospel. The angel too has not escaped remodelling; swirling draperies and the altered pose conceal all but the bare shoulders and arms of the model, clearly a boy in this case.

The priestly congregation reportedly rejected Caravaggio's first *Saint Matthew* for a breach of decorum in his portrayal of the evangelist: Matthew's incredulous expression and hesitant writing betray a dullard's simplicity, and his physical appearance implies low social standing. The masterful illusionism in the painting made Matthew's bare foot appear to project out over the altar in the chapel, but this spatial device here lacked the sacred meaning of Christ's fictive projection in the *Entombment*. As declared at the last session of the Council of Trent in 1563, religious images taught the faithful how to invoke saintly intercession, and so honour and veneration were due to them, especially in ecclesiastical paintings of saints. The Tridentine decree reiterated the role of the saints as reminders of God's grace and as virtuous exemplars of pious conduct and devotion to God. The Council therefore charged bishops to ensure that representations of saints in their churches, as well as those of God and the Virgin Mary, should not be lewd or unbecoming, irreverent or disrespectful. Enforcement of official Church policy is difficult to gauge, but, as stated in Chapter 1, Clement VIII's pastoral visits entailed examination of altarpieces and resulted in the removal of offending works of art. The papal campaign to reform ecclesiastical art was furthered by the revival in 1603 of an earlier edict requiring licences for all new paintings; instigated by Camillo Borghese, then Cardinal Vicar and later Paul V, its intent was to eradicate indecent art. Borghese's action, although postdating by a year the rejection of Caravaggio's first *Saint Matthew*, reflects an ongoing debate about standards for religious art which engaged local congregations as well as those at the highest level within the Church.[33]

**95 Saint Matthew and the Angel**, 1602–3; oil on canvas, 295 × 195 cm, S. Luigi dei Francesi, Rome

182

**96** Gerolamo Romanino, **Saint Matthew and the Angel**, 1521–4; oil on canvas, 205 × 98 cm, S. Giovanni Evangelista, Brescia

Undoubtedly Caravaggio's Roman public considered Matthew's second incarnation as more closely matching their preconceived notions of the evangelist than the unlikely first candidate; he also bore a stronger resemblance to Caravaggio's own portrayal of Matthew as the handsome tax collector in the *Calling* (Pl. 82) and the dignified priest in the *Martyrdom* (Pl. 76). Why, then, did he conceive the first *Saint Matthew* in such a way that it could be construed as 'unbecoming' or 'disrespectful'?

In fact, artistic precedents exist both for Matthew's crossed-legs and bare feet (an engraving of 1518 after Raphael; Figino's altarpiece in S. Raffaele, Milan, *c*.1586; and Peterzano's fresco in the Certosa di Garegnano, 1578–82), and for his lowly social class (Moretto in the Duomo Vecchio, Brescia, 1520–4; Vincenzo Campi, S. Francesco Maggiore, Pavia, 1558; and Romanino (Pl. 96)).

**183**

Unique to Caravaggio's Matthew, however, is his implied illiteracy, for he is apparently incapable of writing without the angel's help. Worse, he is outrageously ignoble by the standards of contemporary Roman painting, epitomized in the pendentive of the dome of St Peter's designed a scant three years before (Pl. 97). Even compared to Caravaggio's earlier sacred figures, Matthew is an anomaly. Coarse types, however, do populate his religious paintings usually in supporting roles such as Peter's executioners, Paul's servant, or Nicodemus. The model for the first *Saint Matthew* is a similarly brutish type, and by flouting custom Caravaggio may have simply hoped to grab attention. But perhaps the painter's conception of Matthew was primarily influenced by his personal religious convictions, to be explored further in the next chapter.

**97** Cesare Nebbia, **Saint Matthew and the Angel**, 1598–9; mosaic, pendentive of dome, St Peter's, Rome

Caravaggio's realistic details. The locus of his discontent were the two pilgrims kneeling in adoration of Mary and the Christ Child; the old woman wears a torn bonnet, and her companion's dirty feet cannot be ignored for they seem to thrust out right above the heads of viewers standing in the chapel. As most pilgrims walked to their holy destination and the most devout of them wore no shoes, Caravaggio might have readily defended his figure's dirty feet as true to fact. But by dwelling on grimy feet and threadbare clothing, he likened his pilgrims to paupers, or worse, the beggars in Rome who were described by one observer in 1601, as 'so numerous that it is impossible to go anywhere in the city without being surrounded by them'. If objectionable on Roman streets, beggars were downright unseemly in a holy altarpiece.[37]

Early commentators neglected to add that Caravaggio's visualization of the *Madonna di Loreto* was no less original. Without knowledge of the dedication of the Cavalletti Chapel it would be hard to associate this altarpiece with the Loretan cult, for most paintings of the theme included the Holy House. Typically, devotional images showed the Madonna and Christ Child seated on its roof, as, for example, in a contemporary Roman altarpiece (Pl. 103). Perhaps impatient with the visual absurdity of a flying building, Caravaggio invented an alternative image which shows Mary standing on the threshold of her house, as if she has just emerged to welcome visitors. The travertine mouldings suggest a Roman façade, and the crumbling stucco on the wall to the right perhaps evokes the poverty in which Christ grew up.[38]

Instead of the apposite pictorial tradition, Caravaggio's novel conception calls to mind prints depicting the cult statue of the Madonna di Loreto in a niche flanked by kneeling pilgrims. By an imaginative leap, however, he transformed those formulaic illustrations into a particularized experience, yet with universal meaning for all believers. So it would seem that the pilgrims' intense faith magically brings the cult statue to life in front of their eyes. Mary is poised on tiptoe with knees crossed, her pose suggesting the weightlessness of an apparition but one so tangible as to cast a shadow on the portal. The Christ Child, exceptionally large, reaches out with his right hand to bless the kneeling couple. Neither saints nor wealthy donors, these anonymous worshippers turn their faces away from the viewer, their

**102 Madonna di Loreto**, *c.*1603–6; oil on canvas, 260 × 150 cm, S. Agostino, Rome

192

whole beings intent on the vision. The miracle lies here, Caravaggio implies, not in the flight of a house. While deploring the pilgrims' lowly appearance, one early critic found poignancy and inspiration in their 'pure simplicity of heart'.[39]

The *Madonna dei Palafrenieri* (Pl. 105), Caravaggio's last Roman altarpiece, is a strangely haunting work. The dark-haired beauty who was the model for the Madonna di Loreto here tenderly bends over to steady her naked son, a curly redhead of about four years, who presses his small foot with hers to crush a serpent's head. Concerned but not interfering, the child's grandmother looks on. A soft light falls on mother and child from an invisible skylight but otherwise does not dispel the encroaching darkness.

As in the *palafrenieri's* earlier altarpiece (Pl. 104), Caravaggio represented their patron saint, Anne, in the company of the Madonna and the Christ Child. But he must have been instructed to omit Peter and Paul, add the serpent and make Anne more conspicuous. With her action, Mary fulfils the prophecy by which, according to the Vulgate Bible (Genesis 3:15), God would send a second Eve to redeem the original sin of the first. Although this passage was exposed as a mistranslation from the Hebrew in the fifteenth century, the post-Tridentine

**103** Domenichino, as assistant to Annibale Carracci, **Madonna di Loreto**, 1604–5; oil on canvas, 250 × 150 cm, S. Onofrio, Rome
**104** Leonardo da Pistoia and Jacopino del Conte, **Madonna dei Palafrenieri**, *c.*1537; Sacristy, St Peter's, Rome

Church upheld the authority of the Vulgate by insisting that the Virgin Mary triumphed over Satan, together with her divine offspring, as Caravaggio indicated in positioning Christ's foot on top of his mother's. The Virgin's role as co-redemptrix was only possible because of her Immaculate Conception.

Saint Anne is present in Caravaggio's painting primarily because of the dedication of the altar. Her inclusion also reflects her association with the Immaculate Conception and the renewed vigour of her cult since the Renaissance; the more exemplary the life led by a mother, the more credence given to the daughter's special status. During the Counter-Reformation in particular, Anne's cult flourished in response to

Protestant attacks, and Gregory XIII extended her feast throughout the Church in 1584. Finally, the vanquished serpent in Caravaggio's painting symbolized for Catholic viewers of the post-Reformation era the Church's victory over the most recent embodiment of Satan: Protestant heresy.

Given its apparently impeccable illustration of Marian devotion, the swift removal of Caravaggio's

*Madonna dei Palafrenieri* from St Peter's is mystifying. A dispute over the Confraternity's rights to the altar may explain their transfer of the painting to their own church of S. Anna. Their sale of it two months later, however, suggests they were either not fully satisfied or found Cardinal Borghese's offer too tempting to refuse. They might also have reconsidered their initial acceptance of the work in the light of its alleged rejection for indecency by the cardinals of the Fabbrica di San Pietro. Practical considerations aside, was Caravaggio's altarpiece judged inappropriate for St Peter's because it was the mother church of Catholicism?

Certainly the *Madonna dei Palafrenieri* shares none of the stylistic characteristics of the works being produced in these years for the principal altars in the transepts of the basilica, such as Roncalli's *Death of Sapphira* (Pl. 87) or Passignano's *Crucifixion of Saint Peter* (Pl. 88). In sharp contrast to these, Caravaggio's painting isolated three figures in the starkest of settings; it further stripped the most sacred beings of their deserved majestic raiments. Instead of the triumphant Mother of God and infant Saviour, Caravaggio evoked a 'peasant woman killing a viper in a barn', to quote from one modern historian.[40] The cardinals of the Fabbrica perhaps frowned upon Mary's attire: instead of her customary matronly veil, mantle and robes, she wears contemporary dress of a simple design and fabric, with skirt hitched up for the work at hand, and her stooping pose reveals rather too much breast. Equally objectionable to prevailing official standards of decency for ecclesiastical art might have been the total nudity of Christ, no longer a baby.

As neither Caravaggio nor any other painter was asked to add a few brushstrokes to cover up the offending details, as often happened in such cases, an additional objection may have blocked acceptance of the work. In an altarpiece dedicated to Saint Anne, Caravaggio surprisingly placed her physically apart from the Madonna and Child and in partial shadow; he was also unsparing in painting a wizened

**105 Madonna dei Palafrenieri**, 1605–6; oil on canvas, 292 × 211 cm, Galleria Borghese, Rome

face and neck and dressing her in mouse-coloured clothing. This singularly unprepossessing Anne has only a passive role in an altarpiece ostensibly meant to honour her. Thus, the Fabbrica, even though possibly numbering two of Caravaggio's patrons (Del Monte and Giustiniani), ejected the *Madonna dei Palafrenieri* from the holiest of basilicas. What was intolerable on public view in St Peter's, however, could be later enjoyed for its artistic merits within the privacy of the papal nephew's home.

Caravaggio's six public commissions catapulted him into the limelight. The unveiling of each painting must have been eagerly awaited by the public – artists and critics, eminent prelates and ordinary Romans alike, whose accolades made Caravaggio famous, if controversial, and his art the talk of Rome. His early easel pictures had already established his originality, but they could never have advanced him to the summit of the Roman artistic scene, because the critical climate did not favour their small dimensions and half-length format, unidealized figures and genre themes. Only in large-scale religious paintings could Caravaggio demonstrate his mastery of complex compositions, the human figure and expression, and historical narrative.

One artistic language unites all of Caravaggio's Roman ecclesiastical paintings. Whether the subject required two or a dozen figures, a shallow foreground space set them on the apron of a stage, so to speak, thrusting out towards the spectator beyond the imaginary proscenium formed by the frame. Unlike the insubstantial forms compressed into the airless space of Mannerist paintings, Caravaggio fashioned three-dimensional bodies occupying real space. He refused to describe that space, however, reducing architecture to a window (*Calling of Saint Matthew*, Pl. 82), ceiling beams (*Death of the Virgin*, Pl. 98), or a door-frame (*Madonna di Loreto*, Pl. 102). He swept away extraneous details, highlighting one or just a few striking, and often symbolic, props. Most importantly, he learned to manipulate his artificial lighting system for several ends: to heighten relief, to sharpen focus on the action, to create mood and, at times, to strengthen the spiritual message. Whether he illustrated a disciple's conversion, the death of Christ, Mary, or a saint, or special Marian devotions, the same shadowy backdrop blurs exterior with interior, banishing any glimpse of blue sky as if to deny the presence of the brilliant Roman sun right outside his studio.

In his insistence on the human figure and the human drama, Caravaggio came within reach of realizing a classicizing aesthetic, centred on these very concerns since antiquity. In fact, he appropriated poses from ancient models. Yet his choice of human actors – ordinary individuals whose appearance and behaviour were at odds with the heroic ideal – was irreconcilable with classical principles. Thus, once in the artistic arena of monumental sacred painting, Caravaggio defied its many conventions. Banishing noble protagonists and angelic hosts, lofty architecture and landscapes, he invented anew the grand episodes of sacred history as intimate and fervent dramas enacted by a minimal cast of plebeian players on a near-empty stage.

After his stunning debut in the Contarelli Chapel, orders for other commissions began to multiply. In addition to the ecclesiastical projects already discussed, Caravaggio apparently turned down a number of offers, such as the 1602 commission for an altarpiece in the Roman church of SS. Trinità dei Pellegrini, and one in 1604 for the high altarpiece of the Capuchin church in Tolentino.[41] As will be discussed in Chapter 5, in order to fulfil his contracts and to satisfy his many private clients, he painted with astonishing speed, regularly managing to deliver work on time or close to the deadline. As attested by both the documentary record and the 1605 inventory of his possessions which lists two large canvases to be painted, three small paintings, a large painting on panel, three large and two other stretchers, he evidently worked on several different commissions at the same time. Contrary to the usual artistic practice of a successful painter, he did not establish a workshop and employ apprentices but seems to have got by with the help of one assistant, although he must have hired more once public commissions had begun to accumulate.[42] He surely delegated to others the practical tasks of grinding and preparing pigments, stretching and priming canvases.

No longer a starving artist, Caravaggio earned the same, or similar, fees as other leading painters for most of his ecclesiastical works, except the *Death of the Virgin* for which he was especially well paid at 280 scudi. As prices varied with medium, size and number of figures, Caravaggio never received the handsome sums Cesari was paid for his fresco cycle in the Sala dei Conservatori (5,000 scudi), or that were paid to Roncalli (700 scudi) and Passignano (1,000 scudi) for the vast altarpieces in St Peter's. Still, by 1603 he was well enough off to rent his own house and forgo a regular stipend.[43]

Caravaggio's house, on the Vicolo di S. Biagio, was of course very modest in comparison to the Palazzo Madama, but it surpassed the average urban home in size, boasting two floors and a loggia overlooking a garden with a well. Its contents in 1605 suggest that the artist had by then assembled a motley group of possessions (Appendix VII). Apart from professional paraphernalia, he owned some glassware and earthenware vases, and various pieces of old furniture; the only household objects of any possible value were brass candlesticks, two mirrors, and his bed with two posts. Among the more personal items are the guitar and violin – mentioned in the preceding chapter – as well as a chest with a dozen books and two swords and two daggers. The impression made by this inventory is that Caravaggio spent his money as he earned it. He supposedly bought expensive clothes but then would wear them until they fell apart. He does not seem to have cared much about outward appearances, for he acquired the reputation of being unmindful of personal cleanliness and was alleged to have used an old canvas for his tablecloth.[44]

Dedicating himself to his art, Caravaggio would shut himself up for feverish spurts of activity, as a contemporary witness reported, but then he would drop work altogether and go about Rome, armed and ready for trouble.[45] The snatches of his life glimpsed from historical record bear out this report, as do the allegations of wildness and contentiousness made by his biographers. To the incidents of assault, disturbing the peace, and illegally carrying a sword already mentioned in Chapter 3, can be added a string of further offences. The most notable include his assault on the painter Mao Salini in October 1601, his prosecution in 1603 for slandering Baglione – to be discussed more fully in the next chapter – and his arrest in April 1604 for threatening a waiter with his sword after throwing a dish of artichokes in boiling oil at him. Two months later, Caravaggio appeared in court for cursing at an official and, early in 1605, he brought a suit against a fellow painter, whom he accused of trying to incriminate him for stealing. When arrested again for bearing arms illegally in the spring of 1605, he was forced to pay a steep fine, and soon after, in July, two women charged him with harassment.[46] Not always the only guilty party, he kept company with his great friend Longhi and other rowdy artists looking for a good time but quick to unsheathe their swords; these disaffected delinquents are mirrored by Tybalt and his cronies in Shakespeare's contemporary *Romeo and Juliet.*

Caravaggio's most serious criminal act prior to the murder which ended his Roman career, occurred in the summer of 1605 when he assaulted a Roman notary, Mariano Pasqualone. In his deposition of 29 July, Pasqualone charged Caravaggio with striking him on the head from behind in the Piazza Navona and then escaping into Del Monte's palace. Although he did not see his attacker, he was certain it was Caravaggio because of a fight between them a few nights earlier over 'a woman named Lena who stands ("sta in piedi") in the Piazza Navona …, who is Caravaggio's woman'. According to the later version of the story told by Giovanni Battista Passeri, a painter and artists' biographer, this 'Lena' was Caravaggio's model for the *Madonna di Loreto*. Passeri explained that Caravaggio had taken revenge on the notary for impugning his behaviour to her. Although Passeri described Lena as 'poor but honourable', he was mistaken about her virtue if she was usually to be found 'standing' in the Piazza Navona. It has been proposed she may be one and the same as the courtesan Maddalena di Paolo Antognetti.[47]

Perhaps aided by either of his Genoese patrons, Costa or Giustiniani, Caravaggio eluded arrest by secretly fleeing Rome for Genoa. During his three-week sojourn there, Prince Marcantonio Doria offered him the astronomical sum of 6,000 scudi to fresco a loggia, but Caravaggio flatly refused the commission. Meanwhile, negotiations must have taken place in Rome to smooth his return, and as soon as he got back at the end of August he made an official declaration of guilt and apologized to Pasqualone in the chambers of Cardinal Borghese.

During Caravaggio's absence, the authorities acted against him upon his landlady's charge of arrears in rent. Thus he returned to discover that he was dispossessed of his belongings and evicted from his house. Twelve years after his arrival as a young unknown, the now famous thirty-four-year-old painter again found himself without a permanent address. The very night of his apology to the notary, he vented his anger at his landlady by raising a commotion outside her house and breaking her shutters. He then moved in with a friend, Andrea Ruffetti, staying until he fled the city for good nine months later. The instability in his private life intensified further in late October 1605 when he sustained wounds to the throat and ear, caused by falling on his own sword, or so he claimed.[48]

Caravaggio's public commissions in Rome spread his fame beyond the capital to Tolentino, as we have seen, to the Gonzaga court at Mantua, where Rubens helped send the *Death of the Virgin*, and also to Modena, whose Duke Cesare d'Este vainly sought to obtain a work by Caravaggio for his private chapel. Within Rome itself, the 'most famous painter' met a growing demand for easel pictures from an ever wider circle of patrons keen to have a 'Caravaggio' hanging on the walls of their private galleries.

Chapter 5 **Private Commissions**

Concurrently with the intense spiritual experience expressed in the Cerasi *Conversion of Saint Paul*, Caravaggio conceived his most provocative secular image in the *Cupid* (Pl. 106), painted for Vincenzo Giustiniani in *c*.1601–2. Cocking his head and opening his mouth in a dimpled smile, a nude prepubescent boy half sits on the edge of a table draped with a white sheet. Sharply raising his left knee, he splays his legs as he steadies himself partly on the ball of his right foot. An intense, directed light glows on his silky skin, carves crisp folds in the white material between his legs, reflects off the black armour at his feet, and is absorbed by the warm brown wood of the lute and violin propped up on the floor next to his leg. The bow and arrows brandished in his right hand and the two extended, large brown wings, one of which grazes his left thigh, tell us that Caravaggio's model is impersonating the pagan god of love. Carefully arranged on the table and floor around the impish boy are various still-life objects, including the two musical instruments, each described with naturalistic precision.

*Cupid* immediately brings to mind Caravaggio's early easel pictures with a single figure and still-life elements, and also echoes the musical theme of Giustiniani's *Lute-Player*. Like all of Caravaggio's sensuous youths, his Cupid directly engages the viewer, and his utter lack of inhibition is at once refreshing and disconcerting. Caravaggio's newly mastered control of monumental canvases sets the *Cupid* apart, however, from his earlier works. The dynamic pinwheel composition relates to that of the *Martyrdom of Saint Matthew* (Pl. 76) and the *Crucifixion of Saint Peter* (Pl. 89), and the full-length and life-size nude projects the same commanding presence as the dying Peter.

Caravaggio's depiction of the ancient god, alone, detached from any familiar fable and paired with an unusual grouping of objects, suggests an intended allegorical meaning. The blatant nudity of his model hints that this Cupid's primary concern lies with the flesh and so, not surprisingly, the painting has been interpreted as the triumph of physical passion over the intellectual and cultural pursuits embodied in the still-life objects. Several modern critics have questioned the nature of the passion, reopening the issue first raised by Caravaggio's youthful genre paintings as to whether this painting too was aimed at a homosexual audience.[1]

An early support for this reading is supplied by an English visitor to Rome in 1649–50; after seeing Caravaggio's *Cupid*, Richard Symonds wrote in his diary that the model was Cecco del Caravaggio, the artist's assistant or servant 'that laid with him'. Cecco, whose few known works imitate the master's manner, has only recently been tentatively identified with the Bergamasque painter Francesco Buoneri (born *c*.1589–90?). As Caravaggio had a studio assistant named Francesco, it is tempting to recognize him as 'Cecco', a diminutive of Francesco. But that Cecco was Caravaggio's model or lover rests only on Symonds's testimony dating fifty years later – a thin support at best for the recent contention that the *Cupid* represents a manifesto of a homosexual subculture in Rome centred around Caravaggio and his milieu.[2]

More plausible interpretations of Caravaggio's *Cupid* address its intended meaning for the patron by considering the particular selection of still-life objects in relation to Giustiniani's diverse interests. Thus, the instruments and score refer to his expertise in music, a compass and T-square represent his mastery of architecture, and an open manuscript with a quill pen refers to his writings. The laurel wreath promises immortality, and a sliver of a starry blue sphere behind Cupid's leg suggests Vincenzo's study of astronomy and astrology. The gleaming armour embodies his chivalric ideals and, lastly, a crown and sceptre on the table to the right commemorate the family's former rule over the Mediterranean island of Chios, which they lost to the Turks in 1566 when Vincenzo was only two years old. The pertinence of the imagery to Vincenzo himself is driven home visually by Caravaggio in the large 'V' at the top of the musical score, and in the repeated 'V-shapes' in the intersecting T-square and compass, and the angled pair of musical instruments. Reference to the patron also explains Cupid's unusual brown wings, specifically described as those of an eagle by Sandrart who was well aware that an eagle with outspread wings emblazons the Giustiniani coat of arms.

In sum, Cupid's accessories invoke activities central to Vincenzo's self-fashioning as a gentleman of culture and consequence. As the gleeful god does not trample anything underfoot, in all likelihood the allegory celebrates, rather than disparages, Giustiniani's achievements. In accord with Neoplatonic theory, Earthly Love here acts as the generator and unifying impulse behind creative endeavours; by flattering analogy, Vincenzo does likewise. Caravaggio's image ingeniously plays on Giustiniani's given name by converting the Roman poet Virgil's celebrated phrase 'Omnia vincit Amor' (*Eclogues*, 10:6) into 'Omnia vincit Vincentius'. The proud declaration issues from an impudent Cupid, and Caravaggio's improbable and witty combination of the two, like the marvellous conceits of Baroque poetry, was surely meant to astonish and delight his patron. The eroticism of the image surely contributed to its success but, as with Caravaggio's earlier attractive boys, cannot be regarded as exclusively homo-erotic. The *Cupid* supposedly so enchanted Giustiniani that he became hopelessly enamoured of Caravaggio's works, and no sum of money would induce him to part with the jewel of his collection, which he displayed under a green silk curtain, drawing it aside to surprise his guests.[3]

**106 Cupid**, *c.*1601–2; oil on canvas, 191 × 148 cm, Staatliche Museen, Berlin

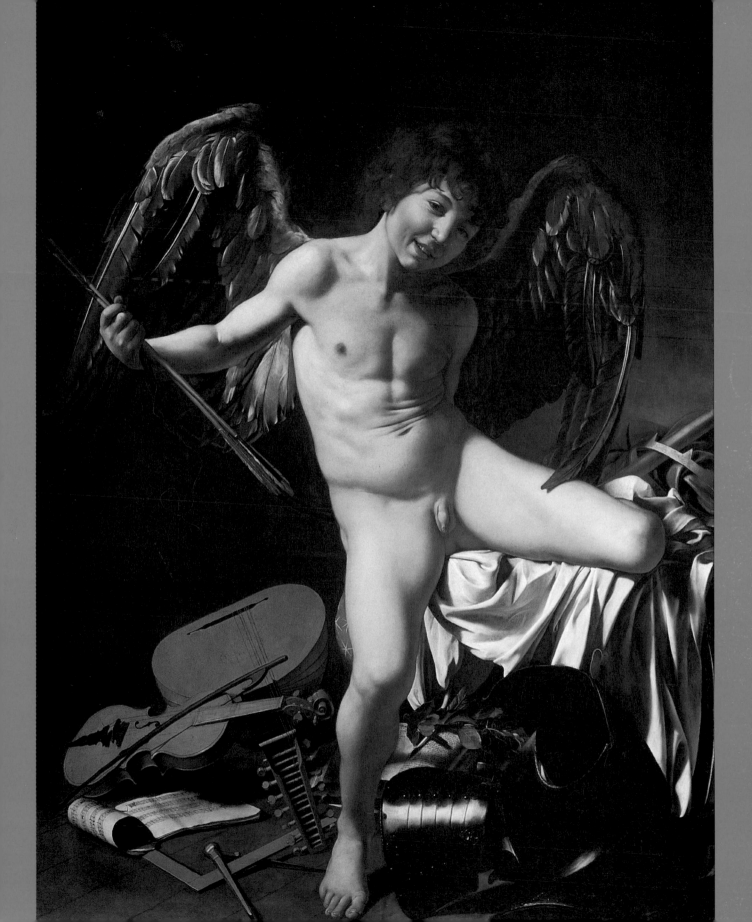

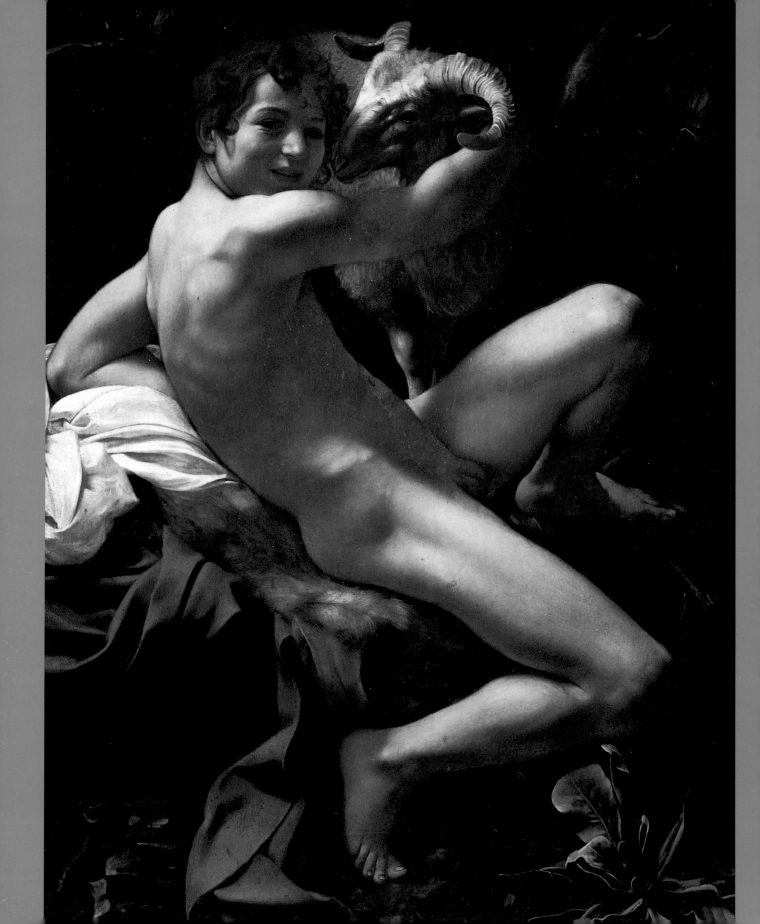

The *Cupid* was probably painted in the Palazzo Mattei, a sprawling complex covering an entire block in the heart of Rome, where Caravaggio was living in June 1601. Marchese Ciriaco Mattei (1542–1614) had also become so enamoured of Caravaggio's painting that he reportedly expended extravagant sums to acquire similar works. Recently discovered evidence sustains Baglione's report of Mattei's patronage and its importance, little understood in the past.[4]

The same model who posed for the *Cupid* reappears as *Saint John the Baptist* (Pl. 107), still wearing no more than the smile he flashes at us from over his shoulder. The canvas can be plausibly linked with two entries in Ciriaco's account books itemizing payments to Caravaggio in June and December 1602. Bequeathed by Ciriaco's son to Del Monte, the painting eventually entered the Capitoline collections, in time disappearing from sight. Only recently has its authenticity been satisfactorily proven. Consensus about the reidentified picture and its outstanding beauty has not yet resolved the debate about the painting's subject and its meaning, however.[5]

Most viewers were prepared to recognize John the Baptist in this unconventional portrayal, although even in the early seventeenth century a few were puzzled by the singularity of the adolescent embracing a ram. Conspicuously missing from the scene are any of John's familiar attributes: reed cross, bowl or lamb. Caravaggio's untraditional ram was re-baptized a lamb in several early citations. But the author of a guidebook who had worked as a painter in the Mattei palace in 1607 and again in 1615 instead affixed a mythological title to the painting, identifying the young man as a pagan shepherd. Although a pagan subject has the merit of justifying the figure's sensuality, the pictorial tradition for the mythological characters proposed thus far has even less in common with the image than Saint John. The problems besetting either a sacred or a profane interpretation have intermittently prompted the tempting conclusion that Caravaggio intended no other subject beyond a 'nude with ram'; however, little evidence exists for a category of paintings without subjects in seventeenth-century Italy.

Although its surprisingly secular tone sets it apart from Caravaggio's two later, indisputable portrayals of John the Baptist (Pls. 124, 179), this canvas also shows a full-length, youthful model sitting on a red cloak. The loins of the saint in the two later paintings, however,

**107** **Saint John the Baptist**, *c.*1602; oil on canvas, 129 × 95 cm, Pinacoteca Capitolina, Rome

are modestly draped. In keeping with legendary accounts of John's life that tell of the camel-skin he wore in the wilderness, an animal fur serves this purpose in the canvas now in Kansas City. The same allusion was probably intended by the soft tawny fur cushioning the model's rocky perch in this picture.[6]

Even more decisive for the identification of Saint John is the ram's reappearance as the Baptist's companion in the latest of the three versions (Pl. 179). In choosing a ram instead of a lamb, Caravaggio exchanged the most common symbol of Christ's crucifixion for the rarer biblical reference to Abraham's sacrifice of a ram in place of his son Isaac, by which he might have intended to juxtapose the old, pre-Christian order with the new. For Christians who read into the Bible signs of Christ's advent, life and death, Abraham's offering foreshadowed Christ's self-sacrifice. Coincidentally, in his *Sacrifice of Isaac* (Pl. 118) dating to a year later than the first *Saint John*, Caravaggio used the same model for Isaac and inserted the head of a ram above that of the boy. Evoking the traditional motif of the infant Baptist hugging a lamb, the model's embrace of a ram would thus emphasize John's origins in the pre-Christian era and imply that the Christian future he prophesied, symbolized by the grapevine in the upper right corner of the canvas, lies removed from him. In sum, Caravaggio surely intended the Capitoline picture to be read as a Saint John, who, it should be remembered, was the name saint of Ciriaco's son and heir, Giovanni Battista.[7]

Most of Caravaggio's audience may also have accepted the saintly label for his painting because of its visual descent from two celebrated John the Baptists by Leonardo da Vinci and Raphael. Departing from an earlier pictorial convention of depicting the Baptist as

**108** Leonardo da Vinci and pupils, **Saint John the Baptist/Bacchus**, *c.*1513–15;  oil on canvas, 177 × 115 cm, Louvre, Paris

**109** Michelangelo, **Ignudo**, 1511;  fresco, Sistine Chapel, Vatican Palace, Rome

mature, bearded, and gaunt, Leonardo introduced the distinctive physical type of a nude adolescent with a soft, rounded body (Pl. 108), a conception which influenced Raphael's equally popular depiction, known in copies. The artistic challenge of representing the male nude in a landscape was one which Caravaggio must have felt compelled to emulate. Balancing this formal concern with the demands of the religious theme was a delicate task, as is proven by the history of both Leonardo's and Caravaggio's depictions of John. In Leonardo's painting, the model's languid pose and ambiguously soft physique disturbed at least one seventeenth-century viewer, who remarked that the image failed to inspire devotion, and the painting was later bowdlerized into a Bacchus, almost presaging the repeated attempts to desanctify Caravaggio's figure.[8]

With the *Saint John* and the *Cupid* Caravaggio continued his earlier study of the single figure, but he now addressed the nude on a life-size scale. The new monumentality projected by the model reflects Caravaggio's concurrent work on large public commissions and also

reveals an animated dialogue with another old master, Michelangelo. Caravaggio used the figural pose of Michelangelo's *Victory* (Palazzo Vecchio, Florence, *c.*1532–4) for the *Cupid* and based his *Saint John* on one of the nude youths (*ignudi*) from the Sistine Ceiling (Pl. 109). However, in the former instance, he discarded the elongated proportions of Michelangelo's statue in favour of his own model's stockier physique, and in both paintings substituted merry faces for the serious expressions of Michelangelo's figures. In short, Caravaggio had his model strike the particular poses of Michelangelo's sculpture and frescoed nude, and then proceeded to paint what he saw in front of him. This approach was diametrically opposed to the faithful imitation of Michelangelo's works practised by Central Italian Mannerist artists, confident that they provided the ideal formula for grace and beauty. Contrary to some modern claims that Caravaggio travestied Michelangelo's art, his prime target was just as likely Michelangelo's epigones and not necessarily the master himself.

Caravaggio's reversion to the live model parallels the Lombard practice whereby pupils drew from models posing expressly in positions derived from a repertory of authoritative examples, Michelangelo foremost among them. Annibale Carracci's contemporary imitation of Michelangelo reached a climax in the frescoes of the Farnese Ceiling (Pl. 58), whose nude youths sitting on the cornice explicitly refer to the Sistine Ceiling. Annibale's nudes owe their vitality to his sessions in the studio observing the live model in poses varying rather than exactly copying any one of the Sistine *ignudi*. Caravaggio's blithe references to Michelangelo are a far cry from the obvious reverence of Annibale, but, as suggested by the latter painter's grinning masks or the peeing cherub tucked discreetly into a corner of the Farnese vault, Caravaggio was joined by his peer in seeking to demystify classical culture and rejuvenate ancient mythology. Caravaggio, and the three Carracci too, asserted the primacy of nature over the slavish imitation of artistic exemplars, a principle essential to the renewal of painting at the start of the seventeenth century. With insight into this very issue, Vincenzo Giustiniani paired Caravaggio with the Carracci in his twelfth and highest category of painting, for they had effected the most challenging alliance between *maniera* practices and the observation of nature.[9]

The *Cupid* and *Saint John* unabashedly revel in the flesh and project an ebullience otherwise absent from Caravaggio's works, which are pervaded by an elegiac tone in the early genre images, by solemnity in the public commissions, and by tragedy in the late paintings. In this respect, the pair of pictures perhaps mirrors Caravaggio's mood during the brief period that he was lionized by Roman society and enjoyed fully the fruits of professional success and fame.[10]

The *Saint John* was neither the first nor the only picture which Caravaggio painted for Ciriaco Mattei. His professional association with the family extended from June 1601 until at least January 1603, when he received his last payment from Ciriaco. As he still identified himself as a member of Del Monte's household in October 1601, perhaps he had kept his fixed residence in the Palazzo Madama, staying intermittently with the Mattei. Head of one of Rome's oldest families, Ciriaco commissioned and bought contemporary art, and amassed a distinguished collection of antiquities for his villa and gardens on the Celian Hill. His younger brother Girolamo (1545–1603), created cardinal in 1586, held various administrative posts in the Curia. Specifically named as Caravaggio's host in June 1601, Girolamo shared quarters with Ciriaco in the older part of the family palace. He also patronized painters, though on a less grand scale than Ciriaco or their younger brother Asdrubale (1554–1638). As all payments for Caravaggio's paintings came from Ciriaco, he must have been the primary patron among the three brothers.[11]

Some form of contractual arrangement probably existed between Ciriaco and Caravaggio, who painted for him the *Supper at Emmaus* (Pl. 110) and *Betrayal of Christ* (Pl. 117), in addition to the *Saint John*, at regularly spaced intervals between 1601 and 1603. As with Del Monte, Caravaggio retained the freedom to satisfy other clients, namely Giustiniani for whom he painted the *Doubting Thomas* (Pl. 114) during this period, and his new collectors Federico Borromeo, who bought the *Still Life With A Basket of Fruit* (Pl. 112), and Maffeo Barberini, who commissioned the *Sacrifice of Isaac* (Pl. 118).

All but one of these five easel pictures illustrate stories from scripture. The *Sacrifice of Isaac* is taken from the Hebrew Bible, and the Christian Gospels provide the source for the *Betrayal of Christ*, *Supper at Emmaus*, and *Doubting Thomas*. Although the group includes a still life, landscape and nocturne, Caravaggio used a horizontal format and close-up view for all and, as in his early easel works, restricted the number of figures in the four narrative paintings, cutting them at three-quarter length. A new monumentality and confidence of design distinguish the *Basket of Fruit* from its antecedents; in the sacred narratives, Caravaggio assembled a fresh cast of mature actors whose vigorous gestures convey a welter of human emotions stirred by treachery, doubt and divine revelation.

In the *Supper at Emmaus*, the earliest of the group and datable to 1601, and *Doubting Thomas* of a year or two later, Caravaggio represented Christological subjects for the first time. These subjects had a long pictorial tradition which Caravaggio reinterpreted in two of his most spellbinding images. The story of the *Supper* derives from Luke (24:30–1) who recounted in his Gospel that, after Christ's Resurrection, Cleophas and another unnamed disciple met a pilgrim on the road to Emmaus. They recognized the stranger as their risen Lord only when he broke and blessed bread at an inn where they had stopped to dine. The Gospel of John (20:19–29) provides the account of Doubting Thomas. Thomas, who was absent at Christ's first appearance to his disciples after the Resurrection and was sceptical of his fellow apostles' report, declared that he could not believe in the miracle until he saw and felt Christ's wounds for

Overleaf **110 Supper at Emmaus**, 1601;  oil on canvas, 141 × 196.2 cm, National Gallery, London

himself. Christ dispelled Thomas's doubt when, upon his next appearance, he invited the apostle to behold the marks of the nails and to thrust his hand into the wound in his side. Envisioning each episode as an intimate gathering, Caravaggio conceived antithetical compositions: in the *Supper*, bold gestures dramatize the climactic moment and link the figures, who seemingly burst out of the painting; in *Doubting Thomas*, by contrast, the apostle's quiet but deliberate gesture draws all attention to Christ's wound and, turning inward,

the figures huddle together.

Adopting the basic scheme of Venetian and Lombard representations of the Supper at Emmaus, such as that of Titian (Pl. 111) and Moretto (Pinacoteca Tosio e Martinengo, Brescia, *c.*1526), Caravaggio showed Christ seated behind a table, flanked by his two disciples and watched by the standing innkeeper. He transformed those restrained scenes, however, into an electrifying drama of recognition. The tightly grouped protagonists are closely framed in a shallow space measured in depth by the extended arms of the apostle on the right. Caravaggio unleashed a battery of illusionistic devices — the cropped chair in the left foreground, the basket perched precariously on the edge of the table, one disciple's jutting elbow and the other's lunging, open hand — all of which make the scene appear to materialize in front of our very eyes. Thus we share in the shock of Cleophas, usually identified as the disciple on the left, who leans forward dumbstruck gripping his chair, while his companion, perhaps the apostle Peter, flings out his arms in astonishment.

**111** Titian, **Supper at Emmaus**, *c.*1540; oil on canvas, 169 × 244 cm, Louvre, Paris

Ingeniously responding to Mark's comment (16:12) that Jesus appeared to the disciples at Emmaus 'in another likeness', Caravaggio chose a round-cheeked, clean-shaven model for Christ, a type perhaps suggested by a few Lombard depictions of an unbearded Christ or by Michelangelo's deity in the Sistine *Last Judgement*.[12] The innkeeper's puzzled expression, as he witnesses the scene at first hand but fails to grasp its meaning, provides a foil to the disciples' agitation. The shadows cast by his figure and by the objects on the table further distinguish the image, as does the uncanny realism with which the food, drink, and vessels are rendered. Rare in Italian painting and used sparingly by Caravaggio, the cast shadows here serve more than one purpose: to reaffirm the corporeality of forms; to project a halo shape on the wall above Christ's head; and to imply the transient nature of the moment represented, for immediately after the theophany, Christ disappeared.[13]

The careful arrangement of food and drink and the absence of plates and utensils announce that this is no ordinary tavern fare but a symbolic meal. Christ's right hand blesses the bread and, at the same time, extends out over the water and wine, evoking the eucharistic offering. Just in front of his left hand lies the platter of chicken. Sandwiched between the bread and the fruit, the dead bird with its inert claws is surely intended as a pointed contrast to the risen Christ promising eternal life to all believers. The basket displays an assortment of ripe fruits that carry traditional allusions to Christ's Passion and Resurrection, despite Bellori's objection that they would have been out of season at Easter-time when the event occurred.[14]

The care which Caravaggio lavished on the design of the basket and its symbolic import are paralleled in the *Still Life With A Basket of Fruit* (Pl. 112), his only known independent still life. Owned by Borromeo by 1607, the painting may have been commissioned by him when he was in Rome between April 1597 and May 1601. Anomalously, then, this still life dates to the period when Caravaggio had stopped representing genre subjects.[15]

In this painting Caravaggio isolated the fruit basket in the middle of a narrow brown ledge against a pale ochre backdrop, and an unusually low viewpoint seemingly sets it overhead. With increased compositional sophistication, he selected a few pieces and arranged them to form a pyramidal grouping, crowned by a peach. Enlivening the controlling geometry are the irregular outlines of the fruit and of the variegated leaves interspersed with the fruit in or reaching out of the basket to trace jagged patterns against the wall. At right an errant grapevine extends seemingly beyond the frame, disrupting the symmetry of the design.

As in the *Supper at Emmaus*, the wicker basket edges out over its ledge which in this instance is flush with the lower border of the canvas. Thus, if hung as an over-door against a like-coloured backdrop, the painted basket would have aped reality with its *trompe-l'œil* illusionism. When conceiving this remarkable exercise in naturalistic observation, Caravaggio perhaps had in mind Pliny the Elder's famous description of an ancient painting by Zeuxis in which the realistically depicted grapes attracted hungry birds.

This still life took its place among others owned by Borromeo, all evoking sacred meaning for they celebrated God's creation in their fidelity to nature. In addition, Caravaggio's blemished apple and pear, and the shrivelled and insect-eaten leaves offered reminders of mortality and the ultimate vanity of earthly things. Imposing in its breadth, the fruit basket defies the modest dimensions of its canvas. Arresting design, surface realism, and elegiac meaning combine in the *Still Life With A Basket of Fruit* to create an outstanding masterpiece of Western still life.

**112 Still Life with a Basket of Fruit**, *c.*1601; oil on canvas, 31 × 47 cm, Pinacoteca Ambrosiana, Milan

In the *Doubting Thomas* (Pl. 114), Caravaggio transformed his artistic precedents in several decisive ways. Previous artists invariably illustrated the episode with full-length figures, at times isolating Christ and Thomas, as did Andrea del Verrocchio in his bronze group of 1483 for the church of Orsanmichele in Florence, but, at other times, enlarging the scene to include the rest of the apostles, as in Albrecht Dürer's woodcut (Pl. 113). Caravaggio multiplied the number of figures and followed Dürer's lead in showing Christ helping Thomas to touch his wound.[16] Caravaggio's unusual, and perhaps unprecedented, choice of a horizontal, three-quarter-length format has the immediate effect of reducing the distance between painted image and spectator, all the better to magnify the object of scrutiny not only for participants within the painted scene but for the viewer too. Thus, we are forced, voyeuristically, to witness the gruesome detail of Thomas's probing finger parting Christ's flesh.

The rigorous design coupled with unflinching observation of detail in the *Doubting Thomas* exemplify the mature Caravaggio's synthesis of artifice and naturalism. A broad arc formed by the bent heads and bent shoulders of the three uppermost figures encloses the figural grouping. Caravaggio centred Thomas's head in the composition and clustered the other three symmetrically above and slightly behind him. Propping up the heavy forms, so it would seem, is an imaginary horizontal line crossing the canvas just below its midpoint, along Christ's right arm and Thomas's pointing hand. Caravaggio also counterbalanced both halves of the composition; occupying the left is the erect form of the semi-nude Christ, and mirroring his general outline are the three stooping, clothed disciples on the right. Their gazes strain towards the wound, underscored visually by the dramatic interplay of hands converging on it and by the zigzagging, lit fold in Christ's mantle directly beneath. While the Lord's profile is veiled by shadow, light exposes the deeply furrowed brows of Thomas and the other apostles. Their poses and expressions, and also their very appearance, grizzled by age and experience, lend truth to this exactingly orchestrated episode.

That the work enjoyed wide critical success is obvious from the early copies recorded in Rome, Genoa and Bologna, and the fact that it inspired versions of the theme by other artists, including Rubens (Koninklijk Museum voor Schone Kunsten, Antwerp, 1614–15), and Guercino, (National Gallery, London, 1621), who without exception diluted Caravaggio's potent image.

217

**113** Albrecht Dürer, **Doubting Thomas**, *c*.1509; woodcut, 12.7 × 9.7 cm

Overleaf **114 Doubting Thomas**, *c*.1602–3; oil on canvas, 107 × 146 cm, Stiftung Schlösser und Gärten, Sanssouci, Potsdam

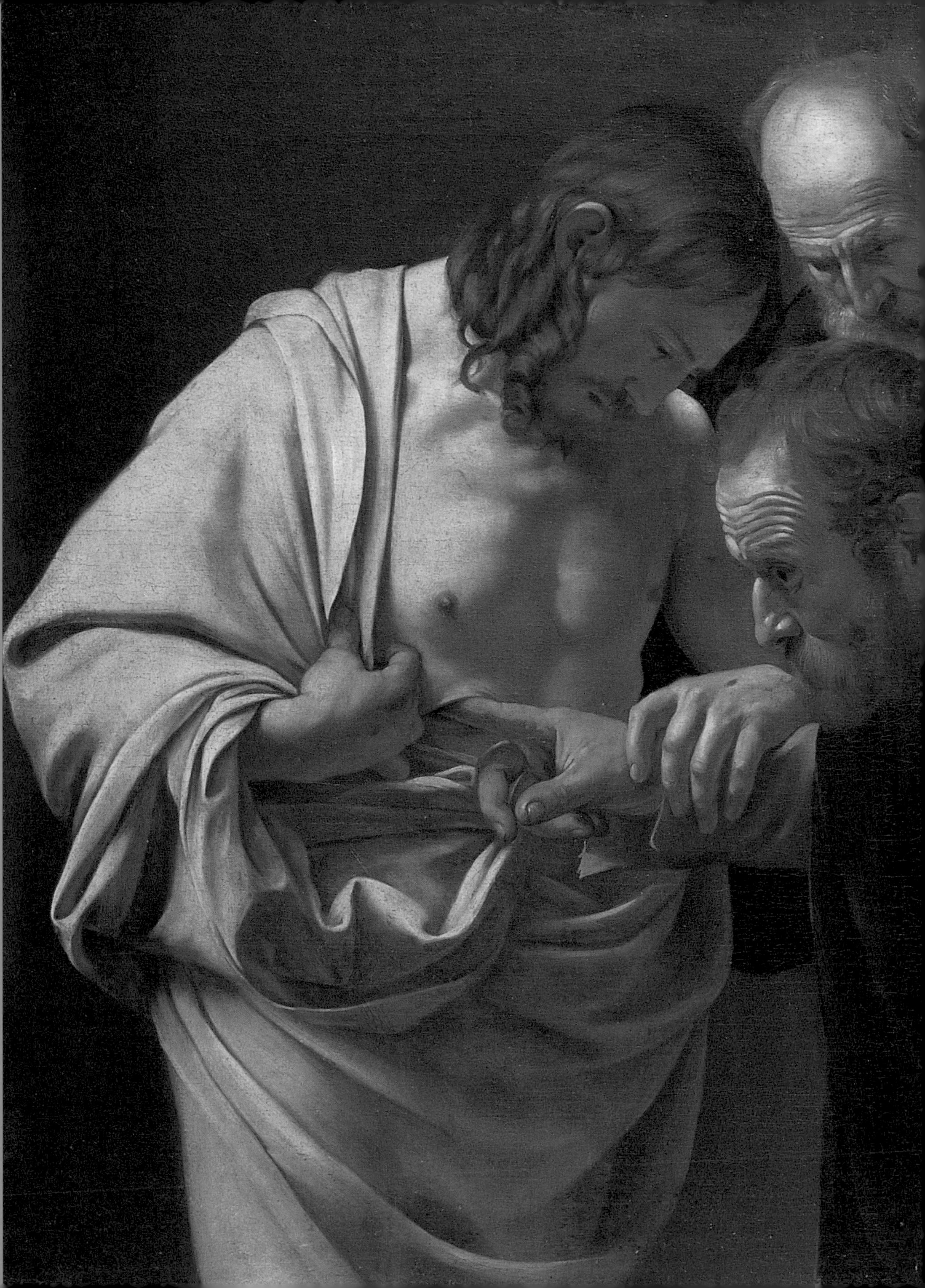

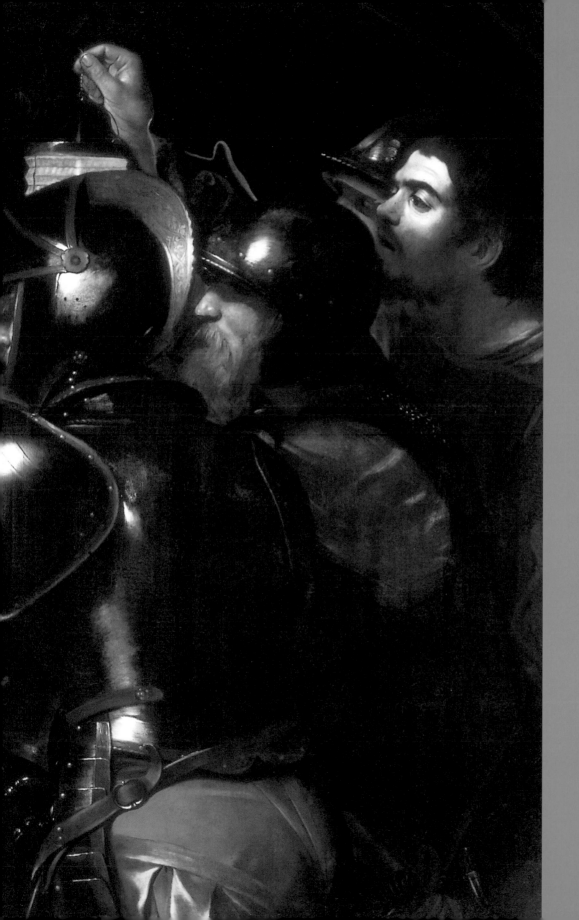

Caravaggio's *Sacrifice of Isaac* (Pl. 118) is the last of this group of religious narratives, from which it stands apart for several reasons: its source in the Hebrew Bible, the bright landscape background, and the fact that its patron was Maffeo Barberini. From a Tuscan family, Maffeo (1568–1644) had been sent to Rome as an adolescent in preparation for an ecclesiastical career, and in 1598 he bought a clerkship in the Apostolic Chamber. His background assured him a place in the Tuscan community in Rome, and conceivably Del Monte put him in touch with Caravaggio, thereby launching his earliest activity as an art patron, which Maffeo consummated stunningly when elected Pope Urban VIII thirty years later.[20]

Taken from Genesis 22:1–19, the *Sacrifice of Isaac* represents the ultimate test of man's blind obedience to, and faith in, God's will. Since the celebrated competition between Brunelleschi and Ghiberti for the Florentine Baptistery in 1401, the subject had afforded artists an ideal opportunity to stage sweeping, suspenseful action and to portray the male nude. Caravaggio confined the action by tightly grouping the three protagonists and toned down the dramatic tension with the overall bright tonality and serene landscape opening at right.

Not only does the clarity of the painting come as a surprise five years after Caravaggio's adoption of a dark manner, but the landscape is equally unexpected. He composed a setting at once naturalistic and allusive. The hazy vista evokes the wooded, hilly terrain of Tuscany with a line of cypresses leading away from a towered villa or monastery on the summit and rustic houses tucked into clearings below. Behind Isaac's head, the stump of a tree-trunk warns of death, while the laurel leaves above the angel's head symbolize eternity, the reward for Christian obedience to God's will. As laurel was one of the Barberini family's emblems, its choice and the Tuscan feel of the view may well have been intentional references to Caravaggio's patron Maffeo.[21]

Most effective in the painting is the interplay of gestures – the angel's pointing finger and his right hand stopping Abraham's wrist, Abraham's fist clenched around the knife blade and his other thumb pressing into the flesh of Isaac's cheek. Caravaggio's concern with eloquent gesture likewise drives the *Supper*, *Doubting Thomas*, and *Betrayal*, but compared to their vehement energy this composition is oddly static, looking ahead to the meditative tone pervading his art after 1605.

At the end of August 1603, two months after accepting Maffeo's commission, Caravaggio was accused of libel by Baglione, who initiated a suit against him and his alleged cohorts, Longhi and the three painters Orazio Gentileschi, Ottavio Leoni and Filippo Trisegni. The depositions of both plaintiff and defendants allow us to reconstruct the essentials of what happened and open a fascinating window on to contemporary artistic life in Rome.

At the heart of the case were doggerel verses scribbled anonymously and circulated throughout the city, denigrating Baglione and his art in scatological and puerile language. According to the testimony of Mao Salini, a witness for the prosecution and the very man assaulted by Caravaggio two years earlier in 1601, the poems were a response to his request, addressed to Filippo Trisegni, for artists' opinions on Baglione's newly unveiled altarpiece, the *Resurrection*, in the Gesù. Trisegni later gave Salini the two defamatory poems, one purportedly written by Caravaggio and Longhi and the other by Gentileschi and Leoni. Implicating Caravaggio in the dissemination of the verses, Salini claimed that copies were given to various painters, including a Mario (surely Caravaggio's friend Minnitti), by Caravaggio's personal servant Bartolomeo and his messenger Giovan Battista. Artistic jealousy, Baglione claimed, had motivated Caravaggio's critical attack on the *Resurrection*, a coveted ecclesiastical commission.

Caravaggio himself testified on 13 September (Appendix VA), two days after his arrest in Piazza Navona, denying all knowledge of the offending poems and taking care to distance himself from anyone named in Salini's testimony: Mario had not lived with him for three years; he did not know any Giovan Battista; his servant Bartolomeo had been away for two months; he had not discussed Baglione's altarpiece with Longhi, and so on. He openly admitted his disdain for Baglione's art, baldly deriding the *Resurrection* as 'clumsy' and the 'worst he has ever done' and adding that the altarpiece was condemned by all but Mao, Baglione's 'guardian angel'.

Questioned generally about painters in Rome, Caravaggio stated tersely what in his view constituted artistic merit: 'a man who can paint well and imitate natural things well'. His list of good, living painters, 'valent'uomini' as he called them, consisted of only five varying in age but sharing public acclaim: Cesari, Zuccaro, Roncalli, Antonio Tempesta and Annibale Carracci.

Caravaggio's deposition is a unique record of his voice. His comments on Baglione are deliciously acerbic, and he pronounces upon contemporary painters with unconcealed arrogance, insisting that any good painter would agree with him; by disagreeing, a painter would betray his incompetence or ignorance. Surprisingly, Baglione's biography of Caravaggio lets slip only a little rancour at this aggressive adversary who was every bit as 'sarcastic and haughty' as Baglione portrayed him.

Caravaggio equivocated about his relationship with Gentileschi, who by this time had dropped his early Mannerist style for a Caravaggesque one. First Caravaggio named Gentileschi among his friends but then contradicted himself, saying they had not spoken for more than three years. A day later, Gentileschi swore they were friends (Appendix VB). According to him, they had not spoken for six to eight months, but he admitted lending Caravaggio some studio props ten days earlier.

Overleaf **118 Sacrifice of Isaac**, 1603; oil on canvas, 104 × 135 cm, Uffizi, Florence

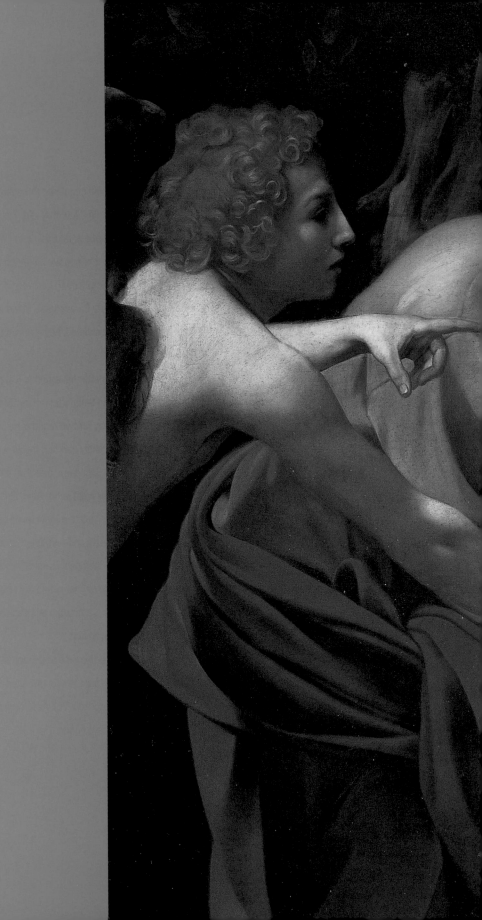

Caravaggio's attempts to avoid self-incrimination failed, he was judged guilty as accused, and was gaoled for two weeks in the Tor di Nona. Upon his release on 25 September, his freedom was still curtailed; for a month he was forbidden to go out without written permission on pain of being condemned to serve on the papal galleys. Caravaggio owed his lenient sentence to the intervention of the French ambassador, at the time Philippe de Béthune (1565–1649); the painter's long-standing Tuscan supporters, above all Del Monte, must have enlisted the influential authority of their French allies. Caravaggio seems to have stayed clear of Baglione and Salini from then on, and his name does not reappear in the criminal records until almost a year later. Longhi, however, was arrested for assaulting their accusers two months after the close of the trial, and in church of all places.[22]

In the early autumn of 1603, Caravaggio entered the last phase in his Roman career. During the three intense years that followed, he produced numerous easel pictures while completing the *Entombment*, *Death of the Virgin*, *Madonna di Loreto*, and the *Madonna dei Palafrenieri*. He painted more pictures for old patrons like Costa and supplied perhaps as many as ten canvases to Vincenzo and Benedetto Giustiniani in addition to the five they already owned. New patrons included not only Cardinal Borghese but also his uncle Paul V, whose portrait by Caravaggio will be discussed in Chapter 6. He gained another new patron in his protector Béthune, whose inventory of 1608 includes four large 'original' works by Caravaggio, acquired most plausibly during his embassy to Rome between September 1601 and June 1605.[23]

Caravaggio also enjoyed the patronage and friendship of two men from the Roman literary world: Giambattista Marino (1569–1625), the greatest Italian Baroque poet, and Marzio Milesi (1570–1637), an all but forgotten writer with Lombard roots who built a reputation in his day as a poet, collector and antiquarian. Milesi dedicated the largest number of his verses on contemporary artists to Caravaggio, whom

**119** Ludovico Cardi, Il Cigoli, **Ecce Homo**, 1607; oil on wood, 175 × 135.5 cm, Palazzo Pitti, Florence
**120** Ludovico Cardi, Il Cigoli, **Study for Ecce Homo**, *c.*1607; pen and wash, 25.2 × 17.5 cm, Louvre, Paris

he hailed as a 'deserving friend' and a 'friend of a singular kind'. Caravaggio presumably returned these warm sentiments in painting *Saints Sebastian and Roch* for Milesi, who bequeathed it to the Roman church of S. Silvestro al Quirinale.[24]

Caravaggio must have met Marino during the latter's prolonged sojourn in Rome between 1600 and 1605. Marino dedicated a sonnet to the portrait Caravaggio painted of him, now lost, along with the one on the *Medusa*, in his famous collection of poems on paintings, *La Galeria* (Milan, 1620).[25]

Marino later referred to his own painting of a 'Susanna and the Elders' by Caravaggio. The title of this lost painting, and the 'Danae' formerly in Béthune's possession both imply a seductive female nude as the protagonist, altogether exceptional for Caravaggio's art. Given Marino's salacious personal reputation, the eroticism of his verse, and his taste for novelty, he may have specially requested this biblical theme from Caravaggio. Although his opinion of Marino does not survive, Caravaggio evidently kept company with him and other poets; he is not, however, portrayed by his biographers as an artist who delighted in poetry or attended Roman literary academies.[26]

Another Roman gentleman, Massimo Massimi, has been associated with Caravaggio ever since the seventeenth century when he

allegedly set up an artistic competition between Caravaggio and the two Florentines Domenico Passignano (1559–1638) and Ludovico Cardi, called Cigoli (1559–1613), for a painting of the 'Ecce Homo', the episode in Christ's Passion when Pilate presents him to the crowd. Owner of the celebrated Palazzo Massimo alle Colonne, designed by Baldassare Peruzzi in 1532, Massimi belonged to the elevated social milieu of the Giustiniani and Mattei, and, like Cherubini, held office in the municipal government. An *Ecce Homo* attributed to Caravaggio (Pl. 121) and Cigoli's painting of the same subject (Pl. 119) have often been connected with this competition in the present century.

A fresh documentary discovery confirms that Massimi did commission paintings from both Caravaggio and Cigoli. On 25 June 1605 Caravaggio contracted with Massimi to paint and deliver by 1 August: 'a painting of the

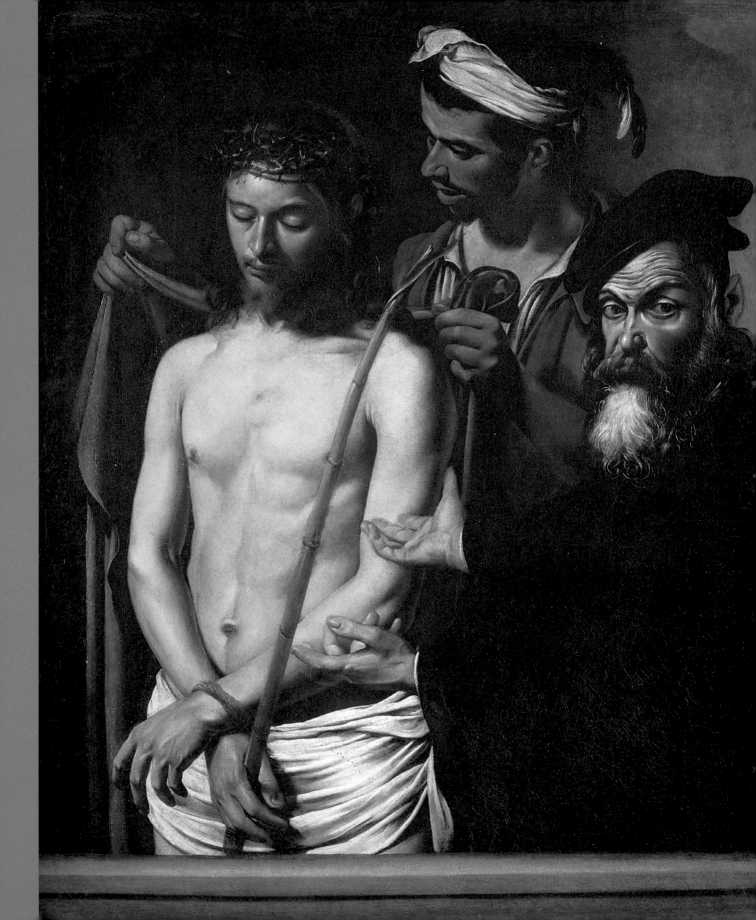

same value and size as the one I have already made of Christ's Crowning [with Thorns]'. This rare autograph receipt (Pl. 122; Appendix VI) establishes that Caravaggio had completed a 'Crowning with Thorns' for Massimi by late June 1605, and that he was commissioned to paint a second work of equal size for him that same summer.[27]

A later receipt, of 1607, discloses that Massimi waited two years before commissioning Cigoli to produce a companion painting for one of these pictures. Cigoli's *Ecce Homo*, convincingly identified with this commission, offers valuable information as to the format, size, and general composition of Caravaggio's two paintings, which must have been approximately 175 x 135 cm, with a few, three-quarter-length figures in a vertical format. An idea of one of Caravaggio's compositions perhaps survives in Cigoli's preparatory drawing for his own painting in which he noted a 'Crowning with Thorns' (Pl. 120) in a small, marginal sketch.[28]

A *Crowning with Thorns* (Pl. 123) has been attributed to Caravaggio which fits the specifications of Massimi's commission and follows Cigoli's thumbnail sketch closely, without replicating it. Although several specialists claim it to be the original, its autograph status is questionable, and it is probably a copy that at most reflects the lost work.[29]

As for Massimi's second commission of 25 June 1605, Caravaggio may never even have had the time to complete it because of his unexpected flight and sojourn in Genoa following the Pasqualone affair. In any case, the second work could not have been the proposed *Ecce Homo*; apart from its inferior quality, the dimensions are too small. By the time Massimi turned to Cigoli two years later, he may

**121 Ecce Homo** (attributed), 1605;  oil on canvas, 128 × 103 cm, Galleria Civica di Palazzo Rosso, Genoa

**122** Caravaggio, autograph receipt, 25 June, 1605; Family Archives, Palazzo Massimo, Rome

**123 Crowning with Thorns** (attributed), *c.*1603–5; oil on canvas, 178 × 125 cm, Cassa di Risparmio e Depositi, Prato

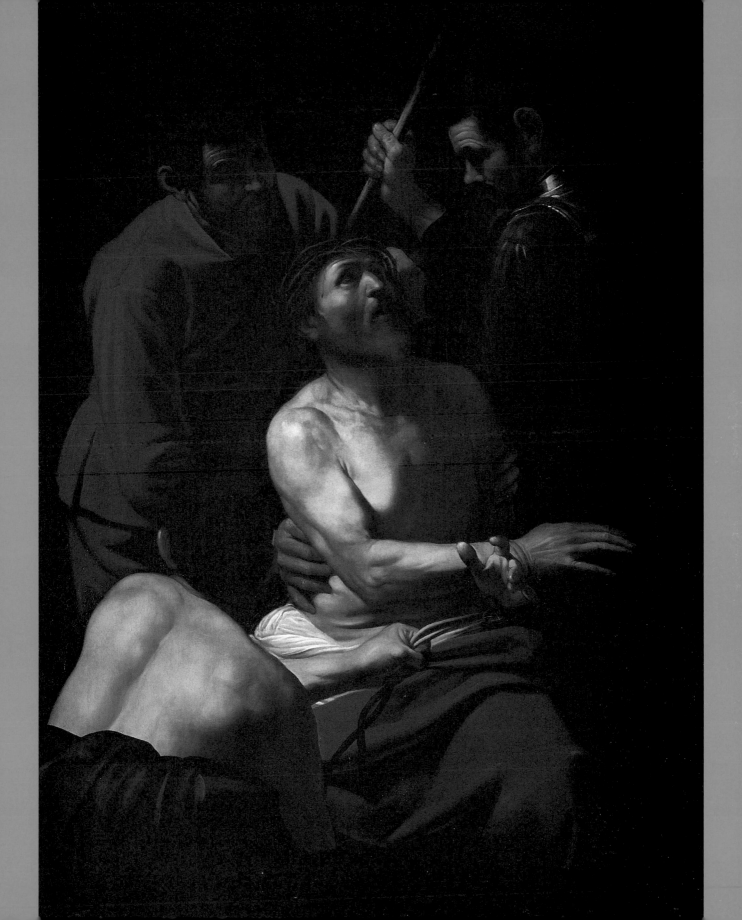

have abandoned hope of another picture from Caravaggio. As for the supposed competition, it seems to have been no more than a literary invention.[30]

The most representative easel pictures from Caravaggio's last Roman years are three devotional images of single saints: *Saint John the Baptist* (Pl. 124), *Saint Jerome* (Pl. 129), *Magdalen in Ecstasy* (Pl. 132), and another version of the *Supper at Emmaus* (Pl. 130). In these mature works, he extended and redefined his conception of the single saint meditating, writing and in ecstasy, and radically rethought his interpretation of the *Supper at Emmaus*.

The *Saint John the Baptist* inaugurates the series of solitary saints which Caravaggio painted towards the end of his Roman career and during his exile. Costa perhaps originally ordered this picture for the newly refurbished Oratory of St John, on his estate outside Genoa. Certain stylistic features – the seated figure's broad compass and his angular limbs, the ample red drapery falling in long vertical folds, the carnivorous shadows encroaching upon the figure and masking the eyes – support a dating between 1603 and 1605, contemporaneous with Caravaggio's late Roman works. His method of composing directly on the canvas remained constant, however, as attested by the presence of incisions visible to the naked eye fixing the contours of the model's head, eyes, back and foreshortened left knee (Pl. 126).[31]

Just a few years separate Caravaggio's earlier, jaunty saint (Pl. 107) from this brooding John. By eliminating the ram, adding the reed

**124 Saint John the Baptist**, *c.*1603–5;  oil on canvas, 173.4 × 132.1 cm, Nelson-Atkins Museum of Art, Kansas City

236

cross, and partially clothing the model, Caravaggio clarified any ambiguity in the subject-matter, yet his new image has little else in common with traditional representations. This mute John belies his scriptural identity as the voice crying out in the wilderness, as typically shown in Francesco Albani's *Saint John the Baptist in the Wilderness* (Pl. 125). Instead Caravaggio intrudes upon the saint in a private moment, at rest and deep in thought. John's slouching pose and shrouded eyes, and his isolation in a dark wood, convey the utter solitude of the prophet's existence, burdened with bearing the truth to an incredulous society. His thoughts focus on Christ's death instead of on his coming; the Crucifixion is alluded to symbolically in the juxtaposition of the reed cross with the autumn leaves of the oak tree directly behind him, oak being traditionally associated with the wood used for Christ's cross. A universal message can also be read into the portrayal of the saint for, as Costa's son presiding as bishop over the Oratory observed in 1624, Caravaggio's Saint John was 'mourning human miseries'. The singularity of the image perhaps discouraged imitators in the seventeenth century, and Caravaggio's melancholic and darkly handsome John has his closest cousin in a contemporary dramatic hero, Shakespeare's Hamlet.

**125** Francesco Albani, **Saint John the Baptist in the Wilderness**, *c.*1603; oil on copper, 49.2 × 37.1 cm, John and Mable Ringling Museum, Sarasota
**126 Saint John the Baptist** (Pl. 124), detail of incisions

Solitude and intimations of mortality also weigh upon Caravaggio's *Saint Jerome* (Pl. 129), possibly commissioned by its later owner, Borghese. In July 1605, two months after his arrival in Rome, Scipione had been appointed cardinal by the newly elected Paul V. The artist's growing criminal record put no damper on the cardinal's admiration of his work, for he happily bought the rejected *Madonna dei Palafrenieri* in 1606, and in 1607, with his uncle's confiscation of Cesari's collection, he acquired two Caravaggios at one swoop. At least two others were painted expressly for Scipione: Caravaggio's last *Saint John the Baptist* (Pl. 179) and his *David With the Head of Goliath* (Pl. 180).

Stylistically *Saint Jerome* is typical of the late Roman works: the breadth of the geometrically ordered composition and the positioning of the figure well back from the picture plane in an enveloping shadowed interior; the restricted palette; the rapid execution visible in the long, summary strokes defining the saint's mantle and the white hanging cloth; the deft brushwork highlighted with dabs of impasto and a wet-on-wet technique used for Jerome's wispy beard. The bald, elderly man who posed for Jerome had already modelled for Caravaggio's second *Saint Matthew and the Angel* (Pl. 95) and *Sacrifice of Isaac* (Pl. 118). Especially characteristic is the saint's air of introspection, so different from Caravaggio's earlier figures who directly involve us with their glances and gestures or by their sheer physical force.

While acknowledging both historical and artistic tradition, Caravaggio's portrayal of Jerome as a scholar in his study strays from the mainstream of contemporary representations. Doctor of the Latin Church, Jerome's greatest work was his translation of the Bible from Hebrew and Greek into the Vulgate, the Latin edition officially sanctioned by the Council of Trent. Inspired by a vision in which God

**127** Alessandro Bonvicini, Il Moretto, **Saint Jerome**, *c.*1550; oil on canvas, 89 × 111 cm, collection of Prince Borromeo, Isola Bella (Novara)

commanded him to put aside Cicero for Christian texts, Jerome withdrew from society to live the life of an ascetic penitent and to devote himself to biblical scholarship.

The theme inspired many Renaissance artists before Caravaggio. Most significant as a precedent for his interpretation is Moretto's *Saint Jerome* (Pl. 127), in which the half-length format centres on the semi-nude saint to the exclusion of the setting. By the start of the seventeenth century, however, Jerome as scholar had been virtually replaced by other personae: Jerome as penitent hermit, as visionary hearing the angel trumpeting the Last Judgement, or receiving communion for the last time.[32] However, the saintly scholar did figure in the Mancini Chapel dedicated to Jerome in S. Giovanni dei Fiorentini, for which Cigoli painted *Saint Jerome in his Study* (Pl. 128) in 1599. In contrast to Cigoli's dignified cardinal kept company by his faithful lion and heavenly visitors, Caravaggio imagined a man physically frail from self-denial whose bony arm reaches out from a sunken chest upon which the skin hangs loosely. Utterly absorbed in his work, he has no company except for the watching skull, positioned by Caravaggio as a deliberate grim counterpart to the saint's lowered head.

**128** Ludovico Cardi, Il Cigoli, **Saint Jerome in His Study**, 1599; oil on wood, 412 × 206 cm, S. Giovanni dei Fiorentini, Rome
Overleaf **129 Saint Jerome**, *c*.1605; oil on canvas, 112 × 157 cm, Galleria Borghese, Rome

Caravaggio's anti-heroic portrayal of Jerome, whose study is as bare as his frame, captures the description in *The Golden Legend* of his long years of tireless labour on the Scriptures, day and night, until he died at the advanced age of ninety-eight. Not interested in endowing Jerome with the trappings befitting his high rank in Church history, Caravaggio focused on an individual's single-minded dedication to a vocation unviolated by social intercourse and subject only to death. He returned to this theme in at least two other paintings, varying his conception somewhat, as in the unfortunately lost picture for Benedetto Giustiniani showing the saint beating his breast with a stone even while reading and writing, and in the later canvas done in Malta (Pl. 141). Caravaggio's very personal view of Jerome had marginal impact on later representations of the saint, except in Naples where Ribera and his workshop made a speciality of images of the haggard saint; Ribera became so closely identified with the theme that Caravaggio's canvas was wrongly attributed to him at the end of the eighteenth

century.[33]

The *Saint Jerome* was perhaps the last picture Caravaggio produced in Rome; he reportedly painted the *Supper at Emmaus* and *Magdalen in Ecstasy* on the Colonna estates outside Rome, perhaps taking the latter canvas with him to Naples but selling the former to Costa to help finance the trip.[34]

The meditative mood present in the *Saint John the Baptist* and *Saint Jerome* also envelops the *Supper at Emmaus* (Pl. 130), whose protagonists share little in common with their ardent counterparts in the version painted four years earlier (Pl. 110). The differences Caravaggio introduced in the second painting suggest fundamental changes in attitude towards illusionism, still life, and even artistic tradition. Although the disciple on the left sits on the near side of the table, his shadowed profile remains within the picture frame, respecting the barrier between fiction and reality. The sparse and simple food betrays a loss of interest in demonstrating virtuosic artistic skill, and a fruit basket finds no place on this table. Instead the main stylistic links lie with Caravaggio's late Roman works, including the spacious composition and the spreading darkness blotting out the background, partially masking forms and dulling colours. Moreover, as in the *Madonna dei Palafrenieri* (Pl. 105) or the *Saint Jerome*, the paint is laid on rapidly in thin layers, leaving the coarse weave of the canvas exposed in places.

Caravaggio here concentrated attention on the individual human responses to the sacred event. The leathery disciple on the right reaches a tanned hand to touch Christ's pale one as if to confirm the truth of what he sees. The female servant, not present in the earlier canvas, witnesses the scene with compassion. Head bowed wearily and face scrunched by age, she represents Caravaggio's latest and most touching revision of a type of old woman first seen in the ugly crone in *Judith Beheading Holofernes* (Pl. 69), shown sympathetically in the devout pilgrim in the *Madonna di Loreto* (Pl. 102), and with the lightest veneer of ceremony in Saint Anne of the *Madonna dei Palafrenieri*. Caravaggio's ennobled, bearded Christ transforms this gathering into a more conventional meal than its antecedent.

The nod to tradition in the second *Supper at Emmaus* might indicate a deliberate ploy on the part of Caravaggio to secure a quick sale, especially if he needed to raise money, as Mancini tells us, and was not certain of a buyer. Arguing against this pragmatic rationale are the painter's fame and the demand for his works, however unconventional. More likely the restraint and retreat from iconoclastic imagery reflect Caravaggio's state of mind during the summer months of 1606, when he first faced the numbing fact of exile. Working within artistic tradition may also signal Caravaggio's mature confidence in the uniqueness of his art, irrespective of novel iconography. Despite its

243

Overleaf **130 Supper at Emmaus**, 1606; oil on canvas, 141 × 175 cm, Brera, Milan

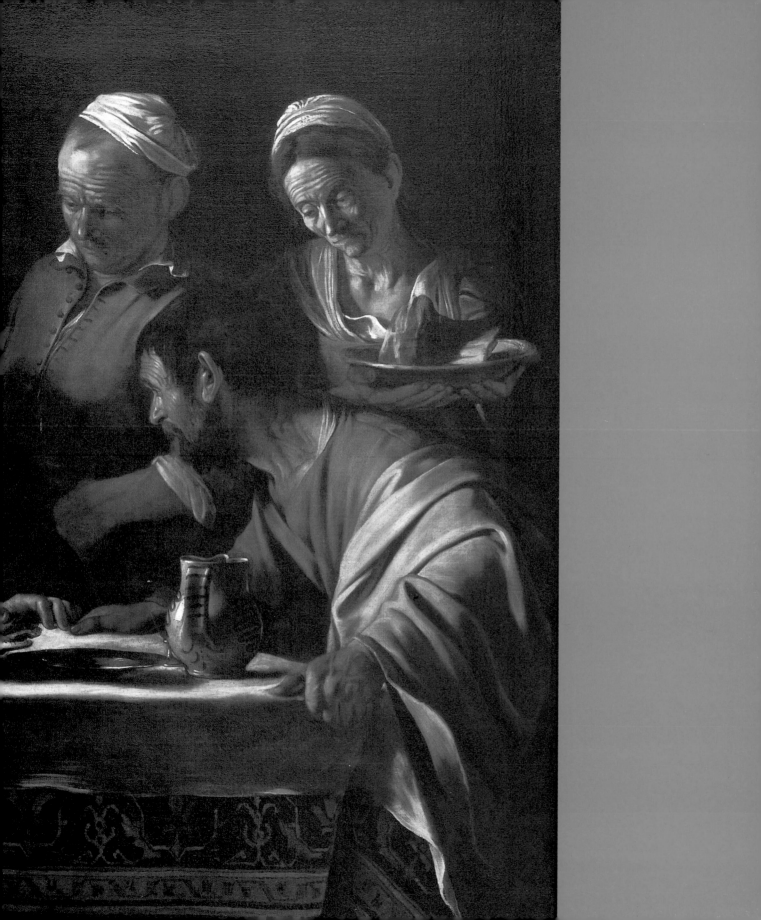

unexpected traditional elements, this *Supper at Emmaus* shares the aching loneliness of Caravaggio's other late Roman pictures.

Caravaggio's *Magdalen in Ecstasy* (Pl. 132), showing a young woman with head flung back, bared neck and shoulder, and flowing auburn hair, presented his contemporaries with a new image of the penitent saint, one elaborating on his own youthful interpretation (Pl. 32). Whereas he had earlier pictured the former sinner's dawning enlightenment, he now imagined her already converted, shorn of finery, and

rapt in divine contemplation. Gone are her ointment jar and jewellery, and by not replacing them with any penitential aids – skull, book or crucifix – he altogether detached her from worldly concerns. In the late Roman works, this conception displaces Caravaggio's earlier portrait-like presentations of saints who project a public persona and directly engage the viewer. The *Magdalen in Ecstasy* represents the culmination of his move towards a starker religious imagery, stripped of all extraneous details of clothing and setting and reduced to essentially two colours, white and red. As a result, our attention is riveted on the saint immersed in a vision invisible to us yet discernible in its physical impact on her body, described by Caravaggio in the subtle observation of the creased forehead, rolled back pupil, swollen upper lip and tightly clasped fingers.[35]

The *Magdalen* enjoyed great critical success if judged by the number of copies, exceeding any other of Caravaggio's pictures with the possible exception of the *Cardsharps*. His persuasive evocation of an individual saint in the throes of an intense spiritual experience served as a model not only for subsequent depictions of the Magdalen, from Orazio Gentileschi's (Pinacoteca Nazionale, Lucca, *c.*1616) to Simon Vouet's (Pl 131), but also for the most famous expression of saintly ecstasy in the seventeenth century, Bernini's *Ecstasy of Saint Teresa* (S. Maria della Vittoria, Rome, 1647–52).

From 1600 to 1606 Caravaggio primarily painted sacred subjects. The reversal in the ratio of secular to sacred themes dividing Caravaggio's Roman works before and after 1600 finds explanation in more than one factor. His public success led to further ecclesiastical commissions which were time-consuming but rewarding professionally and financially. Individual requests for easel pictures with religious

**131** Simon Vouet, **Magdalen in Ecstasy**, *c.*1630; oil on canvas, 100 × 80 cm, Musée des Beaux-Arts, Besançon

**132 Magdalen in Ecstasy** (attributed), 1606; oil on canvas, 106.5 × 91 cm, private collection, Rome

subjects multiplied once it was recognized that Caravaggio's talents exceeded those of minor specialists whose small-scale canvases with genre themes were readily and cheaply available on the market. None the less, given the popularity of his musicians and card-players, and the increasing fashion for such pictures in private galleries, the sharp drop in the number of his secular images implies that he welcomed and encouraged the growing demand for sacred scenes.

The imagery of Caravaggio's ecclesiastical and private religious paintings elicited a mixed reception from his contemporaries. His biographers record an enthusiastic reaction to his naturalism but they note official censure, too. Although his untraditional religious imagery offended the ecclesiastical authorities more than once, individual patrons continued to request pictures with religious subjects for both public and private spaces. These avid clients give the impression of having been pious and cannot be linked singly or as a group to any progressive circles that would have countenanced libertine or unorthodox religious attitudes. Therefore, the appeal of Caravaggio's religious paintings to a spectrum of distinguished ecclesiastical and lay patrons suggests that his novel sacred imagery did not attack their Catholic beliefs; on the contrary, it struck some sympathetic chord.

The exact nature of the relationship between contemporary life in post-Tridentine Rome and Caravaggio's original interpretation of traditional sacred themes has exercised those studying the painter and his work during recent decades. Contradictory explanations have failed, however, to solve the fundamental and perhaps insoluble puzzle of pinpointing the wellspring and essence of Caravaggio's beliefs. The key arguments and counter-arguments require a brief summary here, for they have drawn irreconcilable profiles of the painter as a champion of orthodox faith or as a rebellious non-conformist. Caravaggio's source of inspiration for any or all of the essential elements in his religious works – the sensory realism, humble types, and absence of heavenly visions – has been repeatedly traced to contemporary religious institutions, and especially to the Jesuits and the Oratorians, the two most influential Counter-Reformatory orders. A case has also been made for the significance of the older religious establishment of the Augustinians and, most recently, possible Franciscan spirituality has been suggested.

To date, discussion of Franciscan influence on Caravaggio's imagery has been the most circumscribed. Thus, in Costa's *Saint Francis of Assisi in Ecstasy* (Pl. 61), Caravaggio's emphasis on the saint's imitation of Christ accords with Franciscan hagiography, while in Mattei's *Betrayal of Christ* (Pl. 117), Christ's submissiveness evokes a specifically Franciscan ideal. Investigation of conceivable affiliations between this Order and either of these patrons has failed to uncover supporting evidence for Costa's sympathies, but Mattei held rights to two chapels in the Franciscan church of S. Maria in Aracoeli in Rome. Moreover, Girolamo Mattei served as Cardinal Protector of the Observant Franciscans, and his and Ciriaco's devotion to Francis is reflected in frescoed scenes of the saint's life in the Palazzo Mattei. The Mattei, then, may well have asked Caravaggio to endow Christ with Franciscan humility. By the end of the sixteenth century, however, the revival of Franciscan piety was so widely disseminated that he could also have absorbed its message from the friars' own preaching and work among the people.[36]

Parallels have often been drawn in modern studies of the painter between Caravaggio's ability to set the past vividly before viewers and the Jesuit method of meditative prayer contained in the *Spiritual Exercises*, the enormously influential tract by the Order's founder, Ignatius Loyola. Basic to the method is the 'composition of place' in which the individual contemplates the meaning of a sacred event by reconstructing its physical setting down to the last detail. Yet Caravaggio's representations of conversions and martyrdoms are striking for their minimalist, non-descriptive settings and therefore have nothing in common with the didactic 'composition of place' pictured in the martyrdoms decorating Jesuit churches in Rome, namely S. Stefano Rotondo or S. Vitale. And if his art embodied Jesuit devotions, some official recognition on the part of the fathers would provide confirmation, such as the extensive work commissioned from Rubens for the Order's church in Antwerp. Instead, Caravaggio neither supplied any altar paintings for Jesuit churches nor painted any Jesuit subjects; in fact, he may have been passed over in favour of Baglione for a Gesù altarpiece. Nor is he recorded as having contact with any members of the Order, unlike Bernini who became a close friend of the Society's general and who, as an elderly man, attended daily vespers at Il Gesù.[37]

Among all the sixteenth-century religious orders, the Oratorians have often been cited as the single most important ecclesiastical influence on Caravaggio. Their founder, Philip Neri, who died in May 1595 three years after the painter's arrival in the city, made a profound impact on Roman religious life. Affectionately known as the 'Roman Apostle', Neri was remembered for his charismatic appeal to all levels of Roman society from Clement VIII to the anonymous poor he met on the streets and invited regularly to dine with him. Down to earth, quick to deflate pretentious ceremony, suspicious of mystical experiences, Neri's personality would seem to embody several key elements in Caravaggio's sacred imagery: the unceremonious presentation of sacred subject-matter, the humble apostles and saints, and the near-absence of visionary phenomena. No direct contact between Caravaggio and Neri is recorded, however, and the painter never portrayed the saint as did his fellow artists Roncalli, Reni, and Rubens, to name only three of many. Neri himself preferred sweet and intimate canvases, responding in particular to Barocci's *Visitation* (Pl. 19).[38]

Caravaggio did have ample opportunity to be exposed to the saint's personality and Oratorian devotions through several of his patrons – such as the Crescenzi and Mattei families, and his lifelong protectors, the Colonna family – who were intimately connected with both Neri's inner circle and his congregation. These patrons themselves do not seem to have recognized any particular affinity between Caravaggio's art and Oratorian practices, however; the Crescenzi ordered family portraits from Caravaggio, while the Mattei asked for devotional works whose subjects lack any special Oratorian associations.[39]

Caravaggio did, of course, receive a commission to decorate an altar in the Chiesa Nuova, the Oratorians' mother church in Rome. But his patron Girolamo Vittrice had no demonstrable ties to the congregation, which in any case is not known to have played any role in commissioning the *Entombment*.

By the time Caravaggio painted the altarpiece, the Oratory was led by Cardinal Cesare Baronio, whose influence on the imagery of the altarpiece has insistently been propounded. The proposal rests on the presupposition that Caravaggio was indebted to Baronio's study of Early Christian art for one of the motifs in the *Entombment*; the 'orant' or praying gesture found in catacomb painting would be the artist's visual source for the up-flung arms of his female figure in the background of the composition. This woman, however, looks more swayed by uncontrollable anguish than by thoughts of prayer, and her gesture is a traditional one of grief with a superficial resemblance at best to its putative source.[40]

No documentary evidence confirms whether Caravaggio ever met Baronio, and the recent attribution to him of a portrait of the cardinal is far-fetched. Baronio's well-defined artistic outlook otherwise offers fallow ground for interpreting Caravaggio's works. His role as Church historian shaped his concept of a didactic religious art celebrating the unbroken authority of the Church under papal rule over the centuries. This conception was realized in the decorations he oversaw in the Lateran transept, the Clementine altars in St Peter's, and in his own titular churches of SS. Nereo e Achilleo and S. Gregorio Magno for which his favourite artist, Roncalli, painted pietistic, naturalistic, and above all decorous images. Caravaggio's *Entombment* apparently did not offend his orthodox views, for the altarpiece in the Chiesa Nuova was installed without any dissent.[41]

Caravaggio received no further commissions from Baronio or the Oratorians either for the Chiesa Nuova or for their other foundations. Significantly, the one surviving testimony of an Oratorian's appraisal of the art of Caravaggio, a well-known letter written in August 1603 by Baronio's former pupil, Cardinal Ottavio Paravicino, censures the painter's religious works as being 'between sacred and profane'.[42] Given this conflicting and inconclusive body of evidence, the suggestive links between Caravaggio's religious imagery and Oratorian piety remain a tantalizing theory, and the Order's influence on him would seem more apparent than real.

Whereas some have explained Caravaggio's sacred art in relation to the Roman Oratory, others have interpreted certain aspects of his imagery in terms of Augustinian philosophy. The Cerasi *Conversion of Saint Paul* and the *Crucifixion of Saint Peter* and *Madonna di Loreto* were painted for Augustinian churches. Although the commissions originated with private individuals, respect for the Augustinian Order might well have motivated their patronage of these churches, and so it is reasonable to assess the painted decoration against Augustinian beliefs. In fact the dedication of the Cerasi Chapel to Paul as well as to Peter honours the apostle instrumental in Saint Augustine's own conversion as well as the writer of the epistles that informed Augustinian doctrine.[43]

Essential elements in Caravaggio's religious art can be associated with Augustinianism: the symbolic use of light as embodying divine grace, the visual emphasis on the individual's direct encounter with God, and the implication that salvation is achieved through faith. In the *Conversion of Saint Paul*, Caravaggio's singular interpretation of the saint's epiphany as an inner and passive acceptance of grace signalled by divine illumination closely accords with the Augustinian belief in predestination. During the reigns of Clement VIII and Paul V, the respective roles of grace and free will in salvation occupied Catholic theologians in Rome as a result of the heated debate between the Dominicans, adherents of an Augustinian-Thomist doctrine of predestination, and the Jesuits, who promoted the Molinist view of an individual's free will as a decisive factor in personal salvation.[44]

In the *Madonna di Loreto*, the Augustinian concept of justification by faith can be read into Caravaggio's visualization of the Marian devotion: the pilgrims' intense belief justifies the gift of divine grace, embodied in the privileged vision of Madonna and Child. As in the case of Cerasi, any role that Cavalletti's widow and sons may have played in Caravaggio's formulation of the theme for the family chapel in S. Agostino is simply unknown.

Augustine's belief in the bestowal of divine grace as an inscrutable act of God, irrespective of an individual's good works, is also applicable to paintings by Caravaggio without any direct link to the Augustinian Order. For example, the Contarelli *Calling of Saint Matthew* places pointed emphasis on Matthew's utter surprise at divine choice and on his unworthiness. Furthermore, Caravaggio's late Roman pictures project a sombre and brooding mood that shares the essentially pessimistic Augustinian view of humanity after the Fall.

Affinities with the spirituality of contemporary religious Orders can thus be found to varying degrees in Caravaggio's art, but his adherence to any one in particular cannot be sustained. Similarly, Michelangelo's Sistine Ceiling has eluded a definitive conclusion as to its dependence on Neoplatonism, Augustinianism, or Franciscan piety; likewise, Rembrandt's religious works cannot convincingly be categorized in terms of one Protestant sect, be it Mennonite or Calvinist. More plausibly, Caravaggio evolved the religious attitudes expressed in his paintings from a range of sources. In post-Tridentine Lombardy and Rome he had ample exposure to the charitable works of lay confraternities among the poor and to the popular piety of the anonymous masses manifested in votive processions and pilgrimages, especially conspicuous around the papal Jubilee of 1600. He need not have practised Loyola's *Spiritual Exercises* to be familiar with the aim of meditative prayer to bring alive sacred events. Likewise, he did not have to frequent Oratorian or Franciscan churches to develop empathy for Christian poverty and humility, preached by virtually all the sixteenth-century reformers, including Carlo Borromeo in his native Lombardy. Nor did he have to read Saint Augustine's *Confessions* to imbibe Augustinianism, by then a venerable philosophy with widespread influence on Church doctrine. Furthermore, even within his restricted circle of Roman patrons, Caravaggio had contact with diverse prelates, with any one of whom he could have discussed ideas and consulted on theological fine points.[45]

Assessing Caravaggio's personal religious beliefs and defining the essence of those beliefs are therefore daunting tasks. He was baptized and brought up as a Catholic in a household in which his uncle was a priest, but his attitudes towards his faith and the Church as a mature painter in Rome can be sketched only summarily. Although his denial that he had a brother – who also became a priest – might suggest an anti-clerical bent, it was just as likely fired by an old fraternal grudge. The single surviving testimony of Caravaggio's religious observance from the Roman years is a parish record that he took communion in 1605. Though not necessarily a proof of anything more than the required annual observance, this does reveal that the thirty-four-year-old painter publicly identified himself as a Catholic.[46]

Nothing else from the Roman period testifies to any special devotions, acts of piety, or charitable donations on Caravaggio's part. On the contrary, his own and his friends' 'unchristian' conduct stuck in memory for a long time; Sandrart ascribed to them the impious motto 'nec spe, nec metu' or 'without hope, without fear'. Caravaggio's years in Rome, then, could not be characterized as spent in 'Christian calm', a description that was applied to Roncalli's life. A more serious accusation that he was actually excommunicated from the Church was reportedly made by one of his victims, Pasqualone. This charge, which would have to date to around 1605, must be construed as hyberbolic invective, for if Caravaggio had been an excommunicant, he could never have been received into the Knights of Malta, a religious order, three years later. Although social advancement partly motivated his quest for knighthood, at least outwardly he was perceived as 'burning with zeal for the Order' and, during his year-long stay in Malta, he presumably observed whatever customary rites were demanded of candidates for admission. But his rapid expulsion from the Order indicates that he had not reformed his former mode of conduct.[47]

As to Caravaggio's later state of mind in Sicily, Susinno made the claim that he questioned matters of faith, and relates the poignant anecdote that, when entering a Sicilian church, Caravaggio refused holy water because it only absolved venial sins, whereas his sins were all mortal. Upon Caravaggio's death, Baglione smugly remarked that he died as 'badly as he had lived'; for his contemporaries versed in the 'ars moriendi', or art of dying well in the faith, the immediate comparison would have been with the demise of Annibale Carracci, who died 'most Christianly'.[48]

Based on this historical record, the final conclusion we can draw about Caravaggio's individual faith is limited. His outward observance of Catholicism is only known to have encompassed baptism as a child, partaking of the eucharist on one occasion, and a brief religious knighthood. His antisocial behaviour, equated with unchristian behaviour by the early sources, branded him as a transgressor. But a sinner, even one who has committed murder, is not the same as a disbeliever, and if Caravaggio harboured doubts about his own salvation, this in itself would presuppose belief in God and divine retribution.

Unconventional in both his professional and personal life, Caravaggio is unlikely to have been conventionally pious. Investigation of his great Roman ecclesiastical and easel paintings reveals a willingness to stretch the limits of Tridentine guidelines, without losing sight of the scriptural and hagiographical texts.[49] Clearly not painted by a devout artist, like Guido Reni or Bernini, Caravaggio's religious works none the less convey intense religious experience. The tenor of this experience is not visionary; divinity or sanctitude do not transform earthly matter. In his conception of Christ, the Madonna, and the saints as human and present, Caravaggio imposed a consistent moral vision on his religious art which transcends its own historical period and assumes universal relevance.

Part Three

**Exile** 1606–1610

# Chapter 6  Naples and the Maltese Adventure

On 28 May 1606 Caravaggio killed Ranuccio Tomassoni on the tennis court near the Palazzo Firenze. The earliest reports dating to a few days after the event identify the victim and attribute the fight to a quarrel over a foul call in a tennis match or over a bet on the winner (Appendix X). Fuller information about Tomassoni's personality and a somewhat different reconstruction of the events of that Sunday evening emerge from recent finds in the Roman archives.[1]

A 'well-mannered' young man, as Baglione called him, Ranuccio belonged to a notable family of Roman citizens. Both his father and brothers had served with distinction in the papal armies and, in 1605, his brother Giovan Francesco was elected 'caporione' or local officer in the Campo Marzio, the family's neighbourhood. Both Ranuccio and his brother, who had appointed him a captain of the local militia, are documented as volatile men, quick to draw their swords. Serving élite households in the city, Ranuccio had carved out a sleazy niche for himself in Roman society, protecting the professional and financial interests of high-class courtesans, including Fillide Melandroni whose portrait Caravaggio painted.[2]

The historical record suggests that the fight between the two men was not a spontaneous incident but rather a prearranged duel. The versions of both the Modenese ambassador and of Mancini, in the first draft of the painter's biography, imply that Tomassoni had challenged Caravaggio, who reacted in self-defence for fear of his life. The opponents arrived at the tennis court carrying swords, and each was accompanied by three 'seconds', also armed; this was not the first time this site had proved to be a convenient and secluded duelling ground. When Ranuccio fell wounded, his brother and two brothers-in-law attacked Caravaggio, who was relieved by Onorio Longhi and two Bolognese soldiers. At the end of the clash, Ranuccio lay dead, and all fled the scene except one of Caravaggio's party who was taken to gaol in a critical condition; the painter himself suffered a severe head wound.

Despite the fact that news of the incident quickly circulated, a criminal investigation was not conducted until a month later when arrest warrants and capital sentences were issued for the fugitives. The process of justice may have been intentionally delayed to allow the parties time to get far away and secure safety nets. Although Tomassoni's brother and Longhi successfully petitioned for pardons, a capital sentence continued to hound Caravaggio until his death four years later, largely owing to the social standing and political clout of Tomassoni's family – Ranuccio had been no waiter, notary or artisan.[3]

Conflicting reports circulated in Rome as to the whereabouts of Caravaggio after the murder. According to Baglione and Susinno, he took refuge in Palestrina, but both Mancini and Bellori name Zagarolo, a fiefdom of Marzio Colonna. However, in a letter written four months after the crime, the ambassador to Rome of the Duke of Modena advised his court that Caravaggio had fled to Paliano, ruled at the time by Filippo Colonna. Caravaggio could have been hidden in any of these three towns and possibly moved from one to the other, with the aid of the Colonna family. His decision to go on to Naples surely also depended on Colonna support, for the family had both official and personal ties there: Marzio Colonna was a member of the vice-regal advisory council in Naples, where he maintained his principal residence; Ascanio Colonna, his brother, was Cardinal Protector of the Kingdom of Naples, and one of his sisters, Costanza, the Marchesa di Caravaggio, kept a palace there, while another sister had married into the Neapolitan Carafa family. The Colonna most probably secured Caravaggio's safe arrival in Naples, possibly smoothed his later passage to Malta, and indisputably housed him before his ill-fated return to Rome.[4]

If Caravaggio had died at Tomassoni's hand in May 1606, his historical significance as the founder of a new style of art would be just as great. He had already created masterpieces in the *Calling of Saint Matthew*, *Conversion of Saint Paul* and *Death of the Virgin*, but the works he painted in exile add another dimension to his painting. Despite adversity and perhaps partly because of it, he unleashed a flood of extraordinary paintings – the *Seven Works of Mercy* (Pl. 133), *Beheading of Saint John the Baptist* (Pl. 151), *Burial of Saint Lucy* (Pl. 160), *Raising of Lazarus* (Pl. 162), *David and Goliath* (Pl. 180) and *Martyrdom of Saint Ursula* (Pl. 178). No longer pressed to demonstrate technical wizardry, he concentrated his energy on his subjects, creating imagery to express profound and universal themes of love and compassion, death and grief, hope and redemption. In a career spanning only some sixteen years, the last four years, which he spent in exile from the Papal States, saw his genius realize an original vision that admits him into the company of the greatest artists in the Western tradition.

After hiding near Rome throughout the summer of 1606, Caravaggio surfaced in Naples, where he signed a contract for a new commission on 6 October. Nine months later he moved on to Malta where he lived for a little over a year in Valletta. This stay ended with imprisonment, but he escaped precipitously by night and sailed to Sicily, landing at Syracuse by October 1608. During 1609 he shifted his residence on the island from Syracuse to Messina and finally to Palermo, fulfilling commissions in each city. Back in Naples by late October of that year, he set out for Rome the following July, evidently confident of his papal pardon and perhaps intent on re-establishing himself there.

During these turbulent years, Caravaggio produced as many as thirteen altarpieces and possibly a dozen easel pictures. His Neapolitan, Maltese, and Sicilian paintings are the least well known to the general public today, partly because of their less accessible locations and partly because of their subordinate status in early studies of the painter. In addition, some of these works have physically suffered as a result of the historic problem of the South, especially its economic underdevelopment: the *Burial of Saint Lucy* is a partial ruin; inadequate surveillance resulted in the theft of the *Nativity With Saints Lawrence and Francis* (Pl. 167) from its church in Palermo in 1969; more recently, the *Saint Jerome* (Pl. 141) was stolen but recovered in Malta, and an attempt to steal the *Beheading of Saint John the Baptist* was thwarted in 1989 but Caravaggio's signature was vandalized. Happily, as a result of the increased interest in the artist in the past decade, local historians in Naples, Malta and Sicily have intensively investigated his late works and have uncovered much fresh information, shedding light on issues of attribution, chronology and patronage.

Though a criminal in the Papal States, Caravaggio could live and work freely in his first new home in Naples; like the Milan of his childhood, Naples had lain under the jurisdiction of Spain since the beginning of the sixteenth century. Viceregal capital of the Spanish kingdom stretching across Southern Italy, Naples had grown by Caravaggio's day to three times the size of Rome and had become the largest city in Europe after Paris. At the top of its stratified society resided the Spanish grandees attached to the viceregal court, the Neapolitan nobility, and the international merchants and bankers involved in the busy commerce of the largest port in the Mediterranean. The city also harboured many poor people who crammed into high-rise buildings in densely populated neighbourhoods or lived on the streets. The wealthy professional community founded lay confraternities to dispense private charity and minister to the urgent needs of this destitute class. Extremes of rich and poor thus prevailed in Naples, and a newcomer to the city would have confronted a crowded, noisy and chaotic place, as colourful then as it is now.[5]

In Naples, Caravaggio quickly found patrons who extended him a warm welcome by offering handsome fees for public and private commissions. He drew his clientele from the court, the nobility, and the professional class in the city. During his two Neapolitan sojourns, the Spanish noble Juan Alonso Pimentel y Herrera, eighth Conde de Benavente, ruled as viceroy (1603–10). An inept and corrupt ruler, Benavente enriched himself at the expense of the Neapolitan poor and collected art to send home to Valladolid, including Caravaggio's *Crucifixion of Saint Andrew* (Pl. 173). Benavente's successor, Pietro Fernandez di Castro, the Conde de Lemos, acted quickly to secure any of the painter's unclaimed works for himself after Caravaggio's death; he delayed consigning the *Saint John the Baptist* (Pl. 179) to its intended owner, Borghese, until he could have a copy made. Another Spanish noble, Don Juan de Tasis y Peralta, second Conde de Villamediana, owned a half-length 'David and Goliath' by Caravaggio, presumably acquired during his stay in Naples from 1611 to 1617; he also tried to buy the *Seven Works of Mercy* but had to settle for a copy.[6]

Most of Caravaggio's patrons in Naples were not from the Spanish court, however, but belonged to the commercial and professional community. These included his first client in the city, the Radulovic family, money-changers and silk merchants of Bosnian origin, and the Bergamasque merchant Alfonso Fenaroli whose family chapel in the national Lombard church Caravaggio was asked to decorate. Among the professional Neapolitan families who forged ties with the Spanish rulers, assumed administrative offices and themselves bought land and noble titles, were the De Franchis, who commissioned the *Flagellation of Christ* (Pl. 137) . Also allied to the viceregal court was the local nobility, who had moved into urban palaces from their feudal estates. Caravaggio's own protectors, the Colonna, and their relatives the Carafa, belonged to this upper echelon of Neapolitan society which mixed with the financiers. Italian princes in other parts of the country also kept track of Caravaggio's Neapolitan activity, as attested by the correspondence between Naples and the Mantuan court and by the commission for the *Martyrdom of Saint Ursula* from Prince Marcantonio Doria in Genoa shortly before the painter's death.

Caravaggio encountered a bustling yet disunified, *retardataire* and provincial artistic scene in Naples. Seventeen years before his arrival, in 1589, Cesari had been invited from Rome to fresco the choir vault of the Certosa di S. Martino, the richest ecclesiastical establishment in the city. His graceful Mannerism influenced the leading local artist, Belisario Corenzio (*c.*1560–*c.*1646), who secured a near-monopoly of fresco commissions which he executed in a persistently old-fashioned style. Corenzio had become familiar with Caravaggio's work on a visit to Rome in 1599 and was perhaps responsible for introducing it to his pupil Giovan Battista Caracciolo, called Battistello (1578–1635).[7]

Caravaggio's first Neapolitan commission, from Niccolò Radulovic, which he agreed on 6 October 1606 to deliver within two months, was for a large altarpiece (*c.*360.8 x 224.4 cm). On the same day, he opened a bank account with his advance of 200 ducats. His withdrawal of most of that sum later in the month suggests that he needed money to establish himself in his new city; as well as food and lodging, he probably bought supplies to begin work on the altarpiece. The record of payment also provides the only source for the subject requested by Radulovic: a 'Madonna with the Christ Child in her arms and encircled by an angelic choir and below, Saints Dominic and Francis embracing at centre, flanked by Saint Nicholas on the right and Saint Vito on the left'.[8]

Radulovic's commission was soon overshadowed by a new, grander one for the *Seven Works of Mercy* (Pl. 133), which proved to be Caravaggio's most important Neapolitan altarpiece. The exact date of the contract is not known, but the painting must have been completed between October 1606, when Caravaggio arrived in Naples, and 9 January 1607, the day he received the balance of his fee. Work on this monumental canvas perhaps assumed priority because of the lavish payment and the prestige of the commission. Caravaggio's patron was the Pio Monte della Misericorida, a charitable institution founded by several Neapolitan nobles as recently as 1601. Young, rich, and aware of the latest artistic currents in Rome, the deputies of the Pio Monte swiftly engaged Caravaggio to ensure that the high altar of their new church would boast the most modern and illustrious work of art in the city. At 400 ducats, the altarpiece earned Caravaggio his highest fee yet, even more than the expensive *Death of the Virgin*.[9]

Strangest and most disconcerting of all his ecclesiastical paintings, Caravaggio's *Seven Works of Mercy* presents an allegory of Christian charity. What at first appears to be a bewildering jumble of figures gathered on a dark street corner assumes meaning when examined in light of the activities of the Pio Monte, the textual source for the theme, and artistic tradition. By its statutes, the confraternity undertook those charitable works deemed necessary for salvation on the authority of the Gospel of Matthew (25:31–46): feeding the hungry, giving drink to the thirsty, clothing the naked, sheltering pilgrims, and visiting both the sick and those in prison. To these six obligations was added burial of the dead, included routinely among the works of mercy since the Middle Ages. Inviting other painters to illustrate an individual work of mercy in each of the six side altarpieces, the confraternity evidently asked Caravaggio to combine all the acts in one scene which would function as the centrepiece of a unified decorative programme in the church.[10]

Despite its rarity, the theme of the works of mercy had a consistent artistic tradition in the Renaissance; altarpieces of the Last Judgement sometimes included independent depictions of the acts within their frames. The Tridentine reaffirmation of good works as

**133 Seven Works of Mercy**, 1606–7; oil on canvas, 390 × 260 cm, Pio Monte della Misericordia, Naples

essential to redemption encouraged the foundation of many charitable confraternities like the Pio Monte, and Italian painters continued to interpret the works of mercy within a religious context. The frontispiece of a Jesuit didactic tract of 1586 portrays the Last Judgement, while successive individual prints show each act as a contemporary lay scene with a related biblical episode in the background. For example, the Miracle at Cana serves as the backdrop to a group of well-dressed laymen giving drink to the thirsty (Pl. 134).[11]

Although Caravaggio dropped the traditional reference to Judgement Day he did not secularize his image, for a heavenly vision fills the upper half of his composition. X-rays of the canvas reveal, however, that he altered this part of the painting to insert the Madonna and Child, undoubtedly at the request of the confraternity whose church was dedicated to Our Lady of Mercy. Essential to Caravaggio's original conception are the embracing angels, who offer a celestial model of fraternal charity; the extended hand of the angel on the left appears to generate the good works on earth. In the earthly scene, Caravaggio conflated the scriptural and secular sources in at least two instances: a man in the rear at left, who slakes his thirst from a jawbone, is meant to be the biblical Samson; and a man in a plumed hat preparing to cut his mantle in order to share half with the naked man seated on the ground refers to Saint Martin dividing his cloak to clothe a poor beggar.

**134** Mario Cartaro, **Giving Drink to the Thirsty**, 1586; engraving from Giulio Roscio Ortino, *Icones Operum Misericordiae*, Rome, 1586
**135** Federico Barocci, **Madonna del Popolo**, 1579; oil on wood, 359 × 252 cm, Uffizi, Florence

Few painters before Caravaggio had combined the works of mercy in one scene. A notable exception was Barocci in his *Madonna del Popolo* (Pl. 135). Commissioned by an Umbrian Confraternity also devoted to Our Lady of Mercy, Barocci initially expressed doubts about the theme which to him was 'not suitable for creating a beautiful painting'. He managed none the less to compose a lyrical display of Christian charity in a sunny urban square crowded with joyful mothers, children, beggars, cripples and members of the Confraternity, some of whom marvel at a radiant vision of the Madonna interceding with Christ on behalf of humanity. Barocci, however, alluded to only four out of the customary seven works.[12]

Familiar or not with Barocci's painting, Caravaggio visualized the allegory in antithetical terms. Neither blessing nor interceding, the infant Christ and his mother silently bear witness as the acts of mercy are performed with grim urgency and, paradoxically, in utter ignorance of any inducement from heaven. Caravaggio restricted the figures on earth to the minimum number necessary to explicate all seven works and excluded portraits of the noble members of the Confraternity.

Caravaggio ingeniously resolved the logistical problem of incorporating so many independent actions in one composition by means of

various formal devices. For instance, two figural groups do double duty and illustrate four acts. Saint Martin not only clothes the naked but also aids the sick, a crippled man crouching next to his crutch in the shadows of the lower left corner. Similarly the vignette at right, derived from the classical story of Pero nursing her starving father Cimon, refers to both feeding the hungry and visiting prisoners. Caravaggio also reduced the number of figures required in two other acts of mercy by the use of visual ellipsis. In illustrating burial of the dead he restricted the scene to the dead man's feet and part of the attending deacon, implying that the humble cortège is just emerging around the corner of the prison. In depicting the giving of water to the thirsty he dispensed with the usual two-figure group by making Samson, whose thirst was quenched by divine intervention, the recipient of mercy. Finally, he condensed the act of sheltering pilgrims to a group comprising an innkeeper (the man pointing at left margin) and two men, one wearing a pilgrim's hat with a scalloped shell and holding a staff and the other signalled only by an ear and staff, to the right of Saint Martin's head.[13]

Conceived and completed in three months at the very most, the complexity and sophistication of *Seven Works* reveal an experienced artist who worked swiftly and confidently. The numerous *pentimenti* attest both to Caravaggio's usual practice of composing directly on the canvas and to the exceptionally challenging theme. But, unlike the radical revisions to his earlier *Martyrdom of Saint Matthew* (Pl. 184), the subsequent changes were solely concerned with the placement and interrelationship of the figures. Caravaggio moved the figure of Samson to the left from its original place in the centre and adjusted, here and there, the position of a head or hand. In the lower half of the painting, he loosely aligned most of the figures' heads along an invisible horizontal line midway up the canvas, a solution first arrived at in the *Death of the Virgin*. He then redivided this lower half to determine the placement of the head belonging to the man seated on the ground, while he did likewise in the upper segment of the canvas to fix the position of the angels' heads. The corner of the dark wall in the left background and the lit street-opening with the prison on the right supply a vertical axis running down the middle of the composition. This simple schema imposes a roughly geometric order on the potentially chaotic gathering. To animate the heavenly vision, Caravaggio created great sweeping rhythms with the gesture and arching drapery of the angel on the left and the extended wings of the one on the right; he enlivened the action on earth by the contrasting curves of the deacon's sleeve and Pero's dress, and by the downward arc of water cascading into Samson's mouth.

In the *Seven Works* light descends characteristically along a diagonal from the upper left, selectively illuminating focal points and concealing areas where Caravaggio did not have enough space to define relationships among figures. As in the *Betrayal of Christ* (Pl. 117), he also introduced an internal light source, the torch held by the deacon. He did not exploit the luministic effects of torchlight, however; the motif instead became a favourite of his North Italian followers. Besides ensuring formal unity, the lighting strengthens dramatic unity, especially crucial for a non-narrative theme. He boldly cast the head of the man carrying the corpse into shadow, thereby creating at the very centre of the composition a void around which the action swirls.

Certain visual passages in the *Seven Works* derive from Caravaggio's translation of artistic tradition into his personal idiom. The striking image of a daughter nursing her father must have stuck in Caravaggio's memory from Perino del Vaga's fresco in the Palazzo Doria which he had visited the previous summer while in Genoa. He revamped Perino's elegantly conceived prototype into an immediate, even disquieting image of a woman anxiously fulfilling her filial duty. Another Renaissance model suggested the pose for the left-hand angel: Michelangelo's Christ in the *Conversion of Saint Paul*, 1542–5, in the Pauline Chapel of the Vatican Palace. As he had done earlier in his career, Caravaggio studied the pose afresh from the live model; the angel's flattened hand implies the surface upon which the model rested as he leaned down over a chair or some other support in the studio, and its redness realistically records the rush of blood caused by holding the pose.[14] The looming shadows cast by the wings of the right-hand angel on the upper wall of the prison are a further indication of Caravaggio's continued, intense observation of nature.

In its illustration of a fundamental Counter-Reformatory doctrine, the *Seven Works of Mercy* appears to be ideologically orthodox. The image, however, emphasizes first and foremost the moral imperative of fraternal charity, ignoring any institutional context. Caravaggio's painted donors are drawn, like the recipients of their charity, from the lower walks of Neapolitan society rather than from any historical charitable entity. By combining personages from ancient history, the Bible, saintly legend and contemporary life, Caravaggio seemingly asserts that earthly misery compels each individual to be his brother's keeper, no matter who, when or where, and even without open divine recognition. While the Pio Monte might have held some such philanthropic philosophy, Caravaggio clothed this Neapolitan altarpiece with the quintessential humanity of his mature sacred works. The sombre mood of his last Roman years is even more evident in the *Seven Works of Mercy*. Guilty of murder, living in exile and under a capital sentence, Caravaggio may well have expressed in this work his own personal stake in the evangelical lesson of Christian love and redemption.

Caravaggio's altarpiece must have fully satisfied the Pio Monte, for its members refused to part with the painting despite more than one extravagant offer. Fifty years later, when it had become too small for its congregation, the interior of the rebuilt church was designed to give visual primacy to the high altarpiece.[15] The unveiling of the *Seven Works* provided a ready and influential example of Caravaggio's naturalism among local artists. The whole composition engendered few imitations because of its rare theme, but individual motifs inspired

Caracciolo's *Allegory of the Immaculate Conception*, (S. Maria della Stella, Naples, 1607), Manfredi's *Roman Charity* (private collection, Milan, *c.*1615–20) and Luca Giordano's *Madonna and Child* (private collection).

The success of the *Seven Works of Mercy* directly led to the commission for the *Flagellation of Christ* (Pl. 137), Caravaggio's only other documented Neapolitan work. Whereas the former stands out for its original, complex imagery and dynamic composition, the *Flagellation* is traditional, straightforward and quiet. None the less Caravaggio infused expressive force into the suffering Christ and cruel torturers, imparting a chilling immediacy into this Gospel narrative.

According to Bellori, the canvas originally decorated the Di Franco Chapel in the church of S. Domenico Maggiore. The commission came from the Di Franco or rather De Franchis, a Neapolitan family of magistrates who had already climbed high on the social ladder by 1607 through their official appointments in the viceregal administration. Lorenzo de Franchis's position as one of the deputies of the Pio Monte was perhaps an influential factor in the family's choice of Caravaggio for the commission. The total fee, beyond his advance of 290 ducats, and the date of consignment are not known – only that Caravaggio received payments from Lorenzo's brother Tommaso on 11 and 25 May 1607.[16]

For his composition, Caravaggio turned to a well-known prototype in High Renaissance painting, Sebastiano del Piombo's mural of 1524–5 (Pl. 136). By reducing the number of figures, obliterating any architecture, and directing the lighting, he concentrated attention on Christ, whose muscular torso reproduces the idealism of Sebastiano's figure. Caravaggio lengthened even further the horizontal line extending from the model's bent head to his shoulder, a figural pose he had already favoured in his earlier *Rest on the Flight* (Pl. 59) and *Madonna of Loreto* (Pl. 102). The positioning of the figure's lower body, however, diverges from the classically balanced stance of his predecessor's; the legs twist sharply to the left and bend at the knees as if the model were stumbling forward.

**268**

**136** Sebastiano del Piombo, **Flagellation**, 1524–5; oil on plaster, S. Pietro in Montorio, Rome
**137 Flagellation of Christ**, 1607; oil on canvas, 266 × 213 cm, Museo Nazionale di Capodimonte, Naples

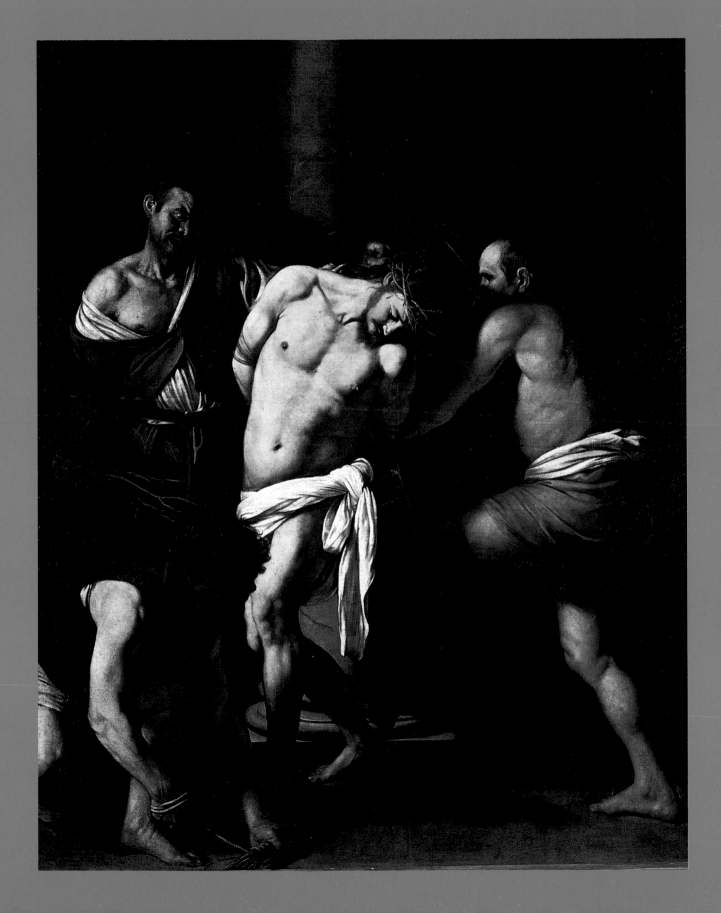

Not only is Christ's utter exhaustion thus realistically captured, but Caravaggio also chose to portray the moment preceding the flagellation so as to explain the immaculate state of his body. The tormentor on the right is still tying Christ's hands to the column, while the second man has stooped to finish fashioning his weapon. Although the latter's pose recalls that of the ancient statue popularly known as the 'Scythian Slave', unclassical shadow completely masks his features and his profile etches a dark silhouette on Christ's illuminated thigh.[17] Darkness also partially conceals both the lower part of the man's head on the right and the movement with which his foot brutally pushes down on the victim's right calf. The torturer on the left has not yet raised his flay, but, tightening his grip on it, grabs Jesus by the hair and screws up his face in anticipation; his expression, which emerges more fully than that of his accomplices, betrays a frightening viciousness. Caravaggio's *Flagellation* retells the Gospel narrative without the tragic grandeur of Sebastiano's fresco, its impact relying instead on the raw exposition of man's cruelty as an anonymous business carried out in secret with cold-blooded efficiency.

The *Flagellation* inspired a beautiful variation on the theme in a three-quarter-length easel picture (Pl. 138), perhaps ordered by a private client impressed with the De Franchis painting. Its dating to the first Neapolitan period is most convincing because of its obvious relation to the Pio Monte altarpiece, the use of the same models for Christ and the man at right, and the Neapolitan provenance of two of its versions. The incisions in the paint around the heads of the three figures and in other key places reflect Caravaggio's practice of establishing the rough outline of the design directly on the canvas, most likely fixing poses drawn directly from the model in the studio.

An important change, however, distinguishes the easel version from the altarpiece. Dispensing with the latter's traditional centralized composition, Caravaggio devised an asymmetrical one: Christ and the column are pushed off centre to the left, and the two tormentors occupy the rest of the canvas. His choice of the same narrative moment is similar, but Caravaggio seized the opportunity to rethink the subject-matter, producing a more studied work in which passages of sharp naturalistic observation are contained by artifice, as in the sweeping arc determining the disposition of the figures and in the showy blazing red drapery in one corner. Dispelling the atmosphere of quiet menace stalking his oppressed Christ in the altarpiece, Caravaggio here conceived a tragically heroic figure, lingering on his powerful, sculpted torso and describing handsome facial features softened by curls framing the face. Posed on the very brink of the canvas, Christ directs his burning gaze beyond the scene as if to imply that freedom from pain can only lie outside the material world.

During the four months between the completion of the *Seven Works of Mercy* and the start of work on the *Flagellation of Christ*, Caravaggio most likely undertook the *Madonna of the Rosary* (Pl. 139), probably the only other major painting of the first Neapolitan period. Comparable to the *Seven Works* in its large scale and number of figures, the *Madonna of the Rosary* also presents a non-narrative subject; unlike the former's near hermetic theme it depicts the familiar devotional image of Madonna and Christ Child enthroned and adored by saints.

Overleaf **138 Flagellation of Christ**, *c.*1607; oil on canvas, 134.5 × 175.5 cm, Musée des Beaux-Arts, Rouen

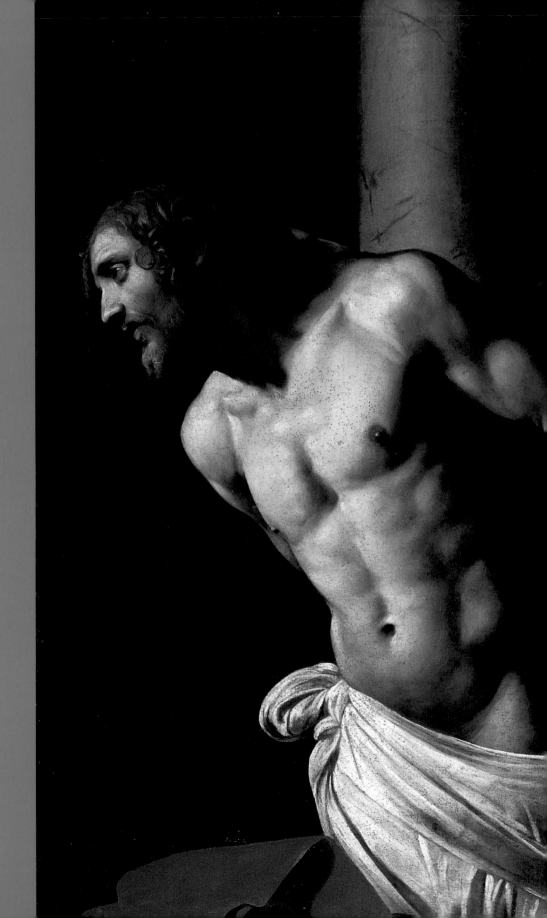

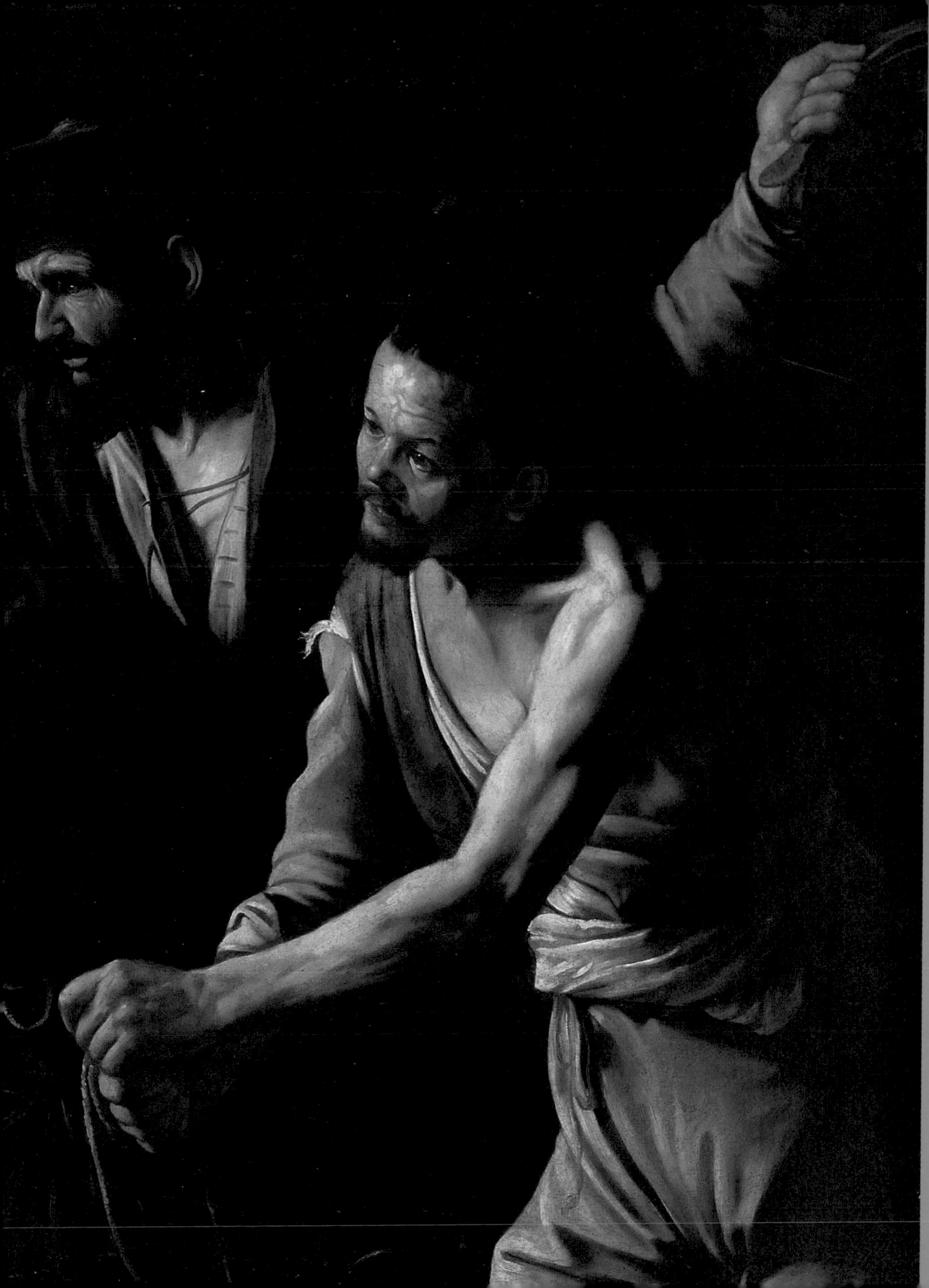

The finished *Madonna of the Rosary* is first documented as being for sale in Naples on 25 September 1607, just over two months after Caravaggio had left for Malta. He had reportedly painted the work in Naples for an altar, and its value was the same as assessed for the *Seven Works*. How the painting came to be on the market in 1607 is not known, however, let alone the circumstances behind its genesis. Despite the lack of any hard evidence, the most often-repeated proposal associates the *Madonna of the Rosary* with a painting which the Duke of Modena had ordered from Caravaggio some time before August 1605. Discrepancy in price, the identity of the donor portrait, and the dating, however, all argue against this proposal.[18]

That Caravaggio portrayed a member of the Colonna family and not the Duke of Modena is supported by visual and circumstantial evidence: the altarpiece celebrates the cult of the Rosary, venerated by the Colonna, and it includes a visual pun on their name and emblem in the fluted column vertically aligned on axis with the donor portrait. The most plausible suggestion to date identifies this as a posthumous portrait of Marcantonio II Colonna, whose victory at Lepanto in 1571 was credited to the Madonna of the Rosary's miraculous intervention. Caravaggio's patron for the altarpiece might then have been his grandson Luigi Carafa-Colonna (1567–1630), and its intended destination, the family funerary chapel dedicated to the 'Santissimo Rosario' in the Neapolitan church of S. Domenico Maggiore. Some as yet unknown mysterious circumstance might have induced him to abandon his plans and sell the altarpiece.[19]

Stylistic analysis of the work itself offers the strongest indication that Caravaggio painted the canvas during his first Neapolitan sojourn.

**139 Madonna of the Rosary**, c 1606–7; oil on canvas, 364.5 × 249.5 cm, Kunsthistorisches Museum, Vienna

Although some motifs do echo his mature Roman paintings – the kneeling men posed like the pilgrims in the *Madonna di Loreto*, the mother's braids arranged like the Magdalen's and the red curtain in the *Death of the Virgin* – the overwhelming impression is of a break with his Roman ecclesiastical paintings. Caravaggio set his assembly within a shadowed, yet defined architectural setting of an apse bounded on one side by the column; he used a cast of models unfamiliar from his Roman works, such as the woman who posed for the Madonna, possibly the same model for the nursing woman in the *Seven Works*, and unmistakably the protagonist in another Neapolitan picture, the *Salome with the Head of Saint John the Baptist* (Pl. 171). Finally, the palette boasts both an uncustomary range and unusual combination of colours – blue, green, yellow and cream – in addition to his usual black, white and earth tones. The closest parallel for this colouring and for the articulation of the interior space exists, not in Caravaggio's previous Roman period, but rather in his *Beheading of Saint John the Baptist* (Pl. 151), executed in Malta within the next year.

Caravaggio did not entirely succeed in breathing life into the conventional composition of the *Madonna of the Rosary*. The holy Mother and Child are both drawn awkwardly and, moreover, their faces look strangely blank, creating an emotional void at the heart of the scene, which jars with the desperate attitudes struck by the humble devotees. X-rays of the canvas betray unusually extensive changes in the placement of figures, hinting at difficulties the artist encountered with his design. Despite the problems that may have plagued the original commission and the failure of the work to attract a buyer in September 1607, the painting enjoyed an illustrious later history. By 1617, the *Madonna of the Rosary* belonged to the artist Louis Finson and his colleague Abraham Vinck, Flemish friends and followers of Caravaggio in Naples, who presumably shipped the altarpiece to Amsterdam along with their possessions when they returned north. Soon after Finson's death, Vinck sold the work to a committee of Flemish painters, including Rubens and Jan Brueghel the Elder, who bought it to adorn the Dominican church in Antwerp, as an example of a 'most extraordinarily grand work of art' and one which Bellori later claimed 'brought Caravaggio's brush great fame'.

Finson (before 1580–1617), who had settled in Naples from 1604 to 1612, copied Caravaggio's *Magdalen in Ecstasy*, *Madonna of the Rosary* and *Crucifixion of Saint Andrew*. In 1607, the original *Madonna of the Rosary* and a 'Judith and Holofernes' by Caravaggio were available for sale in his studio. One local commentator asserted in 1613, by which time Finson had moved to France, that he 'had entirely Caravaggio's style and had long nourished himself on him'. The other Neapolitan painters who responded early to Caravaggio's presence in the city were Battistello and his contemporary Carlo Sellitto (1580–1614). According to Bernardo de Dominici, the biographer of Neapolitan artists, Battistello in particular had '[been] nursed on the new manner [of Caravaggio] … [and] abandoned all of his former models, entirely turned to it and determined absolutely to follow it'. Both Battistello and Finson seem to have enjoyed direct access to Caravaggio and his studio, and are the closest the master ever came to having disciples.[20]

Caravaggio left behind from both his sojourns in Naples a body of mature religious work that determined the strong naturalistic and tenebrist orientation of Neapolitan art for much of the next half-century. This legacy also laid the foundation for a Neapolitan school of painting, shaping the stylistic formations of artists such as Jusepe de Ribera (1591–1652), in Naples from 1616 until his death, and of the masters of the younger generation, Mattia Preti (1613–99), and Luca Giordano (1634–1705).

On 12 July 1607, Caravaggio arrived in Malta on one of the galleys of the Order of Saint John of Jerusalem. For the next fifteen months he settled on this Mediterranean island between Sicily and North Africa that had been ruled by the Knights Hospitallers of Saint John since 1530. Drawing its knights from European nobility, the brotherhood continued to fulfil medical responsibilities throughout the sixteenth and seventeenth centuries, and, most importantly, served as a naval force harrying Turkish vessels and creating a bulwark against Ottoman imperialism.

Arriving in the sweltering summer heat, Caravaggio must have been awed by the massive stone bastions of Valletta, rising on a promontory between two harbours. The Knights' fortified capital had been founded by the Grand Master of the Order Jean de La Valette, who had successfully resisted the Turkish invasion in the Great Siege of 1565. Newly built, regular in its grid layout, and hemmed in by the sea, Valletta would have presented an exotic physical environment to Caravaggio. Although then ruled by the Grand Master Alof de Wignacourt (1547–1622), chosen from the French constituency of the Order, Valletta maintained close ties with Rome and Naples, and so its society and politics would have been more familiar to him than its topography. The Grand Master deferred to the Pope on certain issues, such as special dispensation of the rules for admission into the Order. The population, though small, was cosmopolitan, comprising seven different European nations or 'Langues' into which the Order was divided.[21]

A Sicilian Knight, Fra Giacomo Marchese, who had been Caravaggio's travelling companion, was his host on the island. The arrangements for the painter's voyage, however, were more likely made by the same network of influential protectors who had expedited his flight from Rome and his Neapolitan sojourn. It is difficult to pinpoint exactly who aided him in the Maltese venture because, as with many wealthy Italian noble families, several of his patrons were well connected to the Knights. The Marchesa di Caravaggio's brother, Cardinal

Ascanio, served as Co-Prior of the Knights' convent in Venice, while her son Fabrizio Sforza-Colonna, Co-Prior of Venice with his uncle, commanded the very fleets of the Order that transported Caravaggio. Alternatively, Costa might have recommended Caravaggio to his wife's uncle, Ippolito Malaspina (1540–1624), patron of the *Saint Jerome* (Pl. 141). Conventual Bailiff or high officer in the Order, Malaspina was a good friend of Wignacourt, whom he had helped elect Grand Master, and had arrived in Malta only a few months earlier than Caravaggio.[22]

The artist's move to Malta was surely motivated by his desire for a knighthood, as Bellori claimed; not only did the eight-pointed Maltese cross bestow honour on its wearer (Pl. 140) but it also offered the promise of smoothing the way for a papal pardon and repatriation. Over a year had passed since Tomassoni's death, but despite ongoing negotiations for clemency the capital sentence on Caravaggio still prevailed. The Order had previously proven a refuge for an older Florentine painter Filippo Paladini (*c.*1544–*c.*1616) who had committed a crime for which he was condemned to the galleys. In exchange for years of artistic service to the Knights, Paladini finally attained freedom and was eventually pardoned in 1610. Caravaggio must have also known the case of the Marchesa di Caravaggio's son Fabrizio, who was convicted of a crime and turned over to the Order for trial in 1602. After serving a prison sentence on Malta, Fabrizio soon vaulted to the important post of admiral of the Order's fleet.[23]

On 14 July 1608, a year after his arrival on the island, the Order dubbed Caravaggio a Knight of Obedience. The decree and the type of knighthood indicate that he was so recognized because of his great artistic merits. Unlike the knighthoods of Justice, reserved for

candidates demonstrating proof of noble genealogy, knighthoods of Obedience were awarded for merit and normally conferred at the Grand Master's discretion alone. Caravaggio's criminal status patently posed a formidable obstacle to his candidature because a statute forbade admission to anyone convicted of murder, but this did not deter Wignacourt who in fact knew of his capital sentence. Recently discovered correspondence between Wignacourt and Rome, spanning December 1607 to February 1608, concerns admitting an unnamed 'virtuous' and 'worthy' candidate who had committed murder in a brawl. Paul V approved the petition on 15 February 1608, waiving the rules in this one exceptional instance (Appendix VIII). Another five months elapsed before Caravaggio's reception into the Order in July, a delay possibly occasioned by the customary requirement of a year-long residency for novices.[24]

Caravaggio's desire for a knighthood dovetailed with Wignacourt's desire to patronize a famous artist. The language of the magisterial bull conferring his knighthood likens the honour to that accorded the ancient painter Apelles by the island of Cos. By extension, Wignacourt could cast himself in the role of Apelles's patron Alexander the Great, as had the emperor Charles V in his patronage of Titian more than half a century earlier. Indeed, he commissioned a full-length portrait of himself from Caravaggio, his 'new Apelles', as Alexander had had himself portrayed by the ancient painter. Wignacourt also oversaw Caravaggio's most important official commission in Malta, the *Beheading of Saint John the Baptist*. The success of the work reportedly induced him to reward the painter with two slaves and a gold chain, the latter gift emblematic of princely largesse.[25]

Caravaggio's portrait of Wignacourt (Pl. 142), the *Beheading of Saint John the Baptist* (Pl. 151), *Saint Jerome* (Pl. 141) and a *Sleeping Cupid* (Pl. 148), also painted in Malta, form a distinctive group that sets the Maltese period apart as an artistic peak within his years of maturity. Although the two religious subjects represent themes of saintly devotion and martyrdom familiar from his earlier career, both stand out for the classical designs that at once masterfully integrate figure and ambience, and aggrandize their respective subjects. The

**140** Anonymous, **Portrait of Caravaggio**, 17th century; oil on canvas, 80 × 50 cm, Collezione Ecclesiastica, Malta

*Beheading of Saint John the Baptist*, moreover, is Caravaggio's largest work and the only one he seems ever to have signed (Pl. 153). The two other Maltese canvases have particular significance among his secular works: the painting of Wignacourt for its value as Caravaggio's sole full-length portrait of secure attribution, and the *Sleeping Cupid* for its mythological subject, rare among his late works. One other picture attributed in modern times to Caravaggio can also be assigned to his year in Malta: *Portrait of a Knight of Malta* (Pl. 145). Given the amount of time he spent on the island, the normally speedy painter produced a comparatively small number of works there. The nature of his daily life may account for the slowed pace. Novices were required to serve in the hospital, undergo instruction on the Order's statutes and history, and regularly attend religious devotions; on top of such demands on his time, he also had to organize a studio from scratch.[26]

Caravaggio's *Saint Jerome* was reported to have hung originally as an overdoor in the Chapel of the Italian Langue, one of the side chapels that were richly endowed by each of the main nations of the Order in their conventual church, now the Co-Cathedral of Malta. Given the inclusion of his escutcheon in the lower right-hand corner, Malaspina most likely commissioned the canvas. The painting was apparently installed after his death, and he perhaps had planned for it to be a bequest for the chapel, the intended site of his tomb which is prominently placed in the centre of the pavement.[27]

The harmonious correspondence between the *Saint Jerome* and its location is a general characteristic of Caravaggio's public commissions. The painted light entering from the left corresponds with the natural light in the chapel from a window over the altar; the table tilts up for better viewing from below; and the saint extends his right leg towards the altar, while turning his head and torso towards the nave. Caravaggio executed the canvas with unusual polish, more common in his easel pictures than his altarpieces. If Malaspina had in fact recommended Caravaggio for a knighthood, perhaps he arranged this commission as a demonstration for Wignacourt not only of Caravaggio's art but of the best in contemporary Italian painting. With the foreshortened crucifix projecting illusionistically out of the picture, the composition pointedly exhibited the artist's acclaimed naturalism in depicting still-life objects. The five-month period separating his arrival on the island in July and Wignacourt's petition to the Pope in December 1607 provided an ample span of time for its execution.

As in his earlier version of the theme (Pl. 129), Caravaggio represented Jerome as the old scholar engrossed in writing the Vulgate. Although he designed carefully structured horizontal, three-quarter-length compositions in each, here he centred the figure, moving him behind the table. Both works share very similar colouring limited to the saint's skin tone, deep red robe, some white drapery, and the brown table, but in the later work borders of colour are less sharply separated, a softer interplay of colour and lighting creating a new atmospheric ambience for the figure. For example, the brightly lit red of Jerome's cloak is echoed in the muted red of his hat shown in half-shadow, and the brown of the table likewise is toned down in the brownish-grey of the bed-covers behind. Exceptionally, this Jerome sits in a defined interior, whose rear and side walls are defined by the bed and cardinal's hat, its middle ground by the saint and the table, and its foremost plane by the projecting crucifix and open door at right. Apart from serving a spatial function, the door leaf acts as a narrative device — left ajar, it grants us an intimate glimpse of the scholar at work — and it also provides a support for the Malaspina arms, thereby resolving the artificiality of the crest and its placement.

The cardinal's hat and the objects resting on the table suggest that the saint has not yet severed all ties with the world outside his cell. In contrast to the three oversize folios swamping the tabletop in the earlier canvas, the one book Jerome writes in frees up the rest of the

Overleaf **141 Saint Jerome**, *c*.1607–8; oil on canvas, 117 × 157 cm, Co-Cathedral of St John, Valletta

surface for the inclusion of a few, neatly-laid-out objects. The stone and crucifix are Jerome's customary attributes, referring to his penitential retreat in the wilderness. Tipped on its side and next to an unlit candle, the skull acts as a traditional 'vanitas' emblem alluding to the transitory nature of material things. The unlit candle, whose shaft reflects the light entering from the left, makes another symbolic point: the divine origin of the illumination flooding on to Jerome and enlightening his work. The darkness pressing around the radiant saint protects him from outside distraction, conveying the quiet, meditative mood of Caravaggio's late works.

Less frail than in the earlier picture, Jerome holds erect his gaunt but still strong frame, retaining the dignity of his station even while engaged in his solitary study. As has often been noted, his features bear a striking resemblance to those recorded by Caravaggio in his portrait of Wignacourt. The flattering analogy between the doctor of the Church and the Grand Master, a religious as well as military leader, could only have encouraged a favourable reception from Wignacourt.[28]

Caravaggio's official full-length portrait of Wignacourt (Pl. 142), 'standing and armed' as Bellori noted reputedly earned him his knighthood. As in contemporaneous engraved portraits of the Grand Master, the subject displays the same receding hairline, heavy eyebrows, prominent nose and squarely trimmed beard. Unfortunately, a heavy-handed restoration in the eighteenth century has flattened the paint surface of the canvas, raising occasional but unfounded doubts about its authenticity in the past. Typical of Caravaggio are the familiar tenebrist lighting and characteristic reddish-brown palette, the distinctive emphasis on the man behind the office, and the North Italian artistic sources of the work.[29]

For Wignacourt's pose and the full-length format, Caravaggio drew primarily on a sixteenth-century Venetian tradition of images of the

142 **Portrait of Alof de Wignacourt**, c.1607–8; oil on canvas, 194 × 134 cm, Louvre, Paris

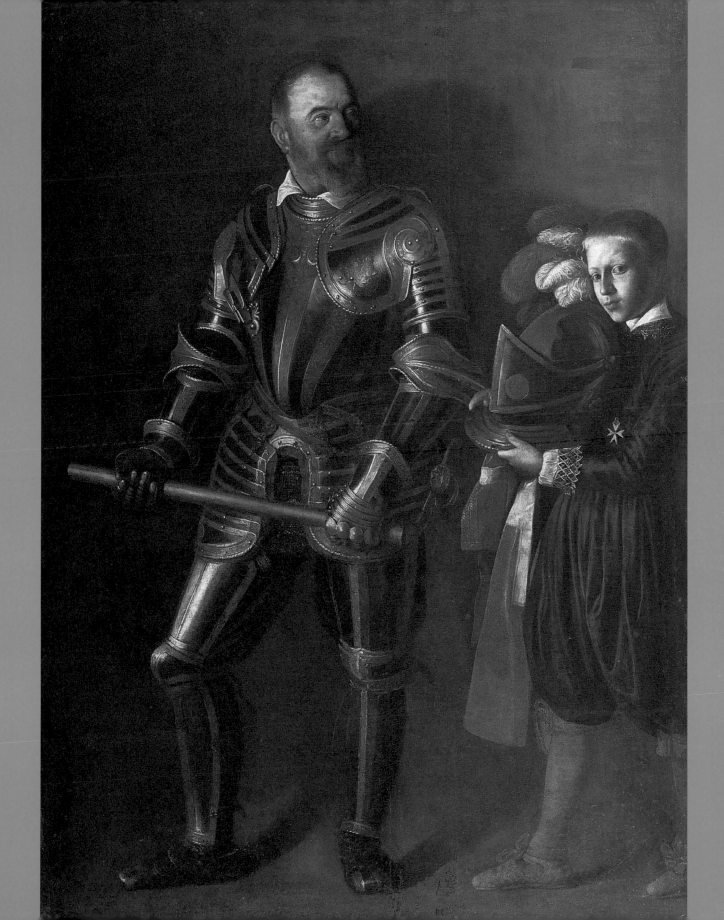

triumphant warrior. Although the portrait does not copy any one prototype, elements such as the figure's averted gaze, the luministic rather than meticulous description of armour, and the inclusion of a young page holding his master's helmet, recall Titian's *Allocution of Alfonso d'Avalos* (Pl. 143) and *Portrait of Alfonso d'Avalos with a Page* (on loan to the Louvre, Paris, *c.*1535), and the Veronesian *Pase Guarienti* (Pl. 144). In following this established type, Caravaggio emphasized Wignacourt's princely authority as head of the oldest chivalric order.

The Grand Master's damascened armour dates to an earlier epoch and had possibly belonged to one of his predecessors, perhaps even Jean de la Valette. For Wignacourt and his knights, well-versed in such fine distinctions, this would have stirred memories of heroic victories over the Turks, in the Great Siege repelled by La Valette in 1565 and at Lepanto in 1571, where Wignacourt himself had served as a young knight. Caravaggio's image thus affirms the past valour of Grand Masters and the present vigilance of Wignacourt, who scans the horizon for the perennial Ottoman threat.[30]

The blond boy, one of several of the youngest aspiring knights, must have been Wignacourt's page. He is clad in soft fabric instead of glinting metal; the feathers of the helmet brush against his smooth-cheeked face; warm reds suffuse his hose, along with his master's cloak and the plumed helmet he holds close against him. Beyond the contrast between august personage and humble acolyte which was customary within this class of portraiture, Caravaggio's portrayal of Wignacourt and his page evokes the universal opposition between age and youth: the mature man who faces the future and his own mortality in contrast with the young boy whose direct gaze forever fixes him in the viewer's present.[31]

Caravaggio impresses his subject's physical presence upon us with the large shadow cast on the back wall and the head-on viewpoint. Although he somewhat flattered Wignacourt – the turned head conceals a large wart – he rejected any of the visual trappings that other painters employed to aggrandize sitters of high rank: columns, swags of drapery, allegorical emblems, or background vignettes of raging battles. In its intimacy and sobriety, Caravaggio's portrait looks back to Lombard precedents in Moretto's and Moroni's portraits of standing gentlemen, and is matched later in the seventeenth century only by Velázquez's images of Philip IV and the Spanish Habsburg court.

**143** Titian, **Allocution of Alfonso d'Avalos**, *c.*1541; oil on canvas, 223 × 165 cm, Prado, Madrid

**144** School of Veronese, **Pase Guarienti**, 1556; oil on canvas, 200 × 115 cm, Museo di Castelvecchio, Verona

The man portrayed in the impressive *Portrait of a Knight of Malta* (Pl. 145), bears a striking physical resemblance to Wignacourt, and the original conception of the portrait, its tenebrism, and the masterful handling of details such as the white collar and shimmering giant cross accord with Caravaggio's late style, sustaining his authorship. The Grand Cross emblazoned on the sitter's chest, worn only by the highest-ranking officials, affirms his status as an important dignitary in the Order. This knight differs from Caravaggio's portrayal of Wignacourt in the Louvre portrait in small details such as the shape of his ear and the style of his beard – which can be explained by the slightly altered pose of the head and a lapse in time between the two works.[37]

The distinctive requirements of each commission are evident from the fact that the official nature of the Louvre portrait called for a more formal presentation than the private Pitti portrait which captures an intimate view of the sixty-year-old subject. Whereas the standing, armed Wignacourt in the Louvre projects the Grand Master's military valour, the Pitti portrait depicts him not only as a knight, hand on the hilt of his sword, but also as the head of a religious Order, fingering rosary beads in his right hand, the faint light reflecting off the white cross barely illuminating the face of the shadowy figure. The aged soldier does not fix his gaze on the horizon but appears lost in thought, like his holy counterpart Saint Jerome meditating on the passage of time and the inevitability of death.

The *Portrait of Wignacourt* and the *Portrait of a Knight*, if the latter's attribution is accepted, are the only extant, relatively secure examples of Caravaggio's portraiture. Yet Caravaggio reportedly painted well over a dozen portraits mentioned by his biographers and

**145 Portrait of a Knight of Malta**, *c.*1608, oil on canvas, 118.5 × 95.5 cm, Palazzo Pitti, Florence

listed in seventeenth-century inventories. Among the various candidates proposed in modern times for these lost works, two stand out as likely attributions: a seated three-quarter length *Portrait of Monsignor Maffeo Barberini* (Pl. 146), *c.*1598, and a full-length *Portrait of Paul V* (Pl. 147).

In the former, Maffeo appears as a young prelate, before being named cardinal and over two decades before he ascended the papal throne as Urban VIII. The paper he clutches in his left hand and the rolled parchment propped up against his chair suggest that the portrait may celebrate his appointment as Apostolic Clerk in 1598.

Arguing for Caravaggio's authorship are certain stylistic features characteristic of his art towards 1600: sharply contrasted lighting, the smooth modelling of the face, the mostly three-colour scheme, and the handling. The brightest areas, in the face and hands, are emphasized by the white collar and sleeves, and set off against the dark green clerical robe. The same green, toned down a notch by the addition of black, covers the chair back, seat, and the dangling, tasselled cord tying up the official document. Narrow red piping emerging in places along Maffeo's robe at the shoulder, neck and along the front opening accentuates the broad areas of green; on the sleeve itself near the top a touch of red over the white paint captures the reflection of the piping. Free and sure brushstrokes create volume in Maffeo's right sleeve, a single thin loaded brushstroke marks its hem at the wrist, and long, uninterrupted strokes, done wet on wet, describe the visible strip of alb in front. But most convincing is the portrayal of Maffeo himself, turning in his chair to fix his animated gaze and jab his finger at someone just beyond the frame. Maffeo projects a lively, physical immediacy, and acceptance of this engaging portrait would extend the range of Caravaggio's portraiture.

290

146 **Portrait of Monsignor Maffeo Barberini** (attributed), *c.*1598; oil on canvas, 124 × 90 cm, private collection

Paul V must have posed for Caravaggio between May 1605, when he became Pope at the age of fifty-three, and May 1606, when Caravaggio left Rome. First assigned to Caravaggio in an early guidebook to the Villa Borghese, the *Portrait of Paul V* shows the Pope at about the appropriate age, and stylistically it resembles Caravaggio's late Roman paintings, such as the *Madonna dei Palafrenieri* (Pl. 105) or the *Saint John the Baptist* (Pl. 124). The existence of complete and partial copies of its composition indicates that this imposing representation served as the official image of the pontiff, who had supposedly expressed his satisfaction with his new portrait by rewarding Caravaggio handsomely. Definitive judgement about the *Portrait of Paul V*, however, must await cleaning and restoration to resolve the question of whether it is the lost original or a copy.[33]

Caravaggio's early critics are unhelpfully reticent on the subject of his portraiture. The exception is Mancini, who evidently thought little of his efforts to capture a likeness. His assessment of them as examples of poor portraits produced by a great artist is surprising: given Caravaggio's reputation for slavish 'truth to nature', of all painters one would have expected an objective portrait from his brush. In view of the number of portraits he was alleged to have painted and the fact that his prestigious sitters evince considerable respect for his achievement, the subsequent loss of so many is also puzzling. Maybe over time, as the sitters' identities faded, the new owners of the portraits grew indifferent to their preservation. But that the portraits also lost their labels as Caravaggios implies that this aspect of his *œuvre* was less well known and appreciated than his narrative and devotional paintings.[34]

Despite the high regard which Ingres, a remarkable portraitist himself, expressed for the *Portrait of Alof de Wignacourt* in the nineteenth century, recent commentators have been reserved about Caravaggio's portraits, some even questioning generally their originality and historical significance. But the compositions of the *Alof de Wignacourt*, and the convincing *Portrait of a Knight of Malta* and *Portrait of Maffeo Barberini* reinterpret rather than merely imitate their artistic prototypes. These works, along with the early *Portrait of Fillide* (Pl. 66), constitute a select gallery of distinct personalities, all of them authoritative, contemplative, active, and coolly poised. Caravaggio's corpus of surviving portraits is too small to be judged as crucial to the course of seventeenth-century portraiture; none the less, the dynamic *Maffeo Barberini* prefigures the 'speaking likenesses' of Bernini or Simon Vouet; the *Alof de Wignacourt* and *Fillide* match the objective sobriety of Velázquez's portraits, and the *Knight of Malta* the introspection of Rembrandt's.[35]

**147 Portrait of Paul V** (attributed), *c.*1605–6; oil on canvas, 203 × 119 cm, collection of Prince Camillo Borghese, Rome

In Malta, Caravaggio also produced the *Sleeping Cupid* (Pl. 148), his last-known mythological work. Alongside the other Maltese pictures, this canvas is the smallest and most unassuming. Its iconology and non-Maltese destination create a broader context for the work than previously suspected, however, and one with unexpected theoretical implications.

The recent archival discovery of a letter of 1609 confirms the old inscription on the back of *Sleeping Cupid* stating that Caravaggio executed it in Malta in 1608 (Appendix IX). This letter was written by Fra Francesco Buonarroti, a knight of Malta, to his brother Michelangelo Buonarroti the Younger (1568–1646), dramatist and poet at the Grand-ducal Court in Florence. Reporting on Caravaggio's picture as the latest island news, Fra Francesco identified its patron as a fellow knight and compatriot, Francesco dell'Antella (1567–1624), the very same *commendatore* of the Order whom Wignacourt had enlisted to help secure the papal dispensation for Caravaggio's admission. Fra Francesco announced to his brother that Dell'Antella had just shipped 'a painting by Michelangelo da Caravaggio, with a sleeping Cupid' from Malta to Florence and mentioned having been shown the painting and a sonnet dedicated to it, adding that he was eager to display the picture in Florence.[36]

The enthusiastic early reception of the *Sleeping Cupid* contrasts with the generally adverse reactions of modern critics who have seen the figure as more dead than asleep, as a perversely unlovely god of love, or even as a clinical record of the pathology of an infant suffering from rheumatoid arthritis.[37] Caravaggio's first mythological painting in six years, the *Sleeping Cupid* presents the antithesis of his earlier *Cupid* (Pl. 106): sleeping and not grinning at us, about four or five and not twelve years old, plump not lithe, homely not beautiful, and accompanied only by his own identifying attributes — quiver, bow and arrow. Some of the discrepancies in this depiction derive, however, from a distinct artistic tradition, which Caravaggio jolted as much in the *Sleeping Cupid* as he had done previously.

The sleeping Cupid, a motif in ancient poetry and sculpture, enjoyed an artistic revival in the sixteenth century after the young

**148  Sleeping Cupid**, 1608;  oil on canvas, 71 × 105 cm, Palazzo Pitti, Florence

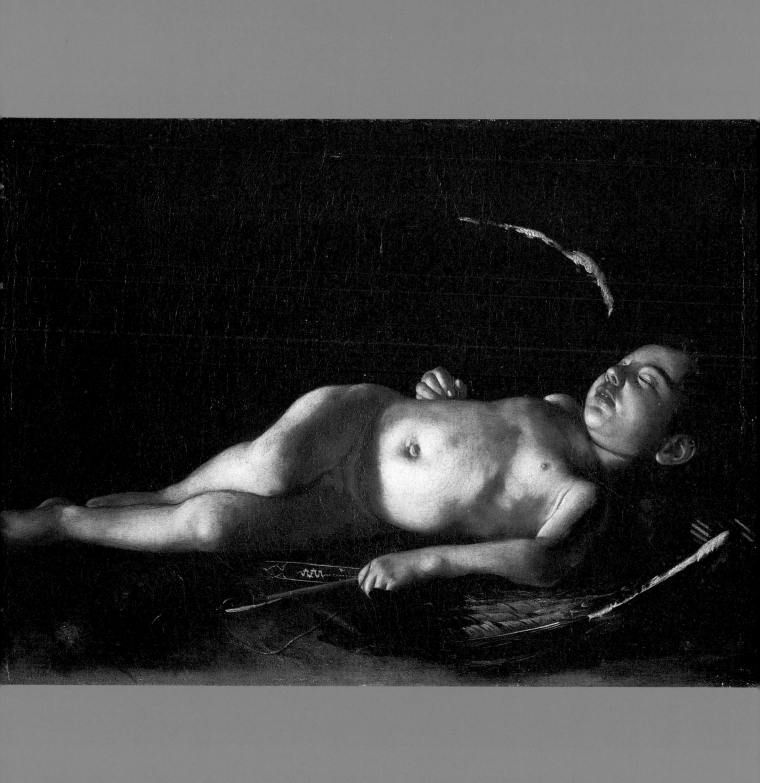

Michelangelo had so expertly carved the subject in imitation of the antique that his work actually passed as a classical piece. Though lost since the seventeenth century, the sculpture was in Mantua during Caravaggio's lifetime. Early accounts describe it as depicting the god 'between six and seven years of age, lying asleep' and with his head resting on one hand; it most likely bore a close resemblance to a Hellenistic piece in the Medici collections (Pl. 149).[38]

Whether he knew the original or a copy or knew of it from a description, Caravaggio could not have helped thinking of the famous sculpture when he took up the theme, especially as he had earlier shown himself ambivalent towards Michelangelo's art. Knowing that the destination of his *Sleeping Cupid* was Florence, did Caravaggio and his patron plan a pictorial re-creation of a famed carving by the city's most illustrious native son? The fact that, before sending the painting to Florence, Dell'Antella particularly wanted to show it to his friend (as it so happened the sculptor's great-nephew), who in turn hastened to notify his brother Michelangelo the Younger (a connoisseur with an ardent devotion to their great-uncle's memory), strongly suggests that Caravaggio's patron valued his new acquisition as a 'modern Michelangelo'.

In imitating Michelangelo's work, Caravaggio isolated the sculptural motif of the sleeping Cupid for an independent painting. His pot-bellied and toothy, snoring child surely flouted the probable classical proportions and cherubic repose of Michelangelo's slumbering figure. Caravaggio's deliberate conception of the work as a rival to its sculpted antecedent is suggested by the ways in which he enhanced the three-dimensionality of his painted Cupid: drastically reducing the range of colour and intensifying the contrast of lights and darks. He knew that for fellow artists, and for Dell'Antella and his cultivated circle too, comparison of the *Sleeping Cupid* with Michelangelo's or any antique sculpted version would surely evoke the *paragone*, the theoretical debate about the relationship of painting and sculpture and their respective merits. Some sixty years earlier, in Florence and in regard to Michelangelo's works, the *paragone* had dominated art theory, and it continued to influence artists into the seventeenth century. As if also arguing for the supremacy of painting, Caravaggio exploited the

**149 Sleeping Cupid**, Roman, 2nd century AD; black marble, length 135 cm, Uffizi, Florence

*chiaroscuro* in the *Sleeping Cupid* to give relief to his figure and to create a nocturnal setting; he thereby demonstrated the painter's illusionistic skill in simulating the actual volume of sculpture and reaffirmed the 'universality' of painting and its unique capacity to describe natural phenomena.[39]

Despite the modest nature of this commission, its links with the *paragone*, Michelangelo's art and classical tradition betray a concern on Caravaggio's part with contemporary critical issues that is surprising in a painter who is more usually viewed as anti-theoretical. Dell'Antella's pleasure in the *Sleeping Cupid* mirrors Giustiniani's in his *Cupid*. But unlike the earlier triumphant god, this Cupid has temporarily stepped out of the game of love; although the arrow he fingers in his left hand warns us of his power, his folded wings, his quiver serving as a pillow, and his unstretched bow all signal a temporary respite for his victims. For its patron, Dell'Antella, vowed to chastity as well as celibacy, Cupid's sleep bespoke the peace of mind attainable through freedom from physical passion.[40]

Caravaggio's *Sleeping Cupid* inspired poets and painters to take up the motif as an independent theme, but none of them caught the humour of his all-too-human deity. Caracciolo's *Sleeping Child* (Galleria Nazionale, Palermo, *c* 1618) most closely apes Caravaggio in posing his subject on the ground in the dark, but in a prettier image. By contrast, Caravaggio's *Sleeping Cupid* betrays an irreverence towards ancient mythology, already blatant in his *Bacchus* and *Cupid*, that is both precocious and rare in Italian art, and recurs only later in the seventeenth century and typically outside Italy in Velázquez's anti-heroic *Mars* (Madrid, Prado, *c*.1640) and Rembrandt's outrageous *Ganymede* (Gemäldegalerie, Dresden, 1635).

In the months immediately preceding the *Sleeping Cupid*, Caravaggio expended tremendous energy on one of his grandest and most classical works, the *Beheading of Saint John the Baptist* (Pl. 151), whose unveiling was probably planned to coincide with the feast of the decapitation of the Baptist, patron saint of the Knights of Malta, on 29 August 1608. Wignacourt had not only conferred the knighthood on Caravaggio but also

*for the church of S. Giovanni he had him paint the beheading of the saint fallen to the ground, while the executioner, as though he had not quite killed him with the sword, takes a knife from his side, seizing him by his hair to cut off his head. Herodias [sic] looks on intently, and an old woman with her is horrified by the spectacle, while the prison warden, in a Turkish garment, points to the atrocious slaughter. In this work, Caravaggio used all the force of his brush, having worked with such boldness that he left the priming of the canvas in half-tones.*[41]

This well-known description testifies to the impact the *Beheading* made in the seventeenth century. For modern pilgrims to Malta, seeing the painting in its original setting is an unforgettable experience (Pl. 150). The monumental work, the largest Caravaggio ever painted, decorates the altar of a large Oratory now reached by a passageway from the nave of the Co-Cathedral. Covering the far wall, the *Beheading* with its over-life-size figures still dominates the room despite Mattia Preti's later lavish embellishment of the altar recess and ceiling. Centred in the composition, caught in the strongest light, and accented by the scarlet swath of drapery, the Baptist and his executioner draw the viewer's gaze across the space of this tranquil retreat, today a museum but formerly set aside for the knights' devotions.

Completed in or around 1605, the Oratory provided the setting for both the religious education of the Order's novices and the private prayers of the knightly Confraternity of Misericordia, committed to the spiritual succour of criminals condemned to death. In all likelihood the initial plans for the Oratory included an altarpiece; Caravaggio's timely arrival in Malta and Wignacourt's vigorous pursuit of a papal dispensation for his admission into the Order suggest that the painter's knighthood was linked to this important commission. Caravaggio's acceptance of the commission may well have satisfied a requirement for knighthood: 'passage money' paid by each novice upon his reception, and on occasion made in kind instead of cash. If this was the case, the *Beheading* would naturally have been discussed and launched before Caravaggio's initiation as a knight in July 1608.[42]

The story of John the Baptist's death is told in the Gospels of Matthew and Mark. King Herod had imprisoned the prophet for denouncing his marriage to his brother's wife, Herodias. Captivated by his stepdaughter's dance at a banquet, Herod promised to grant her any wish; at her mother's instigation, she asked for the Baptist's head. The king then 'sent and had John beheaded in the prison, and his head was brought on a platter and given to the girl, and she brought it to her mother' (Matthew, 14:3–11). Unnamed in the Bible, the girl came to be identified with Salome, though she was often mistakenly called by her mother's name, Herodias, as in Bellori's description quoted above.

**299**

**150** Interior view of Oratory of Saint John, Co-Cathedral of St John, Valletta

Overleaf **151 Beheading of Saint John the Baptist**, 1608; oil on canvas, 361 × 520 cm, Co-Cathedral of St John, Valletta

Before Caravaggio, artists invariably illustrated one of two moments in Saint John's execution: either the instant when the headsman prepares to strike the saint, or after the decapitation as he hands the head to Salome waiting with her platter. From his youth in Milan, Caravaggio certainly knew Antonio Campi's altarpiece of 1571 (Pl. 7) portraying the Baptist kneeling at the executioner's block; in Rome, he could easily have seen examples of the second type, such as the fresco depicting the already beheaded John from the Mannerist cycle in the Oratory of S. Giovanni Decollato (Pl. 152).

Caravaggio disregarded artistic precedent, however, imagining an altogether different moment in the saint's death: John lies bleeding on

the ground next to the sword of the executioner who is pulling out his knife to deliver the *coup de grâce*. Unlike his earlier, gory *Judith Beheading Holofernes* (Pl. 69), he did not paint the actual severing of John's neck, but showed him more dead than alive, sprawling head down with hands tied behind his back. And in contrast to the screaming murderer in his *Martyrdom of Saint Matthew* (Pl. 76), restraint prevails here while the executioner mutely terminates an incomplete job. It is as if, where once he wanted to shock viewers, Caravaggio now elicited their compassion by dwelling on the inexorability of the helpless saint's death.

Action in the *Beheading* unfolds in front of an archway closed by a wooden gate in what appears to be the prison courtyard, as the Gospels dictated. To the right, two figures, presumably prisoners in a dungeon, look on from behind a barred window. Caravaggio here constructed the most clearly articulated of all his painted settings, continuing a trend he had begun in Naples. The stark courtyard is still far from the characteristic elaborate architectural backdrop found in his artistic sources. But, as has often been remarked, the rectilinear and austere building, especially the stone arch, most evokes the Grand Master's Palace in Valletta itself; this marked the first time in Caravaggio's career that he acknowledged his actual physical environment in a painting. Scripturally suitable, the architecture in the

302

**152** Roviale Spagnuolo (attributed), **Martyrdom of Saint John the Baptist**, 1555; fresco, Oratory of S. Giovanni Decollato, Rome

*Beheading* establishes a convincing locale for the story, which for the Knights held the added resonance of restaging the saint's martyrdom in their own time and place.

The limited detail supplied by the Gospels allowed Caravaggio to dispense with the crowds present in earlier depictions of the subject, reducing the *dramatis personae* to five principals and two supporting actors. He arranged the main figures into a tightly-knit semicircle around the saint's prone body, adjusting their poses so that the outline of the group forms an arc echoing the larger archway of the portal behind them. Within the group the two women are juxtaposed with the two men; Salome's pose mirrors the executioner's, and her slim, bared arms are purposefully contrasted with his thick, sinewy arm. An imaginary horizontal extending from Salome's knotted belt to the headsman's knife further unites the protagonists. Caravaggio daringly pushed this main group off-centre, directing dramatic focus along the middle vertical axis of the composition where the dying saint's head is pinned down at the bottom by the full weight of the hand, left arm, head, back and right bent elbow of the executioner. Continuing the axis and the oppressive load above the saint are the massive stone quoins of the archway.

Avoiding conventional symmetry, Caravaggio none the less devised a visual balance whereby the main figural group fills the lower left quadrant, and the window barring the pair of prisoners occupies the upper right quadrant. The two men strain to look towards what is happening, thereby leading the viewer's attention back to the centre. Suspended at right in front of the window is a thick, doubled rope that loops away through a metal ring attached to the wall beneath and then snakes back towards the saint's foot; now lying uselessly on the ground, the rope must have served, Caravaggio forces us to imagine, to tie John in an earlier moment.

As was his usual practice, Caravaggio lit the work with a shaft of light falling from the upper left of the composition on to the main event. Moreover, he calibrated colour with the lighting to reinforce the visual climax. Colour intensifies from the brown of the exposed ground of the canvas, through the black-clad women to a crescendo in the startling blue of the warden's gold-trimmed cape and the burning red of the saint's mantle, and then diminishes to the same dull browns at right. Masterful and new in the *Beheading* is the close interdependence of figural design, light, colour and background setting that makes the work Caravaggio's most classicizing composition.

Classical too are the reduced number of the participants and the restraint. The prison warden, with his ominous keys a sign of his office, impassively orders the job to be finished off. Other than tensing his muscles as he bends to comply, the executioner proceeds with professional detachment. Salome extends the platter with no more expression than if she were expecting it to be filled with fruit or vegetables. The old lady alone reacts emotionally; her whole body appears to shudder as she hunches her shoulders and presses her raised hands to her cheeks. She represents a type – grey-haired, face lined with age, humbly dressed – that Caravaggio conceived beginning with the second version of the *Supper at Emmaus* (Pl. 130). Her compassionate presence at wondrous or tragic events, which she is powerless to change, serves as an affective touchstone for the viewer. Her horror in this instance disrupts the eerie stillness of the scene in which violence is matter-of-fact, and no one but she protests when a man is butchered in cold blood.

For Caravaggio's fellow novices who viewed the *Beheading* hanging directly above the original altar, the sight of the saint's blood seemingly spilling on to the tabernacle of the host below presented a lesson about the religious significance of martyrdom, especially pertinent to their vocation as Christian knights. The martyred John's death at once prefigured that of Christ and of all who were ready to die for the faith. Caravaggio made explicit the symbolic association of the Baptist with Christ by laying John on top of a conspicuous lamb's skin with its two feet oriented towards the exact centre of the composition. His audience would have easily recognized the reference in John to the sacrificial lamb, slaughtered above the altar.[43]

The representation of the novices' martyred patron saint also dramatized the mission of their Order. Those knights who had died as 'martyrs' to the Turks in the Great Siege now lay buried in the cemetery under the Oratory. During that battle, as throughout their history, the cry 'Saint John, Saint John' led the knights' charge. In the recently constructed crypt of the Oratory, all newly deceased knights were entombed. The young novices studied and prayed, then, over the very bones of their forebears and beneath Caravaggio's image of their saintly model.[44]

The altarpiece imparted one additional sacred lesson to the novices. The Baptist's blood, prefiguring Christ's, evoked the eucharistic wine that promised remission of sins. Patristic writings also held that water as well as blood had poured from the wound in the side of the crucified Christ and, whereas the blood sanctified martyrdom, the water symbolized baptism. Caravaggio had already alluded to this connection between baptism and a martyr's death in his *Martyrdom of Saint Matthew* in which Matthew's blood flows into the baptismal pool below the altar. This symbolism is all the more potent in the Malta altarpiece, commemorating John who had baptized Christ. That the blood had sacramental, and not simply narrative, connotations is implied by its gathering in a pool under the saint's head, leaving the executioner's blade strangely clean. For the aspirant knights about to embark upon a new life in the Order of Saint John, the blood signalled spiritual rebirth.[45]

For the first and only instance in his career, Caravaggio proclaimed his own pride in the *Beheading* by affixing his signature (Pl. 153). At a time when painters seldom signed their works, the presence of a signature can commemorate a specific circumstance in the painter's life or

**153 Beheading of Saint John the Baptist** (Pl. 151), detail of artist's signature

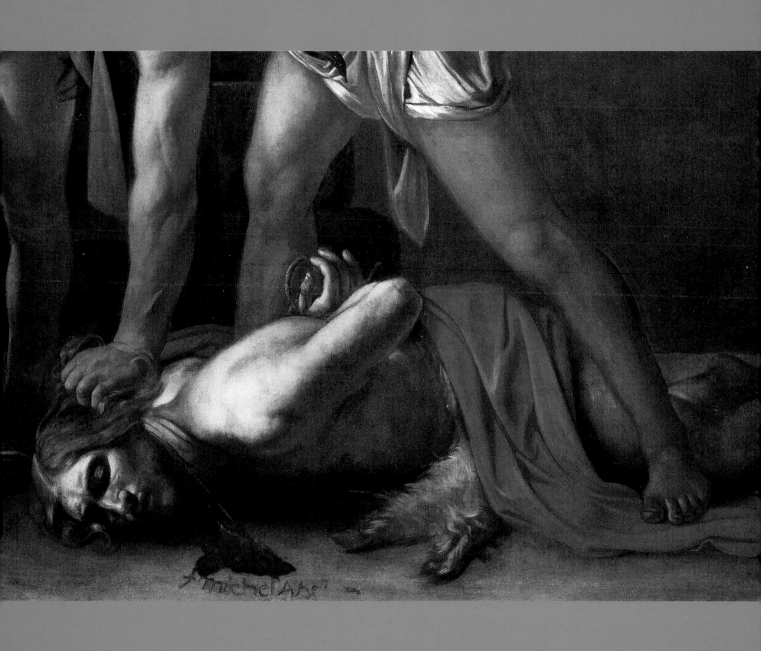

during a commission. The 'F.' which Caravaggio placed before his name stands for 'Fra' or brother; he thus used the occasion to mark the fulfilment of his novitiate and his new knightly rank. But if he had wanted to make only those points, he might have painted his signature in one of the customary places: a corner of the canvas or some other unobtrusive spot. That he intended it to have further meaning is hard to escape, for he chose a highly idiosyncratic place in which to sign his name: in the saint's blood.

Caravaggio's macabre choice has provoked various interpretations among modern viewers, foremost among them psychoanalytical. The nature of the signature would then betray Caravaggio's state of mind following Tomassoni's murder: bordering on the pathological, suffering from a Cain complex, and harbouring a death wish.[46] Although a stimulating exercise, attempts to psychoanalyse a person who lived almost four hundred years ago in a pre-Freudian age present obvious drawbacks. What chills our sensibilities today may have elicited a different response from viewers then, accustomed as they were to public executions and the spectacle of malefactors' heads displayed at the city gates or on the façade of the city prison.

Pictorial tradition and contextual evidence offer the most persuasive interpretation of Caravaggio's unusual signature: a penitential attitude and a desire for expiating his crime. Caravaggio would probably have been familiar with two famous and accessible Lombard works which set artistic precedents for the motif of writing a message with a martyr's blood: Vincenzo Foppa's fresco of the *Martyrdom of Saint Peter Martyr* (Pl. 154), and Moretto's canvas of the same subject (Pinacoteca Ambrosiana, Milan, *c.*1530–5). Both painters had illustrated a saintly legend in which the fatally wounded Peter wrote 'credo in unum deum' ('I believe in one God') in his own blood.

In replacing the dying martyr's prayer with his own name, Caravaggio transposed the motif and, in so doing, altered its meaning. What in the earlier paintings had been a pious affirmation of faith can be construed as the painter's personal statement of faith and salvation. For the commingling of Caravaggio's signature and John's blood must be considered in the religious context of those very associations, explained above, that linked the saint's beheading with the eucharist and baptism. The prefixing of 'Fra' to his baptismal name 'Michelangelo' suggests that Caravaggio saw his own reception into the Order of Saint John as a symbolic baptism; the blood of the Order's patron saint would wash away his mortal sin of murder and furthermore offer the possiblity of spiritual rebirth and a new beginning, with the hope of repatriation.[47]

307

This private expression of atonement also had its public face; for the Grand Master and his Council not only countenanced the singular signature by accepting the *Beheading* but would have interpreted its inclusion in the work as an open act of expiation by their newest member, a known and convicted killer. For his part, Caravaggio the novice addressed a message of religious renewal to his fellow novices. A condemned criminal, he expressed repentance to the members of the Confraternity of Misericordia who also worshipped in the Oratory and whose sacred charge, as he well knew, would have made them members of the cortège accompanying him to his execution. Hope of a papal pardon no doubt preoccupied the painter throughout his Maltese sojourn, and his thoughts must have turned to Rome on 29 August 1609, the Baptist's feast day, when annually the local Confraternity of Misericordia freed one condemned prisoner and carried the happy soul with pomp and circumstance through the city.[48]

The *Beheading of Saint John the Baptist* can rightly claim to be the climactic work of Caravaggio's career. In praising the painter for having 'used all the force of his brush' Bellori acknowledged Caravaggio's own personal and professional stake in the work. Despite its rapid

**154** Vincenzo Foppa, **Martyrdom of Saint Peter Martyr**, 1466–8; fresco, Sant'Eustorgio, Milan

execution, evident from the areas in which he left the ground exposed, the altarpiece looks anything but hurried. The rigorous composition must have demanded careful planning, and technical analysis confirms that only two minor changes were made.[49] Caravaggio's inspired and compelling interpretation of the theme was not new to his art, but in describing the appalling reality of murder while investing it with tragic solemnity he succeeded here in wedding his naturalism to a grandiose conception. His signature, with its amalgam of pride, piety and penance, lends autobiographical poignancy to the Malta altarpiece, marking the moment of brightest optimism in Caravaggio's exile when social and professional rehabilitation seemed within reach.

Caravaggio's knighthood lasted all of four and a half months. Some time before 6 October 1608, the Order had him thrown into the dungeon of the Fort St Angelo, a fortress on a promontory across the grand harbour from Valletta. What crime merited this punishment was not recorded; Baglione and Bellori later claimed that he had insulted a noble knight. If Caravaggio had duelled with another knight, this would in fact have constituted a serious violation of the Order's rules, punishable in other contemporary instances by excommunication and imprisonment.[50]

By 6 October Caravaggio had already escaped from prison, and a criminal commission was set up to trace his whereabouts, conduct an investigation into his escape, and submit a report. The commission presented its findings to the Grand Master and his Council at the end of November. Condemning Caravaggio's gaolbreak and his illegal departure from the island without Wignacourt's permission, the Council

**155 Defrocking of a Knight of Malta**, 1650;  engraving from Christian von Osterhausen, 12.7 × 7.5 cm, *Eigentlicher und gründlicher Bericht …*, Augsburg, 1650

called a public assembly for the purpose of depriving him of his habit. This body of high officials and knights of the Order duly convened on 1 December 1608 and, after verifying that the accused had failed to appear before the Council although summoned four times, voted unanimously to have him 'expelled and thrust forth like a rotten and fetid limb'. The actual defrocking of a knight, which from the start of the seventeenth century customarily took place in the Oratory of St John under the *Beheading*, is recorded in a print from mid-century (Pl. 155). In Caravaggio's case, a symbolic ceremony was enacted in which the Maltese habit was ripped off an empty chair. Whatever had been his original offence, his unsanctioned departure from Malta officially justified the expulsion.[51]

The criminal inquiry established only that Caravaggio had escaped from the dungeon 'by means of ropes'. Either the commission had not discovered or was not inclined to say who had unlocked his cell, provided the ropes, and had a getaway boat waiting below the bastions of the massive fortress. Quick and unimpeded, Caravaggio's flight must have been orchestrated by powerful allies. Perhaps not coincidentally, the Procurator of Prisons at the time was one Giovanni Girolamo Carafa, presumably a relative of the Neapolitan family which had protected Caravaggio in the past. As the painter fled to nearby Sicily and lived for as long as a year in its major cities

which maintained close contacts with Malta, he could easily have been apprehended by the Order's agents. Instead, unpursued, he seems to have enjoyed the continued protection of highly placed friends with the possible tacit consent of the Grand Master himself. Caravaggio later sent a peace-offering to Wignacourt in the form of a painting appropriately depicting *Salome with the Head of Saint John the Baptist*; the present may have simply been a vain ploy for reconciliation but the painter might just as likely have had reason to think that reinstatement in the Order was possible.[52]

By the date of his expulsion from the Knights of Malta, Caravaggio had been in Syracuse for almost two months. Despite his dangerous personal predicament, he still possessed remarkable artistic resources and had already inaugurated a series of altarpieces, his last major works.

Chapter 7    **Final Years**

Caravaggio divided the last two years of his life between Sicily, where he stayed for about a year from early October 1608 until the following autumn, and Naples, his home for the second time until his death in the summer of 1610. His Maltese transgression, imprisonment, flight and expulsion from the Order of Saint John had shattered the year-long reprieve from judicial pursuit and raised a fresh threat to his physical safety which hounded him for the remainder of his exile. Nervous and restless, he changed cities in Sicily twice within a year before departing for Naples. Nevertheless, he threw himself into work, and in contrast to his almost leisurely professional schedule in Valletta, he quickened his pace and fulfilled numerous requests for large-scale and cabinet pictures. Astonishing productivity and a final burst of creative vitality characterize this closing phase of activity.

In Sicily, Caravaggio painted four major ecclesiastical works: the haunting *Burial of Saint Lucy* (Pl. 160) and *Raising of Lazarus* (Pl. 162), and the tender *Nativity with Saints Lawrence and Francis* (Pl. 167) and *Adoration of the Shepherds* (Pl. 165). The prestige, visibility and generous fees of these public commissions – two of which came from the local governments of Syracuse and Messina, each earning him 1,000 scudi – attest to his welcome on the island as a famous artist regardless of his fugitive status. His four public paintings decorated high altars, two in the island's most prosperous city of Messina and one in the viceregal capital of Palermo.

Despite his professional success, Caravaggio had reason to worry about the precariousness of his position now that the Maltese débâcle had effectively destroyed any hope of an imminent papal pardon. Given the close proximity of Sicily to Malta and the many ties linking the two islands, his whereabouts could not have remained a secret from the Order of Saint John. The Knights made no effort, however, to detain him nor, so far as is known, did they issue an arrest warrant. After 1 December 1608, the date of the decree of expulsion, the news might have easily been carried to Sicily by the Order's galleys. Yet even Caravaggio's patron Giovanni Battista de' Lazzari, who had commercial dealings with the Knights, honoured his contract and accepted the knightly honorific in the consignment note of the altarpiece.[1]

For his part, Caravaggio continued to style himself a knight and to receive major commissions. But if the Grand Master and his council turned a blind eye to Caravaggio's presence in Sicily, why did he move fearfully from place to place – as Bellori and his Sicilian biographer Francesco Susinno describe – going to bed fully dressed and armed with a dagger? Granting some credence to these early reports, we can only guess he was menaced by some other enemy, possibly as a result of his wrongdoing in Malta. That he was the target of a personal vendetta rather than threatened by official sanctions is supported by subsequent events in Naples. His mental state in Sicily must therefore have been strained, approaching, if not exceeding as Susinno imagined, the turbulence of the rough Straits of Messina. The length of his stay and the prestige of his commissions, however, suggest that the painter's Sicilian hosts and patrons offered him a relatively secure haven as he reconstructed his professional and personal life.

In escaping to Sicily, Caravaggio once again took refuge in Spanish territory, removing himself from both Maltese and papal jurisdiction. After the regimented and circumscribed life he had led in Valletta, Sicily offered him a very different political, economic, spiritual and cultural prospect.[2] At the time of Caravaggio's arrival in 1608, the Spanish Marchese de Vilhena had recently begun his three-year term as viceroy (1607–10) under King Philip III (1598–1621). Vilhena lived in the capital, Palermo, but was obliged to move his court for half the year to Messina, which had enjoyed this royal privilege since the end of the sixteenth century. The two major cities regularly clashed over such issues of precedence: Palermo, the larger city, was the opulent seat of Spanish power, while Messina boasted a more thriving mercantile trade. Dominating this maritime commerce was a large community of Genoese merchants, like Caravaggio's patron Lazzari, although many Genoese also made their homes in Palermo. The aristocratic capital tended to be more culturally conservative than its commercial sister where the Senate displayed an enlightened attitude toward official art patronage, forming its own gallery and financing artists' study abroad. The relative political and economic insignificance of Syracuse, Caravaggio's first port of entry, may partly explain the brevity of his stay there and his decision to move on to Messina.

Although freed from the religious regimen of the Order of Saint John, Caravaggio could not have evaded the pervasive impact of ecclesiastical reform and spiritual renewal in post-Tridentine Sicily, especially since all his paintings were religious in theme and his four altarpieces were intended for public settings. The spread of the Catholic reform movement in Sicily nurtured the expansion of the religious orders, in particular the Jesuits and Franciscans who, respectively, dedicated themselves to the education and material welfare of Sicilians. Care of the ill was the specific vocation of the Order of Ministers of the Sick, for whose church Caravaggio painted the *Raising of Lazarus*; these fathers were newcomers to Sicily, sent there in 1599 by the Order's founder Saint Camillus of Lellis (1559–1614). Intense popular piety also made a practical contribution to social needs in this period, finding formal expression in the burgeoning number of lay associations that tendered public assistance to the urban poor in Palermo. Burial of the indigent was the primary responsibility of one such group, the Company of Saint Francis which commissioned Caravaggio's *Nativity*.[3]

Two of Caravaggio's Sicilian altarpieces and supposedly one devotional image were intended for Franciscan establishments. Recent studies have emphasized the importance of this mendicant Order in Sicily and speculated about the significance of its ideals for Caravaggio. In Palermo the various branches of Franciscan friars enjoyed particular favour under Viceroy Vilhena, and in Messina the reigning archbishop, the Franciscan Fra Bonaventura Secusio (1605–9), likewise enhanced the role of the friars during his tenure. In the mid-sixteenth century the Capuchins had already been granted a prime site on the outskirts of Messina for their church and monastery of S. Maria la Concezione. The magnanimous sum which the Senate expended on Caravaggio's *Adoration of the Shepherds* for the Capuchins' high altarpiece is evidence of the prestige this Order continued to enjoy in the city.

A specifically Franciscan iconography may have guided the choice of subjects for the *Adoration* and the *Nativity*. In both works celebrating Mary's bearing of Christ, a favourite Franciscan theme, Caravaggio evoked the friars' ideals of humility and poverty by representing the Virgin seated on the ground, and in the *Nativity* by laying the divine baby directly on to the bare earth. Although the evidence is too slight to determine whether the Order itself oversaw the content of either painting, Caravaggio's interpretation of the subject-matter accords well enough with Franciscan spirituality to suggest a conscious sensitivity on his part. The presence of these two altarpieces in churches controlled by, or affiliated with the Franciscan Order may turn out to be no more than coincidental, yet in Sicily, as in Rome, Caravaggio did not get any commissions from the Jesuits; his paintings were instead intended for the religious Order most associated with a social mission to the poor.[4]

Caravaggio encountered a much richer artistic heritage in Sicily than in Malta, and particular visual details in his Sicilian paintings indicate that during his chance sojourn he drew inspiration from the island's noteworthy features. While in Syracuse he visited the imposing Greek ruins in the company of the antiquarian Vincenzo Mirabella, who credited him with dubbing one of the oddly-shaped caves in the limestone quarries the 'Ear of Dionysus' after the city's ancient tyrant. Mirabella may have shown him as well the Early Christian catacombs which also figure prominently in his later guidebook. The quarries, with their awesome natural and man-made formations, and the catacombs with their labyrinthine corridors and chambers, might well have fired Caravaggio's pictorial imagination, for the backgrounds he introduced into the *Burial of Saint Lucy* and the *Raising of Lazarus* seem to echo the soaring, shadowed recesses of the one and the subterranean, vaulted alcoves of the other.[5]

Surely Caravaggio also took note of early Renaissance masterpieces by the one great native painter, Antonello da Messina (*c.*1430–79), and by the Dalmatian sculptor Francesco Laurana (*c.*1430–1502?). That he travelled beyond the limits of Syracuse, Messina and Palermo is probable; a seventeenth-century tradition in Caltagirone, to the west above Catania, holds that he praised a Madonna in one of its churches.[6]

Unfortunately Caravaggio's comments went unrecorded concerning a much greater work in a church in Palermo from at least the 1530s: Raphael's *Way to Calvary*, the so-called *Spasimo di Sicilia* (Pl. 157), whose fame, Vasari claimed, outstripped that of Mount Etna. But his positive reaction to this grand and dramatic work is suggested by the seeming relationship between the two sisters and the open-mouthed bystander in the *Raising of Lazarus* (Pl. 162) and the grieving Mary and the screaming soldier in Raphael's composition. While in Messina

itself, Caravaggio must have been curious to see the paintings of his renowned compatriot, Polidoro da Caravaggio, who had made his way to Sicily after the Sack of Rome in 1527. Settling in the port until his murder in 1543, Polidoro produced many altarpieces in an anti-classical and expressive mode. While Caravaggio was working on the *Adoration of the Shepherds* (Pl. 165), the earnest and humbly dressed shepherds in Polidoro's altarpiece of the same subject in a local church (Pl. 156) presented a model that influenced his own conception; a short time later he referred even more closely to the same work for the appearance of his Madonna in the *Nativity* (Pl. 167) for Palermo: an attractive, unveiled woman, whose hair is gathered up on either side of her lowered face.[7]

Late sixteenth-century painting in Sicily, however, had little to offer Caravaggio. In the spiritual climate following the Council of Trent, numerous iconic and pious altarpieces were installed in the island's churches and, stylistically, Tuscan late Mannerism commanded a privileged position that persisted in the interior of the island even as late as 1630. The prolific native painter Antonio Catalano the Elder (1560–*c.*1605) had decorated many altars with conventional and orthodox religious works, sweetened by Barocci's soft colouring. When confronted by one of his altarpieces in Messina, Caravaggio supposedly dismissed it as no more consequential than playing cards.[8]

In the ranks of the all but forgotten provincial masters active upon Caravaggio's arrival two painters stood out: his friend Minniti, back

**156** Polidoro da Caravaggio, **Adoration of the Shepherds**, 1533; oil on wood, 257 × 200 cm, Museo Regionale, Messina

The *Burial of Saint Lucy* was probably finished before 6 December 1608, when Caravaggio seems to have already left Syracuse for Messina. There he contracted with Lazzari to paint the *Raising of Lazarus* for the high altar of the church of the Ministers of the Sick. Documents published at the beginning of this century, but soon destroyed in the earthquake at Messina of 1908, reveal that Lazzari had initially requested an altarpiece depicting 'the Madonna with Saint John and others'. A marginal note on the delivery notice of 10 June 1609 records the subsequent change in subject and names the painter as 'fra Michelangelo Caravaggio militis Gerosolimitanus'.[12]

If a vivid anecdote reported by Susinno has any grain of truth, Caravaggio possibly started by painting his patron's originally intended subject. According to Susinno, when the canvas was unveiled – presumably showing the 'Madonna with Saint John' – some flippant criticism provoked Caravaggio to draw his dagger and cut it to ribbons, whereupon he promised to produce another, more beautiful picture. This second work would have been, of course, the *Raising of Lazarus* (Pl. 162). Susinno's other claim was that Caravaggio himself lit on the Gospel story of Lazarus in reference to his patron's family name, preferring to illustrate this narrative with its sensational climax rather than a static, Marian devotional image.

Either while working on the *Raising of Lazarus*, or after completing it, Caravaggio began the *Adoration of the Shepherds* (Pl. 165). Susinno reported that the *Adoration* was commissioned for the Capuchin church by the city Senate. The painting remained *in situ* until the Napoleonic closing of ecclesiastical institutions at the end of the eighteenth century, despite repeated offers to buy it from private amateurs.[13]

Caravaggio also painted a few easel pictures for Messinese patrons including a lost cycle of Christ's Passion for a Nicolao di Giacomo. In early August 1609, Di Giacomo recorded he had commissioned four paintings of the Passion from Caravaggio, 'of which he has finished one, depicting Christ shouldering the cross, the sorrowful Virgin, and two soldiers, one of whom is sounding a trumpet'. Di Giacomo added that he expected the other three by the end of the month, as well as the bill from the painter, who, he observed, 'has a deeply disturbed mind' (*cervello stravolto*). While this curt character sketch sounds a familiar leitmotif, the passion cycle remains a mystery, and whether Caravaggio ever delivered the outstanding pictures is not known.[14]

If Caravaggio stayed in Messina during August 1609 to complete the Di Giacomo commission, he could have moved on to Palermo at the beginning of September before departing for Naples in mid-October. Whereas Susinno specifically explained that the artist was forced to leave there after his assault on a teacher, Bellori more generally attributed the move to Caravaggio's fear of arrest. While in Palermo,

**319**

**160 Burial of Saint Lucy**, 1608; oil on canvas, 408 × 300 cm, Museo di Palazzo Bellomo, Syracuse

Caravaggio painted the *Nativity with Saints Francis and Lawrence* (Pl. 167) for the Oratory of S. Lorenzo. The responsibility for the commission probably rested with the Company of Saint Francis because this lay group had recently initiated renovations in the Oratory, which had been under their control since 1569. Significantly, their patron saint, Francis, is paired with the traditional protector of the Oratory, Lawrence, in Caravaggio's altarpiece.[15]

The subject-matter of all four Sicilian altarpieces was new to Caravaggio and, as in the past, he rethought each theme, stimulated but unbound by artistic tradition. Three called for subjects familiar from the Gospels and frequently represented in art while the fourth, the *Burial of Saint Lucy*, featured a rare episode in the life of an often depicted Early Christian saint. Each painting tells its story simply and directly to convey the impact of momentous events on the lives of ordinary people.

The Senate's choice of subject for Caravaggio's *Burial of Saint Lucy* was influenced both by civic devotion and by the location of the Basilica of S. Lucia on the very spot of the saint's death and burial. The body of Lucy — Syracuse's most sacred relic — had been spirited away somewhere in northern Europe in the tenth or eleventh century, and by representing the saint's burial on their high altar over her original grave, the citizens of Syracuse not only proclaimed the sanctity of her Basilica but also reaffirmed the priority of the Syracusan cult of Lucy.

**161** Jacobello del Fiore, **Burial of Saint Lucy**, *c.*1410; tempera on wood, 70 × 52 cm, Pinacoteca Civica, Fermo

X-rays of the canvas reveal a *pentimento* in Lucy's neck; originally a deep gash severed her head from her body but Caravaggio painted this over to show a small wound instead. Whereas Caravaggio's first idea subscribed to the account in an early Greek manuscript, recently discovered by a Syracusan Jesuit, relating that Lucy was decapitated, his definitive version reverts to the authoritative Latin account that she was stabbed in the throat. After initial disagreement as to how the martyrdom should be described, in the end the local authorities must have instructed Caravaggio to uphold custom.[16]

In visualizing the saint's interment, Caravaggio had little in the way of artistic precedent to steer him. If he was not familiar with any of the rare earlier representations, such as Jacobello del Fiore's depiction in a narrative cycle on an early-fourteenth-century polyptych (Pl. 161), he could have remembered analogous scenes from pictorial cycles dedicated to other saints, such as, for example, Giulio Campi's *Burial of Saint Agatha* (S. Agata, Cremona, 1537). But his conception of a saint's burial departs radically from conventional illustrations. Wholly unprecedented is the visual prominence accorded the two gravediggers, whose hulking shapes loom over and frame Lucy's body. They go unmentioned in accounts of Lucy's martyrdom, which tell succinctly how she finally died on the spot where she was stabbed after the bishop and deacons had administered communion in the presence of the populace. In the right foreground, a crozier, mitre, and blessing hand identify the bishop whose form is otherwise blocked from view by an armed Roman soldier raising his gauntlet as if to direct the diggers.

By pushing the representatives of Church and State to the sidelines, Caravaggio effectively eliminated any pomp and circumstance from the scene and instead focused attention on Lucy and her mourners, a knot of anonymous men and elderly women. At the centre of the composition, a young man cloaked in warm red and rising directly behind and above the corpse forms the only uninterrupted vertical in the composition. This man, sometimes called a deacon though he is not wearing vestments, contemplates the saint with meditative calm, suspending his folded hands protectively over her prone form. His lowered glance guides the viewer's attention to the body, which rests directly on the bare earth but will lie beneath it once the gravediggers have finished their work. His and the saint's youthfulness sets them apart from the old and middle-aged participants, and this distinction in age-groups is perhaps meant to stir the viewers' compassion in the face of untimely death. Lighting Lucy's face from below, Caravaggio filled the eye-sockets with pools of shadow, as if in reference to the legend that she had torn out her eyes and sent them to her pagan suitor; as they were miraculously restored and more beautiful than before, she became the patron saint of sight and, in art, often bears a plate with two eyes.

Lucy, humbly dressed in drab brown, is pointedly not laid to rest in a sarcophagus but is buried like any common poor person. This visual detail conforms to the legend recounting how she cast off her riches before her arrest and gave away her material goods to the poor. Apart from lending historical accuracy, the saint's embrace of poverty and charity relates Caravaggio's interpretation of the subject to the movement within the contemporary Church to renew itself by reaching back to the fundamental values of the early Christian community. His portrayal of Lucy's slight body seemingly dissolving into the dirt evokes, moreover, the central biblical passage on death: 'You are dust and to dust you shall return' (Genesis 3:19). A martyr's demise is meant, of course, to signify the soul's victory over bodily death, but missing from the scene are the very allusions – the palm or an angelic host – which customarily convey the redemptive promise of Christian burial. Relying on the ecclesiastical setting of the painting to supply that message, Caravaggio here dwelt on human bereavement before the abyss separating the living and the dead, as he had done earlier in the *Death of the Virgin*.

Christian resurrection is the subject of the *Raising of Lazarus*, taken from the Gospel of John (11:1–44). The Saviour and his disciples arrive in Bethany only to be met by Martha and Mary bearing news of the recent death of their brother and Christ's friend, Lazarus. Ordering the stone to be removed from the tomb, Jesus calls upon God as witness and commands Lazarus to come out.

The miracle of Lazarus, which attested to Christ's divinity and Christian salvation, was an obvious theme for funerary art from early Christian times. From the long pictorial tradition Caravaggio remembered in particular an easel painting by Giuseppe Cesari, his old employer in Rome (Pl. 21). Following Cesari's example, he depicted Lazarus nude and not bandaged and bound according to Jewish custom; he also imitated the pose of Lazarus stretching one hand towards Christ while rising at an oblique angle from a grave located beneath the floor, which reflected current burial practices.[17]

Cesari's work, however, only served as a point of departure for Caravaggio's own interpretation of the subject. Whereas Cesari stressed the reverential awe which the miracle elicited in the faces and gestures of the large crowd spread across a wide stage, Caravaggio concentrated on Lazarus himself whose right hand is fixed at the very centre of the composition. Distinctive, too, are Lazarus's acclamatory

**162 Raising of Lazarus**, 1608–9; oil on canvas, 380 × 275 cm, Museo Regionale, Messina gesture and the horizontal extension of his arms from his torso, suggestive of a cross: an allusion that would have been especially appreciated by the Ministers of the Sick, who wore a red cross emblazoned on their habits.[18]

Caravaggio's brilliant conceit carried yet deeper meaning. Because the raising of Lazarus encouraged alarming popular support for Christ, this miracle not only precipitated his arrest but set in motion the events leading up to his Crucifixion. Lazarus's death and rebirth thus directly foreshadowed Christ's sacrifice and the Resurrection, thereby embodying the Christian belief in the soul's immortality.

The distinguishing details in the portrayal of Christ, Lazarus and the sisters Martha and Mary suggest that Caravaggio thought hard about the symbolic content in this Gospel incident. He placed Christ in front of a door whose darkened opening may allude to the door of death, a motif from Early Christian funerary art. Light enters the scene from behind Jesus, however, striking his shoulder and grazing the wrist and the fingertips of his pointing hand. While one open-mouthed man stares at him, two others appear to look past him towards the light. The interplay of Christ, door and light calls to mind verses found elsewhere in John's Gospel: Christ as the door to salvation (10:9) and his God-appointed role to illuminate the world (6:28; 8:12).

Although Caravaggio showed Lazarus groping towards the light, he still remains suspended between the realms of life and death.[19] Stiff in *rigor mortis*, Lazarus's left hand has not shaken free of the grave, as is made explicit by the skull and bones below. Resting her cheek against Lazarus's (Pl. 163), Martha almost appears to breathe life into her brother. In perfect accord with the Gospel, Caravaggio implies that love and faith wrought the miracle, which in turn testifies that eternal life is the reward for those who believe.

**163 Raising of Lazarus** (Pl. 162), detail of heads of Lazarus and Martha

The ardent expressiveness of the *Raising of Lazarus* may well reflect Caravaggio's personal preoccupations at the time. To be sure, his choice of this subject over the patron's original request favours a narrative rather than a devotional image, but the story of Lazarus also embraces the themes of death and Christian salvation he examined in other contemporaneous works. Some have interpreted Lazarus's struggle against death's powerful grip as a metaphor for Caravaggio's despair of his own salvation.[20] But an equally viable alternative reading can be inferred from the visual evidence, for Caravaggio apparently included a self-portrait in the man whose face appears in profile above Christ's hand (Pl. 164). The short dark hair, low forehead, beard and moustache bear striking similarity to the figure who has been widely identified as Caravaggio in the earlier *Betrayal of Christ* (Pl. 117) and the later *Martyrdom of Saint Ursula* (Pl. 178). His face bathed in light, the man looks towards the Saviour. Caravaggio both oriented and aligned this head with Lazarus's awakening hand, as if to identify himself with Lazarus whose resurrection, however hard the contest, is never in doubt.

The closely related subjects of Caravaggio's last two Sicilian altarpieces, the *Adoration of the Shepherds* (Pl. 165) and the *Nativity With Saints Lawrence and Francis* (Pl. 167), derive from the well-known narrative of Christ's birth in the Gospel of Luke (2:7–16). Given the popularity of representations of events around the birth of Jesus, it is surprising that Caravaggio had never been asked to paint the theme before. In these works he conceived the Holy Family with comparable simplicity and intimacy to his youthful *Rest on the Flight into Egypt* (Pl. 59) but supplanted the lyricism of the former with the sombre mood prevalent in his art since his last years in Rome.

**164 Raising of Lazarus** (Pl. 162), detail of head of Christ and witnesses at left, showing self-portrait

On a first impression, the *Adoration of the Shepherds* and the *Nativity* appear to respect both the general outlines of Luke's Gospel and the rich artistic tradition. As in Cigoli's roughly contemporary altarpiece (Pl. 166), Caravaggio included the staple ingredients of stable, manger, hay, ox and ass, and even, in one of his two scenes, an angel brandishing a banderole inscribed with the words exalting Christ's birth, 'Gloria in excelsis Deo'. Yet he arranged these elements and conceived his individual figures in an utterly original way.

Instead of a reverential Madonna kneeling in adoration before her divine child, Caravaggio's Mary behaves like any ordinary new mother She hugs her baby in the altarpiece for Messina, while she gazes on him tenderly in the work for Palermo. In the latter scene, her bared shoulder and loosened chemise suggest that she is resting after having just nursed the baby; her semi-recumbent pose in Messina recalls the tradition of the Madonna del Parto, or Madonna of childbirth, and the placement of both Madonnas on the ground suggests images of the Madonna of Humility.[21] Caravaggio presented two distinct Marys, however: in Messina, veiled, haloed and traditionally robed, as opposed to her counterpart in Palermo, bareheaded with loosely pinned-up hair, without a halo and wearing contemporary dress. His two Josephs likewise belong to separate worlds; the one shown as an old man, haloed, barefooted and wrapped in a brown cloak, and the other as a younger man with a full head of hair, even though white, and muscular legs. Unlike the weary Joseph in Messina, the unhaloed Joseph of the Palermo canvas twists vigorously on his seat and is wearing modern hose and footwear. These divergent conceptions can perhaps be best explained by the fact that the Messina altarpiece was destined for a Capuchin monastery and the Palermo altarpiece for a lay Oratory. Caravaggio probably received specific instructions from each patron and himself took into account their respective audiences.

**165  Adoration of the Shepherds**, 1608–9;  oil on canvas, 314 × 211 cm, Museo Regionale, Messina

330

In the Messina altarpiece, following custom, Caravaggio portrayed the shepherds paying homage to the infant Christ. They have apparently left their sheep outside the stable and only a shepherd's crook, held by the partially clad man in the centre, identifies their occupation. The Palermo *Nativity* adds a devotional element to the Christmas story with the insertion of two later saints; this common, ahistorical conflation was not Caravaggio's invention but rather reflected his patrons' wishes. Saint Francis assumes a reverential attitude behind the Madonna's shoulder, while Lawrence, patron saint of the Oratory, occupies a conspicuous position in the left foreground. The yellow satin of his deacon's vestment shimmers softly in the penumbra with its magnificent tassel dangling in space, a striking reminder of Caravaggio's powers of naturalistic painting. The artist completed his translation of the miraculous event into a vernacular idiom by showing Joseph unexpectedly turning away from the scene to speak to an old man, presumably to announce the birth of his son.

Pervasive in both altarpieces is Caravaggio's seeming determination to ground the event in reality even at the expense of disregarding the universal jubilation at the Messiah's coming, so intrinsic to Luke's account. Cigoli's representation and other contemporary versions picture music-making hosts on high, and smiling, awestruck humans on earth. Painters further imagined shepherds bringing simple presents to celebrate new life. Finally, the infant Christ is typically portrayed as divine, most often by the celestial light emanating from his body.

Caravaggio's view of the Saviour's birth clashes with these pictorial conventions. His omission of angels in the Messina canvas and the inclusion of a single one in the Palermo altarpiece instead recall the sobriety of sixteenth-century North Italian depictions by artists such as Jacopo Bassano (Pl. 18) or Savoldo (Civica Pinacoteca, Brescia, 1540). But his spare interpretation goes well beyond these precedents. Having earlier demonstrated his expertise in painting musicians, Caravaggio now preferred to banish music altogether from the gatherings. A master at describing expressive extremes, he here restrained any display of emotion even to the extent of denying the animals in the Messina canvas a sentient response to the miraculous happening in their stable. He also dispensed with anecdotal embellishment, letting

the shepherds come to pay their respects empty-handed. Unlike the grieving and excited throngs in the *Burial of Saint Lucy* and the *Raising of Lazarus*, the few people present in the *Adoration of the Shepherds* and the *Nativity* almost efface themselves in order not to disturb the tender intimacy of mother and baby. Nothing intrinsic in this baby signals divinity; without a halo or celestial radiance on its body, it looks much like any newborn child. By emphasizing Christ's human incarnation, Caravaggio perhaps intended the oppressively sombre mood to remind the devout viewer of the future Passion. The singularity of these two *Nativities* also invites reference to Caravaggio's personal tragedy. Pessimism at his protracted exile might have inhibited his willingness or ability to communicate joy. His melancholic versions of Christ's birth would then reflect an essentially bleak attitude towards human existence.

The Sicilian altarpieces reflect Caravaggio's new formal concerns. In the great Maltese *Beheading of Saint John the Baptist* (Pl. 151), he had begun to devise compositions and handle space, lighting and the human figure differently from his Roman altarpieces. In the design of the *Beheading*, which he completed only two months at most before starting work on the *Burial of Saint Lucy*, he had aligned the principal figures in a plane set slightly back from the front edge of the picture and placed them within a measurable architectural space. This general schema also applies to three of the Sicilian altarpieces, the *Burial of Saint Lucy*, *Raising of Lazarus*, and *Adoration of the Shepherds*, all of which are characterized by an unaccustomed interdependence of figures and space. Whereas in works such as the *Martyrdom of Saint Matthew* (Pl. 76) Caravaggio allowed the figures to generate just as much room as necessary in which to move, here the ambient space has swelled and assumes an active role in determining their size and placement.

333

As for backgrounds, Caravaggio not only conceived settings separately but also described them, varying the degree of definition from one work to another. He constructed his most complete space for the *Adoration of the Shepherds*, for which he designed an interior with a ceiling and floor, a back and side wall. In both the *Burial of Saint Lucy* and the *Raising of Lazarus*, an expanse of darkness looms over the figures, leaving the upper half of the canvas empty. These two settings evoke, rather than precisely delineate, caverns. An early copy of the *Burial* reveals that Caravaggio had delimited the now-darkened background with a double-arched opening and a door which he articulated by stone mouldings and metal studs.[22] Similarly in the *Raising*, a grand portal opens at the left behind Christ, and the presence of mouldings, no longer visible, can be ascertained from infrared reflectography. In both works, the half-open doors imply that space extends beyond the visible boundaries of the scene, unlike the narrow stages sealed off by neutral backdrops or walls in the pictures of Caravaggio's Roman period.

Previously, the artist had brought his models to the brink of the foreground, often seeming to breach the picture plane with dramatic foreshortenings, but now he had his figures take a step backward and turned them parallel to the picture plane. For example, Christ in the *Raising of Lazarus* is shown strictly in profile in contrast to his representation in the earlier *Calling of Saint Matthew* (Pl. 82), where he appears to be striding out of the canvas directly towards the spectator even though his head and pointing arm are in profile. As in the Roman paintings, the figural groupings are tightly framed at the bottom and sides and, above, by the darkness seemingly pressing down on them. Intersecting vertical and horizontal axes anchor the central pair of Lucy and mourner in the *Burial of Saint Lucy* while, in the *Adoration of the Shepherds*, a steep diagonal dividing the canvas from upper right to lower left guides the placement of the figures. Caravaggio had always structured his compositions carefully but in the Sicilian works, as in the *Seven Works of Mercy* in Naples or the *Beheading of Saint John* in Malta, geometry not only determines the disposition of figures but controls their integration into the expanded setting. In the *Burial of Saint Lucy*, Caravaggio suggested an unexpectedly deep as well as lofty space by the disproportion in scale between the mourners grieving over Lucy's body in the background and the over-life-size gravediggers, bishop and soldier occupying the foreground.

Rejecting the stark contrast of dark and light he first employed in the Contarelli Chapel, Caravaggio introduced a modified system of lighting in his Sicilian altarpieces. Because of their poor condition and a general tendency for dark pigments to darken with time, these works convey a mistaken impression, reinforced by photographs taken before recent restoration efforts, of being very sombre and monochromatic.[23] At first hand, a surprising range of colour is still visible in all but the *Burial of Saint Lucy*, whose rapid execution perhaps precluded other than a limited palette of browns with one central accent of red on the young man's mantle. In the three other altarpieces, Caravaggio also reserved saturated reds to isolate a principal figure against the earthen tones of the background – Christ in the *Raising*, and the Madonna in the two Nativity scenes – while blues, greens, yellows, and orange imbue the clothing of the main supporting figures, distinguishing them from the drab crowd. Despite this unexpected chromatic variety, Caravaggio toned down individual hues by veiling them with brownish glazes. Conversely, he repeated white across each canvas in accessories and swaths of drapery, especially next to bare skin, so that it brightens as well as unifies the composition.

Directed light illumines the scene from an invisible source outside the composition, but Caravaggio dispensed with an explicit wedge and instead touched faces and hands with a dim glow that even reaches to the background, thus accounting for the greater visibility of the settings. In the *Raising*, the light atypically enters from the side, behind Christ's back, and not from above. None the less, Caravaggio affirmed its divine origin and miraculous power by denying any light source from the conspicuously open door. Although he still endowed light with a symbolic role, he manipulated it with greater pictorial subtlety. The attenuated contrast of light and dark also flattens the relief-life projection of forms and, together with the cursory handling, in this painting Caravaggio moved away from his earlier fully modelled and convincingly rendered surfaces. Moreover, he applied short, loaded brushstrokes of white or lightened pigment to the exposed ground to suggest forms materializing from the shadows: for example in the few, summary dashes delineating Saint Lucy's features or the myriad touches spreading a web across Lazarus's body. By diminishing the sculptural force of individual forms and containing them within the picture plane, he acknowledged the traditional physical gulf between fictive and real space. Yet, at the same time, the new integration of figures and the ambient space from which they seem mysteriously to emerge invests the overall scene with perhaps greater pictorial realism than in his earlier works.

Emerging, phantom-like at times, from their shadowy amplified settings, the actors in the Sicilian pictures take the stage less as soloists than as ensemble players. For his protagonists, Caravaggio probably worked from life, as is suggested by both the individualization of faces and the presence of incisions – recorded in the *Raising of Lazarus* and the *Adoration of the Shepherds* – to transfer contours from the models to the canvas. The impression his life painting made on his Sicilian contemporaries still resonated over a century later in a macabre anecdote related by Susinno: having disinterred a cadaver to use as a model for Lazarus, the obsessed Caravaggio threatened his assistants at knifepoint to make them support the stinking corpse.[24]

The models for other, supporting figures in his Sicilian cast seem to have posed for earlier paintings by Caravaggio. The *Burial of Saint Lucy* provides the best examples: the old lady kneeling next to the saint's body and the male mourner pressing a handkerchief to his cheek closely resemble characters in the *Beheading of Saint John* (Pl. 151). As for Lucy, Caravaggio barely described her face but repeated its tilted position from two Roman works: *Death of the Virgin* (Pl. 98) and *Magdalen in Ecstasy* (Pl. 132). A seeming assortment of imagined faces and live models also characterizes the *Raising of Lazarus*, wherein generalized types – Christ and the veiled sister of Lazarus – stand next to individualized ones – the witnesses and workmen. Yet even among the latter group, the man appearing directly in front of Christ's pointing finger looks familiar from the two earlier Neapolitan paintings of the *Flagellation* (Pls. 137, 138); his physical traits by now belonged to the painter's visual baggage. Conversely, the Messinese woman portraying Lazarus's other sister, Mary Magdalen, is

336

**168** Mario Minniti, **Miracle of the Widow of Naim**, *c.*1625; oil on canvas, 205 × 330 cm, Museo Regionale, Messina

recognizable as the Madonna in the Palermitan *Nativity* and as the heroine in the *Martyrdom of Saint Ursula* (Pl. 178), painted during Caravaggio's return visit to Naples.[25]

To reinforce the dramatic unity of his late work, Caravaggio repeated several salient gestures from previous paintings instead of inventing new, individualized ones. The old lady in the *Burial of Saint Lucy* clutches her head in the same way as the witness in the *Beheading of Saint John*. But what earlier registered as horror at violence here conveys anguish because the woman's action is not viewed in isolation but as one more note in a dirge also sounded by a veiled woman resting her bowed head on clasped hands and the man lifting a handkerchief to his eyes. In contrast to Caravaggio's multifigured Roman compositions, a unified ensemble subsumes assertive, independent personalities. He was less concerned, it would seem, with cataloging multiple reactions to a momentous event, as in the *Martyrdom of Saint Matthew* or the *Death of the Virgin*, than to evoke a few, basic human emotions – grief, wonder, faith – in the face of the universal cycle of birth and death.

The success of the Sicilian altarpieces earned Caravaggio acclaim from local critics and painters. All but the *Adoration of the Shepherds* were copied, and prints of the *Adoration* and of the *Burial of Saint Lucy* illustrated guidebooks to Messina and Syracuse. And such was the esteem in which the *Raising of Lazarus* was held that the painter charged with its restoration in the late seventeenth century was alleged to have died from depression over his disastrous attempts at cleaning the canvas.[26] Despite this high regard, geographic rather than qualitative factors restricted the historical significance of these works to Sicily and they never became as well known as Caravaggio's canvases executed on the mainland. However, the old view that Caravaggio's sojourn on the island had only slight and fleeting importance for Sicilian art needs revision in the light of recent research.[27]

Caravaggio's monumental altarpieces and his presence in Sicily's major artistic centres had an immediate impact on resident painters, such as the established artists Minniti and Paladini. Minniti adopted Caravaggesque motifs and stylistic features in his late works produced in Syracuse and also in Messina, where he stayed far longer than Caravaggio. For example, his *Miracle of the Widow of Naim* (Pl. 168), painted *c*.1625 for the same church as Caravaggio's *Adoration of the Shepherds*, displays the hallmark features of Caravaggio's style; strong light gives relief to contemporary-looking figures, who gesture emphatically. Minniti's own artistic identity reveals itself in the slender figural proportions, his soft lighting that smooths and rounds forms, and the landscape background. Paladini, for his part, later grafted Caravaggesque elements on to a Mannerist style, regenerating his art by introducing live models and a strongly contrasting lighting, as seen in the *Beheading of Saint John the Baptist* (S. Jacopo in Campo Corbolini, Florence, 1608), and the *Stigmatization of Saint Francis of Assisi* (Museo Regionale, Messina, *c.*1610).[28]

A third painter, the Messinese Alonso Rodriguez (1578–1648), who was Minniti's contemporary, also closely imitated Caravaggio, although he may never have met him in person. Rodriguez's few documented works, such as the *Meeting of Saints Peter and Paul* (Pl. 169), display a keener understanding of the emotional intensity of Caravaggio's late paintings than Minniti's or Paladini's.[29]

The early response of these painters to Caravaggio helped to nurture a taste for Caravaggism, creating a favourable, even enthusiastic, climate for its reception among both public and private patrons, especially in Palermo and Messina. Though other stylistic trends were also introduced in Sicily during the first half of the seventeenth century, notably by Anthony Van Dyck's visit to Palermo in 1624, Caravaggism flourished there as a major cultural phenomenon longer than in Rome. Active in Palermo and Messina from the 1630s to 1650s, a second generation of Caravaggisti who came of age after the master's death painted predominantly in his naturalistic language, though alternatively coarsening or refining it: the Sicilian painter Pietro Novelli (1603–47), and two Flemish visitors Mattias Stomer (*c.*1600–50) and Jan van Houbracken (*c.*1600–65). The most eminent Sicilian collector at mid-century, Don Antonio Ruffo of Messina, sought out naturalistic works by contemporary South Italian painters including Mattia Preti, but also by northerners, like Guercino, and surprisingly, Rembrandt; his request to Guercino in 1660 for a painting in his early, forceful manner attests to a taste influenced by the ever-vigorous current of Caravaggism.[30]

Exactly a year after he had disembarked in Sicily, Caravaggio sailed for Naples, arriving there before the end of October 1609. Reportedly pursued by some unnamed enemy or enemies, he had fled Sicily to wait out the negotiations for his pardon closer to Rome. If eluding pursuit, he may have sought the relative safety of Naples because here he could call on former protectors and lose himself amidst the teeming population. His plans went terribly awry, however, and a harsh welcome awaited him. At a tavern in the port assailants attacked him, injuring him so seriously that news of his alleged death reached Rome on 24 October. His face was slashed and scarred beyond recognition.[31]

The armed thugs may have been discharging the vendetta of whomever Caravaggio had offended in Malta a year earlier. Although the lapse of a year between the Maltese incident and the eventual settling of the score is puzzling, a simple explanation may be that his knightly enemy had been occupied elsewhere in the intervening months. After the attack, Caravaggio stayed on in Naples for the

**169** Alonso Rodriguez, **Meeting of Saints Peter and Paul**, *c.*1609–10;  oil on canvas, 261 × 191 cm, Museo Regionale, Messina
Overleaf  **170  Salome with the Head of Saint John the Baptist**, *c.*1609–10;  oil on canvas, 116 × 140 cm, Palacio Reale, Madrid

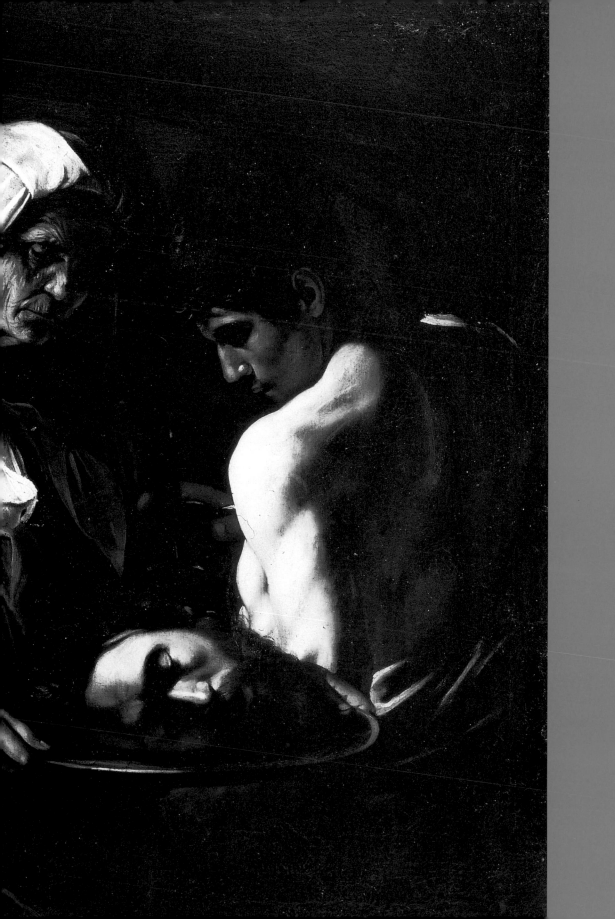

final nine months of his life; depending upon the length of his convalescence, he had some seven or eight months left in which to paint.[32]

When he finally set out for his final trip to Rome, Caravaggio was living at the home in Chiaia of none other than his lifelong protector Costanza Sforza-Colonna, the Marchesa di Caravaggio. It so happened that she was in residence at the time, taking care of family business. Whether Caravaggio spent all nine months in Chiaia is not known, but it is tempting to believe he did; this seaside resort, a fashionable suburb of Naples, enjoyed the reputation of a place for anyone seeking 'to recover from some indisposition', and who 'in a brief time ... becomes almost resuscitated from death to life'. An address with the influential Sforza-Colonna family may also have granted him protection from his enemies. No more attacks disturbed him, as far as is known, and he recovered sufficiently to satisfy a steady stream of both public and private commissions before his ill-fated departure for Rome.[33]

During these months, Caravaggio carried out at least two large-scale works: the *Crucifixion of Saint Andrew* (Pl. 173), and the lost decoration for the Fenaroli Chapel consisting of an altarpiece depicting the 'Resurrection of Christ' and lateral canvases of the 'Stigmatization of Saint Francis of Assisi' and 'Saint John the Baptist'. The Lombard merchant Alfonso Fenaroli had bought the rights to a chapel in S. Anna dei Lombardi, his national church in Naples, in late 1607. Upon his return from Sicily, Caravaggio must have immediately been sought out by Fenaroli for the pictorial decoration, which disappeared in an earthquake at the beginning of the nineteenth century.[34]

342

The *Crucifixion of Saint Andrew* was perhaps commissioned by Don Juan Alonso Pimentel y Herrera, Conde de Benavente, who presumably took the work home with him to Spain at the end of his term as viceroy of Naples in July 1610. A mid-seventeenth-century inventory of paintings in the Benavente palace at Valladolid described the *Crucifixion*, assessing its value as the highest in the collection. Characteristic of Caravaggio's late works are the summary brushwork and the fragmented light reducing the sculptural modelling on Andrew's torso and arms, and on the executioner's back, both of which are typical stylistic features of the Sicilian paintings, especially the *Raising of Lazarus*.[35]

Caravaggio also painted perhaps as many as seven easel pictures before his death, among them two of his most unforgettable, the *Martyrdom of Saint Ursula* and *David with the Head of Goliath*. Bellori mentioned a half-length 'Salome' which the painter sent to Grand Master Wignacourt as a peace-offering; this is to be identified either with the canvas now in Madrid (Pl. 170) bearing an old attribution to Caravaggio, or a version with a different design in London (Pl. 171). Both are ostensibly late, authentic works by the master, presenting complementary variations on a theme. For the Madrid version, Caravaggio devised an original composition with a compact, elliptically disposed figural group pushed off-centre. The London picture derives its design from a Leonardesque prototype and, with the *David with the Head of Goliath*, shares the grisly motif of one figure thrusting a severed head towards the viewer. Each Salome turns her head away from the victim, but the woman in the London canvas averts her gaze while her twin in Madrid stares unflinchingly at the viewer. Whereas a wider ranger of colour accents the brightest passages of the latter image, the palette of the former is starkly restricted to black and white. Both *Salomes* inspired imitations, and the London picture spawned a number of copies, especially in Neapolitan circles.

To the final months of Caravaggio's life belong the *Martyrdom of Saint Ursula* (Pl. 178), painted for Prince Marcantonio Doria of Genoa, and *Saint John the Baptist* (Pl. 179), painted for Cardinal Scipione Borghese. A letter to Prince Doria from his Neapolitan agent on 11 May 1610 announced that the awaited painting had just come off Caravaggio's easel but the varnish had not yet dried sufficiently for shipment. The Prince and the painter already knew each other from at least the summer of 1605 when Caravaggio had taken temporary refuge in Genoa. At that time, the painter had dashed Doria's hopes for a frescoed loggia; now, four years later, he was ready to present him with something more in character, an easel picture with a half-length religious narrative, which had 'stunned' its Neapolitan viewers. The Prince was advised by Caravaggio's agent to think up a subject for a second commission from his 'friend', but once again he ended up disappointed — not, this time, by the painter's refusal but by his early death.[36]

**343**

Around the time that he finished Doria's canvas, Caravaggio must have painted the *Saint John the Baptist*. Letters written immediately after his death reveal that Caravaggio was carrying this painting, as well as another picture with the same theme and a Magdalen, when he embarked on a felucca bound for Rome in July 1610 (Appendix XI). All three works were intended for Cardinal Borghese, and as no mention is made of money, the paintings might have been presents for the Cardinal and part of the conditions for granting Caravaggio's pardon.[37]

Stylistic evidence favours the assignment of one further pair of easel pictures to Caravaggio's last year: the *Denial of Saint Peter* (Pl. 175), a recent rediscovery, and the famous *David with the Head of Goliath* (Pl. 180). Closely related to the *Martyrdom of Saint Ursula*, the *Denial of Saint Peter* shares a similar composition and lighting, similar motifs (the apostle's gesture and the soldier's ornate helmet) and the same extremely cursory handling.

The summary treatment and exposed ground of the *David with the Head of Goliath*, combined with the reduced corporeality of the hero's head and torso, relate it closely to Caravaggio's Sicilian works and his last period of activity. Incisions around the contours of David's head and raised arm suggest Caravaggio's posing of the model, the same thin and angular young man seen in the *Saint John the Baptist*.

Overleaf **171 Salome with the Head of Saint John the Baptist**, *c.*1609–10; oil on canvas, 91.5 × 106.7 cm, National Gallery, London

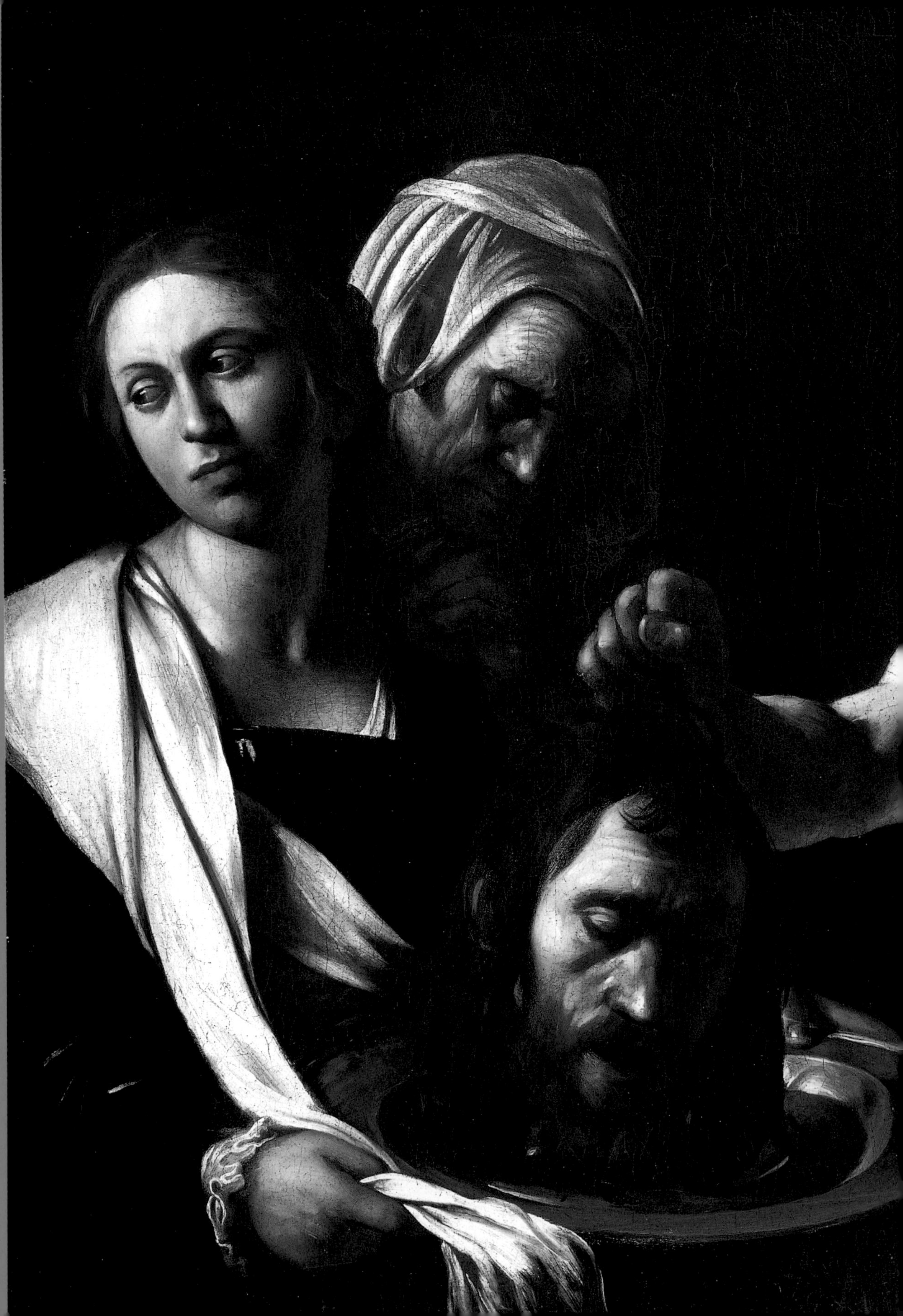

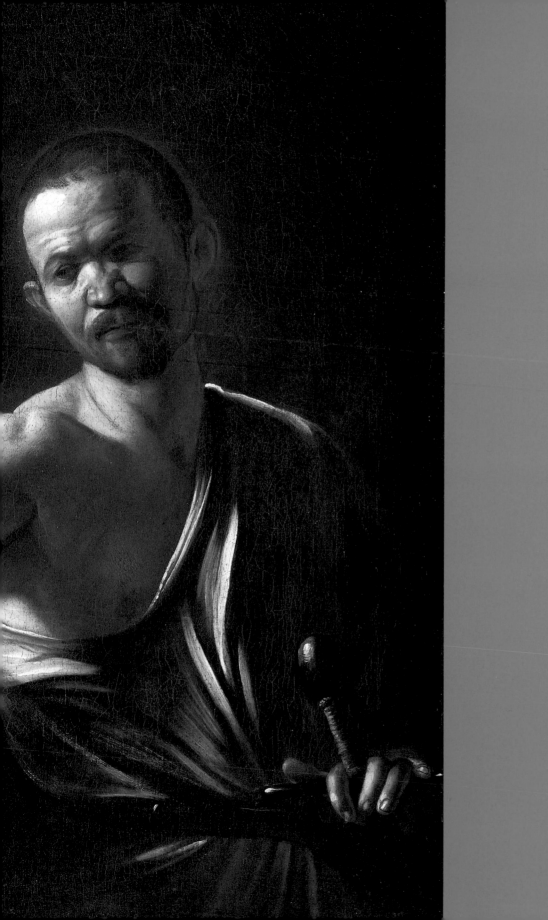

As X-rays of the latter canvas reveal, the faces of the two protagonists resembled each other even more closely before the curl on the Baptist's forehead was added. Not known, however, are the circumstances behind the *David*. Like the *Saint John*, it might have been intended for Cardinal Borghese, who could have bought it after Caravaggio's death.

One final picture bears mention in the context of Caravaggio's last works: the controversial *Toothpuller* (Pl. 172), which though first attributed to him in 1637 has only recently been seriously reconsidered as autograph. Although unexpected so late in his career, its genre subject *per se* does not preclude his authorship, and the mordantly comic tone even seems in tune with his personality. Yet the old lady looks like a sorry caricature of her prototypes in the *Crucifixion of Saint Andrew* (Pl. 173) or the *Salome* (Pls. 170, 171), the three men shown in profile are unfamiliar types, and the child's presence is rare in Caravaggio's *œuvre*. Most compromising are the many stylistic weaknesses: for example, the 'dentist' and 'patient' betray awkward figural proportions, incompetent foreshortening, and faulty draughtsmanship in the hands; equally disturbing are the stilted objects on the table and the mechanical decorative design along the border of the canvas. These glaring shortcomings cannot easily be explained away and argue against Caravaggio's responsibility for the *Toothpuller*.

The public and private commissions with Caravaggio carried out during his final months in Naples testify to his undiminished reputation, despite his fugitive status, among new as well as old patrons. These ranged from the wealthy middle class – the Lombard merchant Fenaroli – to the apex of contemporary society – the Spanish viceroy Benavente, Prince Doria and the papal nephew Borghese. For someone in a weakened physical state, the number of paintings issuing from his studio in the last year of his life represents a prodigious output.

Compared to the stylistic unity of his Sicilian works, these final pictures are notable for variety, in some cases harking back to earlier approaches and in others introducing fresh solutions. As in his pre-Maltese works, figures dominate the compositions, filling the large,

**172  The Toothpuller** (attributed), *c.*1608–10;  oil on canvas, 139 × 194.5 cm, Palazzo Pitti, Florence

empty overhead spaces and masking the background settings which had distinguished his most recent altarpieces. At times, Caravaggio again violated the boundaries of painted space, posing his models on the brink of the picture plane and pushing their foreshortened limbs – even truncated heads – towards the beholder. In the Fenaroli 'Resurrection', Christ 'seemed to come out of the painting', as one seventeenth-century Neapolitan commentator remarked.[38] Conversely, in other works, such as the *Crucifixion of Saint Andrew* (Pl. 173), the viewer is drawn into the action. Gathering the witnesses to the martyrdom around the foot of the cross, Caravaggio cut them off at hip-length with the bottom edge of the frame, without however adopting the irrational proportions and spatial ambiguity of similar Mannerist *repoussoir* figures. Instead he maintained a consistent figural scale both for the bystanders and for the apostle and executioner, linking them through gesture and glance. A gap next to the Roman officer opens up as if the viewer were invited to close the circle. The sense of immediacy intrinsic to Caravaggio's images is even more urgent because of the stripped-down compositions, with few figures, sparing props, and little if any scenery. One or two striking details, transcribed naturalistically, ensure credibility: the old woman's goitre in the *Crucifixion of Saint Andrew*, the soldier's parade helmet in the *Denial of Saint Peter*, and the gilt ornaments on the murderer's breastplate in the *Martyrdom of Saint Ursula*. But otherwise the reduced modelling simplifies faces, hands and clothing, and the contrasted lighting strengthens this generalizing tendency by creating patterns of bright and shadowed areas, as on the maidservant in the *Denial of Saint Peter* or the headsman in the London *Salome*. In these last Neapolitan works, Caravaggio concentrated his attention on the psychological states of his characters, focusing repeatedly on compassion (the old lady in the *Salomes* and the *Crucifixion of Saint Andrew*), and on ambivalence (Ursula's killer, Peter, Salome, John the Baptist, and David).

In this final phase of activity, as throughout his mature career, Caravaggio depicted saints, martyrdoms and biblical subjects. Not surprisingly yet remarkable none the less, he invented another group of original and memorable interpretations of traditional themes. In the

**173 Crucifixion of Saint Andrew**, *c.*1609–10; oil on canvas, 202.5 × 152.7 cm, Cleveland Museum of Art (Purchase, L. C. Hanna Jr. Bequest)

lost 'Resurrection', he startled his contemporaries by his singular Christ, who steps out of the tomb emaciated and frightened amidst the sleeping soldiers, instead of soaring triumphantly into the heavens. Although complaints about decorum crept into descriptions of the altarpiece, its novelty immediately inspired imitations by artists in Naples, such as Finson's *Resurrection* (St Jean de Malte, Aix-en-Provence, *c.*1613), and influenced Caracciolo's representation of *Saint Peter Delivered from Prison* (Pio Monte della Misericordia, Naples, 1615).[39]

In at least two other works from these months, the choice of a rarely depicted moment in scripture gave Caravaggio a similar chance to portray the apostles Andrew and Peter as human beings and not superheroes. At first glance, the *Crucifixion of Saint Andrew* seems to depict the apostle being tied to the cross for his crime of converting the wife of Aegeas, the Roman proconsul, the details of which were told in *The Golden Legend*. Aegeas had ordered ropes instead of nails to prolong Andrew's agony, and for two days Andrew preached to huge crowds who clamoured for his release from suffering, until Aegeas fearfully yielded to their demands. Instead of showing the moment when Andrew was bound to the cross, Caravaggio portrayed the heavenly miracle which occurred when heaven intervened to grant Andrew's wish for martyrdom and miraculously stopped the executioner from untying the saint. When the divine radiance signalling the miracle vanished, the apostle died.[40]

Dramatic as the tale is, it presented obvious practical challenges to a painter, which may explain its rarity in works of art. Caravaggio's contemporaries typically depicted episodes leading up to the apostle's crucifixion, or celebrated the saint's martyrdom as a heavenly triumph replete with angelic choir. To be sure, Caravaggio respected the legend and painted irregular bright streaks at right to signal the fading celestial effulgence announcing the apostle's death. By the symbolic use of light and by omitting any bodily manifestations of the divine, Caravaggio again implied that saintly martyrdom guaranteed no *deus ex machina* to lessen human torment. Short and broken brushstrokes capture the marks of physical exhaustion on Andrew's face with its glazed look and slack mouth, and on his left hand, bent in pain.

Of the five supporting characters, Caravaggio singled out the lone woman, turning her illuminated head towards the viewer. A *pentimento*, visible in X-rays, reveals that he painted her with hands held up to partly cover her neck before deciding to expose her prominent goitre, then a widespread malady among the poor in the countryside around Naples. Quite apart from reflecting an obvious fascination with transcribing this abnormality, the work conveys the moral lesson that, despite her own misery, the old woman knew compassion for another's suffering. Whether or not Caravaggio himself was responsible for choosing the particular incident in Andrew's martyrdom, he adapted it to his own preoccupation with death, making a dying man's final moments the real subject of his painting. Once again, the striking composition and the saint's agonized but quiet end impressed painters both in Naples (Caracciolo's *Crucifixion* of *c.*1610, Museo Civico, Naples), and later in Spain (Francisco de Zurbarán's *Crucifixion with Self-Portrait*, Prado, Madrid, 1635–40).

The *Denial of Saint Peter* (Pl. 175) also exposes an apostle's human vulnerability, in this case to fear and betrayal. Instead of showing Peter's tearful repentance, a favourite post-Tridentine subject painted by the Carracci and their pupils, the canvas illustrates the earlier point in the Gospel narrative when the apostle renounced the arrested Christ. While warming himself by the fire in the courtyard of the high priest's house, Peter was accused of being a disciple by women who recognized him. Just as Jesus had predicted, he denied knowing the Lord three times before the cock crowed.

Caravaggio's paramount interest in the tense confrontation and Peter's inner emotional conflict shaped his visualization of the episode. Eliminating any anecdotal incidentals, he restricted the cast to Peter, one accusing woman, and one guard, the cock being evoked by the suggestive silhouette of the soldier's crested helmet and bushy moustache. The painting isolates one instance of Peter's disavowal of Christ in what resembles a pantomime: the maid indicating Peter to the soldier; the soldier lifting a questioning finger at Peter; and Peter drawing back and pointing to himself with both hands. The saint's gesture apparently declares negation but its double-handed emphasis is self-accusatory at the same time. In contrast to Caravaggio's sensitive conception of the subject, his followers used it as a pretext for a lively guardroom spectacle in which the apostle plays a minor role, as in the *Denial of Saint Peter* attributed to Manfredi (Pl. 174).

**174** Bartolomeo Manfredi, **Denial of Saint Peter**, *c.*1620;  oil on canvas, 166 × 232 cm, Herzog Anton-Ulrich Museum, Braunschweig
Overleaf **175 Denial of Saint Peter**, *c.*1609–10;  oil on canvas, 94 × 125.5 cm, Metropolitan Museum of Art, New York

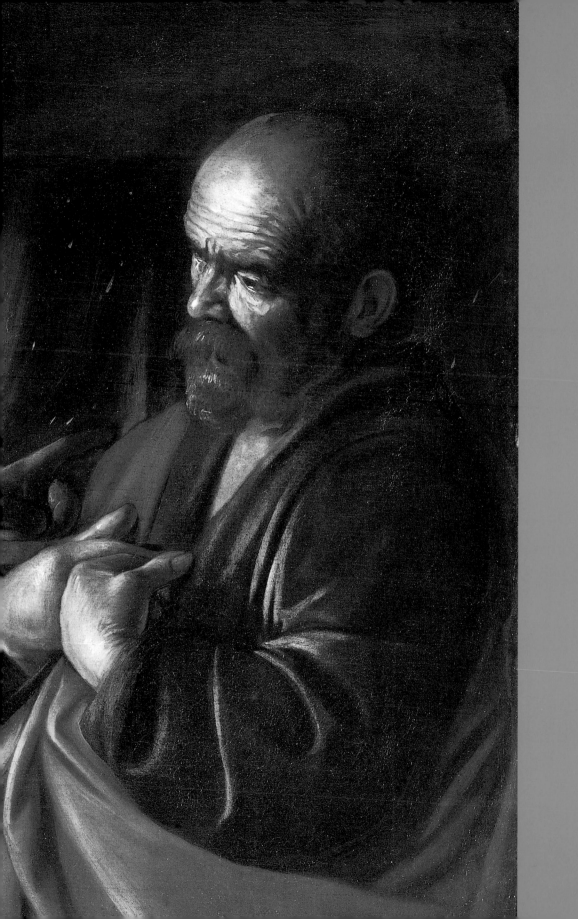

353

354

Caravaggio distilled narrative to its essentials even further in the *Martyrdom of Saint Ursula* (Pl. 178). The theme was probably chosen by the patron Doria who had a special affection for his stepdaughter, the nun 'Sister Ursula'.[41] Frequently depicted in art since the early Renaissance, the medieval legend told the story of the princess Ursula of Brittany who refused to marry the pagan prince of the Huns and was slaughtered in Cologne by his men along with her companions, eleven thousand virgin pilgrims. Ludovico Carracci's altarpiece of 1600 (Pl. 176) can be taken as a representative illustration of the subject in Caravaggio's day: beneath a heavenly apparition, a panorama unfolds showing a tumultuous massacre swirling around Ursula who beatifically awaits her own death from an arrow aimed by a soldier standing in the rear at left.

Caravaggio transposed the event from an epic to a personal scale involving only five people – Ursula, a soldier, two bystanders, and the bowman. So unusual is his conception of the theme that when the canvas was first rediscovered, its subject was vaguely labelled as an allegory. Without a historical setting or transcendental references, the horrific action at first looks like the bloody reckoning at the climax of some private drama of revenge. Ursula's murder is particularly shocking because she is shot at point-blank range before our eyes. Moreover,

**176** Ludovico Carracci, **Martyrdom of Saint Ursula**, 1600; oil on canvas, 380 × 240 cm, S. Domenico, Imola

the arrow has just hit its mark and, for an instant, time seems suspended. By dressing up the assassin in a feathered cap and ornamental armour, Caravaggio specifically identified him as the aggrieved prince of the legend. Glowing against the dark surround, broad areas of saturated red confined to the prince's tunic and Ursula's cloak irrevocably bind the would-be suitor and his intended, but Caravaggio made plain their disastrous incompatibility through *contrapposto*: the aged prince's ugly features and leathery skin are as much at odds with the young saint's classicizing profile and smooth face as is his glinting breastplate with her soft bosom draped with thin fabric. Caravaggio deftly controlled the emotional key of the scene by increasing the pitch for the prince whose expression registers unexpected dismay, and lowering it for Ursula who stares impassively at the wound which she gently presses with her hands. This subtlety was lost on Bernardo Strozzi, who saw Caravaggio's original in Genoa and produced a histrionic imitation (Pl. 177). Strozzi also omitted the pair of bystanders who, in Caravaggio's scene, are shown partially emerging from the shadows behind the saint with their gazes focused on the murderer.

In the second man, who is straining to look over Ursula's shoulder, Caravaggio represented himself. Seven years earlier he had put himself in an almost identical position in the *Betrayal of Christ* (Pl. 117), and he included himself as a bystander in at least two other religious paintings: the Sicilian *Raising of Lazarus* (Pl. 164) and the much earlier *Martyrdom of Saint Matthew* (Pl. 79). In each instance, he pictured himself as a witness not only of a dramatic event but of situations fraught with violence or matters of life and death.

**177** Bernardo Strozzi, **Martyrdom of Saint Ursula**, *c.*1615;  oil on canvas, 104 × 130 cm, private collection
Overleaf **178 Martyrdom of Saint Ursula**, 1610;  oil on canvas, 154 × 178 cm, Banca Commerciale Italiana, Naples

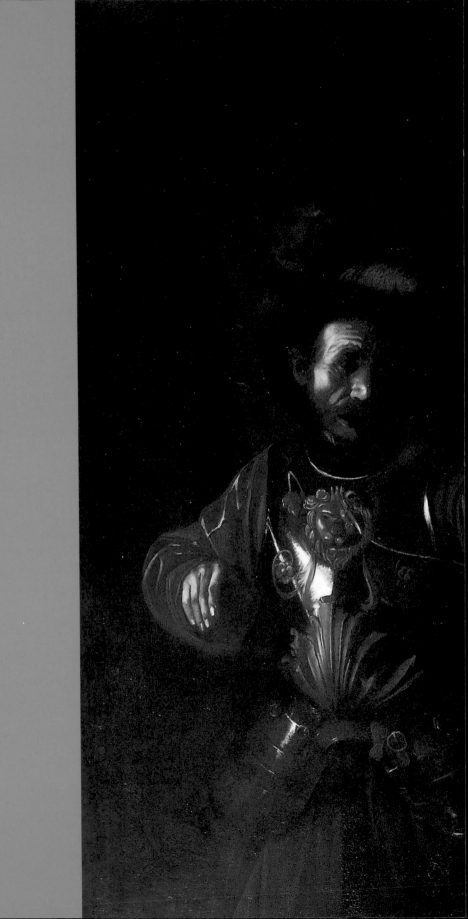

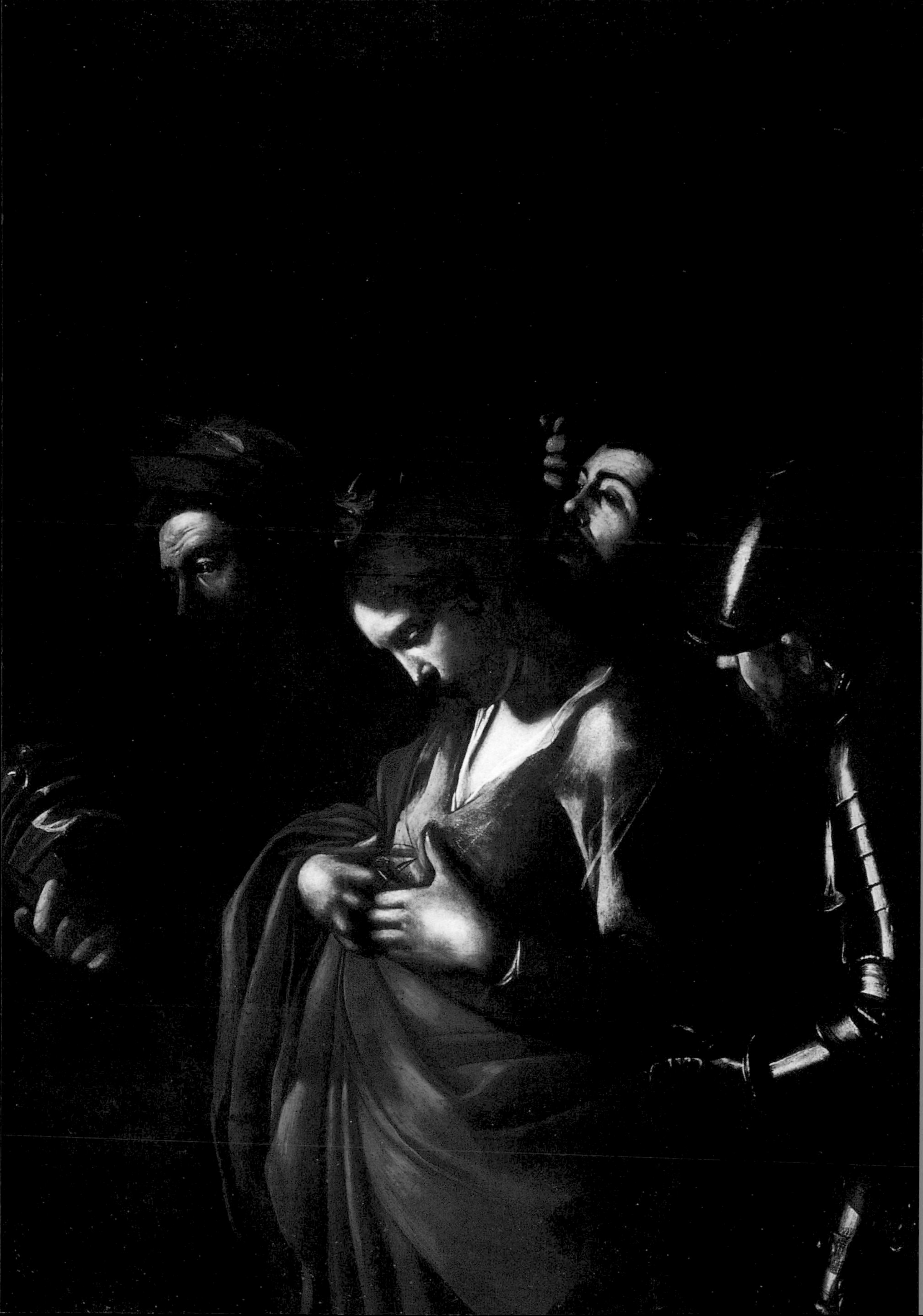

The *Saint John the Baptist* (Pl. 179) represents Caravaggio's third full-length treatment of the biblical figure and his last image of a solitary saint. As in the two previous versions (Pls. 107, 124), an adolescent John sits on a voluminous red drapery against a darkened backdrop. Caravaggio's model in Naples, with a homely face and a slight, ungainly body, embodies a very different type from the sinuous nude and the lanky athlete of the Roman works. Like the earliest John, he looks at the viewer but without a twinkle in his eye or a broad smile, and he appears oblivious to the ram nibbling grape leaves behind him. It is as if the grim future depicted in the intervening *Beheading of Saint John the Baptist* and the two *Salomes* has lowered a pall over this boy, making him older than his years. The evolving conception of the saint belongs to distinct moments in Caravaggio's career, and the change in mood might mirror his own state of mind by 1610, no longer flushed with the success of his first public commissions but worn out by subsequent events and awaiting their resolution.[42]

Since the seventeenth century when the giant's features were recognized as the painter's own, Caravaggio's *David with the Head of Goliath* (Pl. 180) has overwhelmed viewers with its tragic implications, and its complex allusions and associations have inspired numerous interpretations. The familiar biblical story (I Samuel 17:20–58) recounts the victory of the young shepherd, armed only with his slingshot and his faith in God, over the formidable Philistine warrior who had been terrorizing the Israelite forces. Caravaggio illustrated the final episode in the story when, after killing and beheading Goliath, David presented his prize to King Saul.

**179 Saint John the Baptist**, 1610; oil on canvas, 159 × 124 cm, Galleria Borghese, Rome

Behind the representation of the isolated figure of David bearing Goliath's head lies a distinguished artistic tradition launched in fifteenth-century Florence by the marble and bronze statues of Donatello (Bargello, Florence). In this instance, however, Caravaggio did not emulate sculptural precedents from the past but looked to a Giorgionesque prototype (Pl. 182) for the three-quarter-length composition, showing a clothed David holding his sword in his right hand and Goliath's head in his left. As in that work, the slingshot is not included, but Caravaggio managed to allude to it in the shirtsleeve gathered up and hanging down in a loop from the belt. True to the biblical description, his David wears no breastplate, and he captured the narrative action more effectively than his predecessor by omitting the stone ledge under Goliath's head. Instead, he depicted the head dangling and dripping blood. Also suspended, the sword is inscribed with letters spelling out an abbreviation in the groove of the blade. Difficult to read, the markings may stand simply for the swordsmith's or Caravaggio's own signature, but they have lately been interpreted ingeniously, if not conclusively, as deriving from an Augustinian commentary on the Psalms which equates David's triumph over Goliath with Christ's over Satan and, symbolically, with humility over pride.[43]

Although moral right and victory clearly belong to David, Caravaggio and some earlier artists did not portray him as a jubilant hero but rather invested him with unexpected emotions – pensive in both Donatello's bronze and the Giorgionesque painting, and brooding in Giorgione's lost 'Self-Portrait as David'.[44] Caravaggio also drew upon the human qualities of the Jewish king who, as shepherd, fighter, ruler, lover, poet and sinner, displays the full range of feelings in the Bible. Gazing upon his bloody handiwork, David looks perturbed, his expression mingling sadness with compassion. Almost a decade earlier the virtuous heroine of *Judith Beheading Holofernes* (Pl. 69), had betrayed similar ambivalence in destroying her ungodly adversary.

360

**180 David with the Head of Goliath**, *c.*1610;  oil on canvas, 125 × 101 cm, Galleria Borghese, Rome

**181** Cristofano Allori, **Judith and Holofernes**, *c.*1610–12; oil on canvas, 139 × 116 cm, Palazzo Pitti, Florence

Like Giorgione a century before and Bernini twelve years later in his marble *David* (Galleria Borghese, Rome, 1623–4), Caravaggio inserted himself into the biblical story. But his decision to act the villain and not the hero is both startling and enigmatic. Certainly he had masqueraded as the beheaded monster in the early *Medusa* (Pl. 54), if that was indeed a self-portrait, but then he more than likely used his own features for an intense scrutiny of extreme facial expression with bulging eyes and screaming mouth. He had also identified himself with the dying saint in the *Beheading of Saint John the Baptist* by signing his name in the pool of blood. On this occasion, however, he did not lend his own features to the martyred Baptist but reserved them for Goliath, the very embodiment of evil.

Distinctive as is the individual portrayal of each figure, Caravaggio also created an unusual psychological bond between David and Goliath: a bond that is elusive and complicated by a cryptic phrase from Jacomo Manilli in the mid-seventeenth century pointing out that his model for David was 'his Caravaggino' (*il suo Caravaggino*). The ambiguous Italian wording can be translated variously as a reference to a specific person's name, as an inhabitant from the town of Caravaggio, or as a diminutive for 'little Caravaggio'. Perhaps most plausibly the phrase refers to Caravaggio's studio assistant, Cecco del Caravaggio. That this assistant did pose for the master in Rome was commonly believed by the mid-seventeenth century, and gossip circulated that painter and model were lovers.[45] These old reports are impossible to verify; independent portraits of Cecco are not known, and his presence in Caravaggio's Neapolitan workshop is not documented. Debatable also is the premiss that the same person posed for both Caravaggio's *Cupid* and for the David; if Cecco was not David, then some other young 'Caravaggino', a compatriot employed as an assistant in Naples, posed for the master. A sexual intimacy between David/model and Goliath/painter seems an inescapable conclusion, however, given that Caravaggio made David's sword appear to project upward, suggestively, between his legs and at an angle that echoes the diagonal linking the protagonist's gaze to his victim.

363

**182** Follower of Giorgione, **David with the Head of Goliath**, *c.*1510; oil on wood, 65 × 74 cm, Kunsthistorisches Museum, Vienna

Caravaggio now commands an exalted place in the tradition of Western art, yet he took no active role in ensuring his artistic legacy. Although he spurned the professional custom of setting up a workshop with assistants and apprentices, his art inspired imitation from an early stage in his career. Fellow painters like Minniti and Orazio Gentileschi among his circle in Rome and Caracciolo later in Naples resolved to follow his example. Even more remarkably, painters who were not friends or who never knew him adopted his subjects and tried to reproduce his naturalism. Within a decade of his death a self-declared following had mushroomed, and its constituents – the Caravaggisti – were as distinctive for aping Caravaggio as for their diversity in nationality, age and training. Launched in Rome, the movement spread to wherever Caravaggio had travelled, and even further afield to where his cabinet pictures and copies were sent. Whereas his mature sacred imagery transformed Neapolitan art and also made an indelible impression in Sicily, his genre scenes held greater appeal for painters across Northern Europe. Caravaggism was a dominant artistic trend throughout the seventeenth century, waxing and waning at different times in different places.[1]

Given the historical importance of this artistic phenomenon, an examination of Caravaggio's working methods may then appear a surprising departure from the expected discussion of his followers in an epilogue. But Caravaggism has been thoroughly discussed in other books and articles as well as in exhibitions, and our understanding of its scope and character has not drastically altered in recent years. Conversely, recent research on Caravaggio has not only affected our very definition of his *œuvre* in terms of its chronology, patronage and content, but it has also opened up a dynamic view of his working processes. I therefore want to consider Caravaggio's innovative techniques from the combined perspectives of the seventeenth-century sources and the latest studies of both visual and technical data.

In his own day, Caravaggio's success, fame and notoriety rested on his radically new artistic practices. Strongly contrasted lighting and painting from the model were seen by early critics as his most significant contributions to the art of painting. Paradoxically, the same voices damned these practices as leading to the ruination of painting, whereas fellow artists enthusiastically embraced the new practices, imitating his lighting effects and trying their hand at painting directly from life – a reminder of how divorced critical theory and practice can be.

Caravaggio's biographers and critics attributed the unprecedented naturalism of his art to his manipulation of lighting in his studio, to his control of colour, and above all to his painting directly from the model without intermediary drawings. Although they took unusual care in describing how his methods deviated from what was then standard studio practice, their comments are most eloquent about the surface aspects of Caravaggio's art, explaining the methods he devised to achieve the strongly contrasted lighting and life-like colour. On the subject of his mode of composition, however, his biographers offer little comment beyond emphasizing his utter dependence upon the model. But this very issue has come to dominate modern criticism, especially in the decades since the sensational results of the first X-rays taken of the canvases in the Contarelli Chapel during the 1950s. The discovery of an entirely different composition beneath the *Martyrdom of Saint Matthew* (Pl. 184) inaugurated a new, technical phase in studies of Caravaggio's work. X-radiography and infra-red reflectography have provided many insights about his compositional processes, revealing the way in which he built up layers of paint and made changes in the course of painting. The growing, impressive body of technical data for individual paintings has stimulated renewed interest in all aspects of Caravaggio's studio practices. My discussion will begin with light and colour, the most immediately striking elements in his art, before moving on to the more complex and speculative issue of composition.[2]

Seventeenth-century descriptions of Caravaggio's mature method of lighting explained that he directed an overhead light on to his models whom he posed in a dark interior. Exactly how he organized his studio is more difficult to reconstruct, especially as he moved at least five times in Rome. In the different cities to which his exile took him, his precise addresses are not documented. The 1605 inventory of the contents of the house he rented for two years affords only meagre clues about his studio there; the compiler did not specify which room contained what, the number of windows or the height of the ceilings. The observations of Caravaggio's biographers thus remain our best clues to his general approach. Whereas Mancini thought the studio had blackened walls, Sandrart and Bellori referred to a cellar or some other dim, closed room. Apart from minor differences in their characterization of the light as daylight entering from a high window

**184 Martyrdom of Saint Matthew** (Pl. 76), X-radiograph

(Mancini), or, alternatively, as the artificial light emanating from a lamp (Sandrart, Bellori), the three writers agreed that this directed lighting, creating a sharp contrast between the lit forms and shadows on the model, imparted strong relief or three-dimensionality to Caravaggio's figures.[3]

The evidence of the works themselves, especially Caravaggio's bright early paintings such as the *Cardsharps* (Pl. 35) or the *Fortune-Teller* (Pl. 37), generally bear out Mancini's description of the lighting system. The distribution of lights and darks indicates that strong light falling from the upper left, conceivably sunlight from a high-placed window, accentuated the heads and limbs of the figures and cast slanting rays on the back wall. The window reflected in the vase (Pl. 185) in the *Boy Bitten by a Lizard* suggests, too, that sunlight entered the studio, then located in Del Monte's palace, from at least one other window in the wall behind Caravaggio.

The sunny appearance of some of these early pictures can also be explained by Caravaggio's exploitation of a grey ground. Although contested, the results of visual examination and technical analyses have confirmed that this is the case in the *Cardsharps* and in the earlier of the two versions of the *Fortune-Teller*. A grey ground also appears to be present in the *Self-Portrait as Bacchus*, *Boy with a Basket of Fruit* and the *Penitent Magdalen*, but pigment analysis is still needed to confirm its use in these and other early pictures. Caravaggio soon exchanged it for a dark, reddish-brown ground, however, which he adopted from standard Roman practice. X-rays further reveal that from early on in the creative process he blocked out the light and dark areas of his compositions, taking care to leave light areas 'in reserve' when laying in the dark ground.[4]

In his pictures of the late 1590s in which a diagonal shaft of light still crosses the background, but the shadows are intensified, as in the *Lute-Player* (Pl. 47), Caravaggio may have let in sunlight, obtaining the desired contrast by shuttering all but one of the windows in his studio. But after 1600, the signs of directed daylight disappear from his work, with the exception of the *Death of the Virgin* (Pl. 98). The absence of a slanting illuminated wedge on the backdrop, and the antithesis of bright areas and deep shadows in, say, the *Crucifixion of Saint Peter* (Pl. 89) or the *Supper at Emmaus* (Pl. 110), would suggest that Caravaggio had changed his practice and now hung curtains at all the windows and worked beneath an overhead lamp.

Caravaggio strengthened the intensity of the direct light in his mature paintings with the device of cast shadows, previously used infrequently in art. In some instances, a supposedly raised object throws its outline against a figure (the shadow of the sword on the executioner's leg in the *Martyrdom of Saint Matthew*, Pl. 76), or shadows are attached to still-life elements placed on a table (*Supper at*

373

*Emmaus*). At other times, Caravaggio must have suspended his lamp slightly in front as well as to the left of his model, so as to observe the shadow cast on to the wall behind (the innkeeper's shadow in *Supper at Emmaus*; Mary's in the *Madonna di Loreto*, Pl. 102; the angel's in the *Seven Works of Mercy*, Pl. 133; and the Grand Master's in the *Portrait of Alof de Wignacourt*, Pl. 142). Although also occasionally present in his early works, the cast shadows in these mature paintings are projected accurately and reflect an understanding of optical principles which Caravaggio may have gained partly through empirical observation and partly through exposure to the theoretical research of Cardinal Del Monte's brother Guidubaldo, whose treatise on perspective included an advanced discussion of cast shadows. Whereas Caravaggio's strong *chiaroscuro* lent his figures three-dimensionality, his cast shadows conferred physical reality in the manner of the protagonists' experiences in Hofmannsthal's libretto for Strauss's *Die Frau ohne Schatten* or Barrie's *Peter Pan*. Both the frequent use and the accurate transcription of shadows in Caravaggio's *œuvre* surpass earlier and contemporary examples.[5]

By the age of twenty-nine, Caravaggio had mastered the optical properties of light and shadow. Although he followed this system of lighting throughout the rest of his career, the evidence from late works such as the *Raising of Lazarus* (Pl. 162) or the *David with the Head of Goliath* (Pl. 180) reveals that he made a slight but significant modification in his last years in exile. While retaining direct light, he used a less concentrated and intense beam that softened the transitions between bright and dark edges, decreased the number of cast shadows, and allowed light to spread and reach into the background.

As direct light and tenebrism are found in Italian painting before Caravaggio's time, why did his contemporaries hail his system of lighting as new? Before 1600, the most widespread type of lighting in a painting was diffused daylight, spread evenly across figures whether set in a landscape or in an interior. Direct or specific light, as in Caravaggio's work, was also used in certain instances by painters and written about by Leonardo and Lomazzo, who recognized its importance for, on the one hand, creating relief and, on the other, for its expressive force in dramatic themes.[6] Such themes tended to be religious, when the direct lighting might be used to suggest a metaphysical source, such as the brilliant illumination radiating from the infant Christ in Correggio's much admired *Notte* (Gemäldegalerie, Dresden, 1529), or it could combine artificial and natural light to evoke a divine source, as Caravaggio knew from another 'Lombard' example, Antonio Campi's *Saint Catherine Visited in Prison* (Pl. 8). In his own works, direct light still served the same twin ends of conveying sculptural volume of form, as in *Saint John the Baptist* (Pl. 107), and evoking spiritual drama, as in the *Conversion of Saint Paul* (Pl. 86). Unprecedented, however, was his use of direct light to illuminate the entire composition in virtually all of his mature works regardless of subject-matter.

Caravaggio's decision to limit himself exclusively to a system of direct lighting overturned existing artistic theory and practice. He must have been aware of, yet chosen to ignore, Leonardo's warning that a strong light-dark contrast created undesirable, crude extremes.[7] He must also have been familiar with his critics' view that such lighting was unnatural because of the very fact that it excluded natural lighting conditions. But, self-styled naturalistic painter that he was, his study of nature was highly selective, restricted to the human body and a few objects as revealed under artificial lighting conditions and unconcerned with the vast range of natural phenomena in the world outside the studio. Within its confines, he imposed further control on the environment so as to transcribe a convincing illusion of a living person's presence on to his canvas. By reducing the number of compositional variables, he could closely study the fall of direct light on the model, returning again and again, with ever greater experience, to this circumscribed artistic challenge. Caravaggio dropped a dark veil over most of the background beyond the lit model. Thus he arbitrarily set the majority of his scenes in some dark interior, sacrificing other than a minimal setting; where a landscape was unavoidable, he generally did the same thing but hung a vine or planted greenery to evoke the outdoors. By deliberately excluding architectural backdrops or landscapes, those 'other requirements of art' missed by Bellori, this solution allowed him to concentrate on the naturalistic observation of the model alone. In professional terms, his momentous decision to adopt direct lighting with its attendant deep shadows had the decided advantage of differentiating him from his Roman artistic contemporaries.

For the true-to-life look he sought, Caravaggio developed a masterful command of colour, which he wedded to his system of lighting. Contemporary critics unstintingly praised the vividness and forcefulness of his colour. Moreover, its naturalism was seen as a decisive contribution to the reform of Mannerist painting, criticized for its cosmeticized, pale, bleached colour.

Visual and technical analysis of individual paintings reveals that Caravaggio evolved a consistent and limited palette based upon the pigments in use at the time. This generally included lead white, verdigris, carbon black and earths (ochres and umbers). Bellori reported that Caravaggio habitually avoided the too brilliant tones of vermilion (*cinabri*) and blue (*azzurri*) and, when obliged to use them, toned them down. Because of its expense, ultramarine blue was specified in the Contarelli and Cerasi contracts. In the laterals of the first chapel, ultramarine appears in a few, scattered places in the clothing of individual figures. Caravaggio used it more conspicuously in the Cerasi *Crucifixion of Saint Peter* (Pl. 89) for the apostle's mantle occupying the lower right foreground. For the deep, rich tone of Jesus's mantle in the *Betrayal of Christ* (Pl. 117), he layered azurite, a blue more widely available than ultramarine, over a layer of brown. He used blue sparingly elsewhere in his mature works, with the notable exception of the gaoler's striking blue jacket in the *Beheading of Saint John the Baptist* (Pl. 151). Vermilion, on the other hand, reappears regularly throughout his *œuvre*, though toned down with black, as Bellori had observed.[8]

A few distinctive devices have been detected in Caravaggio's application of colour. To sharpen the contours of his figures or to separate two adjacent zones of different colour, he often traced the outline with a thin brush dipped in the same colour as the ground. At other times, he left a narrow strip of ground exposed around the figures for the same purpose – a practice that is not unique to his art, as has been claimed. Although his fundamental binding medium was oil, he applied a thin layer of egg tempera over the still wet oil in at least two known instances, for the *Conversion of Mary Magdalen* (Pl. 67) and the *Supper at Emmaus* (Pl. 110). He may have done this to avoid having to wait for the oil to dry before proceeding to the next layer. Alternatively he perhaps sought the visual effect of increased luminance, or apparent brightness, supplied by mixing the two media in the skin tones of Mary Magdalen and Martha in the former painting and in the white cloth covering the supper table in the latter. Caravaggio also exploited traditional practices in colouring where he wanted special visual accents. For example, he applied gold leaf in the crown and the stars on the globe in *Cupid* (Pl. 106), and along the decorative border of *Medusa* (Pl. 54). And, in several of his early pictures in which he described clothing with embroidery or brocade, he incised guidelines for the later insertion of the patterned neckline, as in the *Conversion of Mary Magdalen* (Pl. 186), or he enhanced the decorative detail by incising its outline in the wet, top layer of paint, probably with the butt-end of the brush, as on the gypsy's collar in the *Fortune-Teller* (Pl. 37), or the saint's dress in *Saint Catherine of Alexandria* (Pl. 63).[9]

Not surprisingly, Caravaggio modified his range and combination of colours over the course of his career. Bellori for one maintained that Caravaggio's early works were characterized by a few 'pure and sweet' colours and tempered shadows, and his mature works by their distinguishing bold colouring and dark shadows. The paintings bear out this general schema, but analysis of the role of colour in the different phases of his activity warns against too simple a linear reconstruction because common threads link youthful and mature works and, at certain moments, 'early' and 'late' practices appear side by side. His Lombard training influenced the choice and range of his early palette, as well as his even application of pigment with its matte finish. Unlike his sixteenth-century predecessors, he avoided gradually modulating his colour from light to dark and instead, within each tone, minimized tonal gradations. Similarly, he laid one saturated colour next to another, effecting abrupt shifts instead of soft chromatic transitions.

The *Cardsharps* (Pl. 35) exemplifies Caravaggio's bright cabinet pictures from the beginning of his Roman years, when he had already

**186 Conversion of Mary Magdalen** (Pl. 67), X-radiograph showing traces of incisions made along upper edge of blouse before addition of painted decoration

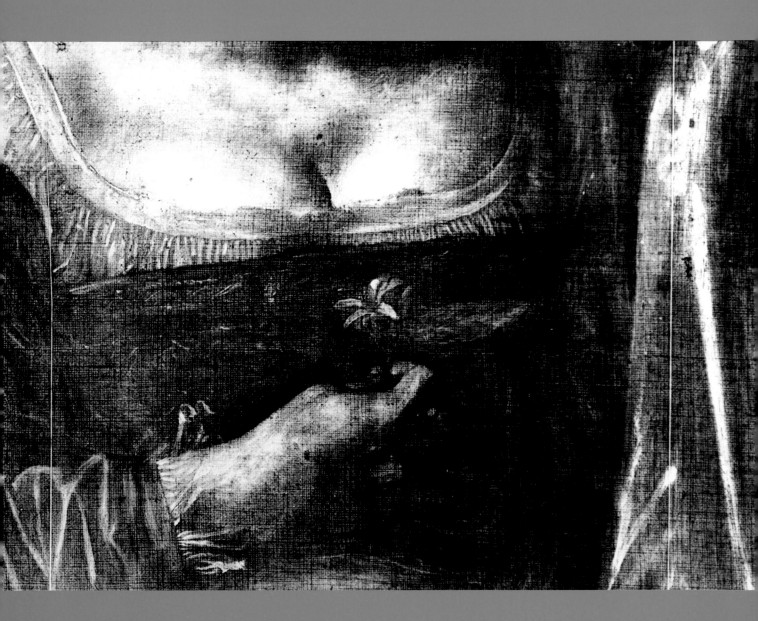

carefully determined his choice and combination of colour. Here he brushed a light yellow ochre on the backdrop, against which he set off the strong and varied tones of the clothing of the three gamblers. Calibrated with the same light value as the backdrop, the older cheat's grey vest and yellow shirt help fix his position spatially behind the two youths. The black mantle thrown over his left shoulder is exploited as a foil for his accomplice's silhouette, which in turn partly masks and so prevents the black from advancing. Taking advantage of the greatest contrast of luminosity on the colour scale, Caravaggio dressed the dupe in deep purple, offsetting his hat and jacket with the cheat's yellow sleeve. The velvety appearance of his jacket is further enhanced by its contrast with the bright whites in his collar, lace cuffs and skin tones.

Caravaggio also chose to pair complementary colours in the clothing of the younger swindler, painting his sleeves greenish-blue and his doublet orange. Through the simultaneous contrast of complementaries, this pairing increases the apparent saturation of the greenish-blue and the orange. In addition, the cool tone of the sleeves reinforces the recession into space of the boy's arms as opposed to the warmth of the orange doublet on his back that appears to project on the near side of the table. Caravaggio conveyed the flashiness of the card-players' garb by accentuating its yellow and orange against contrasting black stripes.[10]

In his first public commission for the Contarelli Chapel, the choice and combination of tones bedecking the company around the table in the *Calling of Saint Matthew* (Pl. 82) directly recall the *Cardsharps*. Buttressing the symbolic role of light in the painting, colour serves to drive home the gulf between the vivid left half and the sombre right half of the painting, embodying the material and spiritual realms respectively. But, generally speaking, the relative variety and weighting towards the bright end of the spectrum in Caravaggio's youthful canvases yield to a reduced and darkened palette by the end of the 1590s.

Once he adopted his strong *chiaroscuro*, Caravaggio refined the practical skills he already possessed in juxtaposing colours and co-ordinated them with

his lighting in order to intensify the tone and luminosity of the focal points, and to heighten spatial illusionism and dramatic mood. As he undertook successive public commissions, their sacred subject-matter and his own evolving sensibility encouraged him to abandon the brilliant brocaded doublets, striped sleeves, and plumed hats of his secular pictures for soberly coloured and styled attire. Beginning with the Cerasi Chapel, Caravaggio shifted from a Lombard-inspired palette to one based on the primary colours and, therefore, on Central Italian tradition. Although the gamut of colour in the *Crucifixion of Saint Peter* (Pl. 89) approximates Roman usage, represented here by Pulzone's *Crucifixion* (Pl. 187) and Annibale Carracci's *Pietà with Saints* (Pl. 188), its red, yellow and blue look the more vivid because each colour retains its apparent saturation even though toned down. Most importantly, Caravaggio subordinated the three

**379**

primary colours and the green on the breeches of one executioner to the brightness of the apostle's luminous nude body, on the one hand, and to the surrounding darkness on the other.

In the *Crucifixion of Saint Peter*, Caravaggio heightened the brilliance in the centre of the composition by using white as a local colour next to the saint's skin. He had already frequently set white shirts, blouses, and draperies against the bared throats, arms, and legs of the models in his earliest easel pictures. But his distinctive and extensive adoption of white assumed its greatest significance in his mature works, after he had darkened his backgrounds and restricted his palette. Usually set against bare skin, white draperies or garments clothe the central figure in altarpieces from the *Entombment* (Pl. 91) to the *Raising of Lazarus* (Pl. 162), and in easel pictures from *Saint Catherine of Alexandria* (Pl. 63) to *David with the Head of Goliath* (Pl. 180). Through the mutual intensification of white and the pale skin tones, Caravaggio created the illusion that the direct light in the painting serves as a spotlight, illuminating most fully the figure centred in its

**187** Scipione Pulzone, **Crucifixion**, 1586; S. Maria in Vallicella (Chiesa Nuova), Rome

**188** Annibale Carracci, **Pietà with Saints**, 1585; oil on canvas, 374 × 238 cm, Galleria Nazionale, Parma

beam. He also exploited two other properties of white: in the first place, its irradiation when set against black which, simply put, means that white appears to pulsate outwards, crossing its own border; and secondly, that it advances against a dark ground and so increases the illusion of relief.[11]

The mature Caravaggio's other favourite colour was red. Sometimes he introduced it as an independent dramatic accent, as in the cushion in *Saint Catherine of Alexandria* or in the Baptist's mantle in the *Beheading of Saint John* (Pl. 151); at other times he paired it with white, intensifying its value for vivid effects, as in the *Supper at Emmaus* (Pl. 110). In a few later instances, when Caravaggio drastically reduced his palette, vermilion supplied the dominant tonality, as in *Saint Jerome* (Pl. 141) or the *Martyrdom of Saint Ursula* (Pl. 178).

In summary, Caravaggio developed an impressive control of lighting and colour in those works built upon his Lombard training and theoretical knowledge, and his empirical observations of their behaviour in his studio. The naturalistic results he achieved depended on his integration of these two pictorial elements into his design process.

The very idea of Caravaggio having a design process is a relatively recent one. Even in his lifetime, the general assumption was that he merely painted what he saw without forethought and added identifying attributes only afterwards. The pictures themselves seemed to argue for this view in that the same models, sometimes wearing the same clothing, reappear in disparate scenes. While energizing the painted figures, the familiar faces demanded the viewer's suspension of disbelief: Was the sad redhead really Mary Magdalen? Was the boy with the dirty fingernails really Bacchus? Shop talk around Rome and Caravaggio's own statements – in the libel deposition, to Giustiniani, and as recorded by his biographers – also fed the conviction that he transcribed unadulterated reality. By 1600, word was out that Caravaggio painted directly from life without making drawings.

For his Roman contemporaries, this approach was tantamount to painting without a composition. Normal studio methods for oil painting at the end of the sixteenth century entailed preparing compositional sketches and figure studies before setting brush to canvas. Drawings thus formed an indispensable part of the creative process. Once the design was established, the painter himself or an assistant could transfer it freehand or by some mechanical means on to the canvas. Caravaggio's reported disregard for this standard practice is born out by the lack of extant drawings by him of any kind, a highly unusual circumstance for an Italian painter of the seventeenth century.

Because elaborate, preliminary preparations were hardly necessary for his early paintings of single figures, such works as *Boy with a Basket of Fruit* (Pl. 24) were conceivably painted directly from the model. Caravaggio's early experience as a portraitist in Milan and Rome may have conditioned his approach to portraying an isolated genre figure. Unlike history paintings with many figures in an expansive setting, portraiture of course did not require elaborate preliminary drawings, and portrait painters also depended upon life sessions to ensure vitality, especially when transcribing the sitter's facial features. Soon, though, Caravaggio was producing images with two and three figures and, as his public career advanced, he tackled narrative subjects with even larger casts. The *Entombment* and the *Raising of Lazarus*, to name just two examples, could not have been painted without any planning. The mechanics of this planning are becoming clearer to us from fresh interpretations of textual and archival evidence coupled with intensive visual and technical analyses. The identifiable techniques Caravaggio evolved constitute an inventive brew of standard studio practices, including rough sketches with the brush, incisions, consultation of contemporary prints, painting in successive layers from the back to the front of the composition, and the use of mirrors.

Even if ill-disposed to making compositional drawings on paper, Caravaggio had certainly been trained in draughtsmanship, and he agreed to present preliminary studies to his patrons for approval on at least three occasions: for the Cerasi Chapel; the lost De Sartis commission; and the *Death of the Virgin*. Although the relevant clause in the contracts may have been a legal formality, the presupposition was that Caravaggio like any other artist could and would satisfy the stipulation. That he did so for the De Sartis altarpiece is proven by the documents stating that his rough sketch (*sbozzo*) had been submitted and accepted.[12] Unfortunately neither the altarpiece nor the drawing has been identified. As for the other two commissions, the contractual circumstances are inconclusive, but Caravaggio's refusal to make preparatory sketches might account for the problems he encountered with the first *Conversion of Saint Paul* and the *Death of the Virgin*; it is also conceivable that objections were raised after his patrons had seen and approved sketches.[13]

The testimony of the sources, the absence of an extant graphic corpus, and perhaps some of the rejections strongly imply that Caravaggio did not customarily make presentation or detailed preliminary drawings for his paintings. This, however, does not necessarily mean he did not draw at all, producing his paintings purely through improvisation. In mature public commissions with many figures, such as the *Seven Works of Mercy* (Pl. 133), or in cabinet pictures with just a few, as the *Doubting Thomas* (Pl. 114), the complex arrangement of figures depends upon a controlling geometric order, as described above. Caravaggio could not have arrived at these sophisticated designs by chance; moreover, his regular recourse to engravings for the poses and gestures of his models reflects advanced planning of individual figures as well as of the overall design. To formulate this design, Caravaggio had various alternatives: he could have made a full-scale drawing ('cartoon'), which he then transferred by mechanical means to the canvas; he perhaps worked out his composition in summary sketches on paper which he then blocked out on the canvas; or he may have roughed out his first idea directly on the canvas, adjusting it to his satisfaction before proceeding.

The theory that he did compose on the canvas itself finds apparent support in the evidence from X-rays of the *Martyrdom of Saint Matthew* (Pl. 184), which record a different composition underneath the visible surface. Yet this initial composition was more than a preliminary rough sketch; it actually represents an abandoned original version that had been well advanced across the whole canvas. Furthermore, its conventional character calling for figures within an architectural setting had probably obliged Caravaggio to follow tradition in this instance and work from a detailed preparatory drawing transferred from paper. The extent of visible revision in the *Martyrdom of Saint Matthew* is unusual for Caravaggio, however. Elsewhere in his work, including early and mature cabinet pictures and ecclesiastical commissions, *pentimenti* typically entail slight modifications to contours or an adjustment of a gesture or a fold of drapery. The relatively small number of *pentimenti* and their marked reduction in large pictures following the Contarelli commission present a puzzle, for they do not record a significant evolution of the original design on the canvas.

Despite its contradictory implications, the evidence concerning *pentimenti* in itself does not rule out the artist's presumed method of composing directly on the canvas. Two other types of data from close examination and scientific analyses can be marshalled to support this practice: rough sketches done with the brush underlying different areas of Caravaggio's paintings, and incisions in the canvas. Sketches blocking out facial features, the placement of an ear, or the edge of a sleeve or fold of drapery have recently been found in a number of Caravaggio's works spanning his Roman and Neapolitan years. The most striking example is the under-sketch for Holofernes' head, revealed in infra-red reflectography of the *Judith Beheading Holofernes* (Pl. 189). Having first blocked out the figure's eyes, nose and mouth with a few, summary brushstrokes, for the sake of verisimilitude Caravaggio later moved the head slightly to the right in the definitive version; this shifting is what makes the sketch beneath so clear. In works of his final years such as the *Burial of Saint Lucy* (Pl. 160) or the *Martyrdom of Saint Ursula* (Pl. 178), Caravaggio had so pared down his application of paint layers that in some places he described figures little beyond the summary sketch.[14]

Fixing the surface features of individual figures, these rough sketches fell short of outlining forms to establish the composition. The question of whether Caravaggio also painted a preliminary, compositional under-drawing on the canvas is still unresolved. Although infra-red reflectography has proven so useful in uncovering Rembrandt's underlying compositional drawings, this technology works best for

**189 Judith Beheading Holofernes** (Pl. 69), infra-red reflectograph of head of Holofernes

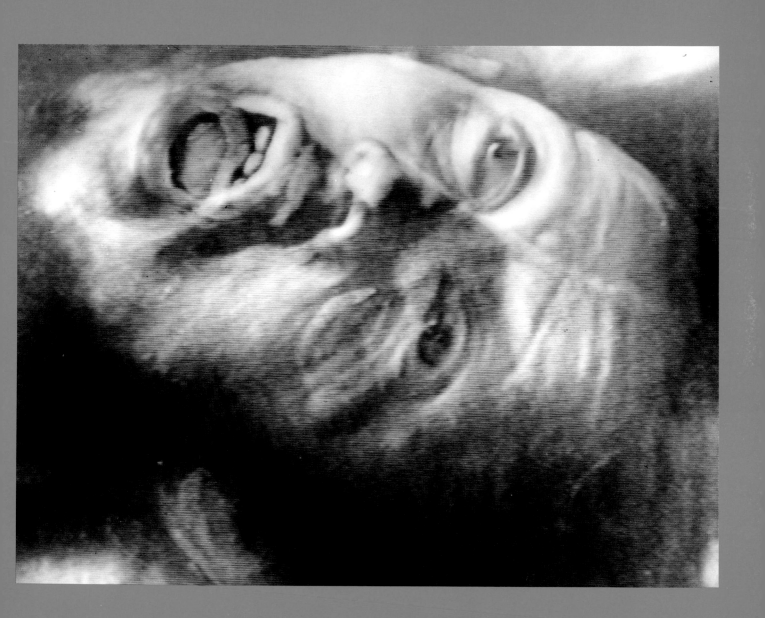

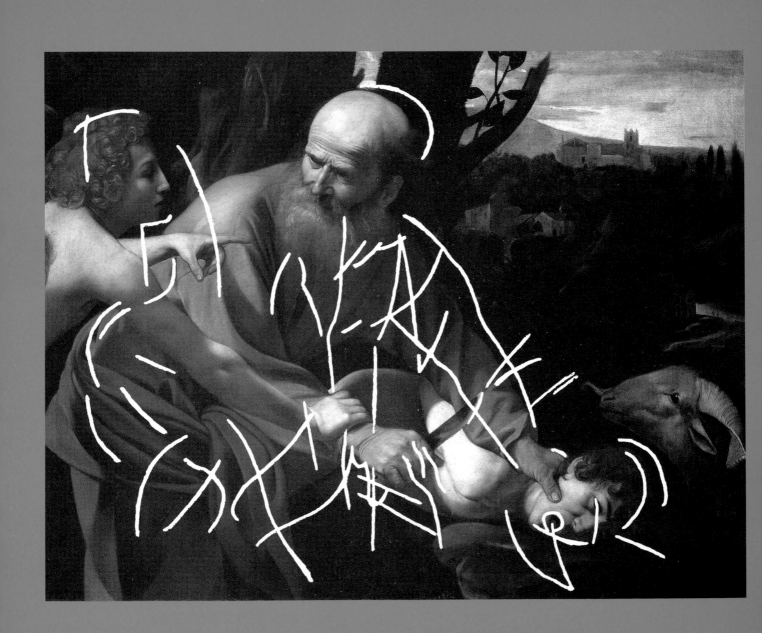

preliminary designs done in black paint on a light ground. Caravaggio used dark grounds in most of his works, and under-drawings in a dark tone would be undetectable to infra-red scanning. This question must therefore remain open until the time when Caravaggio's paintings can be examined with autoradiography, a costly and impractical scientific tool which surpasses infra-red technology in the ability to differentiate paint layers and illuminate the initial stage of execution.[15]

More conspicuous and more extensively documented are the incisions Caravaggio made in his canvases. These were first observed in his works over seventy years ago but only recently has a concerted effort been made to record their presence and explain their function. Visible to the naked eye in raking light, they appear with surprising frequency in single and multi-figured compositions from all phases of his career, beginning with the *Cardsharps* and the first version of the *Fortune-Teller*. Contrary to the assumption that he abandoned the device in his final years, recent investigation of various late paintings has uncovered incisions in paintings from the Sicilian period, such as the *Raising of Lazarus* and *Adoration of the Shepherds*, and in his late *David with the Head of Goliath*. In most instances, Caravaggio selectively incised the contours of figures, usually a head, shoulders, and/or arms. In the *Sacrifice of Isaac*, for example, the diagram recording the location of incisions (Pl. 190) shows that Caravaggio outlined the heads of the angel and Isaac, and the head and extended arms of the prophet. He also noted the placement of Isaac's eyes and open mouth, details crucial to the dramatic effect of the scene. Unlike the underlying rough sketches, then, the incisions mark the contours of figures instead of describing the surfaces of forms.[16]

Caravaggio's use of incisions to outline form had belonged to the artist's repertory of preparatory techniques since the early Renaissance. Originally developed for frescoes, this practice enabled painters to trace cartoons with a stylus on to the freshly plastered wall. By Caravaggio's day, artists had extended the technique to paintings on panel and canvas. Barocci, for one, would first prepare a detailed cartoon and then transfer its design by incising all its outlines on to the ground of the canvas, a method explained by Bellori and confirmed by examination of the works themselves. The art of Caravaggio's early Roman master Cesari reveals at least three different uses for incisions in contemporary studios. In the first, traditional usage, Cesari employed them in transferring the cartoons for his frescoes. A second use, which had also become standard, can be seen in one of his small oil sketches; the incised lines lay out the architectural perspective in the background, presumably established beforehand in a scale drawing. A panel painting with a half-length subject illustrates Cesari's third type of incision, used for silhouetting the figure's contours. In the unlikely event that Caravaggio had not already

**190 Sacrifice of Isaac** (Pl. 118), diagram of incisions

learned about incisions during his Milanese apprenticeship, he must have seen the practice firsthand in Cesari's workshop. It is less certain whether Caravaggio's incisions also functioned to transfer cartoons to the intended support.[17]

The existing evidence advances the theory that Caravaggio used incisions independently of cartoons, thereby departing from convention. In sharp contrast to Barocci's regular network of incisions transcribing every contour and internal detail from his cartoon on to the canvas, Caravaggio's incisions selectively mark figural contours and with a freedom of touch irreconcilable with tracings. As the scored outlines often deviate from the painted forms, the assumption follows that his incisions did not merely copy the already established preliminary design but instead helped him in planning the composition.

The pattern of incisions in the *Sacrifice of Isaac* can again be cited as an example of incisions playing a part in the design process. The marked contours for Abraham's head and left arm indicate that he was first positioned slightly to the right of the painted figure, and scorings in the lower left of the canvas reveal the original outline of Isaac's right thigh, later covered over by his father's mantle. These incisions can therefore be interpreted as substitutes for a painted, preliminary under-drawing that guided but did not necessarily determine the final design. The selective figural contours outlined by incisions in Caravaggio's work appear to be most concerned with anchoring and relating the figures within space rather than sketching a complete composition. This suggests that Caravaggio made use of incisions to note down his observations during life sessions in the studio, working out his design on the canvas by referring to and transposing the figural proportions and spatial interrelationships of posed models. Supporting this proposal is the general absence of incisions in non-figural parts of his compositions, such as the landscape in the *Sacrifice of Isaac* which, of course, he did not paint from life.[18]

Additional incisions of a different character have been detected in X-rays of the *Sacrifice of Isaac*; although less clear-cut in function than those outlining the models' contours, these also appear to establish spatial points of reference. Despite the seeming randomness of the scorings, on closer inspection their placement relates to the three figures: two vertical lines mark the central axis of the composition in Abraham's figure; three short parallel markings descend roughly along his left arm; and several arcs were made in the vicinity of the angel's and Isaac's heads. Caravaggio may have made these incisions as quick and preliminary notations of key positions at the start of the design process before proceeding to the next step of incising actual contours. The regularity of the curving arcs hints that here he used a compass, a supposition given some credence by the entry in the police blotter of 1598 recording a 'pair of compasses' seized by the arresting officer along with Caravaggio's unlicensed sword.[19]

If Caravaggio made incisions during life sessions, are we to picture him staging *tableaux vivants* in his studio, as Derek Jarman so marvellously projected in his film (Pl. 191)? An approach surprisingly like this was used by Barocci, according to Bellori who described how that painter orchestrated harmonious compositions by directing his assistants to test different groupings, gestures and expressions before choosing the most natural yet graceful poses. It is conceivable that Caravaggio devised a similar procedure, but whereas Barocci's observations resulted in a preparatory cartoon, Caravaggio worked directly on the canvas during his studio sessions.[20]

**191** Still from Derek Jarman's film *Caravaggio*, 1986

Renewed examination of the *Judith Beheading Holofernes* (Pl. 69) reveals that during the initial design phase Caravaggio made use of incisions as well as a rough sketch. Using the two techniques to establish the most convincing position for Holofernes's severed head, he had first summarily blocked it out with the brush but subsequently incised its corrected placement to delineate the definitive form. This example suggests that Caravaggio developed his initial idea by posing a model, considering the compositional effect on the canvas, and then repositioning the model to finalize his design. Ever concerned with the dynamic between live model and evolving design on the canvas, Caravaggio developed flexible practices in the studio, varying his procedure as the situation demanded.[21]

The model's crucial role emerges clearly in the *Narcissus* (Pl. 53), which has lately been thoroughly examined. X-rays of the canvas record Caravaggio's modifications to the outline of the boy's reflection in the pool of water. In the underlying first version, he had merely flipped over the figure's profile to create the mirror image. Unsatisfied, he moved up the head and knee, otherwise retaining the same silhouette. The change suggests that Caravaggio, realizing the optical improbability of his first design, checked the appearance of a real reflection by posing a model bending over a mirror, and studied the results with the help of a second mirror set up to the side. His customary selective approach to nature prevailed in the final form of the reflection, however, and although he corrected the figural proportions he chose not to describe the boy's profile from below, thus avoiding the more accurate but less attractive sight of the model's nostrils, throat and armpits.[22]

The probable use of one or more mirrors in designing the *Narcissus* finds support in Baglione's statement that the young Caravaggio 'made a few small paintings after his own reflection in a mirror'. In fact, the one large and one convex mirror included in the inventory of the contents of his house in the later Roman years (Appendix VII) may well have belonged to his studio equipment from an early stage. The paintings from the late 1590s offer the strongest visual evidence for this. A round, convex mirror serves as a narrative prop in the *Conversion of Mary Magdalen* (Pl. 67), and for the *Medusa* (Pl. 54), which is on a similarly shaped support. Caravaggio probably studied his own and/or his model's reflection in a curved mirror, as the play of concavity and convexity in the image implies. Mirrors could have also assisted him in projecting the foreshortening of the two gods seen from below on the ceiling he painted for Cardinal Del Monte. His handling of illusionism was probably partly influenced by late sixteenth-century Lombard perspectival theory which explained figural foreshortening, but it is just as plausible that he availed himself of the practical studio expedient of using mirrors as optical aids. Standing over a slightly tilted mirror laid on the ground, Caravaggio would have seen his own body from the same steep angle as in the painting; did he expose this ruse, tongue in cheek, by portraying Neptune in his own likeness?[23]

There were other optical devices available to Caravaggio for sharpening his transcriptions from life. The most obvious was the *camera obscura*, a form of primitive camera known to Italian painters through prints and theoretical treatises. No textual evidence verifies Caravaggio's use of it; the 'eleven pieces of glass' inventoried among his possessions in 1605 and cited by some as proof that he owned optical lenses, are clearly described in the document as glassware for the table. Examination of the works themselves reveals none of the telltale visual signs of the use of this early form of camera comparable to those in Vermeer's paintings. None the less, Caravaggio may well have been interested in observing the heightened effects of light and colour obtained by the instrument.[24]

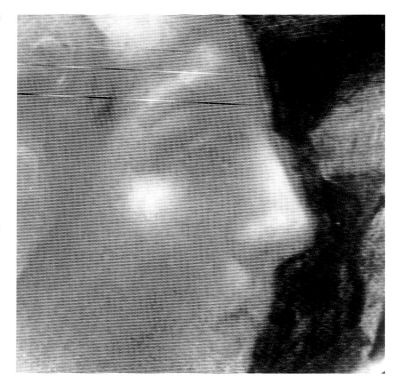

Once he had established the composition on the canvas and proceeded to the actual painting, Caravaggio used the distinctive procedure of layering-in the figural elements in the design from back to front. Visual and technical analyses reveal numerous instances in which he painted an entire figure only to cover it over partially by the person in front; for example, in the *Cardsharps* (Pl. 35), the young cheat's doublet overlaps his partner's left sleeve and glove, and in the *Flagellation* (Pl. 138), the figure of the hatted executioner was first fully laid in and then Caravaggio painted the second executioner's head on top of his shoulder. During the process of painting, he probably still referred to individual models, now posed independently, to ensure the surface naturalism of his figures. At a later stage the model was dismissed, as suggested by an infra-red reflectogram of the *Sacrifice of Isaac* (Pl. 192) which reveals that Caravaggio reworked the model's idiosyncratic features into the angel's more idealized profile. While confirming his use of the model, this instance testifies that

**192  Sacrifice of Isaac** (Pl. 118), Infra-red reflectogram showing face of angel

Caravaggio was not against improving upon nature, an unexpected finding in view of his critics' accusations and his own public stance. At an advanced stage of execution, he introduced the appropriate accessories – sleeves, cloaks, hats, or daggers and swords – painting these over already defined areas: the lutenist's red cloak in the *Musicians* (Pl. 41) lies over his fully painted white sleeve, and the blade is superimposed on Holofernes's chest and cushion in *Judith Beheading Holofernes* (Pl. 69). Finally, to enrich his figures' costumes with decorative details, Caravaggio inserted refinements like the embroidered trim on the saint's dress in the *Conversion of Mary Magdalen* (Pl. 186). He typically softened his protagonists' faces by adding a dangling curl (*Conversion of Mary Magdalen*, Pl. 67, *Narcissus*, Pl. 53, the late *Saint John the Baptist*, Pl. 179) or by attaching beards, as in the *Flagellation* (Pl. 138) in which all three models were clean-shaven.[25]

In summary, Caravaggio's working process can be reconstructed in the following hypothetical but plausible way. With the assistance of posed models, he roughed out the composition and marked key contours on the prepared canvas with his brush and incised outlines. Concurrently, he established fundamental axes and constructed a balanced design by geometrically ordering the canvas. He also decided upon, and blocked out, the overall distribution of lights and darks. Once the composition had been more or less finalized, Caravaggio generally avoided making changes in the actual painting, as the relatively small number of *pentimenti* confirms. He subsequently re-posed models individually or in pairs, according to his guiding design, and then painted each figure successively, proceeding from back to front, using his knowledge of colours and referring back to the model, who was no longer half-undressed but clothed with shirt, sleeves and cloak. Essentially following his original design but honing details, such as the contour of an arm or the border of a mantle, Caravaggio rapidly built up the paint layers, applying finishing touches at the end to embellish the image.

Several essential pieces are still missing from this reconstruction because of the patchiness of available information on any one of Caravaggio's studio techniques. The current state of knowledge about incisions provides a typical example. Although many of Caravaggio's easel pictures have been examined for incisions, to date the results have been diagrammed in only a few instances and with disconcertingly divergent results. As for the ecclesiastical works, critics have occasionally noted incisions over the years, but these have rarely been systematically mapped. Our interpretation of the role of incisions in plotting large-scale, multi-figured compositions must therefore remain tentative, stopping short of any global explanations of Caravaggio's use of this particular technique. In response to such gaps in technical evidence, an ambitious Italian project, Delineavit, is under way to create a comprehensive, computer database that will chart scientific as well as basic factual information for the artist's whole *œuvre*. As the body of technical data grows, two interrelated questions must be kept in mind: how unique and how innovative were Caravaggio's techniques? The first directly bears on assessing the authenticity of paintings, and the second raises the broader issue of the relationship between Caravaggio's practices and his imagery.[26]

Despite the restricted nature of the historical record, the assumption that Caravaggio's techniques were as unique as his art and personality underlies most current discussions of newly discovered or debated canvases. Scientific reports therefore play an important role in verifying individual claims, as recently attested in the cases of the *Cardsharps* (Pl. 35), the *Fortune-Teller* (Pl. 37), and the *Betrayal of Christ* (Pl. 117). Where two identical versions of the same composition exist, technical investigation can help to identify the original. But whereas the canvas in the Galleria Doria Pamphilj has been exposed as a non-autograph copy of the Capitoline *Saint John the Baptist* (Pl. 107), misinterpretations have arisen in other cases which prove that scientific analysis or stylistic evidence viewed in isolation is an inadequate method of backing up an attribution to Caravaggio. For example, the reported use of incisions and the superimposing of paint layers in such debated pictures as the *Ecce Homo* (Pl. 121) and the *Toothpuller* (Pl. 172), fail to confirm Caravaggio's authorship in the face of contrary stylistic evidence. The scientific report is only one factor in assessing an attribution, which also requires judicious consideration of the history of the painting, its form and imagery. The *Narcissus* (Pl. 53) is the latest instructive example of a convincing attribution based on provenance, stylistic and iconographic analyses, and on technical data revealing methods compatible with Caravaggio's.

If techniques used by Caravaggio are found in non-autograph paintings in his style, the implication follows that these methods were known and copied to some extent by his followers. Without an organized studio or apprentices, the means of transmission had to be informal, however. Minniti, with whom he had shared lodgings, surely saw him at work, and other close artist friends in Rome and Naples, such as Prospero Orsi and Caracciolo, had access to his studio, as did his assistant Cecco del Caravaggio. He perhaps also opened his Roman workshop to ardent followers like Gentileschi, Saraceni, and Manfredi. In the small sample of five paintings by Manfredi that have been technically examined, some points in common with Caravaggio's practices can be singled out: accentuation of silhouettes with a border of exposed ground, painting in superimposed layers from the back to the front, and a limited degree of composing on the canvas. But Manfredi used incisions in only one of the five paintings and, demonstrably, for transferring a cartoon.

The exportation of Caravaggism from Rome may also have disseminated some of the master's practices north of Italy. Recent scientific examination of Georges de La Tour's *œuvre* has revealed his use of at least two techniques associated with Caravaggio. Like him, La Tour selectively incised the canvas to fix spatial points of reference, and he also delineated the contours of his figures by leaving exposed an encircling narrow strip of the ground. Unfortunately, this limited sample of comparative material hardly permits any general conclusion to be drawn about the degree to which Caravaggio's followers imitated his practices as well as his compositions.[27]

The single components of Caravaggio's working procedure were not new: composing on the canvas distinguished the Venetian school of painting; incisions served various purposes by the late sixteenth century; the mixing of oil and tempera for painting pale complexions dated back to the early Renaissance. Furthermore, the supports, grounds and pigments employed by Caravaggio were all commonly in use at the time. But Caravaggio modified and combined these practices in unconventional ways, taking a flexible and spontaneous approach to standard methods. From start to finish of the working process, he telescoped studio procedure as if to reduce the number of intermediary steps between the immediate observation of nature and the canvas. The innovation lay less in the technical means than in Caravaggio's guiding principle that practice was a dynamic part of the creative process. The posing of the model, the application of controlled direct light, and the simulation of lifelike colour were central to formulating and realizing the design. The resultant startling verisimilitude created the desired illusion of artlessness – for Caravaggio, the highest art was to forswear any obligation to art.

Caravaggio first arrived in Rome as an unknown, aspiring painter. Exceptionally, within the brief span of six to seven years, he made himself the most talked-about artist in the city, lionized by its urban élite. His emotional instabilty jeopardized his professional success, however, and eventually he wrecked his own career with the murder of Tomassoni and his mysterious crime in Malta, which condemned him to four years in exile. Notwithstanding the turbulence of his life, he transformed himself from a talented painter of simple yet alluring genre scenes to a consummate artist of complex and profound religious imagery.

In his own lifetime Caravaggio's art held a magnetic attraction for other painters. Numerous as his followers were, they merely reproduced the superficial features of his art and none succeeded in capturing its essence. Then as now, his paintings looked like no other artist's. Their originality did not win them ubiquitous applause, however, and in the decades following his death the myth took root among his detractors that he had 'come into the world to destroy painting', as Poussin reputedly inveighed. Less than two centuries later, defamation of Caravaggio all but completely supplanted acclaim, and he was vilified by such as John Ruskin, who held him responsible for all 'horror and ugliness, and filthiness of sin'.

Rescued from malign neglect at the turn of this century, Caravaggio was dubbed 'the first modern artist' by Roger Fry and came to assume the mantle of father to all great realists from Velázquez and Rembrandt to Courbet and Manet. Now, at the close of the twentieth century, Caravaggio is inarguably the best-known and most universally admired Italian Baroque artist. His broad appeal derives from his legendary persona as a revolutionary, iconoclastic painter, a rebel in his personal and professional life, who swept away the cobwebs of Mannerist art and sliced through the cant of his times. Devoid of the distancing patina of age, his paintings address the modern viewer with uncommon directness. The very immediacy of religious intensity, violence and palpable sensuality implicates the viewer, who is tempted to straddle the line between passive observer and voyeur.

Throughout this study of the historical figure of Caravaggio at work in late sixteenth- and early seventeenth-century Italy, I have emphasized his active engagement in the artistic and cultural world of his day, attempting to revise his stereotyped characterization as socially alienated. In examining individual pictures, I have acknowledged the unexpected extent of his dependence on artistic tradition for compositional and iconographical motifs, and even for certain studio practices. The man and his art, however, are not devalued by this reassessment; viewing him in his own historical context more sharply offsets his extraordinary achievement in creating an original body of work that changed the nature of artistic representation. Mirroring the ferment of early Baroque Italy, his art embodies the conflict between past and present that was emerging as a central intellectual issue. While reference to the classical heritage and the heroic artistic legacy of the High Renaissance was as unavoidable for him as for any other artist, Caravaggio challenged and ultimately shattered their canonical authority. Instead he aligned himself with those contemporary forces in the arts and sciences which embraced and promoted innovation and laid the foundations of modernism.

His approach to painting, as his early audience recognized, aggressively pursued naturalism. For some, he defiled the cherished classical–idealist tradition of 'how things ought to look' by substituting the subversive naturalistic principle of 'how things are'. For others, the novelty of his paintings sufficed to recommend them. Neither perspective explains his lasting greatness, which is owed to the originality of his vision. Caravaggio saw beauty in ordinary people and objects and by ordaining them the interpreters of sacred scripture and mysteries of the faith, he transmuted reality into a haunting and transcendent art.

# Checklist of paintings

The checklist includes paintings by, attributed to, or after Caravaggio in chronological order. References to recent, specialized bibliography are given for those works which present problems of connoisseurship or interpretation. Otherwise readers are referred to the standard *catalogues raisonnés* of Caravaggio's works by Cinotti, 1983, and Marini, 1987. The plate numbers and page references in parentheses direct the reader to illustrations and related discussions in the text. All known authentic works by Caravaggio are reproduced in the text, and attributed paintings and copies are illustrated in the Checklist. However, as a rigid dividing line cannot always be drawn between certain and disputed works, several debatable pictures have been included in the text to facilitate discussion (Plates 25, 31, 121, 123, 132, 146, 147, 172) and a few plausible attributions, which could not be fully discussed in the text, only appear in the Checklist, but are reproduced on a larger scale (Plates 200, 204, 210). All works are oil on canvas unless stated otherwise. Dimensions are given in centimetres.

**1**

**Boy Peeling a Fruit**, *c.*1593–4 [pp. 58–9, 66]

**(A)** Private collection, Rome, 75.5 × 64.4 **[Pl. 25]**
**(B)** Phillips, London, sold 10 December 1996, 64.2 × 51.4 **[Pl. 193]**

For a recent discussion of the various versions of the theme and their competing claims to being Caravaggio's original, see S. Macioce, in *Caravaggio: La vita e le opere*, 1996, pp. 123–35, with earlier bibliography. The majority view is that version **(B)**, with the truncated format, most closely resembles the lost original. The Phillips version here illustrated is a very recent addition to the Caravaggio literature, and its autograph status has yet to be tested against that of the other, best version of **(B)**, formerly in the Sabin Collection and exhibited in *The Age of Caravaggio*, 1985, no. 61. The argument of Marini, 1987, no. 4, that **(A)** is the same as the version said to have been confiscated by Borghese from Cesari has been refuted by a re-reading of the documents; see E. Fumigalli, in *Come dipingeva il Caravaggio*, 1996, pp. 143–5. Fumigalli also published a document of 1608 citing Caravaggio's picture and identifying the fruit as a peach; this evidence supports the interpretation of Röttgen, 1974, p. 251, n. 126, that links the boy's action to a popular proverb likening peeling a peach to warding off evil.

**2**

**Self-Portrait as Bacchus**, *c.*1593–4

Galleria Borghese, Rome, 66 × 52
[pp. 52–7, **Pl. 23**]

Contrary to Gilbert, 1995, p. 250, the majority of modern critics continue to recognize the painter's self-portrait in this canvas; see the recent literature by K. Herrmann Fiore, in *Caravaggio. Nuove riflessioni*, 1989, pp. 95–134; and Posèq, 1990.

**3**

**Boy Bitten by a Lizard**, *c.*1593–4 [pp. 53, 61]

**(A)** National Gallery, London, 66 × 49.5 **[Pls. 26, 185]**
**(B)** Roberto Longhi Foundation, Florence, 65.8 × 52.3 **[Pl. 31]**

For a summary of views up to 1991 on each version's autograph status, see Gregori, in *Caravaggio. Come nascono*, 1991, no. 4. For the unconvincing argument that Caravaggio represented a poisonous salamander, see Slatkes, 1976, pp. 148–53; and also see the persuasive counter-argument in Posner, 1981, pp. 387–91. Heimburger, 1990, pp. 8–9, interpreted the work, unconvincingly, as an allegory of all five senses.

**4**

**Boy with a Basket of Fruit**, *c.*1593–4

Borghese Gallery, Rome, 70 × 67
[pp. 53–66, **Pl. 24**]

For the latest discussion, see A. Cottino, in *La natura morta*, 1995, no. 11.

**5**

**Boy with a Vase of Roses**, copy?, *c.*1593–4

The High Museum, Atlanta, 67.3 × 51.8
**[Pl. 194]**

For the fullest recent discussion of the history, attribution, and iconography of this painting, see Gregori, in *The Age of Caravaggio*, 1985, no. 62.

**193** Boy Peeling a Fruit [checklist no. 1 (B)]          **194** Boy with a Vase of Roses [checklist no. 5]

6

**Penitent Magdalen**, *c*.1593–4

Galleria Doria Pamphilj, Rome, 122.5 × 98.5

[pp. 69–71, **Pl. 32**]

For an ingenious but tentative identification of this model, who also posed for the Madonna in *Rest on the Flight into Egypt*, as the red-headed prostitute Anna Bianchini, see Bassani and Bellini, 1994, pp. 50–6, 182–4, who also proposed improbably that her corpse later served as the model for the Madonna in the *Death of the Virgin*. An analogy between the figure's pose and the bride's 'watchful sleep' in the Song of Songs was seen by M. Calvesi, in *La Maddalena*, 1986, pp. 147–51, and seconded by L. Russo, in *Caravaggio. Nuove riflessioni*, 1989, pp. 156–61, who unconvincingly identified the contents of the carafe on the floor as wine.

7

**Cardsharps**, *c*.1594–5

Kimbell Art Museum, Fort Worth, 94.2 × 131.2

[pp. 71–8, **Pl. 35**]

For the full account of the rediscovery of this work, see Gregori, *Caravaggio. Come nascono*, 1991, no. 2, with earlier bibliography.

8

**Fortune-Teller**, *c*.1594–5

Pinacoteca Capitolina, Rome, 115 × 150

[pp. 74–8, **Pl. 37**]

For the fullest discussion of the history of this version and its recent restoration and results, see Gregori, in *Caravaggio. Come nascono*, 1991, no. 1, with further bibliography.

9

**Musicians**, *c*.1595

Metropolitan Museum of Art, New York, 87.9 × 115.9

[pp. 87–95, **Pls. 41, 42**]

10

**Rest on the Flight into Egypt**, *c*.1595

Galleria Doria Pamphilj, Rome, 135 × 166.5

[pp. 116–20, **Pl. 59**]

For a possible Aldobrandini provenance, see M. Cinotti, in *Caravaggio. Nuove riflessioni*, 1989, p. 81 (as Pietro Aldobrandini); but see Bologna, 1992, pp. 301–2 (as Olimpia Aldobrandini). On the music, see Slim, 1983; Trinchieri Camiz, in *Caravaggio. Nuove riflessioni*, 1989, pp. 214–16; and Calvesi, 1990, pp. 201–7. For the interpretation that the scene incorporates Joseph's dream (Matt. 2:19–20), see Barolsky, 1990, pp. 20–1.

11

**Lute-Player**, *c*.1595–6

Hermitage, St Petersburg, 94 × 119

[pp. 94–102, **Pl. 47**]

For a version of this composition which includes the reflection of a window mentioned by Baglione and was formerly in the Duke of Beaufort Collection, see Karin Wolfe, 'Caravaggio: Another "Lute Player"', *BM*, vol. 127 (1985), pp. 451–2.

12

**Lute-Player**, attributed, *c*.1596

Private collection, New York, 100 × 126.5

[pp. 87, 95, **Pl. 195**]

For a summary of the documentary evidence and technical reports on this work, see Gregori, in *Caravaggio. Come nascono*, 1991, no. 5. For its musical theme, a defence of its autograph status, and its relationship to no. 11, see Christiansen, 1990.

13

**Saint Francis of Assisi in Ecstasy**, *c*.1596

Wadsworth Atheneum, Hartford, 92.5 × 127.8

[pp. 120–4, **Pl. 61**]

The former association of this canvas with the listing of a 'Saint Francis in Ecstasy' in Del Monte's 1626 inventory has been cast into serious doubt; see Gilbert, 1995, pp. 107–10, 125; and Bologna, 1992, pp. 237–62, who unconvincingly proposed the Caravaggesque painting in the Barbara Piasecka Johnson Collection as Del Monte's lost picture. Contrary to Askew, 1969, the wound of the stigmata was never present on the saint's right hand; see the restoration report in Cadogan and Mahoney, 1991, p. 84. For the work in relationship to the Franciscans, see Treffers, 1988, pp. 145–71; and Gilbert, 1995, pp. 153–4, 158.

14

**Bacchus**, *c.*1597

Uffizi, Florence, 95 × 85

[pp.103–6, **Pl. 50**]

Current interpretations of the subject-matter include a Christian allegory of
death and resurrection (Calvesi, 1990, pp. 221–4, seconded by Marini, 1987,
pp. 398–9); exclusively homo-erotic content (Posner, 1971, pp. 302–3, 308);
a *tableau vivant* of contemporary Bacchic-inspired banquets (Gregori, in
*The Age of Caravaggio*, 1985, p. 244, and Posèq, 1990); and a celebration
of Horatian frugality and moderation (C. del Bravo, 1985, pp. 162–4).

15

**Narcissus**, *c.*1597

Galleria Nazionale d'Arte Antica, Rome, 113 × 95

[p. 106, **Pl. 53**]

For the restoration report, and discussion of the provenance, attribution and
iconography, see R. Vodret, in *Caravaggio. Nuove riflessioni*, 1989, pp. 222–6;
Vodret, 1996, pp. 9–13; and Vodret, in *Caravaggio: La vita e le opere*, 1996,
pp. 167–83. See also the unconvincing attribution to Spadarino by G. Papi, in
*Caravaggio. Come nascono*, 1991, pp. 359–68.

17

**Calling of Saints Peter and Andrew**, copy?, *c.*1597–8

Royal Collection, Hampton Court Palace, 132 × 163

[**Pl. 197**]

Sometimes called a 'Way to Emmaus' in the past, this work is known in
several versions thought to reflect a lost original (Cinotti, 1983, p. 559), but
its relationship to Caravaggio has been questioned (Hibbard, 1983, p. 294).

16

**Saint John the Baptist**, attributed, *c.*1597–8

Cathedral Museum, Toledo, 169 × 112

[**Pl. 196**]

The controversial attribution was accepted and argued by Gregori, 1989,
pp. 99–142, who had originally assigned it to the Caravaggist Bartolomeo
Cavarozzi (*c.*1590–1625). As Gregori recognized, this is related stylistically
to the *Sacrifice of Isaac* in the Barbara Piasecka Johnson Collection (no.18),
but in both, contours and surfaces are softer than in Caravaggio's art.

18

**Sacrifice of Isaac**, attributed, *c.*1597–8

Barbara Piasecka Johnson Collection, Princeton, NJ, 116 × 173

[**Pl. 198**]

For this recent attribution, see Gregori, in *Caravaggio. Come nascono*, 1991,
no. 6. This work appears to be by the same artist as no.16; Caravaggio's
authorship is very doubtful for either, which resemble more closely works
by Bartolomeu Cavarozzi.

**196 Saint John the Baptist** [checklist no. 16]

**197 Calling of Saints Peter and Andrew** [checklist no. 17]
**198 Sacrifice of Isaac** [checklist no. 18]

### 19
**Medusa**, *c.*1598

Uffizi, Florence, diameter 55
[pp. 106–9, **Pl. 54**]

The work is first recorded in Florence in 1598, where it was probably brought by Del Monte himself; see Waźbiński, 1994, II, p. 350. For the most recent discussions, see Marin, Louis, *Détruire la peinture* (Paris, 1977), pp. 119–44, 191–4; Posèq, 1989, pp. 170–4; Cropper, 1991; and Corradini and Marini, 1993, pp. 167–9.

### 20
**Portrait of Monsignor Maffeo Barberini**, *c.*1598

Private collection, 124 × 90
[pp. 290–3, **Pl. 146**]

For the portrait in Florence, Corsini Collection, formerly proposed but no longer accepted as Caravaggio's lost original, see Friedländer, 1955, no. 44b, Pl. 17.

### 21
**David and Goliath**, attributed, *c.*1598–9

Prado, Madrid, 110 × 91
[**Pl. 200**]

For the fullest discussion of this work, see Gregori, in *The Age of Caravaggio*, 1985, no. 77. For photographs of X-rays of the canvas revealing a *pentimento* in Goliath's head, see Gregori, in *Caravaggio. Come nascono*, 1991, pp. 28–9.

### 22
**Flagellation of Christ**, copy?, *c.*1598–9

Palazzo Camuccini, Cantalupo Sabino (Rieti), 140 × 106
[**Pl. 199**]

**199 Flagellation of Christ** [checklist no. 22]

Known in several versions, this composition was proposed as being after a lost original by Longhi; see Cinotti, 1983, p. 561.

### 23
**Fortune-Teller**, *c.*1598–9

Louvre, Paris, 99 × 131
[pp. 66, 78–9, **Pl. 38**]

Around 1620, Mancini, I, p. 109, saw this version in the collection of Alessandro Vittrici (*c.*1595/6–1650), for whose patronage, see L. Spezzaferro, in *La natura morta*, 1995, pp. 53–4.

### 24
**Conversion of Mary Magdalen**, *c.*1598–9

Detroit Institute of Arts, 97.8 × 132.7
[pp. 131–5, **Pl. 67**]

For the debate over the attribution, see D. Posner, in *BM*, vol. 117 (1975), p. 302; and replies of M. Johnson, and F. J. Cummings, ibid., pp. 302–3; see also the most recent discussion by Papi, in *Caravaggio. Come nascono*, 1991, no. 7.

### 25
**Portrait of Fillide**, *c.*1598–9

formerly Kaiser Friedrich Museum, Berlin (destroyed), 66 × 53
[p. 131, **Pl. 66**]

At Fillide Melandroni's death in 1618, she stipulated in her will that Caravaggio's portrait which was in her possession should be returned to its rightful owner, the Florentine Giulio Strozzi (1583–1660), presumably her noble admirer; see Corradini and Marini, 1993, p. 174, no. 26. By 1638, the portrait had passed into Vincenzo Giustiniani's collection.

### 26.
**Saint Catherine of Alexandria**, *c.*1599

Thyssen-Bornemisza Collection, Madrid, 173 × 133
[pp. 127–9, **Pl. 63**]

### 27
**Judith Beheading Holofernes**, *c.*1599

Galleria Nazionale d'Arte Antica, Rome, 145 × 195
[pp. 135–8, **Pls. 69, 189**]

For the most recent discussion with technical information, see Gregori, in *Caravaggio. Come nascono*, 1991, no. 8.

**200 David and Goliath** [checklist no. 21]

28

**Martyrdom of Saint Matthew**, 1599–1600

Contarelli Chapel, S. Luigi dei Francesi, Rome, 323 × 343
[pp. 154–60, **Pls. 76**, **79**, **184**]

29

**Calling of Saint Matthew**, 1599–1600

Contarelli Chapel, S. Luigi dei Francesi, Rome, 322 × 340
[pp. 160–2, **Pl. 82**]

The chapel stands at the head of the left side of the nave. Contrary to previous claims, Del Monte did not become an official member of the Fabbrica di San Pietro until after its reconstitution as one of the congregations of the Apostolic Chamber in 1605; see Rice, 1997, p. 319. In 1626 Del Monte's funeral was held in S. Luigi. For the Contarelli documents, see Röttgen, 1974, pp. 11–44. For a Franciscan interpretation of the chapel, see Treffers, 1989. The *chiaroscuro* of no. 29 has been related to the language of Clement VIII's bull proclaiming the conversion of King Henri IV of France, solemnized by a Mass in S. Luigi dei Francesi in September 1595; see Calvesi, 1990, pp. 279–84. For the debate about Matthew's identity in no. 29, see Prater, 1985; Kretschmer, 1988; Hass, 1988; Lavin, 1990; Röttgen, 1991; Prater, 1995.

30

**Jupiter, Neptune and Pluto**, *c.*1599–1600

Villa Boncompagni-Ludovisi, Rome, oil on plaster, 500 × 285
[pp. 110–15, **Pl. 55**]

**400**

For the 1990 restoration, see Bernardini, Gaggi, and Marcone, 1991; and for additional iconographical analyses, see Wallach, 1974–5; and Rossi, 1994.

31

**Conversion of Saint Paul**, 1600–1

Private collection, Rome, oil on wood, 237 × 189
[pp. 146–9, 165–6, **Pl. 83**]

For the most recent discussion, see Papi, in *Caravaggio. Come nascono*, 1991, no. 9.

32

**Conversion of Saint Paul**, 1600–1

Cerasi Chapel, S. Maria del Popolo, Rome, 230 × 175
[pp. 166–9, **Pl. 86**]

33

**Crucifixion of Saint Peter**, 1600–1

Cerasi Chapel, S. Maria del Popolo, Rome, 230 × 175
[pp. 169–73, **Pl. 89**]

On the church, see E. Bentivoglio and S. Valtieri, *Santa Maria del Popolo* (Rome, 1976). A painting on canvas in St Petersburg, Hermitage, inv. 28, has been unconvincingly proposed in the past as either a copy or a derivation of the first *Crucifixion of Saint Peter*, see Cinotti, 1983, pp. 560, 635 ill.

34

**Supper at Emmaus**, 1601

National Gallery, London, 141 × 196.2
[pp. 209–13, **Pl. 110**]

For the latest discussion with reference to Mattei's payment, see L. Testa, in *Caravaggio e la collezione Mattei*, 1995, no. 1.

35

**Still Life with a Basket of Fruit**, *c.*1601

Pinacoteca Ambrosiana, Milan, 31 × 47
[p. 215, **Pl. 112**]

For further discussion of the dating, see Gregori, in *The Age of Caravaggio*, 1985, pp. 262–4, who prefers *c.*1599/1600.

36

**Cupid**, *c.*1601–2

Staatliche Museen, Berlin, 191 × 148
[pp. 201–5, **Pl. 106**]

An earlier dating of 1598–9 was proposed by Bissell, 1974, but see Strinati, in *Nuove riflessioni*, 1989, p. 175. The discussion of iconography in the text is indebted to Enggass, 1967; Anita Vitali, 'Caravaggio's *Amore*: A Platonic Visualization in Praise of Vincenzo Giustiniani and the God of Love', Master's Thesis, Rutgers University, 1986; and Pacelli, 1989–90, esp. p. 161. For the proposal that Baglione inserted a visual charge of sodomy against Caravaggio in his *Divine Love and Sacred Love* (Galleria Nazionale, Rome, 1602), see Röttgen, 1993, pp. 326–40. For discussions of the *Cupid* in terms of the *paragone*, see Posèq, 1993, pp. 13–18; and Schröter, 1995, p. 69.

37

**Death of the Virgin**, *c.*1601–3

Louvre, Paris, 369 × 245
[pp. 185–8, **Pls. 98**, **101**]

For the chapel for which this altarpiece was intended and an excellent concise discussion, see Loire and Brejon, 1990. For the range of dating of the altarpiece, compare Cinotti, 1983, no. 41 (1606), and Askew, 1990, pp. 17–18 (1602). On the brown mantle lying across Mary's legs, see Lavin, 1985, who suggested plausibly that it refers to the scapular; also see Askew, 1990, p. 105. Two identifications have been proposed for Caravaggio's model for the Virgin: (a) the rehabilitated prostitute Caterina Vannini (Calvesi, 1990, pp. 341–5); (b) the prostitute Anna Bianchini (Bassani and Bellini, 1994, pp. 181–4).

38

**Saint Matthew and the Angel**, *c.*1602

formerly Kaiser Friedrich Museum, Berlin (destroyed), 223 × 183
[pp. 179–83, **Pl. 94**]

On Matthew's Socratic appearance and the identification of the Hebrew text, see Lavin, 1974, 1974a, 1980.

**39**

**Saint John the Baptist**, *c*.1602

Pinacoteca Capitolina, Rome, 129 × 95
[pp. 204–8, **Pl. 107**]

On the authenticity of the Capitoline version and the exposure of the version in the Doria Pamphilj Gallery as a copy, their respective history, and the technical analyses, see Correale, 1990, with earlier bibliography. Although the 1602 payment by Mattei to Caravaggio is assigned to July by Cappelletti and Testa, 1990, p. 237, June is specified in *Caravaggio e la collezione Mattei*, 1995, p. 120, and in Schröter, 1995, p. 68. The language recording the small payment suggests it may have been a bonus from Ciriaco to Caravaggio, but does not prove the proposal of Gilbert, 1995, p. 279, no. 5, that the painting was a gift. For the unconvincing suggestion that the subject is mythological, see Gilbert, 1995, chapters 1–6, with earlier bibliography. For the view that Caravaggio was parodying Michelangelo, see Friedländer, 1955, pp. 89–94, and Freedberg, 1983, pp. 59–60; and for a Freudian interpretation of Caravaggio's motives, see Hibbard, 1983, pp. 154–9. For discussions of the painting in terms of the *paragone*, see Posèq, 1993; and Schröter, 1995, p. 69.

**40**

**Saint Matthew and the Angel**, 1602–3

Contarelli Chapel, S. Luigi dei Francesi, Rome, 295 × 195
[pp. 178–83, **Pl. 95**]

On the discrepancy in size between the two versions of the altarpiece, see Rotondi, 1966.

**41**

**Betrayal of Christ**, 1602–3

National Gallery of Ireland, Dublin, 133.5 × 169.5
[pp. 220–1, **Pl. 117**]

For the rediscovery of this work in 1990, known previously in copies such as the one in Odessa, for technical information, and for Mattei's patronage, see Benedetti, 1995, 1995a; and Benedetti, in *Caravaggio e la collezione Mattei*, 1995, no. 3.

**42**

**Doubting Thomas**, *c*.1602–3

Stiftung Schlösser und Gärten, Sanssouci, Potsdam, 107 × 146
[p. 216, **Pl. 114**]

Ciriaco Mattei, Benedetto, and Vincenzo Giustiniani have been alternatively proposed as the original owner of this work; see Perini, 1995, p. 200; and Danesi Squarzina, 1997, p. 773. The graphic emphasis on the tangibility of Christ's body may contain an additional allusion to the doctrinal issue of the Real Presence in the eucharistic Host, as was true of earlier Florentine representations; see Kristen van Ausdall, 'The Corpus Verum', *Verrocchio and Late Quattrocento Italian Sculpture*, eds. S. Bule *et al.* (Florence, 1992), pp. 33–49.

**43**

**Entombment**, *c*.1602–4

Pinacoteca Vaticana, Rome, 300 × 203
[pp. 173–6, **Pls. 75, 91**]

On the church popularly called the Chiesa Nuova, see C. Barbieri, S. Barchiesi, and D. Ferrara, *Santa Maria in Vallicella* (Rome, 1995). Pietro's rather than Girolamo Vittrice's patronage is argued by M. Calvesi, in *Caravaggio e la collezione Mattei*, 1995, p. 20. A dating of 1602–4 corresponds best with the style of the work, whose sculptural figures and, above all, masterful composition can only postdate the Contarelli laterals and the second Cerasi laterals. The Madonna's gesture was likened to the priest's consecration of the Host; see Glen, 1988, p. 21.

**44**

**Sacrifice of Isaac**, 1603

Uffizi, Florence, 104 × 135
[p. 224, **Pls. 118, 190, 192**]

For the archival record and technical data, see Gregori, in *Caravaggio. Come nascono*, 1991, no. 11.

**45**

**Still Life with Fruit on a Stone Ledge**, attributed, *c*.1603

Private collection, 87.2 × 135.4
[**Pl. 201**]

This recent attribution was made by Spike, 1995, who dates it to *c*.1602–6 and relates it to an entry in Cardinal Antonio Barberini the Younger's inventory of 1671. Although influenced by Caravaggio, its lighting, composition, execution of details, and blatant sexual symbolism all differ significantly from his known works and argue against the attribution.

**201 Still Life with Fruit on a Stone Ledge** [checklist no. 45]

**46**
**Crowning with Thorns**, attributed, c.1603
Kunsthistorisches Museum, Vienna, 127 × 165.5
[**Pl. 202**]

For the history of the work, discussion of the attribution, and technical
data, see Gregori, in *Caravaggio. Come nascono*, 1991, no. 12. Undeniably
Caravaggesque, the lighting and execution of figures appear to be by another
artist.

**402**

**47**
**Saint John the Baptist**, c.1603–4
Galleria Nazionale d'Arte Antica, Rome, 97 × 132
[**Pl. 204**]

For the most recent discussion of the plausible, albeit debated, attribution, see
S. Alloisi, in C. Strinati and R. Vodret, *Caravaggio and his Italian Followers*,
exh. cat., Wadsworth Atheneum, Hartford (Venice, 1998), no. 2. Supporting the
attribution is the technical evidence that reveals several practices
characteristic of Caravaggio's art.

**48**
**Crowning with Thorns**, attributed, c.1603–5
Cassa di Risparmio e Depositi, Prato, 178 × 125
[p. 231, **Pl. 123**]

For a recent summary of criticism, see Gregori, in *Caravaggio. Come nascono*,
1991, no. 10, who asserts autograph status. In my opinion, the awkward
figural arrangement falls short of Caravaggio's masterful designs, and Christ's
tormentors move like wooden marionettes. Uncharacteristic too is the clumsy
error resulting in the anatomically incorrect hand of the torturer at the upper
border. Furthermore, the smoothed, chiselled features of Christ's face and his
claw-like hands are unparalleled in Caravaggio's *œuvre*.

**49**
**Saint John the Baptist**, c.1603–5
Nelson-Atkins Museum, Kansas City, 173.4 × 132.1
[pp. 235–6, **Pls. 124, 126**]

For the most complete information about the painting with pertinent
bibliography, see Rowlands, 1996, no. 25. A papal bull of 1603 authorizing
refurbishment of the Oratory for which it was probably intended offers a likely
date for Caravaggio's commission.

**50**
**Madonna di Loreto**, c.1603–6
Cavaletti Chapel, S. Agostino, Rome, 260 × 150
[pp. 188–92, **Pl. 102**]

*In situ,* the altarpiece decorates the first chapel in the left nave of the church.
For the most recent discussion, see M. Marini, in *L'iconografia*, 1995, pp.134–7.
Baglione's use of the word 'schiamazzo' to describe popular reaction has
convincingly been interpreted as 'unjustified praise' by Hibbard, 1983, p. 190,
and Bologna, 1992, pp. 230–4. Bassani and Bellini, 1994, pp. 212–14, discussed
Caravaggio's pilgrims in the context of vagabonds in contemporary Rome.

**51**
**Saint Francis**, c.1603–6
S. Maria della Concezione, Rome, 130 × 98
[**Pl. 203**]

For the attribution of the composition to Caravaggio, see Gregori, in *The
Age of Caravaggio*, 1985, nos. 82, 83. Another version in S. Pietro, Carpineto
Romano, has been either called a copy (Christiansen, 1986, p. 442) or, more
improbably, the original (C. Tempesta, in *Caravaggio nei musei romani*, 1986,
pp. 42–3).

403

**204 Saint John the Baptist** [checklist no. 47]

**52**

**Ecce Homo**, attributed, *c.*1605

Galleria Civica di Palazzo Rosso, Genoa, 128 × 103
[pp. 229–31, **Pl. 121**]

Wrongly associated with Massimi's alleged competition in the past (Gregori, in *The Age of Caravaggio*, 1985, no. 86; Barbiellini Amidei, in *Caravaggio. Nuove riflessioni*, 1989, p. 49), this picture neither fits the available historical evidence nor resembles Caravaggio's known works other than superficially, an opinion shared by Christiansen, 1986, p. 438, and 1995, pp. 87–8. For other recent discussion, see also Gregori, 1990, p. 19–20; and Gregori, in *Caravaggio. Come nascono*, 1991, no. 13, with technical data. A painting whose description matches this composition was inventoried as an original in the collection of the Spanish diplomat Juan de Lezcano in 1631; see Antonio Vannugli, 'Orazio Borgianni, Juan de Lezcano and a "Martyrdom of St Lawrence" at Roncesvalles', *BM*, vol. 140 (1998), pp. 5–15, esp. 7, no. 15.

**53**

**Saint Jerome**, *c.*1605

Galleria Borghese, Rome, 112 × 157
[pp. 238–42, **Pl. 129**]

For its provenance, dating, and technical data, see Gregori, in *Caravaggio. Come nascono*, 1991, no. 15, with further bibliography.

**404**

**54**

**Saint Jerome**, attributed, *c.*1605

Museo de Montserrat, Barcelona
110 × 81 [**Pl. 205**]

The modern attribution to Caravaggio is difficult to sustain because of the heavy-handed execution and paucity of invention; but for a summary of divided opinion, see Gregori, in *The Age of Caravaggio*, 1985, no. 84.

**55**

**Agony in the Garden**, attributed, *c.*1605

formerly Kaiser Friedrich Museum, Berlin, 154 × 222
[**Pl. 206**]

Known only in a photograph since its destruction in 1945, the canvas can be identified with a picture inventoried in Benedetto Giustiniani's collection in 1621; see Danesi Squarzina, 1997, p. 773. Its attribution and dating are controversial; see Cinotti, 1983, pp. 411–12.

**56**

**Madonna dei Palafrenieri**, 1605–6

Galleria Borghese, Rome, 292 × 211
[pp. 192–6, **Pl. 105**]

On the Marian imagery, see Mâle, 1972, pp. 30–8, 346–53; and M. Warner, *Alone of All Her Sex: The Myth and the Cult of the Virgin Mary* (New York, 1976), chap. 16; Settis, 1975, pp. 4–18, esp. p. 16. According to Rice, 1997, pp. 44–5, the *palafrenieri* lost the rights to the altar just after the removal of Caravaggio's altarpiece and in vain petitioned for them back. She thus questions Spezzaferro's assertion (in *Colloquio sul tema*, 1974, pp. 129, 136–7) that they were assigned another altar. Despite Calvesi's statement (1990, p. 347) that Del Monte, Giustiniani, and Pietro Paolo Crescenzi were on the Fabbrica di San Pietro in 1605, the first two cardinals were appointed between 1605 and 1612, and the third is unlikely to have been made a member before his elevation to the cardinalate in 1611 (L. Rice, written communication to the author, 21 May 1995). Calvesi's further claim (1990, pp. 347–52) that Paul V was directly responsible for the removal of Caravaggio's painting has been persuasively refuted by Bologna, 1992, pp. 63, 383, no. 15.

**57**

**Portrait of Paul V**, attributed, c.1605–6

Prince Camillo Borghese Collection, Rome, 203 × 119
[p. 293, **Pl. 147**]

On the painting's history and attribution, see Cinotti, 1983, no. 85; Marini, 1987, no. 58. Whereas the stark presentation of the sitter supports attribution of the design to Caravaggio, troubling weaknesses can be spotted in the flattened head, awkwardly positioned right hand, and mechanical description of the papal vestments. These details detract from the overall effect of the painting, eroding the sitter's physical presence and offering an unfavourable comparison with Caravaggio's *Portrait of Alof de Wignacourt*, painted only two to three years later.

**58**

**Supper at Emmaus**, 1606

Brera, Milan, 141 × 175
[pp. 243–6, **Pl. 130**]

For the most recent discussion, see Gregori, in the *The Age of Caravaggio*, 1985, no. 87.

**59**

**Saint Francis in Prayer**, attributed, c.1606

Museo Civico, Cremona, 130 × 90
[**Pl. 207**]

For the latest full discussion of this work whose conception and technique find numerous parallels in Caravaggio's art, see Gregori, in *Caravaggio. Come nascono*, 1991, no. 17, who proposed a date of c.1606.

**60**

**Magdalen in Ecstasy**, attributed, 1606

Private collection, Rome,
106.5 × 91 [p. 246, **Pl. 132**]

For the fullest recent discussion of the different versions of this composition, see Pacelli, 1994, pp. 161–97. This canvas is one of the two replicas of highest quality; unfortunately the other is known only from an old photograph. It has a Neapolitan Carafa-Colonna provenance, and so may be the painting mentioned in the letter from the papal nuncio in Naples to Borghese (Appendix XI). The picture still fails to carry complete conviction as the lost original, because of the uniformity of the tight parallel folds in the Magdalen's blouse, and her boneless hands that look especially weak when compared to the apparent looser execution of fabric and more careful anatomical articulation visible in the photograph of the rival, missing version, published by Longhi in 1947; see Cinotti, 1983, no. 64. Until the latter is traced, judgement is best suspended as to the autograph status of either canvas. The recent arguments that Caravaggio's Magdalen is not in ecstasy, and that he intended an anti-Tridentine stance on the sacrament of Penance are not convincing; for which see Pacelli, 1994, pp. 184–6.

**61**

**Seven Works of Mercy**, 1606–7

Pio Monte della Misericordia, Naples, 390 × 260
[pp. 262–7, **Pl. 133**]

Studies since Pacelli, 1984, include Mormone, 1986, and Tuck-Scala, 1993.

**62**

**Madonna of the Rosary**, c.1606–7

Kunsthistorisches Museum, Vienna, 364.5 × 249.5
[pp. 271–6, **Pl. 139**]

For the most recent discussion of the proposal that this was the painting originally ordered in Rome by Cesare I d'Este, Duke of Modena, see Bologna, 1992, pp. 325–9. Although Caravaggio had promised to consign his 'nearly finished' painting to the ducal agent in mid-November 1605, he still had not done so six months later when he fled Rome, and the agent wrote to him in Naples to recover his advance. The surviving correspondence (Friedländer, 1955, pp. 310–14) neither names the precise subject nor reveals whether the picture was taken to Naples. On the Rosary Chapel in the church of S. Domenico next to the ducal palace in Modena, see J. Southorn, *Power and Display in the Seventeenth Century* (Cambridge, 1988), pp. 14–15. The 400-ducat assessment placed on the *Madonna of the Rosary* in September 1607 far exceeds the very modest fee Caravaggio had quoted to the ducal agent a year and half earlier, a sum disproportionate to a huge and multi-figured altarpiece. Another recent proposal that the original Radulovic painting lies under the *Madonna of the Rosary* was made by Marini, 1987, no. 69, G, but X-rays do not confirm the presence of an underlying design related to Radulovic's commission. For the plausible, though less convincing identification of the donor portrait as the reigning viceroy Benavente, see Brown, 1984. Recently Pacelli, 1994, pp. 56–7, reaffirmed a dating during the first Neapolitan period. For a recent discussion of the space in the painting, see Danto, 1993, pp. 107–8.

**63**

**Flagellation of Christ**, 1607

Museo Nazionale di Capodimonte, Naples, 266 × 213
[pp. 268–70, **Pl. 137**]

For the history of the commission, the De Franchis family, and discussion of whether execution of the work extended over two distinct phases, see Pacelli, 1994, pp. 41–7, and Gregori, in *The Age of Caravaggio*, 1995, no. 93. In my opinion, the unified appearance of the painting and its smooth handling link it most closely to the first Neapolitan period, and given its relatively small size, restricted palette of earth tones, and simple composition, Caravaggio had ample time to finish it before leaving for Malta. X-rays reveal that the torturer replaces an underlying figure, positioned lower down and apparently representing a witness to the scene; for an illustration, see Lapucci, in *Caravaggio. Come nascono*, 1991, p. 43. For the prosposal that the original male figure was a donor portrait, see Pacelli and Brejon, 1985. A possible source for Christ's stumbling pose has been proposed in Romanino's *Flagellation* (Metropolitan Museum of Art, New York) by Christiansen, in *Come dipingeva*, 1996, pp. 26–8. For the influence of the work on Neapolitan painters, see Bologna, in *Battistello Caracciolo*, 1991, no. 2.1.

**64**

**Flagellation of Christ**, *c.*1607

Musée des Beaux-Arts, Rouen, 134.5 × 175.5
[pp. 270–1, **Pl. 138**]

In the manipulation of light and shadow and in the handling of details of modelling, this is the best of the extant versions of the composition. For the history of this version, possibly from Scipione Borghese's collection, and the other four copies, see Papi, in *Caravaggio. Come nascono*, 1991, no. 18.

**65**

**Judith Beheading Holofernes**, copy?, *c.*1607

Banco di Napoli, Naples, 140 × 160
[**Pl. 208**]

For the history of a lost picture with this subject executed by Caravaggio in Naples, and for this painting, proposed as a copy by Louis Finson after the original, see F. Navarro, in *Battistello Caracciolo*, 1991, no. 2.4; and Pacelli, 1994, p. 59.

**66**

**Holy Family**, attributed, *c.*1607

Clara Otero Silva Collection, Caracas, 117.5 × 96
[**Pl. 210**]

Known in at least three versions and a seventeenth-century print, the composition is believed by most experts to reflect a lost original, datable anywhere from Caravaggio's early years to his Neapolitan period. This canvas has not been accessible for first-hand study; none the less it has been judged superior in quality to the other versions on the basis of photographs.

**67**

**Saint Sebastian**, copy?, *c.*1607

Private collection, Rome, 170 × 120
[**Pl. 209**]

For the lost original of this subject, this composition and its three extant versions, see Pacelli, 1994, pp. 64–7.

406

**208 Judith Beheading Holofernes** [checklist no. 65]

**209 Saint Sebastian** [checklist no. 67]

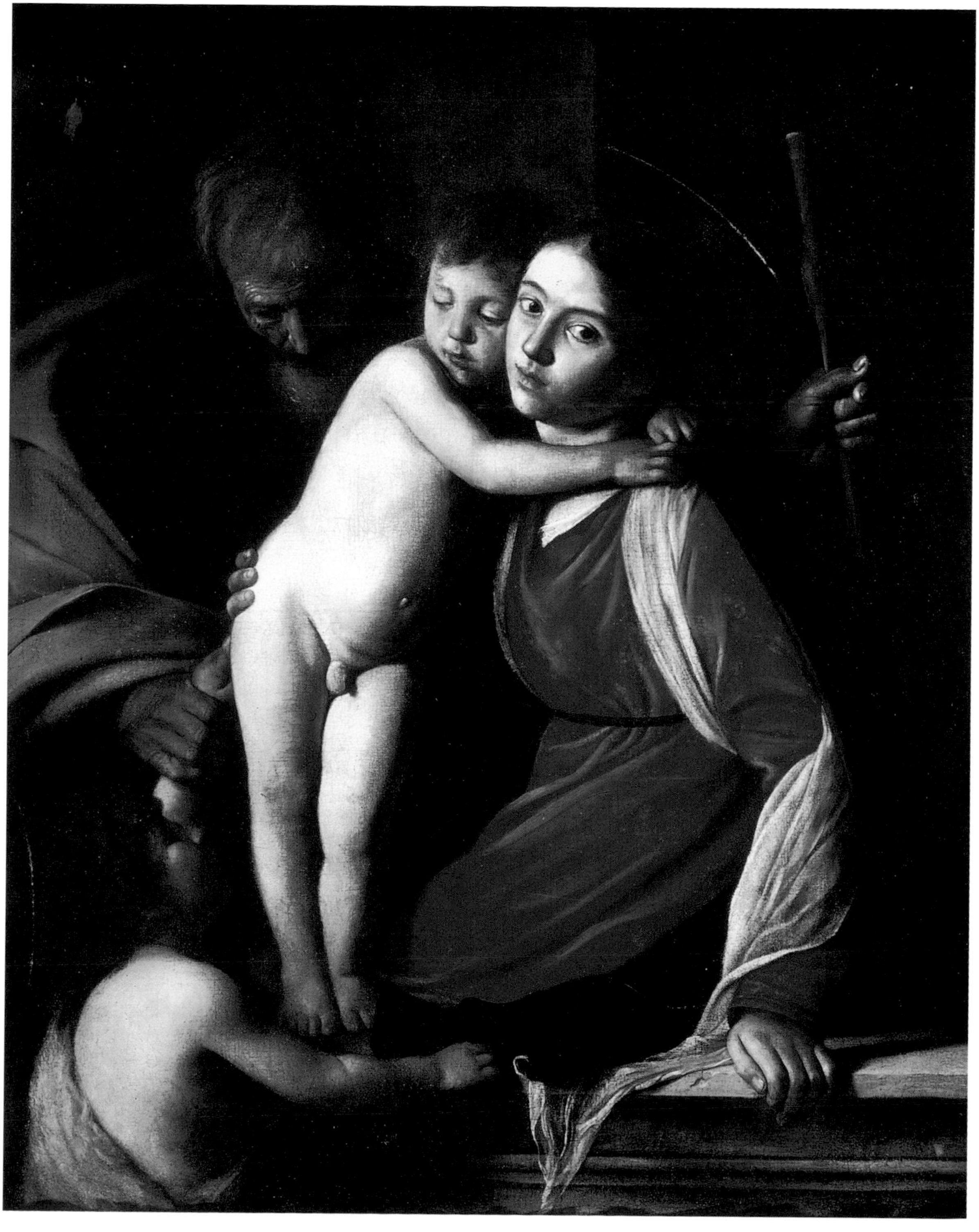



**210 Holy Family** [checklist no. 66]

68
**Saint Januarius**, copy?, c.1607

Mary Jane Harris Collection, New York, 126.5 × 92.5
[**Pl. 211**]

Most recently, Bologna (in *Battistello Caracciolo*, 1991, p. 116) proposed that this is a copy after Tanzio da Varallo and not Caravaggio.

69
**David with the Head of Goliath**, attributed, c.1607

Kunsthistorisches Museum, Vienna, oil on wood, 90.5 × 116.5
[**Pl. 212**]

Although this panel has been tentatively linked to the citation in Bellori, p. 214, of the Conde de Villamediana's 'David', no supporting documentary evidence has been found and the attribution is not widely accepted.

70
**Saint Jerome**, c.1607–8

Co-Cathedral of St John, La Valletta, 117 × 157
[pp. 280–4, **Pl. 141**]

Stolen in 1985, the canvas was recovered two years later and reinstalled in its former position, high on the right wall above a door leading into the next chapel. The 1957 restoration of the canvas confirmed that the door leaf formed part of the original composition and is not a later addition; see Carità, 1957, pp. 41–82, esp. p. 77. For the intriguing proposal that Girolamo Carafa, Prior of Barletta, commissioned the *Saint Jerome*, see Cutajar, 1989, p. 74, and for Maltese copies of the work, see Cutajar, 'Caravaggio in Malta', in *Malta and Caravaggio*, 1989, p. 3. On a supposed 'Magdalen' by Caravaggio in the chapel, see Cutajar, 'Caravaggio in Malta', in *Malta and Caravaggio*, 1989, pp. 3–6.

71
**Portrait of Alof de Wignacourt**, c.1607–8

Louvre, Paris, 194 × 134
[pp. 284–7, **Pl. 142**]

For Wignacourt's engraved portraits, see Maindron, 1908, pp. 241–54, 339–52. In locating the portrait in the Armoury, Bellori, p. 226, may have confused the original with Giulio Cassarino's portrait, not aware that the former had already been shipped to Paris. According to Bellori, p. 226, Caravaggio also portrayed Wignacourt 'seated and unarmed in the habit of Grand Master'. Matching this description is another work by Cassarino, painted a decade after Caravaggio's visit, that has occasionally been proposed as a copy or variation of the lost original. Its composition, the pose, and details of the setting have nothing Caravaggesque about them, however; Cassarino's portrait depends instead upon a conventional prototype by Scipione Pulzone representing an earlier Grand Master; see Cutajar, 'Caravaggio in Malta', in *Malta and Caravaggio*, 1989, p. 15; and Cutajar, 1989, p. 17.

72
**Beheading of Saint John the Baptist**, 1608

Co-Cathedral of St John, La Valletta, 361 × 520
[pp. 297–308, **Pls. 150, 151, 153**]

Prior Stefano Lomellini was not Caravaggio's patron, as wrongly claimed in the past; see Cutajar, in *Malta and Caravaggio*, 1989, p. 13, who points out along with other supporting evidence the fact that Lomellini (d. 1699) was probably not even born at the time. If Caravaggio paid his 'passage money' with a painting, it is more probable that he did so with this large, multi-figured work and not with the *Saint Jerome*, which Macioce had proposed (in *L'ultimo Caravaggio*, 1987, p. 179). On later alterations to the chapel, see Azzopardi and Stone, 1996, and Stone, 1997. In the Order's statute book, a print by Thomassin depicting knights looking out from the barred window of the Order's prison has been proposed as one of Caravaggio's compositional sources; see Stone, 1997, p. 165, fig. 12.

408

73
**Sleeping Cupid**, 1608

Palazzo Pitti, Florence, 71 × 105
[pp. 294–7, **Pl. 148**]

For a recent summary of the painting's history, and the technical report, see Gregori, in *Caravaggio. Come nascono*, 1991, no. 19; and *Caravaggio da Malta a Firenze*, 1996, pp. 40–4. Gregori published a 1538 engraving by Giovanni Battista Scultori as Caravaggio's source but this print is related only in so far as its composition also reflects the antique and Renaissance sculptures. X-rays of the canvas seemingly betray the original presence of a poppy in Cupid's right hand and an owl behind his stomach – traditional references to Sleep (Gregori, in *Caravaggio. Come nascono*, 1991, no. 19). The suggestion that Michelangelo's work aroused Caravaggio's interest in the antique motif was made by Posèq, 1990b, pp. 147–67; see also Posèq, 1987. On Marino's five poems on the same theme in *La Galeria* (Venice, 1619) and the possible exchange of inspiration with Caravaggio, see Cropper, 1991, pp. 199–201. For the frescoed copy of 1619 by Giovanni da San Giovanni (1593–1636) on the façade of the Dell'Antella palace in Piazza Santa Croce, Florence, see Pizzorusso, 1983.

74
**Burial of Saint Lucy**, 1608

Museo di Palazzo Bellomo, Syracuse, 408 × 300
[pp. 317–23, **Pl. 160**]

For the most recent discussions of the painting, see the entry by G. Barbera, and the restoration report by M. Cordaro, in *Caravaggio in Sicilia*, 1984, no. 8, and pp. 269–93; see also A. Zuccari, 'La pala', in *L'ultimo Caravaggio*, 1987, p. 147–73.

75
**Portrait of a Knight of Malta**, *c.*1608

Palazzo Pitti, Florence, 118.5 × 95.5
[p. 289, **Pl. 145**]

For the history of the painting and a summary of scholarly opinions, see Gregori, in *The Age of Caravaggio*, 1985, no. 95, in *Caravaggio. Come nascono*, 1991, no. 20, and in *Caravaggio da Malta a Firenze*, 1996, pp. 36–9. Its rapid execution and seemingly unfinished state, evident in the figure's unmodelled arms, suggest placing this portrait at the very end of the sequence of Maltese works; Caravaggio's imprisonment and escape from the island would have prevented its completion. The sitter's identification as Wignacourt is controversial, and at least two other alternatives have been argued: Niccolò Caracciolo di San Vito (Bologna, 1992, p. 478, no. 23, who questions the attribution to Caravaggio); and Antonio Martelli (Chiarini, 1989, pp. 15–16; Gash, 1997, pp. 156–60).

76
**Raising of Lazarus**, 1608–9

Museo Regionale, Messina, 380 × 275
[pp. 323–7, **Pls. 162, 163, 164**]

For the most recent discussion, see C. Ciolino Maugeri, in *Caravaggio in Sicilia*, 1984, no. 9; and the technical analysis by Lapucci, 1994.

77
**Adoration of the Shepherds**, 1608–9

Museo Regionale, Messina, 314 × 211
[pp. 327–33, **Pl. 165**]

For the most recent discussion, see C. Ciolino Maugeri, in *Caravaggio in Sicilia*, 1984, no. 10; and the technical analysis by Lapucci, 1994. For its possible association with the cult of the 'Madonna del Parto', see E. Natoli, in *L'ultimo Caravaggio*, 1987, p. 224.

78
**Saint John the Baptist at the Source**, attributed, *c.*1608–9

Private collection, Rome, 100 × 73
[**Pl. 213**]

This composition is known in at least three versions. For discussion of this recently restored canvas as the autograph prototype of the others, and datable to *c.*1608–9, see Gregori, 1993, pp. 3–20; and also see pp. 21–3 for T. Schneider's related technical analysis.

409

**79**

**The Toothpuller**, attributed, c.1608–10

Palazzo Pitti, Florence, 139 × 194.5
[p. 346, **Pl. 172**]

For discussion of this controversial attribution, the theme, and technical analysis, see Gregori, in *The Age of Caravaggio*, 1985, no. 98; and Gregori, in *Caravaggio. Come nascono*, 1991, no. 21.

**80**

**Nativity with Saints Lawrence and Francis**, 1609

formerly Oratorio della Compagnia di S. Lorenzo, Palermo, 268 × 197
[pp. 327–33, **Pl. 167**]

For the fullest recent discussion, see C. Ciolino Maugeri, in *Caravaggio in Sicilia*, 1984, no. 11.

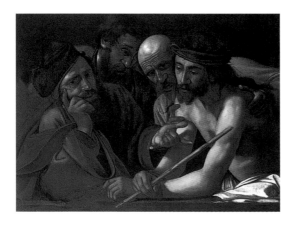

**81**

**Ecce Homo**, copy?, c.1609

Private collection, 77.7 × 101.8
[**Pl. 214**]

Known in at least two extant versions, this composition has been attributed to Caravaggio most recently by Gregori, 1990, pp. 19–27, who associated it with the Passion cycle commissioned by Nicolao di Giacomo in Messina in 1609. The other version, in Arenzano, has been proposed as the autograph lost original by Papi, 1990, pp. 28–48, an opinion not shared by Gregori. Don Juan de Tasis y Peralta, second Conde de Villamediana, owned a copy of this or a related composition; for which see E. Fumigalli, in *Come dipingeva*, 1996, p. 145.

**82**

**Crucifixion of Saint Andrew**, c.1609–10

Cleveland Museum of Art, 202.5 × 152.7
[p. 350, **Pl. 173**]

For the fullest discussion, see Lurie, in *The Cleveland Museum of Art*, 1982, pp. 318–23, with bibliography up to 1982. Even though most modern critics have dated the Cleveland picture to 1607, pointing out stylistic similarities with works from the first Neapolitan period, the later dating proposed here was also argued by Gregori, in *The Age of Caravaggio*, 1985, no. 99.

**83**

**Salome with the Head of Saint John the Baptist**, c.1609–10

National Gallery, London, 91.5 × 106.7
[pp. 342–3, **Pl. 171**]

**84**

**Salome with the Head of Saint John the Baptist**, c.1609–10

Palacio Reale, Madrid, 116 × 140
[pp. 342–3, **Pl. 170**]

The interrelationship and relative dating of these two *Salomes* have elicited varied opinions; see the recent summary in Pacelli, 1994, pp. 62–3. For the Madrid picture, see Cinotti, 1983, no. 28; for the London picture, see Gregori, in *The Age of Caravaggio*, 1985, no. 96. For a variant composition with the same theme attributed recently to Caravaggio, see Bologna, 1992, no. 84, fig. 80.

**85**

**Annunciation**, c.1609–10

Musée des Beaux-Arts, Nancy, 285 × 205
[p. 365, **Pl. 183**]

This painting was given to the Primatiale of Nancy by Henri II, Duke of Lorraine (reigned 1608–24; the Primatiale was founded in 1607 and consecrated in 1609; *Musées de France: Répertoire des peintures italiennes*, Paris, 1988, pp. 72–3). It is generally accepted as a damaged or unfinished original from late in Caravaggio's career; its specific dating is debated. For recent commentaries, see Bologna, 1992, p. 345; and Pacelli, 1994, pp. 81–3. On the patronage, see Calvesi, 1990, pp. 375–8, who suggested that the commission was given to Caravaggio in Malta by one of the Duke's sons. For documentary evidence regarding their presence in Malta, see Macioce, 1994, pp. 209–10, 220, no. 22. The Duke was married to Margherita Gonzaga, the sister of Cardinal Federigo, who negotiated Caravaggio's pardon.

410

86

**Denial of Saint Peter**, *c.*1609–10

Metropolitan Museum of Art, New York, 94 × 125.5
[p. 351, **Pl. 175**]

Attributed to Caravaggio in the 1970s and widely accepted as one of his late
works, the painting was acquired by the museum in 1997. Caravaggio's lost
painting of this theme in the Certosa di S. Martino was cited by Bellori and
praised by De Dominici; for which see Pacelli, 1994, pp. 99–100. See also the
recent discussion of Gregori, in *The Age of Caravaggio*, 1985, no. 100.

87

**Saint John the Baptist**, 1610

Galleria Borghese, Rome, 159 × 124
[p. 359, **Pl. 179**]

For a recent discussion with technical data, see Gregori, in *Caravaggio. Come
nascono*, 1991, no. 22. After Caravaggio's death, the painting was first sent
back to Naples on the same felucca where a copy was made for the Viceroy,
Pietro Fernandez di Castro, Conde de Lemos (1610–16); it reached Scipione
Borghese in Rome in 1611; for this history, see Pacelli, 1994, pp. 119–55,
who also attributed a *Saint John the Baptist* in a German private collection to
Caravaggio, associating it with the second St John recorded on the felucca.

88

**Martyrdom of Saint Ursula**, 1610

Banca Commerciale Italiana, Naples, 154 × 178
[pp. 354–5, **Pl. 178**]

For the fullest, recent discussions of the history of the picture, the relevant
documentary evidence, and the iconography, see Bologna, 1992, pp. 263–80;
and Pacelli, 1994, pp. 100–17.

89

**David with the Head of Goliath**, *c.*1610

Galleria Borghese, Rome, 125 × 101
[pp. 359–65, **Pl. 180**]

For the fullest, recent discussion, with technical information, see Papi, in
*Caravaggio. Come nascono*, 1991, no. 16; and for its copies, see Pacelli,
1994, p. 139. Its dating has previously wavered between the first and second
Neapolitan periods. Recorded in the Borghese collection as early as 1613,
the *David* seems to have been present in Naples in November 1610 when
a Neapolitan painter was paid for making two copies of a work of this subject
by the master. For a recent theory, more ingenious than convincing, that
Goliath's agony is a metaphor for the artist's creative agony, see Posèq,
1990b, pp. 176–7. For a psychoanalyst's opinion of Caravaggio's personality,
see Gedo, 1983, p. 179.

412    **Appendices**

## Appendix I
### Extracts from Mancini's *Considerazioni sulla pittura*, c.1617–21

#### A  Description of the Modern Schools of Painting (pp. 108–9)

[…] having arrived at the century of living artists, the following ideas must be proposed in order to be able to examine them, namely:

That these living painters can be reduced to four categories, classes or, better, schools, one of which is that of Caravaggio, widely followed, and taken up with purpose, care, and knowledge, by Bartolomeo Manfredi, Spagnoletto [Jusepe de Ribera], Francesco, called Cecco del Caravaggio, Spadarino [Giovanni Antonio Galli], and partially Carlo Veneziano [Saraceni]. A characteristic of this school is lighting from one source only, beaming from above without reflections, as would occur from one window in a room with the walls painted black, so that, the light areas being very light and the shadows very dark, they give the picture relief, but in a rather unnatural way, as was never done before or thought of in any other century or by any previous painters, like Raphael, Titian, Correggio or others. In this way of working, the painters of this school are closely tied to nature, which they always keep before their eyes as they work; they do well with one figure alone, but in narrative composition and in interpreting feelings, which depend on imagination and not direct observation, I do not think they are good at portraying nature, which they always keep before their eyes, because it is impossible to put in one room a multitude of people acting out the story with that light from a single window, and having one person that laughs or cries or pretends to be walking, and has to stay still in order to be copied; thus their figures, although forceful, lack movement, feeling, and grace, typical of this way of working, as we shall say. Of this school I do not think that I have seen a more graceful and expressive figure than the Gypsy foretelling good fortune to that young man, by Caravaggio, which is owned by Signor Alessandro Vittrici, a gentleman of Rome; although it is in the same style, none the less the young Gypsy shows her slyness with a false smile while stealing the ring from the young man, who, in his turn, shows his naïveté and his desire for the beauty of the little Gypsy who tells him his fortune while stealing his ring.

#### B  'On Decorum in Art' (p. 120)

… And before proceeding further, one has to consider the appearance of figures, so that the attitude, expression, and movement with which they are depicted is appropriate to the particular action that is being performed. Thus one can understand how badly some modern artists paint, such as those who, wishing to portray the Virgin Our Lady, depict some dirty prostitute from the Ortaccio, as Michelangelo da Caravaggio did in the Death of the Virgin in that painting for the Madonna della Scala, which for that very reason those good fathers rejected it, and perhaps that poor man suffered so much trouble in his lifetime.

#### C  Life of Caravaggio (pp. 223–6)

Our age owes much to Michelangelo da Caravaggio for the manner of colouring he introduced, which is now quite widely followed.

He was born in Caravaggio of most honourable citizens, as his father was major-domo and architect of the Marchese di Caravaggio; when he was still a young boy, he studied diligently for four or six years in Milan although from time to time he would do some crazy thing caused by his hot-tempered nature and high spirits.

Afterwards, at the age of about twenty, he went to Rome where, being poor, he stayed with Pandolfo Pucci da Recanati, a beneficiary of St Peter's, and where he had to work for his keep and perform services which did not befit him; what was worse, in the evening he was given a salad which served as an appetizer, main course and dessert, and, as the saying goes, as accompaniment and toothpick. Having departed greatly dissatisfied after a few months, from then on he called this master benefactor of his 'Monsignor Insalata'.

During this period he made him some copies of devotional images that are in Recanati, and, for sale, a boy crying because he has been bitten by a lizard which he is holding in his hand, and afterwards another boy who is peeling a pear with a knife, and the portrait of an innkeeper at whose house he used to board; and a portrait of a […]

In the meantime he was struck by an illness and, being without money, he had to go to the Ospedale della Consolatione. During his recovery he made many paintings for the prior of the hospital who brought them to Seville [or Sicily?], his home.

I am told that he later stayed in the house of Cavalier Giuseppe [Cesari d'Arpino] and of Monsignor Fantin Petrignani who gave him the use of a room. During this time he painted many pictures and, in particular, a Gypsy telling the fortune of a young man, the Flight into Egypt, the penitent Magdalen and a Saint John the Evangelist.

Then followed the Deposition of Christ in the Chiesa Nuova, the paintings in S. Luigi, the Death of the Virgin in [Santa Maria de] la Scala, which the fathers removed from the church because Caravaggio had portrayed a courtesan as the Virgin and which is now in the possession of the Duke of Mantua, the Madonna of Loreto in S. Agostino, the one for the altar of the *Palafrenieri* in St Peter's, many pictures which are in the possession of the most illustrious Borghese, the Cerasi Chapel in S. Maria del Popolo, as well as many privately owned paintings in the houses of the Mattei, the Giustiniani, and the Sannesio.

Finally, as a result of certain events – having almost lost his life, and having killed his adversary in self-defence with the help of Onorio Longhi – he was forced to flee from Rome. He went first to Zagarolo where he was secretly given sanctuary by the Prince and where he painted a Magdalen, and Christ going to Emmaus, which Costa bought in Rome.

With the money he moved to Naples where he painted various works. From there he went to Malta, where he made some paintings that pleased the Grand Master, who, it is said, gave Caravaggio the habit of his order as a sign of his esteem. Having left there with the hope of being pardoned, he arrived at Porto Ercole where, stricken with a malignant fever, he died alone, in pain and hardship at the height of his glory, at the age of about thirty-five or forty, and was buried nearby.

It is undeniable that he attained a high level of accomplishment for single figures, heads, and the use of colour, and that the profession in this century is greatly indebted to him. However, he brought strange habits to his great knowledge of art. He had only one brother, a priest, a man of letters and of high morals who, when he heard of his brother's fame, wanted to see him and, moved by brotherly love, went to Rome. Knowing that he was staying in the house of the most illustrious Cardinal Del Monte, and being aware of his brother's eccentricities, the priest thought it best to explain everything to the Cardinal first. This he did and he was kindly asked to return in three days' time.

In the meantime the Cardinal called Michelangelo and asked him if he had any relatives; he answered that he had none. Being unable to believe that the priest would tell him a lie about a matter that could be checked, and that would do him no good, the Cardinal had enquiries made among Michelangelo's countrymen to find out if he had any brothers, and who they were, and he found that the viciousness was on Michelangelo's side. The priest returned after the three days and was received by the Cardinal, who sent for Michelangelo. On being confronted with the priest, he said that he was not his brother and that he did not know him. The poor priest, in the presence of the Cardinal, said tenderly, 'Brother, I have come from far away only to see you, and having seen you, I have found what I was looking for, I am, as you know, in such a position, thank God, that I do not need you for myself or for my children.

Instead it was my hope, if God would allow me to arrange a marriage for you, to see you with children. May God help you to do good, as I will implore His Divine Majesty in my prayers, and as I know that your sister will do in her chaste and virginal prayers.'

Michelangelo being unmoved by these words of burning and bright love, the good priest left without even receiving a godspeed from his brother. Thus it cannot be denied that he was extremely crazy and that, owing to this strange behaviour, he shortened his life by ten years or more, and somewhat diminished the glory he had won through his profession. Had he lived longer, he would have grown with his art, to the great benefit of the students of his profession.

### D  The School of Caravaggio (pp. 302–3)

This century is followed by that of those most modern [painters] who, it seems to me, must be preferred to their predecessors for intelligence, style and force of colouring, for landscapes and perspectives. And it is my view that this century can be reduced to four schools, as four different styles of paintings can be recognized in it. [ … ]

It seems to me that the second has to be the school of Michelangelo da Caravaggio, who is very forceful and colours in an excellent way. Many works by him can be seen: the Deposition from the Cross in the Chiesa Nuova, the Madonna dell'Horto [sic] in Sant' Agostino, the chapel of Saint Matthew in San Luigi dei Francesi, and many privately owned pictures, and in particular those in the houses of Signor Marchese Giustiniani and of Signor Alessandro Vittrici; the one on the right, in the [church of the] Madonna della Scala, many things in the room before the chapel in Monte Cavallo, and countless other paintings in private houses. And this [school] is widely followed and taken up in this century, and its characteristic is a certain naturalness.

**414**

**Appendix II**
**Life of Caravaggio by Giovanni Baglione**
(from *Le vite de' pittori*, Rome, 1642, pp. 136–9)

Michelangelo was born in Caravaggio in Lombardy, and was the son of a respectable master builder, named Amerigi. He began to study painting and, because nobody in Caravaggio could teach him in the way he wanted, he went to Milan and lived there for some time. Then he came to Rome with the intention of applying himself diligently to this noble discipline.

At first he settled down with a Sicilian painter who had a shop of crude works of art. Then he went to stay for some months in the house of Cavalier Giuseppe Cesari d'Arpino. After this he tried living by himself, and he made some small pictures of himself drawn from the mirror. The first was a Bacchus with some bunches of various kinds of grapes, painted with great care but a little dry in style. He also painted a boy who was bitten by a lizard as it emerged from flowers and fruits; that head actually seemed to cry out, and it was all done very carefully. Nevertheless, he was unable to sell these works and soon found himself in a pitiable state without money, and very poorly dressed. Fortunately some charitable gentlemen of the profession came to his aid, until Maestro Valentino, an art dealer near San Luigi dei Francesi, arranged to sell a few of the paintings. On this occasion he made the acquaintance of Cardinal del Monte who, being an art lover, took him into his house. Now that he had a home and an allowance, he gathered his courage and reputation, and painted for the Cardinal youths playing music very well drawn from nature, and also a youth playing

a lute. Everything in this picture looked alive and real, most notably a carafe of flowers filled with water in which one could easily distinguish the reflections of a window and other objects in the room. On those flowers was fresh dew, rendered with exquisite accuracy. This, Caravaggio said, was the best picture he had ever made.

He portrayed a gypsy telling a young man's fortune with beautiful colours. He painted a Divine love conquering the profane, and a very terrifying head of a Medusa with vipers for hair and placed on a shield, which was presented as a gift by the Cardinal to the Grand Duke Ferdinand of Tuscany.

On the recommendation of his Cardinal he obtained the commission for the Contarelli Chapel in San Luigi dei Francesi, where, over the altar, he painted Saint Matthew with an Angel. On the right side, the Apostle is called by the Saviour, and on the left side, he is wounded on the altar by the executioner with other figures. The vault of the chapel, however, is very well painted by Cavalier Giuseppe Cesari d'Arpino.

This work, because it contained some paintings drawn from life and was in the company of others made by Cavalier Giuseppe, whose talent had aroused some envy on the part of his colleagues, increased Caravaggio's fame, and was highly praised by malicious persons. But when Federico Zuccaro came to see it, while I was there, he said: 'What is all the fuss about?' and, carefully examining the entire work, added: 'I do not see anything here but Giorgione's conception in the picture of the Saint, when Christ called him to the Apostolate'; and, sneering and marvelling at all this excitement, he turned on his heel and left.

For Marchese Vincenzo Giustiniani he made a seated Cupid drawn from life, so exquisitely coloured that the Marchese admired Caravaggio's works beyond limits; and the painting of a Saint Matthew that he had first made for that altar in San Luigi, which no one had liked, he took for himself because it was Michelangelo's work. The Marchese's opinion of Caravaggio was reinforced by the great fuss which was made of him everywhere by his henchman, Proserpino [Orsi] of the grotesques, who was hostile to Cavalier Giuseppe. Signor Ciriaco Mattei, for whom Caravaggio had painted a Saint John the Baptist, and Our Lord on the road to Emmaus, and the [painting] in which Saint Thomas touches the Saviour's chest with his finger, was likewise seduced by the uproar, and Caravaggio relieved that gentleman of many hundreds of *scudi*.

In the first chapel on the left in the church of S. Agostino he painted a Madonna of Loreto portrayed from life, with two pilgrims, one of them with muddy feet, and the other wearing a torn and soiled bonnet; and because of these frivolities in the details which a great picture must have, the populace made a great fuss over it.

The pictures in the Madonna del Popolo, on the right side of the main altar, in the chapel of the Signori Cerasi, and facing each other on the side walls, the Crucifixion of Saint Peter and the Conversion of Saint Paul are all by Caravaggio. These pictures were first worked by him in another manner, but as they did not please the patron, Cardinal Sannesio took them for himself; and Caravaggio himself made those which can now be seen, painted in oil because he did not work in a different manner; and (so to speak) Fortune and Fame carried him along.

In the Chiesa Nuova on the right side in the second chapel is his Dead Christ about to be buried, with other figures, painted in oil; and this is said to be his best work.

In St Peter's in the Vatican he also made a Saint Anne with the Madonna, who holds the Child between her legs and who, with her foot, is crushing a serpent's head – a work painted for the *Palafrenieri* of the palace – but it was removed on the order of the Cardinals of the Fabbrica [di San Pietro], and then given by the *Palafrenieri* to Cardinal Scipione Borghese.

For the Madonna della Scala in Trastevere he painted the death of the Madonna, but because he had portrayed the Madonna with little decorum, swollen and with bare legs, it was taken away; and the Duke of Mantua bought it and placed it in his most noble gallery.

He painted a Judith cutting off the head of Holofernes for the Signori Costi, and several pictures for others, which I omit because they are not in public places. Instead I will say something of his habits.

Michelangelo Amerigi was a sarcastic and haughty man. He would sometimes speak badly of all the painters of the past and present, no matter how distinguished they were, because he thought that he alone had surpassed all the others in his profession with his works. However, some people consider him to have been the ruination of painting, because many young artists after his example are devoting themselves to imitating a head from life, without studying the rudiments of artistic design and of spatial depth. They are only satisfied with colouring; thus they are incapable of putting two figures together, or of composing any story because they do not understand the value of so noble an art.

Because of the excessive ardour of his spirit, Michelangelo was a little wild, and he sometimes looked for the chance to break his neck or to risk the lives of others. People as quarrelsome as he were often to be found in his company; and having in the end confronted Ranuccio Tomassoni, a well-mannered young man, over some disagreement about a tennis match, they challenged one another to a duel. After Ranuccio fell to the ground, Michelangelo struck him with the point of his sword and, having wounded him in the thigh, killed him. Everyone fled Rome, and Michelangelo went to Palestrina, where he painted a Saint Mary Magdalen. From there he travelled to Naples, where he also made many things.

Then he went to Malta and, being invited to pay his respects to the Grand Master, he painted his portrait; as a sign of merit, that prince then presented him with the habit of Saint John and made him a Knight of Grace. Here, engaged in some sort of dispute with a Knight of Justice, Michelangelo insulted him in some way and ended up in prison. After escaping from the prison by night, he fled from Malta to the island of Sicily where he made some works in Palermo. As he was being chased by his enemy, he decided to return to the city of Naples; but here the enemy finally caught up with him and he was so severely wounded in the face that he was almost unrecognizable. Having given up all hope of revenge, although he had attempted it, he boarded a *felucca* bound for Rome with a few of his belongings, on the assurance that Cardinal Gonzaga was negotiating with Pope Paul V for his pardon. When he got ashore, he was mistakenly captured and put in prison where he was held for two days. On his release, unable to find the *felucca*, he was furious and made his way along the coast in desperation under the cruel heat of the summer sun, trying to catch sight of the vessel at sea that was carrying his belongings. Finally reaching a place of habitation along the shore, he was put to bed with a malignant fever; and after a few days, without human succour, he died as miserably as he had lived.

If Michelangelo Amerigi had not died so soon, he would have accomplished much in his art because of the good style of painting from nature he had taken up, even though he did not have much judgement in selecting the good and avoiding the bad in the things he represented. Nevertheless, he acquired a great reputation, and people paid more for his heads than for the history pictures of others, such is the value of popularity, which does not judge with its eyes but looks with its ears. And his portrait now hangs in the Academy.

## Appendix III
## Life of Caravaggio by Giovanni Pietro Bellori
(from *Le Vite de' pittori, scultori et architetti moderni*, 1672, pp. 211–33)

Demetrius, the ancient sculptor, is said to have been such a student of likenesses that he cared more for the imitation of things than for their beauty; we saw the same thing in Michelangelo Merisi, who recognized no other master than the model, and without selecting from the best forms of nature – astonishing to say – it seems that he imitated art without art. With his birth he doubled the fame of Caravaggio, a noble town in Lombardy, also the home of the celebrated painter Polidoro; both of them exercised the trade of stonemason in their youth, and acted as hod-carriers on buildings. While Michele was employed in Milan by his father, who was a mason, he happened to prepare glue for some painters of frescoes and, driven by the desire to use colours, he remained with them, applying himself totally to painting.

For the next four or five years he went on making portraits, and then, because of his turbulent and contentious nature, having fled Milan on account of certain quarrels, he went to Venice where he came to enjoy Giorgione's colouring so much that he chose him as a guide to imitate. For this reason one can see that his first works are sweet, direct and without those shadows that he later used; and as Giorgione was the purest and the simplest of all the Venetian painters who excelled as colourists in representing natural forms with not many tones, Michele followed the same approach when he first set himself to look closely at nature.

Having moved on to Rome, he did not earn enough to pay his expenses in advance, so he lived there without food and lodgings and unable to afford to pay the models without which he did not know how to paint. Michele was forced by necessity to enter the services of Cavalier Giuseppe d'Arpino, by whom he was employed to paint flowers and fruits so realistically that they began to attain the higher beauty that we love so much today. He painted a carafe of flowers which captured the transparencies of the water and the glass and the reflections of the window of a room, while the flowers were sprinkled with the freshest dew, and he made other excellent pictures of equal realism. But he worked reluctantly at these things, deeply regretting that they kept him away from figure painting, and so he took up the offer of Prospero, a painter of grotesques, and left the house of Giuseppe to compete with him for the glory of painting.

Beginning to paint according to his own inclination, not only ignoring but even despising the most excellent marbles of the ancients and the famous paintings of Raphael, he resolved that nature would be the only subject of his brush. Thus, when the most famous statues of Phidias and Glykon were pointed out to him so that he could use them as models, he made no reply other than extending his hand towards a crowd of people, saying that nature had provided him with enough masters. To lend authority to his words, he called a gypsy who happened to be passing by in the street and, after taking her to his lodgings, he portrayed her in the act of predicting the future, as is the custom of these women of Egyptian race; he made a young man place his gloved hand on his sword and offer her the other hand bare to hold and examine; and in these two half-figures Michele captured reality so purely that he confirmed what he had said. Almost the same story can be read about the ancient painter Eupompos; though this is not the time to consider to what extent such teaching is praiseworthy. And since he aspired only to the glory of colour, so that the complexion, the skin and the blood and the natural surface might look real, he attentively directed his eye and work to this alone, leaving aside all the other concerns of art.

Therefore, in finding and arranging his figures, whenever he came upon someone in town whom he liked, he was satisfied with that invention of nature without further exercising his brain. He painted a young girl seated on a chair, with her hands in her lap in the act of drying her hair; he portrayed her in a room and, adding a small ointment jar, with jewellery and gems, on the floor, he pretended that she was the

Magdalen. She leans her head a little to one side and her cheek, neck, and breast are rendered in pure, simple, and true colours, in keeping with the simplicity of the whole figure; she has her arms in a blouse, and her yellow gown is drawn up to her knees over a white underskirt of flowered damask. We have described this figure in detail to point out Caravaggio's naturalistic practices and imitation of true colour with just a few tones. In a bigger picture he painted the Madonna resting on her flight to Egypt: there is a standing angel who plays the violin, while Saint Joseph, seated, holds the music book for him. The angel is very beautiful, turning his head sweetly in profile to display his winged shoulders and the rest of his nude body except for the part covered by a cloth. On the other side sits the Madonna, bowing her head and seeming to sleep with her baby at her breast.

These pictures can be seen in Prince Pamphili's palace, and another one worthy of the same praise in Cardinal Antonio Barberini's rooms, showing three half-figures playing cards. In this Caravaggio represented a naïve young man holding the cards, a head well portrayed from life in a dark suit, seated opposite a dishonest young man, turned towards him in profile, who leans on the card table with one hand while with the other behind him he takes a false card from his belt; the third figure, close to the young man, looks at the marks on the cards, and with three fingers of his hand reveals them to his companion who, as he bends forward over the table, exposes his shoulder to the light in a yellow jacket striped with black, nor is the colour false in its imitation of life. These are the first strokes of Michele's brush in Giorgione's free manner, with tempered shadows; and Prospero, by acclaiming Michele's new style, increased the renown of his works to his own advantage among the leading persons at the court.

The picture was bought by Cardinal Del Monte who, being a lover of painting, helped Michele out of his difficulties by giving him an honoured place in his house among his gentlemen. For this gentleman he painted youths playing music portrayed from life in half-figures, a woman in a blouse playing a lute with the music before her, and Saint Catherine on her knees leaning against the wheel; the last two are still in the same rooms, but show a more saturated colouring, as Michele was already beginning to strengthen the dark tones. He also painted Saint John in the desert as a naked young boy, seated, who, leaning his head forward, embraces a lamb; and this can be seen in Signor Cardinal Pio's palace.

Caravaggio, as he was already called by everybody after the name of his native town, was making himself more and more renowned for the colouring he was introducing, not as sweet and sparingly tinted as before, but reinforced throughout with bold shadows, using a great deal of black to give relief to the forms. He went so far in this manner of working that he never brought any of his figures out into the daylight, but found a way to paint them against the darkness of a closed room, taking a high lamp that hung vertically over the principal part of the body, and leaving the rest in shadow, so as to give force through the power of light and dark. The painters then in Rome were much taken by the novelty of this approach, and the young ones particularly gathered around him and praised him as the unique imitator of nature. Looking upon his works as miracles, they outdid each other in copying him, undressing their models and raising their lights; and rather than setting out to learn from study and instruction, each readily found in the streets or squares of Rome both master and models for copying nature. As Caravaggio's easy style attracted the other [young painters], only the old painters, accustomed to the old ways, were dismayed by this new study of nature; nor did they cease to attack Caravaggio and his style, spreading word that he never emerged from the cellars and that, lacking invention and design, without decorum or art, he painted all his figures in one light and on one plane without any gradation: but such accusations did not stop the escalation of his fame.

When Caravaggio had painted Cavalier Marino's portrait, both the poet and the painter were rewarded by the praises of the literary men of the Academies; in the same way his Medusa's head, that Cardinal Del Monte gave to the Grand Duke of Tuscany, was particularly praised by Marino himself. Thus Marino, because of his very great love of and delight in Caravaggio's style, introduced him into the house of Monsignor Melchiorre Crescenzi, a clerk of the papal chamber. Michele painted the portrait of this most learned prelate and another of Signor Virgilio Crescenzi who, as an heir of Cardinal Contarelli, chose him to compete with Giuseppino [Cesari] for the paintings in the chapel of San Luigi dei Francesi. Marino, who was a friend of both painters, suggested that Giuseppe, an expert fresco painter, be assigned the figures on the wall above, and Michele the oil paintings. Here something happened that deeply upset Caravaggio concerning his reputation: after he had finished the central picture of Saint Matthew and placed it on the altar, it was taken away by the priests. The figure had neither decorum nor the appearance of a saint, they said, as it was sitting with its legs crossed and its feet rudely exposed to the public.

Caravaggio was in despair at such an outrage over his first work in a church, but Marchese Vincenzo Giustiniani intervened on his behalf and spared him this grief; intervening with the priests, he took the picture for himself, and had him paint a different one, which is the one now seen above the altar; and to honour the first more he took it to his house and later added the other three Evangelists by Guido [Reni], Domenichino, and Albani, the three most celebrated painters of that time.

Caravaggio exerted every effort to succeed in this second picture; and in order to give a natural form to the saint writing the Gospel, he showed him with a knee bent over the stool and his hands on the table, while he is dipping his pen in the inkwell on the book. In so doing he turns his face to the left towards the angel who, suspended on wings in the air, talks to him and makes a sign by touching the index finger of his left hand with his right. The illusionistic colour makes the angel seem far away, and he is suspended on his wings towards the saint, his arms and chest naked, with a fluttering white veil surrounding him in the darkness of the background. On the right side of the altar is Christ calling Saint Matthew to the apostolate, and some heads portayed from nature, among which the saint, who has stopped counting the coins, turns towards the Lord with one hand on his chest; close to him an old man is putting his spectacles on his nose, while looking at a young man seated at the corner of the table who draws the coins to himself. On the other side is the martyrdom of the saint himself in priestly garments, stretched out on a bench; and the nude figure of the executioner is brandishing the sword to strike him, while other figures withdraw in horror. The composition and the movements, however, are not adequate for the story, although Caravaggio painted it twice; and the darkness of the chapel and of the colour makes it difficult to see these two paintings.

He then painted in the church of Sant'Agostino the other picture for the chapel of the Signori Cavalletti, the standing Madonna holding the Child in her arms in the act of giving benediction; two pilgrims with clasped hands are kneeling before her, the first of whom is a poor man with bare feet and legs, with his leather cape and his staff resting on his shoulder, and accompanied by an old woman with a bonnet on her head.

The Deposition of Christ in the Chiesa Nuova of the Oratorians is deservedly regarded as being among the best works of Michele's brush; the figures are placed on a stone in the opening of the sepulchre. The holy body can be seen in the middle, the standing Nicodemus holding it under the knees, and as the thighs are lowered the legs jut out. On the other side Saint John places one arm under the shoulder of the Redeemer, whose deadly pale face and chest are turned upward, one arm hanging down with the sheet; all the nude parts are portrayed with the force of the most precise imitation. Behind Nicodemus we see the mourning Marys rather well, one with her arms upraised, another with her veil raised to her eyes, and the third looking at the Lord. In the church of the Madonna del Popolo, inside the chapel of the Assumption painted by Annibale Carracci, the two pictures on the side are by Caravaggio: the Crucifixion of Saint Peter and the Conversion of Saint Paul, which story is entirely without action.

He continued to be favoured by Marchese Vincenzo Giustiniani, who commissioned some pictures from him, the Crowning with Thorns, and Saint Thomas putting his finger in the wound in the side of the Lord, who holds Thomas's hand and exposes his chest from the shroud, pulling it away from his breast. Besides these half-figures he painted a victorious Love who with his right hand raises an arrow, while arms, books, and other instruments are lying at his feet on the ground as trophies. Other Roman gentlemen were also pleased with Caravaggio's brush, among them Marchese Asdrubale Mattei who had him paint the Taking of Christ in the Garden, also in half-figures. Judas lays his hand on the Lord's shoulder, after the kiss; meanwhile a soldier in full armour extends his arm and his iron-clad hand to the chest of the Lord, who stands patiently and humbly with his hands crossed before him, as, behind, Saint John is running away with outstretched arms. He faithfully depicted the rusty armour of that soldier, with head and face covered by a helmet, his profile partially visible; behind him a lantern is raised, and two more heads of armed men can be seen.

For the Signori Massimi he painted an Ecce Homo that was taken to Spain, and for the Marchese Patrizi the Supper at Emmaus, where Christ is in the centre blessing the bread, and one of the seated apostles stretches out his arms in recognition and the other rests his hands on the table and stares in astonishment; behind are the innkeeper with a cap on his head and an old woman who brings food. For Cardinal Scipione Borghese he painted a somewhat different version of this theme; the first one in deeper tones, and both to be praised for their imitation of natural colour, although they lack decorum, Michele often degenerating into common and vulgar forms. For the same cardinal he painted Saint Jerome who, as he is writing attentively, extends his hand and his pen towards the inkwell, and the other half-figure of David brandishing the sword and holding by the hair Goliath's head, which is his own portrait; he rendered David as a bareheaded youth with one shoulder out of his shirt, painted with a very dark background and shadows that he generally exploited to give strength to his figures and compositions. The cardinal was pleased with these and other works that Caravaggio made for him; he introduced him to Pope Paul V, who was portrayed seated by him, and by whom he was well rewarded. For Cardinal Maffeo Barberini, who later became Pope Urban VIII, he painted, in addition to his portrait, the Sacrifice of Abraham, in which the patriarch holds the knife near the throat of his son, who screams and falls.

But Caravaggio did not at all calm his restless nature by busying himself with painting; after working for a few hours in the day, he would appear in town with his sword at his side and behave as if he were a professional swordsman, seeming to care for anything but painting. Having fought with a young friend of his over a tennis game, they hit each other with their rackets and drew their arms. The young man was killed and Caravaggio himself wounded. Having fled from Rome, without money and being pursued, he took refuge in Zagarolo with Duke Marzio Colonna, where he painted the picture of Christ at Emmaus, sitting between the two apostles, and another half-figure of the Magdalen.

Afterwards he went to Naples, where he immediately found employment, since his style and reputation were already known there. For the church of San Domenico Maggiore he was commissioned to paint the Flagellation of Christ at the column in the chapel of the Signori di Franco, and the Resurrection in Santa Anna dei Lombardi. In Naples, the Denial of Saint Peter in the Sacristy of San Martino is thought to be among his finest works; painted with nocturnal lighting, it depicts a servant girl pointing at Peter, who turns around with open hands in the act of denying Christ, while other figures warm themselves by the fire. In the same city, for the church of the Misericordia, he painted the Seven Acts of Mercy in a picture about ten *palmi* long; one can see the head of an old man sticking out through the bars of the prison sucking milk from the bare breast of a woman bending towards him. Among the other figures can be seen the feet and legs of a dead man being carried to burial; the light of the torch held by one of those carrying the corpse spreads its rays over the priest in a white surplice, and the colour is lit up, thus giving life to the composition.

Caravaggio was eager to receive the cross of Malta, which was usually given as an honour to notable persons for merit and achievement; he therefore made up his mind to go to that island where, when he arrived, he was introduced to the Grand Master Wignacourt, a French gentleman. He painted him standing dressed in armour, and seated without armour, in the Grand Master's habit, the first portrait being in the Armoury of Malta. As a reward this gentleman presented him with the cross, and for the church of San Giovanni he had him paint the beheading of the saint fallen to the ground, while the executioner, as though he had not quite killed him with his sword, takes his knife from his side, seizing him by his hair to cut off his head. Herodias looks on intently, and an old woman is horrified by the spectacle, while the prison warden, in a Turkish garment, points to the atrocious slaughter. In this painting Caravaggio used all the force of his brush, having worked with such boldness that he left the priming of the canvas in half-tones. Besides honouring him with the cross, the Grand Master gave him a precious golden chain and made him a gift of two slaves among other things, as a sign of his esteem and satisfaction with his work. For the same church of San Giovanni, in the Italian chapel, Caravaggio painted two half-figures over two doors, the Magdalen and Saint Jerome writing; and he made another Saint Jerome meditating upon death with a skull, which is still in the palace.

Caravaggio was very happy with the honour of the cross and with the praises received for his painting, and he lived in Malta respectably and lacked for nothing. But all of a sudden his turbulent nature caused him to fall out of this prosperous state and out of the Grand Master's favour; because of a very inopportune quarrel with a most noble knight he was put into prison and reduced to a state of misery and fear. In order to regain his freedom he exposed himself to the gravest danger and, escaping from prison by night, he fled, undetected, to Sicily with such speed that he could not be recaptured. Having arrived in Syracuse he painted for the church of Santa Lucia, which is outside the city on the seashore, a picture of the dead Saint Lucy being blessed by the bishop while two men are digging the ground with shovels to bury her.

Having moved on to Messina, he painted the Nativity for the church of the Capuchins, with the Virgin and Child outside a broken-down shack, with its ramshackle boards and rafters, and Saint Joseph leaning on his staff with some shepherds in adoration. For the same fathers he painted Saint Jerome writing in a book, and in the church of the Ministri degl'Infermi, in the chapel of the Signori Lazzari, the Resurrection of Lazarus in which the saint, being raised out of the sepulchre, opens his arms at the voice of Christ who calls him and extends his hand towards him. Martha is crying, the Magdalen is astonished, and there is a man holding his nose to protect himself from the stench of the corpse. The figures in this huge painting are placed in a grotto, with the strongest light on the nude Lazarus and those who are carrying him, and it is highly esteemed for its powerful verisimilitude. But Michele's misdeed haunted him, and fear drove him from place to place; so that, hurrying across Sicily, he moved from Messina to Palermo, where he painted another Nativity for the Oratory of the Compagnia di San Lorenzo. Here the Virgin contemplates her newborn child together with Saint Francis and Saint Lawrence; there is also the seated Saint Joseph and an angel in the air, while the lights are diffused among the shadows of the night setting.

After this work, feeling that it was no longer safe to remain in Sicily, Caravaggio left the island and sailed back to Naples, where he thought he would stay until he received news of his pardon and could return to Rome. Hoping to placate the Grand Master, he sent him a present of a half-figure of Herodias with the head of Saint John in a basin. These efforts were in vain because, having stopped one day in the doorway of the Osteria del Ciriglio on the quayside, and having been surrounded by some armed men, he was beaten up and wounded in the face. After boarding a felucca as soon as it was possible, suffering the acutest pain, he headed for Rome, having by then obtained his liberation from the Pope through Cardinal Gonzaga's intercession. Upon his arrival ashore, the Spanish guard, who was waiting for another knight, arrested him by mistake and held him prisoner. Although he was soon released, he could no longer see the felucca which had carried him and his possessions. Thus, wretchedly shaken by anxiety and despair, running along the shore in the full heat of the summer sun, [and] having arrived at Porto Ercole, he collapsed and, seized by malignant fever, died within a few days, at about forty years of age, in 1609 [*sic*]. This was a sad year for painting, as it took away Annibale Carracci and Federico Zuccari as well. Thus Caravaggio ended his life and [left] his bones on a deserted shore, and the unexpected news of his death arrived in Rome just when his return was awaited. There was universal sorrow, and Cavalier Marino, his very close friend, mourned his death and honoured his memory with the following verses:

> Death and Nature, Michele, made a cruel plot against you;
> The latter feared to be bested by your hand in every image,
> Which was by you created, rather than painted;
> The former burned with indignation,
> Because with high interest,
> As many people as his scythe cut down,
> Your brush would recreate.

Without doubt Caravaggio advanced the art of painting, for he came upon the scene at a time when, realism being not much in evidence, figures were drawn according to convention and in a mannerist way, and the taste for beauty was better satisfied than that for truth. This man, taking away all artificial ornament and vanity from colour, strengthened his tones and restored flesh and blood to his figures, thus reminding painters once again of what imitation could achieve. However, nowhere did he use vermilions or blues in his figures; and even when he occasionally did so, he toned them down, saying that they were the poison of colours, to say nothing of blue sky and clear air, which he never painted in his pictures. On the contrary, he always used black ground and depths, and black for the flesh, limiting the force of the light to few areas. Moreover, he claimed that he copied his models so closely that he did not take credit for even a single brushstroke; his brushstroke, he said, was not his own, but nature's, and repudiating all other rules, he considered not being bound to art as the highest form of art. He received such great acclaim for this novel approach that some talented and educated artists from the best schools were compelled to follow him; one such was Guido Reni, who adapted himself somewhat to Caravaggio's style and showed himself a naturalistic painter, as can be seen in the Crucifixion of Saint Peter in the [church of the] Tre Fontane, and later on Giovanni Francesco da Cento [Guercino] as well. Despite all this praise, which Caravaggio accepted as his due, claiming to be the only faithful imitator of nature, he nevertheless fell short of the best elements of art in many respects, for he possessed neither invention, nor decorum, nor design, nor any knowledge of painting, and the moment the model was removed from before his eyes, his hand and his mind remained empty. None the less many artists were taken by his style and embraced it gladly, because without further study or effort they could easily copy nature, imitating common forms and without beauty.

With the majesty of art thus suppressed by Caravaggio, everyone did as he pleased. What followed was contempt for beautiful things; the authority of antiquity and Raphael was destroyed; and because it was easy to find models and paint heads from life, these people abandoned the histories which are the particular province of painting, and devoted themselves instead to half-figures, which previously were little used. Then the imitation of vulgar things began, with filth and deformity being assiduously pursued by some: if they have to paint armour, they choose the rustiest, if a vase, they do not present it intact, but chipped and broken. In copying figures they clothe them in stockings, breeches and big caps, and they devote all their attention to the wrinkles and defects of skin and suchlike, depicting gnarled fingers,

and limbs altered by disease.

Owing to his pursuit of this style Caravaggio suffered disappointment: his pictures were taken down from their altars, as we have said at San Luigi. The same thing happened to his Death of the Virgin in the Chiesa della Scala, removed because he had imitated the swollen body of a dead woman too closely. The other picture of Saint Anne was also removed from one of the minor altars of the Vatican Basilica because the Virgin and the nude Christ Child were humbly portrayed, as one can see in the Villa Borghese. In Sant'Agostino one is presented with the dirt of the Pilgrim's feet; and in Naples among the Seven Works of Mercy there is a man who, raising his flask, drinks with his mouth wide open, vulgarly letting the wine flow into it. In the Supper at Emmaus, as well as the rustic character of the two apostles and the portrayal of Christ as young and beardless, the innkeeper is serving with a cap on his head, and on the table there is a plate of grapes, figs, and pomegranates out of season. Thus, like certain herbs which have the power both to heal and to poison, in the same way Caravaggio, although he did some good, was also very harmful in that he turned upside down everything that was beautiful and in the best tradition of painting. Indeed painters, who strayed too far from the imitation of nature, needed someone to set them in the right path again; but just as it is easy, in fleeing from one extreme, to fall into the other, it so happened that, moving away from mannerism to follow nature too closely, painters moved away from art altogether, remaining in error and darkness until Annibale Carracci came to enlighten their minds and restore beauty to the imitation.

Caravaggio's style corresponded to his physiognomy and appearance: he had a dark complexion and dark eyes and black hair and eyebrows; this he reflected naturally in his work. His first style of painting, sweet and pure, was his best and represented his greatest achievement, in which he earned praise and proved himself to be an excellent Lombard colourist. But he soon moved on to the other, dark style, driven to it by his own temperament. Because of his turbulent and contentious nature, he first had to leave Milan and his homeland; then he was compelled to flee from Rome to Malta, to hide in Sicily, to be in danger in Naples, and to die miserably on a beach. We must not forget to mention the way he behaved and dressed. Although his clothes were made of the finest materials and velvets, when he had put on one outfit, he never changed it until it had fallen into rags. He was very negligent in his personal hygiene and he ate for many years on the canvas of a portrait, using it as a tablecloth morning and evening.

His colours are prized wherever painting is esteemed; the picture of Saint Sebastian with two executioners tying his hands behind his back – one of his best works – was taken to Paris. The Count of Benevento, who was Viceroy of Naples, took the Crucifixion of Saint Andrew to Spain, and the Count of Villa Mediana owned the half-figure of David and the portrait of a youth with an orange blossom in his hand. The painting of the Rosary is preserved in Antwerp, in the Church of the Dominicans, and it is a work which brings great praise to Caravaggio's brush. In Rome they attribute to his hand Jupiter, Neptune, and Pluto in the Ludovisi Garden at Porta Pinciana, in the casino which belonged to Cardinal Del Monte who, as a scholar of chemical medicines, adorned with it the small room of his laboratory, associating these gods with the elements, with the globe of the world in their midst. It is said that Caravaggio, hearing himself blamed for not understanding either planes or perspective, placed his figures to be seen from below in order to prove himself equal to the most difficult foreshortenings. It is indeed true that these gods do not retain their proper forms, and are painted in oil in the vault, since Michele had never painted in fresco, just as his followers always prefer the convenience of oil when painting from the model. Many were those who imitated his manner in painting from nature, and were therefore called naturalists; and among them we shall note those who are the most renowned ...

## Appendix IV
## Notice of Caravaggio's Arrest – 4 May 1598
(from Bellini, 1992, p. 65)

[After the night round on the morning of 4 May 1598, Bartolomeo, the deputy of the Chief Constable of Rome, reported as follows to the notary of the director of the Tor di Nona gaol:]

'… yesterday, between the hours of two and three in the night [i.e. between 10 and 11 pm nowadays] making the rounds through Rome, when I was between Piazza Navona and Piazza Madama, I ran into Michelangelo da Caravaggio who was carrying a sword without permission, and a pair of compasses, and so I seized him and imprisoned him in Tor di Nona.'

[Questioned afterwards in the office attached to the prison by the judge, wishing to know 'where, when, and on which occasion he was arrested', Merisi answers:]

'I was seized yesterday at about the hour of two in the night between Piazza Madama and Piazza Navona, because I was carrying the sword I usually carry, being the Painter of the Cardinal Del Monte, and getting a salary for myself and my servant, and lodging in his house as well. I am registered in his service.'

[His deposition ends with the formula 'then …', meaning the end of the questioning and, at the same time, the closing of the proceedings.]

## Appendix V
## Libel Suit Brought by Giovanni Baglione
(from Bertolotti, 1881, II, pp. 58–60)

### A   Caravaggio's Deposition, 13 September 1603

I was seized the other day in Piazza Navona, I do not know why.

I am a painter.

I think I know nearly all the painters in Rome, and beginning with the good artists I know Giuseppe [Cesari], [Annibale] Carracci, [Federico] Zuccari, Pomarancio [Cristoforo Roncalli], [Orazio] Gentileschi, Prospero [Orsi], Giovanni Andrea [Galli], Giovanni Baglione, Gismondo and Giorgio the German, [Antonio] Tempesta, and others.

Nearly all the painters I have mentioned above are my friends, but not all of them are good men.

By a good man I mean someone who can perform well in his art, and by a good painter a man who can paint well and imitate natural things well.

Among those I have mentioned above, neither Giuseppe, nor Giovanni Baglione, nor Gentileschi, nor Giorgio the German are my friends, because they do not speak to me; all the others speak to me and converse with me.

Among the painters I have mentioned above, I consider as good painters Giuseppe, Zuccari, Pomarancio, and Annibale Carracci; I do not consider the others good artists.

Good artists are those who understand painting, and they will judge good painters those I have judged good, and bad [those I have judged bad]; but bad and ignorant painters will judge good those who are ignorant like themselves.

I do not know that any painter praises and regards as a good painter any of those I do not regard as good. I forgot to say that Antonio Tempesta, too, is a good painter.

I do not know anything about there being any painter who praises Giovanni Baglione as a good painter.

I have seen nearly all the works by Giovanni Baglione; namely the High Altar Chapel in the Madonna dell'Orto, a picture in San Giovanni Laterano and, lately, Christ's Resurrection at the Gesù.

I do not like this painting because it is clumsy and I regard it as the worst he has ever done, and I have not heard the said painting being praised by any painter, and of all the painters I have spoken with, none liked it except one who is always with him, and who is called his guardian angel; he was there praising it when it was unveiled, and they call him Mao.

When I saw it, Prospero and Giovanni Andrea were with me, and I have seen it at other times, when I had occasion to go to the Gesù.

It may be that Mao, too, daubs a little, as a pastime; but I have never seen any works by this Mao.

I know Onorio Longhi who is a great friend of mine, and I also know Ottavio Padovano [Leoni], but I have never spoken to him.

With the former I have never spoken about Baglione's Resurrection; and Gentileschi has not spoken to me for over three years.

I know a Lodovico Bresciano and a Mario, painters. The latter once stayed with me, but it is three years since he left me, and I have not spoken to him since; and I have never spoken to Lodovico.

Bartolomeo was formerly my servant: two months ago he went to the Soderini family's estates.

No, sir, I do not amuse myself composing verses, either in Italian or Latin.

I have never heard of the existence of rhymes or prose against Baglione.

### B   Orazio Gentileschi's Deposition, 14 September 1603

I have known all the painters in Rome for some time and, in the first place, all the most important.

These are Giuseppe, Annibale Carracci, Giovanni dal Borgo, Pomarancio, Michelangelo da Caravaggio, Durante dal Borgo, Giovanni Baglione and others whom I do not remember, who belong to the first class.

I am a friend of all these painters; however, there is a certain rivalry among us: for instance, when I placed a picture of Saint Michael the Archangel in San Giovanni dei Fiorentini, Baglione showed his rivalry and placed another picture opposite it, which was a Divine Love he had painted to rival an Earthly Love by Michelangelo da Caravaggio; he had dedicated this Divine Love to Cardinal Giustiniani and, although this picture was not appreciated as much as Michelangelo's, none the less, it was reported that the Cardinal presented him with a chain. This picture had many imperfections, as I told him, as he had made an armed, full-grown man, while it should have been a nude child, and so later he made another, which was entirely nude.

I never spoke to Baglione again after the matter of that Saint Michael, and seldom even before because when walking about Rome he waits for me to lift my cap to him, and I wait for him to lift his cap to me, and Caravaggio, too, although he is a friend of mine, waits for me to greet him first, although we are friends; but it must be six or eight months since I last spoke to Caravaggio, although he sent to my house for a Capuchin habit, which I lent him, and a pair of wings, which he sent back to me about ten days ago […]

## Appendix VI
### Autograph contract, 25 June 1605
(from Barbiellini Amidei, 'Della committenza Massimo', in *Caravaggio. Nuove Riflessioni*, 1989, p. 47)

I Michel Angelo Merisi da Caravaggio undertake to paint for the Most Illustrious Signor Massimo Massimi, having been paid in advance, a painting of the same value and size as the one I have already made of Christ's Crowning [with Thorns] by the first of August 1605. I attest I have written and signed this below in my own handwriting on this the 25 June 1605
I Michel Angelo Merisi.

## Appendix VII
### Inventory of Caravaggio's possessions in Vicolo di San Biagio, Rome, 26 August 1605
(from Bassani and Bellini, 1993, and Corradini and Marini, 1993)

Inventory. The 26th day of August, 1605. This is the inventory of all the personal property of the painter Michelangelo from Caravaggio, which was found [...]
First, a kitchen-dresser made of white poplar wood, with three compartments and an alder frame, containing eleven pieces of glassware, namely glasses, carafes and flasks covered in straw, a plate, two salt-cellars, three spoons, a carving board and a bowl, and on the above-mentioned dresser two brass candlesticks, another plate, two small knives and three terracotta vases.

*Item* a water jug.
Two stools.
*Item* a red table with two drawers.
*Item* a couple of bedside tables. A picture.
*Item* a small coffer covered with black leather, containing a pair of ragged breeches and a jacket.
A guitar, a violin.
A dagger, a pair of earrings, a worn-out belt and a door leaf.
*Item* a rather big table.
*Item* two old straw chairs and a small broom.
*Item* two swords, and two hand daggers.
*Item* a pair of green breeches.
*Item* a mattress. *Item* a shield. *Item* a blanket.
*Item* a foldaway bed for servants.
*Item* a bed with two posts.
*Item* a chamber-pot.
*Item* a stool. *Item* an old chest.
*Item* a majolica basin.
*Item* another chest containing twelve books.
*Item* two large pictures to paint.
*Item* a chest containing certain rags.
*Item* three stools. *Item* a large mirror. *Item* a convex mirror.
*Item* three smaller pictures.
*Item* a small three-legged table.
*Item* three large stretchers. *Item* a large picture on wood.
*Item* an ebony chest containing a knife.
*Item* two bedside tables.

*Item* a tall wooden tripod.
*Item* a small cart with some papers with colours.
*Item* a halberd. *Item* two more stretchers.

## Appendix VIII
### Request and Approval of Caravaggio's Admission into the Knights of Malta
(from J. Azzopardi, 'Caravaggio's Admission into the Order', in *Malta and Caravaggio*, 1989, p. 55)

### Letter of 7 February 1608 from Grand Master Alof de Wignacourt, Malta, to Pope Paul V, Rome

Most Holy Father
Since the Grand Master of the Order of St John of Jerusalem wishes to honour some virtuous and worthy persons, who have a desire and devotion to dedicate themselves to his service and to that of his Order, and since he does not have at the moment any other way of doing so in a more suitable way, he humbly begs Your Holiness to deign to grant to him, by a Brief, the authority and power for one time only to be able to decorate and adorn with the habit of Magistral Knight two persons favoured by him, and to be nominated by him. Despite the fact that one of the two has previously committed homicide in a brawl. And despite the fact that it has been prohibited by the Chapter General of the above mentioned Order that this habit of Magistral Knight can be further granted. He begs to receive it as a very special favour, for the great desire he has to honour such virtuous and worthy persons. And may the Lord preserve you for a long time.

15 February 1608
For Alof de Wignacourt,
Grand Master of the Hospital of St John of Jerusalem

Authority to present the habit of Magistral Knight to two persons favoured by him although one of the two had committed homicide in a brawl.
It pleased the Most Holy Father to approve.

## Appendix IX
### Reception of Caravaggio's *Sleeping Cupid*

**Letter of 20 July 1609 from Fra Francesco Buonarroti, Malta, to Michelangelo Buonarroti the Younger, Florence**
(from Sebregondi Fiorentini, 1982, p. 122)

For your information, let it be known that I happened to talk two or three times to Signor Antella, who tells me he has sent a painting by Michelangelo da Caravaggio, with a sleeping Cupid, to the house of his brother Signor Niccolò, and that the Commendatore considers it very precious, and is very happy that it may be seen so he can have other people's opinions, and because someone who has seen it has composed some sonnets about it, which he showed to me; therefore I suppose that he would like me to see it.

## Appendix X
### Murder of Ranuccio Tomassoni

#### A Report of 31 May 1606
(from Corradini, 1993, p. 71, no. 83)

Caravaggio, the painter, has left Rome badly wounded, after killing a man who had provoked him to quarrel on Sunday night; and I am told that he has headed for Florence, and will perhaps come to Modena, too, where he will be pleased to make as many paintings as will be requested.

#### B Report of 31 May 1606
(from Corradini, 1993, p. 71, no. 84)

Two nights ago Caravaggio, a renowned painter, accompanied by a Captain Petronio Bolognese, confronted Ranuccio da Terni and, shortly after coming to blows, the painter was critically wounded in his head, and the other two died. The quarrel originated from a call over a fault, while playing tennis, towards the [palace of] the ambassador of the Grand Duke.

#### C Report of 31 May 1606
(from Corradini, 1993, p. 71, no. 85)

Rome, on the last day of May, Wednesday. On the aforesaid Sunday night a serious quarrel took place in Campo Marzio with four men on either side, the leader of one being a Ranuccio da Terni who died immediately after a long fight, and of the other Michelangelo da Caravaggio, a painter of some renown in our day, who was reportedly wounded, but whom it is impossible to locate; but one of his companions, called the Captain from Bologna, who was a soldier of Castel [Sant'Angelo], was badly wounded and imprisoned, and they think the reason was a dispute over a game, and ten *scudi* which the dead man had won from the painter.

## Appendix XI
### Caravaggio's Death

**Letter of 29 July 1610 from Fra Deodato Gentile, Bishop of Caserta, Naples, to Cardinal Scipione Borghese, Rome**
(from Pacelli, 1994, p. 121)

Most Reverend Respectable Patron
I deny what had been reported in the letter of the Most Illustrious Lanfranco of the 24th of the present month to Your Most Illustrious Lordship about Caravaggio the painter: which being to me unknown, I immediately tried to get information about it, and I find out that poor Caravaggio has not died in Procida, but at Porto Ercole, because, having arrived at Palo aboard the felucca on which he sailed, he was there put into prison by that captain, and heard that the felucca set sail and returned to Naples; Caravaggio having remained in prison, got his freedom by paying a large amount of money, and by land and perhaps walking, he went as far as Porto Ercole where, having fallen ill, he lost his life; the felucca, on its return voyage, brought back the remaining belongings to the house of the Signora Marchesa of Caravaggio, who lives in Chiaia, from where Caravaggio had left: I have immediately made inquiries to find out if the paintings are there, and I discover that they are no longer there, except three, the two Saint Johns, and the Magdalen, and they are in the aforesaid house of the Signora Marchesa, whom I immediately begged to keep them well guarded, so that they are not ruined, without letting anyone see them, or be taken by anyone, because they were intended and must be kept for Your Most Illustrious Lordship, but until the heirs and creditors of the aforesaid Caravaggio will be dealt with in order to give them due satisfaction, as regards this some have already come, I will see and understand what can be done, and I will manage that in any way the paintings are preserved, and come into the possession of Your Most Illustrious Lordship, to whom I humbly bow in the end.
Naples, on the 29th July 1610
Most Humble Devoted and Obliged Servant and creature Fra Deodato Gentile, Bishop of Caserta

Primary sources are cited by author's name only, and secondary works
appear under author's name and year of publication.
Full references can be found in the Bibliography.

**Abbreviations**

| | |
|---|---|
| *AB* | *Art Bulletin* |
| *ABA* | *Antologia di belle arti* |
| *AD* | *Art e dossier* |
| *AEH* | *Artibus et historiae* |
| *AIV* | *Atti dell'Istituto Veneto di Scienze, Lettere ed Arti* |
| *AL* | *Arte lombarda* |
| *BICR* | *Bollettino dell'Istituto Centrale del Restauro* |
| *BM* | *Burlington Magazine* |
| *DBI* | *Dizionario biografico degli italiani* |
| *GBA* | *Gazette des Beaux-Arts* |
| *MD* | *Master Drawings* |
| *NKJ* | *Nederlands Kunsthistorisch Jaarboek* |
| *RKJ* | *Römisches Jahrbuch für Kunstgeschichte* |
| *RSI* | *Rivista storica italiana* |
| *SA* | *Storia dell'arte* |
| *ZK* | *Zeitschrift für Kunstgeschichte* |

**Chapter 1**
**Lombard Roots**

**1** Cinotti, 1983, p. 234; Calvesi, 1990, p. 113.

**2** Sandrart, p. 275; Baglione, p. 136; Bellori, p. 212; Mancini, I, p. 223; on the question of the Merisi family's noble status, see Cinotti, 1983, p. 206; and M. Calvesi, 'La nobiltà del Caravaggio', *AD*, vol. 68 (1992), pp. 17–18.

**3** See Appendix VII. Further on Caravaggio and grammar school, see Orr, 1982, pp. 18–20.

**4** This chronology is based on the register of documents in Cinotti, 1983, pp. 236–8. On the alleged Milanese criminal act, see Cinotti, 1983, p. 209; Calvesi, 1990, pp. 117–18.

**5** On sixteenth-century Lombardy, see *Storia di Milano*, 1957; M. Gregori, 'Notizie storiche sulla Lombardia', in *Il seicento lombardo*, 1973, pp. 19–46.

**6** On Borromeo, see M. Bendiscioli, in *Storia di Milano*, 1957, chap. 3; M. Certeau, 'Borromeo, Carlo', *DBI*, vol. 20, pp. 260–9; *San Carlo Borromeo e il suo tempo. Atti del convegno internazionale nel IV centenario della morte*, 2 vols. (Rome, 1986).

**7** *Instructiones fabricae et supellectilis ecclesiasticae* (Milan, 1577), reprinted in P. Barocchi, ed., *Trattati d'Arte del Cinquecento*, 3 vols. (Bari, 1977), III, pp. 3–113.

**8** On his uncle and brother, see Cinotti, 1983, pp. 235, 237. On Costanza and Borromeo, see Calvesi, 1990, p. 107.

**9** Bellori, p. 212; Mancini, I, p. 223; Baglione, p. 136. Calvesi, 1990, p. 117, corrected the earlier reading of four to six years in Mancini's manuscript in the Biblioteca Marciana, Venice.

**10** For local artists, see *Dizionario degli artisti di Caravaggio e Treviglio*, eds. E. De Pascale and M. Olivari (Bergamo, 1994); on Bernardino Campi, see R. Armerio Tardito, 'Appunti sugli affreschi restaurati di Bernardino Campi nella Parrocchiale di Caravaggio', *AL*, vol. 51 (1979), pp. 39–41. On Tibaldi in Milan, see P. Mezzanotte, 'Architettura Milanese', *Storia di Milano*, 1957, esp. pp. 586–98.

**11** Cinotti, 1983, p. 236 (6 April 1584).

**12** G. A. Dell'Acqua, 'La pittura a Milano', *Storia di Milano*, 1957, pp. 671–780; R. P. Ciardi, *Giovan Ambrogio Figino* (Florence, 1968), esp. pp. 23–31; S. Freedberg, *Painting in Italy* (Harmondsworth, 1979), pp. 595–6; Gregori, 'Notizie storiche sulla Lombardia', in *Il seicento lombardo*, 1973, pp. 19–46.

**13** For Peterzano, see Baccheschi and Calvesi, 1975.

**14** The proposed identification of Caravaggio as the painter paid for working on frescoes in Milan in 1581–3 is unconvincing, given his age; see S. Macioce, 'Considerazioni su documenti inediti', *SA*, vol. 85 (1995), pp. 359–68, esp. 362–4.

**15** On these aspects of Caravaggio's debt to Peterzano, see M. Gregori, *Gli affreschi della certosa di Garegnano* (Milan, 1973), p. 17; M. T. Fiorio, in *The Age of Caravaggio*, 1985, pp. 73–5; Baccheschi and Calvesi, 1975, p. 484.

**16** On the use of prints in Lombard studios, see K. Christiansen, 'Thoughts on the Lombard Training of Caravaggio', in *Come dipingeva*, 1996, pp. 7–28.

**17** Longhi, 1968, p. 60.

**18** Longhi, 1968, p. 122; Friedländer, 1955, p. 42.

**19** Bora, in *I Campi*, 1985, pp. 184, 196.

**20** On Caravaggio and Leonardo, see Hibbard, 1983, pp. 152, 251; Spear, 1987, p. 60.

**21** J. Shearman, 'Leonardo's Colour and Chiaroscuro', *ZK*, vol. 25 (1962), pp. 13–47; K. Weil Garris Posner, *Leonardo and Central Italian Art: 1515–1550* (New York, 1974); Barasch, 1978, chap. 4; Gregori, and Bertelli, in *The Age of Caravaggio*, 1985, pp. 36–9, 60; and M. Gregori, 'I temi della luce artificiale', in *Giovanni Gerolamo Savoldo tra Foppa, Giorgione, e Caravaggio* (Milan, 1990), pp. 87–91.

**22** On these decorations, see L. Zanzi, *Sacri monti e dintorni. Studi sulla cultura religiosa ed artistica della controriforma* (Milan, 1990). For Borromeo's visit, see M. Rosci, 'Storie del popolo lombardo', in *Il seicento lombardo*, 1973, p. 53.

**23** For two portraits attributed to Peterzano, see Baccheschi and Calvesi, 1975, p. 533.

**24** On Caravaggio and Italian still-life painting, see the essays in *La natura morta*, 1995, with earlier bibliography.

**25** F. Paliaga, in *I Campi*, 1985, pp. 207–10.

**26** Bellori, pp. 212–13. The principal modern views are represented by Longhi, 1968, pp. 135–6 (a strictly Lombard formation); Friedländer, 1955, pp. 48–50 (Venetian influences without the necessity of a trip); Baccheschi and Calvesi, 1975, p. 487 (probability of a Venetian trip).

**27** For the early sources, see Bellori, pp. 212–13, 216; Baglione, p. 137. On Giorgione and 'Lombard' colour, see Y. Zolotov, 'A propos du problème du giorgionisme chez le Caravage', *AIV*, vol. 137 (1978–9), pp. 467–77; and Spear, 1987, p. 63. On Giorgionism, see 'L'influence de Giorgione', *Le siècle de Titien*, exh. cat., Grand Palais, Paris, 1993, pp. 377–430.

**28** On Tintoretto and Caravaggio, see Friedländer, 1955, p. 52; Gregori, in *The Age of Caravaggio*, 1985, p. 246; Del Bravo, 1983, pp. 69–77.

**29** M. T. Fiorio, 'Note su alcuni disegni inediti di Simone Peterzano', *AL*, vol. 19 (1974), pp. 87–100; R. P. Ciardi, 'Giovan Ambrogio Figino e la cultura artistica milanese', *AL*, vol. 7 (1962), pp. 73–84; A. Scotti and G. Bora, in *I Campi*, 1985, pp. 302–9. See further discussion in the Epilogue.

## Chapter 2
## Rome

**1** On Caravaggio's Roman addresses, see Marini, 1990. On Pucci, see Calvesi, 1990, p. 118; Cinotti, 1983, p. 210. For Lorenzo's possible identification, see Bassani and Bellini, 1994, p. 26, n. 20. For Petrignani, see Mancini, I, p. 224; II, n. 887; Cinotti, 1983, p. 212; and J. Hess, 'The Chronology of the Contarelli Chapel', *BM*, vol. 93 (1951), p. 193 n. 63. The document from the summer of 1593 purporting to be the earliest mention of Caravaggio in Rome, published by Bassani and Bellini, 1994, pp. 7–10, has been proven falsified by S. Corradini, 'Nuove e false notizie', in *Caravaggio: La vita e le opere*, 1996, p. 73.

**2** For late sixteenth-century Rome, see L. von Pastor, *History of the Popes*, vols. XXIII, XXIV (London, 1952); Delumeau, 1957; Magnuson, 1982; Nussdorfer, 1992.

**3** Delumeau, 1957, I, p. 358.

**4** For the population, see Delumeau, 1957, I, chap. 4.

**5** On the edicts against prostitutes, see Delumeau, 1957, I, pp. 427–8; Magnuson, 1982, I, pp. 40–3.

**6** On Clement's pastoral visits, see R. Zapperi, 'L'ignudo e il vestito', *Gli amori degli dei. Nuove indagini sulla Galleria Farnese* (Rome, 1987), pp. 49–68, esp. p. 53.

**7** Abromson, 1976; Zuccari, 1984; *Roma 1300–1875*, 1985, pp. 205–9; Macioce, 1990.

**8** For the Academy of St Luke, see N. Pevsner, *Academies of Art, Past and Present* (Cambridge, 1940). The 1593 document was kindly brought to my attention by Maurizio Marini. For the record of the assault in 1600, see Bassani and Bellini, 1994, p. 116.

**9** Mancini, I, pp. 109, 305; Giustiniani, p. 125.

**10** Bellori, p. 213. On Cesari's career, see Röttgen, 1973.

**11** Macioce, 1990, pp. 102–3.

**12** On Caravaggio and Cesari, see Röttgen, 1974, pp. 43–4.

**13** For Bellori's anecdote and Baglione's statement, see Appendix II, III.

**14** Cinotti, 1983, pp. 245–6.

**15** For the most recent assessment of the painter's still lifes, see the essays by M. Gregori, C. Strinati, L. Spezzaferro and A. Cottino in *La natura morta*, 1995. For the *Still Life with a Basket of Fruit*, see Chapter 5. For the lost 'vase', see Bellori, p. 213; Frommel, 1971, p. 31. For a summary of recent attributions of still lifes to Caravaggio, see Bologna, 1992, pp. 287–90; for the recent attribution of a still life in a private collection, see Checklist no. 45.

**16** Bellori, p. 213; for Caravaggio's statement, see Giustiniani, p. 123.

**17** Calvesi, 1990, pp. 224–8, 234–6; seconded by Marini, 1987, p. 112, and Zuccari, 1984, p. 151.

**18** On Bassano's cycles, see *Jacopo Bassano, c.1510–1592*, exh. cat., eds. B. Brown and P. Marini (Bologna, 1993), cat. nos. 50–1, 58–9, 70–1. For Campi's set, see J. Spike, *Italian Still Life Painting from Three Centuries*, exh. cat., National Academy of Design (New York, 1983), pp. 22–6; and B. Wind, 'Vincenzo Campi and Hans Fugger: A Peep at Late Cinquecento Bawdy Humor', *AL*, vol. 47/48 (1977), pp. 108–14.

**19** See Heimbürger, 1990, with earlier bibliography.

**20** For a useful analysis of interpretative approaches, see Spear, in the *Age of Caravaggio*, 1985, pp. 24–7.

**21** Gregori, in *The Age of Caravaggio*, 1985, p. 236.

**22** Longhi, 1968a, p. 14.

**23** See Posner, 1971; Frommel, 1971, pp. 21–56.

**24** For the meanings of *bardassa*, see the *Vocabulario degli Accademici della Crusca* (Florence, 1866), vol. 2, p. 73. For the transcript of the 1603 trial, see Friedländer, 1955, pp. 274–5.

**25** For the 1605 incident, see Friedländer, 1955, p. 283; see also Mancini, I, p. 224.

**26** Susinno, pp. 114–15; see further, Gilbert, 1995, pp. 192–4.

**27** Orgel, 1996, p. 59, with related bibliography.

**28** On Leonardo's presumed homosexuality, see J. Saslow, *Ganymede in the Renaissance*, New Haven, CT, and London, 1986, pp. 65, 75; and Gilbert, 1995, p. 303, n. 96, who discusses androgyny in art at length, pp. 216–20.

**29** Sterling, 1959, p. 59; E. Gombrich, 'Tradition and Expression in Western Still Life' (review of Charles Sterling), in *Meditations on a Hobby Horse* (London, 1963), p. 104; Gregori in *The Age of Caravaggio*, 1985, pp. 264–5; Wind, 1975, p. 72.

**30** See Gregori, in *The Age of Caravaggio*, 1985, p. 200; and further discussion in the Checklist, no. 1.

**31** For the comparison with ancient literature, see Wind, 1975, p. 72; for that with modern poetry, see Salerno, 1966, pp. 106–12.

**32** See Marini, 1987, pp. 346–51; and J. Spike, 'E se Caravaggio avesse avuto una bottega?', *Il Giornale dell'Arte*, no. 99 (1992), p. 5.

**33** Cinotti, 'Vita del Caravaggio', in *Caravaggio: Nuove riflessioni*, 1989, p. 81.

**34** For the tradition of representing the Magdalen, see *La Maddalena*, 1986.

**35** Bellori, p. 215.

**36** D. Mahon, 'Fresh light on Caravaggio's earliest period: his *Cardsharps* recovered', *BM*, vol. 130 (1988), pp. 11–25; Gregori, in *Caravaggio. Come nascono*, 1991, cat. 1, 2.

**37** See Cuzin, 1977, pp. 12–13.

**38** This discussion is indebted to Bell, 1993, and Bell, 1995.

**39** Cuzin, 1977, pp. 16–24.

**40** On the costumes, see S. M. Pierce, 'Costume in Caravaggio's Painting', *Magazine of Art*, vol. 47 (1953), pp. 147–54; Wind, 1974, p. 33; G. Feigenbaum, 'Gamblers, Cheats, and Fortune-Tellers', in Conisbee, 1996, p. 156.

**41** For Campi's and Van Leyden's paintings, see G. Bora, in *I Campi*, 1985, p. 133; E. Lawton Smith, *The Paintings of Lucas van Leyden* (Columbia,

MO, and London, 1992), pp. 45–56. On the theatre's influence, see Wind, 1974, pp. 25–35; on the literary treatments of the theme, see Cuzin, 1977, p. 22. For the copies, see Moir, 1976, pp. 105–7.

**42** Baglione, p. 136; Mancini, I, p. 140. His hospitalization occurred before or after his stay in Cesari's workshop; the Hospital's Prior, more plausibly Sevillian than Sicilian, has been tentatively identified as Camillo Contreras; see Mancini, I, p. 224, II, n. 886.

**43** For Orsi, see Baglione, pp. 299–300; Bassani and Bellini, 1994, p. 40; M. Calvesi, 'Prospero Orsi, *turcimanno* del Caravaggio', *SA*, vol. 85, 1995, pp. 355–8. Orsi's presumed birthdate may now have to be changed to c.1569–72 in light of the documents published by Corradini and Marini, 1998, pp. 25–8. On Minniti, see Susinno, pp. 116–17; C. L. Frommel, 'Caravaggio e il Cardinale Francesco Maria Del Monte', in *Caravaggio: La vita e le opere*, 1996, pp. 18–41. On Longhi, see Bassani and Bellini, 1994, pp. 11–17, 47; but note that the authors' assertion, pp. 7–8, that Caravaggio's and Longhi's names were linked in the police records in 1593 has since been discredited by M. Marino, 'Caravaggio Assassinato', *Il Tempo*, 18 July 1995.

**44** For Maestro Valentino's possible identity, see Bassani and Bellini, 1994, p. 48, nn. 4, 5; and most recently, Corradini and Marini, 1998, p. 25.

## Chapter 3
### In Cardinal del Monte's Household

**1** Corradini and Marini, 1998, pp. 25–8.

**2** For the 1598 incident, see Appendix IV.

**3** Bassani and Bellini, 1994, p. 58, give, without any supporting evidence, a figure of two hundred for Del Monte's retinue, which would have been nearly double that of the wealthiest cardinals. I am grateful to Elena Fumigalli for the notice of Del Monte's residence in the Palazzo Madama.

**4** Bellini, 1992, p. 70; Bassani and Bellini, 1993, p. 70.

**5** On Del Monte, see V. I. Comparato, 'Bourbon Del Monte, Francesco Maria', *DBI*, vol. 13 (Rome, 1971), pp. 523–4; Spezzaferro, 1971, p. 59, quoting a report of 1621; and Ważbiński, 1994.

**6** Cited in Spezzaferro, 1971, p. 59. For the cultural world of princely cardinals, see P. Falguières, 'La cité fictive', *Les Carrache et les décors profanes* (Rome, 1988), pp. 215–333.

**7** For his scientific interests, see Spezzaferro, 1971, pp. 73–80; for his musical interests, see Trinchieri Camiz and Ziino, 1983, pp. 67–90; Trinchieri Camiz, 'La "Musica" nei quadri del Caravaggio', in *Caravaggio. Nuove riflessioni*, 1989, pp. 198–221; Trinchieri Camiz, 1991.

**8** For Del Monte's complete inventory, see Frommel, 1971, pp. 30–49, and on his art patronage, see Heikamp, 1966, pp. 64–6; Spezzaferro, 1971, pp. 80–2.

**9** For Caravaggio's lost pictures for Del Monte – a 'vase of flowers', and 'divine love conquering profane love'– see, respectively, Gregori, in *La natura morta*, 1995, p. 22, and Marini, 1987, no. 14, Bologna, 1992, p. 304.

**10** *Perspectivae Libri Sex* (Pesaro, 1600); for its historical importance, see Spezzaferro, 1971, p. 82.

**11** Frommel, 1971, pp. 32, 36.

**12** On the recovery of the wings and quiver during the 1983 restoration, see Gregori, *Caravaggio. Come nascono*, 1991, p. 110.

**13** See C. Ripa, *Iconologia*, ed. P. Buscaroli (Milan, 1992), pp. 308–9; and on tuning up, see P. Egan, '"Concert" Scenes in Musical Paintings of the Italian Renaissance', *Journal of the American Musicological Society*, vol. 14 (1961), pp. 184–95, esp. p. 188.

**14** For the specific scores, see Trinchieri Camiz, 1991, pp. 216–17; for Del Monte's musical collection, see Frommel, 1971, pp. 44–5.

**15** For Caravaggio's guitar and violin, see Appendix VII.

**16** For the young and old Del Monte, see Spezzaferro, 1971, pp. 59–60, 68; and Haskell, 1980, pp. 28–9; for the 1597 episode, see R. Zapperi, *Eros e controriforma* (Turin, 1994), p. 87, n. 7; Giustiniani's tastes were speculated about by Haskell, 1980, p. 28.

**17** For musical practices, see J. Bowers and Tick, J., eds., *Women Making Music: The Western Art Tradition 1150–1950* (Urbana and Chicago, 1986), especially chaps. 5 and 6. For Cavalieri's work, see C. Strinati, 'Caravaggio nel 1601', in *Caravaggio. Nuove riflessioni*, 1989, pp. 162–78; for the 1605 ballet, see Cinotti, 1983, p. 215.

**18** Trinchieri Camiz, 1988.

**19** Trinchieri Camiz, 1991, p. 218.

**20** This interpretation was proposed by Trinchieri Camiz, '"Per prima cosa"', in *La natura morta*, 1995, pp. 75–9.

**21** For the impact of Rome, see Gregori, in *The Age of Caravaggio*, 1985, p. 244; for Del Monte's antiquities, see Frommel, 1971, pp. 38–41.

**22** For this record, see G. Corti, 'Il "Registro de Mandati"', *Paragone*, no. 473 (1989), pp. 108–46 (18 March 1618).

**23** For Bacchus' androgyny, see Gilbert, 1995, pp. 207–14.

**24** For a similar interpretation to mine, see L. F Bauer, 'Moral Choice in some Paintings by Caravaggio and His Followers', *AB*, vol. 73 (1991), pp. 391–8.

**25** For further discussion, see the Epilogue, and see Checklist no. 15 for related bibliography.

**26** Heikamp, 1966.

**27** For Leonardo's lost work, see G. Vasari, *Le vite dei più celebri pittori, scultori e architetti*, 4th edn., 2 vols., (Florence, 1922), vol. 3, pp. 492–3.

**28** For Murtola's poem, see Salerno, 1966, p. 107; and Cinotti, 1973, p. 51; and for Marino's poem, see Cinotti, 1973, p. 55.

**29** Bellori, p. 233; Zandri, 1969. For the acquisition, sale, and re-acquisition of the property, see Trinchieri Camiz, 1992, pp. 82, 84.

**30** On this medium, see Paolo Bensi, 'La pittura murale a olio', in *Come dipingeva il Caravaggio*, 1996, pp. 91–101, with further bibliography.

**31** Calvesi, 1990, p. 192. On the viewpoint from below, see further, Gregori, in *The Age of Caravaggio*, 1985, pp. 36–7.

**32** For these possible meanings, see Calvesi, 1990, pp. 173–96; and Trinchieri Camiz, 1992, p. 86. For further bibliography, see Checklist no. 30.

**33** For the present, nineteenth-century gilt stuccoed frame, see Marini, 1987, p. 407. For Del Monte's response to the Sala Clementina, see Heikamp, 1966, p. 65.

**34** L. Salerno (*I dipinti del Guercino*, Rome, 1988, p. 42) also noted this parallel.

**35** Bellori, p. 217.

**36** Mancini, I, p. 224; Bellori, p. 215.

**37** See Friedländer, 1955, p. 46, but note that Federico Borromeo only acquired Bassano's painting in Milan in 1612 (Jones, 1993, p. 229). For the iconography, see Mâle, 1972, pp. 257–9.

**38** See Calvesi, 1990, p. 204; and S. Johnson Jordan, 'The iconography of Caravaggio's "Rest on the Flight into Egypt"', *SA*, vol. 61, (1987), pp. 225–7.

**39** Longhi, 1982, pp. 57–8.

**40** This discussion of the iconography is indebted to Askew, 1969; and Treffers, 1988, pp. 145–71.

**41** Frommel, 1971, pp. 24, 51; Gregori, in *The Age of Caravaggio*, 1985, p. 227.

**42** For the provenance, see Gregori, in *The Age of Caravaggio*, 1985, p. 248. For this saintly devotion, see Cinotti, 1983, p. 419; and Gilbert, 1995, p. 127.

**43** See Zuccari, 1984, p. 13, and nn. 14, 15.

**44** On Melandroni, see Bassani and Bellini, 1994, chap. 4.

**45** For Costa's will of 1632, see Papi, in *Caravaggio. Come nascono*, 1991, p. 174; for Olimpia Aldobrandini's 1606 inventory, see Cappelletti and Testa, 1990, pp. 240–1.

**46** See F. Cummings, 'Detroit's "Conversion of the Magdalen" (the Alzaga Caravaggio)', *BM*, vol. 116 (1974), pp. 563–4, 572–8; and more recently, Gregori, in *The Age of Caravaggio*, 1985, pp. 250–1.

**47** For the technical data, see Christiansen, 1986, pp. 436–7; and *Caravaggio. Come nascono*, 1991, no. 7; and further discussion in the Epilogue.

**48** On Caravaggio's use of the traditional device of *contrapposto*, see Hibbard, 1983, p. 67.

**49** The recent description of Judith as an inexpressive mannequin is puzzling; see M. Garrard, *Artemisia Gentileschi* (Princeton, NJ, 1989), p. 291.

**50** On Giustiniani, see Haskell, 1980, pp. 29–30, 94–5; on Costa, see Matthiesen and Pepper, 1970, p. 452; Spezzaferro, 1974, pp. 579–86. For new light on Cardinal Benedetto Giustiniani's patronage, see Danesi Squarzina, 1997 and 1998.

**51** Bassani and Bellini, 1994, pp. 112–13, 116.

**52** For the incident with Caravaggio's brother, see Mancini, I, pp. 225–6. For Giovanni Battista's movements and for Del Monte's remark, see Cinotti, 1983, pp. 239 (15 April; 18 December 1599), 243 (6, 7, and 24 August 1605).

**53** For an *avviso* of 5 May 1601, referring to the 'famosissimo pittore Michel Angelo da Caravaggio', see Marini, 1987, p. 446.

## Chapter 4
## 'Most Famous Painter'

**1** Scannelli, p. 197.

**2** Baglione, p. 136. On Del Monte's francophile attitudes, see Papi, in *The Age of Caravaggio*, 1985, p. 79.

**3** For the tentative proposal that this work is the same as Caravaggio's *Entombment*, see M. Calvesi, 'Riflessioni sul Caravaggio', in *Caravaggio. Nuove riflessioni*, 1989, pp. 8–10.

**4** On Cerasi, see F. Petrucci, in *DBI*, vol. 23, pp. 655–7. On these papal posts, see Nussdorfer, 1992, pp. 46–8.

**5** Baglione, p. 137. For Sannesio, see Papi, in *Caravaggio. Come nascono*, 1991, p. 200; Ważbiński, 1994, I, pp. 142, n. 170, 169.

**6** For examples of rejections, see Hibbard, 1983, pp. 146–7.

**7** For the contract and related documents for the *Death of the Virgin*, see Parks, 1985. For Cherubini, see M. Palma, in *DBI*, vol. 24, pp. 434–5; and Askew, 1990, pp. 11–13. On Roman conservators, see Nussdorfer, 1992, pp. 71–2.

**8** For Cherubini and the Giustiniani, see Askew, 1990, pp. 7–11, 89, 148, n. 15.

**9** Baglione, pp. 100, 137; Bellori, pp. 219–20.

**10** For the documents, see Röttgen, 1974, pp. 57–62. This chronological sequence is based on Hibbard's sensible interpretation; see 'Caravaggio's Two *Saint Matthews*', *RJK*, vol. 20 (1983), pp. 183–91.

**11** See Zuccari, 1983, with earlier bibliography.

**12** On Girolamo Vittrice and Caravaggio, see Bologna, 1992, pp. 110–11; Zuccari, 1983, p. 54; Hibbard, 1983, p. 312.

**13** For Girolamo's *Fortune-Teller*, see Corradini, 1993, p. 96, no. 120; Mancini, I, p. 109; Marini, 1987, p. 464; and Spezzaferro, in *La natura morta*, 1995, pp 53–4.

**14** For the Cavalletti, see Amayden, 1979, I, pp. 288–9.

**15** 'Grooms', the customary translation for *palafrenieri*, inadequately conveys their social status and duties, for which see P. Waddy, *Seventeenth-Century Roman Palaces* (New York, 1990), pp. 7, 32, 33. For the documents and the history of the *palafrenieri*'s altar, see Spezzaferro, 1974, pp. 125–37, and the most recent review of all the surviving evidence by Rice, 1997, pp. 43–5.

**16** Bellori, p. 220; Baglione, p. 137.

**17** For the original Italian text of the memorandum, see Röttgen, 1974, p. 21. Also see *The Golden Legend*, pp. 561–6.

**18** For reproductions and discussion of the X-rays, see G. Urbani, 'Il restauro delle tele del Caravaggio in S. Luigi dei Francesi a Roma', *BICR* (1966), pp. 37–76.

**19** These men are convincingly identified as neophytes in F. Trinchieri Camiz, 'Death and Rebirth in Caravaggio's "Martyrdom of St Matthew",' *AEH*, vol. 11 (1990), pp. 89–105.

**20** For a possible source in Palma Giovane's *Purification of the Temple*, see H. Röttgen, 'Mein Haus soll ein Bethaus heissen, ihr aber habt eine Diebeshöhle daraus gemacht', *Pantheon*, vol. 50 (1992), pp. 55–60.

**21** Bellori, p. 217.

**22** For Roncalli's design, see Cappelletti and Testa, 1994, p. 17.

**23** For bibliography on Matthew's identity, see the Checklist, no. 29.

**24** For the motif of eyeglasses, and other symbolic references, see Hibbard, 1983, pp. 100, 296.

**25** Bellori, p. 222. Roncalli had been asked to set the price for Caravaggio's expenses for pigments in the Contarelli Chapel (Cinotti, 1983, p. 239, under 23 July 1599).

**26** This conclusion was reached by me, the restorer, and another Caravaggio specialist, upon examining the painting in the lab at arm's length, out of its frame and in full light.

**27** Friedländer, 1955, pp. 7–8; Herrmann Fiore, 1995, pp. 24–7.

**28** On the paintings viewed *in situ*, see L. Steinberg, 'Observations in the Cerasi Chapel', *AB*, vol. 41 (1959), pp. 184–90.

**29** His reaction to Annibale's *Saint Margaret* (Rome, Santa Caterina dei Funari) was reported by Francesco Albani, in a letter of 1658 (cited by Mahon, 1951, p. 230, n. 72).

**30** On the confrontation of Caravaggio and Annibale Carracci, see D. Posner, *Annibale Carracci* (London, 1971), I, chap. 11; C. Dempsey, *Annibale Carracci and the Beginnings of Baroque Style* (Glückstadt, 1977), pp. 85–6, n. 59; Hibbard, 1983, pp. 131–2; and Bell, 1993, pp. 103–30.

**31** On the stone, see Friedländer, 1955, p. 128; and on the eucharistic content, see G. Wright, 'Caravaggio's *Entombment* Considered in Situ', *AB*, vol. 58 (1978), pp. 35–42; and Hibbard, 1983, p. 174. See further bibliography in the Checklist, no. 43.

**32** For Rubens's sketch, see Glen, 1988, pp. 19–22.

**33** See Appendix IB, for Mancini on decorum. On censorship, see Askew, 1990, pp. 53–4. For the 1603 edict, see Bassani and Bellini, 1994, pp. 184–5.

**34** *The Golden Legend*, pp. 449–65, collected the various versions of the Virgin's death. Askew, 1990, chap. II, provides a valuable review and illustrations of traditional depictions; my discussion is indebted to her book without accepting all of its interpretations.

**35** On the Virgin's youthfulness, see R. Hinks, *Caravaggio's 'Death of the Virgin'* (London/New York/Toronto, 1953), p. 9, and see the Checklist, no. 37, for further bibliography on the iconography.

**36** Mancini, I, pp. 120, 224; Baglione, pp. 137–8; Bellori, p. 231. On Baronio's writing about the Virgin's death, see Askew, 1990, p. 22.

**37** For contemporary reaction to the altarpiece, see Baglione, p. 137, and Bellori, p. 231. On Rome's beggars and pilgrims, see Delumeau, 1957, I, pp. 136, 407.

**38** Calvesi, 1990, p. 330; but see Marini, in *L'iconografia*, 1995, p. 137.

**39** Scannelli, p. 98. This discussion is indebted to Hibbard, 1983, pp. 186–7, who illustrates a print of the cult statue of the Madonna di Loreto (fig. 121).

**40** The quotation is from Mâle, 1972, p. 39. For the alleged indecency of Caravaggio's Madonna and Child, see Baglione, p. 137; and Bellori, p. 231.

**41** He apparently refused both commissions; see A. Lemoine, 'Caravage, Cavalier d'Arpin, Guido Reni et la confrérie romaine de la SS Trinità dei Pellegrini', *SA*, vol. 85 (1995), pp. 417–29; and Cinotti, 1983, p. 579, n. 165.

**42** For the inventory, see Appendix VII. Documents verify that Caravaggio had a servant in 1598 (Appendix IV), 1603 (testimony at libel suit – Appendix VA), and 1605 (for an assistant's cot listed in inventory – Appendix VII).

**43** For the fee for the *Death of the Virgin*, see Marini, 1987, p. 479; for Cesari's fee, see Röttgen, 1973, p. 87; for Roncalli's fee, see Chiappini di Sorio, 1975, p. 117; for Passignano's fee, see Chappell and Kirwin, 1974, pp. 162–3.

**44** For the inventory, see Appendix VII, and for further discussion, see Bassani and Bellini, 1993, pp. 68–76; and Corradini and Marini, 1993, pp. 161–76.

**45** Van Mander's report of 1603 derived from an earlier Roman source: *Het Schilder-Boeck* (Haarlem, 1604), as translated by Hibbard, 1983, p. 344.

**46** For these incidents, see Friedländer, 1955, pp. 270–3; Bassani and Bellini, pp. 116–17, 222–5.

**47** Passeri, pp. 347–8; for Pasqualone's deposition and Maddalena di Paolo Antognetti, see Bassani and Bellini, 1994, pp. 205–14. However, the authors falsified a documented friendship between Antognetti and Caravaggio.

**48** On the official reconciliation and his eviction, see Bassani and Bellini, 1994, p. 224; Bassani and Bellini, 1993, pp. 68–72.

**Chapter 5**
**Private Commissions**

**1** Frommel, 1971, pp. 49–52; Posner, 1971, p. 314; Hibbard, 1983, pp. 158–60; Röttgen, 1992, pp. 7–8.

**2** M. Wiemers, 'Caravaggios "Amore Vincitore" im Urteil eines Romfahrers um 1650', *Pantheon*, vol. 44 (1986), pp. 59–61. For the diary, see M. Beal, *A Study of Richard Symonds, His Italian Notebooks and their Relevance to Seventeenth-Century Painting Techniques* (New York, 1984). Symonds's remarks are wrongly discredited by Gilbert, 1995, pp. 199–200. On Cecco, see Papi, 1992. For Caravaggio's assistant, see Marini, 1987, pp. 346–7.

**3** Baglione, p. 137; Sandrart, pp. 276–7. Propriety may have also inspired the curtain, a practice recommended for draping erotic paintings by Mancini, I, p. 143.

**4** For the archival finds, see *Caravaggio e la collezione Mattei*, 1995; Cappelletti and Testa, 1994; Marabottini, 1995, pp. 62–72; Schröter, 1995, pp. 62–87. See also Baglione, p. 137.

**5** For the payments and further bibliography, see the Checklist, no. 39.

**6** For other Baptists attributed to Caravaggio, see the Checklist, nos. 16, 48, 76, 87. For the most recent attribution of a *Saint John* in a German private collection, see Pacelli, 1994, pp. 140–55, pl. XXVIII.

**7** For the ram as a typology of Christ, see Röttgen, 1974, pp. 118–19; Calvesi, 1990, pp. 243–4; Gilbert, 1995, chap. 2, presents an unconvincing alternative meaning.

**8** For Leonardo's painting, see C. Pedretti, *Leonardo: A Study in Chronology and Style* (New York and London, 1973), pp. 163ff. For early copies of Raphael's design, see M. Gregori, in *Raffaello a Firenze*, exh. cat., Palazzo Pitti (Florence, 1984), p. 222, no. 19.

**9** On the Carracci and the model, see G. Feigenbaum, 'Practice in the Carracci Academy', *The Artist's Workshop. Studies in the History of Art*, National Gallery of Art, Washington, DC, 1993, pp. 59–76. For Lombard practice, see Chapter 1.

**10** For similar opinions, see Moir, 1982, p. 114, and Calvesi, 1990, p. 242.

**11** For a contrary opinion, see Gilbert, 1995.

**12** Scribner, 1977. The proposal of Gilbert, 1995, pp. 141–50, that the disciples do not recognize Christ strains credibility.

**13** For cast shadows in Italian painting, see E. H. Gombrich, *Shadows: the Depiction of Cast Shadows in Western Art* (New Haven, CT, and London, 1995). The shadow of the basket was read as suggesting a symbolic fish by Scribner, 1977, p. 376, n. 10. For the lighting and colour, see also Bell, 1995, pp. 139–70.

**14** See Warma, 1990.

**15** For the 1607 record and Borromeo's visits to Rome, see Jones, 1993, pp. 241–2.

**16** Friedländer, 1955, p. 162.

**17** See Herrmann Fiore, 1995, pp. 24–7.

**18** Herrmann Fiore, 1995, p. 25.

**19** For John's presence, see Benedetti, 1995, pp. 738–49; Benedetti, 'Letter to the Editor', *BM*, vol. 137 (1995), pp. 37–8; Gilbert, 1995, pp. 135–52.

**20** On Maffeo, see Moroni, 1857, pp. 41–2.

**21** On the symbolism in the landscape, see Marini, 1987, p. 466.

**22** For further excerpts from the trial, see Friedländer, 1955, pp. 270–9. For further discussion, see Hibbard, 1983, pp. 161–2; and R. Ward Bissell, *Orazio Gentileschi* (University Park, PA, and London, 1981), pp. 12–14. For Baglione's lost Gesù altarpiece, see R. Spear, in *The Age of Caravaggio*, 1985, no. 16. On Béthune's intervention, see Bassani and Bellini, 1994, pp. 163–7.

**23** See J.-P. Babelon, 'Les Caravage de Philippe de Béthune', *GBA*, vol. 111 (1988), pp. 33–8; for the Giustiniani collection, see Salerno, 1960; and for new light on Benedetto's role as Caravaggio's patron, see Danesi Squarzina, 1997 and 1998.

**24** On Milesi, see Petrucci, 1956; Fulcro, 1980; Spezzaferro, 1980.

**25** For the portrait, see Cinotti, 1983, p. 571, no. 111.

**26** On Caravaggio and Marino, see Cinotti, 1983, p. 571; Marini, 1987, p. 364, P–12, whose proposed identification for the lost 'Susanna' (no. 46) is unconvincing. See also G. Fulcro, 'Il sogno di una "Galeria"', *ABA*, vol. 3 (1979), pp. 9–12, 84–99; Bologna, 1992, pp. 147, 316; Cropper, 1991 pp. 193–212. New evidence reveals that Caravaggio represented a nude Mary Magdalen for Cardinal Benedetto Giustiniani; see Danesi Squarzina, 1997, p. 771.

**27** The documents were first cited by Marini, 1987, and published in full by R. Barbiellini Amidei, 'Della committenza Massimo', in *Caravaggio. Nuove riflessioni*, 1989, pp. 47–69, with earlier literature on the competition. See also Bellori, pp. 207–8.

**28** For Cigoli's *Ecce Homo*, see M. Chiarini, in *Lodovico Cigoli 1559–1613*, exh. cat., Galleria Palatina (Palazzo Pitti), Florence (Florence, 1992), no. 24, with earlier bibliography; and M. Chappell, 'On Some Drawings by Cigoli', *MD*, vol. 27 (1989), pp. 195–214, esp. pp. 201–2.

**29** See the Checklist, no. 52, for recent literature.

**30** The later shipment of Cigoli's *Ecce Homo* to Spain may have been confused by Bellori with the history of Caravaggio's painting for Massimi (see E. Goldberg, 'Spanish Taste, Medici Politics and a Lost Chapter in the History of Cigoli's "Ecce Homo"', *BM*, vol. 134, 1992, pp. 102–10).

**31** On the incisions, see Christiansen, 1986, p. 438, figs. 30–3. See Checklist no. 49 for further bibliography.

**32** See Mâle, 1972, pp. 500–3.

**33** For the *Saint Jerome* attributed to Caravaggio in the Museo de Montserrat, Barcelona, see Checklist no. 54. For Caravaggio's later *Saint Jerome* in Malta, see Chapter 6. Moir, 1976, no. 28, lists no known copies after *Saint Jerome*. For Giustiniani's lost picture, see Salerno, 1960, p. 135, and Danesi Squarzina, 1997, p. 773.

**34** Mancini, I, p. 225; Bellori, pp. 223, 225.

**35** For the various replicas of the composition and this version, see Checklist no. 60.

**36** On Caravaggio and Franciscan piety, see Treffers, 1988; Treffers, 1989. On the Mattei's ties to the Order, see Benedetti, 1995, pp. 738–40; Gilbert, 1995, pp. 153–4, 158. For other representations of Saint Francis attributed to Caravaggio, see Checklist nos. 51, 59. See Chapter 7 for Caravaggio's Sicilian pictures with Franciscan ties.

**37** The Jesuit thesis was first proposed by Friedländer, 1955, pp. 121–3; and elaborated by J. Chorpenning, 'Another Look at Caravaggio and Religion', *AEH*, vol. 8 (1987), pp. 149–58; Zuccari, 1984, pp. 147–52, saw affinities rather than direct links between the Jesuits and Caravaggio.

**38** On Neri and the Oratory, see Ponnelle and Bordet, 1932; and P. Prodi, 'San Filippo Neri: un'anomalia nella Roma della Controriforma?', *SA*, vol. 85 (1995), pp. 333–9, with recent bibliography. For a positive assessment of Oratorian influence on Caravaggio, see Friedländer, 1955, pp. 123–8; Zuccari, 1981, pp. 77–112; C. Strinati, 'Il corpo', in *La regola e la fama*, 1995, pp. 20–33.

**39** On the Oratorian ties of Caravaggio's patrons, see Ponnelle and Bordet, 1932; see also, Calvesi, 1990, pp. 248, 284–7, and in *Caravaggio e la collezione Mattei*, 1995, pp. 17–28.

**40** For the view that Baronio influenced Caravaggio, see A. Zuccari, 'Cesare Baronio, le immagini, gli artisti', in *La regola e la fama*, 1995, pp. 80–97, esp. pp. 92–3, with earlier bibliography. For the dissenting view, see Bologna, 1992, pp. 12–13, 31–3, 80–1.

**41** On Baronio, see *Baronio e l'Arte. Atti del convegno internazaionale di studi* (Sora, 1985); and Troy, 1988, pp. 74–81. For the attributed portrait, see J. T. Spike, M. Seracini, and B. Schleicher, 'Un ritratto del Cardinale Baronio', in *La regola e la fama*, 1995, pp. 588–93.

**42** For the letter, see G. Cozzi, 'Intorno al cardinal Ottavio Paravicino', *RSI*, vol. 73 (1961), pp. 36–68.

**43** For Augustinian elements in Caravaggio's art, see Hibbard, 1983, pp. 100, 129–31; Calvesi, 1990; C. Strinati, in *Roma 1300–1875*, 1985, pp. 413–4; Del Bravo, 1983, pp. 69–77.

**44** For the Dominican and Jesuit positions, see J. Mourant, 'Scientia Media and Molinism',

*Dictionary of Philosophy*, vol. 7 (New York and London, 1967), pp. 338–9. For Caravaggio's depiction of a Saint Augustine for Giustiniani, see Salerno, 1960, p. 135. In an unpublished lecture, L. Spezzaferro characterized Cerasi as a libertine, though without providing any proof; as cited in Cinotti, 1983, p. 422. Röttgen, 1974, pp. 109–11, recognized the unprecedented emphasis on the direct confrontation between Christ and Paul but did not extrapolate any larger religious implications.

**45** Similar conclusions were reached by Troy, 1988, pp. 81–2; and Bologna, 1992, whose discussion is the most extensive and systematic to date.

**46** For the record of communion, see Marini, 1981, pp. 180–3. Caravaggio's attendance at a Lenten Forty-Hours Devotion was recorded in October 1594; see H. Waga, *Vita nota e ignota dei virtuosi al Pantheon* (Rome, 1992), appendix I, pp. 219, 220ff (as cited in Corradini and Marini, 1998, p. 25, n. 2).

**47** The motto is cited in Sandrart, p. 277; for Pasqualone's charge, see Passeri, pp. 347–9.

**48** For the Sicilian anecdote, see Susinno, p. 114. On Annibale's death, see Baglione, p. 109, and Bellori, p. 87.

**49** For the argument that Caravaggio was polemically opposed to Cardinal Paleotti's Tridentine ideals, see Bologna, 1992, pp. 18–54.

## Chapter 6
## Naples and the Maltese Adventure

**1** Macioce, 1985; Bassani, 1993; Bassani and Bellini, 1994, pp. 65, 67–73, 196–200; Corradini, 1993, nos. 17, 33.

**2** For Filide, see above, chapter 3.

**3** My account of the murder depends on Bassani, 1993, pp. 92, 98. For discussion of Caravaggio's and Tomassoni's enmity in a larger political context of pro-French and pro-Spanish factions, see Bassani and Bellini, 1994, esp. chaps. X, XII; the authors do not consider, however, Caravaggio's ties with pro-Spanish protectors, for which see Calvesi, 1990, pp. 142–3.

**4** On Caravaggio and the Colonna, see especially Calvesi, 1990, pp. 107–9, 119–23; and R. Fuda, 'Note caravaggesche', *Paragone*, nn. 509–11 (1992), pp. 72–85.

**5** On seventeenth-century Naples, see *Storia di Napoli*, 11 vols., Naples, 1967–82; and the essays by C. Whitfield and G. Galasso, in *Painting in Naples*, 1983, pp. 19–30.

**6** On the viceroys, see G. Coniglio, *I vicerè spagnoli di Napoli* (Naples, 1967), pp. 163–73; and for their patronage of Caravaggio, see Pacelli, 1994, pp. 128–34. Villamediana's picture has been linked to the picture in Vienna attributed to Caravaggio; see Checklist no. 69.

**7** P. L. L. de Castri, 'Painting in Naples from Caravaggio to the Plague of 1656', in *Painting in Naples*, 1983, pp. 41–54; R. Causa, 'La pittura a Napoli' (1983), *Civiltà del seicento*, 1984, I, pp. 99–114.

**8** For the documents, see Pacelli, 1977; 'palmi 13 2/3 x 8 1/2' (*palmo napolitano* = 26.4 cm); and further on the bank account, see Pacelli, 1984, p. 102, n. 8. On the lost composition and the patron, see Pacelli, 1984, p. 101, n. 3, with further bibliography; and Pacelli, 1994, pp. 16–20. See further discussion in the Checklist, no. 62

**9** For the documents and on the Pio Monte, see Pacelli, 1984, pp. 102–3, n. 9; and Pacelli, 1994, pp. 21–4.

**10** On the Pio Monte's idiosyncratic definition of the seven works, see Pacelli, 1984, pp. 52–4.

**11** For the artistic tradition, see Pacelli, 1984, chap. 2.

**12** A. Emiliani, *Mostra di Federico Barocci* (Bologna, 1975), no. 106.

**13** For this reading, see Pacelli, 1984, pp. 49–58, who corrects the imprecise earlier reading of Fagiolo dell'Arco, 1968.

**14** Gregori, in *Painting in Naples*, 1983, no. 16.

**15** Gregori, in *Painting in Naples*, 1983, no. 16.

**16** For the controversial dating and further bibliography, see Checklist no. 63.

**17** In Caravaggio's day, the 'Scythian Slave' was displayed in the Villa Medici (Haskell and Penny, 1981, no. 11).

**18** See Cinotti, 1983, no. 36. For the proposal about the Duke of Modena's patronage, see discussion in Checklist no. 62.

**19** Calvesi, 1990, pp. 352–5, first proposed these identifications, which have been accepted by Pacelli, 1994, p. 57. On the Colonna, see F. Petrucci, in *DBI*, vol. 27, 1982, pp. 370–83. For yet another identification of the donor, see Checklist no. 62.

**20** See also D. Bodart, in *Civiltà del seicento*, 1984, p. 142, with earlier bibliography; Pacelli, 1984, pp. 79–85. For Battistello, see De Dominici, *Vite dei pittori, scultori ed architetti napoletani*, Naples, 1844, 3 vols. in 2 (Bologna, 1979), pp. 273–6; F. Bologna, 'Battistello e gli altri', in *Battistello Caracciolo*, 1991, pp. 15–180. On Sellitto, see *Carlo Sellitto*, exh. cat. (Naples, 1977). For the *Judith Beheading Holofernes*, see Checklist no. 65.

**21** For the Order's history, see Sire, 1994. For the date of Caravaggio's arrival in Malta, see Azzopardi, 1978, pp. 16–20.

**22** Macioce, 'Caravaggio a Malta', 1994, pp. 215, 228. On the Colonna's and Malaspina's ties to the Order, see Calvesi, 1990, pp. 132–3; and S. Macioce, 'Caravaggio a Malta: il S. Girolamo e lo stemma Malaspina', in *L'ultimo Caravaggio*, 1987, pp. 177–8.

**23** For Paladini, see Sebregondi Fiorentini, 1982, p. 112, with earlier bibliography; for Fabrizio Sforza-Colonna, see Calvesi, 1990, p. 132.

**24** Azzopardi, 'Caravaggio's Admission', in *Malta and Caravaggio*, 1989, pp. 45–56. For additional letters, see Macioce, 1994, pp. 207–28. On the residency rule, see Calvesi, 1990, p. 133.

**25** For the gifts, see Bellori, pp. 226, 228.

**26** Marini, 1987, p. 64; Gash, 1993, pp. 531–2. The proposal of Pacelli, 1994, chap. 2, that Caravaggio shuttled back and forth from Malta to Naples, has rightly been challenged by Cutajar, 'Caravaggio in Malta', in *Malta and Caravaggio*, 1989, pp. 11–13. For the novitiate, see Sire, 1993, p. 218. The absence of the painter's name from the Order's rolls suggests he did not have to serve on the galleys; see Macioce, 1994, p. 209.

**27** Bellori, p. 226–7; Macioce, 1994, pp. 217, 228.

**28** On the resemblance, see Calvesi, 1990, pp. 365–6; Gash, 1997, p. 160.

**29** See Bellori, p. 226, and Checklist no. 71.

**30** On the armour, see Maindron, 1908, pp. 244, 253; Marini, 1987, no. 82; and Calvesi, 1990, p. 364.

**31** On the Order's pages, see Sire, 1994, p. 83. On Wignacourt and the page, see Gash, 1993, p. 535; Cutajar, 'Caravaggio in Malta', in *Malta and Caravaggio*, 1989, p. 5.

**32** For the history of the picture and debate about the sitter's identity, see Checklist. no. 75.

**33** On the *Portrait of Paul V*, see Bellori, p. 224, and Checklist no. 57. For the recently published *Portrait of a Gentleman*, see Gregori, 1994, p. 137, reproduced in colour. Undocumented, the work looks Caravaggesque; it has been little studied because of the present owner's reluctance to show it.

**34** See Mancini, I, pp. 135–6.

**35** Marini, 1987, pp. 37–8, rightly saw a precedent for Bernini's portraiture in the *Maffeo Barberini*. For Ingres' opinion, see *Ecrits sur l'art*,

ed. R. Cogniat (Paris, 1947), p. 48. For a modern, negative appraisal, see Spear, 1975, p. 7.

**36** On Dell'Antella, who also owned a bust-length portrait of Wignacourt by Caravaggio, see Sebregondi Fiorentini, 1982, pp. 107–22; Macioce, 1994, pp. 208–9.

**37** Hibbard, 1983, p. 331, no. 172; Longhi, 1968, p. 106; the medical analysis is referred to by Cutajar, 1995, pp. 9–13, esp. p. 12.

**38** On Michelangelo's lost work, see M. Hirst and J. Dunkerton, *Making and Meaning: The Young Michelangelo*, exh. cat. (London, 1994), pp. 20–8.

**39** On the *paragone*, see L. Mendelsohn, *Paragoni: Benedetto Varchi's Due Lezzioni and Cinquecento Art Theory* (Ann Arbor, MI, 1982); and Farago, 1991.

**40** First proposed by Marini, 1987, no. 85, and seconded by Pizzorusso, 1983, pp. 50–9.

**41** Bellori, p. 226.

**42** On the history of the Oratory, see Cutajar, 1989, pp. 63, 88–92; Mr Cutajar generously supplied further information to me in a letter of 19 February 1996; and see also Stone, 1997, pp. 161–70. On 'passage money', see Cutajar, 'Caravaggio in Malta', in *Malta and Caravaggio*, 1989, p. 7.

**43** On the religious symbolism of John's beheading and the Knights' veneration of this cult, see Lane, 1978, pp. 662–72. For the identification of John with the sacrificial lamb, see Cutajar, 'Caravaggio in Malta', in *Caravaggio and Malta*, 1989, p. 9.

**44** On the cemetery and crypt, see Stone, 1997, p. 168.

**45** On the symbolic relationship between baptism and John's beheading, see Lane, 1978.

**46** See Fagiolo dell'Arco, 1968, p. 50; Röttgen, 1974, pp. 211–13; Hibbard, 1983, p. 231; Marini, 1987, p. 66.

**47** This interpretation is greatly indebted to, but differs in emphasis from, Calvesi, 1990, p. 367. Further, on the form of the signature, see Cutajar,

'Caravaggio in Malta', in *Malta and Caravaggio*, 1989, pp. 7–8.

**48** For this practice, see D. Gallavoti Cavallero, ed., *Guide rionali di Roma: Rione XII–Ripa*, part 1 (Rome, 1977), p. 96.

**49** For the restoration report, see Carità, 1957, pp. 41–82, esp. p. 56.

**50** Baglione, p. 138; Bellori, p. 227. On duelling, see Macioce, 1994, pp. 209, 219, n. 17.

**51** Azzopardi, 'Documentary Sources', in *Malta and Caravaggio*, 1989, pp. 34–9. For the defrocking, see Stone, 1997, pp. 164–5, who generously supplied the photograph of the print.

**52** For the painter's arranged escape, see Cutajar, 'Caravaggio in Malta', in *Malta and Caravaggio*, 1989, p. 11. The identity of the Procurator of Prisons was established by Macioce, 1994, p. 209.

## Chapter 7
## Final Years

**1** One possible knightly informant was Caravaggio's former host on Malta, Giacomo de Marchese, whose legal affairs brought him to Messina in February 1609; see Cutajar, 'Caravaggio in Malta', in *Malta and Caravaggio*, 1989, p. 11.

**2** For Sicily, see S. Correnti, *La Sicilia del Cinquecento* (Milan, 1980); D. Mack Smith, *A History of Sicily: Medieval Sicily 1300–1713* (New York, 1988); and *Storia della Sicilia*, 1977–81, esp. vol. 6.

**3** On the Ministers of the Sick and the lay companies, see the essays by E. Natoli, 'I luoghi di Caravaggio'; S. La Barbera and A. Mazzè, 'Regesto delle Compagnie a Palermo'; and D. Malignaggi, 'La *Natività* del Caravaggio e la Compagnia di S. Francesco', in *L'ultimo Caravaggio*, 1987, pp. 216–29, 253–77, 279–88.

**4** On Caravaggio and the Franciscans in Sicily, see A. Spadaro, 'Note sulla permanenza di Caravaggio', in *L'ultimo Caravaggio*, 1987, pp. 289–92, esp. p. 290.

**5** See V. Mirabella, *Dichiarazione delle piante delle antiche Siracuse* (Naples, 1613); modern guidebooks still use the same name for this cave, citing Caravaggio. See also Zuccari, 'La pala di Siracusa', in *L'ultimo Caravaggio*, 1987, pp. 154–9; Marini, 1987, no. 88.

**6** The Caltagirone work was sculpted by Antonello Gagini (1478–1536); see Spadaro, 'Note sulla permanenza di Caravaggio', in *L'ultimo Caravaggio*, 1987, pp. 289–92.

**7** On Polidoro's *Adoration of the Shepherds* for S. Maria di Altobasso, see Natoli, 'I luoghi di Caravaggio', in *L'ultimo Caravaggio*, 1987, p. 224.

**8** Susinno, p. 112; on late-sixteenth-century painting in Sicily, see A. Barricelli, 'La pittura in Sicilia', in *Storia della Sicilia*, 1977–81, vol. 10, pp. 3–72; V. Abbate, 'I tempi del Caravaggio', in *L'ultimo Caravaggio*, 1987.

**9** For Paladini, see Susinno, pp. 105, 112; M. G. Paolini and D. Bernini, *Mostra di Filippo Paladini* (Palermo, 1967); V. Abate, in *Caravaggio in Sicilia*, 1984, pp. 54–8, 85–6, 248–55, with further bibliography.

**10** On the style of the Sicilian works, see Pacelli, 1994, esp. pp. 199–205.

**11** G. Barbera, in *Caravaggio in Sicilia*, 1984, no. 8; Zuccari, 'La pala di Siracusa', 1987, pp. 147–73.

**12** Saccà, 1907, pp. 41–79, esp. Appendix, pp. 66–9.

**13** For the Capuchins' further commission of a 'Saint Jerome writing in a book', perhaps commissioned by the Sicilian friar Geronimo Errante, the Capuchins' general in Sicily (1605–11), see Bellori, p. 227; Abbate, 'I tempi del Caravaggio', in *Caravaggio in Sicilia*, 1984, p. 51. For a conflicting report on the possible patronge of the Adonnino family, see Natoli, 'I luoghi di Caravaggio', in *L'ultimo Caravaggio*, 1987, pp. 226–7.

**14** The document was first published by Saccà, 1907, esp. pp. 64–5; see also F. Campagna Cicale, 'Intorno all'attività di Caravaggio', in *Caravaggio in Sicilia*, 1984, pp. 117–18, and 141, n. 76.

**15** La Barbera and Mazzè, 'Regesto delle Compagnie', in *L'ultimo Caravaggio*, 1987, pp. 253–77; D. Malignaggi, '"La Natività" del Caravaggio', in *L'ultimo Caravaggio*, 1987, pp. 216–29.

**16** For Lucy's cult, see M. C. Celletti, 'Lucia di Siracusa', *Bibliotheca Sanctorum*, vol. 8, pp. 242–58. On its textual sources, see A. Zuccari, 'La pala di Siracusa', in *L'ultimo Caravaggio*, 1987, pp. 147–73. For the *pentimento*, see Cordaro, 'Il restauro del *Seppellimento di S. Lucia*', in *Caravaggio in Sicilia*, 1984, p. 270.

**17** R. Spear, 'The *Raising of Lazarus*: Caravaggio and the Sixteenth-Century Tradition', *GBA*, vol. 65 (1965), pp. 65–70.

**18** For Lazarus's gesture and cross-like form, see H. Röttgen, 'La *Resurrezione di Lazzaro*', in *Novità sul Caravaggio*, 1975, pp. 61–74.

**19** Röttgen, 'La *Resurrezione di Lazzaro*', *Novità sul Caravaggio*, 1975, pp. 61–74.

**20** Röttgen, 'La *Resurrezione di Lazzaro*', *Novità sul Caravaggio*, 1975, pp. 61–74.

**21** Friedländer, 1955, pp. 127, 216.

**22** For the copy of the *Burial* now in a Roman private collection, see Marini, 1987, p. 292.

**23** For the most current technical reports on the Sicilian paintings, see Cordaro, 'Il restauro del *Seppellimento di S. Lucia*', in *Caravaggio in Sicilia*, 1984, pp. 269–93; Lapucci, 1994, pp. 17–67.

**24** Susinno, p. 112. For the incisions, see Lapucci, 1994, figs. 4, 25.

**25** For these and additional correspondences, see Pacelli, 1994, figs. 92–120.

**26** Susinno, p. 219. For copies, see Cinotti, 1983, no. 30; Marini, 1987, nos. 88, 89, 90; and Agnello, 1991, pp. 89–97; and for prints of the *Burial of Saint Lucy* and the *Adoration of the Shepherds*, see respectively Zuccari, 'La pala di Siracusa', and Natoli, 'I luoghi di Caravaggio', in *L'ultimo Caravaggio*, 1987, pp. 169, 222.

**27** As a corrective to Moir, 1967, pp. 182–95, see D. Bernini, 'Sugli inizi del caravaggismo', in *L'ultimo Caravaggio*, 1987, pp. 211–16; V. Scuderi, 'Caravaggeschi nordici', in *Caravaggio in Sicilia*, 1984, pp. 183–224; M. Guttilla, 'Caravaggismo a Palermo', and V. Scuderi, 'Il caravaggismo di Pietro Novelli', in *L'ultimo Caravaggio*, 1987, pp. 231–52, 315–35.

**28** For Minniti, see F. Campagna Cicala, in *Caravaggio in Sicilia*, 1984, pp. 110–20, 174–9, with further bibliography. For Paladini, see no. 9 above.

**29** For Rodriguez, see F. Campagna Cicala, in *Caravaggio in Sicilia*, 1984, pp. 121–30, 167–73, with further bibliography.

**30** On Ruffo, see Haskell, 1980, pp. 209–10.

**31** Baglione, p. 138; Bellori, p. 228; J. Orbaan, *Documenti sul barocco a Roma* (Rome, 1920), p. 157.

**32** For the less persuasive hypothesis that Spanish soldiers assaulted him, see Calvesi, 1990, p. 147, seconded by Marini, 1987, p. 80. For a recent discussion of these events, see V. Pacelli, 'Una nuova ipotesi', in *Caravaggio: La vita e le opere*, 1996, pp. 184–94.

**33** For recently published letters written immediately after Caravaggio's death naming Chiaia, see Pacelli, 1994, pp. 119–55, 182, and further discussion below. Calvesi, 1995, pp. 13–14 hypothesized that Caravaggio lived in the Palazzo Cellamare. On Chiaia, see E. Bacco, *Naples, An Early Guide* (Naples, 1616), ed. and trans. by E. Gardiner (New York, 1991), p. 20.

**34** For the Fenaroli Chapel, see Bologna and Pacelli, 1980, pp. 24–40, esp. 29, n.3. Pacelli, 1994, pp. 67–9, later proposed an unconvincing, earlier dating.

**35** On two other possible commissions – the *Circumcision* in the Dominican church of S. Maria della Sanità, completed by another painter, Giovan Vincenzo Forlì, and a 'decapitated bishop saint' in the Benavente inventory – see Marini, 1987, nos. 76, 99.

**36** For the documents of the *Martyrdom of Saint Ursula*, see Bologna and Pacelli, 1980, pp. 24–2.

**37** See Pacelli, 1994, pp. 121–55. The picture in a German private collection, proposed by Pacelli (Pl. XXVIII) as the lost Saint John, looks from the photographs to be by another artist. The other two paintings are lost.

**38** C. Celano, 1692, as cited in Pacelli, 1994, p. 218, n. 42.

**39** For early descriptions of the 'Resurrection', see Pacelli, 1994, pp. 67–8.

**40** For the subject, see Lurie and Mahon, 1977.

**41** Bologna and Pacelli, 1980, p. 28. For the saint, see M. Liverani, 'Orsola', *Bibliotheca Sanctorum*, vol. 9, pp. 1251–71.

**42** Also observed by Gregori, in *Caravaggio. Come nascono*, 1991, no. 22, and Pacelli, 1994, p. 154.

**43** For a summary of interpretations of the inscription and for reproductions of the X-rays, see Papi, in *Caravaggio. Come nascono*, 1991, no. 16.

**44** On Giorgione's 'Self-Portrait', see T. Pignatti, *Giorgione*, 2d rev. edn. (Milan, 1978), p. 147, Gregori, in *The Age of Caravaggio*, 1985, no. 97, associated this with Caravaggio's *David*.

**45** The association of Cecco with Jacomo Manilli's phrase and Symonds' references respectively was made by Christiansen, 1990, p. 52, n. 88; and repeated by Papi, 1992, p. 22. But see Marini, 1993, p. 172, for a contrary opinion.

**46** For discussion of this type, see Posèq, 1990a, pp. 171–2.

**47** For a summary of scholarly interpretations, see Papi, in *Caravaggio. Come nascono*, 1991, no. 16.

**48** This version of Caravaggio's death is greatly indebted to Marini, 1992; see also Calvesi, 1990, pp. 145–50 (on imprisonment); Calvesi, 1995; Pacelli, 1994, pp. 119–29. For the latest, intriguing hypothesis that Caravaggio was murdered, see Pacelli, 'Una nuova ipotesi', in *Caravaggio: La vita e le opere*, 1995, pp. 184–94.

432

### Epilogue

**1** On Caravaggism, the standard surveys are Moir, 1967; Spear, 1975; and Nicolson, 1989.

**2** On scientific methods of analysis, see J. R. J. van Asperen de Boer, 'An introduction to the scientific examination of paintings', *NKJ*, vol. 26 (1975), pp. 1–40; H. von Sonnenburg, in *Rembrandt/Not Rembrandt*, exh. cat., Metropolitan Museum of Art (New York, 1995), pp. 11–23.

**3** Mancini, I, p. 108; Sandrart, p. 275; Bellori, pp. 217–18. For the 1605 inventory, see Appendix VII; Corradini and Marini, 1993, and Bassani and Bellini, 1993, whose hypothetical reconstruction of the studio is misleadingly presented as fact.

**4** On the colour of Caravaggio's grounds, see Christiansen, 1988, pp. 26–7; Christiansen, 1992, pp. 502–3; Christiansen, 1995, p. 89. For the X-ray evidence, see R. Lapucci, 'La tecnica di Caravaggio', in *Caravaggio. Come nascono*, 1991, p. 50.

**5** My discussion of Caravaggio's lighting and cast shadows is indebted to Bell, 1995, pp. 154–8.

**6** On Leonardo's universal and specific light, and Lomazzo's primary light, see Barasch, 1978, pp. 58–62, 148–53.

**7** See Barasch, 1978, p. 61; and on the unnaturalness of Caravaggio's lighting, see Bellori, p. 218.

**8** Bellori, pp. 229. On Caravaggio's palette, see M. Cordaro, 'La tecnica pittorica del Caravaggio', in *L'ultimo Caravaggio*, 1987, pp. 105–38; Lapucci, 'La tecnica del Caravaggio', in *Caravaggio. Come nascono*, 1991, pp. 31–52. For the *Betrayal of Christ*, see Benedetti, 1993.

**9** For these decorative incisions, see Lapucci, 'La tecnica del Caravaggio', in *Caravaggio. Come nascono*, 1991, p. 93; Christiansen, 1986, pp. 436, 440. On the tempera layer over oil, see Greaves and Johnson, 1974, pp. 568–71.

**10** On colour perception, see De Grandis, 1986.

**11** On Caravaggio's use of white in the London *Supper at Emmaus*, see Bell, 1995, p. 153.

**12** G. L. Masetti Zannini, 'Un dipinto del Caravaggio', *Commentari*, vol. 22 (1971), pp. 184–6.

**13** The latter alternative was proposed to me by K. Christiansen, who discusses the dynamics of patronage in his review of Askew, 1990, in *ZK*, vol. 55, 1992, pp. 300–1.

**14** For the under-drawings, see Gregori, 'Come dipingeva il Caravaggio', in *Caravaggio. Come nascono*, 1991, pp. 22–4. For further discussion, and especially of the *Judith Beheading Holofernes*, see Christiansen, 1986, pp. 427–9.

**15** Infra-red reflectography has not revealed compositional under-drawings in the *Cardsharps* and Capitoline *Fortune-Teller*, which do have light-coloured grounds. On autoradiography, see E. V. Sayre and H. N. Lechtman, 'Neutron Activation Autoradiography of Oil Paintings', *Studies in Conservation*, vol. 13, (1968), pp. 161–85.

**16** For the most thorough discussion of incisions up to 1986, see Christiansen, 1986. For more recent data, see the essay and technical reports appended to individual catalogue entries by Lapucci, 'La tecnica del Caravaggio', in *Caravaggio. Come nascono*, 1991. For the late works, see Lapucci, 1994, pp. 17–67, figs. 4, 25.

**17** For Barocci's and Cesari's incisions, see Christiansen, 1986, p. 426. On Cesari's, also see Gregori and Papi, in *Caravaggio. Come nascono*, 1991, pp. 18, 66–8.

**18** The evidence of incisions in the ram is inconclusive: see Lapucci's diagrams, in *Caravaggio. Come nascono*, 1991, p. 237.

**19** On these geometric incisions, see Lapucci, in *Caravaggio. Come nascono*, 1991, pp. 235–6. For the compass, see Appendix IV.

**20** On Barocci, see Bellori, p. 205.

**21** On the re-posing of the model in *Judith Beheading Holofernes*, see Christiansen, 1986, p. 428.

**22** This interpretation is indebted to Vodret, 1996, pp. 9–13, but does not accept either the author's claim that the *Narcissus* is a self-portrait or that the reflection presents what the boy himself sees.

**23** On illusionistic foreshortening, see Kemp, 1990, pp. 71–4.

**24** For further discussion of Caravaggio and optical devices, see Corradini and Marini, 1993, pp. 164–9; Lapucci, 1994a, pp. 160–70, with earlier bibliography.

**25** For a recent summary of Caravaggio's layering, see R. Lapucci, 'Radiografie e riflettografie', in *Come dipingeva il Caravaggio*, 1996, pp. 31–50.

**26** For the Delineavit project, see Correale, 1990, pp. 121–41. On the limits of technical data, see K. Christiansen, 'Thoughts', in *Come dipingeva il Caravaggio*, 1996, pp. 7–28, esp. p. 7.

**27** On Manfredi's practices, see Lapucci, in *Dopo Caravaggio*, 1987, p. 89. On La Tour's, see M. Gifford *et al.*, 'Some Observations' and C. Barry, 'Appendix', in Conisbee, 1996, pp. 240–57, 287–301.

**434** **Selected Bibliography**

This Bibliography is largely limited to works cited in abbreviated form in the Notes and Checklist. Recent literature has been emphasized; complete bibliographies with earlier literature on Caravaggio can be found in Cinotti, 1983, and Marini, 1987.

## Primary Sources

Baglione, Giovanni, *Le vite de' pittori, scultori et architetti* (Rome, 1642)

Bellori, Giovan Pietro, *Le vite de' pittori, scultori et architetti moderni*, Rome, 1672, ed. Evelina Borea (Turin, 1976)

Giustiniani, Vincenzo, 'Discorso sopra la pittura', in G Bottari and S. Ticozzi, *Raccolta di lettere sulla pittura, scultura ed architettura* (Hildesheim and New York, 1976), vol. 6, no. XXXIV, p. 121–9

Mancini, Giulio, *Considerazioni sulla pittura*, ed. Adriana Marucchi and Luigi Salerno, 2 vols. (Rome, 1956–7)

Passeri, Giovanni Battista, Jacob Hess, ed., *Die Künstlerbiographien von Giovanni Battista Passeri* (Leipzig, 1934)

Sandrart, Joachim von, *L'academia todesca della architettura, scultura et pittura*, Nuremberg, 1675, ed. A. Peltzer (Munich, 1925)

Scannelli, Francesco, *Il microcosmo della pittura* (Cesena, 1657)

Susinno, Francesco, *Le vite de' pittori messinesi*, ed. Valentino Martinelli (Florence, 1960)

## Secondary Sources

Abromson, Morton C., *Painting in Rome during the Papacy of Clement VIII (1592–1605)* (New York, 1976)

*The Age of Caravaggio*, exh. cat., Metropolitan Museum of Art, New York (New York, 1985)

Agnello, Santi Luigi, 'Due scolii ad un catalogo', *Archivio storico siracusano*, vol. 5 (1991), pp. 89–97

Amayden, Teodoro, *Storia delle famiglie romane*, ed. Carlo Augusto Bertini, 2 vols., Rome, 1914 (Bologna, 1979)

Askew, Pamela, 'The Angelic Consolation of St Francis of Assisi in Post-Tridentine Italian Painting', *Journal of the Warburg and Courtauld Institutes*, vol. 32 (1969), pp. 280–306

Askew, Pamela, *Caravaggio's 'Death of the Virgin'* (Princeton, 1990)

Azzopardi, John, 'Caravaggio in Malta: an unpublished document', *The Church of St John in Valletta, 1578–1978*, exh. cat. (Malta, 1978), pp. 16–20

Azzopardi, John, and Stone, David, 'Above Caravaggio: the Massacre of the Knights at Fort St Elmo', *Treasures of Malta*, vol. 3, no. 1 (1996), pp. 61–6

Baccheschi, Edi, and Calvesi, Maurizio, 'Simone Peterzano', *I Pittori Bergamaschi dal XIII al XIX Secolo: Il Cinquecento, IV* (Bergamo, 1975), pp. 473–557

Barasch, Moshe, *Light and Color in the Italian Renaissance Theory of Art* (New York, 1978)

Barolsky, Paul, 'The Biblical Poetry of Caravaggio's *Rest on the Flight into Egypt*', *Source*, vol. 10 (1990), pp. 20–1

Bassani, Riccardo, 'Documenti inediti sull'omicidio di Ranuccio Tomassoni da Terni per mano di Michelangelo Merisi da Caravaggio', *Rivista storica del Lazio*, vol. 1 (1993), pp. 87–111

Bassani, Riccardo, and Bellini, Fiora, 'La casa, le "robbe", lo studio del Caravaggio a Roma. Due documenti inediti del 1603 e del 1605', *Prospettiva*, vol. 71 (1993), pp. 68–76

Bassani, Riccardo, and Bellini, Fiora, *Caravaggio assassino* (Rome, 1994)

*Battistello Caracciolo e il primo naturalismo a Napoli*, exh. cat., Castel Sant'Elmo, Naples (Naples, 1991)

Bell, Janis C., 'Some Seventeenth-Century Appraisals of Caravaggio's Coloring', *Artibus et historiae*, vol. 14, no. 27 (1993), pp. 103–30

Bell, Janis C., 'Light and Color in Caravaggio's *Supper at Emmaus*', *Artibus et historiae*, vol. 16, no. 31 (1995), pp. 139–70

Bellini, Fiora, 'Tre documenti inediti per Michelangelo da Caravaggio', *Prospettiva*, vol. 65 (1992), pp. 70–1

Benedetti, Sergio, 'Caravaggio's "Taking of Christ"', *Burlington Magazine*, vol. 135 (1995), pp. 731–46

Benedetti, Sergio, *Caravaggio: The Master Revealed* (National Gallery of Ireland, 1995) [Benedetti, 1995a]

Bernardini, Maria Grazia, Gaggi, Gabriella, and Marcone, Anna, 'Giove, Nettuno e Pluto di Caravaggio nel casino Ludovisi a Roma. Il cosmo in una stanza', *Art e dossier*, no. 6 (1991), pp. 18–21

Bertolotti, Antonio, *Artisti lombardi a Roma nei secoli XV, XVI e XVII*, 2 vols. (Milan, 1881)

*Bibliotheca Sanctorum*, 12 vols. (Rome, 1961–70)

Bissell, R. Ward, 'Concerning the Date of Caravaggio's *Amore Vincitore*', *Hortus imaginum: Essays in Western Art*, eds. Robert Enggass and Marilyn Stokstad (Lawrence, KA, 1974), pp. 113–23

Bologna, Ferdinando, *L'incredulità del Caravaggio e l'esperienza delle 'cose naturali'* (Turin, 1992)

Bologna, Ferdinando, and Pacelli, Vincenzo, 'Caravaggio, 1610: la "Sant'Orsola confitta dal Tiranno" per Marcantonio Doria', *Prospettiva*, vol. 23 (1980), pp. 24–40

Brehm, Margrit, *Der Fall Caravaggio: Eine Rezeptionsgeschichte* (Frankfurt, 1992)

**435**

Brown, Jonathan, 'A New Identification of the Donor in Caravaggio's *Madonna of the Rosary*', *Paragone*, no. 407 (1984), pp. 15–21

Cadogan, Jeanne K., and Mahoney, Michael, eds., *Wadsworth Atheneum Paintings. Vol. 2. Italy and Spain* (Hartford, CT, 1991)

Calvesi, Maurizio, *Le realtà del Caravaggio* (Turin, 1990)

Calvesi, Maurizio, 'Novità e conferme: Ancora sulle carte relative agli ultimi giorni di Caravaggio', *Art e dossier*, vol. 66 (1995), pp. 13–14

*I Campi e la cultura artistica cremonese del Cinquecento*, exh. cat. (Milan, 1985)

Cappelletti, Francesca, and Testa, Laura, 'I quadri di Caravaggio nella collezione Mattei. I nuovi documenti e i riscontri con le fonti', *Storia dell'arte*, vol. 69 (1990), pp. 234–44

Cappelletti, Francesca, and Testa, Laura, *Il trattenimento di virtuosi: Le collezioni secentesche di quadri nei Palazzi Mattei di Roma* (Rome, 1994)

*Caravaggio. Come nascono i capolavori*, exh cat., Galleria Palatina, Palazzo Pitti, Florence, ed. Mina Gregori (Milan, 1991)

*Caravaggio da Malta a Firenze*, exh. cat., Palazzo Vecchio, Florence (Milan, 1996)

*Caravaggio e la collezione Mattei*, exh. cat., Galleria Nazionale, Rome (Milan, 1995)

*Caravaggio in Sicilia: il suo tempo, il suo influsso*, exh. cat., Museo regionale di Palazzo Bellomo, Syracuse (Palermo, 1984)

*Caravaggio: La vita e le opere attraverso i documenti: Atti del convegno internazionale di studi*, Rome 1995, ed. Stefania Macioce (Rome, 1996)

*Caravaggio nei musei romani* (Rome, 1986)

*Caravaggio. Nuove riflessioni*, Quaderni di Palazzo Venezia, 6 (Rome, 1989)

Carità, Roberto, 'Il restauro dei dipinti caravaggeschi della cattedrale di Malta', *Bollettino dell'Istituto Centrale del Restauro*, nos 29–30 (1957), pp. 41–82

Chappell, Miles L., & Kirwin, Chandler W., 'A Petrine Triumph: The Decoration of the Navi Piccole in San Pietro under Clement VIII', *Storia dell'arte*, vol. 21 (1974), pp. 119–70

Chiappini di Sorio, Ileana, 'Cristoforo Roncalli detto il Pomerancio', *I Pittori Bergamaschi dal XIII al XIX secolo: Il seicento*, IV, Part I (Bergamo, 1975)

Chiarini, Marco, 'La probabile identità del *Cavaliere di Malta* di Pitti', *Antichità viva*, vol. 28, no. 4 (1989), pp. 15–16

Christiansen, Keith, 'Caravaggio and "L'esempio davanti del naturale"', *Art Bulletin*, vol. 68 (1986), pp. 421–45

Christiansen, Keith, 'Technical report on the *Cardsharps*', *Burlington Magazine*, vol. 130 (1988), pp. 26–7

Christiansen, Keith, *A Caravaggio Rediscovered. The 'Lute Player'* (New York, 1990)

Christiansen, Keith, 'Caravaggio's second versions', *Burlington Magazine*, vol. 134 (1992), pp. 502–3

Christiansen, Keith, *Le Caravage et 'L'Esempio davanti del naturale'* (Paris, 1995)

Cinotti, Mia, *Caravaggio: tutte le opere* (Bergamo, 1983)

Cinotti, Mia, and Dell'Acqua, Gian Alberto, *Immagine del Caravaggio: Mostra didattica itinerante*, exh. cat. (Milan, 1973)

*Civiltà del seicento a Napoli*, exh. cat., 2 vols., Museo di Capodimonte, Naples (Naples, 1984)

*The Cleveland Museum of Art: Catalogue of Paintings: European Paintings of the 16th, 17th, and 18th Centuries* (Cleveland, 1982)

*Colloquio sul tema Caravaggio e i Caravaggeschi* (Rome, 1974)

*Come dipingeva il Caravaggio: Atti della giornata di studio*, ed. Mina Gregori (Milan, 1996)

Conisbee, Philip, *Georges de La Tour and His World*, exh. cat., National Gallery of Art, Washington, DC, and Kimbell Art Museum, Fort Worth (Washington, DC, 1996)

Corradini, Sandro, *Caravaggio; Materiali per un processo* (Rome, 1993)

Corradini, Sandro, and Marini, Maurizio, '"Inventarium omnium et singulorum bonorum mobilium" di Michelangelo da Caravaggio "pittore"', *Artibus et historiae*, vol. 14, no. 28 (1993), pp. 161–76

Corradini, Sandro, and Marini, Maurizio, 'The earliest account of Caravaggio in Rome', *Burlington Magazine*, vol. 140 (1998), pp. 25–8

Correale, Giampaolo, ed., *Identificazione di un Caravaggio: Nuove tecnologie per un rilettura del 'San Giovanni Battista'* (Venice, 1990)

Cropper, Elizabeth, 'The Petrifying Art: Marino's Poetry and Caravaggio', *Metropolitan Museum Journal*, vol. 26 (1991), pp. 193–212

Cutajar, Dominic, *Malta: History and Works of Art in St John's Church, Valletta* (Valletta, 1989)

Cutajar, Dominic, 'Caravaggio – The Maltese Phase', *Treasures of Malta*, vol. 2 (1995), pp. 9–13.

Cuzin, Jean-Pierre, *La diseuse de bonne aventure de Caravage*, Les dossiers du département des peintures (Paris, 1977)

Danesi Squarzina, Silvia, 'The Collections of Cardinal Benedetto Giustiniani', *Burlington Magazine*, vol. 139 (1997), pp. 766–9, and vol. 140 (1998), pp. 102–18

Danto, Arthur C., 'Caravaggio: the Name of the Rosary', *Art News*, vol. 92 (Sept. 1993), pp. 107–8

de Grandis, Luigina, *Theory and Use of Color*, trans. J. Gilbert (New York, 1986)

del Bravo, Carlo, 'Sul significato della luce nel Caravaggio e in Gianlorenzo Bernini', *Artibus et historiae*, vol. 4, no. 7 (1983), pp. 69–77

del Bravo, Carlo, *Le risposte dell'arte* (Florence, 1985)

Delumeau, Jean, *Vie économique et sociale de Rome dans la seconde moitié du XVIe siècle*, 2 vols. (Paris, 1957)

*Dizionario biografico degli italiani*, vols. 1– (Rome, 1977–)

*Dopo Caravaggio: Bartolomeo Manfredi e la Manfrediana Methodus*, exh. cat., Cremona (Milan, 1987)

Enggass, Robert, 'L'Amore Giustiniani del Caravaggio', *Palatino*, vol. 11 (1967), pp. 13–20

Fagiolo dell'Arco, Maurizio, 'Le "Opere di misericordia": contributo alla poetica del Caravaggio', *L'arte*, vol. 1 (1968), pp. 37–61

Farago, Claire J., *Leonardo da Vinci's 'Paragone'* (Leiden and New York, 1991)

Freedberg, Sydney J., *Circa 1600: A Revolution of Style in Italian Painting* (Cambridge, MA, and London, 1983)

Friedländer, Walter, *Caravaggio Studies*, Princeton, NJ, 1955 (rev. edn., New York, 1969)

Frommel, Christoph Luitpold, 'Caravaggios Frühwerk und der Kardinal Francesco Maria del Monte', *Storia dell'arte*, vol. 9–10 (1971), pp. 5–52

Frommel, Christoph Luitpold, 'Caravaggio und seine Modelle', *Castrum Peregrini*, vol. 96 (1971), pp. 21–56 [Frommel, 1971a]

Fulcro, Giorgio, '"Ammirate l'altissimo pittore": Caravaggio nelle rime inedite di Marzio Milesi', *Ricerche di storia dell'arte*, vol. 10 (1980), pp. 65–89

Gash, John, 'Painting and Sculpture in Early Modern Malta', in *Hospitaller Malta 1530–1798*, ed. V. Mallia-Milanes (Minerva Publications, 1993)

Gash, John, *Caravaggio*, London, 1980 (reprinted London, 1988, and Rizzoli, 1994)

Gash, John, 'The Identity of Caravaggio's *Knight of Malta*', *Burlington Magazine*, vol. 139 (1997), pp. 156–60

Gedo, John, *Portraits of the Artist: Psychoanalysis of Creativity and Its Vicissitudes* (New York and London, 1983)

Gilbert, Creighton E., *Caravaggio and His Two Cardinals* (University Park, PA, 1995)

Glen, Thomas L., 'Rubens after Caravaggio: *The Entombment*', *RACAR: Revue de l'art canadienne*, vol. 15/1 (1988), pp. 19–22

*The Golden Legend of Jacobus de Voragine*, trans. Granger Ryan and Helmut Ripperger (New York, London, Toronto, 1941)

Graeve, Mary Ann, 'The Stone of Unction in Caravaggio's Painting for the Chiesa Nuova', *Art Bulletin*, vol. 40 (1958), pp. 223–38

Greaves, James L., and Johnson, Meryl, 'New Findings on Caravaggio's Technique in the Detroit Magdalen', *Burlington Magazine*, vol. 116 (1974), pp. 568–71

Gregori, Mina, 'Il *Sacrificio di Isacco*: un inedito e considerazioni su una fase savoldesca del Caravaggio', *Artibus et historiae*, vol. 10 (1989), pp. 99–142

Gregori, Mina, 'Sulla traccia di un'altro *Ecce Homo* del Caravaggio', *Paragone*, no. 489 (1990), pp. 19–27

Gregori, Mina, 'Il *San Giovannino alla sorgente* del Caravaggio', *Paragone*, nos. 519–21 (1993), pp. 3–20

Gregori, Mina, *Caravaggio* (Milan, 1994)

Haskell, Francis, *Patrons and Painters*, 2d rev. edn. (New Haven, CT, and London, 1980)

Haskell, Francis, and Penny, Nicholas, *Taste and the Antique* (New Haven, CT, and London, 1981)

Hass, Angela, 'Caravaggio's *Calling of St Matthew* reconsidered', *Journal of the Warburg and Courtauld Institutes*, vol. 51 (1988), pp. 245–50

Heikamp, Detlef, 'La *Medusa* del Caravaggio e l'armatura dello Scià 'Abbas di Persia', *Paragone*, no. 199 (1966), pp. 62–76

Heimburger, Minna, 'Interpretazioni della pitture di genere del Caravaggio secondo il "metodo neerlandese"', *Paragone*, no. 489 (1990), pp. 3–18

Held, Jutta, *Caravaggio: Politik und Martyrium der Körper* (Berlin, 1996)

Herrmann Fiore, Kristen, 'Caravaggio's *Taking of Christ* and Dürer's woodcut of 1509', *Burlington Magazine*, vol. 137 (1995), pp. 24–7

Hibbard, Howard, *Caravaggio* (New York, 1983)

Hinks, Roger, *Michelangelo Merisi da Caravaggio* (London, 1953)

*L'iconografia della Vergine di Loreto nell'arte*, exh. cat., eds. Floriano Grimaldi and Katy Sordi (Loreto, 1995)

Jones, Pamela, *Federico Borromeo and the Ambrosiana* (Cambridge, 1993)

Kemp, Martin, *Art and Science* (New Haven, CT, and London, 1990)

Kitson, Michael, *The Complete Paintings of Caravaggio* (New York, 1969)

Kretschmer, H., 'Zu Caravaggios Berufung des Matthäus in der Cappella Contarelli', *Pantheon*, vol. 46 (1988), pp. 63–6

Lane, Barbara G., 'Rogier's Saint John and Miraflores Altarpieces Reconsidered', *Art Bulletin*, vol. 60 (1978), pp. 655–72

Lapucci, Roberta, 'Documentazione tecnica sulle opere messinesi del Caravaggio', *Quaderni dell'attività didattica del museo regionale di Messina*, vol. 4 (1994), pp. 17–67

Lapucci, Roberta, 'Caravaggio e i "quadretti nello specchio ritratti"', *Paragone*, nos. 529–33 (1994), pp 160–70 [Lapucci, 1994a]

Lavin, Irving, 'Divine Inspiration in Caravaggio's Two *St Matthews*', *Art Bulletin*, vol. 56 (1974), pp. 59–81

Lavin, Irving, 'Addenda to "Divine Inspiration"', *Art Bulletin*, vol. 56 (1974), pp. 590–1 [Lavin, 1974a]

Lavin, Irving, 'A Further Note on the Ancestry of Caravaggio's First *Saint Matthew*', *Art Bulletin*, vol. 62 (1980), pp. 113–14

Lavin, Irving, 'Caravaggio's Roman Madonnas', Paper delivered at the Age of Caravaggio Symposium, Metropolitan Museum of Art (New York, 1985)

Lavin, Irving, 'On the Identity of the Protagonist in Caravaggio's *Calling of Saint Matthew*, Paper delivered at College Art Association Conference (New York, 1990)

Loire, Stéphane, and Brejon de Lavergnée, Arnauld, *Caravage: La mort de la Vierge – Une Madone sans dignité* (Paris, 1990)

Longhi, Roberto, *'Me pinxit' e Quesiti Caravaggeschi* (Florence, 1968)

Longhi, Roberto, *Caravaggio*, trans. B. D. Phillips (Leipzig, 1968) [Longhi, 1968a]

Longhi, Roberto, *Caravaggio*, rev. edn. (Rome, 1982)

Lurie, Alison T., and Mahon, Denis, 'Caravaggio's *Crucifixion of Saint Andrew* from Valladolid', *Bulletin of the Cleveland Museum of Art*, vol. 64 (1977), pp. 3–24

Macioce, Stefania, 'Attorno a Caravaggio. Notizie d'archivio', *Storia dell'arte*, vol. 55 (1985), pp. 389–92

Macioce, Stefania, *Undique splendent. Aspetti della pittura sacra nella Roma di Clemente VIII Aldobrandini (1592–1605)* (Rome, 1990)

Macioce, Stefania, 'Caravaggio a Malta e i suoi referenti: notizie d'archivio', *Storia dell'arte*, vol. 81 (1994), pp. 207–28

Macrae, Desmond, 'Observations on the Sword in Caravaggio', *Burlington Magazine*, vol. 106 (1964), pp. 412–16

*La Maddalena tra sacro e profano*, exh. cat., ed. Marilena Mosco, Palazzo Pitti, Florence (Milan, 1986)

Magnuson, Torgil, *Rome in the Age of Bernini*, 2 vols. (Uppsala, 1982–6)

Mahon, Denis, 'Egregius in Urbe Pictor. Caravaggio revised', *Burlington Magazine*, vol. 93 (1951), pp. 223–34

Maindron, Maurice, 'Le portrait du grand maître Alof de Wignacourt au musée du Louvre, son portrait et ses armes à l'arsenal de Malta', *Revue de l'art ancien et moderne*, vol. 24 (1908), pp. 241–54, 339–52

Mâle, Emile, *L'art religieux de la fin du XVIe siècle* (Paris, 1972)

*Malta and Caravaggio*, ed. Dominic Cutajar, Malta, 1986 (2d rev. edn. 1989)

Marabottini, Alessandro, 'Caravaggio e la collezione Mattei: qualche considerazione e un contributo', *Commentari d'arte*, vol. 1, no. 2 (1995), pp. 62–72

Marini, Maurizio, 'Un estrema residenza', *Antologia di belle arti*, nos. 17–18, 19–20 (1981), pp. 180–3

Marini, Maurizio, *Caravaggio: Michelangelo Merisi da Caravaggio 'pictor praestantissimus'*, Rome, 1987 (2d rev. edn. 1989)

Marini, Maurizio, 'L'ospite inquieto. Le residenze romane di Caravaggio', *Art e dossier*, vol. 42 (1990), pp. 8–9

Marini, Maurizio, 'L'ultima spiaggia: Nuovi documenti sulla drammatica morte di Caravaggio', *Art e dossier*, vol. 66 (1992), pp. 8–11

Matthiesen, Patrick, and Pepper, D. Stephen, 'Guido Reni: An Early Masterpiece Discovered in Liguria', *Apollo*, vol. 91 (1970), pp. 452–62

Moir, Alfred, *The Italian Followers of Caravaggio* (Cambridge, MA, 1967)

Moir, Alfred, *Caravaggio and His Copyists* (New York, 1976)

Moir, Alfred, *Caravaggio* (New York, 1982)

Mormone, Raffaele, 'Per un rilettura delle *Sette Opere di Misericordia*', *Napoli nobilissima*, vol. 25, nos. 3–4 (1986), pp. 91–100

Moroni, Gaetano, *Dizionario di erudizione storico-ecclesiastica*, 109 vols. (Venice, 1840–79)

*La natura morta al tempo di Caravaggio*, exh. cat., Capitoline Museums, Rome (Naples, 1995)

Nicolson, Benedict, *The International Caravaggesque Movement* (Oxford, 1979); 2d rev. edn. retitled, *Caravaggism in Europe* (Turin, 1989)

*Novità sul Caravaggio. Saggi e Contributi*, ed. Mia Cinotti (Milan, 1975)

Nussdorfer, Laurie, *Civic Politics in the Rome of Urban VIII* (Princeton, NJ, 1992)

Orgel, Stephen, *Impersonations: The Performance of Gender in Shakespeare's England* (Cambridge, 1996)

Orr, Lynn Federle, 'Classical Elements in the Paintings of Caravaggio', Ph.D. dissertation (University of California at Santa Barbara, 1982)

Pacelli, Vincenzo, 'New documents concerning Caravaggio in Naples', *Burlington Magazine*, vol. 119 (1977), pp. 819–29

Pacelli, Vincenzo, *Caravaggio. Le sette opere di misericordia* (Salerno, 1984)

Pacelli, Vincenzo, 'Strumenti in posa: novità sull'*Amore Vincitore* del Caravaggio', *Prospettiva*, vols. 57–60 (1989–90), pp. 156–62

Pacelli, Vincenzo, *L'ultimo Caravaggio dalla Maddalena a mezza figura ai due San Giovanni, 1606–1610* (Todi, 1994)

Pacelli, Vincenzo, and Brejon de Lavergnée, Arnauld, 'L'eclisse del commitente? Congetture su un ritratto nella "Flagellazione" di Caravaggio rivelato dalla radiografia', *Paragone*, nos. 419–21–23 (1985), pp. 209–18

*Painting in Naples 1606–1705 from Caravaggio to Giordano*, exh. cat., eds. Clovis Whitfield and Jane Martineau, National Gallery of Art, Washington, DC (London, 1983)

Papi, Gianni, 'Un nuovo *Ecce Homo* del Caravaggio', *Paragone*, no. 489 (1990), pp. 28–48

Papi, Gianni, *Cecco del Caravaggio* (Florence, 1992)

Parks, N. Randolph, 'On Caravaggio's "Dormition of the Virgin" and its Setting', *Burlington Magazine*, vol. 127 (1985), pp. 438–48

438

Perini, Giovanna, 'Caravaggio a Bologna', in *Napoli, L'Europa: Ricerche di Storia dell'Arte in onore di Ferdinando Bologna*, eds. Francesco Abbate and Fiorella Sticchia Santoro (Catanza, 1995), pp. 199–203

Peter, Christine, *Gespräche mit Bildern: Caravaggio in Rom* (Münster, 1994)

Petrucci, Alfredo, 'Amici del Caravaggio: Chi era Marzio Milesi', *Studi romani*, vol. 4 (1956), pp. 123–46

Pizzorusso, Claudio, 'Un "tranquillo dio": Giovanni da San Giovanni e Caravaggio', *Paragone*, no. 405 (1983), pp. 50–9

Ponnelle, Louis, and Bordet, Louis, *St Philip Neri and the Roman Society of His Times (1515–1595)*, trans. R. F. Kerr (London, 1932)

Posèq, Avigdor W. G., 'A Note on Caravaggio's *Sleeping Amor*', *Source*, vol. 6 (1987), pp. 27–31

Posèq, Avigdor W. G., 'Caravaggio's *Medusa Shield*', *Gazette des Beaux-Arts*, vol. 113 (1989), pp. 170–4

Posèq, Avigdor W. G., 'Bacchic Themes in Caravaggio's Juvenile Works', *Gazette des Beaux-Arts*, vol. 115 (1990), pp. 113–21

Posèq, Avigdor W. G., 'Caravaggio's Self-Portrait as the Beheaded Goliath', *Konsthistorik Tidskrift*, vol. 3 (1990), pp. 169–82 [Posèq, 1990a]

Posèq, Avigdor W. G., 'Caravaggio and the Antique', *Artibus et historiae*, vol. 11 (1990), pp. 147–67 [Posèq, 1990b]

Posèq, Avigdor W. G., 'Caravaggio's *Amor Vincitore* and the Supremacy of Painting', *Source*, vol. 12 (1993), pp. 13–18

Posner, Donald, 'Caravaggio's Homo-erotic Early Works', *Art Quarterly*, vol. 34 (1971), pp. 301–24

Posner, Donald, 'Lizards and Lizard Lore, with Special Reference to Caravaggio's Leapin' Lizard', *Art the Ape of Nature* (New York, 1981), pp. 387–91

Prater, Andreas, 'Wo ist Matthäus? Beobachtungen zu Caravaggios Anfängen, als Monumentalmaler in der Contarelli-kapelle', *Pantheon*, vol. 43 (1985), pp. 70–4

Prater, Andreas, *Licht und Farbe bei Caravaggio* (Stuttgart, 1992)

Prater, Andreas, 'Matthäus und kein Ende? Eine Entgegnung', *Pantheon*, vol. 53 (1995), pp. 53–61

*La regola e la fama: San Filippo Neri e l'arte*, exh. cat., Museo Nazionale del Palazzo Venezia, Rome (Milan, 1995)

Rice, Louise, *The Altars and Altarpieces of New St Peter's: Outfitting the Basilica, 1621–1666* (Cambridge University Press, 1997)

*Roma 1300–1875. L'arte degli anni santi*, eds. Maurizio Fagiolo and Maria Luisa Madonna (Milan, 1984)

Rossi, Luigi, 'Riflessioni e proposte per una nuova lettura del dipinto sul muro eseguito da Caravaggio nel Casino Del Monte', *Arte documento*, vol. 8 (1994), pp. 181–4

Rotondi, Pasquale, 'Una nuova proposta per il Caravaggio nella Cappella Contarelli', *Bollettino dell'Istituto Centrale del Restauro*, vol. 46 (1996), pp. 11–44

Röttgen, Herwarth, *Il Cavalier d'Arpino*, exh. cat., Palazzo Venezia, Rome (Rome, 1973)

Röttgen, Herwarth, *Il Caravaggio. Ricerche e interpretazioni* (Rome, 1974)

Röttgen, Herwarth, 'Da ist Matthäus', *Pantheon*, vol. 49 (1991), pp. 97–9

Röttgen, Herwarth, *Caravaggio: Der Irdische Amor oder Der Sieg der fleischlichen Liebe* (Frankfurt, 1992)

Röttgen, Herwarth, 'Quel diavolo è Caravaggio. Giovanni Baglione e la sua denuncia satirica dell'*Amore terreno*', *Storia dell'arte*, vol. 79 (1993), pp. 326–40

Rowlands, Eliot W., *The Collections of the Nelson-Atkins Museum of Art: Italian Paintings 1300–1800* (Kansas City, 1996)

Saccà, Virgilio, 'Michelangelo da Caravaggio pittore. Studi e ricerche', *Archivio storico messinese*, vol. 8 (1907), pp. 41–79

Salerno, Luigi, 'The Picture Gallery of Vincenzo Giustiniani', *Burlington Magazine*, vol. 102 (1960), pp. 21–7, 93–104, 135–48

Salerno, Luigi, 'Poesia e simboli nel Caravaggio', *Palatino*, vol. 10 (1966), pp. 106–12

Schroeder, Veronika, *Tradition und Innovation in Kabinettbilden Caravaggios* (Munich, 1988)

Schröter, Elizabeth, 'Caravaggio und die Gemäldesammlung der Familie Mattei: Addenda und Corrigenda zu den jungsten Forschungen und Funden', *Pantheon*, vol. 53 (1995), pp 62–87

Scribner, Charles, III, '"In Alia Effigie": Caravaggio's London *Supper at Emmaus*', *Art Bulletin*, vol. 59 (1977), pp. 375–82

Sebregondi Fiorentini, Ludovico, 'Francesco dell'Antella, Caravaggio, Paladini e altri', *Paragone*, nos. 383–5 (1982), pp. 107–22

*Il seicento lombardo*, exh. cat., Palazzo Reale and Pinacoteca Ambrosiana, Milan (Milan, 1973)

Seong-Doo, Noh, *Übernahme und Rhetorik in der Kunst Caravaggios* (Münster, 1993)

Settis, Salvatore, 'Immagini della meditazione, dell'incertezza e del pentimento nell'arte antica', *Prospettiva*, vol. 2 (1975), pp. 4–18

Sire, H.J.A., *The Knights of Malta* (New Haven, CT, and London, 1994)

Slatkes, Leonard 'Caravaggio's *Boy Bitten by a Lizard*', *Print Review*, vol. 5 (1976), pp. 148–53

Slim, H. Colin 'Music in and out of Egypt: A little-studied Iconographical Tradition', *Musica disciplina*, vol. 37 (1983), pp. 289–326

Spear, Richard *Caravaggio and His Followers*, exh. cat., Cleveland Museum of Art, rev. edn. (New York, 1975)

Spear, Richard 'Leonardo, Raphael, and Caravaggio', in *Light on the Eternal City*, eds. H. Hager and S. Scott Munshower, *Papers in Art History from The Pennsylvania State University*, vol. 2 (University Park, PA, 1987), pp. 59–90

Spezzaferro, Luigi 'La cultura del cardinal Del Monte e il primo tempo di Caravaggio', *Storia dell'arte*, vols. 9–10 (1971), pp. 57–92

Spezzaferro, Luigi, 'The Documentary Findings: Ottavio Costa as a Patron of Caravaggio', *Burlington Magazine*, vol. 116 (1974), pp. 579–86

Spezzaferro, Luigi, 'Il testamento di Marzio Milesi: tracce per un perduto Caravaggio', *Ricerche di storia dell'arte*, no. 10 (1980), pp. 90–9

Spike, John T., 'Ephemera/Rediscovery', *FMR*, vol. 75 (1995), pp. 14–22

Sterling, Charles, *Still Life Painting* (Paris, 1959)

Stone, David M., 'The Context of Caravaggio's *Beheading of St John* in Malta', *Burlington Magazine*, vol. 139 (1997), pp. 161–70

*Storia della Sicilia*, 10 vols. (Naples and Palermo, 1977–81)

*Storia di Milano. X. L'età della riforma cattolica (1559–1630)* (Milan, 1957)

Treffers, Bert, 'Il Francesco Hartford del Caravaggio e la spiritualità francescana alla fine del XVI sec.', *Mitteilungen des Kunsthistorisches Institutes in Florenz*, vol. 32 (1988), pp. 145–71

Treffers, Bert, 'Dogma, esegi e pittura: Caravaggio nella Cappella Contarelli in San Luigi dei Francesi', *Storia dell'arte*, vol. 67 (1989), pp. 241–55

Treffers, Bert, *Caravaggio, genie in opdracht: een Kunstenaar en zijn opdrachtgevers in het Rome van rond 1600* (Nijmegen, c.1991)

Trinchieri Camiz, Franca, 'The Castrato Singer: From Informal to Formal Portraiture', *Artibus et historiae*, vol. 18 (1988), pp. 171–86

Trinchieri Camiz, Franca, 'Music and Painting in Cardinal Del Monte's Household', *Metropolitan Museum Journal*, vol. 26 (1991), pp. 213–16

Trinchieri Camiz, Franca, '"Luogo molto vago et delitioso …": il casino del cardinal Del Monte ed un suo soffitto dipinto da Caravaggio', *Ricerche di storia dell'arte*, no. 47 (1992), pp. 81–8

Trinchieri Camiz, Franca, and Ziino, Agostino, 'Caravaggio: Aspetti musicali e committenza', *Studi musicali*, vol. 12 (1983), pp. 67–90

Troy, Thomas, 'Caravaggio and the Roman Oratory of Saint Philip Neri', *Studies in Iconography*, vol. 12 (1988), pp. 61–89

Tuck-Scala, Anna, 'Caravaggio's "Roman Charity" in the *Seven Acts of Mercy*', *Parthenope's Splendor: Art of the Golden Age in Naples*, Papers in Art History from the Pennsylvania State University, vol. 7 (University Park, PA, 1993), pp. 126–63

*L'ultimo Caravaggio e la cultura artistica a Napoli, in Sicilia, e a Malta*, Atti del convegno, Syracuse-Malta, April 1985, ed. Maurizio Calvesi (Syracuse, 1987)

Vodret, Rossella, 'Ritratto di artista allo specchio', *Art e dossier*, vol. 109 (1996), pp. 9–13

Wallach, Nancy C., 'An Iconographic Interpretation of a Ceiling Painting Attributed to Caravaggio', *Marsyas*, vol. 17 (1974–5), pp. 101–12

Warma, Suzanne J., 'Christ, First Fruits, and the Resurrection: Observations on the Fruit Basket in Caravaggio's London "Supper at Emmaus"', *Zeitschrift für Kunstgeschichte*, vol. 53 (1990), pp. 583–6

Ważbiński, Zygmunt, *Il cardinale Francesco Maria del Monte 1549–1626*, 2 vols. (Florence, 1994)

Wind, Barry, 'Pitture Ridicole: Some Late Cinquecento Comic Genre Paintings', *Storia dell'arte*, vol. 20 (1974), pp. 25–35

Wind, Barry, 'Genre as Season: Dosso, Campi, Caravaggio', *Arte Lombarda*, vol. 42/3 (1975), pp. 70–3

Wind, Barry, 'Gesture and Meaning in Two Paintings by Caravaggio', *Source*, vol. 16 (1997), pp. 9–11

Zandri, Giuliana, 'Un probabile dipinto murale del Caravaggio per il Cardinale Del Monte', *Storia dell'arte*, vol. 3 (1969), pp. 338–43.

Zuccari, Alessandro, 'La politica culturale dell' Oratorio romano nella seconda metà del cinquecento', *Storia dell'arte*, vol. 41 (1981), pp. 77–112

Zuccari, Alessandro, 'La cappella della "Pietà" alla Chiesa Nuova e i committenti del Caravaggio', *Storia dell'arte*, vol. 47 (1983) pp. 53–6

Zuccari, Alessandro, *Arte e committenza nella Roma di Caravaggio* (Rome, 1984)

440

**Photographic Acknowledgements**

Alinari, Florence 2, 14, 17, 130, 135, 151, 180, 195

Amministrazione Borromeo, Milan 127

Canon John Azzopardi, Malta 140

Barbara Piasecka Johnson Collection Foundation, New Jersey 198

Biblioteca Comunale, Fermo 161

Bildarchiv Preussischer Kulturbesitz, Berlin 4, 66, 94, 106, 206

Bridgeman Art Library, London 145

British Library Map Library, London 39

Canali Photobank, Capriolo 72

Keith Christiansen, New York 49

Cleveland Museum of Art, 1997, Leonard C. Hanna Jr. Fund 173

Courtauld Institute of Art, Witt Library, London 116

Detroit Institute of Arts, Michigan 67, 186

Editech SRL, Florence 189, 192

Foto Saporetti, Milan 5, 8, 10, 154

Foto Vasari, Rome 20, 22, 55, 57, 73, 74, 75, 77, 81, 83, 87, 99, 100, 106, 136, 152, 156, 159, 162, 163, 164, 168, 169, 203

Fotoflash, Venice 78

Fundación Colección Thyssen-Bornemisza, Madrid 63

Graphische Sammlung Albertina, Vienna 80

Gruppo Banca Commerciale Italiana, Milan 178

Mary Jane Harris, New York 211

Herzog Anton Ulrich-Museum, Braunschweig 174

High Museum of Art, Atlanta 194

Index, Florence 76, 95, 119, 128, 176

Institut Amatller D'Art Hispanic, Barcelona 196

Instituto Centrale per il Restauro, Rome 184

John and Mable Ringling Museum of Art, Sarasota 40, 125

Kimbell Art Museum, Fort Worth 35

Kunsthistorisches Museum, Vienna 139, 182, 202, 212

Maurizio Marini, Rome 25, 132, 147, 210

Matthiesen Gallery, London 177

Metropolitan Museum of Art, New York, Marquand Fund 1912 9; Rogers Fund 1952 41; Gwynne Andrews Fund 1991 166; purchase Lila Acheson Wallace Gift 1997 175

Monumenti Musei e Gallerie Pontificie, Vatican City 57, 97, 103, 104

Musée de la Ville de Strasbourg 30

Musée des Beaux-Arts et d'Archéologie, Besançon 131

Musée des Beaux-Arts de Rouen 138

Musei Civici, Turin 36;

Museo del Prado, Madrid 11, 64, 157

National Gallery of Art, Washington DC, Ailsa Mellon Bruce Fund 1997 Board of Trustees 33; Bequest of Lors Heinemann in memory of her husband, Dr Rudolf J. Heinemann, 1997 Board of Trustees 45

National Gallery of Canada, Ottawa 93

National Gallery of Ireland, Dublin 117

National Gallery, London 26, 110, 171

Nelson-Atkins Museum of Art, Kansas City 124, 126, 201

Palacio Real, Madrid 170

Luciano Pedicini, Naples 6, 7, 21, 28, 51, 71, 208

Philadelphia Museum of Art, Pennsylvania, John G. Johnson Collection 43

Phillips, Son and Neale, London 193

Photocity, Valletta 150

Publifoto SNC, Palermo 158, 160

Antonio Quattrone, Florence 54, 82, 133

Rijksmuseum, Amsterdam 27

RMN, Paris 98, 101, 108, 111, 120, 142

Ronald Grant Archive, London 191

Royal Collection, © Her Majesty the Queen, Hampton Court Palace 197

San Diego Museum of Art, Gift of Anne R. and Amy Putnam 68

Scala, Florence 1, 18, 19, 23, 24, 31, 32, 34, 37, 38, 39, 46, 47, 50, 53, 54, 56, 58, 59, 60, 69, 70, 79, 82, 84, 86, 89, 90, 91, 92, 102, 105, 107, 109, 112, 118, 121, 123, 137, 141, 143, 144, 146, 148, 155, 162, 167, 172, 179, 181, 183, 187, 188, 196, 200, 204, 205, 207, 213

Snite Museum of Art, University of Notre Dame, Gift of Mrs Fred J. Fisher 65

Soprintendenza per I Beni Artistici e Storici, Florence 149

Soprintendenza per I Beni Artistici e Storici, Urbino 62

Staatliche Kunstsammlungen, Dresden 48

Stiftung Preussische Schlösser und Garten, Potsdam 114

Studio Fotografico Il Girasole, Milan 12, 13, 16, 85, 96

Wadsworth Atheneum, Hartford 61

442

**Index of Works**
**&**
**General Index**

445

448